The Sociology of Dissent

The Sociology of Dissent

EDITED BY
R. SERGE DENISOFF
Bowling Green State University

UNDER THE GENERAL EDITORSHIP OF
Robert K. Merton
Columbia University

Harcourt Brace Jovanovich, Inc.
New York   Chicago   San Francisco   Atlanta

ISBN: 0-15-582364-7
Library of Congress Catalog Card Number: 74-5589
Printed in the United States of America

To Ray B. Browne, a gentle revolutionary in the ivory tower

PREFACE

Dissent, protest, revolution. The events of the 1960s gave these enduring terms a new urgency. Although the questions raised in that period are still fresh, enough time has elapsed for reflection about them. We now have an opportunity to analyze and interpret some of the issues underlying the spectrum of dissent, from political disagreement to violent revolution.

Many of the specific issues of the 1960s are still with us. We have yet to deal adequately, for example, with the claims presented by minority groups, the alienation of our youth (especially among the privileged strata), and the abuse of power by constituted authority. The problems posed by these substantive issues deserve the best analysis sociology can provide as do their broader theoretical and methodological underpinnings. The latter concern problems of approach, questions of objectivity, difficulties in utilizing appropriate concepts for ongoing events. The effort to understand the specific and general problems posed by the dissent that came to a head in the late 1960s may well illuminate both the recent past and the nature of sociological inquiry itself.

The Sociology of Dissent brings together twenty-three essays that, in my view, represent the best current thinking on the enduring problems given new urgency by recent events. Articles by Blumer, Turner, Smelser, Zygmunt, Douglas, and Pettee, for example, deal with the theoretical and methodological issues raised by dissent, from the vantage point of both recent and distant history. Mauss, Flacks, Killian, Ferkiss, and Stark, among others, discuss the particular issues raised by dissent, on both the Left and the Right. There are, of course, many excellent and pertinent discussions that could not be included in this collection of readings, for such obvious reasons as limitations of space, duplication of approach and subject, or difficulty of discourse. At all times, in making my selections and writing my commentary, I have kept in mind that my expected readers are students.

Indeed, this book is intended as an introduction for students to the sociological aspects of dissent. It is designed primarily for use in such courses as collective behavior, social movements, and political sociology. It can be used as well, however, in introductory sociology courses that focus on selected problem areas or explore a variety of sociological approaches to the discipline. Serious studies have been placed in a framework that will make them readily accessible to a wide variety of students.

The Sociology of Dissent opens with the theories and methods pertinent to an inquiry into the subject, then considers dissent on the extreme Left and the extreme Right, and concludes with discussions of revolution and the repression of dissent. In every instance I tried to choose works that are interesting in their own right and at the same time relevant to that portion of the subject under review. For example, in considering the function of ideology, students will have an opportunity to read about the radicalization of the middle class in the selection by Harvey Molotch; while dealing with the extreme Left they can read a discussion of the women's liberation movement by Jo Freeman; and studying the Radical Right they can read the excellent analysis of Right-Wing thought by Gary Rush. My hope, finally, is that the selections in *The Sociology of Dissent* will be provocative enough to lead students who use this book to read further in the subject.

A number of people made helpful suggestions and provided constructive criticisms during the development of this book. I especially wish to thank Robert K. Merton, Richard Flacks, Joseph R. Gusfield, Harvey Molotch, and Ralph H. Turner for their invaluable assistance. As always, my gratitude is extended to Lauretta Lahman, Phyllis Eaton, Karen Cody, and Dawn Mc-Caghy for their help in clerical and editorial matters.

R. SERGE DENISOFF

CONTENTS

The Sociology of Dissent

1: Introduction to Social Movements

Sociology is a product of the political and economic turmoil that convulsed the European continent during the eighteenth and nineteenth centuries. The Industrial Revolution tore apart the social and economic fabric of feudalism and replaced it with a cold new economic garment. People tied to the soil were driven from rural estates into overcrowded cities to compete for jobs in factories, where they worked 16 hours a day for an impersonal "management" instead of a particular, paternalistic nobleman. The conditions of life made the inequities between the "haves" and the "have-nots" more visible; injustices were enormous.

The Industrial Revolution also sharpened earlier questions about the existing political system. Writers and philosophers wondered aloud about the function and value of the monarchy and aristocracy when the merchant class possessed most of the economic if not political power in Western Europe. Although they did not agree on solutions, social critics suggested that something was seriously wrong with society. Rather than pointing to technology as the culprit, these critics singled out various political, economic, and even religious institutions as creating poverty, inequality, and a lack of personal freedom or fulfillment.[1]

The French Revolution expressed past discontent and represented a search for a better future. The Revolution, the ensuing Reign of Terror, and the rise and fall of Napoleon generated considerable intellectual furor. The debate focused on a score of issues that dealt chiefly with the social and human cost of progress. Only the staunchest conservatives opposed change, which was usually associated with progress. A number of observers, like the English politician and writer Edmund Burke, considered the French Revolution an essentially ineffective and costly means of bringing about change. Others, like the German philosopher Georg Wilhelm Friedrich Hegel, viewed the French Revolution as necessary to the progress of history. It was along these lines that the issue was drawn.

Revolution or evolution? This was the issue that intrigued early-nineteenth-century social thinkers, such as the French political economist Jerome Adolphe Blanqui. In order to reach some answer, social thinkers—many of whom had strong political beliefs—examined the conditions leading to the rise of industrialism and the French Revolution. It is in this context that Danish historian Lorenz von Stein published, in 1852, **The History of the Social Movement in France from 1789–**

---

[1] See Robert Nisbet, *The Social Philosophers: Community and Conflict in Western Thought*, (New York: Thomas Y. Crowell Co., 1973).

1

1850. He argued that society was divided into two camps, proletariat and ruling class, and that social transformation was no longer merely a theoretical question. Change was "to become the substance of present and future developments."[2] The most important element in social change was the people, or the masses, gathered together in order to realize the goals of "liberty and equality." Von Stein defined a **social movement** as people joined together in order to change conditions in society. This definition, based on the model of the French Revolution, was tied to the view, shared by supporter and foe alike, that the mob (the masses) was the volatile element in society that could lead to social disruption and political change.[3]

In this conceptual frame, a social movement is a vehicle for political change. Although a hundred years have passed and von Stein is generally forgotten, his original terminology has stood the test of time. Sociologists may no longer link the concept of "social movement" to mobs or any specific social class, but they still use the concept as well as the term. Other properties have been added to the concept, such as the type of change desired and the tactics used, yet nearly all descriptions of social movements include the factors discussed by von Stein: a perceived social problem, a proposed solution, some form of collective action, and some type of structural change.[4]

The concept has also been expanded to include other types of groups besides those bent on storming the palace gates. Although American sociologists studied the so-called "grand revolutionary" movements that appeared in France in 1789 and Russia in 1917, they found little in these movements that was applicable to the American experience. Instead, they investigated native groups, such as the Know Nothing, Suffragette, Progressive, and Populist Movements. Members of these movements did not want complete social change and generally worked within the established social system. They were quite conservative by comparison to the epic-making revolutionaries. The rise of the Nazi Party in Germany during the 1930s raised new questions about the revolutionary model. This event generated as much interest among sociologists as the storming of the Bastille and the Czar's palace.

Herbert Blumer, using tactics as his frame of reference, introduced several new types into the description of social movements. He envisioned two distinct political types: the revolutionary and reform movements. The **revolutionary** movement desires total change, including the prevailing moral values, and therefore, Blumer said, is not socially respectable and is subject to severe public attack. The **reform** movement, in contrast, works for limited change by influencing public opinion through an appeal to established moral values. It is respectable and not subject to repressive measures.

Blumer's list included several other movements, which he classified on the basis of goals. He described **expressive** movements as unconcerned with social change, inwardly oriented, and more concerned with the values of their own members than the objective conditions of the outside world. **Revivalist** and **nationalist** movements are in some ways similar, since they too are inwardly directed, but they have revolutionary potential. These movements have been called **resistance** or **regressive** movements by other sociologists, such as Louis Wirth, who used these labels to

---

2 Lorenz von Stein, *The History of the Social Movement in France, 1789–1850*, trans. and ed. by Kaethe Mengelberg (Totowa, N.J.: The Bedminster Press, 1964). Von Stein, according to many historians of thought, was a major influence on Karl Marx's thinking about social movements and the political potential of the proletariat. See Herbert Marcuse, *Reason and Revolution: Hegel and the Rise of Social Theory*, rev. ed. (Boston: Beacon Press, 1960), pp. 374–88.

3 See Irving M. Zeitlin, *Ideology and the Development of Sociological Theory* (Englewood Cliffs, N.J.: Prentice-Hall, 1968), pp. 35–82; Robert A. Nisbet, *Tradition and Revolt: Historical and Sociological Essays* (New York: Random House, 1968), pp. 73–142; and Frank Manuel, *The Prophets of Paris* (Cambridge, Mass.: Harvard University Press, 1962).

4 A review of social movement definitions is presented in Gary B. Rush and R. Serge Denisoff, *Social and Political Movements* (New York: Appleton-Century-Crofts, 1971), pp. 180–82.

describe those groups of people organized together to maintain "racial purity" and ultra nationalism.[5] In time, the labels, resistance or regressive, would be used to describe ethnocentric and conservative movements ranging from the Daughters of the American Revolution to the German Nazi party. In general, students of social movements have accepted three basic designations for social movements: revolutionary, regressive, and reform. These are classified on the basis of goals and tactics.[6]

But events in the 1960s caused some sociologists to reexamine their definitions. The student protests, the antiwar demonstrations, and the "counterculture" did not fit traditional concepts of a social movement. Student protest was addressed to myriad grievances by many unrelated groups and unaffiliated individuals. Hippies, sometimes known as "flower children," presented themselves as free-floating spirits concerned more with otherworldliness than social change. "Turn on, tune in, and drop out" was a universe away from "workers of the world unite!" Even the black-power umbrella covered many different programs. The Black Panthers' cry of "all power to the people" meant something quite different from the NAACP spokesman's use of the black power slogan. The NAACP saw black power as a voting block or a force to be reckoned with in the courts. The Panthers tended to see black power as coming through direct street action or even by way of the gun. In the 1960s a rainbow array of tactics, programs, and goals required sociological inquiry; classification on the basis of tactics and goals alone was not sufficient. Although they did not fit the sociological concept, these "movements" could scarcely be dismissed for that reason.

Ralph Turner was one of the first American sociologists to bring the analytical problem posed by these movements to the attention of his colleagues. Turner concluded that the goals and tactics of the social movements of the 1960s in many cases were linked to individual feelings. Feelings of despair and alienation were previously considered personal rather than social problems by most people. Turner contended personal malaise was seen by the protestors of the sixties as a social problem and reflected a new perception of social justice. In their view, society as a whole is responsible for remedying personal, psychological ills. In 1970, Turner asserted that modern social movements were in the process of identifying the problem and taking collective action that expressed their perception of the problem, but they were not yet in agreement on a solution to the problem.

Turner's thesis suggests that the protest movements of the sixties were symbolic or expressive rather than ameliorative. As will be seen in Chapter 2, much of the social-psychological literature dealing with movements has adopted this view. Any reexamination of the sociological aspects of the political arena will lead to the conclusion that the concept of expressive movements has considerable relevance to the protest activity of the sixties and early seventies. We can no longer ignore the concept of an expressive movement and must grant it status equal to the more traditional categories of revolutionary, regressive, and reformist movements.

---

[5] Louis Wirth, "Types of Minority Movements," in Ralph Turner and Lewis Killian, *Collective Behavior* (Englewood Cliffs, N.J.: Prentice-Hall, 1957), pp. 321–26.

[6] See *ibid.*; Rudolf Heberle, *Social Movements* (New York: Appleton-Century-Crofts, 1951); C. Wendell King, *Social Movements in the United States* (New York: Random House, 1956); and Lewis Killian, "Social Movements," in *Handbook of Modern Sociology*, ed. Robert E. L. Faris (Chicago: Rand McNally and Co., 1964), pp. 426–55.

Social Movements

HERBERT BLUMER

Social movements can be viewed as collective enterprises seeking to establish a new order of life. They have their inception in a condition of unrest, and derive their motive power on one hand from dissatisfaction with the current form of life, and on the other hand, from wishes and hopes for a new scheme or system of living. The career of a social movement depicts the emergence of a new order of life. In its beginning, a social movement is amorphous, poorly organized, and without form; the collective behavior is on the primitive level, . . . and the mechanisms of interaction are the elementary, spontaneous mechanisms. . . . As a social movement develops, it takes on the character of a society. It acquires organization and form, a body of customs and traditions, established leadership, an enduring division of labor, social rules and social values—in short, a culture, a social organization, and a new scheme of life.

Our treatment of social movements will deal with three kinds—general social movements, specific social movements, and expressive social movements.[1]

GENERAL SOCIAL MOVEMENTS

By general social movements we have in mind movements such as the labor movement, the youth movement, the women's movement, and the peace movement. Their background is constituted by gradual and pervasive changes in the values of people—changes which can be called cultural drifts. Such cultural drifts stand for a general shifting in the ideas of people,

---

[1] Attention is called, in passing, to spatial movements, such as nomadic movements, barbaric invasions, crusades, pilgrimages, colonization, and migrations. Such movements may be carried on as societies, as in the case of tribal migrations; as diverse peoples with a common goal, as in the case of the religious crusades of the Middle Ages; or as individuals with similar goals, as in most of the immigration into the United States. Mechanisms of their collective operation will be dealt with in the following discussion of social movements. In themselves, such movements are too complicated and diversified to be dealt with adequately here.

particularly along the line of the conceptions which people have of them-selves, and of their rights and privileges. Over a period of time many people may develop a new view of what they believe they are entitled to—a view largely made up of desires and hopes. It signifies the emergence of a new set of values, which influence people in the way in which they look upon their own lives. Examples of such cultural drifts in our own recent history are the increased value of health, the belief in free education, the extension of the franchise, the emancipation of women, the increasing regard for chil-dren, and the increasing prestige of science.

Indefinite images and behavior

The development of the new values which such cultural drifts bring forth involves some interesting psychological changes which provide the motivation for general social movements. They mean, in a general sense, that people have come to form new conceptions of themselves which do not conform to the actual positions which they occupy in their life. They acquire new dispositions and interests and, accordingly, become sensitized in new directions; and, conversely, they come to experience dissatisfaction where before they had none. These new images of themselves, which people be-gin to develop in response to cultural drifts, are vague and indefinite; and correspondingly, the behavior in response to such images is uncertain and without definite aim. It is this feature which provides a clue for the under-standing of general social movements.

Characteristics of general social movements

General social movements take the form of groping and unco-ordinated efforts. They have only a general direction, toward which they move in a slow, halting, erratic yet persistent fashion. As movements they are un-organized, with neither established leadership nor recognized membership, and little guidance and control. Such a movement as the women's move-ment, which has the general and vague aim of the emancipation of women, suggests these features of a general social movement. The women's move-ment, like all general social movements, operates over a wide range—in the home, in marriage, in education, in industry, in politics, in travel—in each area of which it represents a search for an arrangement which will answer to the new idea of status being formed by women. Such a movement is episodic in its career, with very scattered manifestations of activity. It may show considerable enthusiasm at one point and reluctance and inertia at another; it may experience success in one area, and abortive effort in an-other. In general, it may be said that its progress is very uneven with set-backs, reverses, and frequent retreading of the same ground. At one time the impetus to the movement may come from people in one place, at another time in another place. On the whole the movement is likely to be carried on by many unknown and obscure people who struggle in different areas without their striving and achievements becoming generally known.

A general social movement usually is characterized by a literature, but the literature is as varied and ill-defined as is the movement itself. It is likely to be an expression of protest, with a general depiction of a kind of utopian existence. As such, it vaguely outlines a philosophy based on new values and self-conceptions. Such a literature is of great importance in spreading a message or view, however imprecise it may be, and so in implanting suggestions, awakening hopes, and arousing dissatisfactions. Similarly, the "leaders" of a general social movement play an important part— not in the sense of exercising directive control over the movement, but in the sense of being pace-makers. Such leaders are likely to be "voices in the wilderness," pioneers without any solid following, and frequently not very clear about their own goals. However, their example helps to develop sensitivities, arouse hopes, and break down resistances. From these traits one can easily realize that the general social movement develops primarily in an informal, inconspicuous, and largely subterranean fashion. Its media of interaction are primarily reading, conversations, talks, discussions, and the perception of examples. Its achievements and operations are likely to be made primarily in the realm of individual experience rather than by noticeable concerted action of groups. It seems evident that the general social movement is dominated to a large extent by the mechanisms of mass behavior, such as we have described in our treatment of the mass. Especially in its earlier stages, general social movements are likely to be merely an aggregation of individual lines of action based on individual decisions and selections. As is characteristic of the mass and of mass behavior, general social movements are rather formless in organization and inarticulate in expression.

The basis for specific social movements

Just as cultural drifts provide the background out of which emerge general social movements, so the general social movement constitutes the setting out of which develop specific social movements. Indeed, a specific social movement is usually a crystallization of much of the motivation of dissatisfaction, hope, and desire awakened by the general social movement and the focusing of this motivation on some specific objective. A convenient illustration is the antislavery movement, which was, to a considerable degree, an individual expression of the widespread humanitarian movement of the nineteenth century. With this recognition of the relation between general and specific social movements, we can turn to a consideration of the latter.

SPECIFIC SOCIAL MOVEMENTS

The outstanding instances of this type of movement are reform movements and revolutionary movements. A specific social movement is one which has a well-defined objective or goal which it seeks to reach. In this effort it develops an organization and structure, making it essentially a society. It develops a recognized and accepted leadership and a definite membership characterized by a "we-consciousness." It forms a body of traditions, a guiding set of values, a philosophy, sets of rules, and a general body of expectations. Its members form allegiances and loyalties. Within it there develops a division of labor, particularly in the form of a social structure in which individuals occupy status positions. Thus, individuals develop personalities and conceptions of themselves, representing the individual counterpart of a social structure.

A social movement, of the specific sort, does not come into existence with such a structure and organization already established. Instead, its organization and its culture are developed in the course of its career. It is necessary to view social movements from this temporal and developmental perspective. In the beginning a social movement is loosely organized and characterized by impulsive behavior. It has no clear objective; its behavior and thinking are largely under the dominance of restlessness and collective excitement. As a social movement develops, however, its behavior, which was originally dispersed, tends to become organized, solidified, and persistent. It is possible to delineate stages roughly in the career of a social movement which represent this increasing organization. One scheme of four stages has been suggested by Dawson and Gettys.[2] These are the stage of social unrest, the stage of popular excitement, the stage of formalization, and the stage of institutionalization.

Stages of development

In the first of these four stages people are restless, uneasy, and act in the random fashion that we have considered. They are susceptible to appeals and suggestions that tap their discontent, and hence, in this stage, the agitator is likely to play an important role. The random and erratic behavior is significant in sensitizing people to one another and so makes possible the focusing of their restlessness on certain objects. The stage of popular excitement is marked even more by milling, but it is not quite so random and aimless. More definite notions emerge as to the cause of their condition and as to what should be done in the way of social change. So there is a sharpening of objectives. In this stage the leader is likely to be a prophet or a reformer. In the stage of formalization the movement becomes more clearly organized with rules, policies, tactics, and discipline. Here the leader is likely to be in the nature of a statesman. In the institutional stage, the movement has crystallized into a fixed organization with a definite personnel and structure to carry into execution the purposes of the movement. Here the leader is likely to be an administrator. In considering the development of the specific social movement our interest is less in considering the stages through which it passes than in discussing the mechanisms and means through which such a movement is able to grow and become organized. It is convenient to group these mechanisms under five heads: (1) agitation, (2) development of *esprit de corps*, (3) development of morale, (4) the formation of an ideology, and (5) the development of operating tactics.

---

[2] C. A. Dawson and W. E. Gettys, *Introduction to Sociology* (Rev. ed.; New York: Ronald Press Co., 1935, chap. 19).

The role of agitation

Agitation is of primary importance in a social movement. It plays its most significant role in the beginning and early stages of a movement, although it may persist in minor form in the later portions of the life-cycle of the movement. As the term suggests, agitation operates to arouse people and so make them possible recruits for the movement. It is essentially a means of exciting people and of awakening within them new impulses and ideas which make them restless and dissatisfied. Consequently, it acts to loosen the hold on them of their previous attachments, and to break down their previous ways of thinking and acting. For a movement to begin and gain impetus, it is necessary for people to be jarred loose from their customary ways of thinking and believing, and to have aroused within them new impulses and wishes. This is what agitation seeks to do. To be successful, it must first gain the attention of people; second, it must excite them, and arouse feelings and impulses; and third, it must give some direction to these impulses and feelings through ideas, suggestions, criticisms, and promises.

Agitation operates in two kinds of situations. One is a situation marked by abuse, unfair discrimination, and injustice, but a situation wherein people take this mode of life for granted and do not raise questions about it. Thus, while the situation is potentially fraught with suffering and protest, the people are marked by inertia. Their views of their situation incline them to accept it; hence the function of the agitation is to lead them to challenge and question their own modes of living. It is in such a situation that agitation may create social unrest where none existed previously. The other situation is one wherein people are already aroused, restless, and discontented, but where they either are too timid to act or else do not know what to do. In this situation the function of agitation is not so much to implant the seeds of unrest, as to intensify, release, and direct the tensions which people already have.

Agitators seem to fall into two types corresponding roughly to these two situations. One type of agitator is an excitable, restless, and aggressive individual. His dynamic and energetic behavior attracts the attention of people to him; and the excitement and restlessness of his behavior tends to infect them. He is likely to act with dramatic gesture and to talk in terms of spectacular imagery. His appearance and behavior foster the contagion of unrest and excitement. This type of agitator is likely to be most successful in the situation where people are already disturbed and unsettled; in such a situation his own excited and energetic activity can easily arouse other people who are sensitized to such behavior and already disposed to excitability.

The second type of agitator is more calm, quiet, and dignified. He stirs people not by what he does, but what he says. He is likely to be a man sparing in his words, but capable of saying very caustic, incisive, and biting things—things which get "under the skin" of people and force them to view things in a new light. This type of agitator is more suited to the first of the social situations discussed—the situation where people endure hardships or discrimination without developing attitudes of resentment. In this situation, his function is to make people aware of their own position and of the inequalities, deficiencies, and injustices that seem to mark their lot. He leads them to raise questions about what they have previously taken for granted and to form new wishes, inclinations, and hopes.

The function of agitation, as stated above, is in part to dislodge and stir up people and so liberate them for movement in new directions. More specifically, it operates to change the conceptions which people have of themselves, and the notions which they have of their rights and dues. Such new conceptions involving beliefs that one is justly entitled to privileges from which he is excluded, provide the dominant motive force for the social movement. Agitation, as the means of implanting these new conceptions among people, becomes, in this way, of basic importance to the success of a social movement.

A brief remark relative to the tactics of agitation may be made here. It is sufficient to say that the tactics of agitation vary with the situation, the people, and the culture. A procedure which may be highly successful in one situation may turn out to be ludicrous in another situation. This suggests the problem of identifying different types of situations and correlating with each the appropriate form of agitation. Practically no study has been conducted on this problem. Here, one can merely state the truism that the agitator, to be successful, must sense the thoughts, interests, and values of his listeners.

The development of esprit de corps

Agitation is merely the means of arousing the interest of people and thus getting them to participate in a movement. While it serves to recruit members, to give initial impetus, and to give some direction, by itself it could never organize or sustain a movement. Collective activities based on mere agitation would be sporadic, disconnected, and short-lived. Other mechanisms have to enter to give solidity and persistency to a social movement. One of these is the development of *esprit de corps*.

Esprit de corps might be thought of as the organizing of feelings on behalf of the movement. In itself, it is the sense which people have of belonging together and of being identified with one another in a common undertaking. Its basis is constituted by a condition of rapport. In developing feelings of intimacy and closeness, people have the sense of sharing a common experience and of forming a select group. In one another's presence they feel at ease and as comrades. Personal reserve breaks down and feelings of strangeness, difference, and alienation disappear. Under such conditions, relations tend to be of co-operation instead of personal competition. The behavior of one tends to facilitate the release of behavior on the part of others, instead of tending to inhibit or check that behavior; in this sense each person tends to inspire others. Such conditions of mutual sympathy and responsiveness obviously make for concerted behavior.

Esprit de corps is of importance to a social movement in other ways. Very significant is the fact that it serves to reinforce the new conception of himself that the individual has formed as a result of the movement and of his participation in it. His feeling of belonging with others, and they with him, yields him a sense of collective support. In this way his views of himself and of the aims of the movement are maintained and invigorated. It follows that the development of *esprit de corps* helps to foster an attachment of people to a movement. Each individual has his sentiments focused on, and intertwined with, the objectives of the movement. The resulting feeling of expansion which he experiences is in the direction of greater allegiance to the movement. It should be clear that *esprit de corps* is an important means of developing solidarity and so of giving solidity to a movement.

How is *esprit de corps* developed in a social movement? It would seem chiefly in three ways: the development of an in-group–out-group relation, the formation of informal fellowship association, and the participation in formal ceremonial behavior.

The in-group–out-group relation. The nature of the in-group–out-group relation should be familiar to the student. It exists when two groups come to identify each other as enemies. In such a situation each group regards itself as the upholder of virtue and develops among its members feelings of altruism, loyalty, and fidelity. The out-group is regarded as unscrupulous and vicious, and is felt to be attacking the values which the in-group holds dear. Before the out-group the members of the in-group not only feel that they are right and correct, but believe they have a common responsibility to defend and preserve their values.

The value of these in-group–out-group attitudes in developing solidarity in a social movement is quite clear. The belief on the part of its members that the movement is being opposed unjustly and unfairly by vicious and unscrupulous groups serves to rally the members around their aims and values. To have an enemy, in this sense, is very important for imparting solidarity to the movement. In addition, the "enemy" plays the important role of a scapegoat. It is advantageous to a movement to develop an enemy; this development is usually in itself spontaneous. Once made, it functions to establish *esprit de corps*.

Informal fellowship. *Esprit de corps* is formed also in a very significant way by the development of informal association on the basis of fellowship. Where people can come together informally in this way they have the opportunity of coming to know one another as human beings instead of as institutional symbols. They are then in a much better position to take one another's roles and, unwittingly, to share one another's experience. It seems that in such a relationship, people unconsciously import and assimilate into themselves the gestures, attitudes, values, and philosophy of life of one another. The net result is to develop a common sympathy and sense of intimacy which contributes much to solidarity. Thus, we find in social movements the emergence and use of many kinds of informal and communal association. Singing, dancing, picnics, joking, having fun, and friendly informal conversation are important devices of this sort in a social movement. Through them, the individual gets a sense of status and a sense of social acceptance and support, in place of prior loneliness and personal alienation.

Ceremonial behavior. The third important way in which social movements develop *esprit de corps* is through the use of formal ceremonial behavior and of ritual. The value of mass meetings, rallies, parades, huge demonstrations, and commemorative ceremonies has always been apparent to those entrusted with the development of a social movement; the value is one that comes from large assemblages, in the form of the sense of vast support that is experienced by the participant. The psychology that is involved here is the psychology of being on parade. The individual participant experiences the feeling of considerable personal expansion and therefore has the sense of being somebody distinctly important. Since this feeling of personal expansion comes to be identified with the movement as such, it makes for *esprit de corps*. Likewise, the paraphernalia of ritual possessed by every movement serves to foster feelings of common identity and sympathy. This paraphernalia consists of a set of sentimental symbols, such as slogans, songs, cheers, poems, hymns, expressive gestures, and uniforms. Every movement has some of these. Since they acquire a sentimental significance symbolizing the common feelings about the movement, their use serves as a constant reliving and re-enforcement of these mutual feelings.

Esprit de corps may be regarded, then, as an organization of group feeling and essentially as a form of group enthusiasm. It is what imparts life to a movement. Yet just as agitation is inadequate for the development of a movement, so is mere reliance on *esprit de corps* insufficient. A movement which depends entirely on *esprit de corps* is usually like a boom and is likely to collapse in the face of a serious crisis. Since the allegiance which it commands is based merely on heightened enthusiasm, it is likely to vanish with the collapse of such enthusiasm. Thus, to succeed, especially in the face of adversity, a movement must command a more persistent and fixed loyalty. This is yielded by the development of morale.

The development of morale

As we have seen, *esprit de corps* is a collective feeling which gives life, enthusiasm, and vigor to a movement. Morale can be thought of as giving persistency and determination to a movement; its test is whether solidarity can be maintained in the face of adversity. In this sense, morale can be thought of as a group will or an enduring collective purpose.

Morale seems to be based on, and yielded by, a set of convictions. In the case of a social movement these seem to be of three kinds. First is a conviction of the rectitude of the purpose of the movement. This is accompanied by the belief that the attainment of the objectives of the movement will usher in something approaching a millennial state. What is evil, unjust, improper, and wrong will be eradicated with the success of the movement. In this sense, the goal is always overvalued. Yet these beliefs yield to the members of a movement a marked confidence in themselves. A second conviction closely identified with these beliefs is a faith in the ultimate attainment, by the movement, of its goal. There is believed to be a certain inevitability about this. Since the movement is felt to be a necessary agent for the regeneration of the world, it is regarded as being in line with the higher moral values of the universe, and in this sense as divinely favored. Hence, there arises the belief that success is inevitable, even though it be only after a hard struggle. Finally, as part of this complex of convictions, there is the belief that the movement is charged with a sacred mission. Together, these convictions serve to give an enduring and unchangeable character to the goal of a movement and a tenacity to its effort. Obstructions, checks, and reversals are occasions for renewed effort instead of for disheartenment and despair, since they do not seriously impair the faith in the rectitude of the movement nor in the inevitability of its success.

It is clear from this explanation that the development of morale in a movement is essentially a matter of developing a sectarian attitude and a religious faith. This provides a cue to the more prominent means by which morale is built up in a movement. One of these is found in the emergence of a saint cult which is to be discerned in every enduring and persisting social movement. There is usually a major saint and a series of minor saints, chosen from the popular leaders of the movement. Hitler, Lenin, Marx, Mary Baker Eddy, and Sun Yat-sen will serve as convenient examples of major saints. Such leaders become essentially deified and endowed with miraculous power. They are regarded as grossly superior, intelligent, and infallible. People develop toward them attitudes of reverence and awe, and resent efforts to depict them as ordinary human beings. The pictures or other mementos of such individuals come to have the character of religious idols. Allied with the saints of a movement are its heroes and its martyrs. They also come to be regarded as sacred figures. The development of this whole saint cult is an important means of imparting essentially a religious faith to the movement and of helping to build up the kind of convictions spoken of above.

Similar in function is the emergence in the movement of a creed and of a sacred literature. These, again, are to be found in all persisting social movements. Thus, as has been said frequently, *Das Kapital* and *Mein Kampf* have been the bibles respectively of the communist movement and of the National Socialist movement. The role of a creed and literature of this sort in imparting religious conviction to a movement should be clear.

Finally, great importance must be attached to myths in the development of morale in a social movement. Such myths may be varied. They may be myths of being a select group or a chosen people; myths of the inhumanity of one's opponents; myths about the destiny of the movement; myths depicting a glorious and millennial society to be realized by the movement. Such myths usually grow out of, and in response to, the desires and hopes of the people in the movement and acquire by virtue of their collective character a solidity, a permanency, and an unquestioned acceptance. It is primarily through them that the members of the movement achieve the dogmatic fixity of their convictions, and seek to justify their actions to the rest of the world.

The development of group ideology

Without an ideology a social movement would grope along in an uncertain fashion and could scarcely maintain itself in the face of pointed opposition from outside groups. Hence, the ideology plays a significant role in the life of a movement; it is a mechanism essential to the persistency and development of a movement. The ideology of a movement consists of a body of doctrine, beliefs, and myths. More specifically, it seems to consist of the following: *first*, a statement of the objective, purpose, and premises of the movement; *second*, a body of criticism and condemnation of the existing structure which the movement is attacking and seeking to change; *third*, a body of defense doctrine which serves as a justification of the movement and of its objectives; *fourth*, a body of belief dealing with policies, tactics, and practical operation of the movement; and, *fifth*, the myths of the movement.

This ideology is almost certain to be of a twofold character. In the first place, much of it is erudite and scholarly. This is the form in which it is developed by the intellectuals of the movement. It is likely to consist of elaborate treatises of an abstract and highly logical character. It grows up usually in response to the criticism of outside intellectuals, and seeks to gain for its tenets a respectable and defensible position in this world of higher learning and higher intellectual values. The ideology has another character, however—a popular character. In this guise, it seeks to appeal to the uneducated and to the masses. In its popular character, the ideology takes the form of emotional symbols, shibboleths, stereotypes, smooth and graphic phrases, and folk arguments. It deals, also, with the tenets of the movement, but presents them in a form that makes for their ready comprehension and consumption.

The ideology of a movement may be thought of as providing a movement with its philosophy and its psychology. It gives a set of values, a set of convictions, a set of criticisms, a set of arguments, and a set of defenses. As such, it furnishes to a movement (*a*) direction, (*b*) justification, (*c*) weapons of attack, (*d*) weapons of defense, and (*e*) inspiration and hope. To be effective in these respects, the ideology must carry respectability and prestige—a character that is provided primarily by the intelligentsia of the movement. More important than this, however, is the need of the ideology to answer to the distress, wishes, and hopes of the people. Unless it has this popular appeal, it will be of no value to the movement.

The role of tactics

We have referred to tactics as the fifth major mechanism essential to the development of a social movement. Obviously the tactics are evolved along three lines: gaining adherents, holding adherents, and reaching objectives. Little more can be said than this, unless one deals with specific kinds of movements in specific kinds of situations. For, tactics are always dependent on the nature of the situation in which a movement is operating and always with reference to the cultural background of the movement. This functional dependency of tactics on the peculiarity of the situation helps to explain the ludicrous failures that frequently attend the application of certain tactics to one situation even though they may have been successful in other situations. To attempt revolutionary tactics these days in terms of the tactics of two centuries ago would be palpably foolish. Similarly, to seek to develop a movement in this country in terms of tactics employed in a similar movement in some different cultural setting would probably bring very discouraging results. In general, it may be said that tactics are almost by definition flexible and variable, taking their form from the nature of the situation, the exigencies of the circumstances, and the ingenuity of the people.

We can conclude this discussion of the five mechanisms considered merely by reiterating that the successful development of a movement is dependent on them. It is these mechanisms which establish a program, set policies, develop and maintain discipline, and evoke allegiance.

Reform and revolution

Mention has been made of the fact that specific social movements are primarily of two sorts: reform and revolutionary movements. Both seek to effect changes in the social order and in existing institutions. Their life-cycles are somewhat similar, and the development of both is dependent on the mechanisms which we have just discussed. However, noteworthy differences exist between the two; some of these differences will now be indicated.

The two movements differ in the *scope of their objectives*. A reform movement seeks to change some specific phase or limited area of the existing social order; it may seek, for example, to abolish child labor or to prohibit the consumption of alcohol. A revolutionary movement has a broader aim; it seeks to reconstruct the entire social order.

This difference in objective is linked with a *different vantage point of attack*. In endeavoring to change just a portion of the prevailing social order, the reform movement accepts the basic tenets of that social order. More precisely, the reform movement accepts the existing mores; indeed, it uses them to criticize the social defects which it is attacking. The reform movement starts with the prevailing code of ethics, and derives much of its support because it is so well grounded on the ethical side. This makes its position rather unassailable. It is difficult to attack a reform movement or reformers on the basis of their moral aims; the attack is usually more in the form of caricature and ridicule, and in characterizing reformers as visionary and impractical. By contrast, a revolutionary movement always challenges the existing mores and proposes a new scheme of moral values. Hence, it lays itself open to vigorous attack from the standpoint of existing mores.

A third difference between the two movements follows from the points which have been made. A reform movement has *respectability*. By virtue of accepting the existing social order and of orienting itself around the ideal code, it has a claim on existing institutions. Consequently, it makes use of these institutions such as the school, the church, the press, established clubs, and the government. Here again the revolutionary movement stands in marked contrast. In attacking the social order and in rejecting its mores, the revolutionary movement is blocked by existing institutions and its use of them is forbidden. Thus, the revolutionary movement is usually and finally driven underground; whatever use is made of existing institutions has to be carefully disguised. In general, whatever agitation, proselytizing, and maneuvers are carried on by revolutionary movements have to be done outside the fold of existing institutions. In the event that a reform movement is felt as challenging too seriously some powerful class or vested interests, it is likely to have closed to it the use of existing institutions. This tends to change a reform movement into a revolutionary movement; its objectives broaden to include the reorganization of the institutions which are now blocking its progress.

The differences in position between reform and revolutionary movements bring in an important distinction in their *general procedure and tactics*. A reform movement endeavors to proceed by developing a public opinion favorable to its aims; consequently, it seeks to establish a public issue and to make use of the discussion process which we have already considered. The reform party can be viewed as a conflict group, opposed by interest groups and surrounded by a large inert population. The reform movement addresses its message to this indifferent or disinterested public in the effort to gain its support. In contradistinction, the revolutionary movement does not seek primarily to influence public opinion, but instead tries to make converts. In this sense it operates more like a religion.

This means some difference as to the groups among which the two movements respectively conduct their agitation and seek their adherents. The reform movement, while usually existing on behalf of some distressed or exploited group, does little to establish its strength among them. Instead, it tries to enlist the allegiance of a middle-class public on the outside and to awaken within them a vicarious sympathy for the oppressed group. Hence, generally, it is infrequent that the leadership or membership of a reform movement comes from the group whose rights are being espoused. In this sense a revolutionary movement differs. Its agitation is carried on among those who are regarded as in a state of distress or exploitation. It endeavors to establish its strength by bringing these people inside of its ranks. Hence, the revolutionary movement is usually a lower-class movement operating among the underprivileged.

Finally, by virtue of these characteristic differences, the two movements diverge in their functions. The primary function of the reform movement is probably not so much the bringing about of social change, as it is to reaffirm the ideal values of a given society. In the case of a revolutionary movement, the tendency to dichotomize the world between those who have and those who have not, and to develop a strong, cohesive, and uncompromising group out of the latter, makes its function that of introducing a new set of essentially religious values.

A concluding remark may be made about specific social movements. They can be viewed as societies in miniature, and as such, represent the building up of organized and formalized collective behavior out of what was originally amorphous and undefined. In their growth a social organization is developed, new values are formed, and new personalities are organized. These, indeed, constitute their residue. They leave behind an institutional structure and a body of functionaries, new objects and views, and a new set of self-conceptions.

EXPRESSIVE MOVEMENTS

The characteristic feature of expressive movements is that they do not seek to change the institutions of the social order or its objective character. The tension and unrest out of which they emerge are not focused upon some objective of social change which the movement seeks collectively to achieve. Instead, they are released in some type of expressive behavior which, however, in becoming crystallized, may have profound effects on the personalities of individuals and on the character of the social order. We shall consider two kinds of expressive movements: religious movements and fashion movements.

Religious movements

Genuine religious movements are to be distinguished from reform movements and factional splits that take place inside of an established religious body. Religious movements begin essentially as cults; they have their setting in a situation which, psychologically, is like that of the dancing crowd. They represent an inward direction of unrest and tension in the form of disturbed feelings which ultimately express themselves in movement designed to release the tension. The tension does not then go over into purposive action but into expression. This characteristic suggests the nature of the situation from which religious movements emerge. It is a situation wherein people are upset and disturbed, but wherein they cannot act; in other words, a situation of frustration. The inability to release their tension in the direction of some actual change in the social order leaves as the alternative mere expressive behavior.

It is well to recall here the most prominent features of the dancing crowd. One of these is a feeling of *intense intimacy* and *esprit de corps*. Another is a heightened feeling of *exaltation* and ecstasy which leads individuals to experience personal expansion and to have a sense of being possessed by some transcendental spirit. Individuals feel inspired and are likely to engage in prophetic utterances. A third mark is the *projection of the collective feelings on outside objects*—persons, behavior, songs, words, phrases, and material objects—which thereby take on a sacred character. With the recurrence and repetition of this crowd behavior, the *esprit de corps* becomes strengthened, the dancing behavior formalized and ritualized, and the sacred objects reinforced. It is at this stage that the sect or cult appears. Since the growth of a religious movement is patterned after that of the sect, let us consider some of the important features of the sect.

First it should be noted that the members of a sect may be recruited from a heterogeneous background, showing differences in wealth, rank, education, and social background. These differences and distinctions have no significance in the sect. In the milling and in the development of rapport everyone is reduced to a common level of brotherhood. This fact is shown not only by the feelings and attitudes which the members have for one another, but also by the manner in which they refer to one another and the way in which they address one another.

Around the feelings of exaltation and the sacred symbols in which these feelings become crystallized, there grow up a series of beliefs and rites which become the *creed and the ritual of the sect*. The whole life of the sect becomes centered around this creed and ritual which, in themselves, come to acquire a sacred character. Since they symbolize the intense feelings of the group, they become absolute and imperative. The prophet plays an important role here. He is a sacred personage and he tends to symbolize in himself the creed and ritual of the group. Also, he is the primary guardian of this creed and ritual.

The creed of the group becomes elaborated into an extensive body of doctrine as the sect becomes cognizant of criticisms made by outsiders and as it seeks to justify its views. It is in this way that a *theology* arises; a large part of it is in the form of an apologia. Accompanying this is some change in the ritual. Those features of its practices and modes of living which subject the sect to criticism and even persecution at the hands of outsiders are likely to be cherished by the sect as the marks of its own identity and thus acquire a special significance.

Another important feature of the sect that arises from its peculiar experience and sacred character is the belief that it is divinely favored, and that it consists of a *select group of sacred souls*. The personal transformation experienced by members of the sect and the new moral and communal vistas that it yields, readily lead them to this conviction. People on the outside of the sect are regarded as lost souls; they have not been blessed with this rectifying experience.

The feeling which the sect has of itself as a community of saved souls easily disposes it to aggressive proselyting of outsiders. Frequently, it feels it has a divine mission to save others and to "show them the light." Hence it seeks *converts*. In order to become a member, an outsider has to have a conversion experience—a moral transformation similar in character to that of the original members. The public confession is a testimonial of such an experience, and is a sign that the individual is a member of the select. These remarks point to a particularly significant characteristic of the sect—the intense conflict relation in which the sect stands with reference to the outside world. The sect may be said to be at war with the outside world, yet it is a peculiar kind of conflict relation, in that the sect is not concerned with seeking to change the institutions or the objective social order, but instead seeks the moral regeneration of the world. It aims, at least originally, not to change the outside existence, but to change the inner life. In this sense, the sect might be thought of as profoundly revolutionary, in that it endeavors to inculcate a new conception of the universe instead of merely seeking to remake institutions or the objective structure of a social order.

A religious movement tends to share these features of the sect. Its program represents a new way of living and it aims at a moral regeneration of the world. As it develops from the amorphous state that it is likely to have in the situation of the dancing crowd, it tends to acquire a structure like that of the sect, and so develops into a society. In this way it becomes analogous to specific social movements except that its aims are of a profoundly different nature.[3]

Fashion movements

While fashion is thought of usually in relation to clothing, it is important to realize that it covers a much wider domain. It is to be found in manners,

[3] There are political as well as religious sects. The difference is that the political sect seeks to bring about political revolution as well as change in the fundamental philosophy of life.

the arts, literature, and philosophy, and may even reach into certain areas of science. In fact, it may operate in any field of group life, apart from the technological and utilitarian area and the area of the sacred. Its operation requires a class society, for in its essential character it does not occur either in a homogeneous society like a primitive group, or in a caste society.

Fashion behaves as a movement, and on this basis it is different from custom which, by comparison, is static. This is due to the fact that fashion is based fundamentally on differentiation and emulation. In a class society, the upper classes or so-called social elite are not able to differentiate themselves by *fixed* symbols or badges. Hence the more external features of their life and behavior are likely to be imitated by classes immediately subjacent to them, who, in turn, are imitated by groups immediately below them in the social structure. This process gives to fashion a vertical descent. However, the elite class finds that it is no longer distinguishable, by reason of the imitation made by others, and hence is led to adopt new differentiating criteria, only to displace these as they in turn are imitated. It is primarily this feature that makes fashion into a movement and which has led one writer to remark that a fashion, once launched, moves to its doom.

As a movement, fashion shows little resemblance to any of the other movements which we have considered. While it occurs spontaneously and moves along in a characteristic cycle, it involves little in the way of crowd behavior and it is not dependent upon the discussion process and the resulting public opinion. It does not depend upon the mechanisms of which we have spoken. The participants are not recruited through agitation or proselyting. No *esprit de corps* or morale is built up among them. Nor does the fashion movement have, or require, an ideology. Further, since it does not have a leadership imparting *conscious* direction to the movement, it does not build up a set of tactics.[4] People participate in the fashion movement voluntarily and in response to the interesting and powerful kind of control which fashion imposes on them.

Not only is the fashion movement unique in terms of its character, but it differs from other movements in that it does not develop into a society. It does not build up a social organization; it has no personnel or functionaries; it does not develop a division of labor among its participants with each being assigned a given status; it does not construct a set of symbols, myths, values, philosophy, or set of practices, and in this sense does not form a culture; and finally, it does not develop a set of loyalties or form a we-consciousness.

Nevertheless, the movement of fashion is an important form of collective behavior with very significant results for the social order. First, it should be noted that the fashion movement is a genuine expressive movement. It does not have a conscious goal which people are trying to reach through collective action, as is true in the case of the specific social movements. Nor does it represent the release of excitement and tension generated in a dancing crowd situation. It is expressive, however, of certain fundamental impulses and tendencies, such as an inclination toward novel experience, a desire for

---

[4] This discussion may appear to be contradicted in the area of clothes fashions by the existence of a large fashion industry which depends heavily on massive, well-organized promotional campaigns. The appearance is delusory. Tastes may be manipulated but only within limits. The fashion industry serves the process; it does not create it.

distinction, and an urge to conform. Fashion is important especially in providing a means for the expression of developing tastes and dispositions; this feature establishes it as a form of expressive behavior.

The latter remark provides a cue for understanding the role of fashion and the way in which it contributes to the formation of a new social order. In a changing society, such as is necessarily presupposed for the operation of fashion, people are continually having their subjective lives upset; they experience new dispositions and tastes which, however, are vague and ill-defined. It seems quite clear that fashion, by providing an opportunity for the expression of dispositions and tastes, serves to make them definite and to channelize them and, consequently, to fix and solidify them. To understand this, one should appreciate the fact that the movement and success of fashion are dependent upon the acceptance of the given style or pattern. In turn, this acceptance is based not merely upon the prestige attached to the style but also upon whether the style meets and answers to the dispositions and developing tastes of people. (The notorious failures that attend efforts to make styles fashionable upon the basis of mere prestige provide some support for this point.) From this point of view, we can regard fashion as arising and flourishing in response to new subjective demands. In providing means for the expression of these dispositions and tastes, fashion acts, as suggested before, to shape and crystallize these tastes. In the long run fashion aids, in this manner, to construct a *Zeitgeist* or a common subjective life, and in doing so, helps to lay the foundation for a new social order.

REVIVAL MOVEMENTS AND NATIONALIST MOVEMENTS

In our discussion so far, we have been treating separately specific social movements, religious movements, and fashion movements. Yet it should be clear that they can be merged, even though in very different degrees. Thus a revolutionary movement may have many of the features of a religious movement, with its success dependent to some extent upon the movement's becoming fashionable.

Revival movements

Revival movements and nationalist movements are particularly likely to have this mixed character. We shall devote a few remarks to them. In revival movements people idealize the past, venerate the ideal picture that they have, and seek to mold contemporary life in terms of this ideal picture. Such movements are explainable, apparently, as a response to a situation of frustration. In this situation people are experiencing a loss of self-respect. Since the future holds no promise for them to form a new respectful conception of themselves, they turn to the past in an effort to do so. By recalling past glories and achievements they can regain a modicum of self-respect and satisfaction. That such movements should have a strong religious character is to be expected. Nationalist movements are very similar in these respects.

Nationalist movements

Movements of nationalism are exceedingly pronounced in our current epoch. They represent efforts of a given people sharing some sense of common identity and historical lineage to gain independent status inside of an international order of sovereign bodies. They seek to guide their own destiny in place of being subservient to the control of an alien group. "Liberty" and "freedom" thus become both the goal and the inspiring clarion calls of nationalist movements. This type of movement has its source in distressing personal experiences in which individuals are made to feel inferior because of the subordinate status of the people to which they belong. They seek accordingly, to raise the status of their group. While usually beginning as reform movements nationalist movements generally become revolutionary in character. Barred from the institutions and channels of the dominant group they resort to the use of revolutionary tactics, carrying on their agitation and planning inside of their own separate institutions, frequently their native church. At the same time, like a reform movement, they solicit the favorable opinion of outside peoples. Thus, nationalist movements rely on the use of the mechanisms previously discussed in the case of specific social movements. One should note, in addition, the strong revivalistic slant that nationalist movements usually take; such movements seek to glorify the past of the people and eulogize the distinctive culture of the people, particularly their language. Where there is no sense of a common past or the sharing of a common language, as in the case of many recent nationalist movements in present-day Africa, a nationalist movement has to depend primarily on cultivating and using the in-group–out-group mechanism as the means of developing unity and persistence.

The Theme of Contemporary Social Movements

RALPH H. TURNER

Two main points are preliminary to the analysis that is to follow. First, any major social movement depends upon and promotes some normative revision. In case of movements having the greatest significance for social change this normative innovation takes the form of a new sense of what is *just* and what is *unjust* in society.[1] This is quite different from merely saying that the leaders and followers of a movement discover a problem and seek to do something about it. The problem may have existed for a long time or it may be of relatively recent origin, and awareness of the problem may predate the movement by centuries. The change we are speaking of is represented in the difference between conceiving of a problem as a *misfortune* and conceiving of it as a state of *injustice*. Man has been intensely aware of misfortune throughout recorded history. He has established many institutional procedures to soften the impact of misfortune. He has always recognized the sympathy due to those who suffer misfortune, and he has always held a high opinion of charitable activities directed toward the relief of many types of misfortune. But misfortune is not the same thing as injustice. Death and illness are misfortunes. We are deeply upset over the prospect of a young man dying of incurable cancer, but we do not conceive it as a deep injustice which provokes a sense of outrage against a system productive of such misfortunes.

The sense of misfortune and the sense of injustice can be distinguished by the difference between *petition* and *demand*. The victims of misfortune petition whoever has the power to help them for some kind of aid. The victims of injustice demand that their petitions be granted. The poor man appealing for alms is displaying his misfortune. The Poor People's March on Washington to demand correction of their situation expressed a sense of injustice.

Another way to indicate the distinction is by speaking of *charity* as compared with *what people have a right to expect*. The poor man asking for alms appeals to the good will of those who have the resources to do some-

"The Theme of Contemporary Social Movements" is reprinted from the *British Journal of Sociology*, Vol. XX, No. 4 (1969). Copyright 1969 by the London School of Economics and Political Science. Reprinted by permission of the publisher and the author.

thing for him. The poor who marched on Washington *demanded* what they claimed as their right. The labor movement of the 1930's answered Henry Ford's declaration that he already paid higher wages than his competitors by insisting that the principle be established that a favorable wage structure was theirs by right rather than because of an employer's generosity.

A significant social movement becomes possible when there is a revision in the manner in which a substantial group of people look at some misfortune, seeing it no longer as a misfortune warranting charitable consideration but as an injustice which is intolerable in society. A movement becomes possible when a group of people cease to petition the good will of others for relief of their misery and demand as their right that others ensure the correction of their condition.

INJUSTICE AND HISTORICAL ERAS

The second preliminary point is that major eras in history have differed in the dominant sense of injustice which underlay the major movements of the time and dictated the main direction of social change. Karl Mannheim has offered one cogent characterization of the sequence of major movements during modern times.[2] He proposes that there have been four major waves of movements beginning with chiliastic developments expressed most dramatically in the peasant revolts; continuing with the liberal humanitarian movements which found their fullest expression in the French and American revolutions; followed by a conservative movement; and culminating in the socialist movements which were not only found in international communism but gave the main coloring to the New Deal and the welfare state in the United States and Britain.[3]

In the analysis to follow we shall dwell primarily upon two of these, namely, the *liberal humanitarian* and the *socialist* movements. We believe that the chiliastic movement is a rather special case reflecting a preliminary stage of discontent, which is to some degree recapitulated at the beginning of each new era. It lacks the relatively clear image of the nature of reform to be brought about by the movement. We shall also disregard the so-called conservative movement, feeling that here Mannheim was misled in assigning to these reactions against the liberal humanitarian movement the prominence of a major group of movements in the reform of society. We shall speak of the era dominated by the liberal humanitarian movements giving way to the more recent era shaped by the socialist movements. We suggest that the power of both the liberal humanitarian and the socialist conceptions of injustice has been largely exhausted.[4] We shall seek to identify a 'utopia' or a new central theme which is capable of arousing the enthusiasm and focusing the energies of discontent in the era that is only now beginning to take shape.

Within each of these major eras there are one or two movements that color the preoccupations and the social change effected during the era. These are the movements that embody the main theme most completely. Many other movements are lesser expressions of the same goal, or movements seeking a more limited goal which is consistent with the principal movements. And there are also movements directed toward other problems that do not seem at first to be directly concerned with the era's central preoccupations. However, the emerging conception of injustice does color all other important themes in the same era. The main themes also persist from one era to the next so that major movements in the next era retain much of the language and much of the symbolism of the preceding era, but only insofar as they can be incorporated into and subordinated to the newly emerging conception of injustice.

Two features of these eras must be observed. First, the sequence may start later or proceed more slowly in some places than in others, while the essential development order persists. For example, if 1848 marks the emergence of the socialist utopia as a leading factor in European history, it is probably not until 1932 that socialist conceptions of justice became vital in the United States. Second, subsidiary issues—the troublesome side-problems in society from the point of view of the large population—are especially likely to continue to be viewed through the lens provided by the older sense of justice, at the same time that central problems are being viewed with the new perspective.

If we look at the two eras specifically in terms of the major new conception of injustice which dominated the movements, we see first that in the American and French revolutions people asserted the right to be ensured the opportunity to participate in ruling themselves. Such specifics as freedom of speech, freedom of assembly, freedom of the press, were all incident to and justified by insistence that people should no longer merely petition to be heard, but that institutional arrangements should be so revised as to ensure that all people could be heard and participate in governing themselves in some tangible and dependable way. It is characteristic that the fundamental injustice of denying some people a full voice in determining their own destiny was the touchstone which would supply solutions to all the other important problems of the era. Give people the right to vote and the freedom to speak, to read and write and discuss their respective interests, and the problems of poverty and other avoidable misfortunes would be well on the way to correction.

The socialist movements retain the symbolism of freedom and participation but subordinate them to a new sense of injustice. For the first time the fundamental right of people to demand that the essential material needs of life be provided for them was recognized. To the liberal humanitarians of the late eighteenth and early nineteenth centuries poverty was a misfortune and gross inequalities in material wealth and comfort might be regarded as unfortunate. But they were certainly not to be treated as injustices. The arguments of the New Deal era in American history incorporate the difference between the older liberal humanitarian philosophy and the newer socialist conception of fundamental injustice. The New Deal was essentially a victory, albeit a limited victory, for the view that freedom of the liberal humanitarian sort without an underpinning of material security is meaningless. The New Deal incorporated reforms reflecting the assumption that a society is obligated to provide for the material wants of its people, and that its people have a right to demand that these wants be met. The changed view of what is just and unjust is reflected in Franklin Roosevelt's Four Freedoms. By adding the *freedom from want* and the *freedom from fear*, Roosevelt departed drastically from the liberal humanitarian conception and acknowledged the right of people to demand that their society provide them with material needs.[5]

Different movements in both eras varied in the extent to which they demanded total equality or the provision of some kind of minimum for all. The more extreme movements in each era held that any condition other than complete equality of representation or complete equality of material comforts and possession was unjust. The more moderate views usually won out in both eras, holding only that society must guarantee every citizen a minimum opportunity to participate in determining his own destiny and that every society must provide each citizen with the minimum necessities for a decent living.

It is easy to see how the main conceptions of injustice shaped the objectives of secondary movements. Two of the major secondary movements in the liberal humanitarian era in American society were the movement for women's suffrage and the abolition movement. The abolition movement was dominated by the conviction that freeing the slaves and granting them the same minimum political participation that was ensured for all other people would resolve the injustice of slavery. There was no recognition that it might be necessary to go further. Anything further that would be done for the slaves would be in the nature of charity rather than provision of what they could claim by right. Similarly, the problems of woman's role in modern society were viewed as soluble through the provision of political equality with men. Once women were given the vote and granted the same rights to speak and read and write, the injustice of woman's position would have been corrected.

The post-depression era in the United States has been dominated by the socialist's conception of injustice and our approach to a variety of problems has been colored accordingly. Ever since the Second World War, one main approach to the problem of minority groups in our society has been to ensure the economic base for their existence. It is true that we have been involved in voter drives, and have been cleaning up the left-over business from the liberal humanitarian era in this respect. However, we have not been slow to recognize that the right to vote is not an end in itself, but merely a means, and we are not surprised that minority problems are not resolved merely by extending the franchise. Government commissions approaching the problem of urban riots consistently took the right of the population to demand provision for their minimum physical needs as the fundamental basis for recommendations regarding the prevention of rioting.

INJUSTICE IN THE CONTEMPORARY ERA

If we look at the contemporary era consisting of roughly the second half of the twentieth century, I think it has become quite clear that the liberal humanitarian ideology no longer has the vitality to rouse great populations to the active pursuit of reform or revolution. This is a discovery that seems to be coming last in our foreign policy. The contention that the socialist's conception of injustice, the demand for assurance of material wants or even for material equality is declining in its vitality, may be more difficult to substantiate. Nevertheless, a rather strong impression can be drawn from events in many spheres to suggest that as an accepted principle, the injustice of material want has become commonplace so that it draws ready assent without arousing excitement and enthusiasm for its implementation.

Neither aspect of the last observation should be overlooked. There is no contradiction in asserting that a principle that has become nearly consensual often fails to evoke enough enthusiasm to stimulate a drive toward alleviating the remaining injustices. The consensus is like that of many moral and religious doctrines, accepted as verbally unchallengeable truths that exercise declining influence over actual behavior after they cease to be a feature of intergroup conflict.

The new conception of injustice

It is the central thesis of this paper that a new revision is in the making and is increasingly giving direction to the disturbances of our era. This new conception is reflected in a new object for indignation. Today, for the first time in history, it is common to see violent indignation expressed over the fact that people lack a sense of personal worth—that they lack an inner peace of mind which comes from a sense of personal dignity or a clear sense of identity. It is not, of course, a new thing that people have wondered who they are, nor that people have wondered whether man and man's life are worthwhile. The Old Testament contains poetic complaints about the meaninglessness of life, and the insignificance of man. Although this concern has been before us for millennia, the phenomenon of a man crying out with indignation because his society has not supplied him with a sense of personal worth and identity is the distinctive new feature of our era. The idea that a man who does not feel worthy and who cannot find his proper place in life is to be pitied is an old one. The notion that he is indeed a victim of injustice is the new idea. The urgent demand that the institutions of our society be reformed, not primarily to grant man freedom of speech and thought, and not primarily to ensure him essential comforts, but to guarantee him a sense of personal worth is the new and recurrent theme in contemporary society.

Heretofore, the discovery of a purpose and a sense of worth in one's life was considered to be an individual problem. It was, of course, the concern of one's friends simply because any intimate is concerned with the well-being of a friend. But the idea that people have a right to demand that society provide them with a sense of personal worth still appears strange and incredible to most people. In the prevalent view, one who has not found his place in society, one who has no sense of personal worth, ought to conceal this deficiency from others, lest they think less of him for it. The picture of young people proclaiming to the world that they have not found themselves and expressing consequent indignation is simply incomprehensible in terms of traditional conceptions of justice.

These new views are perhaps most fully embodied in the doctrines of today's New Left. Well before the Vietnam war became the central preoccupation there were expressions of outrage against the depersonalizing and demoralizing effect of modern institutions, ranging from the family to the university and the state.

The main symbol of the new era is *alienation*. Here is a fine example of the way in which a term is borrowed from an earlier era but assigned new meaning. We know that the socialist movements borrowed the term democracy, but when we examine what they mean by a democratic government it is quite clear that it has little to do with the conception employed by the liberal humanitarians. Similarly, the concept of alienation is borrowed from Marx. It had original reference to the specific relationship of the laboring man to his work. In one way or another it meant simply that a man's work no longer mattered to him as it had in a handicraft era when he could take pride in his accomplishments, with various psychological overtones that made it more than simple job dissatisfaction. But the new meaning refers to a deeply psychological state. Man's alienation is now a divorcement of the individual from himself or the failure of the individual to find his real self, which he must employ as a base for organizing his life. Alienation has thus been transformed into the designation for a psychological or psychiatric condition which is quite different from the most important usage during the socialist era.

Each emergent conception of injustice has been associated with a major approach in philosophy. The philosophy provides the elaborated rationalization for the new sense of injustice and supplies the conceptual vehicles through which persons may reflect about the burning injustice which they must seek to correct. The liberal humanitarian era is clearly associated with rationalism in philosophy. The socialist era is associated with dialectical materialism and some of its more modern variations. American pragmatism might be considered a very watered down form, but one which clearly played a major part in setting the stage for the New Deal and the associated development of progressive education. The philosophy of the New Era is clearly *existentialism* in its many forms and variations. Existentialism focuses on the problem of man's alienation, on the problem of man's existence and the dilemma of his efforts to uncover a viable sense of self.[6]

In a sense each of these philosophies and each of these conceptions of injustice is focused in a different area of human concern. The liberal humanitarian movements with their rationalist philosophy focus in the realm of politics. The solutions to man's problems are to be found in the political sphere and the reforms that are sought are primarily reforms in political institutions. The socialist sense of injustice, with dialectical materialism, concentrates upon the economic sphere. It is, of course, necessary to work through the political system; but the main aim is to achieve total reform in the economic system. The doctrine of the withering away of the state epitomizes the subordination of politics to economics in this view. The contemporary preoccupation falls initially in the psychological and the psychiatric spheres. But insofar as these internal problems are externalized, the attention is turned upon the social order which encompasses and transcends the merely economic and the merely political. The preoccupation then is with the social psychological and the social psychiatric and increasingly the sociological realm.

The nature of the constituency

In each major era the fundamental circumstance that has made possible the development of a revised sense of justice has been the rise in power and general standing of some major class. None of the great movements has been the product of groups who were moving downward nor of groups in abject powerlessness, poverty, or despair. There is a theory about earthquakes which says that there is a slow but imperceptible movement deep beneath the ground which continues for a period of time without compensating adjustments at the surface. Eventually so great a tension is built up that there is a sudden slippage at the surface, along an established fault line, releasing the accumulated tension in the violence of an earthquake. The important feature of this theory is that the underlying change has already occurred unnoticed and that the earthquake is merely a corrective adjustment. This is an apt model to describe what happens in our major social movements. The liberal humanitarian movements were movements of the rising industrial and business classes. They had been growing in economic power and in wealth, but their resources could not be fully converted into commensurate power and social status because of the traditional power of landowning and aristocratic classes. The liberal humanitarian movements may be regarded, first and foremost, as the readjustment through which industrial and business classes were able to throw off the traditional power of the aristocracy and the landed gentry and to assume the station in society toward which national developments had been moving them. The specific way in which injustice was defined reflected the nature of impediments to realization of their full status by these rising classes. They already had the economic resources: all they needed was the freedom to capitalize on them. Hence, they had no occasion to think of economic deficiencies as a matter of injustice. The solution to their problem lay in undermining the monopoly of political power in the hands of the aristocracy. Hence, it appeared from their own perspective that the fundamental injustice in society was the failure to grant full participation by all the people in self-government. Of course "all the people" initially had a rather limited meaning and was likely to be restricted to substantial citizens. Once the idea caught hold it had its own career and was extended from one group to another. But the basic notion that this was the fundamental injustice arose out of the peculiar set of conditions which at that time were preventing the rising business and industrial classes from realizing their full status in society.

The socialist movements seem to have been associated with the rising status of working classes in the societies where they prevailed. The conditions of industrial life had in fact improved the position of the laboring man. But at the same time by making him an employee of large concerns that might lay him off whenever it suited their concerns, the system had created a fundamental insecurity about economic conditions which prohibited the worker from exploiting to the full the relative wealth which he was in fact experiencing. The fact that the idea once established was then extended to the impoverished does not change the observation with regard to the source of this kind of thinking.

If my interpretation of what is happening in contemporary society is correct, we are seeing a new type of entity in society as the constituency for the dominant movements of our era. In the two previous eras the constituencies have been largely socio-economic classes, though this has been by no means clear-cut and exclusive, especially in the case of socialist movements. In the contemporary era, however, the major readjustments which are being made in society no longer concern socio-economic classes but concern *age groups*. The most striking phenomenon of the last quarter-century has been the increasing authority and independence and recognition accorded the youthful generation. There has been a reduction of parental authority and of institutional adult authority over adolescents and young adults in all spheres of life. There has been increasingly earlier introduction of children and adolescents to the major problems of our time. The rapid changes in society have meant that the technical expertise of the young is often superior to that of the more mature. Having gained considerable power and autonomy and comfort, young people now demand that the system be changed so as to remove the last restrictions to their assumption of an appropriate condition in society. In Herbert Marcuse they find a prophet who seems to declare that they are most fitted to bring about the needed transformation in society.[7]

The problem of alienation and the sense of worth is most poignantly the problem of a youthful generation with unparalled freedom and capability but without an institutional structure in which this capability can be appropriately realized. Adolescence is peculiarly a 'non-person' status in life. And yet this is just the period in which the technical skills and the new freedom are being markedly increased. The sense of alienation is distinctively the sense of a person who realizes great expectations for himself yet must live in a non-status.

For the movement to effect pervasive change in the institutions of society the new sense of justice must make substantial inroads outside of the movement's constituency. For this to happen, the problem at issue must not appertain exclusively to one class or age group. Political participation and economic justice had wide relevance in the eighteenth and nineteenth centuries. Today alienation is understandable to other groups than youth. The new sense of injustice can become the leaven for vast social changes because adults, the elderly, minority groups, and other organizable segments of society can see many of their own problems in the terms set forth by youthful activists.

From chaos to focused movements

It is crucial to observe that the new movements have not yet discovered or formulated solutions to their problem. The liberal humanitarian movements formulated the solution to their problem as one of seeking political representation with related guarantees of freedom of speech, assembly, and press. The socialist movements defined their problem and identified the solution as either the dictatorship of the proletariat in the communist version or some form of welfare state in more moderate socialist versions. The contemporary movement is discovering the problem of alienation, is expressing indignation against society as the source of that alienation, but has not yet discovered or agreed upon a solution to the problem. . . .

REFERENCES

1. This statement represents an extension of the *emergent norm* approach to collective behavior, applied earlier to crowd behavior. Cf. "Collective Behavior" in R. E. L. Faris (ed.) *Handbook of Modern Sociology,* Chicago, Rand McNally, 1964, pp. 382–425.
2. Karl Mannheim, *Ideology and Utopia,* trans. Louis Wirth and Edward Shils, New York, Harcourt Brace Jovanovich, 1946.
3. See Norman Cohn, *The Pursuit of the Millennium.* 2nd ed. New York: Harper & Row, 1961; see also Eric C. Wolf, *Peasant Wars of the Twentieth Century.* New York: Harper & Row, 1969. [Editor's note.]
4. Daniel Bell's classical study, *The End of Ideology,* Glencoe, Ill., Free Press, 1960, documents the exhaustion of these traditional ideas as spurs to political action.
5. Roosevelt's Four Freedoms were freedom of speech and worship and freedom from want and fear. [Editor's note.]
6. Existentialism is a twentieth-century philosophy. The leading figures in this school of thought are Martin Heidegger, Karl Jaspers, Jean-Paul Sartre, and Albert Camus. [Editor's note.]
7. See Herbert Marcuse, *One-Dimensional Man: Studies in the Ideology of Advanced Industrial Society.* Boston: Beacon Press, 1964. [Editor's note.]

2: Two Approaches to Social Movements

Since the French Revolution, some observers have been concerned with the social conditions that give rise to social movements, while others have stressed the types of people who join social movements. A more succinct distinction would be between sociologists interested primarily in social structures and those interested in psychological factors. The structuralists see man fundamentally as the product of society and history. For them, institutions, customs, values, and events all determine the behavior of man. In contrast, social psychologists place greater emphasis on individual variability. According to this view, individual motives, both rational and irrational, play a significant role as determinants of social change. Social psychologists frequently probe the "motivation" of participants in a movement, while structuralists rarely do so. The two theoretical perspectives, however, are not totally at odds with one another but rather direct attention to different aspects of a social movement.

Structuralists pose a fundamental question: "What social factors cause a group of people to come together in a social movement?" The question is not as simple as it may seem. The Great Depression of the thirties affected almost every man, woman, and child in the United States, yet only a minute percentage of the population joined or formed a social movement. It is therefore difficult to say the Depression caused this or that social movement. Furthermore, women, blacks, and other groups have long held social positions inferior to those accorded to white males. Can we then say discrimination was a major component leading to the formation of the Black Panthers, the National Organization for Women (NOW), or the Gay Liberation Movement (GLM)? The sociologist must also account for the fact that only a very small number of people affected by injustice actually do something about it. Why, for example, is the percentage of women engaged in the liberation movement so small? Moreover, sociologists must account for the time in which a social movement arises. Why did "inequality" become so important an issue in the 1960s and not the 1950s?[1] These are complicated questions.

One approach to answering these questions has been the serial or sequential method. This method posits a developmental pattern for all social movements and thus focuses on historical processes.[2] More than a generation ago, C. A. Dawson and

[1] See Robert Ross and Graham L. Staines, "The Politics of Analyzing Social Problems," *Social Problems* 20 (Summer 1972): 18–40.
[2] Examples of the serial method can be found in Mayer N. Zald and Roberta Ash, "Social Movement Organizations: Growth, Decay and Change," *Social Forces* 44 (March 1966): 327–

W. E. Gettys presented five stages of development through which a movement must pass.[3] These were identified by Herbert Blumer as agitation, esprit de corps, morale, ideology, and operating tactics.[4] While useful for descriptive purposes, serial studies were without much theoretical or predictive significance. Little headway has been made since 1937 when Theodore Abel noted that "in order to make valid statements about a particular movement, an adequate **theory** of social movements is necessary. . . . As yet we have no such theory. In fact, only few attempts have been made at a typological analysis of movements."[5]

Neil Smelser, a student of Talcott Parsons, has provided a typological analysis. In his "Theoretical Issues of Scope and Probems," he applies the economic theorem of value-added increments to social movements. The term, "value-added" refers to the cumulative effect of necessary determinants in the development and behavior of a social movement. "The key element," according to Smelser, "is that the earlier stages must combine **according to a certain pattern** before the next stage can contribute its particular value to the finished product."[6] Smelser introduced five determinants that affect social movements:

1. **Structural conduciveness:** a necessary condition that permits a movement to be formed.
2. **Structural strains:** disruptive situations in social life that lead to social movements only when they occur within a context of structural conduciveness.
3. **Generalized belief:** a belief system (ideology) that interprets the disruptive situation and suggests solutions to the problems posed by it. **Precipitating factors,** which can be thought of as subordinate determinants, provide immediate confirmation for the generalized belief and also provide targets for indignation.
4. **Mobilization:** the process by which members of a movement are motivated to take specific actions in response to the precipitating factors.
5. **Social control:** the countermeasures taken by those in power to either repress a movement or disarm it through co-optation.

Smelser presents valuable material correlating specific social problems with movements, ideologies, and societal reaction. All these factors are important.[7] However, several critics have taken issue with Smelser, suggesting that his theory is so general it cannot be tested. Currie and Skolnick note that Smelser's lack of specific criteria must lead to considerable confusion for anyone attempting to employ his analysis of collective behavior.[8] Fred Thalheimer also asserts: "The general level at which all the determinants are phrased helps to make them applicable to the entire range of collective behavior but at the same time seriously limits their utility for prediction."[9]

41; Rex Hopper, "The Revolutionary Process," *Social Forces* 28 (March 1950): 270–79; and John Wilson, *Introduction to Social Movements* (New York: Basic Books, 1973).

3 Charles A. Dawson and William E. Gettys, *Introduction to Sociology*, rev. ed. (New York: Ronald Press, 1935).

4 See H. Blumer, "Social Movements," pp. 4–20. Other sociologists who have made serial studies are Theodore Abel, "The Pattern of a Successful Political Movement," *American Sociological Review* 2 (June 1937): 347–52; William Bruce Cameron, *Modern Social Movements* (New York: Random House, 1969); and C. Wendell King, *Social Movements in the United States* (New York: Random House, 1956).

5 Abel, *op. cit.*, p. 347.

6 Neil J. Smelser, *Theory of Collective Behavior* (New York: The Free Press, 1963).

7 Ralph Turner and Lewis Killian, *Collective Behavior*, 2nd ed. (Englewood Cliffs, N.J.: Prentice-Hall, 1973).

8 Elliot Currie and Jerome H. Skolnick, "A Critical Note on Conceptions of Collective Behavior," in *Collective Violence*, ed. James F. Short, Jr., and Marvin E. Wolfgang (Chicago: Aldine, 1972), p. 64.

9 Fred Thalheimer, "Some Observations on the Sociology of Social Movements." Paper read at the Pacific Sociological Association Meetings, April 1, 1967, at Long Beach, Calif. Mimeographed.

Despite various theoretical attempts to account for social movements, most discussions remain descriptive rather than analytical. Useful approaches have been developed by such scholars as Bendix, Gusfield, Lipset, Kornhauser, and Pinard, who have employed selected sociological concepts, such as class, status, and mass society to explain the rise of specific social movements.[10] In **Symbolic Crusade,** for example, Joseph R. Gusfield shows how the declining status of small town white Protestants led to the rise of the Prohibition movement. In addition, the decline of middle-class prestige has been used to account for the emergence of the Nazis in Germany as well as the Radical Right in America during the 1950s and 1960s.[11] In such studies, the work of social psychologists frequently complements the schemas developed by structuralists.

In distinction from the structuralists, social psychologists ask the basic question: "Why do people protest?" Moreover, why does a particular person or group join and participate in a social movement? Social psychologists, as Joseph F. Zygmunt suggests, are concerned with "identifying the psychological factors which render people susceptible to the appeals of movements and which motivate and sustain affiliation with them."[12] These concerns in turn can be reduced to three questions: (1) What types of people are attracted to social movements? (2) Why are they attracted? (3) What are the techniques of recruitment?

Inherent in the question of why people join movements is the notion that the joiners are among the malcontent and emotionally disturbed members of society. Some social psychological studies have presented this idea quite seriously.[13] The rise of the Third Reich in Germany, for example, furthered the notion that leaders and members of social movements are emotionally unstable. Writers such as Erich Fromm and Theodore Adorno asserted the Nazi movement appealed to people with "authoritarian" personality structures.[14] The authoritarian personality has frequently been presented since then as the foundation of Right-Wing and conservative politics.

Studies indicating that some people who joined radical movements were psychologically better adjusted than some outside of protest politics did little to counter the belief that radicals were emotionally unstable.[15] By contriving a portrait of the "true believer," Eric Hoffer, a popular writer of the fifties, helped disseminate the notion that there indeed was a "radical" personality type. According to Hoffer, social problems and their solutions were not important for the true believer, only movement participation was. Hoffer identified eleven categories of people who could become true believers, including "the poor," "misfits," "minorities," "youth," "the ambitious," and "sinners."[16] Very few contemporary social psychologists, however, now maintain that a specific personality type will support specific kinds of movements.

Explanations for the attractiveness of social movements are still somewhat speculative. It was long held that movement affiliation is related to an unconscious

10 See Gary B. Rush and R. Serge Denisoff, *Social and Political Movements* (New York: Appleton-Century-Crofts, 1970), pp. 37–102.

11 See Joseph R. Gusfield, *Symbolic Crusade* (Urbana, Ill.: University of Illinois Press, 1963); and Daniel Bell, *The Radical Right* (Garden City, N.Y.: Anchor Books, 1964).

12 An excellent summary of this approach is Stanley Milgram and Hans Toch, "Collective Behavior: Crowds and Social Movements," in *The Handbook of Social Psychology,* 2nd ed., vol. 4, ed. Gardner Lindzey and Elliot Aronson (Reading, Mass.: Addison-Wesley Publishing Co., 1969), pp. 584–610.

13 See Thelma H. McCormack, "The Motivation of Radicals," *American Journal of Sociology* 56 (July 1950): 17–24; and Christian Bay, "Political and Apolitical Students: Facts in Search of Theory," *Journal of Social Issues* 23 (July 1967): 76–91.

14 Erich Fromm, *Escape From Freedom* (New York: Holt, Rinehart and Winston, 1941); and Theodore Adorno, et. al., *The Authoritarian Personality* (New York: Harper and Bros., 1950).

15 Maurice Krout and Roger Stagner, "Personality Development in Radicals: A Comparative Study," *Sociometry* 2 (January 1939): 31–46; Kenneth Keniston, *The Uncommitted: Alienated Youth in American Society* (New York: Harcourt Brace Jovanovich, 1965); and *Young Radicals: Notes on Committed Youth* (New York: Harcourt Brace Jovanovich, 1968).

16 Eric Hoffer, *The True Believer* (New York: Mentor Books, 1951), p. 25.

need of the members.[17] This conception was later modified by Harold Lasswell and Hadley Cantril. Cantril and Lasswell argue that in periods of rapid social change discrepancies between individual norms and social values occur, creating individual discontent.[18] Individuals experiencing this state of unhappiness can either accept the transformations occurring around them or seek shelter with like-minded people. Cantril suggested that it is in the movement that the discontented individual finds understanding and support. The movement, therefore, becomes a source of need fulfillment. This means that like-minded people band together for support, solace, and political effectiveness. Cantril also recognized that the original purposes of a movement can be subverted because of its need fulfillment functions.[19]

Cantril's thesis, though, could not explain why individuals chose one social movement rather than another. In recent years Lawrence Kohlberg's "moral response" scale has become popular among social psychologists trying to deal with this question.[20] The Kohlberg scale assumes that individuals have certain levels of maturity and that this is reflected in their moral judgments. According to the scale, persons of low maturity will choose relatively simple, self-centered answers to problems, while more mature people will choose a moral imperative they feel is right regardless of the personal consequences. Kohlberg introduced a six-stage scale ranging from simple to complex that opposes internal individual gain to social value. When Norma Haan and her associates applied the moral reasoning scale to the Berkeley student protests, they found a strong correlation between activism and mature reasoning.[21] Follow-up studies seem to indicate that the reliance of student activists on "internal mechanisms," such as conscience, was greater than for nonparticipants. It was also found that individuals who chose external factors, such as "law and order," tended to be highly conservative.[22]

There are a number of objections to social psychological explanations of participation in social movements. Perhaps the most widely noted is the objection to the assumption of irrationality or maladjustment associated with personality types or need fulfillment. There is, however, ample evidence that irrationality is not a necessary ingredient of the personality structures of individuals attracted to social movements. For example, Keniston, Flacks, and Haan found that demonstrators in the student protests of the sixties could rationally explain their participation. Another objection is that social psychological explanations do not adequately account for the type of movement one is likely to join. As Edward Shils and others have indicated, the authoritarian personality can be found in Left-Wing movements as well as in Right-Wing ones. The question then remains, Why does an authoritarian personality type affiliate with one group rather than another? During the 1930s, for example, literally hundreds of groups formed on the Right and Left to cure the ills of the Great Depression just as during the 1960s, civil rights and antiwar groups and their ideological opposites abounded. In an attempt to deal with this difficult question social psychologists have examined the conversion process involved in motivating "susceptible" people to join specific social movements.

17 McCormack, *op. cit.*
18 Hadley Cantril, *The Psychology of Social Movements* (New York: John Wiley & Sons, 1941); and Harold Lasswell, *The Psychopathology of Politics* (Chicago: University of Chicago Press, 1930).
19 For further development of Cantril's thought, see Hans Toch, *The Social Psychology of Social Movements* (Indianapolis: Bobbs-Merrill, 1965), p. t.
20 See Lawrence Kohlberg, "Development of Moral Character and Moral Ideology," in *Review of Child Development Research*, vol. I, ed. M. L. Hoffman and L. W. Hoffman (New York: Russell Sage Foundation, 1964), pp. 383–431.
21 Norma Haan, "Activism as Moral Protest: Moral Judgment of Hypothetical Moral Dilemmas and an Actual Situation of Civil Disobedience," in *The Development of Moral Judgment and Action*, ed. L. Kohlberg and E. Turiel (New York: Holt, Rinehart and Winston, 1972).
22 See James Fishkin, Kenneth Keniston, and Catharine McKinnon, "Moral Reasoning and Political Ideology," *Journal of Personality and Social Psychology* 27 (July 1973): 109–19.

Early studies stressed the propaganda appeal of social movements.[23] The assumption underlying many of these studies, which was much discussed in the literature on collective behavior, was that the cunning of the agitator exploited such psychological factors as "emotional contagion" and "herd instinct."[24] Person-to-person appeals were somewhat different. Studies of individual members and their reasons for joining a specific movement seem to suggest that most decisions were made on the basis of familiarity and propinquity. That is, people joined a movement because their friends were already in it, thus providing easy accessibility, and the ideological position was already known and to some degree accepted. This formulation, while it evades the central issue, does have the virtue of explaining subtle ideological discriminations. For example, in the 1930s one could become a member of the Socialists, Communists, Trotskyites, and a number of other Left-Wing movements, all of which were oriented toward the same general political goals. A similar array of politically parallel organizations was available to the socially concerned student of the 1960s.

Examining scholarly treatments of the student protests of the 1960s, Jack Douglas provides an excellent example of the problems encountered in studying social movements. Douglas suggests that many observers of student protests were quite biased for or against the demonstrators. Furthermore, many social scientists labored under a priori, or preconceived, notions derived mainly from the psychological or structural approaches. Psychologists ignored the basic issues generating the dissent, while structuralists ignored the individual motivation of student activists.

In light of the analytical one-sidedness of both the structural and social psychological approaches to social movements, efforts have been made to wed the strengths of both.[25] Perhaps the most successful attempt was made by Egon Bittner, who examined both the structural aspects of movements and the "common sense" world of their membership.[26] He suggests that radical movements enjoy a unique relationship to the rest of society. This relationship imposes on the movement a number of problems that it must cope with in order to survive both internally and externally.

Bittner's formulation was supported in a study of the propaganda and tactics of the American Communist party.[27] The adherence to a radical definition of reality did fulfill the organizational needs of a movement. However, as these needs were satisfied, those outside of the Left were alienated. An example of this process was the adoption of rural folk songs by the Communist party as the ideal form of "proletarian," or worker's, music. The rural folk song nicely fit the Party's conception of "real" proletarian culture. But the urban proletariat at the time was involved with swing and jazz, preferred crooners like Bing Crosby and Frank Sinatra, and was generally unaware of folk songs. A union leader once told a group of Leftist folksingers: "What do we need these hillbillies for? We have work to do."[28]

Bittner presents an important question: "How does a social movement succeed while maintaining its deviant perspective?" The implications of this question are important in any consideration of both structural determinants and psychological variables.

---

23 See Leo Lowenthal and Norbert Guterman, *Prophets of Deceit: A Study of the Techniques of the American Agitator*, 2nd ed. (Palo Alto: Pacific Books, 1970).

24 See Charles W. Lomas, *The Agitator in American Society* (Englewood Cliffs, N.J.: Prentice Hall, 1968).

25 See Arthur G. Neal, "On the Transferability of Ideological Commitments." Mimeographed (Bowling Green, Ohio: Bowling Green State University, 1973).

26 Egon Bittner, "Radicalism and the Organization of Radical Movements," *American Sociological Review* 28 (December 1963): 928–40.

27 R. Serge Denisoff, *Great Day Coming: Folk Music and the American Left* (Urbana University of Illinois Press, 1971).

28 *Ibid.*

Theoretical Issues
of Scope
and Problems

NEIL J. SMELSER

In this paper I shall set down a few ideas that I consider central in the study of collective behavior and conflict, and indicate a few similarities and differences between my views on these subjects and the views of others. I shall organize my remarks around the following questions. (1) What are the defining characteristics of collective behavior? In addressing this question I shall simultaneously be talking about what I consider to be the scope of the field. (2) What are the central problems in this field? (3) What are the ways in which these problems can be most adequately handled? Here I shall outline the "value-added" approach to explaining collective outbursts and movements. (4) To conclude, I shall focus on social movements with political aims, and ask two questions: When is a movement likely to become revolutionary? When is a revolutionary movement likely to become violent? In discussing these final questions, I shall apply some of the variables of the value-added scheme, and introduce the subject of conflict explicitly.

THE DEFINING CHARACTERISTICS OF COLLECTIVE BEHAVIOR

The first question that has to be asked of any phenomenon under study is: By what criteria do we recognize an instance of this phenomenon? In seeking to define the identifying criteria for collective behavior, various scholars have come up with different answers. Perhaps the most common criteria have been psychological. Writers like LeBon and Freud[1] viewed crowds in terms of a certain type of mentality that grips the participants;

[1] Gustave LeBon, *The Crowd: A Study of the Popular Mind* (New York: Viking, 1960), Books I and II; Sigmund Freud, *Group Psychology and the Analysis of the Ego* (London: The Hogarth Press, 1955).

"Theoretical Issues of Scope and Problems" is reprinted from *The Sociological Quarterly*, Vol. 5, No. 1 (Spring, 1964). Copyright 1964 by the Publications Committee of the Midwest Sociological Society. Reprinted by permission of the publisher and the author.

more recently, Brown,[2] a social psychologist, identifies collective behavior in terms of how frequently group attention is polarized and how permanent is the participants' identification. Other investigators have tended to identify collective episodes in terms of a distinctive kind of communication or interaction—imitation, milling, social contagion, for example. Blumer[3] uses these criteria to set off some types of collective behavior from other kinds of behavior. While I agree that these phenomena frequently accompany collective episodes, I have chosen to identify and classify collective behavior on a different basis. I view collective behavior as purposive behavior, in which people are trying to reconstitute their social environment. (In this assertion, incidentally, I am in agreement with those many investigators who distinguish between structured, institutionalized behavior and spontaneous, undefined, creative behavior.) Furthermore, people in collective episodes are trying to reconstitute this environment on the basis of a certain type of belief, which I call a generalized belief. Generalized beliefs are very much like magical beliefs; the world is portrayed in terms of omnipotent forces, conspiracies, and extravagant promises, all of which are imminent. It is uninstitutionalized action taken in the name of such a belief that constitutes an episode of collective behavior. No one special motive or mentality (such as psychological regression), above and beyond this belief, necessarily characterizes the participants; no one special means of communicating this belief (e.g., circular reaction) necessarily operates. While individual motives, as well as patterns of communication and mobilization, influence the timing, content, and intensity of an episode, they are not its necessary defining characteristics.

Having selected these criteria of uninstitutionalized action to reconstitute some part of the social environment in the name of a generalized belief, I then ask: What are the relevant parts of the social environment that are reconstituted? Working within a theoretical framework evolved by Talcott Parsons and his associates, I identify the following central components of social action: (a) values, or general sources of legitimacy, (b) norms, or regulatory standards for interaction, (c) mobilization of individual motivation for organized action in roles and collectivities, and (d) situational facilities, or information skills, tools, and obstacles in the pursuit of concrete goals. Generalized attempts to reconstitute these components result in a classification of collective behavior including (a) the value-oriented movement, (b) the norm-oriented movement, (c) the hostile outburst, and (d) craze and panic, respectively. Such are the defining characteristics, the scope, and the internal divisions of the field of collective behavior as I envision it.

CENTRAL PROBLEMS IN THE FIELD

The questions raised so far have been definitional and classificatory. The central explanatory question for the sociologist is to account for variations

---

[2] Roger Brown, "Mass Phenomena," in Gardner Lindzey, ed. *Handbook of Social Psychology* (Cambridge, Mass.: Addison-Wesley, 1954), pp. 833–40.

[3] Herbert Blumer, "Collective Behavior," in Joseph B. Gittler, ed., *Sociology: Analysis of a Decade* (New York: Wiley, 1957), pp. 129–30.

in the occurrence of the different types of collective behavior. Why do they cluster in time and in certain parts of the social structure? This general question breaks down into several parts: What distinctive conditions give rise to generalized beliefs? Under what conditions are generalized beliefs translated into collective action? Once collective episodes appear, what conditions govern their spread, duration, and intensity? These questions take the collective episode itself as the primary object of analysis. This focus differs from that of some approaches, which take the individual participant (and especially his psychological state) as the primary unit of analysis; it also differs from other approaches, which focus on the internal processes of communication and mobilization of collective outbursts and movements. While these aspects play a role in the spread, duration, and intensity of collective episodes, I do not approach them nearly so much as subjects in themselves. Some of the apparent disagreements between others working in the field and myself no doubt stem from this initially different emphasis in posing questions.

VALUE-ADDED AS AN EXPLANATORY MODEL

These central questions in the field of collective behavior necessarily have complicated answers, because so many different kinds of determinants bear on the occurrence of these episodes. An intellectual apparatus is required to sort out and arrange these determinants, if we are to advance beyond eclectic identification of determinants from one individual case to another. The intellectual apparatus I have chosen to employ is the "value-added" approach; this approach is a way of ordering determinants in a scale from general to specific. Each determinant is seen as logically—though not necessarily temporally—prior to the next. Each determinant is seen as operating within the scope established by the prior, more general determinant. Each determinant is viewed as a necessary but not a sufficient condition for the occurrence of an episode of collective behavior; taken together the necessary conditions constitute the sufficient condition for its occurrence. Let me illustrate the several determinants of the value-added scheme with reference to financial panic.

The first necessary condition for the occurrence of panic is *structural conduciveness*. An example of structural conduciveness is the ability of actors to dispose of their resources rapidly at will. If property is closely tied to kinship and can be disposed of only on the death of the father, panic is ruled out as impossible; the property is locked into the social structure and cannot be moved unless the institutional framework is altered. If, on the other hand, free and rapid disposal is permitted—as it is in the stock exchange—panic becomes possible. The word "possible" must be stressed; mere structural conduciveness does not cause panics; it merely establishes a range of situations within which panic can occur and rules out other situations in which it cannot. As a determinant, therefore, structural conduciveness is not very specific.

The second determinant is some kind of *strain*. The most obvious kind of strain in the determination of financial panic is the threat of financial loss. The threat of financial loss alone, however, can give rise to many other kinds of behavior than panic (scapegoating, reform movements, etc.); consequently this strain must be seen as operating within the context of conduciveness. It is now possible to see the logic by which the several determinants are organized; each time a new determinant is introduced, it is seen as operating within the scope of the previous determinant, and an increasingly great number of alternative behaviors are ruled out. The process of determination becomes progressively more specific.

The third necessary condition involves the growth of a *generalized belief*, in which the threat is exaggerated and seen to be imminent. The result, in the case of panic, is a hysterical belief—a cognitive structuring of an uncertain threat into a definite prognostication of disaster. Various precipitating events (such as the closing of a bank) give focus to this belief and provide "evidence" that the terrible threat is at work.

The fourth necessary condition is to *mobilize* people for action in the name of the generalized belief. In the case of the panic this may be realized by a single dramatic event, such as a rumor of a "panic sell" by a leading holder of securities. In more complicated social movements leadership may be more deliberate and highly organized.

Finally, it is necessary to mention *social control* as a determinant. In its more general sense, social control refers to the activation of counterdeterminants for the conditions just listed. It is helpful, however, to distinguish between counterdeterminants of a preventive sort (dealing with conduciveness and strain) and counterdeterminants which appear only when the collective episode has made its appearance. In the case of panic, social control is effected, for instance, by spiking scare rumors or by actually preventing potential sellers from selling. This last measure is sometimes employed by governments attempting to stop an international flight of capital.

The value-added approach, in sum, is a logical patterning of determinants, each seen as contributing its "value" to the explanation of the episode. One moral that emerges from utilizing this model is that in studying collective behavior it is of limited value to attempt to find correlations between one type of determinant (e.g., threatened financial loss) and one type of collective outburst (e.g., panic). Threatened financial loss gives rise to other things than panic, and panic requires many more determinants than the threat of financial loss. Only if such correlations are observed within the scope of other more general determinants do they become meaningful.

THE GROWTH OF REVOLUTIONARY MOVEMENTS

To conclude, I shall sketch a process by which social movements become oriented to values (and thus become a potential "cause" in the name of which an ideological revolution may be perpetrated); and how, once this value-orientation has risen, revolutionary violence erupts. Though it would be possible to document my remarks extensively from the major ideological revolutions of the West, as well as many of the nationalistic revolutions of the underdeveloped areas of the world, I shall have to hold empirical illustration to a minimum.

The type of strain that can potentially give rise to revolutionary sentiment is so varied as to be bewildering. If an investigator is interested in establishing a relation between a type of strain (e.g., status disequilibrium) and revolutionary movements, he will be able to illustrate his case extensively in the historical record, but he will also be able to find an endless number of other types of strain in the background of these movements. In order to determine whether institutional strains will work their way into a value-oriented ideology or some other form of protest, we must turn to the variable of structural conduciveness.

The rise of many value-oriented ideologies in the colonial countries during the first half of the twentieth century was preceded by a period of the colonial powers' "closing the door" on various kinds of protest against colonial domination. The colonial powers were relatively successful in "pacifying" the colonies, i.e., ruling out hostile outbursts, and they were relatively unresponsive to modest kinds of institutional reform demanded by the colonials. (The British provide an exception to this generalization in some of their colonies, e.g., Ceylon.) The history of many colonies before nationalism is one of "reminding" the colonials, sometimes with force, that the colonial powers were both effective in imposing their will and inflexible in the face of demands for reform. It was in this context of closing off other alternatives—combined with a multiplicity of strains—that various nativistic and other value-oriented forerunners of aggressive nationalism made their appearance in the colonies.

The appearance of a value-oriented ideology, however, does not necessarily lead to an aggressive revolutionary outburst. Indeed, some of the colonial value-oriented movements experienced a long existence either as underground groups harried by colonial authorities or as bizarre cults of withdrawal (the growth of the Peyote religion among the permanently repressed American Indians is perhaps the most striking example of the latter). The subsequent career of these value-oriented ideologies depends above all on the behavior of agencies of social control. If authorities continue to be effective in crushing opposition, unresponsive to demands, and repressive of expressions of value-oriented sentiments, the movement tends to drift toward the cult form. If, however, the agencies of control suddenly lose their effectiveness, the movement turns in a revolutionary direction. It is not so much the nature of the ideology of the movement as the behavior of the authorities that determines this change of direction. The ineffectiveness of the authorities may take many forms—division among the ruling classes themselves, weakening through military defeat (the British and Dutch defeats at the hands of the Japanese in World War II are examples), or the fraternization or defection of the rulers' military forces. In sum, then, we call upon separate sets of determinants to account for the rise of a value-oriented ideology and its expression in revolutionary form. The rise of the generalized value-oriented belief is accounted for mainly by a specific combination of strain and conduciveness, whereas its translation into action depends above all on the behavior of the agencies of social control.

Movements and Motives: Some Unresolved Issues in the Psychology of Social Movements

JOSEPH F. ZYGMUNT

Of the several lines of endeavor to clarify the nature and functions of social movements, various styles of motivational analysis have been pursued with special vigor and have achieved considerable currency among students in the field.[1] Typically, motivational analysis has aimed at identifying the psychological factors which render people susceptible to the appeals of movements and which motivate and sustain affiliation with them. While this approach has been pursued most avidly by psychologists, it has by no means been confined to them. Sociologists, historians, political scientists, and others have often ventured interpretations which are basically 'motivational' in emphasis (cf. Tilly, 1963–64). In some instances they have borrowed their motivational concepts from psychological theory, in others they have drawn upon the common sense vocabularies of motives extant in their own society and, occasionally, have attempted to make more or less 'original' motivational assessments.

Motivational interpretations have varied considerably in theoretical scope. Some have been movement-specific, venturing assessments of particular historical instances, such as the Nazi or the Communist movements (Almond, 1954; Fromm, 1941; Gilbert, 1950; Krugman, 1953; MacRae, 1951; Reich, 1946). Others have taken the form of 'middle-range' theories, covering a more general class of movements, such as revolutionary, millenarian, or youth movements (Aberle, 1962; Cohn, 1957; Davies, 1962; Feuer, 1969; Keniston, 1965; Lowenthal & Guterman, 1949). A few attempts have been made to develop even more inclusive theories, intended to supply frame-

[1] Representative instances would include: Cantril (1941), Flugel (1945), Fromm (1941), Hoffer (1951), Krugman (1953), Lasswell (1930), Toch (1965). Additional examples are cited below.

works for interpreting movements of a variety of types (Cantril, 1941; Flugel, 1945; Hoffer, 1951; Toch, 1965; Wallace, 1956b).

As a general approach to the study of social movements, the motivational type of analysis may be distinguished particularly from two others currently in use: the structural-functional and the interactional. Structural-functional theorists have focused mainly upon the structural conditions within social systems as such, which are conducive to the emergence of movements, treating these in terms of such sociological concepts as 'structural strain,' 'societal disequilibrium,' 'cultural malintegration,' and the like. In this perspective, movements would be seen as explicitly collective, and sometimes concerted, endeavors to restore equilibrium within the system through some kind of reconstitution of social values and/or norms (Gusfield, 1963; Heberle, 1951; Johnson, 1966; Parsons, 1954; Selznick, 1951; Smelser, 1963; Wallace, 1956). Interactional theorists, while generally taking some condition of socio-cultural disorganization as their point of departure, would give more explicit attention to the collective interactional processes through which movements arise, develop, maintain themselves, and change (Blumer, 1946, 1957; Lang & Lang, 1961; Lofland, 1966; Turner & Killian, 1957).

The relevance of considering psychological variables in analyzing social movements would generally be acknowledged by proponents of the latter two approaches. The major issues which continue to divide such theorists from the more vigorous champions of the motivational approach, and to some extent from one another as well, pertain to the manner in which such variables are to be conceptualized and especially the specific functions to be assigned to them in the genesis and sustenance of movements (cf. Inkeles, 1959; Johnson, 1966; Smelser, 1963). Accusations of 'psychological reductionism' may still be heard on the one side, countered by allegations of 'abstract sociologism' on the other. The broader and more fundamental dispute really concerns the future form and direction which a social psychology of movements is to take.

While motivational analyses of social movements are often appended as supplements to other levels of theoretical interpretation, they are sometimes offered as more discerning substitutes of allegedly superior explanatory power. Abstract delineations of 'objective' socio-cultural arrangements, it would be argued, do not adequately define the psychological worlds in which 'real people' live and act. Nor do derangements in such abstractly conceived 'systems' represent sufficiently definitive specifications of the experiential and motivational preconditions of movement support (cf. Toch, 1965, pp. 7–10). Advocates of the motivational approach have often contended that other levels of interpretation bypass some of the most fundamental questions in the social movements area—in particular, how or why, under a given set of objective conditions, some people are attracted to a movement while others are not. Joiners must differ from non-joiners in some discernible ways. Given a predilection for explaining behavioral differences in terms of differences in motivational predisposition, a sanguine attitude toward the motivational assessment of joiners becomes quite understandable.[2]

---

[2] It needs to be noted in this connection that the use of non-joiners as control groups to check on motivational generalizations has been quite rare (see Krout & Stagner, 1939).

The purpose of this paper, however, is not to review the ongoing quarrels among psychologists, sociologists, and others concerning the relative merits of their respective approaches to social movements. The usefulness, and indeed the indispensability, of explicitly sociological interpretations and of alternative social-psychological analyses are here assumed to have been demonstrated. It is, however, also conceded that some lines of motivational analysis may illuminate some aspects of the life of movements which other approaches leave in the dark. The major intent of the discussion which follows is to try to appraise the realism of the motivational approach as it is commonly applied in this field and to suggest some ways in which its proponents might sharpen and extend their inquiries to maximize their theoretical yield. The present paper is furthermore concerned mainly with some of the more important theoretical questions raised by certain types of motivational analysis. The methodological adequacy of specific pieces of research undertaken in this tradition deserves more attention than is possible here.[3]

THE MOTIVATIONAL MODEL OF ANALYSIS

Although there is no inherent reason why motivational analysis should be limited to the general question of why people *join* social movements, this has, in fact, tended to be its central concern. The approach, in other words, has focussed the bulk of its attention on the recruitment problem. Generally starting with movements which have already been launched, most of the theoretical writing and research in this tradition have been concerned with movement growth or diffusion, rather than movement origin.[4]

While styles of motivational analysis have varied greatly, they have generally taken the form of attempts to establish psycho-functional connections between the properties of social movements (usually construed as 'appeals'), on the one hand, and the social-psychological characteristics of potential or actual recruits (generally construed as motivational predispositions), on the other. These connections have been commonly treated in terms of some variant of the idea of functional complementarity and elaborated in various theories of 'conversion susceptibility' or movement 'attraction.' The dominant imagery has been essentially 'psycho-economic,' depicting a situation of psychological 'supply and demand.' The 'demand' side of the psychological equation would be represented by the personality structure, with its 'needs,' 'drives,' and other motivational predispositions; and the 'supply' side,

[3] For a more detailed discussion of some of the methodological problems involved in motivational assessment of movements, see Almond (1954), Gundlach & Riess (1954), Heberle (1951), Krugman (1953, 1954), Toch (1965). For some additional cautions regarding motivational assessment in general, see Burke (1936, 1945, 1950), MacIver (1940), Mills (1940).

[4] Illustrative of a broader concern with 'origins' as well as 'diffusion' would be Wallace's (1956) analysis of 'revitalization movements' and Gilbert's (1950) analysis of the Nazi movement. Since some motivational theorists seem to believe that, in dealing with the diffusion or recruitment problem, they are also clarifying the problem of origins, Bittner's caution deserves notice: '. . . the discovery of discriminable types or classes of persons who are appropriately motivated to accept some pattern of belief as true and some pattern of conduct that accords with this belief as right, does not yet constitute an adequate explanation for the existence of these patterns in the first place' (Bittner, 1963, pp. 928–929; cf. Smelser, 1963).

by the movement itself, with its promises and opportunities for need-gratification, tension-reduction, catharsis, predispositional expression, etc. Motivational theorists have tended to emphasize the functional importance of various states of psychic disequilibrium in rendering people susceptible to the influence of movements. Complementing this emphasis has been a correlative stress upon the psychologically expressive and re-equilibrating functions of movements themselves—their appeal to individuals on the basis of the opportunities they afford for restoring psychological equilibrium by compensating for frustrations, helping to resolve personal conflicts, etc.

The establishment of such psycho-functional relationships between personal motives and movement traits is generally the terminal point of motivational analysis and is often assumed to provide the definitive and complete answer to the recruitment problem. Since social movements seem to arise and develop through the accretion of converts, it is often further assumed that the answer to the original question, 'Why do people join?,' provides the major key to the life of movements.

There have been significant variations in the relative weight assigned to historical, situational, and characterological factors in rendering people susceptible to the influence of movements. Illustrative of a strong historical emphasis would be Erich Fromm's (1941) endeavor to identify the factors shaping predispositions toward affiliation with movements of an authoritarian type. Hadley Cantril's (1941) and Hans Toch's (1965) theoretical formulations would exemplify a more social-situational accent. Such psychoanalytically oriented theorists like Dicks (1950), Jones (1941), Flugel (1945), Krugman (1952, 1953), Lasswell (1930) and Rinaldo (1921) illustrate the tendency to lay stress upon deeply rooted, mainly unconscious, characterological factors.[5] Some scholars, like Gabriel Almond (1954), have followed a more eclectic approach which considers all three classes of factor.

One of the points of lingering contention among motivational theorists concerns the generality or specificity of predispositions to join movements. The 'generalists' have argued in favor of the 'interchangeability' or psycho-functional equivalence of movements, taking the position that an essential feature of conversion susceptibility is its diffuse character. The predisposition to join is regarded not as movement-specific but rather as in the nature of a generalized need for reorientation and an openness to new influences which may be supplied by a variety of alternative movements. Thus, for example, Hoffer (1951, p. 25) has argued that "when people are ripe for a mass movement, they are usually ripe for any effective movement, and not solely for one with a particular doctrine or program." This is also implicitly the position taken by those theorists who have conceived of these predispositions in terms of such traits as 'radicalism,' 'authoritarianism' and the like (Flugel, 1945; Adorno et al. 1950).[6] On the other hand, some theorists,

---

[5] Psychoanalytically derived formulations vary considerably in the extent to which they explicitly consider the role of social processes and cultural contexts in structuring predispositions and in conditioning their linkage with movements. The observations of Gilbert (1950) on the Nazi movement illustrate an attempt to situate psychoanalytic interpretations within such broader frames.

[6] On the other hand, one of the criticisms of the famous 'Authoritarian Personality' study has been that the researchers conceived of their personality type too narrowly, restricting their attention to authoritarian ideologies of a politically conservative sort

while conceding that movement susceptibilities may have a degree of dif-fuseness, would go on to observe that these generalized predispositions operate within certain limits, defined partly by other personal attributes and partly by situational factors. Arguing that what needs to be explained is why a given person joins a particular movement, they would be disposed to urge focussing simultaneously upon general predispositions and upon chan-nelizing traits and conditions.[7]

SOME STANDARDS OF EVALUATION

In seeking to appraise the theoretical adequacy of motivational inter-pretation, we might begin with a brief statement of what our current knowl-edge of social movements suggests ought to be included, as a bare minimum, in any acceptable analysis of the recruitment process. With this set of mini-mal requirements in view, we can evaluate the extent to which motivational theorists have actually met them in their analyses.

To be of most use, motivational analysis must first be grounded in a realistic conception of social movements. Such a conception ought to in-clude an explicit recognition of several generic movement-properties, whose implications for motivational interpretation may not be immediately ap-parent but which nevertheless have important bearings on how the recruit-ment process is likely to be approached (Blumer, 1946; Heberle, 1951; King, 1956; Lang & Lang, 1961; Smelser, 1963; Turner & Killian, 1957).

1. Social movements originate within concrete historical contexts and are conditioned in their development by the socio-cultural systems within which they seek to operate.
2. Social movements tend to flourish under conditions of social disor-ganization. Such conditions are likely to be accompanied by, or to produce, some degree of psychological disturbance within individuals and groups in the form of alienation, disorientation, deranged motiva-tions, etc.
3. Social movements have a set of distinctly collective dimensions. Al-though they vary greatly in degree of coordination, they have inter-individual, relational, and interactional properties which cannot be reduced to purely intra-individual terms.
4. If they are to endure and operate effectively, social movements are obliged to develop organizational provisions for meeting their own functional requirements as collective enterprises. These would gener-ally include some kind of organizational structure and symbolic system designed to coordinate their operations and to maintain the continuity of their endeavor.
5. Social movements are change-seeking enterprises. While showing con-siderable diversity in both the explicitness and the content of their

and overlooking the fact that there is also an 'authoritarianism of the left.' See Shils (1954). For a critical review of the early literature on the psychological correlates of 'radicalism' as a personality trait, see McCormack (1951).
[7] For a fuller discussion of the generality-specificity issue, see Hoffer (1951, pp. 25–29), Lang & Lang (1961, pp. 257–289), Lofland (1965), Toch (1965), Weiss (1963).

goal-structures, they typically seek, in however groping a fashion, to bring about modifications in prevailing institutions, practices, or views.

6. Social movements live and operate in the dimension of time and are, themselves, subject to transformations in their ideological and structural designs, as well as in their relations to the broader society.

Proponents of the motivational approach have not always given these several dimensions the recognition they deserve. In this respect, their working concepts of social movements have ranged from barely adequate to clearly inadequate.

More specifically, a realistic analysis of the recruitment process must further include, or be grounded in, an adequate theory of: (1) alienation, (2) attraction, (3) conversion and (4) membership management, with special attention to the problems of fortification and control. Schemes of motivational interpretation have not given equally satisfactory attention to these several processes or, more reprehensibly, have often simply assumed that in concerning themselves with one, they were providing an adequate treatment of the others. Our knowledge of the dynamics of recruitment, however, suggests that, while these several processes overlap and condition one another, they are not quite the same in their elements or their dynamics, making it necessary to give all of them due consideration.

Alienation

If it be true that a crucial aspect of an individual's continued support of prevailing institutional arrangements is his socially mediated relatedness to them, then it would seem to follow that a comparably crucial aspect of his questioning and challenging them is some derangement in these mediating relations. While the degree, scope, and qualitative character of prior alienation may be expected to vary from individual to individual, it would seem fruitful to hypothesize that a background of alienation is an important common denominator of all potential recruits. This suggests that the student of motivation working in the social movements field must have at his disposal some more or less adequate theory of alienation.

Indeed, such a theory would seem to be the logical starting point for any attempt to deal with susceptibility to movement influence. Affiliation with a social movement usually means identification with a collective enterprise which challenges some aspect(s) of the institutional *status quo*. By definition, a social movement is negatively disposed toward the prevailing sociocultural system to some degree. It enunciates new views, values, or norms and competes with existing institutions and groupings for attention, faith, and loyalty. Its recruitment of adherents is significantly contingent upon the weakening of attachments at least to those arrangements which it is trying to change. The processes through which institutional and group ties are attenuated, deranged, or broken are, therefore, of quite direct concern to the student of movements.

Most of the investigators who have tried to deal with the problem of recruitment in motivational terms have, in fact, recognized alienation in some form as an important facet of conversion susceptibility. The predominantly 'negative' character of most of the motivational profiles of movement recruits brings this out quite clearly. Potential recruits are variously described as 'anomic,' 'estranged,' 'neurotic,' 'discontented,' 'disoriented,' 'frustrated,' 'anxiety-ridden,' 'self-rejecting,' in a state of 'stress,' 'malaise,' 'relative depri- vation,' 'identity-diffusion,' 'internal conflict,' 'powerlessness,' 'meaningless- ness,' 'normlessness,' etc. While, perhaps, most of these characteristics might be regarded as symptoms of alienation, the selective focus on one or a few of them in many theories of susceptibility has led to rather incomplete appreciation of the nature and role of alienation as a predisposing factor in movement attraction. The clearest examples are to be found in those theories of susceptibility which have been phrased more or less exclusively in terms of individual psychopathologies, such as neurotic character distortions, psychopathic states, and psychotic tendencies. While such psychopatho- logical manifestations of alienation certainly deserve recognition, a theory of susceptibility that is limited to them can hardly do justice to the broader range of alienative phenomena which seem to be involved in movement formation and growth.[8]

It is not our purpose here to try to adjudicate among the conflicting con- ceptions of alienation implicit in various theories of movement susceptibility. Nor can we undertake to present a fully worked-out alternative conception of alienation which might be more realistic in dealing with the recruitment problem.[9] We merely wish to make the general observation that the theories of alienation implicit in motivational assessments of movements have been of variable adequacy and to point out a few of their shortcomings. Among the major weaknesses have been: (1) oversimplified views of alienation as a process, (2) a common failure to appreciate its broader socio-cultural di- mensions and its social-interactional character, and (3) a frequent disregard of the active role of movements themselves in generating, sustaining, and intensifying it.

The process which motivational theorists have most often indicated as the key agency, estranging individuals from the socio-cultural establishment and predisposing them to the appeals of movements, has been the frustra- tion of basic needs or socially-derived drives. There is a common tendency to equate such frustration with alienation or to regard the latter as the more or less automatic resultant of the former (cf. Maier, 1942). It seems clear, however, that alienation, far from being simply reducible to frustra- tion, may condition it to an important degree. While frustration certainly deserves to be included in any analysis of alienation, the relationships be- tween these two processes appear to be considerably more complicated than is usually recognized. Facile invocations of the psychoanalytic formula of 'frustration-hostility-displacement-alienation' have unfortunately discouraged the search for intervening variables that might clarify these relationships more fully.[10]

---

[8] For a more extended discussion of the role of psychopathology in social movements, see Gilbert (1950), Heberle (1951).

[9] The growing theoretical and research literature on alienation *per se* contains many use- ful suggestions along this line (see, e.g., Clark, 1959; Kornhauser, 1959; Merton, 1957; Papenheim, 1959; Seeman, 1959; Selznick, 1951).

[10] The attempts which have been made to refine the concept of 'frustration' through

Another important failure has been the relative neglect of the interaction of disaffected individuals as a factor in the development of alienative predispositions. Although individuation and social estrangement are often accompaniments of alienation, these processes cannot be treated adequately in purely intra-individual terms. Nor can they be realistically considered simply in relation to such restricted social contexts as those represented by family circles. A broader view is clearly required, recognizing the society-wide scope and character of the process and the involvement of more embracing categories and groups within it. While individuals are obviously involved, the major "units" of alienation would typically seem to be such broader collectivities as social classes, generations, ethnic groups, interest groups, etc. Not only must the collective dimensions of alienation be recognized in this sense, but its essentially interactional nature must also be appreciated. In this respect, individuals must be seen as becoming 'alienated together.'

In this connection, one of our starting premises might be recalled: movements tend to arise and flourish under conditions of social discoordination and cultural malintegration—a fact which has considerable social-psychological significance. Its relevance for motivational assessments, though not always fully acknowledged, should be clear. Motivational patterns become deranged under such conditions. Not only are new individual and collective currents of motivation likely to be activated, but the very character of motivational dynamics may be altered. People are thrust quite literally into motivational quandaries. In their unstable conditions, they may be prone to make novel and sometimes bizarre linkages between their predicaments and proposed 'solutions' (cf. Leighton, 1949). Periods of chaos are likely to be periods of motivational fluidity and unpredictability. This *fluidity* of motives, rather than their structure, may indeed be the more relevant aspect to consider when looking for motivational sources of movement support.

As might be expected, sociologists and sociologically oriented social psychologists have observed these cautions rather more fully than have psychologists. Sociologically-grounded motivational assessments, whether conjectural or empirical, are more likely to be structurally framed and culturally situated. Motives prompting movement affiliation are more commonly traced to societal stress and treated in terms of group derangements, status inconsistencies, role strains, and the like. Yet the need for a fuller and clearer specification of the connections between 'societal disequilibrium' and alienation continues to be as pressing here as in other quarters.

A related omission has been failure to consider the role of movements themselves as alienating agencies and not merely as vehicles through which already existing alienation may be expressed and remedied. More specifically, many motivational analyses have given insufficient attention to a movement's agitational endeavor as an unrest-producing and unrest-defining medium. It seems abundantly clear, however, that agitation must be seen not only as tapping predeveloped disaffections but also as creating them, in-

---

the development of the auxiliary concept of 'relative deprivation' would seem to be promising. Their potential usefulness and some of the analytical directions in which they might be carried are illustrated in Davies' (1962) work on revolutionary movements and Aberle's (1962) on millenarian movements.

tensifying them and, especially, giving them more specific forms and targets (Blumer, 1946, 1957; Lang & Lang, 1961; Turner & Killian, 1957; Lowenthal & Guterman, 1949). Pre-existing estrangements are certainly important factors in the probable success of agitational endeavor itself. The point is that the 'alienative' part of recruitment susceptibility must be treated in emergent and interactional terms, not merely as a prestructured disposition.

It would seem necessary to recognize further that alienation may function, not only as an antecedent and intervening variable, but also as a post-affiliation variable. Membership in some movements, particularly those which have come to be defined negatively by a society, may have widespread negative repercussions for a recruit's relations with non-members, along the line of estrangements, rebuffs, conflicts, and the like. Such alienating consequences deserve recognition since they may either make continued adherence to a movement problematic or accelerate and deepen the recruit's attachment to it.

Attraction

Although a background of alienation would seem to constitute a significant aspect of susceptibility to movement affiliation, it is in the nature of a necessary, but not sufficient, condition for actual involvement. Alienation may be expressed or coped with in alternative ways. Persons who share an alienated disposition may remain uninvolved in any movement or may gravitate toward different types of movement. A satisfactory theory of recruitment must make some provisions for bridging such possible discontinuities. Some theory of 'attraction,' as distinct from 'alienation,' is therefore also required. Motivational interpretations of movements, irrespective of analytical style, generally include some theory along this line, and indeed assign to it a central place. It is in this core area, however, that some of the most serious issues and problems arise.

The problem of 'attraction' is obviously a relational one, calling for some explanation of how individuals come within the social-psychological orbit of a movement's influence and respond positively by choosing to remain within it. As indicated above, while motivational solutions to this problem have varied in their particulars, most of them have taken the form of attempts to establish psycho-functional linkages between individual predispositions and movement traits, generally spelled out in some kind of theory of movement 'appeal.' The concept of 'appeal' is really a psychologically 'conjunctive' concept, in the sense that it refers to a movement's properties as perceived and responded to positively by a potential recruit. The key proposition here would be that movement characteristics become 'appeals,' not merely because they exert direct influence upon the people who are exposed to them, but rather because individuals are motivationally predisposed to perceive, evaluate, and respond to them selectively. Analyses of movement appeals have, in one way or another, sought to identify such psychological conjunctions between individual needs and a movement's perceived promises of satisfying them.[11]

[11] Toch (1965, p. 17) regards this as the 'crux of the social psychology of social movements.'

The actual analytic operations, through which such conjunctions are established, have not always fulfilled the methodological requirements which seem to be called for by this line of theoretical reasoning. Quite frequently, for example, attempts are made to infer the appeals of a movement directly from some of its characteristics, generally its ideological pronouncements, with the aid of some abstract psychological theory but with little or no empirical inquiry into how recruits themselves perceive and define these characteristics (Lowenthal & Guterman, 1949; MacRae, 1951; Brown, 1943). In this sort of deductive operation, the interpreter's assumptions about basic human motives would be tacitly introduced as major, but untested, premises. 'Appeals' derived in this manner, of course, would remain hypothetical unless verified by data relating to actual recruits. If any supporting data are presented, these often consist of a few selectively drawn and selectively interpreted cases which, at best, illustrate rather than test the interpretation. The cases selected, furthermore, are often not those of individuals who are in the process of being attracted to the movement but rather of recruits who have already undergone the fuller process of indoctrination, and even occasionally those who have defected from the movement. Cases of this sort, of course, pose the rather difficult problem of disentangling the psychological products of participation in the movement from predispositions to participate in it.

Supporting data often take the alternative form of some kind of supplementary observations about the social categories or groups among whom the movement is trying to make, or is known to have made, headway—e.g., youth, women, minority group members, or a particular social class. The social, economic, or political situations of such people, especially the problematical aspects of their status, are translated into psychological terms, an attempt being made to infer the outstanding patterns of needs, wants, discontents, and anxieties which presumably define their susceptibilities.[12] Such generalized predispositional profiles are then juxtaposed to the characteristics of the movement and an attempt is made to establish relationships of congruence or complementarity between the two. Although sometimes executed with considerable sensitivity and insight, such lines of supplementary analysis still provide, at best, conjectural bases for a theory of attraction. Perhaps their major point of vulnerability is that the important step of translating social predicaments into psychological predispositions may still suffer from the intrusion of untested motivational assumptions.[13]

The 'appeals' approach to the problem of attraction has been attended by several other questionable tendencies. In some quarters it has encouraged a style of analysis which not only fails to do justice to the properties of move-

---

[12] See, e.g., Hoffer's (1951) profiles of potential converts and also Riezler's (1943) typology of revolutionary supporters.

[13] Some of the research done on right-wing movements illustrates the hazards of drawing psychological inferences about recruits directly from ideology. Wolfinger's (1964) study of the supporters of the Christian Anti-Communist Crusade, for instance, revealed them to be quite heterogeneous with respect to their socio-political attitudes. He challenges the common assumption 'that supporters of the radical right have a consistent set of attitudes far outside the normal political system' and warns that 'attempting to deduce their attitudes from radical-right ideology would be no more valid than would deducing the opinions of a group of Republicans from the Republican platform' (pp. 274–275).

ments but comes close to being a kind of 'psychological debunking' of them. There is, for instance, the rather common tendency, especially among those who follow psychoanalytic theory, to treat the ideological appeals of a movement in a reductive manner. Writers showing this inclination might regard the ideological presentations of a movement suspiciously as 'motivational cryptograms' whose 'secret psychological codes' have to be broken. The avowed aims of the movement may thus be discounted as disguises deliberately or unconsciously adopted by the leaders and adherents of a movement to satisfy 'deeper' needs or to achieve ulterior objectives. A recruit's identification with the ideologically defined goals of the movement, and even his claim that he joined the movement 'because' its avowed aims articulated with his own personal values, are thus often given a 'beside-the-point' treatment as rationalized symptoms of more sinister motives.

It seems reasonable to ask, however, whether anyone interested in fathoming the psychology of a movement is not obliged to try to understand it, at least in part, on its own terms. I am not urging that all ideological pronouncements be taken at their face value as faithful expressions of a movement's aims or as the sole source of appeals. Appreciating that the 'latent' content of ideologies deserves attention, the major point of my argument is that serious attention needs also to be given to their manifest content as a possible source of direct 'appeals' and that ideologically derived convictions may operate as potent motives for participation in movements (cf. Toch, 1965, pp. 20–24). A recruit's support of the change-seeking program of a movement presupposes his acceptance of the movement's definition and diagnosis of prevailing conditions and arrangements, generally conveyed through its ideology. It is in this ideologically mediated definitional process, furthermore, that at least a part of the answer to a theoretically important question probably lies, viz., why people who share a general condition of alienation turn out to be differentially susceptible to alternative movements. The key factor may be the relative meaningfulness of the 'diagnoses' of people's predicaments purveyed by different movements largely through their ideological presentations. Thus, in terms of his general condition of alienation, an individual might be a potential candidate for either religious or political conversion but undergo the one rather than the other mainly because he finds his problems more meaningfully defined in one set of ideological symbols than the other. His acceptance of a particular movement's 'cures' is contingent on his acceptance of its 'diagnoses.'[14]

While ideological appeals form an important basis for attraction, it would be a mistake to assume that they are the only basis. A movement is more than an ideological conveyance and champion of change; it is also a circle of interaction, a network of social relationships, a social microcosm. At the bare minimum, this general aspect of a movement's character deserves attention as a possible source of attraction in its own right, over and above any explicitly ideological considerations. Indeed, in many instances, ideological

---

[14] Focussing analysis more or less exclusively on the manner in which internal predispositions structure an individual's perception of a movement has also distracted attention from potentially important external influences. How a movement is defined, evaluated, and responded to publicly, for example, must be recognized as a significant conditioner of the process through which recruits are won and their participation in the movement sustained (see Turner, 1964).

appeal may be a relatively minor factor prompting affiliation with a movement. The alleviation of the pangs of loneliness, the offer of a defined and secure place within an organizational structure, the opportunity for an enlarged, interesting, and even exciting set of social experiences, etc. may be potent 'motives' for joining a movement.[15]

The adequacy of treating the process of attraction simply in terms of some 'isomorphic' model, which tries to match personal motives and movement traits, can be seriously questioned on still another ground. While there are, no doubt, convergences and continuities between the characteristics of recruits and the ideological and other properties of movements which recruits find 'attractive,' there are also discrepancies and discontinuities. The latter may indeed be possible sources of 'attraction.' Writing about the sectarian recruit many years ago, Ellsworth Faris (1937, p. 55) pointed out that psychological candidacy for conversion consists not so much in a person's being endowed with certain characteristics which, in some sense, dovetail the characteristics of the movement which attracts him, but rather in perceiving or sensing that his own characteristics are different and in aspiring to acquire these new qualities. As Faris put it, 'the new convert does not come in because he was of like mind, but . . . because he changes his mind. . . . The sect attracts him because he wants to be different and it takes him and makes him into a different type as he comes to enter the cultural life.'[16]

In view of the discontinuities that are obviously present in the recruitment situation and the common failure to give them adequate consideration, it becomes all the more necessary to add still another dimension to recruitment theory—viz., some theory of 'conversion' as distinct from simple 'attraction.'

Conversion

In a broad sense, of course, the conversion process would include 'alienation' and 'attraction.' The major point to be made here is that an adequate theory of conversion must include more than is usually considered under the latter two headings.[17]

Recruitment is more than a selective ingathering of alienated and propitiously motivated individuals. In its most significant social-psychological sense, recruitment entails not only winning recruits but also moulding them into 'members.' This means involving recruits in some process of conversion, resocializing them, shaping their predispositions to meet the movement's

---

[15] Some theorists do explicitly recognize some kind of need for affiliation and incorporate it within their concept of susceptibility (see, e.g., Almond, 1954; Fromm, 1941; Lang & Lang, 1961, pp. 272–275).

[16] Hoffer (1951) makes a similar observation in emphasizing the importance of the search for a 'substitute self' as a motive in movement affiliation. A similar point could be made regarding the aspects of a movement's ideology or program which recruits find 'appealing.' Their appeal may not derive from any specific ideas or proposals but rather simply from the fact that they are novel, iconoclastic, promissory of change, etc. (cf. Almond, 1954; Converse, 1964).

[17] Some social psychological analyses of movements do provide fairly ample discussions of the conversion process (see, e.g., Toch, 1965).

own organizational requirements. What Faris (1937, pp. 56–57) wrote about the sect applies to most other organized movements:

> . . . The sect is not a safe refuge where the temperament and desires of an outsider can be comfortably expressed and realized; it is rather a formative force or set of forces; and the motives which lead a man to join a sect may be quite different from those which assure his continuance in it. No one on the outside can fully know what the experience on the inside is. Being a sectarian may be more satisfying than was at first imagined, or it may be less so, but it is never exactly anticipated. . . . The sectarian is, therefore, in some sense a new creature (cf. Bittner, 1963, p. 940; Walzer, 1963).

Every organized movement develops some kind of symbolic, normative, and structural framework to synchronize and coordinate its collective endeavors. A vital and indispensable phase of the recruitment process is the incorporation of the recruit into this group framework. Motivational predispositions, including those that have been awakened or implanted through prior alienation and agitational appeal, may help to bring the recruit into the movement's orbit, but they do not obviate the necessity for the movement's exerting influence over him. Predispositions must be ordered, put into the service of the movement, linked with its values, harnessed to its goals, intermeshed with its own internal requirements as an organized collectivity. Pre-existing motives become relevant mainly as points of departure for a process of unlearning and relearning, which the movement must direct. Personal motives are not necessarily extinguished in this process, but they come to be linked with new patterns of conduct which are relevant to, and supportive of, the collective enterprise which the movement represents.

Complete motivational homogeneity among recruits is not required for concerted, organizationally supportive, collective action.[18] What is required is a kind of 'motivational orchestration,' involving the linkage of multifold motives at the individual level with the movement's collective identity at the organizational level. The symbolic framework of a movement provides not only the shared ground for concerted action but also the context in which redefinitions of self and reorientations toward the world occur at the individual level. It seems reasonable to suggest that the essential features of conversion might best be treated in terms of the manner in which individual recruits are led to redefine themselves in terms of, or in relation to, the movement's collective identity, thus achieving a share in it. It is mainly in this way that a movement can operate as a more or less organized collectivity, despite motivational diversity at the private individual level.

Any realistic treatment of the conversion process in motivational terms, however, would have to recognize the active role of the movement itself not only in rechanneling prior motives but also in generating new sources of motivation. Following the leads of Kenneth Burke (1936, 1945, 1950),

[18] Devereux (1961) makes somewhat the same point when he indicates that 'both organized and spontaneous social movements and processes are possible not because all individuals participating in them are identically . . . motivated, but because a variety of authentically subjective motives may seek and find an ego syntonic outlet in the same type of collective activity' (cf. Spiro, 1961; Wallace 1961a, b).

C. Wright Mills (1940), and others, one might hypothesize that an important aspect of the conversion of recruits into members is their acquisition of new, organizationally salient 'vocabularies of motives.' The convert learns a new set of 'reasons for acting,' for acting in ways required by the movement. While this involves acquiring a symbolic framework of 'rationalizations,' it also involves the formation of a new set of 'purposes' (cf. Devereux, 1961; Lofland & Stark, 1965).

Post-conversion management

Although conversion, thus construed, might be said to complete the process of recruitment, it would seem desirable to recognize the importance of the recruit's post-conversion experience within the movement as a conditioner of the *kind* of member he becomes or continues to be. Whether or not this is explicitly treated as an additional phase of recruitment *per se,* it does invite further attention to the interactional dimensions of movements which have been emphasized in this paper. It suggests, in particular, the desirability of following up one's analysis of alienation, attraction, and conversion with some inquiry into the movement's system of membership management, especially its systems of fortification and control (cf. Blumer, 1946, 1957).

To state this in another way, conversion is an elongated process, some aspects of which do not become clearly visible until the member has undergone a process of testing and seasoning. Membership in a movement is not a fixed or static category, of course. It is a source of emergent social experience as rich and varied and as potentially influential as membership in any other kind of group, possibly more so. Membership in movements ought to be thought of in 'career' terms. Whether the career pattern be one of continued adherence and progressively deeper involvement, or one of wavering participation, weakening attachment, and possibly eventual defection, knowledge of it is likely to be an invaluable source of additional information about the dynamics of the movement-member relationship. The movement's role in maintaining, renewing, and possibly changing the member's 'motivations' to assure continued participation in the face of adversity, disappointment, boredom, etc. is especially likely to be illuminated by extending analysis in this direction (cf. Blumer, 1946, pp. 208–210; Hoffer, 1951, pp. 57–118).

CONCLUSIONS

Because of the frequent failure to observe the cautions mentioned above, our knowledge of the dynamics of recruitment in social movements is presently quite limited. While significant progress has been made in clarifying the social-psychological nature of 'susceptibility' to movement influence, it remains incompletely understood. The several components of susceptibility—the characterological, the situational, the socio-cultural, and the interactional—have been only partially explored. Their interrelationships and their roles within the broader recruitment process are still in need of clarification.

Perhaps the most serious shortcoming of the motivational approach as commonly applied has been its tendency to blunt and short-circuit analysis of the complexities of 'attraction' as an interactional process. If we are to think of recruitment in terms of 'attraction,' we must recognize that it involves both attraction *to* and attraction *by* a movement. We must, above all, recognize that attraction is typically not a 'one-shot' affair but an elongated and many-faceted process, in the course of which the potential recruit *develops* a positive orientation toward a movement. While 'susceptibilities' are involved, so are external influences. The latter have not always been adequately considered.

Implicit in the critical observations made in this paper has been a plea which might be made explicit at this point, viz., that the problem of movement affiliation be approached through the study of the broader *recruitment process*, with explicit recognition of its socio-cultural context, its interactional character, and its typically longitudinal span. While motivational assessment has a place in the study of this process, it must be executed with due recognition of the other elements involved.

REFERENCES

Aberle, D. F. (1962). A note on relative deprivation theory as applied to millenarian and other cult movements. In Thrupp, S. L. (ed.), *Millenial dreams in action* (Supplement II, *Comparative Studies in Society and History*). The Hague: Mouton & Co.

Adorno, T. W. *et al.* (1950). *The authoritarian personality.* New York: Harper & Bros.

Almond, G. (1954). *The appeals of communism.* Princeton: Princeton University Press.

Apter, D. E. (ed.) (1964). *Ideology and discontent.* New York: Free Press.

Bittner, E. (1963). Radicalism and the organization of radical movements. *American Sociological Review 28*, 928–940.

Blumer, H. (1946). Collective behavior. In Lee, A. M. (ed.), *New outline of the principles of sociology.* New York: Barnes & Noble.

Blumer, H. (1957). Collective behavior. In Gittler, J. B. (ed.), *Review of sociology*, pp. 128–158. New York.

Brown, H. G. (1943). The appeal of communist ideology. *American Journal of Economics and Sociology 2*, 161–174.

Burke, K. (1936). *Permanence and change.* New York: New Republic.

Burke, K. (1945). *The grammar of motives.* New York: Prentice-Hall.

Burke, K. (1950). *The rhetoric of motives.* New York: Prentice-Hall.

Cantril, H. (1941). *The psychology of social movements.* New York: Wiley.

Clark, J. P. (1959). Measuring alienation within a social system. *American Sociological Review 24*, 849–852.

Cohn, N. (1957). *The pursuit of the millennium.* London: Secker & Warburg.

Converse, P. E. (1964). The nature of belief systems in mass publics. In Apter, D. E. (ed.), *Ideology and discontent.* New York: Free Press.

Davies, J. C. (1962). Toward a theory of revolution. *American Sociological Review 27*, 5–19.

Devereux, C. (1961). Two types of modal personality models. In Kaplan, B., *Studying personality cross-culturally.* New York: Harper & Row.

Dicks, H. V. (1950). Personality traits and national socialist ideology. *Human Relations 3*, 111–154.

Faris, E. (1937). The sect and the sectarian. In Faris, E. *The nature of human nature*. New York: McGraw-Hill.

Feuer, L. S. (1969). *The conflict of generations*. New York: Basic Books.

Flugel, J. C. (1945). *Man, morals, and society*. London and Baltimore: Penguin Books.

Fromm, E. (1941). *Escape from freedom*. New York: Farrar and Rinehart.

Gilbert, G. M. (1950). *The psychology of dictatorship*. New York: Ronald Press Co.

Gundlach, R. H. & Riess, B. F. (1954). A critique of the sampling, method, and logic of Krugman's article on Communism. *Psychiatry 17*, 207–209.

Gusfield, J. (1963). *Symbolic crusade: status politics and the temperance movement*. Urbana: University of Illinois Press.

Heberle, R. (1951). *Social movements*. New York: Appleton-Century-Crofts.

Hoffer, E. (1951). *The true believer*. New York: The New American Library.

Inkeles, A. (1959). Personality and social structure. In Merton, R. K., Broom, L. & Cottrell, L. S., Jr. (eds.), *Sociology today*. New York: Basic Books.

Johnson, C. (1966). *Revolutionary change*. Boston: Little, Brown, & Co.

Jones, E. (1941). Evolution and revolution. *International Journal of Psycho-Analysis 22*, 193–208.

Keniston, K. (1965). *The uncommitted*. New York: Dell.

King, C. W. (1956). *Social movements in the United States*. New York: Random House.

Kornhauser, W. (1959). *The politics of mass society*. Glencoe, Ill.: Free Press.

Krout, M. H. & Stagner, R. (1939). Personality development in radicals: a comparative study. *Sociometry 2*, 1–46.

Krugman, H. E. (1952). The appeal of communism to American middle-class intellectuals and trade unionists. *Public Opinion Quarterly 16*, 331–355.

Krugman, H. E. (1953). The role of hostility in the appeal of communism in the U.S. *Psychiatry 16*, 253–261.

Krugman, H. E. (1954). Rejoinder to Gundlach and Riess. *Psychiatry 17*, 209–210.

Lang, K. & Lang, G. E. (1961). *Collective dynamics*. New York: Crowell.

Lasswell, H. D. (1930). *Psychopathology and politics*. Chicago: University of Chicago Press.

Leighton, A. (1949). Beliefs under stress. In Snyder, R. C. & Wilson, H. H. (eds.), *Roots of political behavior*. New York: American Book Co.

Lofland, J. (1966). *Doomsday cult*. Englewood Cliffs, N.J.: Prentice-Hall.

Lofland, J. & Stark, R. (1965). Becoming a world-saver: a theory of conversion to a deviant perspective. *American Sociological Review 30*, 862–875.

Lowenthal, L. & Guterman, N. (1949). *Prophets of deceit, a study of the techniques of the American agitator*. New York: Harper & Bros.

Maier, N. R. F. (1942). The role of frustration in social movements. *Psychological Review 49*, 586–599.

McCormack, T. H. (1950). The motivation of radicals. *American Journal of Sociology 56*, 17–24.

MacIver, R. M. (1940). The imputation of motives. *American Journal of Sociology 46*, 4–6.

Macrae, D. G. (1951). The Bolshevik ideology. *The Cambridge Journal 5*, 164–177.

Merton, R. K. (1957). Social structure and anomie. In Merton, R. K., *Social theory and social structure*. Glencoe, Ill.: Free Press.

Mills, C. W. (1940). Situated actions and vocabularies of motive. *American Sociological Review 5*, 904–913.

Pappenheim, F. (1959). *The alienation of modern man.* New York: Monthly Review Press.

Parsons, T. (1954). Some sociological aspects of the Fascist movements. In Parsons, T., *Essays in sociological theory.* Rev. ed. Glencoe, Ill.: Free Press.

Reich, W. (1946). *The mass psychosis of Fascism.* New York: Orgone Institute Press.

Riezler, K. (1943). On the psychology of the modern revolution. *Social Research 10,* 320–336.

Rinaldo, J. (1921). *Psychoanalysis of the reformer.* New York: Lee Publishing Co.

Seeman, M. (1959). On the meaning of alienation. *American Sociological Review 24,* 783–791.

Selznick, P. (1951). Institutional vulnerability in mass society. *American Journal of Sociology 56,* 320–331.

Shils, E. A. (1954). Authoritarianism: right and left. In Christie, R. & Jahoda, M. (eds.), *Studies in the scope and method of the authoritarian personality.* Glencoe, Ill.: Free Press.

Smelser, N. J. (1963). *Theory of collective behavior.* New York: Free Press.

Spiro, M. E. (1961). Social systems, personality, and functional analysis. In Kaplan, B. (ed.), *Studying personality cross-culturally.* New York: Harper & Row.

Tilly, C. (1963–64). The analysis of a counter-revolution. *History and Theory 3,* 30–37, 45–58.

Toch, H. (1965). *The social psychology of social movements.* Indianapolis: Bobbs-Merrill Co.

Turner, R. H. (1964). Collective behavior and conflict: new theoretical frameworks. *Sociological Quarterly 00,* 122–128.

Turner, R. H. & Killian, L. M. (eds.) (1957). *Collective behavior.* Englewood Cliffs, N.J.: Prentice-Hall.

Wallace, A. F. C. (1956). Revitalization movements. *American Anthropologist 58,* 264–281.

Wallace, A. F. C. (1961a). *Culture and personality.* New York: Random House.

Wallace, A. F. C. (1961b). The psychic unity of human groups. In Kaplan, B. (ed.), *Studying personality cross-culturally.* New York: Harper & Bros.

Walzer, M. (1963). Puritanism as a revolutionary ideology. *History and Theory 3.*

Weiss, R. F. (1963). Defection from social movements and subsequent recruitment to new movements. *Sociometry 26,* 1–20.

Wolfinger, R. E. *et al.* (1964). America's radical right: politics and ideology. In Apter, D. E. (ed.), *Ideology and discontent.* New York: Free Press.

The Theories
of the American Student
Protest Movements

JACK DOUGLAS

In the end, one must judge whether the student radicals fundamentally represent a better world that can come into being, or whether they are not committed to outdated and romantic visions that cannot be realized, that contradict fundamentally other desires and hopes they themselves possess and that contradict even more the desires of most other people. I am impressed by Zbgniew Brzezinski's analysis of the student revolution:

> *Very frequently revolutions are the last spasms of the past, and thus are not really revolutions but counterrevolutions, operating in the name of revolutions. A revolution which really either is non-programmatic and has no content, or involves content which is based on the past but provides no guidance for the future, is essentially counterrevolutionary.*

The student radicals come from the fields that have a restricted and ambiguous place in a contemporary society. They remind me more of the Luddite machine smashers than the Socialist trade unionists who achieved citizenship and power for workers. This is why the universities stand relatively unchanged—because despite their evident inadequacies the student radicals have as yet suggested nothing better to replace them with.

> Nathan Glazer,
> " 'Student Power' in Berkeley"

One of the most striking things about student protest movements over the last several years has been the great profusion of explanations of the movements, especially of those in the United States. There has, of course, been a vast literature written on the student protest movements precisely be-

"The Theories of the American Student Protest Movements" is reprinted from *Youth in Turmoil* by Jack Douglas, published in 1970 by the U.S. Government Printing Office. Reprinted by courtesy of the Center for Studies of Crime and Delinquency, National Institute of Mental Health, Alcohol, Drug Abuse, and Mental Health Administration, U.S. Department of Health, Education, and Welfare.

cause the people most directly affected by them—the academics and the intellectuals—are the people who do most of the writing in this society. In addition, the journalists who do most of the rest of the writing have become increasingly oriented toward the academic and intellectual world in the last few decades. It would sometimes appear that every journalist and every academic in every individual interview by the mass media has his own favorite explanation of the student protest movements. They have been attacked—or joined—where they live and they have responded by writing about it.

Sometimes it is quite apparent that particular individuals are using the protest movements for their own political purposes—that is, they prefer to see in the protest movements things which they themselves have long been in favor of. This has been especially true in some of the romantic statements about the student protest movements that one finds expressed by certain radical or extremely liberal intellectuals. In many instances these "analysts" warmly identify with the protesters. In a few instances, they have joined the students. To them the student protest movements appear to be the dawning of a new day, the realization at last of their long dreamed of utopian movements, a new Children's Crusade, only this time destined for greater success. Lewis Feuer has described some individual instances of this identification among the Berkeley faculty:

> For a while the elders of the faculty subscribed to a New Cult of Youth, according to which the student activist was the Community's Prophetic Conscience. A professor of English poetry departing on a leave of absence delivered a farewell address in which he spoke of the "beautiful and strong Mario Savio." A chairman of a department of science, who happened to be a member of a religious sect, became convinced that Mario Savio was a reincarnation of Jesus; even his militant colleagues were discomfited by this unusual theology. The philosophers were not far behind the scientists; their chairman told an excited student assemblage after the Greek Theater microphone seizure that they had all the power. Professors of biochemistry included such questions as the definition of "civil disobedience" on their examinations.[1]

We can see this strong identification with the protesters and a rather unanalytical acceptance of anything they allege in such statements as that by John Seeley, who has long taken similar positions concerning American society:

> The more finicky of my friends send me, with their approval, just as they did during the 1964 Great Overture at Berkeley, columns and clippings critical of the behavior of Columbia students: not, of course, those students who violently sought to starve out the occupants of the citadel, but those who, momentarily at least, sat down in the seats of power. "How," one good lady asked me in horror, "are we going to save a free society now?"
>
> That's a good question, though belated. But it's a tricky one and misdirected: tricky because it assumes we have a free society now to "save"; misdirected because its address should not be through me to

[1] Feuer, Lewis, *The Conflict of Generations,* New York: Basic Books, Inc., 1969, p. 463.

the students, but through Grayson Kirk to Mr. Kirk's "military-indus-
trial-intellectual complex" . . .

The leading issues are crystal clear, and no amount of diversionary
chatter about purloined and copied documents should make us glance
away from them for even a footnote-instant. . . . Where is the showing that Columbia—potentially more fully informed than most as to the
criminality in substance and form of the war, the evils of the draft and
selective service, and the adverse effect on education of Mr. Hershey's
"manpower channeling"—moved earnestly, actively and massively to
clear its skirts, in fact and appearance, of all involvement in what many
judge to be crimes against humanity? "Where?" I ask, and Echo answers, "Where?"

People always ask, "even though mistakes have been made, doesn't
such a great center of learning deserve to survive?" My answer is "Yes,
if . . ." Yes, if it can now, in sackcloth and ashes, having rid itself of
its administration and board, go to the students it proposes to impugn,
not merely with amnesty and guarantee of safe passage, but with bay
and laurel, its highest accolades, its gratitude forever, its most hon-
orary degree. When Columbia holds a new Commencement awarding
these its new LL.D's (Doctors of Liberties), only then will we know
it has commenced anew and aright, and deserves the tentative support
of those who love what a university ought to be.[2]

But even those who apparently agree completely with the student protest
movements, and identify with "the cause," see very different things in it and
very different causes. This is very apparent in the article written by Bernard
Steinzor that appeared in the same journal as that by Seeley. Steinzor, a
psychiatrist, sees a mental health message—and justification—in the Columbia movement:

This is again a decade of reformation, especially compared with the
'50's, when we castigated the students for their apathy. Today's students are making a heady mix of the values we have stood for and the
current condition of men. Raised on Spock, they have been joined by
him in civil disobedience—a rather lovely happening. The generation
gap was thus overcome; the father and son together were doing a self-
less thing. This is a new and stirring development: young activists are
risking much in a cause for others. Helping the individual climb out
of his self-centeredness is what we psychotherapists try to do. We
recognize that narcissistic careers are expressions of a deep sense of
helplessness. And powerlessness, we know, precludes love . . .

. . . The protesting students at the universities, and those who joined
the so-called "Children's Crusade," do not require referral; the aura of
violence which surrounds their ideology and tactics must be understood as the reaction of people who have been taken for granted too
long, treated like babies, when, indeed, they had outdistanced their
elders in sensibility and understanding of the vital issues of the times.
We cannot ignore the lessons of our own history: social justice never
has been attained without some damage to aspects deemed worthy by
authorities. . . .

The Students have been doing our thing. Partly because of the faith
we and our parents have placed in the possibility of a progressive

[2] Seeley, John R., "Plantation Politics," pp. 16–21, in *Psychiatry and Social Science Review,* July 1968, Vol. 2, No. 7.

order ever expanding the coordinates of love and justice, they do it better. We certainly can become slightly nervous at their audacity, but —let us hope—so will they when the next generation comes of age.[3]

When we then consider all of the descriptions and analyses of the same protest movements that do not involve this kind of agreement and identification with the protesters, but are either neutral, which is unusual, or antagonistic, we find that the variety of both descriptions and analyses is extremely great. When the different people with different orientations to the events look at "the same thing," if it even makes sense to assume this, they "see" different things and their analyses of those things they see take them to completely different conclusions about the goals, values, and significances of the protesters. For example, Sidney Hook, looking at the same events at Columbia and writing in the same journal, sees and understands completely different things from those things seen and understood by Seeley and Steinzor:

> Not many weeks ago, as Dr. David Truman, Provost of Columbia University, walked to his office on the campus, one of the striking students strode up to him and spat in his face. Nothing happened to that student. No protest was heard from the other students. None of the faculty members who pleaded for complete amnesty for the students rebuked the action when it became known. It was received in almost the same matter-of-fact way as the streams of abuse, of profane and foul language that the rebellious students have hurled at those who expressed disagreement with them.
>
> In some ways it is events of this character which are more significant than the differences over the specific issues, like the building of a gymnasium or the nature of legitimate academic research. For they reveal a situation altogether incompatible with the idea of the university as conceived until now.
>
> The unspoken allegiance of the community of scholars has been to civility of mind. Respect for the rights of teachers and students to differ with each other and among themselves has been taken for granted together with the presumption of good faith and goodwill on the part of intellectual dissenters and heretics. All this has been fractured at Columbia by violence, obscenity and hysterical insult. The language and behavior of the gutter have invaded the academy.[4]

However, when we look at these many different explanations more carefully and begin to more systematically compare them, we find that these apparently vast differences, this apparent profusion of individual explanations, is more apparent than real. We find there are actually a number of basic dimensions to these analyses and basic factors which most of those involved in the academic world and the intellectual world have made use of in many different ways with many different nuances to explain the basic aspects of student protest movements. The important differences in the explanations seem to be primarily differences in the perspectives adopted and in the ordering and emphases on factors, rather than in the factors that are seen as relevant. It is especially the differences in perspectives that are of

---

[3] Steinzor, Bernard, "Coordinates of Power and Intimacy," pp. 24–26, *Ibid.*, p. 25.
[4] Hook, Sidney, "Symbolic Truth," pp. 22–23, *Ibid.*, p. 22.

basic importance to anyone trying to explain the student protest movements, especially since the perspective problems must be solved at the beginning, before one can decide on how to go about handling the factors considered important.

THE EVASION OF THE ISSUES

The theoretical perspectives adopted to explain the movements show all too clearly the ways in which professional disciplines determine one's views of such concrete events and the ways in which theoretical perspectives are adopted long before one comes to such concrete events, so that the theorists have already assumed that they know the general nature of the phenomena and their causes before they come to the concrete phenomena. In the great majority of these works there is an academic presumption that the analyst knows the general truth before he begins. Indeed, in all too many instances there is not merely the assumption that one knows the general nature of the truth, which is certainly more defensible in terms of the impossibility and undesirability of always starting from ground level in trying to understand the world, but there is also the assumption that a great deal is known about the specific nature of the phenomena to be studied. For example, when a structural sociologist comes to study the events of student protest he is very apt to assume completely implicitly that the only valid explanation of the events will be found in the family backgrounds, class associations, or in some other traditionally recognized "structural" factors. In the same way, when a psychologist comes to study the events he is very apt to assume completely implicitly that the only valid explanation of the events will be found in the earlier, especially childhood sexual, family relations of the protesters. The only thing that saves us from a complete war of theoretical perspectives is the willingness of many of the theorists to adopt a multi-factored approach by which they recognize the partial, if subordinate, validity of other perspectives. In this way we get a live-and-let-live approach to the theoretical explanations of the phenomena, but we do not get any closer to the phenomena. The events are forced into the Procrustean bed of pre-established theories and all too often neither the theory nor the events leads to any improvement in the other.

One of the crucial results of this whole approach to the events has been an apparent *evasion of the issues*. The students are in some cases profoundly angry about certain aspects of American society and policy and they talk endlessly about what they see as the sources of their anger. But in many of the theories there is a complete evasion of this anger and of the issues which the students argue lie behind their anger. In a review of two of the better known books on the student protest movement, Michael Rossman, one of the members of the Free Speech Movement Steering Committee, has expressed very well the strong feeling of the students that the academics have consistently evaded the "real issues":

> "What do you feel about the FSM Books?" I asked my friend Steve Weissman, who was on the FSM Steering Committee with me.
> "The Academics are at the dungheap with their forceps again."

"You can tell the bird by his droppings?" I suggested.

"Maybe. But you can't tell the way he flies."

Those who were FSM will understand this, will understand how I struggle without poetry to say something about these books, which is not in their image and dead names, missing the point as they miss theirs; to articulate the indelible sense of unreality, of irrelevance they leave me with. The sense is familiar, the conflict was cloaked in fog: were these writers talking to us, hearing us, even seeing us? How ironic, how fitting, to find it again, from the same sources and for the same reasons. I can only say—with the same strange Chaplin humor that infused every action of the FSM, yet finds no notice in these books—that the Failed Seriousness Quotient is very high.

FSM happened at the locus of Modern Scholarship. The entire armament of analysis hung poised and desperately avoiding contact with the Perfect Chance that shook a fist in its face; while we sang, "I write theses/ about fesces/ and it greases/ my way up the line."[5]

The tendency to *evade the phenomena* is itself so powerful that we find it a dominant tendency even in those cases in which the analysts are trying very hard to deal with the issues as defined by the students. There are almost innumerable articles and many books that purport to deal with the "way students see it today," or "why they do it," that make almost no reference to *concrete, living-and-breathing, real-life students*. The students, even the very vocal activist students, become *the silent subject generation*, an object of aloof adult discussion and argument, a *cause célèbre* for many different points of view—but unheard, unseen. In some peculiar way, the analysts, even some of the best and some of those most interested in the student points of view, take other analysts as the official spokesmen of the younger generation. As unbelievable as it may seem to some of us, this evasion of the phenomena has gone to the extreme of taking Edgar Friedenberg and Paul Goodman, two of the more unusual and romantic critics of American society in the name of "youth," as such official spokesmen of "youth," even though they have often provided excellent documentation of their lack of experience with the youth they were trying to write about.[6] There is almost never reference to what a concrete student has said, but there are often concrete references to what Friedenberg and Goodman have said.

Part of the reason for this lack of explicit reference to real students is probably the scholarly bias that sees more *reality in print* than in what can be seen or heard in everyday life. Paul Goodman has *print-reality;* the student at the lunch table does not. Closely related to this is the greater *hierarchical reality-value* attributed to the "recognized authority," the "professor," or any other man of authority. For both reasons, as well, the analysts would want to avoid giving the impression of "being journalistic" that would come from using the "human-interest" style of "as one distraught freshman at Stoney Brook put it over a Coke."

But it is probably most important that the evasion of the phenomena, in-

---

[5] Rossman, Michael, "Barefoot in a Marshmallow World," in *The New Radicals,* Jacobs, Paul, and Landau, Saul, eds., New York: Vintage Books, 1966, p. 209.

[6] Friedenberg, Edgar Z., *The Vanishing Adolescent* (Preface), New York: a Delta Book, 1964.

cluding the issues, has been so complete that until recently there were almost no published *real-word statements* by real students. There were plenty of surveys and attitude studies of the sort done by Coleman or Katz, in which real students were collapsed into the 12 percent who responded in a given way to a multiple-choice question and got scaled-up very neatly, all methodologically prearranged to screen the reader from the real-person, the real-student. But only after the student revolts made some students saleable in print did we get any real-word statements by students. While some of these are helpful, and will be used in some of our descriptive and explanatory sections, there is now the grave danger that these print-realities, carefully screened by the saleability criterion, will come to be taken as representative of *the* students, whereas in fact the writing and publishing of a book or essay is itself such an unusual situation, so removed from the "barricades of student revolt," that the writer himself is probably in many cases screening his own thoughts and recollections to such an extent that they become distortions of what actually happened, what could have been observed to happen and be said had one been on the scene.

In some of the better instances we do find, fortunately, that this evasion of the phenomena is only partial. In a work such as Martin Meyerson's essay on "The Ethos of the American College Student: Beyond the Protests"[7] we find no explicit reference to what real-students said, though we do find some good uses of slogans taken from buttons. But there is clearly a great deal of experience with real-students lying behind most of his statements. Nevertheless, the dangers of evading the phenomena are apparent even in this work. For example, Meyerson argues that the present college students suffer from a "strain of being part of neither the elect nor the electorate," presumably because they recognize the way in which the vast increases in college enrollment have decreased their elite status. But from my own experience I would suspect that this is a complete "misreading" of the way the students today define their situation. I have heard graduates and seniors looking at their job possibilities express such feelings, but the vast majority of undergraduates seem oblivious of this state of affairs. They seem quite convinced that college is absolutely necessary in order to have any chance of being in the elite and they generally seem to feel that having made college they have gone a long way toward making it all the way. This is certainly very much the case in the elite schools where college is seen as *the* beginning of a whole new life. For example, this is excellently described in a rare essay by a student on how it looks to him:

> The first task in trying to understand college students is necessarily to consider the context in which they play out their undergraduate years. For Harvard students—and a good many others around the country—that context is undeniably clear. They conclude very early in college that society asks of them a fixed role in life, a career in which they will become specialists—for the whole of society appears to their newly opened eyes to be built out of small, die-cast parts. And they conclude soon thereafter that almost any career with passably attractive possibilities will require a graduate degree, in some size, shape, or

[7] Meyerson, Martin, "The Ethos of the American College Student: Beyond the Protests," pp. 266–291, in *The Contemporary University: USA*, Robert S. Morison, ed., Boston: The Houghton Mifflin Company, 1966.

form—for the chance of finding an interesting career without such credentials seems hopelessly slight. . . . Many come to see their four years as only a brief respite before their serious work begins. Others search frantically for that proverbial "last fling" before their "real" lives get underway. Whatever the results, the attitudes with which a student looks ahead to graduate school can have an immense impact on his attitudes as an undergraduate. It would be superficial to tackle the substance of those four years of college without some sense of the shades of student approaches to graduate school.[8]

While this is an important point in itself, the importance of it here is that the analysts have a strong tendency to substitute their own understandings of the "real situation" for the students' understandings of those situations and, thereby, to quite misunderstand how the students see it and why they do anything, such as revolt.

But the social scientists and other analysts of the student protest movements have found it possible to evade the phenomena and the issues even when they gave some consideration to the kinds of things students say and do, simply by insisting on imposing their preconceived theories on whatever phenomena or issues they do consider, so that they come up with "real" meanings for what the students say and do that just happen to fit the general ideas held by the analysts before there were any protest movements. The most common of these unintended strategies for evading the issues and phenomena are the psychologistic and structural theories.

THE PSYCHOLOGISTIC THEORIES

The first half of the twentieth century has been an Age of Psychology in Western societies, especially in American society in which the traditional commonsense ideas of individualism fit in very nicely with the individualistic perspective of psychology. In the last few decades this psychologistic bent, this insistence on explaining everything people do in terms of "psychological factors," has crested and has definitely begun to recede and be replaced by an opposite tendency, that of structuralism or sociologistic theories; but in the interim the mass media have continued to be dominated by the psychologistic theories. As we should expect in this situation, there have been many different psychologistic theories proposed to explain the student protest movements.

One of the more extreme "psychologistic" theories of the student protest movements is that of Bruno Bettelheim.[9] Bettelheim makes use of some very important observations of the kinds of things the radicals have to say in their everyday lives, at least when they are being observed in those lives by outsiders, but he uses them to show that it all goes back to the parents, and that the "messages" emitted by the radicals are "really" only messages from their own inner "chaos" and "need for external controls" (which is a

[8] Gordon, David M., " 'Rebellion' in Context: A Student's View of Students," pp. 292–313, in Morison, op. cit., p. 294.
[9] Bettelheim, Bruno, "Student Revolt: The Hard Core," pp. 405–10 in Vital Speeches of the Day, April 15, 1969.

typical psychological description of paranoid schizophrenics, a label which Bettelheim graciously refuses to invoke).

He notes first of all that, as a Harvard senior had earlier observed, SDS members very frequently respond to questions about "the sickness of society" with remarks about "well, take my father for example. . . ." He concludes from this that ". . . it is indeed in the changed ways of rearing children in the upper-middle class home that we have to look for some additional answers." I suggest there are two completely different reasons for this frequent reference to one's family members. First of all, and most obviously, the radicals, like any other young people, know their parents far better than they know any other adults. Indeed, in many instances, their parents are the *only* adults they have seen to any significant degree *behind the public fronts* which are so essential for successfully navigating the enemy-filled territory of highly competitive social groups found in the American upper-middle class. Their parents, then, are some of the only good evidence they have about the strains, hypocrisies, etc., which they are talking about. When they are concerned with things about which they have other "good examples" (as they see it) from the public domain of the mass media, they refer to those at least as often. For example, the extreme radicals were concerned with ridiculing Lyndon Johnson in *MacBird* and in other statements of their great hatreds, rather than with ridiculing their parents. Secondly, when the radicals refer to their parents as the "causes" of their own anguish, being "mixed up," and so on, they are generally simply making use of the psychologistic theories of the aetiological causation of emotional states and of behavior which they and the general public have learned from the psychologists, especially from the psychoanalysts. Surely it could not have escaped Bruno Bettelheim's attention that this is the Great Age of Psychoanalysis in American society and that the upper-middle class, especially the highly educated of the large urban centers, are precisely the people who have dedicated themselves to psychoanalyzing every aspect of life. Surely he could not be ignorant of the fact that psychoanalysis has for years been the One True Religion for the upper and upper-middle class people of our great cities, especially of New York City, which has long been the worshipped Mecca of psychoanalysis. Surely he could not be ignorant of the fact that even many of the mass media, especially the movies, have been suffused with the psychologizing of personal problems. And surely he could not be ignorant of the fact that many of these radicals themselves, like many other college students in the wealthy universities, have themselves "been through analysis" of one sort or another where they have been patiently taught (by indirection, or nondirectively, of course) to analyze the most minute childhood experience, especially those in which they experienced any hatred, animosity, distaste, or petty pique against their parents, especially their fathers, to see what the "real causes" of their "symptoms" are.

Bettelheim is using a very blatant form of *ex post facto validation* to "prove" his point. That is, he and thousands of other psychologizers, in and out of the universities, have taught the educated, upper-middle class to explain their adult feelings and behavior in terms of their childhood relations with their parents, especially their animosities against their parents. And then the psychologizers have used the fact that their "patients" and the children of their "patients" have learned their lessons well enough to repeat almost verbatim these theories as *proof* that the theories were right all along. In a very and important sense, these psychologizers have taught the present generation to believe in the essentials of the "generation gap," the all important element of animosity, and then have helped further to expand it by now arguing that "Yes! Yes! Now you can see that we were right all along, that Oedipal conflicts really are necessary, that sons must inevitably turn against their fathers."

The psychologizers have taught the upper-middle class the *Oedipal perspective* on their problems in precisely the same way that sociologists and other social scientists have taught them to look at our society almost entirely in terms of the *social problems perspective*, the narrow view of our society which focuses entirely on the problems and excludes consideration of the beauties and virtues (which even the radicals would agree are beauties and virtues in other contexts). This teaching has been so highly effective in this increasingly education oriented society that today even the least educated militant talks about his problems and ideas in terms of the sociological jargon of "power structure," "institutional racism," "bourgeois way of life," "social system," and so on; and radical proclamations about "black power" take time out in the early parts of the call to arms to discuss the sociological distinction between "social structure" and "social system." It is clearly time for all social theorists to become aware of how powerful the *ex post facto bias* has become in our society. In a very real sense our entire society has become so "tuned in" to the mass media and "turned on" by the "scientific experts," who teach the mass-mediaists and who in turn teach the masses through the trickle-down system, that our whole society has become a "biased sample," or one in which the expert's teaching methods and observation become a primary determinant of what he will observe: the expert winds up studying himself and what he has created!

Bettelheim goes on to argue that:

> The mainspring of their action is their wish to prove themselves strong, rather than any particular political convictions, which are superimposed on their self-doubts and a hatred of a society they feel has left them out in the cold.
> In many ways, at the same time, a student who revolts is reflecting a desperate wish to do better than the parent, especially in areas where the parent seemed weak in his beliefs. In this sense revolt also represents a desperate desire for parental approval. Even more, it is a desperate wish that the parent should have been strong in his own convictions.
> This is the reason why so many of our radicals embrace Maoism, why they chant in their demonstrations "Ho Ho Ho Chi Minh." Both Mao and Ho are strong father figures, with strong convictions, who powerfully coerce their "children" to follow their commands. While consciously they demand freedom and participation, unconsciously the commitment of rebelling students to Mao and other dictators suggests their deep need for controls from the outside, since without them they are unable to bring order into their inner chaos.[10]

We can see from this example that Bettelheim has chosen to draw in the

10 *Ibid.*

"unconscious" forces to explain what appear to him to be "irrational" contradictions between calling for freedom and supporting Mao and Ho Chi-Minh, rather than seeking any "rational" explanation in terms of the messages they are consciously communicating, such as their political beliefs. There is a perfectly obvious political explanation of their support of Ho and Mao: they support them, and wave Vietcong flags, and resist the draft, and attack the Pentagon, and spill blood on draft board records, and ban ROTC from the campuses, and do a great many other things in good part because, remarkable as it might seem to Bettelheim, they are in fact very angry at the United States over the Vietnamese war and because they see Ho and Mao as their best hope for defeating the United States in that war. They attack their political enemies and support their friends in precisely the same way that a rational psychologist, such as Bettelheim undoubtedly is (in spite of what the radicals would say), might do; and this in itself is not really a remarkable fact requiring the immense machinery of the unconscious, the id, the superego, the ego, and various other mechanisms and complexes to explain it.

There are also a large number of obvious facts that could not be explained by this supposed paranoid need for "external controls" to "bring order into their inner chaos." For example, the insistence of SDS on an almost totally unstructured "non-organization" to carry on the movement is in total contradiction to this paranoid symptom theory. The lives of the individuals, the way they have unstructured their nearly "non-group," and the way they try to arrive at non-group decisions through universal consent makes the whole movement more like a celebration of anarchy than a celebration of Mao-tyranny.

The psychologistic theories are singularly given to a venting of the analyst's own darkest fears, his nightmare anxieties, and his own antagonisms toward the youth, perhaps because they involve such a total evasion of the issues resulting from the almost universal insistence of the "irrational forces," the "unconscious forces" which the actor himself must be unaware of by their very nature. (Declaring your opponent-subject to be "irrational" and to be "necessarily unconscious of the truth" before you begin attacking-analyzing him is extremely effective in undercutting his inevitable counter-attacks, at least for all of those who see the attack-analysis as "scientific" and who are not put off by the unfairness of such a tactic.) Bettelheim's analyses of youth seem to have been haunted primarily by the nightmarish fear that we are witnessing a return of the Nazi Youth (though we must avoid getting too psychologistic in our own analyses). But the most important psychologistic theory of the protest movements, that proposed by Lewis Feuer in *The Conflict of Generations*,[11] is haunted more by ancient Freudian forces, the dark forces of Oedipal conflicts which are so infinitely subtle that they can be found lurking in the shadows behind the most far-flung and opposite forms of conflicts between groups of youth and groups of adults, from Tokyo to Buenos Aires, from Lagos to Ithaca.

Lewis Feuer's work on *The Conflict of Generations* is not only the most scholarly work yet published on student protest movements, but is also probably the most scholarly psychoanalytic theory of universal historical

[11] Feuer, *op. cit.*

forces yet published. It will undoubtedly receive wide attention from scholars and the general public on both counts. While it certainly deserves this wide consideration, and while some aspects of it are excellent, it suffers from most of the same things that Bettelheim's unscholarly work does. It, too, is fundamentally an evasion of the issues, an evasion based from the very beginning on the psychologistic insistence on the irrationality of the other person's point of view.

Taken as a whole, Feuer's theory is a rich and convoluted one, with many open ends and many dangling hypotheses. But its central points are very few and very simple. In fact, they can probably very fairly be reduced to four basic points: (1) generational conflict is universal because of the nature of Oedipal conflicts and the nature of adolescence (the young must give up a part of themselves, which is necessarily painful); (2) generational conflict only breaks out into youth revolt when the older generation has been de-authorized by some crucial, symbolic events (which is the most important and original of his particular points); (3) the students are the ones who revolt in more complex, civilized societies because they form an intellectual elite of the young; (4) youth revolts are always a mixture of youthful love and hate, and ambivalent reaction full of unconscious emotions which the young cannot face, providing the motivating force for the movements, so they are always largely destructive.

The basic problem which any universal theory of any such thing faces is that of explaining why it is that something that is universal only pops up here and there in history, rather than being there all the time. Michael Miller, who lived inside the student movements at Berkeley, made this point very well when he accepted the theory, but then pointed out that it could not explain what happened at Berkeley: "Generational conflict, however, is so ancient and archetypal a social mechanism—certainly it functions in almost every revolution, political or artistic—that it affords little insight into the campus turmoil."[12] Recognizing this obvious difficulty far better than almost any other psychologistic theorist, Feuer proposed to explain the relatively rare outbreaks of active revolt from the young by the crucial social mechanism of *de-authorization* of the elders: "Every student movement is the outcome of a de-authorization of the elder generation. This process can take place in small colleges as well as impersonal universities, in industrialized countries as well as underdeveloped ones, in socialist as well as capitalist ones."[13]

Yet it is clear that de-authorization does not simply happen. Feuer argues that there must be some *dramatic event* that de-authorizes the elder generation:

> As we have seen, a struggle of generations, in and of itself, however, will not give rise to a massive student movement. What is always required, in addition, is some signal event in which the de-authorization of the older generation, as a collective whole, is vividly dramatized. The May Fourth Movement, the turning point in modern Chinese history, arose from such a conjunction of generational conflict with the de-authorization of the elders.[14]

[12] *Ibid.*, p. 59.
[13] *Ibid.*, p. 528.
[14] *Ibid.*, p. 184.

But the danger of any such ex post facto analysis is that one can always find something after-the-fact that looks like de-authorization unless he is very clear about what constitutes de-authorization. What does produce de-authorization in Feuer's analysis? Unfortunately, Feuer is never very clear about this. But a few examples of his analysis appear to make it clear. In the Chinese case just referred to, it is clearest of all, for he immediately concludes after the above statement that it was the acceptance of a humiliating defeat by the elders that served as this dramatic event that de-authorized the elders:

> The immediate incidents which ignited the May Fourth Movement brought about a crisis in the relations of the generations. It was at the end of April 1919 that the news reached Peking of the humiliation of the Chinese government at the Paris Conference. The elders had submitted abjectly to the Japanese; they had acquiesced in the surrender of Shantung to Japan. A group of student study circles resolved to call a mass demonstration on May 7, National Humiliation Day, the fourth anniversary of Japan's so-called Twenty-One Demands. These student circles were small; the influential New Tide Society, for instance, had only thirty-seven members, all of them students at Peking University. They became leaders, however, in the May Fourth Movement. Then the official student bodies of the colleges and universities in Peking voted to join the demonstration—25,000 in all, according to their own claims, probably exaggerated.[15]

From this example it is apparent that the de-authorization of the Chinese elders came from their "unmanliness," something Feuer keeps talking about, in accepting a humiliating defeat from the Japanese. But does this mean that de-authorization generally follows only from lack of strength and courage in battle? Apparently not, for Feuer finds the "same kind" of de-authorization taking place in generation after generation of Russian fathers and sons:

> It was not the strength of fathers which made their sons react by becoming revolutionary activists. Rather it was their weakness, their failure, their femininity. . . .
> It was this de-authorization of the older generation (this dethronement of the superego) which was the root cause of the Russian student movement. The inventory of grievances, usually adduced, the restrictions on student political action, the formality of the university, were all secondary. Angelica Balabanoff, as a student revolutionary, was dismayed, for instance, by the absence of a German student movement when by all her Russian criteria there should have been a most militant one. . . .
> But the basic fact was that the German elder generations enjoyed a series of political successes in the Bismarckian era which gave them pride and prestige in the students' eyes.[16]

De-authorization, then, takes place when there is a lack of prestige, manliness, strength, victory, and so on, among the elders. The same theme is repeated for the American Jews of the early part of the twentieth century:

[15] *Ibid.*
[16] *Ibid.*, pp. 152–154.

The young students inhabited a cultural universe which their parents could not comprehend. Often their mothers and fathers were illiterate; and if they could read Yiddish, they were still alien to the American culture and language of Emerson, Bryant, Whitman. With their lack of dignity and their seeming acquiescence to persecution and poverty, with their lack of manliness and resistance, they were depreciated by the standards of the new literary-philosophical culture which the sons imbibed in school. They were at the lowest rung of society, defeated, always fleeing, and their lips could not form the words that school-teachers spoke. The sons were ashamed of their parents and prone to accept a redemptive philosophy which would acknowledge the claim of intellect to leadership and which would usher in social justice.[17]

But when is a group collectively a failure or a success? When is a group taken-as-a-whole, across all of life's vicissitudes, a victor or a victim? A winner or loser? Most groups' lives are made up of some of both, this-and-that. If we are to have a universal, cross-cultural explanation, then we must have a universal way of knowing when it is there and when it is not, the positive and negative cases of "de-authorization" and, if this formal theory is to be anything more than an *ex post facto argument of plausibility*, then it must specify for us when it will occur and when it will not. Feuer not only does not do this, while purporting to do so, but does not even look at all of the obvious negative cases. In a world of superpowers, or even a world of imperial powers, which is the way our world has been for the last several centuries, most national groups of elders are losers, bad losers. And, relatively speaking, those losers are certainly not the United States, Great Britain, the Soviet Union or most other nations of the Western world—all of which have student protest movements, according to Feuer. In a world of hierarchical societies and competitive struggles, most groups within any given society are losers. And, relatively speaking, those losers are not the fathers of the middle and upper class students—whom Feuer tries in this first chapter to show are the fathers of the students and the protesters. Feuer has even asserted that these sons-of-losers are not the ones who give way to generational conflict: "The engineering and working-class students, who so often have been immune to the revolt-ardor of middle class humanistic students, stand as dissenters to the doctrine of generational privilege. They have held more fast their sense of reality. . . ."[18]

The problems become even worse when Feuer gets around to considering the one case he knows best of all, the place where it all started for him and for most of the rest of us—Berkeley. Feuer has a whole section (from page 462 to page 466) devoted to the "Elder Generation De-authorized" at Berkeley, but, unfortunately, he has no significant mention of just what constituted this de-authorization. We can only conclude that he wishes us to determine what constituted de-authorization at Berkeley from the earlier discussions of unmanliness, etc. And, indeed, this does fit his discussion. This is even shown in the title of the section: "The Berkeley Faculty Capitulates: An Elder Generation De-authorized."[19] He then goes on to give details on the "capitulation," speculates on the various reasons for doing this, and so

[17] *Ibid.*, p. 425.
[18] *Ibid.*, p. 530.
[19] *Ibid.*

on. But there is something profoundly disturbing about this argument. For all that we may join him in denouncing the kind of "unmanly, emasculated" faculty who cave in under such threats (or however one might wish to put it), any de-authorization resulting from that cave-in can hardly be used to explain why there were those threats—that student protest movement—to begin with. It might lead to further de-authorization, but it could hardly be the beginning. Most especially, it could not be the beginning because the Berkeley faculty were mainly winners, men of great academic and worldly prestige—and income and power. Their only defeat was at the *hands of the students.* Moreover, why would the faculty or the administration be significant in creating their sense of de-authorization anyhow? Why not their fathers? After all, Feuer has argued very strongly, and rightly, that a large percentage of the student rebels came to Berkeley "looking for a generational battlefield." Many of them were already rebels, so surely it would have had to be their fathers who were de-authorized. Yet it couldn't be their fathers in general, since Feuer knows as well as anyone else that their fathers were very generally successful men, not lonely failures skulking around skid-row. Their fathers were often significant participants in the machinery of the most powerful nation in the history of the world, men of financial success in the most wealthy nation in the world, men of power in a mighty nation that had won two world wars and innumerable little ones, men who could be heard in a nation that could destroy the world. What could these men or the faculty and administration at Berkeley possibly have in common in the way of collective "unmanliness," "failure," "effeminency," and "demeaning poverty" with the Chinese losers, the inept Russian fathers, and the Jewish immigrant fathers (who had shown the courage to move their families half-way around the world to start a new life in a difficult world of intense competition and who had shown the decency of raising their children to want something better)?

The whole theory fails on this crucial point, this inability to specify just what constitutes de-authorization, the crucial independent variable in the theory. In the end, the implicit meaning of de-authorization is circular: de-authorization comes to mean "whatever mental state it is that precedes student rebellion." What Feuer fails to see is that the fundamental problem is precisely that of specifying *why* they no longer are willing to accept the authority of the older generation. Why, for example, do they choose one kind of group or standard in terms of which they judge their fathers and the collective older generation rather than another group or standard? Why do they see them as failures or successes? Feuer has avoided the fundamental problem of specifying the reasons for the meanings given by the students to their elders' situations and actions. The work is based on the assumption that some way has been found to solve problems of specifying why things mean what they do to some group, and that this can even be done cross-culturally; but what this way might be is never stated. It seems clear from an analysis of the details of the work that in fact no way has been found.

It also seems clear that any psychologistic approach, either cross-cultural or intra-cultural, will face the same basic inability to deal with the meaning of things to the participants. The approach seems inevitably to lead to an evasion of the phenomena, and, consequently, an evasion of the issues that are important to the participants. The same thing seems true of the sociologistic, or structural, theories that have been proposed by so many sociologists.

THE STRUCTURAL THEORIES

Most sociologists are inveterate structuralists, in the same way that psychologists are inveterate individualizers: they have built structuralism into the very basic public rationales for their professional existence and they have trained generations of students to look at any given events in the world in those terms. When they come to explain events such as student protest movements, they automatically adapt a structural point of view. In the case of the student protest movements, this has meant that they try to provide the structural background of the movement and the participants and implicitly assume that these constitute an "explanation." For example, they commonly put great effort into determining by "scientific" methods the family backgrounds of the participants in any protest event, and then they provide just any old speculation that they happen to like to "explain" how it is that these backgrounds, which are never anything more than rough statistical sharings of factors, can produce these events, these protest actions. Lipset,[20] Flacks,[21] and others, for example, argue that those who were involved in very specific protests at Berkeley and Chicago tend to come from upper-middle-class families with liberal values; and they try to show that, indeed, more of those involved report such backgrounds than do those who are not involved (some lesser structuralists don't even provide control samples). They then concentrate on "speculating" about the relations between this one most frequent background factor and the kinds of meaningful definitions they might give to the situations that would lead them to engage in the protest movement at that time. Some of them then treat this one factor *as if* it were explaining the whole thing (all the variance), even though they know on methodological grounds that it could not possibly explain more than a small part of the variance and that such correlations can never validly be assumed to be causal relations without evidence that there is no more general causal factor(s) producing both of them, which can only be done by far more extensive and detailed investigations of the many things taking place in the situation and in the backgrounds. (For example, it is perfectly possible and plausible to argue that those of higher status are far more apt to take part in public demonstrations simply because being thrown out of school seems less important to them—and less likely—than it would to students with lower family status, for whom expulsion would be far more costly over the long run. The nature of their families may have little more to do with it than this. Structural correlations cannot prove it one way or the other, especially when they take into consideration so very few factors as they normally do in these studies of student demonstrators.) Again, such structural speculations are based on only two or three such studies at the most "elite institutions," a sample that is not very likely to

---

[20] See Lipset and Altbach, *op. cit.*, Lipset, "The Activist: A Profile," *op. cit.*
[21] Flacks, Richard, "The Liberated Generation: An Exploration of the Roots of Student Protest," *Journal of Social Issues,* Vol. XXIII, No. 3, 1967.

prove representative. Most of the structuralists, and certainly the more sophisticated of them, such as Flacks and Lipset, do not try to explain everything by any one structural variable, such as the status of one's family of origin. At the very least, they consider a number of "structural variables." But they do tend strongly to take one of these structural variables, generally the status of one's family, as the starting point around which they build their theories. This one variable then becomes the cornerstone upon which the rest of the theory is built. In some cases it even becomes the basis for formulating all the other basic questions, and, thence, the basic hypothesis of the theory. This, for example, is true of Flack's work on the student protesters. After presenting his evidence on some protesters at the University of Chicago, he then asks:

> How, then, can we account for the emergence of an obviously dynamic and attractive radical movement among American students in this period? Why should this movement be particularly appealing to youth from upper-status, highly educated families? Why should such youth be particularly concerned with problems of authority, of vocation, of equality, of moral consistency? Why should students in the most advanced sector of the youth population be disaffected with their own privilege?[22]

In addition, such structural points of view face the terrible problem of not being able to deal with the "positive negatives," those who fall in the one category but not the "right" one. For example, what of all those high-status students at Vassar and Wellesley, at Williams and Haverford? After all, the average status of students at USC makes Berkeley students look like AFDC specimens. Why did protest not start and become most virulent at the schools with the highest status students—such as Princeton or USC? Why Berkeley, years before Harvard? The structuralists will argue that there are "other" structural factors—there always are. Berkeley before Harvard because of the "West Coast effect"? But, then, why Berkeley rather than Stanford or USC? Or is it because there are more liberal Jewish students at Berkeley? The structuralists who insist on finding some common background factors will no doubt go on searching for some set of factors that will provide a "plausible explanation" of the events, but they will be plausible only to those who are true believers in the structural point of view to begin with.

Certainly there are some structural factors of crucial importance in explaining these events. That is, there must be some patterning of events that lies behind the observed pattern of student protest movements; for surely such a mass of similar events does not just suddenly appear on the historical scene by chance or by some random confluence of events. But the crucial question is what kinds of structural events or factors? The traditional structuralists in sociology are also generally traditional positivists, especially those who do research rather than "general systems analysis." As a result they implicitly start their investigations with the assumption that those structural factors that will be of crucial importance in explaining the events will in fact be precisely those factors which the researcher can *count*, or get quantitative measures on a beautifully simple, linear, and monotonic scale that can very

---

[22] *Ibid.*, p. 59.

easily be analyzed by the simplest forms of mathematical thought devised for handling functions of a real variable. (The whole thing is terribly convenient and every positivistic structuralist of this sort must be eternally grateful to the Great Artificer who so graciously built the world with the researcher's convenience in mind.) Since so many of these positivistic structuralists studying student protest movements have also been deeply concerned with stratification, some from the Marxist standpoint and some from a more conventional standpoint, they have implicitly assumed that the stratification "variables" that are subject to simple counting procedures will be the crucial ones—hence self-reports on family income and occupation, rather than self-reports on fears of death, love of life, and so on. But, since they do recognize in some way that such variables can hardly be expected to "explain" more than a small part of the variance, they generally use a multi-factored approach, throwing in any other variables that meet the *convenience test*, without trying to see how the various structural elements might be related to each other.

What they almost always fail to see is that the crucial (historical) structural factors are (1) the existence of certain general subcultures, specifically, the youth culture and the student culture, which form the general background for all students of the protest movements and provide much of the meaning for the students of such things as their parental status, and (2) the "structural," nonnegotiable aspects of their situation as students in our society today, that is, the racial situation, the Vietnam situation and their draft status, and many lesser aspects of their situation which most members of our society, or government officials, are not willing to negotiate in determining the individual situations of students. In addition, they apparently fail to see that, even with these general structural factors existing, there is certainly no guarantee, no certainty, that student protest will appear at a given university, at a given time, or in any given form. There are a great number of important factors in the immediate situations, that is, in the situations faced by students and others involved at the time any series of events occurs, that are very much negotiable. These factors are negotiated by the various participants, and determine whether a protest movement arises, whether protests occur, what they are like, what their effects are, whether they recur, and so on.[23] These immediate-situational, concrete phenomena are the ones which are very much determined by the free choices of the individuals involved. It is undoubtedly true that as the situations encountered in protests become typified—especially as they become stereotyped by the structured communications that take place through the mass media—and as the sides become increasingly polarized into "enemy" camps, the amount of freedom of choice, of individual negotiation, that can take place in any given situation involving that typified protest is greatly decreased. The participants in such typified, polarized situations come increasingly to respond to what "everyone in this kind of situation knows is true," very largely because the existence of such a typified set of beliefs puts a frame around the activities which no one can easily go around because anyone involved is likely, and is known to be likely, to be thinking in those terms. But even in such typified,

[23] Douglas, Jack D., "The Social Construction of Moral Meanings," in *Deviance and Respectability*, Jack D. Douglas, ed., New York: Basic Books, Inc., 1970.

polarized situations, which the student protest movements have been rapidly approaching and which have given recent confrontation that aura of inevitability, of necessity, found in Greek tragedies, there is still an important element of free choice that helps to determine the direction and intensity of events, even when they cannot be reversed or prevented.

EVADING THE THEORY

But there is another danger faced in explaining student protest movements, one that is the opposite of evading the phenomena. There are some social scientists today who would argue that we must not "give" any meanings to social phenomena. To them the entire purpose of "social science" is to determine only how the members involved see such events. To try to go beyond this is, they believe, only to impose our own meanings on them and, thus, to distort them. This is the opposite point of view, to those who evade the issues; this point of view *evades the explanation,* at least to the extent of evading any explanation other than those which the involved members give for the events. This point of view submerges any "social science" in commonsense, makes "social science" the captive of commonsense, and denies that it is possible to achieve any form of knowledge or understanding that goes beyond the *cultural wisdom* of the members. While this point of view is in many ways a valuable corrective to the rampant structuralism and assumptions of irrationalism of ordinary people made by earlier social scientists, it has its own fundamental weaknesses. Most importantly, it undercuts the whole idea of a "social science." Without any adequate justification, it denies the efficacy of human reason in gaining a better understanding of human affairs through systematic studies and analyses of the sort that the man acting within commonsense never has time for, even if he has an inclination for it.

What is needed is a more middle range approach. It is of vital concern to the social scientist to determine what the members of society think and feel, for without this there is no source of information. Human actions are the result of the meanings of things to the individuals involved: human action is meaningful action. Few of us would doubt that there is a great deal of subconscious motivation, rhetoric, lying, and so on in ordinary human action. Certainly we must not take everything the members say or do at face value. For example, it is certainly true that in many instances student protesters are "playing to the galleries," "motivated by box office," "simulating commitment to liberal causes" in order to "radicalize" the rest of the students, and lying to the press. But we must carefully observe all of their activities that we can in order to determine what is "substance" and what is "shadow," what is simulation or lie, and what is sincere commitment and concern. To sweep all of this aside by declaring that it is all "really" irrationalism, "really determined by forces beyond the conscious realization" of the participants, or that it is all merely the epiphenomena of basic structural determinants that only the social scientist can divine, is the most rampant form of irrationalism and overweening expertise. Without closely studying what the participants say and do, and using this to unravel the truth about their internal states, the true meanings of things to them, where is the social scientist to get any information on the real world—any "data"? If he does not do this, he is left with nothing other than his own speculations and his own irrationalisms.

Rather than evading the issues, we must recognize that the issues are of vital concern to the participants, that they have real significance in leading them to undertake protests. The important question is not whether we should be concerned with what they say about their own actions, but what they "really" mean; not whether the issues are important, but what the "real" issues are. This is a fundamental problem for which there are no easy solutions and for which, as yet, we can hope for little more than partial solutions.

While I have concentrated thus far on the important failings of certain fundamental perspectives that have been involved in most of the previous theories of the student protest movements, it must not be concluded that these earlier explanations are irrelevant to constructing an adequate explanation of these events. This would be far from the truth. . . . These various works have provided us with what I believe are the crucial elements in explaining the protest movements; and there are few of them that have not been at least partly right, for the simple reason that most of them are very much mixed theories, multifactored theories. The primary problem has been in not seeing these various factors in the right historical context, especially the context of the basic changes taking place in the social positions and meanings of youth and college students, and the political context of youth today.

3: Ideology and Social Movements

The term "ideology" derives from an eighteenth-century group of French thinkers who desired to create a "science of ideas" or a "philosophy of the mind." Antoine Louis Destutt de Tracy, a leading spokesman of this group, saw ideology as involving the proposition that "political principles are derived from knowledge of the mind, and from the study of sensations."[1] Acting on this view, the **ideologues** were concerned with the study of the mind and its functions. The prominent role played by ideologues in the French Revolution created a backlash and they came to be seen as radical troublemakers. In 1812, Napoleon voiced this view of ideology, writing: "It is to ideology, that obscure metaphysic, . . . that we are to attribute all the calamities that our beloved France has experienced."[2] During the Napoleonic period, ideology came to represent any belief system that was hostile to the existing social order.[3]

Karl Marx and Friedrich Engels enlarged and complicated the notion of ideology, arguing that generally accepted ideologies were the dominant belief systems supporting the interests of the ruling class. Marxism conceived of ideologies as containing either "false consciousness" or "true consciousness." In the Marxist view, true consciousness was opposed to the capitalist ruling class. In contrast, false consciousness was any ideological position that supported the exploitative social system. Workers without a revolutionary ideology were imbued with false consciousness because their world view did not fit their life situation and did tend to support the interests of the ruling class.

In **Ideology and Utopia,** the German sociologist Karl Mannheim further developed the Marxist distinction between true and false consciousness. Concerned with the meanings contained in the concept of ideology, Mannheim posited two senses for the term. When one regards an opponent's ideas or arguments as serving the purposes of self-interest, whether consciously or unconsciously, one is applying what Mannheim called "a particular conception of ideology." In this view, the ideological component is only part of a larger conceptual framework and is a distortion of a "truth" that can be validated by reference to a common belief system. However, when one views an entire belief system of a historical period or a socioeconomic class as distinct from one's own, then one is applying what Mannheim

---

[1] Quoted in Richard H. Cox, ed., *Ideology, Politics, and Political Theory* (Belmont, Calif.: Wadsworth Publishing Company, 1969), p. 15.
[2] *Ibid.,* p. 14.
[3] Henry D. Aiken, *The Age of Ideology* (New York: Mentor Books, 1956), pp. 16–17.

called "a total conception of ideology." In this instance structural relations between the total system of thought and its social setting are analyzed without regard for individual motivation. Given the adversary relation implicit in the term "ideology," Mannheim further distinguishes the two conceptions by noting that an antagonist will try to "annihilate" specific beliefs from the vantage point of a particular conception and will try to destroy the intellectual basis for these beliefs from the vantage point of a total conception.[4]

The total assault on established belief systems informs most radical critiques of society. In an effort to transform society, the radical ideologue seeks to convince nonbelievers that the accepted interpretation of reality is "false" and that his own is "true." The **Communist Manifesto** is perhaps one of the earliest instances of a political effort to create a new ideological sense of reality. Lenin emphasized the role of radical movements in the conflict between true and false ideologies. In "What Is to Be Done?" he indicated that the proletariat is only capable of "outbursts of desperation" or at best "trade union consciousness." The latter, of course, was false ideology in Lenin's view. The communist vanguard, he further argued, possessed true political consciousness based on the science of Marxism, and must therefore inculcate this ideology in the exploited masses.[5] The consciousness of a radical movement transcends the total ideology of a society and "breaks the bonds of existing order,"[6] as Mannheim noted. Many social movements see themselves as the possessors of the truth, while outsiders are perceived as either wholly unaware or victims of false consciousness.

The two major types of radical ideologies—the Right and the Left—each have their own basic set of assumptions. As Silvan Tomkins points out in considerable detail, the Left-Right polarity contains certain conflicting assumptions about the nature of man and society.[7] The ideology of the Right assumes that man is essentially evil and in need of control, and that it is the role of traditional social institutions to accomplish this task. Society, in this view, is basically sound. In contrast, the Left sees man as basically good. However, man's potential is hampered by society and it is only by changing social institutions that man's potential can be realized.[8]

Although there are many variations on these basic themes, nearly all sociopolitical ideologies possess a fairly uniform set of assumptions about man and society. Despite the differences between the Right and Left ideologies, both revolutionary and regressive movements place a considerable amount of emphasis on correct ideology. Daniel Bell, discussing the Marxist Left in America, suggests:

> A social movement can rouse people when it can do three things: simplify ideas, establish a claim to truth, and in the union of the two demand a commitment to action. . . . The nineteenth century ideologies (Marxism, Syndicalism), by emphasizing inevitability and by infusing passion into their followers, could compete with religion. By identifying inevitability with progress they linked up with the positive values of science.[9]

4 Karl Mannheim, *Ideology and Utopia* (New York: Harcourt Brace Jovanovich, 1936), p. 56. See also Robert K. Merton, *Social Theory and Social Structure* (New York: The Free Press, 1968).

5 V. I. Lenin, "What Is to Be Done?" in *Collective Works*, vol. 4 (New York: International Publishers, 1929).

6 Mannheim, *op. cit.*, p. 192.

7 See also T. B. Bottomore, *Critics of Society: Radical Thought in North America* (New York: Vintage Books, 1966); and Winston White, *Beyond Conformity* (New York: The Free Press, 1961).

8 Mannheim, *op. cit.*, p. 192.

9 Daniel Bell, *The End of Ideology: On the Exhaustion of Political Ideas in the Fifties*, rev. ed. (New York: Collier Books, 1962); and Herbert Blumer, "Social Movements," in *Principles of Sociology*, ed. Alfred M. Lee (New York: Barnes and Noble, 1946).

Ideological movements, as Nahirny indicates, make very specific demands on their members. In Nahirny's terms, "ideas and beliefs become 'personalized' and human beings 'ideologized.' " Ideological groups, according to Nahirny, demand total adherence to a particular world view.

Following the Second World War, there arose a debate on the role of ideological commitment in America centering on the "end of ideology" thesis presented by Daniel Bell and Seymour Martin Lipset.[10] Bell argued that ideology, once a "road to action," had come to a dead end. The passion of ideology, which led to radical action, had been extinguished by the misadventures of the Stalin purges, the Russo-German nonaggression pact, concentration camps, the suppression of Hungary, and the cold war. Given these events, which contradicted certain fundamental premises of the Left, Marxist ideology, Bell argued, had lost its "truth claim" and its power to persuade. Concurrently, Bell asserted, the rise of the "welfare state" abolished, at least in the West, the need for an ideology based on the perception of class exploitation and struggle. Lipset, in **Political Man,** by and large supported this thesis, adding:

> . . . democracy . . . is the good society itself in operation. . . . The democratic class struggle will continue, but it will be a fight without ideologies, without red flags, without May Day parades.[11]

As Chaim Waxman correctly notes, "the end of ideology" controversy centered on two premises: (1) that the truth-value of ideological politics is no longer believed in, and (2) that America has reached or is well on its way to reaching the "good society." The latter premise is violently disputed by a host of writers. Critics such as Aiken and Mills deny the good society notion posited by Bell.[12] Equally, Lipset's glorification of pluralism is rejected by these same critics. C. Wright Mills, for one, suggested in **Causes of World War III** that the domination of the "power elite" prohibits pluralism in America.[13] Other social thinkers contended that the socioeconomic conditions in the West required innovative ideologies for the achievement of the "good life."[14]

Joseph R. Gusfield argues that pluralism, seen by proponents of the end of ideology thesis as an ideal, may in fact lead to political extremism and the rise of radical ideologies.[15] Gusfield suggests that five conditions in pluralism may radicalize individuals: (1) certain groups, such as Negroes and young people, are excluded from political participation, (2) other groups, such as white southerners, see the future as far less satisfying than the past, (3) an imbalance exists among competing pluralistic groups, (4) some groups may find the compromises required by successful pluralism too great a cost on a given issue, and (5) crises that are outside of the pluralistic rules of the game, such as depressions and wars, may erupt. In this view, pluralism does not appear to possess all of the advantages claimed by Bell and Lipset.

The reemergence of ideological groups, both Right and Left, was coupled with the politicalization of segments of society previously seen as relatively free of ideological politics. A classic example of this process, reported by Harvey Molotch,

10 Seymour Martin Lipset, *Political Man: The Social Bases of Politics* (Garden City: N.Y., Anchor Books, 1963).
11 *Ibid.*, pp. 439, 445.
12 See Chaim I. Waxman, *The End of Ideology Debate* (New York: Funk and Wagnalls, 1968).
13 C. Wright Mills, *Causes of World War III* (New York: Ballantine Books, 1958).
14 See especially Irving Louis Horowitz, Robert A. Haber, Stephen W. Rousseas, and James Farganis, in Waxman, *op. cit.;* Michael Harrington, *The Accidental Century* (New York: Macmillan, 1965); and Gary B. Rush and R. Serge Denisoff, *Social and Political Movements* (New York: Appleton-Century-Crofts, 1971), pp. 421–96.
15 Joseph R. Gusfield, "Mass Society and Extremist Politics," *American Sociological Review* 27 (February 1962): 19–30.

is the temporary radicalization of the upper-middle class in Santa Barbara following the oil spillage of 1969. Similar processes of politicalization have also been reported in reference to opposition to the Vietnam war and opposition to federally sponsored integration programs in housing, education, and occupations. With an ever increasing number of social strains, it appears that ideology may be on the rise once again.

The meaning of ideology has shifted from the relatively simple notions of de Tracy to the complexities of Marx, Engels, and Mannheim. The ideologies of the thirties, as many have observed, are no longer relevant. In their place other radical ideologies appeared on both the Right and Left during the sixties. The Progressive Labor party, Gay Lib, Women's Lib, the Black Panthers, the John Birch Society, and the Minutemen all fit Nahirny's definition of an ideological group: "groups which make their members relate to one another in the light of ideas and belief rather than in the light of personal qualities or specific functions which they perform."

Left and Right: Assumptions of Ideological Polarity

SILVAN TOMKINS

The first and most important pair of assumptions which underlies the polarity [of extreme right-, middle-, and left-wing ideologies] is: Man is an end in himself versus man is not an end in himself: the valuable exists independent of man. The major assumption from which most of the other forms of the polarity may be derived is this belief of man about man. No question with which man confronts himself engages him more than the question of his own worth. On the left he conceives himself to be an end in himself, to be of ultimate value; he wishes to be himself and to realize the potentialities which are inherent in him. On the right man is at best neutral, without value. There exists a norm, an objective value, independent of him, and he may become valuable by participation in, conformity to, or achievement of this norm. On the left, as a derivative, whatever perpetuates man's existence is valuable and whatever destroys or threatens it is of negative value. On the right, anything which harms or threatens man is neutral. It may be considered positive if it changes his wishes or behavior in the direction of positive values or if it punishes him for seeking negative values or failing to achieve positive value. It will be negative if it changes his wishes or behavior in the direction of negative values or if it punishes him for seeking positive values or rewards him for failing to achieve positive value.

From this basic postulate there are a number of derivatives which are essentially variants of the affirmation or denial of the value of man, or man is good versus man is evil. The first variant on the affirmation of man's value, in general, concerns his moral value. The left-wing ideology not only affirms his general significance but, as a special case, affirms man's inherent goodness in contrast to the extreme right-wing affirmation of man's essential

From "Left and Right: A Basic Dimension of Ideology and Personality" (Editor's title: "Left and Right: Assumptions of Ideological Polarity") is reprinted from Robert W. White, editor, *The Study of Lives* (New York: Atherton Press, 1963); copyright © 1963 by Atherton Press. Reprinted by permission of the author and Aldine Publishing Company.

badness. Whereas the left affirms that man must be corrupted to become bad, i.e. to violate his own nature, the right affirms that he must labor by the sweat of his brow to become good. In the more extreme right-wing ideologies man is so bad that he can never completely attain a state of goodness.

Man should be the object of love versus man should be loved if he is worthy. A second derivative concerns the appropriate personal positive affects toward man. The left urges man to love man because he is an end in himself, whereas the right makes love conditional upon his conformity and his achieved value. If he fails to meet the norm, the right urges hate rather than love.

The third derivative is: man should be the object of respect and approbation versus man should be respected if he is respectable. The left urges unconditional glorification and respect and approbation for man as well as unconditional love, whereas the right urges a conditional respect dependent on norm achievement or compliance.

The fourth variant is: unconditional and unlimited versus conditional and limited approbation toward the achievements of man. The left urges unconditional and unlimited respect, not only for man per se, but for all his works. These are the glory of man. The right urges not only an approbation conditional upon norm achievement but an approbation limited by an awareness of the essential discrepancy between man and the norm. Instead of joy, pride, and confidence in future achievement as extensions of glory, the right urges restraint and a temperate enthusiasm for the future achievements of the human race, with a hint of contempt for the inevitable human frailty which may endanger future achievement and with some skepticism about the inherent recalcitrance of nature to man's purposes.

Approbation of man's affects versus disapprobation of man's affects is the fifth derivative. Nowhere is the polarity between the right and left sharper than in the attitudes toward man's affects. The left has positive affects toward affects per se and is at home in the realm of feeling. The right is uneasy about and intolerant of affect per se, lest it endanger norm attainment. Approval of human affect is limited and contingent on its utility in enabling compliance, or as a reward for norm achievement. More often affect is portrayed as intruding and jeopardizing rational control of behavior.

Approbation versus disapprobation of man's reason is the sixth derivative. For the left, reason is another instance of the glory of man for which there should be approbation. In its relationship to the world perceived through the senses, reason guarantees man a certain distance between himself and the potentially excessive pressure of the immediacy of the senses. This is the position of the left. In contrast, the right wing views reason in this same context as overweening and a source of much error, which can be held in check only by the authority of the world external to the individual, the external norm which impresses itself through the senses.

The seventh, and last, derivative of the first major assumption is: disapprobation versus approbation of reason as a restraining force on affects. There is no clearer example of the ambiguity of concepts in ideology than the various roles in which reason has been cast by both the right and the left. Although the left approves of reason when it enhances man's independence of brute empiricism and although the right disapproves of reason when it sets itself in overweening opposition to the weight of authority and tradition as these are communicated over the sensory channels, the left is as hostile to reason as the right is approving when reason is viewed as a function controlling the drives and affects. When reason is viewed as limiting and restraining the feelings and drives, the left views this as a violation of the nature of the human being, but the right under these same conditions views reason as the representative of the norm within the human being and therefore as an object of approbation. This reversal of position between the right and left with respect to reason is evidence for our belief that the underlying assumption in the polarity of the right and left is the acceptance of the human being as an end in himself versus the glorification of a normative realm and the essential derogation of man. When one understands the fundamental role which these oversimplified, strongly positive and negative affects toward man play in the ideological polarity, one can account for a variety of apparent inconsistencies in the status assigned to various of man's functions and characteristics.

The second major assumption underlying the polarity, which is, however, rarely made explicit, is that of the identity of the real and the valuable. The real and the valuable are identical: man is real versus man is unreal. Theoretically it would have been possible to assume that man might be the most important entity in nature, but that he was not as real as the world in which he lived because it existed before him and would continue to exist after there were no men; or that man was insignificant and of no value, but that he was real, as evil is real, and even that he created the world as an idea out of the depths of his willfulness, as his plaything. In fact, however, there appears to be an extraordinary correlation within all ideologies, whether of the left or of the right, that if man is the most valuable phenomenon, he is also the most real entity and that if the norm or essence is the most valuable phenomenon, it is also the entity of greatest reality, in comparison with which, as in Plato, both man and nature are poor copies. Psychologically it is obvious enough that what is important must be real and what is real must be important, but the philosophic generalization of such an assumption is theoretically unwarranted despite its psychological persuasiveness.

The Greek legacy to Western civilization was in fact a double one. First was the left-wing ideology of man as the measure, in the sense of creator, and second was the right-wing ideology of the Platonic essence, independent and prior to man. Historians have emphasized one or the other of these ideologies according to their own ideological postures. In contrast to the emphasis on the significance of the legacy of Platonism, Hadas has stressed the left-wing legacy:

> The most striking single feature of the Homeric ethos is the enormous importance attached to individual prowess, individual pride, individual reputation. . . . The Homeric hero may not compromise loyalty to his own being with loyalty to any other, human or divine. . . . Achilles actually prays for the defeat of his own side in war, to enhance his own glory, and he allows his comrades to die in battle when it is in his power to protect them. . . . He and others like him earn the title of hero because they enlarge mankind by demonstrating man's capacity for greatness, by endowing the commonplace things of life, food and weapons and clothing, with an aura of glory, by pushing back the boundaries of what is possible to man. . . . His super-

human stature is officially recognized, after his death, and he receives annual offerings on his particular day and his mediation is invoked in realms of activity appropriate to his heroism. . . . The Homeric ideal is summarized in a single line "To strive always for excellence and to surpass all others."[1]

The third major polarity is that values are what man wishes versus values exist independent of man. Inherent in the assumption that man is or is not an end in himself is an implicit definition of the nature of values. For the left wing, a value is a human wish; we would say, a human affect. If what he wishes defines the valuable, man can become an end in himself insofar as man wishes to be himself and loves himself. For the right wing, values are independent of man and therefore men may or may not wish for the good, the true, and the beautiful. Wishing per se cannot make it so, and wishing neither adds nor subtracts from the value or reality of anything. The left wing's theory of value is essentially an affect theory of value. As Ralph Barton Perry defined value, it is any object of any interest. We should generalize his use of the word interest, however, if we wish to describe the typical value theory of the left-wing ideologist, since the latter in fact believes in and defends the entire spectrum of affects.

The fourth polarity is that man should satisfy and maximize his drives and affects—hunger and sex, himself and others, work and play, novelty, risk, and familiarity, intimacy and detachment—versus man should be governed by norms which in turn modulate his drives and affects. The left-wing ideologist urges maximal satisfaction of the full spectrum of the drives and the positive affects. He regards the satisfaction of both sex and hunger as natural and good. As Bertrand Russell, among many others, has expressed it: "The source of all the harm is that the good life has been sought in obedience to a negative imperative, not in broadening and developing the natural desires and instincts."[2]

In contrast, John Locke: "As the strength of the body lies chiefly in being able to endure hardships, so also does that of the mind. And the great principle and foundation of all virtue and worth is placed in this; that a man is able to deny himself his own desires, cross his own inclinations, and purely follow what reason directs as best, though appetite lean the other way."[3]

The right-wing ideologist urges the control of all the drives and the affects by reason, in the interest of some norm. The left-wing ideologist stresses man's natural affective investment in himself as well as in others. He presents man as naturally both self-interested and socially responsive. The right-wing ideologist is more likely to stress man's natural egoism to the disadvantage of his social responsiveness. The latter, he is likely to argue, is a by-product of control of natural egoism by norms, through the exercise of reason. The left-wing theorist portrays man as equally excited by work as by play. The right-wing theorist makes work a more serious, more alien demand upon the human being and rejects play as utterly childish. The left-wing theorist portrays man drawn to novelty and risk and to familiarity, excited

---

[1] M. Hadas, *Humanism* (New York: Harper & Brothers, 1960), p. 132.
[2] B. Russell, *On Education* (London: Allen and Unwin, 1930), p. 250.
[3] J. Locke, *Some Thoughts Concerning Education* (New York: Charles Scribner's Sons, 1928), p. 350.

by the new and addicted to the old. Thus Camus, in *The Myth of Sisyphus:* "Delicious anguish of being, exquisite proximity of a danger we do not know, it is to live then to run to our death. . . . I have always had the impression that I lived on the high seas, threatened, at the heart of royal happiness."[4]

The quest for the familiar in the novel is more explicit in Fromm:

> There is no innate "drive for progress" in man; it is the contradiction in his existence that makes him proceed in the way he set out. Having lost paradise, the unity with nature, he has become the eternal wanderer (Odysseus, Oedipus, Abraham, Faust); he is impelled to go forward and with everlasting effort to make the unknown known by filling in with answers the blank spaces of his knowledge. He must give account to himself of himself, and of the meaning of his existence. He is driven to overcome this inner split, tormented by a craving for "absoluteness," for another kind of harmony which can lift the curse by which he was separated from nature, from his fellow men, and from himself. . . . This split in man's nature leads to dichotomies which I call existential because they are rooted in the very existence of man: they are contradictions which man cannot annul but to which he can react in various ways, relative to his character and his culture. . . .
>
> If he faces the truth without panic he will recognize that there is no meaning to life except the meaning man gives his life by the unfolding of his powers, by living productively; and that only constant vigilance, activity, and effort can keep us from failing in the one task that matters—the full development of our powers within the limitations set by the laws of our existence. . . .
>
> There is only one solution to his problem: to face the truth, to acknowledge his fundamental aloneness and solitude in a universe indifferent to his fate, to recognize that there is no power transcending him which can solve his problem for him. Man must accept the responsibility for himself and the fact that only by using his powers can he give meaning to his life. But meaning does not imply certainty; indeed the quest for certainty blocks the search for meaning.[5]

The right-wing ideologist is committed neither to novelty and risk, nor to familiarity, but to the norm, be it an achievement norm, a norm of morality, or a norm of manners. These may demand that the individual risk his life in the interest of the norm, but they may also demand that he conform to tradition as the carrier of the norm. The fact that human beings are excited by risk and by novelty and that they enjoy the familiar is irrelevant.

Finally, the left-wing ideologist urges both intimacy and detachment as basic human needs. In his stress on intimacy he is captivated by all those modes of knowing in which the distinction between the subject and the object is lost. He believes there is no better way to acquaint oneself with the other than to coalesce with that other, be it human, impersonal, or divine. Even within the doctrine of mysticism there are important variations in the degree of intimacy permitted the subject. Thus in the so-called throne

[4] A. Camus, *The Myth of Sisyphus* (New York: Knopf, 1955), p. 215.

[5] E. Fromm, *Man for Himself* (New York: Holt, Rinehart and Winston, Inc., 1947), pp. 41, 44–45.

mysticism the worshipper maintains a respectful distance from the object of adoration. At the same time the left-wing theorist urges the importance of detachment, perspective, and rational analysis to understand the object better and to see it in its relatedness to other objects. Thus the left-wing philosopher is likely to be one who spends much of his life in reflection on the value of immediacy. Whether a left-wing ideologist stresses one or the other, as he may do, depends in part on what he takes for granted and what is the most visible enemy. Thus if he lives in an age of superstition, he is apt to glorify rational analysis. If he lives in an age of science he is apt to stress, as do the existentialists today, the value of intimate surrender to the object.

The right-wing ideologist is indifferent about these distinctions, so long as there is norm attainment and compliance. However, he rejects mysticism and too great intimacy, lest it be too orgiastic and too emotional and lest the distinction between the worshipper and the worshipped become too attenuated. In science he is contemptuous of any doctrine of intuition, lest it weaken the demands of rigorous proof. But he is equally suspicious of too great an emphasis on detachment and theoretical activity, for fear that the authority of the real world be undermined or derogated.

The right-wing ideologist in science is likely to urge a middle course, eschewing the Scylla of seduction by the object and the Charybdis of alienation of the object through overweening pride in the power of reason. In contrast, the left-wing ideologist is hostile to a stable marriage between the self and the object, preferring both the passion of a love affair and the detachment of the uncommitted bachelor. In terms of psychoanalytic ideology, left-wing science oscillates between the oceanic communion of the womb, or the oral stage, and the overweening pride of the phallic stage, whereas right-wing science is a derivative of the anal stage, in which the emphasis is on successfully duplicating the directives of the model and, above all, in making no mistakes.

The fifth major polarity is that man should minimize drive dissatisfaction and negative affects—hunger and sex, fear, shame, distress and aggression —versus man should maximize norm conformity and norm realization. The left urges first of all the sanctity of human life. It is an absolute which is not to be surrendered. In the American credo the human being has first of all the right to life, as well as to liberty and happiness. The right-wing thinker is not indifferent to the maintenance of life. He may be troubled by the taking of life, either one's own or another's, but mainly because it is a norm violation or violation of the will of God. He is not, however, troubled by the lives which must be surrendered in the name of the norm, be it God or State.

The left-wing ideologist urges that the frustration of either hunger or sex be minimized, whereas the right-wing ideologist regards them as either neutral or as impediments to the attainment or maintenance of piety, achievement, or whatever the norm that is affirmed. The left urges that the human being has the right to freedom from fear, from being humiliated, from distress, and from reason for anger. He defends however the right of the human being to be angry and to protest. As Camus expressed it in *The Myth of Sisyphus,* revolt is "the impulse that drives an individual to the defense of a dignity common to all men." The right urges control of aggression by the individual but urges its use for the punishment of norm violators. The use of aggression is, however, most often reserved to authority which represents the norm.

Contempt for the norm offender is urged upon all by the right. The left under similar circumstances counsels empathy and understanding and the imposition of negative sanctions only as a last resort in the interests of saving the lives and minimizing the suffering of others. Since the right is concerned only with the maintenance and achievement of norms, any violation of norms is appropriately punished through increasing the suffering of the offender. The right-wing ideologist defends the use of contempt as an agent of social control and is indifferent to the negative consequences of hierarchical relationships. The left-wing ideologist rejects contempt as a technique of social control lest it alienate and jeopardize social solidarity and egalitarian sentiments. All men are born free and equal, and should remain so. Shaming is therefore minimized and no man should bend the knee to another. Nor should anyone be terrorized, according to the ideology of the left. According to the right, beginning with the fear of God, it is appropriate that authority be the object of fear and trembling, particularly if insurrection is at question. According to the left, distress and suffering are to be outlawed and as minimized as humiliation and terror. Life should be made as tolerable as the imagination of man can so contrive it. For the right, offenders should suffer, and whether the pious are distressed is a matter of indifference. It is more often assumed that the way of both the blessed and the sinner are necessarily hard, since there is a permanent gap between the individual and the norm.

In the attitude of the left- and right-wing ideologists of science there is a differential sensitivity to the negative and positive affects. The left urges imagination and the maximizing of excitement and enjoyment in the pursuit of truth. Shame should occur only if the main chance has been missed. The right urges discipline and rigor and the minimizing of error, lest one be the proper object of contempt. Shame should occur if one has been shown to be in error or if one has had overweening pride and overreached himself. One stresses the logic of discovery, whereas the other stresses the logic of verification.

The sixth major polarity is: affect inhibition should be minimized versus affects should be controlled by norms. The left-wing theorist stresses the toxicity of affect control and inhibition, and it therefore becomes a special case of the principle of minimizing negative affect that such control should be kept to a minimum. The left-wing theorist is more alarmed at the cost to the individual of defending himself against the expression of distress, shame, aggression, excitement, or enjoyment than he is at the cost of freely expressing his affects. He is likely to stress the value both to the individual and to society of an openness and tolerance for intrusions of the irrational, of the Dionysian, of the *Weltschmerz*, of the *fin de siècle*. The right-wing ideologist sets himself sternly against such intrusions and argues for the importance of controlling affects in the interests of morality, achievement, piety, or classic beauty. It is not that he is necessarily, in Nietzsche's term, an apologist for the Apollonian rather than the Dionysian. It is rather that he is for some norm, which may require heroic mobilization of affect and energy to achieve or which may require unrelenting hostility against those who challenge the good, the true, or the beautiful. If that challenge is seen to be from within, then the most severe inhibition of the offending affects may be required; and, at the same time that positive affects toward the norm may be demanded, it may also be necessary not to inhibit all negative affects but to direct them against the self.

The seventh major polarity is that power should be maximized in order to maximize positive affects and to minimize negative affects versus power should be maximized to maximize norm compliance and achievement. All ideologists invoke a power postulate in which the ability of the individual to realize values is urged. The difference lies in which values the means-end power should maximize. The left wing is, first of all, an ideology of individualism. Although it does not set the individual into necessary conflict with society (since it urges that man is at once a self-interested and a social animal), nonetheless it has usually set itself against any subordination of the individual to the society, since society is conceived to be a set of individuals rather than the representative of some normative authority. During those historical periods when social and political authority is seen as violating the rights and dignity of man, the left-wing ideologist, as we have seen in the case of Homeric hero, is apt to set himself in violent opposition to tradition and even to the needs of others with whom he may in large measure identify himself. The same left-wing ideologist, confronted with mass misery, such as that which followed in the wake of the industrial revolution, may reject the robber baron and identify with the masses to such an extent that one may overlook the communality of these two pictures. What is common, first in identification with and glorification of the hero, and then in identification with and glorification of the masses against the exploiting, individualistic capitalist, is the belief in maximizing the power of human beings to control their own destiny, to maximize their positive affect, and to minimize their negative affect. It is a bias in favor of humanity, both the individual human being and groups of human beings. Historical circumstances dictate whether the heroic individual is pitted against society or whether society is pitted against the tyrant.

At another time the power of the creative individual to refuse the cake of custom, the pressures of the group toward conformity, is the message of the left-wing ideology. Whatever limits the power of human beings to maximize their positive affects and to minimize their negative affects—whether this limitation be internal or external, in the masses or in an elite class, in a corrupting or an exploiting individual—that limiting force will be opposed by the left-wing ideologist, depending on where the major threat is seen at the particular historical moment.

The idea of the importance of freedom is a derivative of the idea of power, since it has been supposed that without the freedom for each individual to grow in his own way there could be no development of individuals who differ from each other.

The emphasis on the full development of the human personality has dominated Western ideology since Leonardo. This was the ideal from the Renaissance artists, through the Elizabethans, through Locke, Voltaire, and Rousseau. As Bronowski maintained:

> The vision of the freely developing man, happy in the unfolding of

his own gifts is shared by men as different in their conceptions as Thomas Jefferson and Edmund Burke. . . . The Renaissance ideal of man had an element of condottiere brutality, which has lingered on in Western thought; it is perhaps inseparable from the Western admiration for power, over nature and over men. Something of this sense of power, of mastering the techniques and desires of the earthly life, is present in the ideal men of the Reformation—in Calvin's 'new man' and in the Puritan soldiery. . . . A different direction was set by the Tudor ideal of a gentleman and by the seventeenth-century ideal of the virtuoso. This direction leads from the humanist of the sixteenth century to the philosophe of the eighteenth and is seen at its best in the tolerant, rational, free, and yet convinced and single-minded men of English dissent and of the American Revolution.[6]

We agree with Bronowski's affirmation of the continuity of the idea of power as a fulfillment of the potentiality of the human being, but we would stress more than he does what each ideologist thought was the proper use of this power. For the right-wing ideologist it is not to maximize man's enjoyment and excitement and to minimize distress, fear, and shame, but to examine his power to achieve, to be a gentleman, to be virtuous, to be pious, to be perfect, or to amass wealth.

In the interests of power the left-wing ideologist affirms the desirability of power of the self (1) over the self, if and when any part of the self threatens to restrict the freedom of the self as a whole, as in the perpetuation of an infantile conscience or as in the swamping of the self by panic, grief, rage, or humiliation; (2) over other selves, including the state, if and when others threaten to restrict the freedom of the self; (3) over nature, if and when it is recalcitrant to the attainment of human purposes.

The eighth major assumption is the polarity between the principle of pluralism versus the principle of hierarchy. The left ideology assumes that conflict between affects within the individual and between individuals should be minimized. This is a derivative of the more general strategy of maximizing the positive affects and of minimizing the negative affects. Since all satisfactions are desirable, limitation by conflicting satisfactions is to be minimized. The right-wing ideology ordinarily orders all wishes according to a norm and according to the necessity of the particular wish or behavior in furthering maintenance or achievement of the norm. No attempt is made to minimize conflict per se.

The ninth major assumption is the polarity between the principle of selectivity by maximizing positive and minimizing negative affect versus the principle of selectivity by maximizing normative behavior. Not only is there a difference between the strategy of pluralism versus that of hierarchy, in which the left tries to minimize conflict as much as possible, while the right is indifferent to conflict per se, but when restrictions on maximizing strategies cannot be avoided, i.e. when the principle of pluralism breaks down, the left-wing ideology bases the choice between competing interests, either within the individual or between individuals, on the same principle as that which dictated pluralism. Thus if an individual is confronted with the necessity of surrendering one of his satisfactions in the interest of another, accord-

---

[6] J. Bronowski and B. Mazlish, *The Western Intellectual Tradition* (New York: Harper & Brothers, 1960), p. 522.

ing to the left this selectivity should be governed by the general strategy of maximizing positive and minimizing negative affects. Freud's reality principle by which the pleasure principle is governed is a familiar example. The right-wing ideology has another criterion: that should be surrendered which is lower in the normative hierarchy or which will most threaten some higher member of the hierarchy.

In a conflict of interests between men, resolution should be governed by the principle of maximizing wish fulfillment and minimizing wish frustration of every party to the conflict, according to the ideology of the left. According to right-wing ideology, in a conflict of interests between men resolution should be governed by the principle of maximizing norm achievement or conformity. When the norms were those of an aristocratic society, that basic conflict of interests perpetuated in the institution of slavery was solved in favor of the slave owner and rationalized on the grounds that he was the more worthy of the competing human beings and that the slave was a barbarian or in some way inferior.

The tenth major polarity is that of tolerance and amelioration of weakness versus intolerance and punishment of weakness. All ideologies of both the right and left, however much they may glorify man, have also taken notice of man's imperfections and frailties. The left-wing ideologist counsels forgiveness and indulgence and offers nurture. One should try to change the imperfect one by example, by love, and by the lure of identification. For hate return love. Toward those who sin by failure to do something, offer forgiveness, give yet another chance, offer support and inspire by exciting interest. When man is weak he most needs love. If man is not perfect, he is perfectible. Stress his positive qualities.

The right-wing ideologist has a complementary set of injunctions. Towards man's weakness man should be unrelenting, unforgiving, and punitive. If a man is weak, he should not be helped, he should help himself. Toward man's weakness, do not offer love, but demand reform and atonement. Against the will of the offender every pressure should be brought to bear to break that will. The weak should be toughened and the strong-willed should be curbed. Man should never be permitted to forget his imperfection, his sins, and his weaknesses. He is not perfect and there are limits to his perfectibility. For these discrepancies between the ideal and the actual, the appropriate response is to terrorize, to shame, and to distress the offender.

Let us examine Russell and Locke again, on the subject of education. First Russell:

> A thousand ancient fears obstruct the road to happiness and freedom. But love can conquer fear, and if we love our children nothing can make us withhold the great gift which it is in our power to bestow.[7]

Contrast this with Locke:

> Esteem and disgrace are, of all others, the most powerful incentives to the mind, when once it is brought to relish them. If you can once

[7] B. Russell, *On Education* (London: Allen and Unwin, 1930), p. 250.

get into children a love of credit and apprehension of shame and disgrace, you have put into them the right principle, which will constantly work and incline them to the right.[8]

Although the right-wing ideologist stresses negative sanctions, such as
shame and disgrace for weakness and error, he may also stress positive sanctions as a reward for norm maintenance or achievement. As we see in Locke,
the love of right principles is a shield against the shame and disgrace of
norm violation. Nonetheless, in response to actual norm violation the primary sanctions urged by right-wing ideologists are negative.

The details of the difference in socialization which ultimately produce
resonance to one or the other ideological posture we have considered elsewhere.[9] These concern differences in tolerance for, or intolerance of, the
several primary human affects: excitement, enjoyment, surprise, distress,
contempt, shame, fear, and anger.[10]

---

[8] *Loc. cit.*
[9] S. S. Tomkins, *Affect, Imagery, Consciousness* (New York: Springer, 1962).
[10] [The paper from which our selection is taken] was originally written in honor of
Henry A. Murray and delivered at the thirtieth anniversary celebration of the Harvard Psychological Clinic in 1957. This is a revised and expanded account of that
address.

Some Observations on Ideological Groups[1]

VLADIMIR C. NAHIRNY

Undue reliance has been placed in the sociological literature upon the common dichotomies *Gemeinschaft* [group-oriented] and *Gesellschaft* [self-oriented] and their many contemporary variations; yet ample evidence suggests that these antithetical types present "conceptual obstacles" to the fruitful analysis of a myriad of social groups and, indeed, impede the development of a satisfactory group taxonomy. This condition is in part derived from the tacit assumption that these logically exclusive schemes are also empirically exhaustive: they supposedly establish outer limits within which all other transitional and intermediate social entities fall.

To be sure, no such refined ordering and comprehending of intermediate social relationships and groups was ever accomplished. Something patently different occurred: all imaginable social groups—kinship and friendship, religious orders and ideological circles, corporate bodies and large-scale associations, totalitarian movements and political parties—came increasingly to approach either *Gemeinschaft* or *Gesellschaft*-like formations. The shifting images of a society as a whole are in many ways the outgrowth of this tradition of typing social groups antithetically. Suffice it to recall a handful of such terms as "atomization," "depersonalization," "bureaucratization," "mass culture," and "mass society" that loomed so large in sociology some two decades or so ago. These and similar expressions evoke an image of modern society characterized by an increased division of labor and specialization of functions, by rootlessness and anonymity of many of its members. More recently, with the "rediscovery" of small primary groups, the allegedly mounting tide of *Vergesellschaftung* [pseudo-group oriented] has been successfully averted. Relationships formerly considered to be impersonal and formal were found to be intricately interwoven with an infinite network of personal and intimate ones. Conditions previously viewed as

[1] Grateful acknowledgment is made for the encouragement and counsel of Professor Edward A. Shils.

disorganized and anomic were then found to be permeated by small personal groups—cliques and gangs. Even mass culture was personalized by intervening variables of personal influence and primary contacts. In brief, the wasteland of anonymity and anomie was more and more likened to one big playground filled with "peers," "buddies," or simply friends ever eager to respond to sociometric queries. The reader of sociological literature may also learn that the ties binding the members of religious sects and ideological movements are not unlike those found in small personal groups. In analyzing, for example, the relationship between the intensity of conflict and the frequency of interaction in personal primary groups, on the one hand, and formal associations on the other, Coser resorts to the following argument:

> In groups that appeal only to a peripheral part of their members' personality, or, to use Parson's terminology, in groups in which relations are functionally specific and affectively neutral, conflicts are apt to be less sharp and violent than in groups wherein ties are diffuse and affective, engaging the total personality of their members. In effect, this suggests that conflicts in groups such as Rotary Clubs or Chambers of Commerce are likely to be less violent than in groups such as religious sects or radical parties of the Communist type.[2]

The main thesis of this essay is that there are distinct social groups which are qualitatively different from personal and functional ones. These are groups which make their members relate to one another in the light of ideas and beliefs rather than in the light of personal qualities or specific functions which they perform. If this assumption is correct, neither the traditional dichotomies nor the more recent pattern variables can adequately account for them. To the extent that the pattern variables are but an elaboration upon *Gemeinschaft* and *Gesellschaft* they pertain at best to personal groups and functional associations. A serious difficulty emerges as soon as one applies the same conceptual tools to the analysis of ideological groups and totalitarian movements of the Communist type. To suggest that the ties which bind the members of ideological groups are diffuse, that they are "strongly affective, intimate, 'organic'"[3] is to equate them inadvertently with such personal groups as friendship or the family. Would it not be more proper to question the adequacy of these concepts rather than to apply them indiscriminately to an ever widening range of social phenomena?

Such a difficulty was faced by this writer in his study of the small ideological circles that mushroomed on the Russian social scene during the second half of the nineteenth century. These circles have also been traditionally conceived as small friendship cliques of young men and women carrying on an uneven struggle against the autocracy and working disinterestedly for the liberation of *narod* (Russian word for "people") and proletariat. A careful scrutiny of biographies, memoirs, programs, and other sources reveals a strikingly different picture. They neither were, nor were they meant to be by their founders and members, personal cliques of political and social outcasts. What were they then?

[2] Lewis A. Coser, *The Functions of Social Conflict* (Glencoe, Ill.: Free Press, 1956), pp. 68–69.

[3] Michael S. Olmstead, *The Small Group* (New York: Random House, 1959), p. 59.

IDEOLOGICAL RELATIONSHIPS

It is one of the most striking and general features of ideological groups that they frown upon and oppose vehemently any display of personal affective attachments among their members. Ideally, members of ideological groups are expected to avoid familiarity and to forego willingly all familial attachments and personal ties for the sake of some such central symbols and collectivities as socialism, revolution, people, or proletariat. The few individuals who tend to form personal ties within and without the ideological group are suspected and, indeed, find themselves standing apart from the rest of the members. They belong, to cite one writer, to the category of those to whom the ideological group cannot become "country, family, everything."[4] One such member in the Land and Freedom organization [an agrarian reform movement] was characterized in this way:

> Many features of his character were the cause of it, his sarcastic and sometimes haughty bearing. . . . But the main reason, it seems to me, was the fact that Alexander Ivanovich underestimated the moral qualities of those he was in contact with and this was felt instinctively by others. He loved some, but *not all;* valued some, but *not all.* In the meantime, if I am correct, all of us in our friendly relations did not *individualize*—for us the knowledge that one is a man totally committed to the revolutionary cause and is ever ready to offer for it his liberty and life—evoked love to him, created a certain emotional nimbus around him.[5]

Continuing on the same theme, the same writer deemed it necessary to add that "between him and other distinguished revolutionists there did not exist close relations . . . he could not fuse with them and did not admit of *full revolutionary intimacy.*"[6]

A mere glance at such expressions as "individualize" and "full revolutionary intimacy" points to the unique type of relationship supposed to exist among the members of Land and Freedom. Basically, they all relate to that particular individual's failure to make his attachment to other members transferable and universalistic. Yet love and close friendly relationship entail individualization; they presuppose that an attachment be particularized. In the Land and Freedom organization, however, this same differential response and the accompanying tendency to individualize undermined "full revolutionary intimacy" and also precluded the establishment of close friendly relations. May it not be that the so-called revolutionary intimacy has nothing in common with the intimate interpersonal relationship between friends or between husband and wife? That this is the case can be gauged by the attitude toward those few individuals who, like one of them, "loved women and was loved in turn,"[7] or like another who "loved all the passions and charms of life" and followed the dictum: "life was given to us in order

[4] S. Kravchinsky (Stepniak), *Underground Russia* (New York: Chas. Scribner's Sons, 1892), p. 68.
[5] Vera Figner, *Polnoe Sobranie Sochinenii* (Moscow, 1928), V, 215.
[6] *Ibid.*
[7] Kravchinsky, *op. cit.*, p. 96.

to live it."[8] Significantly enough, these few individuals of "unusual spiritual physiognomy" were singled out because their relationship to "women-revolutionists was completely different from other friends."[9] Whereas most of the members displayed "simple friendship," these exceptional ones "dispersed sparkles, followed and pursued, attempted to satisfy whims, evoked caprices and laughter."[10] To put it succinctly, their uniqueness lay in the fact that they responded to women as women, that they introduced spontaneity and permitted personal feelings to enter into the relationship. Because of this they were scarcely desirable individuals in those circles. "One such man can be in our party, two is still possible to retain, but three of them is impossible."[11] It is far from paradoxical, therefore, that the exemplary type of individual who best fitted those "close" and "friendly" relations was a young man who was cold and indifferent to the people surrounding him and burned only with "social passion," who "had no family and whom love did not disturb";[12] a young woman who did not have the "slightest trace of the desire which almost every woman has of displaying her beauty" and was "incapable of the spontaneous friendship of young and inexperienced minds."[13] Indeed, they were expected to forget "all ties of kinship and all personal sympathies, love and friendship,"[14] to be emptied of all affective dispositions toward other human beings and of all personal needs and inclinations. It is for this reason that some observers were struck by the very slight account they took of "personal interests connected with their profession, their future, and even of the pleasures which are said to grace the morning of life."[15]

One encounters here an extremely significant phenomenon: the terms "intimacy" and "close" and "friendly" relations connote complete lack of personal intimacy, or personal and affective attachments. More than that, the same intimate and friendly relationships demand that their subjects be deprived of all "romanticisms, all sensitivity and enthusiasms," that they be inimical to all private considerations, "personal hatred," that they refuse to allow themselves to be guided by personal impulses, that they obliterate "all the soft and tender affections arising from kinship, friendship, and love,"[16] so much so that the members of the same "fraternal groups" should have "no personal inclinations, no business affairs, no emotions, no attachments, no property, and no name."[17]

---

[8] Figner, *op. cit.*, I, 191.

[9] *Ibid.*

[10] *Ibid.*

[11] *Ibid.*

[12] Kravchinsky, *op. cit.*, p. 231.

[13] *Ibid.*, p. 109.

[14] Vera Figner, *Memoirs of a Revolutionist* (New York: International Publishers, 1927), p. 180.

[15] Kravchinsky, *op. cit.*, p. 231.

[16] These and similar demands contained in the *Revolutionary Catechism* should in no way be attributed, as has been traditionally done, to the personal aberrations of Nechaev and his elderly friend Bakunin. In fact, the by-laws of the Executive Committee of the Will of the People organization consist of well-nigh identical requirements (see Robert Payne, *The Terrorists: The Story of the Forerunners of Stalin* [New York: Funk & Wagnalls Co., 1957], p. 22).

[17] *Ibid.*, p. 21.

Formulated in general terms, ideological groups require, first of all, that their members divest themselves of all personal ties and attachments. More specifically, they demand that their members obliterate completely the sphere of privacy and lay bare all their innermost feelings and desires. This is achieved through the revolutionary intimacy which makes it possible to control "every little weakness, every lack of devotion to the cause."[18] There reigns thus a complete internal publicity and a total secrecy with reference to the surrounding world. One of the leading members of the Will of the People organization [a nineteenth century Russian terrorist group] left this injunction in his testament:

> I enjoin you, brothers, to keep guard over each other in every practical activity, in all the small concerns of everyday life. It is necessary that this guarding should enter into the conscience and thus turn itself into a principle, that it should cease to seem offensive, that personal considerations should be silenced before the demands of reason. It is necessary for all the closest friends to know how a man lives, what he wears, how he takes notes and what kind of notes he takes, how careful, observant, and resourceful he is—in this is our power, in this is the perfection of the activities of our organization.[19]

It is not surprising, then, that ideological groups preclude any manifestation of personal sentiment, any display of genuine intimacy and affectivity. These are most likely to thrive in the sphere of privacy. Indeed, the more intense the "revolutionary intimacy" between the members of ideological groups, the less likelihood there is that personal sentiments of liking or disliking will appear. The personal intimacy is thus inversely related to the ideological one, that is to say, the reassertion of the former is indicative of the weakening of the latter.

The same observations may be recast somewhat differently in terms of the interrelations between interaction and sentiment. It is well known that Homans has advanced several "analytical statements" about the behavior of human groups based on these and one additional concept, activity. One of them, for example, states "that the more frequent the interaction between people, the stronger in general their sentiments of liking or affection for one another."[20] A positive relationship, in other words, exists between interaction and the sentiment of affection. In ideological groups, on the other hand, the personal sentiment tends to increase with the decrease of in-group interaction. For it is precisely those individuals to whom the ideological group cannot become "country, family, everything," who cannot merge themselves completely with other members of the ideological group, who do not admit of "full revolutionary intimacy," who form personal affective attachments with outsiders, are prone to individualize, to stand aloof, to like some and dislike others, and, indeed, to display personal sentiments of affection toward other members of the same ideological group. Those individuals, in

[18] Kravchinsky, *op. cit.*, p. 119.

[19] B. Basilevich (ed.), *Literature Partii Narodnoi Voli* (Paris, 1905), p. 972. In addition to spying, the ideological groups resort also to public confessions, e.g., the technique of *éruption* and purification employed by the Jacobins.

[20] George C. Homans, *The Human Group* (New York: Harcourt Brace Jovanovich, 1950), p. 444.

contrast, who intensely interact with other members of an ideological group, who, in fact, confine their whole relationship to the small circle of zealots and are completely isolated from the surrounding world, are least prone to individualize and thus evolve sentiments of personal affection for one another. They are, in effect, those who develop "full revolutionary intimacy."

One may continue arguing along these lines by selecting other similar "analytical statements" about human groups. But even this single illustration clearly shows that at best they summarize some of the uniformities found in personal groups—be they those in the Bank Wiring Room or in some other friendship cliques. Moreover, it also suggests that the very concepts which enter into the formulation of such hypotheses as (1) the greater the interaction, the greater the sentiments of affection, or (2) the closer the relationship, the more intense the conflict, will have to be redefined and clarified anew. This clarification and redefinition are necessary because the nature of interaction, cohesion, conflict, and, indeed, sentiments of affection in small personal groups is most likely to be qualitatively different from that in ideological groups or even religious sects. Unless this takes place, sociologists will undoubtedly continue to argue that the splits and disruptions in both the family and ideological groups are to be explained by close affective and diffuse relationship. In doing so, they will disregard the distinction that ideologists themselves draw between their own brand of "simple friendship" and personal friendship, between their own "revolutionary intimacy" and genuine intimacy. Even more, they will be unable to account for the extreme suspicion and hatred that ideological groups display toward any manifestation of personal affectivity among their members.

MODALITIES OF IDEOLOGICAL ORIENTATION

In what follows an attempt will be made to identify tentatively the basic components of ideological orientation and also to show wherein they differ from personal and functional ones. First, ideological orientation is *total*—involving a response to the whole person as nothing but a belief-possessed being. Phrased differently, members of ideological groups respond to ideas and beliefs as if these were qualities of persons rather than objects of cognitive or appreciative orientation and, conversely, conceive of themselves as solely the carriers of ideas, not the possessors of various personal qualities. The end result of this orientation is of far-reaching consequence: ideas and beliefs become "personalized" and human beings "ideologized."

Ideological orientation is thus total in a twofold sense. It is total because it is all-inclusive and requires that the individuals empty themselves of all personal interests and identifying attributes, forgetting even their names, and act and respond to one another solely in terms of their symbolic significance. It is also total because it is exclusive of multiple-group loyalty and, as such, demands that the individuals sever all personal ties and primordial attachments and, indeed, stand outside all normal social ramifications.[21]

[21] It is evident that membership in an ideological group presupposes a particular type of man. On the level of personality he is an individual completely integrated and unconditioned. Whenever he acts he acts not to satisfy his "personal passions, but for mankind in general," whatever he says he says "from principle and not from passion,

Second, ideological orientation is *dichotomous*. This dichotomy is deeply imbedded in ideological orientation and is expressed on several levels. It is expressed, first of all, in the so-called authoritarian syndrome characterized by the intolerance of ambiguity and rigid all-or-nothing formulas. More basically, it is a dichotomous orientation because it conceives of the social universe in terms of black and white, hopelessly divided into two irreconcilable parts—one part of it to be collectively saved, another collectively destroyed. Consequently, it gives rise, as one member of the Will of the People remarked, to a kind of primitive morality, to two sets of directly opposed rules for approaching and judging the people.

> In a moral sense I discover plainly that the ideas of Lavrov lead merely in some degree to a revival of a quite primitive, imperfect kind of morality. Instead of a universal brotherhood and a higher justice which governs all private interests (including those of the circles), Lavrov revives the Old Testament circlelike solidarity. According to this, within the circle (or party) the closest relations develop, but all the rest, the external world so to speak, represents some *goys* and *giaours;* it comes about that they are looked upon as enemies, as *nemtsy, nemy* (the dumb) with whom the Lavrovs cannot communicate (there is no common language). No doubt, this external world they have in mind to save, but in the first place, as a collectivity, as mankind, while individuals who come under the heading of "enemies of socialism" have no right to expect justice. In their attitude towards the latter, as is evident from the above, the revolutionists permit themselves to drop all ideas of honor. In the matter of "saving," neither honesty nor regard is shown to the external world.[22]

The persistent attempts made by ideological groups to draw clear-cut bounds between themselves and the hostile world reflect this dualistic orientation. The clearer such a line of demarcation, the more intense are the hatred and suspicion of the outside world and, consequently, the more cohesive the ideological group. This external world to be hated *in toto* is identified, as a rule, in terms of social entities (*narod,* proletariat) destined to be collectively saved. It is as if ideological groups could thrive only as long as there were objects to be hated—be they real or imaginary.

Third, ideological orientation precludes seeing a human being as a composite of personal ascribed qualities and performances. These aspects of individual human beings have no meaning in ideological relationships. In other words, ideologists neither value each other for what they are nor for what they achieve as individual persons. Ideally, they are completely deindividualized, and by renouncing all personal qualities, conceive of themselves as nothing but the carriers of beliefs. To the extent that they do this, the most important criterion is *commitment.* Once it is known that an in-

---

from conviction and not from personal desire." On the level of interaction, in turn, such a man is one and indivisible. He is "throughout his life, in all the spheres of his life and activity, in all his acts decisively consistent and devoid of conflicting qualities." To speak metaphorically, an ideologist is dressed on all occasions in one and the same attire, and, as a result, is bent on playing only one master role—that of a man of convictions. He may, of course, change his article of faith, he may also worship different deities—mankind, *narod,* proletariat—but he is nonetheless intensely attached to his faith, boundlessly devoted to his gods, and totally committed to their service.

[22] Lev Tikhomirov, *Pochemu ia perestal byt Revolutsionerom* (Moscow, 1896), pp. 108–9.

dividual is totally committed to a set of beliefs and is ever ready to die for them, he is showered, as has been pointed out, with "love" and also endowed with an "emotional nimbus."

Finally, ideological orientation precludes a direct affective disposition toward human beings. Tyrannical to themselves and to others, the individuals in an ideological relationship attempt to subdue, if not entirely to eliminate, any direct expression of personal affection. At the same time, it is not an affectively neutral orientation. In fact, ideologists channel all personal passions and emotions on to the collective cause they cherish. Human beings share in this *displaced* and *collective affectivity* to the extent to which they are its vessels. It is thus a profoundly antipersonalist orientation, characterized by an all-pervasive insensitivity to the needs and sufferings of concrete human beings—be they peasants or workers. "Not the concrete and real peasant," observed one populist writer, "attracted all our attention, was liked by us, made us ready to sacrifice everything decisively for the sake of improving his life—we wished well to and loved the abstract peasant. More than that, we feared the peasant closest to us, and so to speak perceptible."[23] Far from being the Christian *caritas,* this kind of love for collective entities —*narod* or proletariat—may go hand in hand with extreme contempt for individual peasants and workers. It is safe to assert, indeed, that in terms of the displaced affectivity described above, ideologists are not inconsistent when they suffer and die for people, and also exclaim in the same breath that concrete human beings are nothing to them, that the cause of the "people" is everything. It is even doubtful whether they are inconsistent when, on the one hand, they deceive individual peasants by forging manifestoes, and terrorize human beings en masse, and on the other hand, convince themselves and others that they are servants of the same "people," working disinterestedly for their welfare and liberty.

The four components of ideological orientation have been tentatively identified by way of a contrast with the well-known conceptual scheme of the pattern variables. Thus, totality and displaced-collective affectivity are contrasted with the two "attitudinal" variables of diffuseness-specificity and affectivity-neutrality; dichotomy and commitment, in turn, with the two "object categorization" variables of particularism-universalism and quality-performance. Whatever the implications of this procedure, the significant point is that the very decision to introduce the four key concepts named above was based primarily on hard facts brought to light in the process of studying several ideological groups and movements. These facts could be neither meaningfully interpreted nor coherently related in terms of the pattern variables. Needless to add, the value of this ideal model is that of any constructive typology—the capacity to relate in a meaningful fashion hitherto unrelated facts.

INFORMAL AND FORMAL IDEOLOGICAL GROUPS

The four components of ideological orientation can be most likely expressed through diverse organizational structures. This is readily recognized

[23] Lev Deich, *Za Polveka* (Berlin, 1923), II, 67.

when one compares, for example, the internal structure of a small group of belief-ridden zealots with that of a centralized ideological movement of the Communist type. Wherein does this difference lie?

One way of approaching this structural differentiation is to specify the basic difficulty that constantly besets small ideological groups. Evidence exists that such groups are impelled from within to degenerate with time into friendship cliques in which the spontaneous flow of emotion and personal likes and dislikes reassert themselves. It is known, for example, that ideologists indulge recurrently in so-called little banquets at which they pour out their hearts to each other. "This need of giving unrestrained expression to feeling, so natural among people allied more by community of effort, ideas and dangers, than by ties of blood, communicated to these rare gatherings something poetical and tender, which rendered them beyond measure attractive."[24] It is also known that behind the façade of ideological asceticism there tend also to evolve personal ties between men and women who are members of the same circles. As one of them readily admitted a few decades later: "When I look back at that period of my life, I recall that among the people surrounding me there were quite a few couples in love and that many of those couples culminated their intimate relations in marriage."[25] Finally, this same personal factor is manifest in the mode of recruitment of new members into small ideological circles. Available evidence suggests that they cannot but rely exclusively upon mutual confidence and individual acquaintance and contacts.

To obviate the danger of relapse into the sphere of privacy and thus secure ideological identity and organizational continuity, small ideological circles resort to what might be called "bureaucratization." It is of interest here to note that this very move split the Land and Freedom organization into two opposing factions. One of them contended that new members ought to be recruited on the basis of personal acquaintance and confidence; the other insisted that impersonal consideration of the individual's integrity and usefulness should suffice for acceptance into the organization. Underlying this particular disagreement, however, was the central problem of the "progressive elaboration of the superior type of organization" upon which "revolutionary continuity" and the successful accumulation of "revolutionary experience" depend.[26] This superior type of organization was to recruit new members not on the basis of personal confidence but on the basis of prescribed rules for expressing confidence or lack of it; it was to regulate, in an explicitly stated manner, the duties of its members; it was to be centralized and thus capable of co-ordinating the activities of dispersed circles; and finally, it was also to be hierarchically structured and disciplined.[27]

---

[24] Kravchinsky, *op. cit.*, p. 74.

[25] N. A. Morozov, *V Nachale Zhizni* (Moscow, 1907), p. 176.

[26] Figner, *Polnoe Sobranie Sochinenii, op. cit.*, I, 107; see also O. V. Aptekman, *Obshchestvo "Zemlia i Volia" 70-kh Godov* (2d. ed.; Moscow, 1924), pp. 194–98.

[27] Viewed from this vantage point, Lenin's organizational proposal was merely an elaboration on that of Land and Freedom. He referred to it with approval on several occasions and explicitly acknowledged his indebtedness to its authors. "But the magnificent organization that the revolutionists had in the seventies and which should serve us all as a model, was not formed by the *Narodovolists*, but by the adherents of *Zemlya i Volya.* . . . And only a gross failure to understand Marxism . . . could give

Such "bureaucratization" of the organizational structure notwithstanding, the ideological character of the groups remains intact. True enough, they are built upon the principle of hierarchy and a consistent system of formalized rules, but they are most certainly different from any functional associations. It matters little, of course, what names one gives to these two types of ideological groups. They may be conveniently called here, respectively, ideological informal and ideological formal groups. The important point is that they not be confused with personal groups or functional associations. Ideological formal groups do not admit in the fashion of the latter either the separation of public and private spheres of life, or the clear-cut segregation of the individual's roles. Their members do not participate in them merely in the capacity of one narrowly defined and functionally specific role of "official." They continue to demand, like informal ideological groups, a total commitment to the cause, which is now authoritatively defined and institutionalized. It is here that they differ strikingly from ideological informal groups. Members of ideological informal groups are recruited on the basis of individual contacts and mutual confidence, members of ideological formal groups on the basis of formal requirements and regulations. The former groups are held together by "inner convictions" of their members, the latter by the organizational structure which has come to embody them. By establishing, as it were, an "immediate rapport" with their ideas, members of ideological informal groups are inwardly compelled to conform to them. Members of ideological formal groups, in the fashion of Lenin's "tribunes," conform primarily to organizational principles. What we witness here is both "formalization" of the organizational structure and "institutionalization" of ideas. The former leads to the rise of professional ideologists; the latter results in the establishment of a doctrine.

CONCLUDING REMARKS

The foregoing analysis provides us with a vantage point from which we can put into new perspective one type of human group. It hardly needs to be added that no conceptual scheme at present available to sociology can account plausibly for the nature of the relations extant in ideological groups, religious orders and sects. The very fact that sociologists still continue placing these groups on the continuum of *Gemeinschaft* and *Gesellschaft* lends credence to our contention. The same observation applies with even greater force to such an historical phenomenon as the Russian intelligentsia. It is not without good reason that at least one student of Russian history recently voiced the following complaint: "No recognized system of social analysis, either those known to the intelligentsia itself, or those elaborated since by modern sociology, makes provision for a 'class' held together only by the bond of 'consciousness,' 'critical thought,' or 'moral passion.' "[28]

It remains to be seen what other implications and additional lines of in-

---

rise to the opinion that the rise of a mass movement *relieves* us of the duty of creating as good an organization of revolutionists as *Zemlya i Volya* had in its time, and even a better one" (V. I. Lenin, *Collected Works* [New York: International Publishers, 1929], IV, 208–9).

[28] Martin Malia, "What Is the Intelligentsia," *Daedalus*, Summer, 1960, p. 445.

quiry the approach indicated by this paper may harbor. From what has been said, however, it can be argued on a priori grounds that the category of individuals best fitted to join ideological formations would have to be looked for among those who have no personal responsibility, who have severed for one reason or another all personal attachments and primordial ties, and who are not bound, as adults are, by specific obligations to corporate groups and associations. Ideally, they would be individuals who have left the family of orientation but have not yet established the family of procreation; who have ceased to be dependent children but have not yet become responsible citizens. In short, the category of least responsible people most closely approximating this model is youth. On this point there can be hardly any doubt that ideological groups are well-nigh completely monopolized by young people. Yet it is evident also that not every youth in any conceivable social condition is psychologically prepared to substitute love of mankind, *narod,* or some other collective entity for personal affection; that not every youth is ready to accept commitment to the cause and give up, in exchange, attachment to individual persons. Ideally, then, the recruits for ideological groups should not only be young but should also stand outside normal social ramifications. They should be individuals who have lost the sense of personal identity and belonging; that is, they should be socially uprooted and alienated from the surrounding world.

Implicit in the argument above is the assumption that ideological relations provide an ersatz to those people whom the world has deprived of, or made insensitive to, personal ones. And although in the present state of our understanding of ideological relations and groups, we are unable to pin down all the ersatz qualities they possess, two of them—total immersion within a society of belief-ridden brethren and the accompanying feeling of belonging and meaningfulness—are readily evident.

Oil in Santa Barbara and Power in America*

HARVEY MOLOTCH

More than oil leaked from Union Oil's Platform A in the Santa Barbara Channel—a bit of truth about power in America spilled out along with it. It is the thesis of this paper that this technological "accident," like all accidents, provides clues to the realities of social structure (in this instance, power arrangements) not otherwise available to the outside observer. Further, it is argued, the response of the aggrieved population (the citizenry of Santa Barbara) provides insight into the more general process which shapes disillusionment and frustration among those who come to closely examine and be injured by existing power arrangements.

A few historical details concerning the case under examination are in order. For over fifteen years, Santa Barbara's political leaders had attempted to prevent despoilation of their coastline by oil drilling on adjacent federal waters. Although they were unsuccessful in blocking eventual oil leasing (in February, 1968) of *federal* waters beyond the three-mile limit, they were able to establish a sanctuary within *state* waters (thus foregoing the extraordinary revenues which leases in such areas bring to adjacent localities —e.g., the riches of Long Beach). It was therefore a great irony that the one city which voluntarily exchanged revenue for a pure environment should find itself faced, on January 28, 1969, with a massive eruption of crude oil— an eruption which was, in the end, to cover the entire city coastline (as well as much of Ventura and Santa Barbara County coastline as well) with a thick coat of crude oil. The air was soured for many hundreds of feet inland and the traditional economic base of the region (tourism) was under

* This paper was written as Working Paper No. 8, Community and Organization Research Institute, University of California, Santa Barbara. It was delivered at the 1969 Annual Meeting of the American Sociological Association, San Francisco. A shorter version has been published in *Ramparts*, November 1969. The author wishes to thank his wife, Linda Molotch, for her active collaboration and Robert Sollen, reporter for the *Santa Barbara News-Press*, for his cooperation and critical comments on an early draft.

threat. After ten days of unsuccessful attempts, the runaway well was brought under control, only to be followed by a second eruption on February 12. This fissure was closed on March 3, but was followed by a sustained "seepage" of oil—a leakage which continues, at this writing, to pollute the sea, the air, and the famed local beaches. The oil companies had paid $603,000,000 for their lease rights and neither they nor the federal government bear any significant legal responsibility toward the localities which these lease rights might endanger.

If the big spill had occurred almost anywhere else (e.g., Lima, Ohio; Lompoc, California), it is likely that the current research opportunity would not have developed. But Santa Barbara is different. Of its 70,000 residents, a disproportionate number are upper class and upper middle class. They are persons who, having a wide choice of where in the world they might live, have chosen Santa Barbara for its ideal climate, gentle beauty and sophisticated "culture." Thus a large number of worldly, rich, well-educated persons—individuals with resources, spare time, and contacts with national and international elites—found themselves with a commonly shared disagreeable situation: the pollution of their otherwise near-perfect environment. Santa Barbarans thus possessed none of the "problems" which otherwise are said to inhibit effective community response to external threat: they are not urban villagers (cf. Gans, 1962); they are not internally divided and parochial like the Springdalers (cf. Vidich and Bensman, 1960); nor emaciated with self-doubt and organizational naiveté as is supposed of the ghetto dwellers. With moral indignation and high self-confidence, they set out to right the wrong so obviously done to them.

Their response was immediate. The stodgy *Santa Barbara News-Press* inaugurated a series of editorials, unique in uncompromising stridency. Under the leadership of a former State Senator and a local corporate executive, a community organization was established called "GOO" (Get Oil Out!) which took a militant stand against any and all oil activity in the Channel. In a petition to President Nixon (eventually to gain 110,000 signatures), GOO's position was clearly stated:

> . . . With the seabed filled with fissures in this area, similar disastrous oil operation accidents may be expected. And with one of the largest faults centered in the channel waters, one sizeable earthquake could mean possible disaster for the entire channel area. . . .
> Therefore, we the undersigned do call upon the state of California and the Federal Government to promote conservation by:
>   1. Taking immediate action to have present offshore oil operations cease and desist at once.
>   2. Issuing no further leases in the Santa Barbara Channel.
>   3. Having all oil platforms and rigs removed from this area at the earliest possible date.

The same theme emerged in the hundreds of letters published by the *News-Press* in the weeks to follow and in the positions taken by virtually every local civic and government body. Both in terms of its volume (372 letters published in February alone) and the intensity of the revealed opinions, the flow of letters was hailed by the *News-Press* as "unprecedented." Rallies were held at the beach, GOO petitions were circulated at local shopping centers and sent to friends around the country; a fund-raising dramatic spoof of the oil industry was produced at a local high school. Local artists, playwrights, advertising men, retired executives and academic specialists from the local campus of the University of California (UCSB) executed special projects appropriate to their areas of expertise.

A GOO strategy emerged for a two-front attack. Local indignation, producing the petition to the President and thousands of letters to key members of Congress and the executive would lead to appropriate legislation. Legal action in the courts against the oil companies and the federal government would have the double effect of recouping some of the financial losses certain to be endured by the local tourist and fishing industries while at the same time serving notice that drilling would be a much less profitable operation than it was supposed to be. Legislation to ban drilling was introduced by Cranston in the U.S. Senate and Teague in the House of Representatives. Joint suits by the city and County of Santa Barbara (later joined by the State) for $1 billion in damages [were] filed against the oil companies and the federal government.

All of these activities—petitions, rallies, court action and legislative lobbying—were significant for their similarity in revealing faith in "the system." The tendency was to blame the oil companies. There was a muckraking tone to the Santa Barbara response: oil and the profit-crazy executives of Union Oil were ruining Santa Barbara—but once our national and state leaders became aware of what was going on, and were provided with the "facts" of the case, justice would be done.

Indeed, there was good reason for hope. The quick and enthusiastic responses of Teague and Cranston represented a consensus of men otherwise polar opposites in their political behavior: Democrat Cranston was a charter member of the liberal California Democratic Council; Republican Teague was a staunch fiscal and moral conservative (e.g., a strong Vietnam hawk and unrelenting harasser of the local Center for the Study of Democratic Institutions). Their bills, for which there was great optimism, would have had the consequence of effecting a "permanent" ban on drilling in the Channel.

But from other quarters there was silence. Santa Barbara's representatives in the state legislature either said nothing or (in later stages) offered minimal support. It took several months for Senator Murphy to introduce Congressional legislation (for which he admitted to having little hope) which would have had the consequence of exchanging the oil companies' leases in the Channel for comparable leases in the under-exploited Elk Hills oil reserve in California's Kern County. Most disappointing of all to Santa Barbarans, Governor Reagan withheld support for proposals which would end the drilling.

As subsequent events unfolded, this seemingly inexplicable silence of the democratically elected representatives began to fall into place as part of a more general problem. American democracy came to be seen as a much more complicated affair than a system in which governmental officials actuate the desires of the "people who elected them" once those desires come to be known. Instead, increasing recognition came to be given to the "all-powerful oil lobby"; to legislators "in the pockets of Oil"; to academicians "bought" by Oil and to regulatory agencies which lobby for those they are supposed to regulate. In other words, Santa Barbarans became increasingly *ideological,* increasingly *sociological,* and in the words of some observers, increasingly *"radical."*[1] Writing from his lodgings in the area's most exclusive hotel (the Santa Barbara Biltmore), an irate citizen penned these words in his published letter to the *News-Press:*

> We the people can protest and protest and it means nothing because the industrial and military junta are the country. They tell us, the People, what is good for the oil companies is good for the People. To that I say, Like Hell! . . .
> Profit is their language and the proof of all this is their history (*SBNP*[2], Feb. 26, 1969, p. A-6).

As time wore on, the editorials and letters continued in their bitterness.

THE EXECUTIVE BRANCH AND THE REGULATORY AGENCIES: DISILLUSIONMENT

From the start, Secretary Hickel's actions were regarded with suspicion. His publicized associations with Alaskan Oil interests did his reputation no good in Santa Barbara. When, after a halt to drilling (for "review" of procedures) immediately after the initial eruption, Hickel one day later ordered a resumption of drilling and production (even as the oil continued to gush into the channel), the government's response was seen as unbelievingly consistent with conservationists' worst fears. That he backed down within 48 hours and ordered a halt to drilling and production was taken as a response to the massive nationwide media play then being given to the Santa Barbara plight and to the citizens' mass outcry just then beginning to reach Washington.

Disenchantment with Hickel and the executive branch also came through less spectacular, less specific, but nevertheless genuine activity. First of all, Hickel's failure to support any of the legislation introduced to halt drilling was seen as an *action* favoring Oil. His remarks on the subject, while often expressing sympathy with Santa Barbarans[3] (and for a while placating local sentiment) were revealed as hypocritical in light of the action not taken. Of further note was the constant attempt by the Interior Department to minimize the extent of damage in Santa Barbara or to hint at possible "compromises" which were seen locally as near-total capitulation to the oil companies.

Volume of Oil Spillage. Many specific examples might be cited. An early (and continuing) issue in the oil spill was the *volume* of oil spilling into the Channel. The U.S. Geological Survey (administered by Interior), when queried by reporters, broke its silence on the subject with estimates which struck

---

[1] See the report of Morton Mintz in the June 29, 1969 *Washington Post.* The conjunction of these three attributes is not, in my opinion, coincidental.

[2] *SBNP* will be used to denote Santa Barbara News Press throughout this paper.

[3] Hickel publicly stated and wrote (personal communication) that the original leasing was a mistake and that he was doing all within discretionary power to solve the problem.

[the residents of Santa Barbara as incredible]. One of the extraordinary attributes of the Santa Barbara locale is the presence of a technology establishment among the most sophisticated in the country. Several officials of the General Research Corporation (a local R & D firm with experience in marine technology) initiated studies of the oil outflow and announced findings of pollution volume at a "minimum" of ten fold the Interior estimate. Further, General Research provided (and the *News-Press* published) a detailed account of the methods used in making the estimate (cf. Allan, 1969). Despite repeated challenges from the press, Interior both refused to alter its estimate or to reveal its method for making estimates. Throughout the crisis, the divergence of the estimates remained at about ten fold.

The "seepage" was estimated by the Geological Survey to have been reduced from 1,260 gallons per day to about 630 gallons. General Research, however, estimated the leakage at the rate of 8,400 gallons per day at the same point in time as Interior's 630 gallon estimate. The lowest estimate of all was provided by an official of the Western Oil and Gas Association, in a letter to the *Wall Street Journal*. His estimate: "Probably less than 100 gallons a day" (*SBNP*, August 5, 1969:A-1).

Damage to Beaches. Still another point of contention was the state of the beaches at varying points in time. The oil companies, through various public relations officials, constantly minimized the actual amount of damage and maximized the effect of Union Oil's cleanup activity. What surprised (and most irritated) the locals was the fact that Interior statements implied the same goal. Thus Hickel referred at a press conference to the "recent" oil spill, providing the impression that the oil spill was over, at a time when freshly erupting oil was continuing to stain local beaches. President Nixon appeared locally to "inspect" the damage to beaches, and Interior arranged for him to land his helicopter on a city beach which had been cleaned thoroughly in the days just before, but spared him a close-up of much of the rest of the County shoreline which continued to be covered with a thick coat of crude oil. (The beach visited by Nixon has been oil stained on many occasions subsequent to the President's departure.) Secret servicemen kept the placards and shouts of several hundred demonstrators safely out of Presidential viewing or hearing distance.

Continuously, the Oil and Interior combine implied the beaches to be restored when Santa Barbarans knew that even a beach which looked clean was by no means restored. The *News-Press* through a comprehensive series of interviews with local and national experts on wildlife and geology made the following points clear:

(1) As long as oil remained on the water and oil continued to leak from beneath the sands, all Santa Barbara beaches were subject to continuous doses of oil—subject only to the vagaries of wind change. Indeed, all through the spill and up to the present point in time, a beach walk is likely to result in tar on the feet. On "bad days" the beaches are unapproachable.

(2) The damage to the "ecological chain" (a concept which has become a household phrase in Santa Barbara) is of unknown proportions. Much study will be necessary to learn the extent of damage.

(3) The continuous alternating natural erosion and building up of beach sands means that "clean" beaches contain layers of oil at various sublevels under the mounting sands; layers which will once again be exposed when

the cycle reverses itself and erosion begins anew. Thus, it will take many years for the beaches of Santa Barbara to be completely restored, even if the present seepage is halted and no additional pollution occurs.

Damage to Wildlife. Oil on feathers is ingested by birds, continuous preening thus leads to death. In what local and national authorities called a hopeless task, two bird-cleaning centers were established to cleanse feathers and otherwise administer to damaged wild-fowl. (Oil money helped to establish and supply these centers.) Both spokesmen from Oil and the federal government then adopted these centers as sources of "data" on the extent of damage to wild-fowl. Thus, the number of dead birds due to pollution was computed on the basis of number of fatalities at the wild-fowl centers.[4] This of course is preposterous given the fact that dying birds are provided with very inefficient means of propelling themselves to such designated places. The obviousness of this dramatic understatement of fatalities was never acknowledged by either Oil or Interior—although noted in Santa Barbara.

At least those birds in the hands of local ornithologists could be confirmed as dead—and this fact could not be disputed by either Oil or Interior. Not so, however, with species whose corpses are more difficult to produce on command. Several observers at the Channel Islands (a national wildlife preserve containing one of the country's largest colonies of sea animals) reported sighting unusually large numbers of dead sea-lion pups—on the oil stained shores of one of the islands. Statement and counter-statement followed with Oil's defenders arguing that the animals were not dead at all—but only appeared inert because they were sleeping. Despite the testimony of staff experts of the local Museum of Natural History and the Museum Scientist of UCSB's Biological Sciences Department that the number of "inert" sea-lion pups was far larger than normal and that field trips had confirmed the deaths, the position of Oil, as also expressed by the Department of the Navy (which administers the stricken island) remained adamant that the sea animals were only sleeping (cf. *Life,* June 13, 1969; July 4, 1969). The dramatic beaching of an unusually large number of dead whales on the beaches of Northern California—whales which had just completed their migration through the Santa Barbara Channel—was acknowledged, but held not to be caused by oil pollution. No direct linkage (or non-linkage) with oil could be demonstrated by investigating scientists (cf. *San Francisco Chronicle,* March 12, 1969:1–3).

In the end, it was not simply Interior, its U.S. Geological Survey and the President which either supported or tacitly accepted Oil's public relations tactics. The regulatory agencies at both national and state level, by action, inaction and implication had the consequence of defending Oil at virtually every turn. Thus at the outset of the first big blow, as the ocean churned with bubbling oil and gas, the U.S. Coast Guard (which patrols Channel waters regularly) failed to notify local officials of the pollution threat because, in the words of the local commander, "the seriousness of the situation

---

[4] In a February 7 letter to Union Oil shareholders, Fred Hartley informed them that the bird refuge centers had been "very successful in their efforts." In fact, by April 30, 1969, only 150 birds (of thousands treated) had been returned to the natural habitat as "fully recovered" and the survival rate of birds treated was estimated as a miraculously high (in light of previous experience) 20 per cent (cf. *SBNP,* April 30, 1969, F-3).

was not apparent until late in the day Tuesday and it was difficult to reach officials after business hours" (*SBNP*, January 30, 1969: A-1, 4). Officials ended up hearing of the spill from the *News-Press*.

The Army Corps of Engineers must approve all structures placed on the ocean floor and thus had the discretion to hold public hearings on each application for a permit to build a drilling platform. With the exception of a single *pro forma* ceremony held on a platform erected in 1967, requests for such hearings were never granted. In its most recent handling of these matters (at a point long after the initial eruption and as oil still leaks into the ocean) the Corps changed its criteria for public hearings by restricting written objections to new drilling to "the effects of the proposed exploratory drilling on *navigation or national defense*" (*SBNP*, August 17, 1969:A-1, 4). Prior to the spill, effects on *fish and wildlife* were specified by the Army as possible grounds for objection, but at that time such objections, when raised, were dismissed as unfounded.

The Federal Water Pollution Control Administration consistently attempted to understate the amount of damage done to waterfowl by quoting the "hospital dead" as though a reasonable assessment of the net damage. State agencies followed the same pattern. The charge of "Industry domination" of state conservation boards was levelled by the State Deputy Attorney General, Charles O'Brien (*SBNP*, February 9, 1969:A-6). Thomas Gaines, a Union Oil executive, actually sits as a member on the State Agency Board most directly connected with the control of pollution in Channel waters. In correspondence with complaining citizens, N. B. Livermore, Jr., of the Resources Agency of California refers to the continuing oil spill as "minor seepage" with "no major long-term effect on the marine ecology." The letter adopts the perspective of Interior and Oil, even though the state was in no way being held culpable for the spill (letter, undated to Joseph Keefe, citizen, University of California, Santa Barbara Library, on file).

With these details under their belts, Santa Barbarans were in a position to understand the sweeping condemnation of the regulatory system as contained in a *News-Press* front page, banner-headlined interview with Rep. Richard D. Ottenger (D-NY), quoted as follows: "And so on down the line. Each agency has a tendency to become the captive of the industry that it is to regulate" (*SBNP*, March 1, 1969:A-1).

THE CONGRESS: DISILLUSIONMENT

Irritations with Interior were paralleled by frustrations encountered in dealing with the Congressional establishment which had the responsibility of holding hearings on ameliorative legislation. A delegation of Santa Barbarans was scheduled to testify in Washington on the Cranston bill. From the questions which Congressmen asked of them, and the manner in which they were "handled," the delegation could only conclude that the Committee was "in the pockets of Oil." As one of the returning delegates put it, the presentation bespoke of "total futility."

At this writing, six months after their introduction, both the Cranston and Teague bills lie buried in committee with little prospect of surfacing.

Cranston has softened his bill significantly—requiring only that new drilling be suspended until Congress is convinced that sufficient technological safeguards exist. But to no avail.

SCIENCE AND TECHNOLOGY: DISILLUSIONMENT

From the start, part of the shock of the oil spill was that such a thing could happen in a country with such sophisticated technology. The much overworked phrase, "If we can send a man to the moon . . ." was even more overworked in Santa Barbara. When, in years previous, Santa Barbara's elected officials had attempted to halt the original sale of leases, "assurances" were given from Interior that such an "accident" could not occur, given the highly developed state of the art. Not only did it occur, but the original gusher of oil spewed forth completely out of control for ten days and the continuing "seepage" which followed it remains uncontrolled to the present moment, seven months later. That the government would embark upon so massive a drilling program with such unsophisticated technologies, was striking indeed.

Further, not only were the technologies inadequate and the plans for stopping a leak, should it occur, nonexistent, but the area in which the drilling took place was known to be ultrahazardous from the outset. That is, drilling was occurring on an ocean bottom known for its extraordinary geological circumstances—porous sands lacking a bedrock "ceiling" capable of containing runaway oil and gas. Thus the continuing leakage through the sands at various points above the oil reservoir is unstoppable, and could have been anticipated with the data *known to all parties involved*.

Another peculiarity of the Channel is the fact that it is located in the heart of earthquake activity in that region of the country which, among all regions, is among the very most earthquake prone.[5] Santa Barbarans are now asking what might occur in an earthquake: if pipes on the ocean floor and casings through the ocean bottom should be sheared, the damage done by the Channel's *thousands* of potential producing wells would be devastating to the entire coast of Southern California.[6]

Recurrent attempts have been made to ameliorate the continuing seep by placing floating booms around an area of leakage and then having workboats skim off the leakage from within the demarcated area.[7] Chemical dispersants, of various varieties, have also been tried. But the oil bounces over the sea booms in the choppy waters; the work boats suck up only a drop in the bucket and the dispersants are effective only when used in quantities

---

[5] Cf. "Damaging Earthquakes of the United States through 1966," Fig. 2, National Earthquake Information Center, Environmental Science Services Administration, Coast and Geodetic Survey.

[6] See Interview with Donald Weaver, Professor of Geology, UCSB, *SBNP*, Feb. 21, 1969, p. A-1, 6. (Also, remarks by Professor Donald Runnells, UCSB geologist, *SBNP*, Feb. 23, 1969, p. B-2.) Both stress the dangers of faults in the Channel, and potential earthquakes.

[7] More recently, plastic tents have been placed on the ocean floor to trap seeping oil; it is being claimed that half the runaway oil is now being trapped in these tents.

which constitute a graver pollution threat than the oil they are designed to eliminate. Cement is poured into suspected fissures in an attempt to seal them up. Oil on beaches is periodically cleaned by dumping straw over the sands and then raking up the straw along with the oil it absorbs.

This striking contrast between the sophistication of the means used to locate and extract oil compared to the primitiveness of the means to control and clean it up was widely noted in Santa Barbara. It is the result of a system which promotes research and development which leads to strategic profitability rather than to social utility. The common sight of men throwing straw on miles of beaches within sight of complex drilling rigs capable of exploiting resources thousands of feet below the ocean's surface, made the point clear.

The futility of the clean-up and control efforts was widely noted in Santa Barbara. Secretary Hickel's announcement that the Interior Department was generating new "tough" regulations to control off-shore drilling was thus met with great skepticism. The Santa Barbara County Board of Supervisors was invited to "review" these new regulations—and refused to do so in the belief that such participation would be used to provide the fraudulent impression of democratic responsiveness—when, in fact, the relevant decisions had been already made. In previous years when they were fighting against the leasing of the Channel, the Supervisors had been assured of technological safeguards; now, as the emergency continued, they could witness for themselves the dearth of any means for ending the leakage in the Channel. They had also heard the testimony of a high-ranking Interior engineer who, when asked if such safeguards could positively prevent future spills, explained that "no prudent engineer would ever make such a claim" (SBNP, February 19, 1969:A-1). They also had the testimony of Donald Solanas, a regional supervisor of Interior's U.S. Geological Survey, who had said about the Union Platform eruption:

> I could have had an engineer on that platform 24 hours a day, 7 days a week and he couldn't have prevented the accident.

His "explanation" of the cause of the "accident": "Mother earth broke down on us" (SBNP, February 28, 1969:C-12).

Given these facts, as contained in the remarks of Interior's own spokesmen, combined with testimony and information received from non-Interior personnel, Interior's new regulations and the invitation to the County to participate in making them, could only be a ruse to preface a resumption of drilling. In initiating the County's policy of not responding to Interior's "invitation," a County Supervisor explained: "I think we may be falling into a trap" (SBNP, April 1, 1969).

The very next day, the Supervisors' suspicions were confirmed. Interior announced a selective resumption of drilling "to relieve pressures." (News-Press letter writers asked if the "pressure" was "geological or political.") The new tough regulations were themselves seriously flawed by the fact that most of their provisions specified those measures, such as buoyant booms around platforms, availability of chemical dispersants, etc., which had proven almost totally useless in the current emergency. They fell far short of minimum safety requirements as enumerated by UC Santa Barbara geologist Robert Curry who criticized a previous version of the same regulations as "relatively trivial" and "toothless"[8] (*SBNP*, March 5, 1969:C-9).

On the other hand, the new regulations did specify that oil companies would henceforth be financially responsible for damages resulting from pollution mishaps. (This had been the *de facto* reality in the Union case; the company had assumed responsibility for the clean-up, and advised stockholders that such costs were covered by "more than adequate" insurance.[9]) The liability requirement has been vociferously condemned by the oil companies—particularly by those firms which have failed to make significant strikes on their Channel leases (*SBNP*, March 14, 1969). Several of these companies have now entered suit (supported by the ACLU) against the federal government charging that the arbitrary changing of lease conditions renders Channel exploitation "economically and practically impossible," thus depriving them of rights of due process (*SBNP*, April 10, 1969:A-1).

The weaknesses of the new regulations came not as a surprise to people who had already adapted to thinking of Oil and the Interior Department as the same source. There was much less preparation for the results of the Presidential Committee of "distinguished" scientists and engineers (the DuBridge Panel) which was to recommend means of eliminating the seepage under Platform A. Given the half-hearted, inexpensive and primitive attempts by Union Oil to deal with the seepage, feeling ran high that at last the technological sophistication of the nation would be harnessed to solve this particular vexing problem. Instead, the panel—after a two-day session and after hearing testimony from no one not connected with either Oil or Interior—recommended the "solution" of drilling an additional 50 wells under Platform A in order to pump the area dry as quickly as pos-

[8] Curry's criticism is as follows:
"These new regulations make no mention at all about in-pipe safety valves to prevent blowouts, or to shut off the flow of oil deep in the well should the oil and gas escape from the drill hole region into a natural fissure at some depth below the wellhead blowout preventers. There is also no requirement for a backup valve in case the required preventer fails to work. Remember, the runaway well on Union Platform A was equipped with a wellhead blowout preventer. The blowout occurred some 200 feet below that device.
Only one of the new guidelines seems to recognize the possible calamitous results of earthquakes which are inevitable on the western offshore leases. None of the regulations require the minimization of pollution hazards during drilling that may result from a moderate-magnitude, nearby shallow-focus earthquake, seismic sea wave (tsunami) or submarine landslide which could shear off wells below the surface.
None of the regulations state anything at all about onshore oil and gas storage facilities liable to release their contents into the oceans upon rupture due to an earthquake or seismic seawave.
None of the new regulations stipulate that wells must be cased to below a level of geologic hazard, or below a depth of possible open fissures or porous sands, and, as such, none of these changes would have helped the present situation in the Santa Barbara Channel or the almost continuous blowout that has been going on since last year in the Bass Straits off Tasmania, where one also finds porous sands extending all the way up to the sea floor in a tectonically active region—exactly the situation we have here."
[9] Letter from Fred Hartley, President of Union Oil, to "all shareholders," dated February 7, 1969.

sible. The process would require ten to twenty years, one member of the panel estimated.[10]

The recommendation was severely terse, requiring no more than one and a half pages of type. Despite an immediate local clamor, Interior refused to make public the data or the reasoning behind the recommendations. The information on Channel geological conditions was provided by the oil companies; the Geological Survey routinely depends upon the oil industry for the data upon which it makes its "regulatory" decisions. The data, being proprietary, could thus not be released. Totally inexplicable, in light of this "explanation," is Interior's continuing refusal to immediately provide the information given a recent clearance by Union Oil for public release of all the data. Santa Barbara's local experts have thus been thwarted by the counter-arguments of Oil-Interior that "if you had the information we have, you would agree with us.

Science was also having its non-neutral consequences on the other battle-front being waged by Santa Barbarans. The chief Deputy Attorney General of California, in his April 7 speech to the blue-ribbon Channel City Club of Santa Barbara, complained that the oil industry

> is preventing oil drilling experts from aiding the Attorney General's office in its lawsuits over the Santa Barbara oil spill (*SBNP*, Aug. 8, 1969).

Complaining that his office has been unable to get assistance from petroleum experts at California universities, the Deputy Attorney General further stated:

> The university experts all seem to be working on grants from the oil industry. There is an atmosphere of fear. The experts are afraid that if they assist us in our case on behalf of the people of California, they will lose their oil industry grants.

At the Santa Barbara Campus of the University, there is little Oil money in evidence and few, if any, faculty members have entered into proprietary research arrangements with Oil. Petroleum geology and engineering is simply not a local specialty. Yet it is a fact that Oil interests did contact several Santa Barbara faculty members with offers of funds for studies of the ecological effects of the oil spill, with publication rights stipulated by Oil.[11] It

[10] Robert Curry of the geography department of the University of California, Santa Barbara, warned that such a tactic might in fact accelerate leakage. If, as he thought, the oil reservoirs under the Channel are linked, accelerated development of one such reservoir would, through erosion of subterranean linkage channels, accelerate the flow of oil into the reservoir under Platform A, thus adding to the uncontrolled flow of oil through the sands and into the ocean. Curry was not asked to testify by the DuBridge Panel.

[11] Verbal communication from one of the faculty members involved. The kind of "studies" which oil enjoys is typified by a research conclusion by Professor Wheeler J. North of Cal Tech, who after performing a one week study of the Channel ecology under Western Oil and Gas Association sponsorship, determined that it was the California winter floods which caused most of the evident disturbance and that (as quoted from the Association Journal) "Santa Barbara beaches and marine life should be back to normal by summer with no adverse impact on tourism." Summer came

is also the case that the Federal Water Pollution Control Administration explicitly requested a UC Santa Barbara botanist to withhold the findings of his study, funded by that Agency, on the ecological consequences of the spill (*SBNP*, July 29, 1969:A-3).

Except for the Deputy Attorney General's complaint, none of these revelations received any publicity outside of Santa Barbara. But the Attorney's allegation became something of a statewide issue. A professor at the Berkeley campus, in his attempt to refute the allegation, actually confirmed it. Wilbur H. Somerton, Professor of petroleum engineering, indicated he could not testify against Oil

> because my work depends on good relations with the petroleum industry. My interest is serving the petroleum industry. I view my obligation to the community as supplying it with well-trained petroleum engineers. We train the industry's engineers and they help us. (*SBNP*, April 12, 1969, as quoted from a *San Francisco Chronicle* interview.)

Santa Barbara's leaders were incredulous about the whole affair. The question—one which is more often asked by the downtrodden sectors of the society—was asked: "Whose University is this, anyway?" A local executive and GOO leader asked, "If the truth isn't in the universities, where is it?" A conservative member of the State Legislature, in a move reminiscent of SDS demands, went so far as to ask an end to all faculty "moonlighting" for industry. In Santa Barbara, the only place where all of this publicity was occurring, there was thus an opportunity for insight into the linkages between knowledge, the University, government and Oil and the resultant non-neutrality of science. The backgrounds of many members of the DuBridge Panel were linked publicly to the oil industry. In a line of reasoning usually the handiwork of groups like SDS, a *News-Press* letter writer labeled Dr. DuBridge as a servant of Oil interests because, as a past President of Cal Tech, he would have had to defer to Oil in generating the massive funding which that institution requires. In fact, the relationship was quite direct. Not only has Union Oil been a contributor to Cal Tech, but Fred Hartley (Union's President) is a Cal Tech trustee. The impropriety of such a man as DuBridge serving as the key "scientist" in determining the Santa Barbara outcome seemed more and more obvious.

TAXATION AND PATRIOTISM: DISILLUSIONMENT

From Engler's detailed study of the politics of Oil, we learn that the oil companies combat local resistance with arguments that hurt: taxation and patriotism (cf. Engler, 1961). They threaten to take their operations elsewhere, thus depriving the locality of taxes and jobs. The more grandiose argument is made that oil is necessary for the national defense; hence, any weakening of "incentives" to discover and produce oil plays into the hands of the enemy.

Santa Barbara, needing money less than most locales and valuing environ-

---

with oil on the beaches, birds unreturned, and beach motels with unprecedented vacancies.

ment more, learned enough to know better. Santa Barbara wanted oil to leave, but oil would not. Because the oil is produced in federal waters, only a tiny proportion of Santa Barbara County's budget indirectly comes from oil, and virtually none of the city of Santa Barbara's budget comes from oil. *News-Press* letters and articles disposed of the defense argument with these points: (1) oil companies deliberately limit oil production under geographical quota restrictions designed to maintain the high price of oil by regulating supply; (2) the federal oil import quota (also sponsored by the oil industry) which restricts imports from abroad, weakens the country's defense posture by forcing the nation to exhaust its own finite supply while the Soviets rely on the Middle East; (3) most oil imported into the U.S. comes from relatively dependable sources in South America which foreign wars would not endanger; (4) the next major war will be a nuclear holocaust with possible oil shortages a very low level problem.

Just as an attempt to answer the national defense argument led to conclusions the very opposite of Oil's position, so did a closer examination of the tax argument. For not only did Oil not pay very much in local taxes, Oil also paid very little in *federal* taxes. In another of its front-page editorials the *News-Press* made the facts clear. The combination of the output restrictions, extraordinary tax write-off privileges for drilling expenses, the import quota, and the 27.5 per cent depletion allowance, all created an artificially high price of U.S. oil—a price almost double the world market price for the comparable product delivered to comparable U.S. destinations.[12] The combination of incentives available creates a situation where some oil companies pay no taxes whatever during extraordinarily profitable years. In the years 1962–1966, Standard of New Jersey paid less than 4 per cent of profits in taxes, Standard of California, less than 3 per cent, and 22 of the largest oil companies paid slightly more than 6 per cent (*SBNP*, February 16, 1969:A-1). It was pointed out, again and again to Santa Barbarans, that it was this system of subsidy which made the relatively high cost deep-sea exploration and drilling in the Channel profitable in the first place. Thus, the citizens of Santa Barbara, as federal taxpayers and fleeced consumers were subsidizing their own demise. The consequence of such a revelation can only be *infuriating*.

THE MOBILIZATION OF BIAS

The actions of Oil and Interior and the contexts in which such actions took place can be reexamined in terms of their function in diffusing local

---

[12] Cf. Walter J. Mead, "The Economics of Depletion Allowance," testimony presented to Assembly Revenue and Taxation Committee, California Legislature, June 10, 1969, mimeo: "The System of Government Subsidies to the Oil Industry," testimony presented to the U.S. Senate Subcommittee on Antitrust and Monopoly, March 11, 1969. The ostensible purpose of the depletion allowance is to encourage oil companies to explore for new oil reserves. A report to the Treasury Department by Consad Research Corp. concluded that *elimination* of the depletion allowance would decrease oil reserves by only 3 per cent. The report advised that more efficient means could be found than a system which causes the government to pay $10 for every $1 in oil added to reserves. (Cf. Leo Rennert, "Oil Industry's Favors," *SBNP*, April 27, 1969, pp. A-14, 15 as reprinted from the *Sacramento Bee*.)

opposition, disorienting dissenters, and otherwise limiting the scope of issues which are potentially part of public controversies. E. E. Schattschneider (1960:17) has noted:

> All forms of political organization have a bias in favor of the exploitation of some kinds of conflict and the suppression of others because *organization is the mobilization of bias.* Some issues are organized into politics while others are organized out.

Expanding the notion slightly, certain techniques shaping the "mobilization of bias" can be said to have been revealed by the present case study.

1. *The pseudo-event.* Boorstin (1962) has described the use of the pseudo-event in a large variety of task accomplishment situations. A pseudo-event occurs when men arrange conditions to simulate a certain kind of event, such that certain prearranged consequences follow as though the actual event had taken place. Several pseudo-events may be cited. *Local participation in decision making.* From the outset, it was obvious that national actions vis-à-vis Oil in Santa Barbara had as their strategy the freezing out of any local participation in decisions affecting the Channel. Thus, when in 1968 the federal government first called for bids on a Channel lease, local officials were not even informed. When subsequently queried about the matter, federal officials indicated that the lease which was advertised for bid was just a corrective measure to prevent drainage of a "little old oil pool" on federal property adjacent to a state lease producing for Standard and Humble. This "little old pool" was to draw a high bonus bid of $21,189,000 from a syndicate headed by Phillips (*SBNP*, February 9, 1969:A-17). Further, local officials were not notified by any government agency in the case of the original oil spill, nor (except after the spill was already widely known) in the case of any of the previous or subsequent more "minor" spills. Perhaps the thrust of the federal government's colonialist attitude toward the local community was contained in an Interior Department engineer's memo written to J. Cordell Moore, Assistant Secretary of Interior, explaining the policy of refusing public hearings prefatory to drilling: "We preferred not to stir up the natives any more than possible."[13] (The memo was released by Senator Cranston and excerpted on page 1 of the *News-Press.*)

Given this known history, the Santa Barbara County Board of Supervisors refused the call for "participation" in drawing up new "tougher" drilling regulations, precisely because they knew the government had no intention of creating "safe" drilling regulations. They refused to take part in the pseudo-event and thus refused to let the consequences (in this case the appearance of democratic decision-making and local assent) of a pseudo-event occur.

Other attempts at the staging of pseudo-events may be cited. Nixon's "inspection" of the Santa Barbara beachfront was an obvious one. Another series of pseudo-events were the Congressional hearings staged by legislators who were, in the words of a local well-to-do lady leader of GOO, "kept men." The locals blew off steam—but the hearing of arguments and the

---

[13] Cranston publicly confronted the staff engineer, Eugene Standley, who stated that he could neither confirm or deny writing the memo. (Cf. *SBNP*, March 11, 1969, p. A-1.)

proposing of appropriate legislation based on those arguments (the presumed essence of the Congressional hearing as a formal event) certainly did not come off. Many Santa Barbarans had a similar impression of the court hearings regarding the various legal maneuvers against oil drilling; legal proceedings came to be similarly seen as ceremonious arrangements for the accomplishing of tasks not revealed by their formally-stated properties.

2. *The creeping event.*   A creeping event is, in a sense, the opposite of a pseudo-event. It occurs when something *is* actually taking place, but when the manifest signs of the event are arranged to occur at an inconspicuously gradual and piecemeal pace, thus eliminating some of the consequences which would otherwise follow from the event if it were to be perceived all-at-once to be occurring. Two major creeping events were arranged for the Santa Barbara Channel. Although the great bulk of the bidding for leases in the Channel occurred simultaneously, the first lease was, as was made clear earlier, advertised for bid prior to the others and prior to any public announcement of the leasing of the Channel. The federal waters' virginity was thus ended with only a whimper. A more salient example of the creeping event is the resumption of production and drilling after Hickel's second moratorium. Authorization to resume *production* on different specific groups of wells occurred on these dates in 1969: February 17; February 21; February 22; and March 3. Authorization to resume *drilling* of various groups of new wells was announced by Interior on these dates in 1969: April 1, June 12, July 2, August 2, and August 16. (This is being written on August 20 [1969].) Each time, the resumption was announced as a safety precaution to relieve pressures, until finally on the most recent resumption date, the word "deplete" was used for the first time as the reason for granting permission to drill. There is thus no *particular* point in time in which production and drilling was re-authorized for the Channel—and full resumption has still not been officially authorized.

A creeping event has the consequences of diffusing resistance to the event by holding back what journalists call a "time peg" on which to hang "the story." Even if the aggrieved party should get wind that "something is going on," strenuous reaction is inhibited. Non-routine activity has as its prerequisite the crossing of a certain threshold point of input; the dribbling out of an event has the consequence of making each of the revealed inputs fall below the threshold level necessary for non-routine activity. By the time it becomes quite clear that "something *is* going on" both the aggrieved and the sponsors of the creeping event can ask why there should be a response "*now*" when there was none previously to the very same kind of stimulus. In such manner, the aggrieved has resort only to frustration and a gnawing feeling that "events" are sweeping him by.

3. *The "neutrality" of science and the "knowledge" producers.*   I have already dealt at some length with the disillusionment of Santa Barbarans with the "experts" and the University. After learning for themselves of the collusion between government and Oil and the use of secret science as a prop to that collusion, Santa Barbarans found themselves in the unenviable position of having to demonstrate that science and knowledge were, in fact, not neutral arbiters. They had to demonstrate, by themselves, that continued drilling was not safe, that the "experts" who said it was safe were the hirelings directly or indirectly of Oil interests and that the report of the DuBridge

Panel recommending massive drilling was a fraudulent document. They had to document that the University *petroleum* geologists were themselves in league with their adversaries and that knowledge unfavorable to the Oil interests was systematically withheld by virtue of the very structure of the knowledge industry. As the SDS has learned in other contexts, this is no small task. It is a long story to tell, a complicated story to tell, and one which pits lay persons (and a few academic renegades) against a profession and patrons of a profession. An illustration of the difficulties involved may be drawn from very recent history. Seventeen Santa Barbara plaintiffs, represented by the ACLU, sought a temporary injunction against additional Channel drilling at least until the information utilized by the DuBridge Panel was made public and a hearing could be held. The injunction was not granted and, in the end, the presiding federal judge ruled in favor of what he termed the "expert" opinions available to the Secretary of the Interior. It was a function of limited time for rebuttal, the disorienting confusions of courtroom procedures, and also perhaps the desire to not offend the Court, that the ACLU lawyer could not make his subtle, complex and highly controversial case that the "experts" were partisans and that their scientific "findings" follow from that partisanship.

4. *Constraints of communication media.*   Just as the courtroom setting was not amenable to a full reproduction of the details surrounding the basis for the ACLU case, so the media in general—through restrictions of time and style—prevent a full airing of the details of the case. A more cynical analysis of the media's inability to make known the Santa Barbara "problem" in its full fidelity might hinge on an allegation that the media are constrained by fear of "pressures" from Oil and its allies; Metromedia, for example, sent a team to Santa Barbara which spent several days documenting, interviewing and filming for an hour-long program—only to suddenly drop the whole matter due to what is reported by locals in touch with the network to have been "pressures" from Oil. Such blatant interventions aside, however, the problem of full reproduction of the Santa Barbara "news" would remain problematic nonetheless.

News media are notorious for the anecdotal nature of their reporting; even so-called "think pieces" rarely go beyond a stringing together of proximate "events." There are no analyses of the "mobilization of bias" or linkages of men's actions and their pecuniary interests. Science and learning are assumed to be neutral; regulatory agencies are assumed to function as "watchdogs" for the public. Information to the contrary of these assumptions is treated as exotic exception; in the manner of Drew Pearson columns, exception piles upon exception without intellectual combination, analysis or ideological synthesis. The complexity of the situation to be reported, the wealth of details needed to support such analyses require more time and effort than journalists have at their command. Their recitation would produce long stories not consistent with space requirements and make-up preferences of newspapers and analogous constraints of the other media. A full telling of the whole story would tax the reader/viewer and would risk boring him.

For these reasons, the rather extensive media coverage of the oil spill centered on a few dramatic moments in its history (e.g., the initial gusher of oil) and a few simple-to-tell "human interest" aspects such as the pathetic deaths of the sea birds struggling along the oil-covered sands. With increasing temporal and geographical distance from the initial spill, national coverage became increasingly rare and increasingly sloppy. Interior statements on the state of the "crisis" were reported without local rejoinders as the newsmen who would have gathered them began leaving the scene. It is to be kept in mind that, relative to other local events, the Santa Barbara spill received extraordinarily extensive national coverage.[14] The point is that this coverage is nevertheless inadequate in both its quality and quantity to adequately inform the American public.

5. *The routinization of evil.* An oft quoted American cliché is that the news media cover only the "bad" things; the everyday world of people going about their business in conformity with American ideals loses out to the coverage of student and ghetto "riots," wars and crime, corruption and sin. The grain of truth in this cliché should not obfuscate the fact that there are *certain kinds of evil* which, partially for reasons cited in the preceding paragraphs, also lose their place in the public media and the public mind. Pollution of the Santa Barbara Channel is now routine; the issue is not whether or not the Channel is polluted, but *how much* it is polluted. A recent oil slick discovered off a Phillips Platform in the Channel was dismissed by an oil company official as a "routine" drilling by-product which was not viewed as "obnoxious." That "about half" of the current oil seeping into the Channel is allegedly being recovered is taken as an improvement sufficient to preclude the "outrage" that a big national story would require.

Similarly, the pollution of the "moral environment" becomes routine; politicians are, of course, on the take, in the pockets of Oil, etc. The depletion allowance issue becomes not whether or not such special benefits should exist at all, but rather whether it should be at the level of 20 or 27.5 per cent. "Compromises" emerge such as the 24 per cent depletion allowance and the new "tough" drilling regulations, which are already being hailed as "victories" for the reformers (cf. *Los Angeles Times*, July 14, 1969:17). Like the oil spill itself, the depletion allowance debate becomes buried in its own disorienting detail, its ceremonious pseudo-events and in the triviality of the "solutions" which ultimately come to be considered as the "real" options. Evil is both banal and complicated; both of these attributes contribute to its durability.[15]

THE STRUGGLE FOR THE MEANS TO POWER

It should (although it does not) go without saying that the parties competing to shape decision-making on oil in Santa Barbara do not have equal access to the means of "mobilizing bias" which this paper has discussed. The same social structural characteristics which Michels has asserted make for an "iron law of oligarchy" make for, in this case, a series of extraordinary advantages for the Oil-government combine. The ability to create pseudo-

[14] Major magazine coverage occurred in these (and other) national publications: *Time* (Feb. 14, 1969); *Newsweek* (March 3, 1969); *Life* (June 13, 1969); *Saturday Review* (May 10, 1969); *Sierra Club Bulletin; Sports Illustrated* (April 10, 1969). The last three articles cited were written by Santa Barbarans.

[15] The notion of the banality of evil is adapted from the usage of Arendt, 1963.

events such as Nixon's Santa Barbara inspection or controls necessary to bring off well-timed creeping events are not evenly distributed throughout the social structure. Lacking such ready access to media, lacking the ability to stage events at will, lacking a well-integrated system of arrangements for goal attainment (at least in comparison to their adversaries) Santa Barbara's leaders have met with repeated frustrations.

Their response to their relative powerlessness has been analogous to other groups and individuals who, from a similar vantage point, come to see the system up close. They become willing to expand their repertoire of means of influence as their cynicism and bitterness increase concomitantly. Letter writing gives way to demonstrations, demonstrations to civil disobedience. People refuse to participate in "democratic precedures" which are a part of the opposition's event-management strategy. Confrontation politics arise as a means of countering with "events" of one's own, thus providing the media with "stories" which can be simply and energetically told. The lesson is learned that "the power to make a reportable event is . . . the power to make experience" (Boorstin, 1962:10).

Rallies were held at local beaches: Congressmen and state and national officials were greeted by demonstrations. (Fred Hartley, of Union Oil, inadvertently landed his plane in the midst of one such demonstration, causing a rather ugly name-calling scene to ensue.) A "sail-in" was held one Sunday with a flotilla of local pleasure boats forming a circle around Platform A, each craft bearing large anti-oil banners. (Months earlier boats coming near the platforms were sprayed by oil personnel with fire hoses.) City-hall meetings were packed with citizens reciting "demands" for immediate and forceful local action.

A City Council election in the midst of the crisis resulted in the landslide election of the Council's bitterest critic and the defeat of a veteran Councilman suspected of having "oil interests." In a rare action, the *News-Press* condemned the local Chamber of Commerce for accepting oil money for a fraudulent tourist advertising campaign which touted Santa Barbara (including its beaches) as restored to its former beauty. (In the end, references to the beaches were removed from subsequent advertisements, but the oil-financed campaign continued briefly.)

In the meantime, as a *Wall Street Journal* reporter was to observe, "a current of gloom and despair" ran through the ranks of Santa Barbara's militants. The president of Sloan Instruments Corporation, an international R & D firm with headquarters in Santa Barbara, came to comment:

> We are so God-damned frustrated. The whole democratic process seems to be falling apart. Nobody responds to us, and we end up doing things progressively less reasonable. This town is going to blow up if there isn't some reasonable attitude expressed by the Federal Government—nothing seems to happen except that we lose.

Similarly, a well-to-do widow, during a legal proceeding in Federal District Court in which Santa Barbara was once again "losing," whispered in the author's ear:

> Now I understand why those young people at the University go around throwing things. . . . The individual has no rights at all.

One possible grand strategy for Santa Barbara was outlined by a local public relations man and GOO worker:

> We've got to run the oil men out. The city owns the wharf and the harbor that the company has to use. The city has got to deny its facilities to oil traffic, service boats, cranes and the like. If the city contravenes some federal navigation laws (which such actions would unquestionably involve), to hell with it.
>
> The only hope to save Santa Barbara is to awaken the nation to the ravishment. That will take public officials who are willing to block oil traffic with their bodies and with police hoses, if necessary. Then federal marshals or federal troops would have to come in. This would pull in the national news media (*SBNP*, July 6, 1969, p. 7).

This scenario has thus far not occurred in Santa Barbara, although the use of the wharf by the oil industries has led to certain militant actions. A picket was maintained at the wharf for two weeks, protesting the conversion of the pier from a recreation and tourist facility to a heavy industrial plant for the use of the oil companies.[16] A boycott of other wharf businesses (e.g., two restaurants) was urged. The picket line was led by white, middle-class adults—one of whom had almost won the mayorality of Santa Barbara in a previous election. Hardly a "radical" or a "militant," this same man was several months later representing his neighborhood protective association in its opposition to the presence of a "Free School" described by this man (somewhat ambivalently) as a "hippie hotel."

Prior to the picketing, a dramatic Easter Sunday confrontation (involving approximately 500 persons) took place between demonstrators and city police. Unexpectedly, as a wharf rally was breaking up, an oil service truck began driving up the pier to make delivery of casing supplies for oil drilling. There was a spontaneous sit-down in front of the truck. For the first time since the Ku Klux Klan folded in the 1930's, a group of Santa Barbarans (some young, some "hippie," but many hard-working middle-class adults), was publicly taking the law into its own hands. After much lengthy discussion between police, the truck driver and the demonstrators, the truck was ordered away and the demonstrators remained to rejoice in their victory. The following day's *News-Press* editorial, while not supportive of such tactics, found much to excuse—noteworthy given the paper's long standing *bitter* opposition to similar tactics when exercised by dissident Northern blacks or student radicals.

A companion demonstration on the water failed to materialize; a group of Santa Barbarans was to sail to the Union platform and "take it"; choppy seas, however, precluded a landing, causing the would-be conquerors to return to port in failure.

It would be difficult to speculate at this writing what forms Santa Barbara's resistance might take in the future. The veteran *News-Press* reporter who has covered the important oil stories has publicly stated that if the government fails to eliminate both the pollution and its causes "there will, at best be civil disobedience in Santa Barbara and at worst, violence." In

---

[16] As a result of local opposition, Union Oil was to subsequently move its operations from the Santa Barbara wharf to a more distant port in Ventura County.

fact, talk of "blowing up" the ugly platforms has been recurrent—and is heard in all social circles.

But just as this kind of talk is not completely serious, it is difficult to know the degree to which the other kinds of militant statements are serious. Despite frequent observations of the "radicalization"[17] of Santa Barbara, it is difficult to determine the extent to which the authentic grievances against Oil have generalized to a radical analysis of American society. Certainly an SDS membership campaign among Santa Barbara adults would be a dismal failure. But that is too severe a test. People, especially basically contented people, change their world-view only very slowly, if at all. Most Santa Barbarans go about their comfortable lives in the ways they always did; they may even help Ronald Reagan to another term in the statehouse. But I do conclude that large numbers of persons have been moved, and that they have been moved in the direction of the radical left. They have gained insights into the structure of power in America not possessed by similarly situated persons in other parts of the country. The claim is thus that some Santa Barbarans, especially those with most interest and most information about the oil spill and its surrounding circumstances, have come to view power in America more intellectually, more analytically, more sociologically —more *radically*—than they did before.

I hold this to be a general sociological response to a series of concomitant circumstances, which can be simply enumerated (*again!*) as follows:

1. *Injustice.* The powerful are operating in a manner inconsistent with the normatively sanctioned expectations of an aggrieved population. The aggrieved population is deprived of certain felt needs as a result.

2. *Information.* Those who are unjustly treated are provided with rather complete information regarding this disparity between expectations and actual performances of the powerful. In the present case, that information has been provided to Santa Barbarans (and only to Santa Barbarans) by virtue of their own observations of local physical conditions and by virtue of the unrelenting coverage of the city's newspaper. Hardly a day has gone by since the initial spill that the front page has not carried an oil story; everything the paper can get its hands on is printed. It carries analyses; it makes the connections. As an appropriate result, Oil officials have condemned the paper as a "lousy" and "distorted" publication of "lies."[18]

3. *Literacy and Leisure.* In order for the information relevant to the injustice to be assimilated in all its infuriating complexity, the aggrieved parties must be, in the larger sense of the terms, literate and leisured. They must have the ability and the time to read, to ponder and to get upset.

My perspective thus differs from those who would regard the radical response as appropriate to some form or another of social or psychological freak. Radicalism is not a subtle form of mental illness (cf. recent statements of such as Bettelheim) caused by "rapid technological change," or increasing "impersonality" in the modern world; radicals are neither "immature," "underdisciplined," nor "anti-intellectual." Quite the reverse. They

---

[17] Cf. Morton Mintz, "Oil Spill 'Radicalizes' a Conservative West Coast City," *Washington Post,* June 29, 1969, pp. C-1, 5.

[18] Union Oil's public relations director stated: "In all my long career, I have never seen such distorted coverage of a news event as the *Santa Barbara News-Press* has foisted on its readers. It's a lousy newspaper." (*SBNP*, May 28, 1969, p. A-1.)

are persons who most clearly live under the conditions specified above and who make the most rational (and moral) response, given those circumstances. Thus radical movements draw their membership disproportionately from the most leisured, intelligent and informed of the white youth (cf. Flacks, 1967), and from the young blacks whose situations are most analogous to these white counterparts.

THE ACCIDENT AS A RESEARCH METHODOLOGY

If the present research effort has had as its strategy anything pretentious enough to be termed a "methodology," it is the methodology of what could be called "accident research." I define an "accident" as an occasion in which miscalculation leads to the breakdown of customary order. It has as its central characteristic the fact that an event occurs which is, to some large degree, unanticipated by those whose actions caused it to occur. As an event, an accident is thus crucially dissimilar both from the pseudo-event and the creeping event. It differs from the pseudo-event in that it bespeaks of an authentic and an unplanned happening; it differs from the creeping event in its suddenness, its sensation, in the fact that it brings to light a series of preconditions, actions and consequences all at once. It is "news"—often sensational news. Thresholds are reached; attentions are held.

The accident thus tends to have consequences which are the very opposite of events which are pseudo or creeping. Instead of being a deliberately planned contribution to a purposely developed "social structure" (or, in the jargon of the relevant sociological literature, "decisional outcome"), it has as its consequence the revelation of features of a social system, or of individuals' actions and personalities, which are otherwise deliberately obfuscated by those with the resources to create pseudo- and creeping events. A resultant convenience is that the media, at the point of accident, may come to function as able and persistent research assistants.

At the level of everyday individual behavior, the accident is an important lay methodological resource of gossipers—especially for learning about those possessing the personality and physical resources to shield their private lives from public view. It is thus that the recent Ted Kennedy accident functioned so well for the purpose (perhaps useless) of gaining access to that individual's private routines and private dispositions. An accident such as the recent unprovoked police shooting of a deaf mute on the streets of Los Angeles provides analogous insights into routine police behavior which official records could never reveal. The massive and unprecedented Santa Barbara oil spill has similarly led to important revelations about the structure of power. An accident is thus an important instrument for learning about the lives of the powerful and the features of the social system which they deliberately and quasi-deliberately create. It is available as a research focus for those seeking a comprehensive understanding of the structure of power in America.

FINALE

Bachrach and Baratz (1962) have pointed to the plight of the pluralist students of community power who lack any criteria for the inevitable *selecting* of the "key political decisions" which serve as the basis for their research conclusions. I offer accident as a criterion. An accident is not a decision, but it does provide a basis for insight into whole series of decisions and non-decisions, events and pseudo-events which, taken together, might provide an explanation of the structure of power. Even though the local community is notorious for the increasing triviality of the decisions which occur within it (cf. Schulze, 1961; Vidich and Bensman, 1958; Mills, 1956), accident research at the local level might serve as "micro"-analyses capable of revealing the "second face of power" (Bachrach and Baratz), ordinarily left faceless by traditional community studies which fail to concern themselves with the processes by which bias is mobilized and thus how "issues" rise and fall.

The present effort has been the relatively more difficult one of learning not about community power, but about national power—and the relationship between national and local power. The "findings" highlight the extraordinary intransigence of national institutions in the face of local dissent, but more importantly, point to the processes and tactics which undermine that dissent and frustrate and radicalize the dissenters.

The relationship described between Oil, government, and the knowledge industry does not constitute a unique pattern of power in America. All major sectors of the industrial economy lend themselves to the same kind of analysis as Oil in Santa Barbara. Where such analyses have been carried out, the results are analogous in their content and analogous in the outrage which they cause. The nation's defeat in Vietnam, in a sense an accident, has led to analogous revelations about the arms industry and the manner in which American foreign policy is waged.[19] Comparable scrutinies of the agriculture industry, the banking industry, etc., would, in my opinion, lead to the same infuriating findings as the Vietnam defeat and the oil spill.

The national media dwell upon only a few accidents at a time. But across the country, in various localities, accidents routinely occur—accidents which can tell much not only about local power, but about national power as well. Community power studies typically have resulted in revelations of the "pluralistic" squabbles among local sub-elites which are stimulated by exogenous interventions (cf. Walton, 1968). Accident research at the local level might bring to light the larger societal arrangements which structure the parameters of such local debate. Research at the local level could thus serve as an avenue to knowledge about *national* power. Sociologists should be ready when an accident hits in their neighborhood, and then go to work.

---

[19] I have in mind the exhaustively documented series of articles by I. F. Stone in the *New York Review of Books* over the course of 1968 and 1969, a series made possible, in part, by the outrage of Senator Fulbright and others at the *mistake* of Vietnam.

REFERENCES

Allen, Allan A.
    1969   "Santa Barbara oil spill." Statement presented to the U.S. Senate Interior Committee, Subcommittee on Minerals, Materials and Fuels, May 20, 1969.
Arendt, Hannah
    1963   Eichmann in Jerusalem: A Report on the Banality of Evil. New York: The Viking Press.
Bachrach, Peter and Morton Baratz
    1962   "The two faces of power." American Political Science Review 57 (December): 947–952.
Boorstin, Daniel J.
    1961   The Image. New York: Atheneum Press.
Engler, Robert
    1961   The Politics of Oil. New York: Macmillan.
Flacks, Richard
    1967   "The liberated generation." Journal of Social Issues 22 (December): 521–543.
Gans, Herbert
    1962   The Urban Villagers. New York: The Free Press of Glencoe.
Mills, C. Wright
    1956   The Power Elite. New York: Oxford University Press.
Schattschneider, E. E.
    1960   The Semisovereign People. New York: Holt, Rinehart & Winston.
Schulze, Robert O.
    1961   "The bifurcation of power in a satellite city." Pp. 19–81 in Morris Janowitz (ed.), Community Political Systems. New York: The Free Press of Glencoe.
Vidich, Arthur and Joseph Bensman
    1958   Small Town in Mass Society. Princeton: Princeton University Press.
Walton, John
    1968   "The vertical axis of community organization and the structure of power." Pp. 353–367 in Willis D. Hawley and Frederick M. Wirt (eds.), The Search for Community Power. Englewood Cliffs, N.J.: Prentice-Hall.

The End of Ideology? [1]

SEYMOUR MARTIN LIPSET

A basic premise of this [essay] is that democracy is not only or even primarily a means through which different groups can attain their ends or seek the good society; it is the good society itself in operation. Only the give-and-take of a free society's internal struggles offers some guarantee that the products of the society will not accumulate in the hands of a few power-holders, and that men may develop and bring up their children without fear of persecution. And, as we have seen, democracy requires institutions which support conflict and disagreement as well as those which sustain legitimacy and consensus. In recent years, however, democracy in the Western world has been undergoing some important changes as serious intellectual conflicts among groups representing different values have declined sharply.

The consequences of this change can perhaps be best illustrated by describing what happened at a world congress of intellectuals on "The Future of Freedom" held in Milan, Italy, in September 1955. The conference [2] was attended by 150 intellectuals and politicians from many democratic countries, and included men ranging in opinions from socialists to right-wing conservatives. Among the delegates from Great Britain, for example, were Hugh Gaitskell and Richard Crossman, socialists, and Michael Polanyi and

[1] I have taken the chapter heading from the title of Edward Shils' excellent report on a conference on "The Future of Freedom" held in Milan, Italy, in September 1955, under the auspices of the Congress for Cultural Freedom. See his "The End of Ideology?" *Encounter*, 5 (November 1955), pp. 52–58; for perceptive analyses of the nature and sources of the decline of ideology see Herbert Tingsten, "Stability and Vitality in Swedish Democracy," *The Political Quarterly*, 2 (1955), pp. 140–51; and Otto Brunner, "Der Zeitalter der Ideologien," in *Neue Wege der Sozialgeschichte* (Göttingen: Van den Hoeck and Ruprecht, 1956), pp. 194–219. For a prediction that the "age of ideology" is ending see Lewis S. Feuer, "Beyond Ideology," *Psychoanalysis and Ethics* (Springfield: Charles C. Thomas, 1955), pp. 126–30. Many of these topics are discussed in detail by Daniel Bell in *The End of Ideology* (Glencoe: The Free Press, 1960) and by Ralf Dahrendorf in *Class and Class Conflict* (Stanford: Stanford University Press, 1959).

[2] My original report on this conference which I attended was published as "The State of Democratic Politics," *Canadian Forum*, 35 (November 1955), pp. 170–71. It is interesting to note the similarities of the observations in it and the report by Edward Shils, *op. cit.*

Colin Clark, conservatives. From the United States came Sidney Hook, then the vice-chairman of the Union for Democratic Socialism, Arthur Schlesinger, Jr., of Americans for Democratic Action, and Friedrich A. Hayek, the arch-conservative economist. The French representatives included André Philip, a left-socialist leader, Raymond Aron, once active in the Gaullist movement, and Bertrand de Jouvenal, the conservative philosopher. Similar divergencies in political outlook were apparent among the delegates from Scandinavia, Germany, Italy, and other countries.

One would have thought that a conference in which so many important political and intellectual leaders of socialism, liberalism, and conservatism were represented would have stimulated intense political debate. In fact, nothing of the sort occurred. The only occasions in which debate grew warm were when someone served as a "surrogate Communist" by saying something which could be defined as being too favorable to Russia.

On the last day of the week-long conference, an interesting event occurred. Professor Hayek, in a closing speech, attacked the delegates for preparing to bury freedom instead of saving it. He alone was disturbed by the general temper. What bothered him was the general agreement among the delegates, regardless of political belief, that the traditional issues separating the left and right had declined to comparative insignificance. In effect, all agreed that the increase in state control which had taken place in various countries would not result in a decline in democratic freedom. The socialists no longer advocated socialism; they were as concerned as the conservatives with the danger of an all-powerful state. The ideological issues dividing left and right had been reduced to a little more or a little less government ownership and economic planning. No one seemed to believe that it really made much difference which political party controlled the domestic policies of individual nations. Hayek, honestly believing that state intervention is bad and inherently totalitarian, found himself in a small minority of those who still took the cleavages within the democratic camp seriously.

A leading left-wing British intellectual, Richard Crossman, has stated that socialism is now consciously viewed by most European socialist leaders as a "Utopian myth . . . often remote from the realities of day-to-day politics."[3] Few socialist parties still want to nationalize more industry. This objective has been largely given up by the socialist parties of the more industrialized states like Scandinavia, Britain, and Germany. The Labor party premier of the Australian state of Queensland, defending the retention of socialization as an objective at the party's 1950 convention, clearly acknowledged that its significance was largely ritualistic when he said:

> "I point out that there are serious implications in any way altering our platform and objectives. In the first place it is a bad thing to break ground in attack if we can avoid it, and I think we should not duck around corners and pretend we do not want socialization of industry. It is a long term objective in the Labor movement, exactly in the same way that there is a long term objective in the Christian movement. The people who espouse Christianity have been struggling for over 2,000 years and have not arrived at it."[4]

[3] Richard Crossman, "On Political Neurosis," *Encounter*, 3 (May 1954), p. 66.
[4] Cited in T. C. Truman, *The Pressure Groups, Parties and Politics of the Australian*

The rationale for retaining long-term objectives, even those which may not be accomplished in 2,000 years, was well stated by Richard Crossman:

> A democratic party can very rarely be persuaded to give up one of its central principles, and *can never afford to scrap its central myth*. Conservatives must defend free enterprise even when they are actually introducing state planning. A Labour Government must defend as true Socialism policies which have very little to do with it. The job of party leaders is often to persuade their followers that the traditional policy is still being carried out, even when this is demonstrably not true.[5]

The fact that the differences between the left and the right in the Western democracies are no longer profound does not mean that there is no room for party controversy. But as the editor of one of the leading Swedish newspapers once said to me, "Politics is now boring. The only issues are whether the metal workers should get a nickel more an hour, the price of milk should be raised, or old-age pensions extended." These are important matters, the very stuff of the internal struggle within stable democracies, but they are hardly matters to excite intellectuals or stimulate young people who seek in politics a way to express their dreams.

This change in Western political life reflects the fact that the fundamental political problems of the industrial revolution have been solved: the workers have achieved industrial and political citizenship; the conservatives have accepted the welfare state; and the democratic left has recognized that an increase in over-all state power carries with it more dangers to freedom than solutions for economic problems. This very triumph of the democratic social revolution in the West ends domestic politics for those intellectuals who must have ideologies or utopias to motivate them to political action.

Within Western democracy, this decline in the sources of serious political controversy has even led some to raise the question as to whether the conflicts that are so necessary to democracy will continue. Barrington Moore, Jr., a Harvard sociologist, has asked whether

> . . . as we reduce economic inequalities and privileges, we may also eliminate the sources of contrast and discontent that put drive into genuine political alternatives. In the United States today, with the exception of the Negro, it is difficult to perceive any section of the population that has a vested material interest on behalf of freedom. . . . There is, I think, more than a dialectical flourish in the assertion that

Labor Movement (unpublished M.A. thesis, Department of Political Science, University of Queensland, 1953), Chap. II, p. 82.

[5] Richard Crossman, *op. cit.*, p. 67. (My emphasis.) And in Sweden, Herbert Tingsten reports: "The great controversies have thus been liquidated in all instances. As a result the symbolic words and the stereotypes have changed or disappeared. . . . Liberalism in the old sense is dead, both among the Conservatives and in the Liberal party; . . . and the label of socialism on a specific proposal or a specific reform has hardly any other meaning than the fact that the proposal or reform in question is regarded as attractive. The actual words 'socialism' or 'liberalism' are tending to become mere honorifics, useful in connection with elections and political festivities." Tingsten, *op. cit.*, p. 145.

liberty requires the existence of an oppressed group in order to grow vigorously. Perhaps that is the tragedy as well as the glory of liberty. Once the ideal has been achieved, or is even close to realization, the driving force of discontent disappears, and a society settles down for a time to a stolid acceptance of things as they are. Something of the sort seems to have happened to the United States.[6]

And David Riesman has suggested that "the general increase of wealth and the concomitant loss of rigid distinctions make it difficult to maintain the Madisonian [economic] bases for political diversity, or to recruit politicians who speak for the residual oppressed strata."[7] The thesis that partisan conflict based on class differences and left-right issues is ending is based on the assumption that "the economic class system is disappearing . . . that redistribution of wealth and income . . . has ended economic inequality's political significance."[8]

Yet one wonders whether these intellectuals are not mistaking the decline of ideology in the domestic politics of Western society with the ending of the class conflict which has sustained democratic controversy. As the abundant evidence on voting patterns in the United States and other countries indicates, the electorate as a whole does not see the end of the domestic class struggle envisioned by so many intellectuals. A large number of surveys of the American population made from the 1930s to the 1950s report that most people believe that the Republicans do more for the wealthy and for business and professional people and the Democrats do more for the poor and for skilled and unskilled workers.[9] Similar findings have been reported for Great Britain.

These opinions do not simply represent the arguments of partisans, since supporters of both the left and the right agree on the classes each party basically represents—which does not mean the acceptance of a bitter class struggle but rather an argeement on the representation functions of the political parties similar to the general agreement that trade-unions represent workers, and the Chamber of Commerce, businessmen. Continued class cleavage does not imply any destructive consequences for the system; as I indicated in an early chapter, a stable democracy requires consensus on the nature of the political struggle, and this includes the assumption that different groups are best served by different parties.

The predictions of the end of class politics in the "affluent society" ignore the relative character of any class system. The decline of objective deprivation—low income, insecurity, malnutrition—does reduce the potential tension level of a society, as we have seen. But as long as some men are rewarded more than others by the prestige or status structure of society, men will feel *relatively* deprived. The United States is the wealthiest country in the world,

---

[6] Barrington Moore, Jr., *Political Power and Social Theory* (Cambridge: Harvard University Press, 1958), p. 183.

[7] David Riesman, "Introduction," to Stimson Bullitt, *To Be a Politician* (New York: Doubleday & Co., Inc., 1959), p. 20.

[8] S. Bullitt, *ibid.*, p. 177.

[9] See Harold Orlans, *Opinion Polls on National Leaders* (Philadelphia: Institute for Research in Human Relations, 1953), pp. 70–73. This monograph contains a detailed report on various surveys conducted by the different American polling agencies from 1935–53.

and its working class lives on a scale to which most of the middle classes in the rest of the world aspire; yet a detailed report on the findings of various American opinion surveys states: "The dominant opinion on polls before, during, and after the war is that the salaries of corporation executives are too high and should be limited by the government." And this sentiment, prevalent even among prosperous people, finds increasing support as one moves down the economic ladder.[10]

The democratic class struggle will continue, but it will be a fight without ideologies, without red flags, without May Day parades. This naturally upsets many intellectuals who can participate only as ideologists or major critics of the *status quo*. The British socialist weekly, *The New Statesman*, published a series of comments through 1958–59 under the general heading "Shall We Help Mr. Gaitskell?" As the title suggests, this series was written by various British intellectuals who are troubled by the fact that the Labor party is no longer ideologically radical but simply the interest organization of the workers and the trade-unions.

The decline of political ideology in America has affected many intellectuals who . . . must function as critics of the society to fulfill their self-image. And since domestic politics, even liberal and socialist politics, can no longer serve as the arena for serious criticism from the left, many intellectuals have turned from a basic concern with the political and economic systems to criticism of other sections of the basic culture of American society, particularly of elements which cannot be dealt with politically. They point to the seeming growth of a concern with status ("keeping up with the Joneses"), to the related increase in the influence of advertisers and mass media as the arbiters of mass taste, to the evidence that Americans are over-conformists—another side of keeping up with the Joneses. Thus the critical works about American society in the past decades which have received the most attention have been sociological rather than political, such books as David Riesman's *The Lonely Crowd*, William H. Whyte's *The Organization Man*, Max Lerner's *America as a Civilization,* and Vance Packard's *The Status Seekers.*

Yet many of the disagreeable aspects of American society which are now regarded as the results of an affluent and bureaucratic society may be recurring elements inherent in an equalitarian and democratic society. Those aspects of both American and socialist ideology which have always been most thoroughly expressed in the United States make a concern with status and conformity constant features of the society.

The patterns of status distinction which Lloyd Warner, Vance Packard, and others have documented have been prevalent throughout America's history, as the reports of various nineteenth-century foreign travelers plainly show. These visitors generally believed that Americans were *more* status-conscious than Europeans, that it was easier for a *nouveau riche* individual to be accepted in nineteenth-century England than in nineteenth-century America; and they explained the greater snobbery in this country by suggesting that the very emphasis on democracy and equalitarianism in America, the lack of a well-defined deference structure, in which there is no

---

[10] *Ibid.,* p. 149. The one exception is among the very poor who are somewhat less intolerant of high executive salaries than those immediately above them.

question about social rankings, make well-to-do Americans place more emphasis on status background and symbolism than do Europeans.

> It may seem a paradox to observe that a millionaire has a better and easier social career open to him in England than in America. . . . In America, if his private character be bad, if he be mean or openly immoral, or personally vulgar, or dishonest, the best society may keep its doors closed against him. In England great wealth, skillfully employed, will more readily force these doors to open. For in England great wealth can, by using the appropriate methods, practically buy rank from those who bestow it. . . . The existence of a system of artificial rank enables a stamp to be given to base metal in Europe which cannot be given in a thoroughly republican country.[11]

The great concern with family background (which generation made the money?) that many observers from Harriet Martineau (one of the most sophisticated British commenters on American life in the 1820s) to the contemporary American sociologist Lloyd Warner have shown to be characteristic of large parts of American society may be a reaction to the feelings of uncertainty about social position engendered in a society whose basic values deny anyone the inherent right to claim higher status than his neighbor. As the sociologist Howard Brotz has pointed out in comparing the status systems of Britain and the United States:

> In a democracy snobbishness can be far more vicious than in an aristocracy. Lacking that natural confirmation of superiority which political authority alone can give, the rich and particularly the new rich, feel threatened by mere contact with their inferiors. This tendency perhaps reached its apogee in the late nineteenth century in Tuxedo Park, a select residential community composed of wealthy New York businessmen, which, not content merely to surround itself with a wire fence, posted a sentry at the gate to keep nonmembers out. Nothing could be more fantastic than this to an English lord living in the country in the midst, not of other peers, but of his tenants. His position is such that he is at ease in the presence of members of the lower classes and in associating with them in recreation. For example, farmers [that is, tenants] ride to the hounds in the hunts. It is this "democratic" attitude which, in the first instance, makes for an openness to social relations with Jews. One cannot be declassed, so to speak, by play activities.[12]

The problem of conformity which so troubles many Americans today has been noted as a major aspect of American culture from Tocqueville in the 1830s to Riesman in the 1950s. Analysts have repeatedly stressed the extent to which Americans (as compared to other peoples) are sensitive to the

---

[11] James Bryce, *The American Commonwealth*, Vol. II (New York: Macmillan, 1910), p. 815. Cf. D. W. Brogan, *U.S.A.* (London: Oxford University Press, 1941), pp. 116ff.; see Robert W. Smuts, *European Impressions of the American Worker* (New York: King's Crown Press, 1953), for a summary of comments by many visitors in the 1900s and the 1950s who reported that "social and economic democracy in America, far from mitigating competition for social status, intensified it" (p. 13).

[12] Howard Brotz, "The Position of the Jews in English Society," *The Jewish Journal of Sociology*, 1 (1959), p. 97.

judgments of others. Never secure in their own status, they are concerned with "public opinion" in a way that elites in a more aristocratic and status-bound society do not have to be. As early as the nineteenth century foreign observers were struck by the "other-directedness" of Americans and accounted for it by the nature of the class system. This image of the American as "other-directed" can, as Riesman notes, be found in the writing of Tocqueville and other curious and astonished visitors from Europe."[13] Harriet Martineau almost seems to be paraphrasing Riesman's own description of today's "other-directed" man in her picture of the early nineteenth-century American:

> Americans may travel over the world, and find no society but their own which will submit [as much] to the restraint of perpetual caution, and reference to the opinions of others. They may travel over the whole world, and find no country but their own where the very children beware of getting into scrapes, and talk of the effect of actions on people's minds; where the youth of society determines in silence what opinions they shall bring forward, and what avow only in the family circle; where women write miserable letters, almost universally, because it is a settled matter that it is unsafe to commit oneself on paper; and where elderly people seem to lack almost universally that faith in principles which inspires a free expression of them at any time, and under all circumstances.[14]

It may be argued that in an open democratic society in which people are encouraged to struggle upward, but where there are no clearly defined reference points to mark their arrival, and where their success in achieving status is determined by the good opinion of others, the kind of caution and intense study of other people's opinions described by Martineau is natural. Like Riesman today, she notes that this "other-directed" type is found most commonly in urban centers in the middle and upper classes, where people live in "perpetual caution." Nowhere does there exist "so much heart-eating care [about others' judgments], so much nervous anxiety, as among the dwellers in the towns of the northern states of America."[15] Similarly, Max Weber, who visited the United States in the early 1900s, noted the high degree of "submission to fashion in America, to a degree unknown in Germany," and explained it as a natural attribute of a democratic society without inherited class status.[16]

A society which emphasizes achievement, which denies status based on ancestry or even long-past personal achievements, must necessarily be a society in which men are sensitively oriented toward others, in which, to use Riesman's analogy, they employ a radar to keep their social equilibrium. And precisely as we become more equalitarian, as the lower strata attain citizenship, as more people are able to take part in the status race, to that extent do we, and other peoples as well, become more concerned with the

---

[13] David Riesman, *et al.*, *The Lonely Crowd: A Study of the Changing American Character* (New Haven: Yale University Press, 1950), pp. 19–20.

[14] Harriet Martineau, *Society in America*, Vol. II (New York: Saunders and Otley, 1837), pp. 158–59.

[15] *Ibid.*, pp. 160–61.

[16] Max Weber, *Essays in Sociology* (New York: Oxford University Press, 1946), p. 188.

opinions of others, and therefore more democratic and more American in the Tocquevillian sense.

The politics of democracy are to some extent necessarily the politics of conformity for the elite of the society. As soon as the masses have access to the society's elite, as soon as they must consider mass reaction in determining their own actions, the freedom of the elite (whether political or artistic) is limited. As Tocqueville pointed out, the "most serious reproach which can be addressed" to democratic republics is that they "extend the practice of currying favor with the many and introduce it into all classes at once," and he attributed "the small number of distinguished men in political life to the ever increasing despotism of the majority in the United States."[17]

The same point has been made . . . in regard to much of the discussion about the negative consequences of mass culture. Increased access by the mass of the population to the culture market necessarily means a limitation in cultural taste as compared to a time or a country in which culture is limited to the well to do and the well educated.

The current debates on education reflect the same dilemma—that many who believe in democracy and equalitarianism would also like to preserve some of the attributes of an elitist society. In England, where the integrated "comprehensive" school is seen as a progressive reform, the argument for it is based on the assumption that the health of the society is best served by what is best for the largest number. This argument was used in this country when liberal educators urged that special treatment for the gifted child served to perpetuate inequality and that it rewarded those from better home and class environments at the expense of those from poorer backgrounds. Educators in Britain today argue strongly that separate schools for brighter children (the so-called "grammar schools") are a source of psychic punishment for the less gifted. Many of us have forgotten that liberals in this country shared similar sentiments not too long ago; that, for example, Fiorello La Guardia, as Mayor of New York, abolished Townsend Harris High School, a special school for gifted boys in which four years of school work were completed in three, on the ground that the very existence of such a school was undemocratic, that it gave special privileges to a minority.

What I am saying is simply that we cannot have our cake and eat it too. We cannot have the advantages of an aristocratic *and* a democratic society; we cannot have segregated elite schools in a society which stresses equality; we cannot have a cultural elite which produces without regard to mass taste in a society which emphasizes the value of popular judgment. By the same token we cannot have a low divorce rate and end differentiation in sex roles, and we cannot expect to have secure adolescents in a culture which offers no definitive path from adolescence to adulthood.

I do not mean to suggest that a democratic society can do nothing about

[17] Alexis de Tocqueville, *Democracy in America*, Vol. I (New York: Vintage Books, 1954), pp. 276, 277. Of course, Plato made the same points 2500 years ago when he argued that in a democracy, the father "accustoms himself to become like his child and to fear his sons, and the son in his desire for freedom becomes like his father and has no fear or reverence for his parent. . . . The school master fears and flatters his pupils . . . while the old men condescend to the young and become triumphs of versatility. . . . The main result of all these things, taken together, is that it makes the souls of the citizens . . . sensitive." *The Republic of Plato*, ed. by Ernest Rhys (London: J. M. Dent and Co., 1935), pp. 200–26.

reducing conformity or increasing creativity. There is considerable evidence to suggest that higher education, greater economic security, and higher standards of living strengthen the level of culture and democratic freedom. The market for good books, good paintings, and good music is at a high point in American history.[18] There is evidence that tolerance for ethnic minorities too is greater than in the past. More people are receiving a good education in America today than ever before, and regardless of the many weaknesses of that education, it is still true that the more of it one has, the better one's values and consumption patterns from the point of view of the liberal and culturally concerned intellectual.

There is a further point about the presumed growth of conformity and the decline in ideology which has been made by various analysts who rightly fear the inherent conformist aspects of populist democracy. They suggest that the growth of large bureaucratic organizations, an endemic aspect of modern industrial society, whether capitalist or socialist, is reducing the scope of individual freedom because "organization men" must conform to succeed. This point is sometimes linked to the decline in the intensity of political conflict, because politics is seen as changing into administration as the manager and expert take over in government as well as in business. From James Burnham's *Managerial Revolution* to more recent restatements of this thesis by Peter Drucker and others, this trend has been sometimes welcomed, but more often in recent years deplored.

The growth of large organizations may, however, actually have the more important consequences of providing new sources of continued freedom and more opportunity to innovate. Bureaucratization means (among other things) a decline of the arbitrary power of those in authority. By establishing norms of fair and equal treatment, and by reducing the unlimited power possessed by the leaders of many non-bureaucratic organizations, bureaucracy may mean less rather than greater need to conform to superiors. In spite of the emergence of security tests, I think that there is little doubt that men are much less likely to be fired from their jobs for their opinions and behavior today than they were fifty or even twenty-five years ago. Anyone who compares the position of a worker or an executive in a family-owned corporation like the Ford Motor Company when its founder was running it to that of comparably placed people in General Motors or today's Ford Motor Company can hardly argue that bureaucratization has meant greater pressure to conform on any level of industry. Trade-unions accurately reflect their members' desires when they move in the direction of greater bureaucratization by winning, for example, seniority rules in hiring, firing, and promotion, or a stable three-year contract with detailed provisions for grievance procedures. Unionization, of both manual and white-collar workers, increases under conditions of large-scale organization and serves to free the worker or employee from subjection to relatively uncontrolled power. Those who fear the subjection of the workers to the organizational power of unionism ignore for the most part the alternative of arbitrary management power. In many ways the employee of a large corporation who is the subject

---

[18] See Daniel Bell, "The Theory of Mass Society," *Commentary*, 22 (1956), p. 82 and Clyde Kluckhohn, "Shifts in American Values," *World Politics*, 11 (1959), pp. 250–61, for evidence concerning the growth rather than the decline of "genuine individuality in the United States."

of controversy between two giant organizations—the company and the union —has a much higher degree of freedom than one not in a large organization.

Although the pressures toward conformity within democratic and bureaucratic society are an appropriate source of serious concern for Western intellectuals, my reading of the historical evidence suggests that the problem is less acute or threatening today than it has been in the past, if we limit our analysis to domestic threats to the system. There is reason to expect that stable democratic institutions in which individual political freedom is great and even increasing (as it is, say, in Britain or Sweden) will continue to characterize the mature industrialized Western societies.

The controversies about cultural creativity and conformity reflect the general trend discussed at the beginning of the chapter—the shift away from ideology towards sociology. The very growth of sociology as an intellectual force outside the academy in many Western nations is a tribute, not primarily to the power of sociological analysis but to the loss of interest in political inquiry. It may seem curious, therefore, for a sociologist to end on a note of concern about this trend. But I believe that there is still a real need for political analysis, ideology, and controversy within the world community, if not within the Western democracies. In a larger sense, the domestic controversies within the advanced democratic countries have become comparable to struggles within American party primary elections. Like all nomination contests, they are fought to determine who will lead the party, in this case the democratic camp, in the larger political struggle in the world as a whole with its marginal constituencies, the underdeveloped states. The horizon of intellectual political concerns must turn from the new version of local elections—those which determine who will run national administrations— to this larger contest.

This larger fight makes politics much more complex in the various underdeveloped countries than it appears within Western democracies. In these states there is still a need for intense political controversy and ideology. The problems of industrialization, of the place of religion, of the character of political institutions are still unsettled, and the arguments about them have become intertwined with the international struggle. The past political relations beween former colonial countries and the West, between colored and white peoples, make the task even more difficult. It is necessary for us to recognize that our allies in the underdeveloped countries must be radicals, probably socialists, because only parties which promise to improve the situation of the masses through widespread reform, and which are transvaluational and equalitarian, can hope to compete with the Communists. Asian and African socialist movements, even where they are committed to political democracy (and unfortunately not all of them are, or can be even if they want to), must often express hostility to many of the economic, political, and religious institutions of the West.

Where radicals are in power—in India, Ghana, Ceylon, Burma, and other countries—they must take responsibility for the economic development of the country, and hence must suffer the brunt of the resentments caused by industrialization, rapid urbanization, bad housing, and extreme poverty. The democratic leftist leader must find a scapegoat to blame for these ills— domestic capitalists, foreign investors, or the machinations of the departed imperialists. If he does not, he will lose his hold on the masses who need the hope implicit in revolutionary chiliastic doctrine—a hope the Communists are ready to supply. The socialist in power in an underdeveloped country must continue, therefore, to lead a revolutionary struggle against capitalism, the western imperialists, and, increasingly, against Christianity as the dominant remaining foreign institution. If he accepts the arguments of Western socialists that the West has changed, that complete socialism is dangerous, that Marxism is an outmoded doctrine, he becomes a conservative within his own society, a role he cannot play and still retain a popular following.

The leftist intellectual, the trade-union leader, and the socialist politician in the West have an important role to play in this political struggle. By virtue of the fact that they still represent the tradition of socialism and equalitarianism within their own countries, they can find an audience among the leaders of the non-Communist left in those nations where socialism and trade-unionism cannot be conservative or even gradualist. To demand that such leaders adapt their politics to Western images of responsible behavior is to forget that many Western unions, socialist parties, and intellectuals were similarly "irresponsible and demagogic" in the early stages of their development. Today Western leaders must communicate and work with non-Communist revolutionaries in the Orient and Africa at the same time that they accept the fact that serious ideological controversies have ended at home.

. . . Ideology and passion may no longer be necessary to sustain the class struggle within stable and affluent democracies, but they are clearly needed in the international effort to develop free political and economic institutions in the rest of the world. It is only the ideological class struggle within the West which is ending. Ideological conflicts linked to levels and problems of economic development and of appropriate political institutions among different nations will last far beyond our lifetime, and men committed to democracy can abstain from them only at their peril. To aid men's actions in furthering democracy in then absolutist Europe was in some measure Tocqueville's purpose in studying the operation of American society in 1830. To clarify the operation of Western democracy in the mid-twentieth century may contribute to the political battle in Asia and Africa.

4: The Extreme Left

Any discussion of the American Left must take into account a wide variety of ideologies, tactical programs, and groups ranging from reform-minded democratic socialists to militant advocates of permanent revolution. Leftists may adopt a diverse amalgam of tactics, from parliamentary participation to urban guerrilla activity. Because of this variety of tactics it is very difficult to define the American Left.

In their study of American socialism, Donald D. Egbert and Stow Persons classify Left-Wing movements on the basis of goals, attitudes toward change, and institutional focus.[1] The most widely accepted classification of the Left distinguishes between liberals, democratic socialists, communists, and anarchists.[2] Liberals and democratic socialists generally do not propose radical or revolutionary programs.[3] Instead, they generally urge gradual and orderly forms of change that have the effect of increasing governmental control over the socioeconomic affairs of the country. Communists and anarchists advocate more comprehensive forms of social change at a more rapid pace. Both movements want to transform all social relations throughout a society and argue for immediate fundamental change.

A less precise but more contemporary way of discussing the Left, especially in America, is chronological: the Old Left and the New Left. The "Old Left" generally refers to the working class movements of the twenties and thirties, such as the socialists and various competing groups of communists. As Bell suggests, it followed a "foreign ideology" that was rigid and inflexibly devoted to elevating the "common worker" to a position of socioeconomic supremacy.[4] The Old Left in part derived from the few radical immigrants who came to America from Europe and had participated in the abortive strikes and revolutions of the mid-nineteenth century. They were joined later in the century by other dispossessed political activists, particularly from Eastern Europe, who spread the doctrines of Marx and Engels, Lassalle, and Bakunin. Although the various groups comprising the American Left rarely agreed, they all tended to idealize the working class as the destined vehicle of change

---

[1] Donald D. Egbert and Stow Persons, "Terminology and Types of Socialism," in *Socialism and American Life*, vol. 1, ed. D. Egbert and S. Persons (Princeton: Princeton University Press, 1952), pp. 1–20.

[2] See Lyman T. Sargent, *Contemporary Political Ideologies: A Comparative Analysis* (Homewood, Ill.: The Dorsey Press, 1969).

[3] In totalitarian states opposition is not tolerated, consequently in these societies even liberals and democratic socialists may be suspect and subject to repression.

[4] Daniel Bell, "The Background and Development of Marxian Socialism in the United States," in Egbert and Persons, *op. cit.*, pp. 213–406.

leading to the abolition of private property and capitalism. They also agreed that modern technology made a better world possible for all, not for just a privileged few.

Beyond these shared beliefs the Old Left has historically been divided by various factors, such as language, ethnicity, and two major issues: tactics and "correct ideology." These two issues revolved around the controversy of revolution versus evolution. One position or the other intermittently came to the fore as "tendencies" supported by different factions within Leftist movements. The Socialist party of America spent years debating whether it should use "the gun or the ballot box" to achieve its goals.[5] The Industrial Workers of the World (IWW) underwent similar internal dissension, in time leaning toward the tactics of violence and the general strike.[6] The Bolshevik success of 1917 temporarily ended this debate, by seeming to "prove" the superiority of revolution over evolution.[7]

The success of the October Revolution had a profound impact on communist and socialist organizations around the globe. Leftists of many persuasions identified their efforts with the achievements of the Bolsheviks. One IWW leader exclaimed "Bolshevism was but the Russian name for the I.W.W."[8] More moderate democratic socialists also rushed to support the first successful Marxist revolution, since "all the talk, the dreams, the theories, everything that to even the least doubting or least contemplative of socialist minds must sometimes have seemed dim and elusive now took on the force of reality."[9] Most important, the Russian Revolution became the model for other aspiring "revolutionary" movements in the world, especially those affiliated with the Communist International. These movements were rocked by the conflicts and controversies that took place behind Kremlin walls. In America, the Communist Party of the United States (CPUSA) emerged as the dominant Left-Wing movement of the late twenties and was soon confronted with the battle over Lenin's succession.

This conflict centered on the role of the Soviet Union in the international communist movement and was further complicated by the personalities involved: Stalin and Trotsky in Russia; William Foster, James Cannon, and Jay Lovestone in America. One faction supported Stalin's notion of one socialist state. These "Stalinists," as they were known, asserted that all communists must follow the Kremlin leadership and support the Soviet Union against the threat of counter-revolution and "bourgeois" subversion. The U.S.S.R., it was argued, would in time become the model socialist state and export the revolution to other countries. Other communist parties therefore had to act in the interests of the Kremlin, even at the sacrifice of their own immediate needs and goals. Stalin's unsuccessful antagonist, Leon Trotsky, formed the "Opposition Left," which contended that there must be a "permanent revolution" in every country and that no one country could become a truly socialist state by itself. "Trotskyites," as his followers were known, rejected Stalin's fear of "encircling capitalist countries" and his insistence that the Soviet Union must be strengthened before socialism could take place elsewhere. In the United States this ideological split was defined in terms of a Kremlin orientation as opposed to a more native Marxist orientation. The Trotskyites, who advocated the nationalist orientation, lost this power struggle and were expelled from the CPUSA, forming the Socialist Workers Party (SWP). The SWP, in time, split in amoeba fashion into a number of contending groups.

5 See Albert Fried, *Socialism in America: From the Shakers to the Third International* (Garden City: Anchor Books, 1970); also David Shannon, *The Socialist Party of America* (New York: Macmillan Co., 1955).
6 Patrick Renshaw, *The Wobblies* (New York: Anchor Books, 1967).
7 See Theodore Draper, *The Roots of American Communism* (New York: Viking Press, 1957).
8 Harold Lord Varney, "Left Wing or I.W.W.—The Way to Unity," *Revolutionary Age* (April 19, 1919): 8.
9 Irving Howe and Lewis Coser, *The American Communist Party: A Critical History* (Boston: Beacon Press, 1957), pp. 25–26.

In 1927 the Communist Academy in Moscow was told "There is no revolutionary situation in America."[10] The CPUSA was charged with failing to overcome the "false consciousness" produced by the "illusions" American capitalism fostered. The main reason for this lack of success, the Communists believed, was the foreign composition and outlook of the movement. As one member recalled, "We had great difficulties because most of our members could not write English."[11] Much concerned with the American party's ineffectiveness, the Communist International issued an open letter to its American members indicating that the CPUSA "has been for many years an organization of foreign workers not much connected with the political life of the country."[12] The "popular front against fascism" was inaugurated by the Kremlin in the mid-thirties and communist parties were urged to form broadly based alliances with native Left-Wing movements. In the United States the CPUSA employed what Lowenthal and Guterman call the "simple Americans" technique, which utilized many nationalist symbols and helped reinforce the identification of Party members with the "people."[13] This device enabled the Stalinists to appeal to some non-Marxists and reduce somewhat the isolation of the CPUSA. The membership, which until 1936 was predominantly European in outlook and interest, felt itself a part of the American working class. The Party slogan became "Communism Is Twentieth Century Americanism."

During this era, the Party reached the height of its political popularity and potential (although at no time did it have more than 70,000 members and approximately one million sympathizers). The fledgling Congress of Industrial Organizations (CIO) welcomed Party members as labor organizers, and a substantial number of Americans, particularly intellectuals and artists, supported the CPUSA's opposition to fascism in Germany, Italy, and Spain. The Stalin-Hitler nonaggression pact of 1939, however, alienated many of these intellectuals and began the decline of American Communism. The CPUSA suspended political activity during the Second World War, and Communist hopes of returning to the successes of its popular front days were blunted by the cold war and Stalin's reasserting the doctrine of "one socialist state." Dissenting Communists, like Earl Browder, the General Secretary of the Party, who urged further Americanization of the movement, were expelled. Increasing international tensions resulted in a series of political setbacks for the American Left, such as the Smith Act trials and the investigations by Joseph McCarthy, Pat McCarren, and Robert Wood. Finally, Khruschev's de-Stalinization speech of 1956 finally split the CPUSA, and the Party declined into political oblivion.[14] Throughout the late forties and fifties the American Left fought a losing battle for self-preservation.

In the early sixties protest groups began to emerge once again. They began by advocating some of the political causes previously endemic to the Old Left, but this time with a difference. The term "New Left" arose in the 1960s to distinguish these new groups from the earlier Left Wing. The "New Left" generally defies definition. It refers to an amorphous collection of personalities and small groups weakly tied together by common concerns such as opposition to racial inequality and the Indochina war. There are, however, several distinctive features of this loose association of protest groups. Originally, the New Left disavowed foreign allegiances and rigid ideological postures. Moreover, they lacked a permanent infra-structure associated with Stalinist and Trotskyite organizations. New Left organizations were in

---

10 Quoted in Nathan Glazer, *The Social Basis of American Communism* (New York: Harcourt Brace Jovanovich, 1969), p. 60.

11 *Ibid.*, p. 61.

12 Draper, *op. cit.*, p. 386.

13 See Leo Lowenthal and Norman Guterman, *Prophets of Deceit* (New York: Harper and Bros., 1949). A biased but interesting view of the 1930s is Eugene Lyons, *The Red Decade* (New Rochelle: Arlington House, 1970).

14 See David Shannon, *The Decline of American Communism* (New York: Harcourt Brace Jovanovich, 1959).

the beginning primarily evolutionary and parliamentary. For example, the Students for a Democratic Society (SDS), founded in 1961, urged a form of Jeffersonianism, which they called "participatory democracy."[15] SDS opposed the establishment of a permanent leadership, fearing the co-optation described by Armand L. Mauss. The tactics of New Left groups were largely derived from the southern civil rights movement. In due course, their tactics of nonviolence and occupation of forbidden territorial space were adapted by dissident students to the situations on campus.[16] The Free Speech Movement (FSM) at the University of California at Berkeley was the first of many instances in which students employed the tactics and rhetoric their leaders had learned from the voter-registration drives in the South.

In 1966, the focus, tactics, and rhetoric of the Left were drastically altered because of the Vietnam war. In the South and on the campus, the New Left was partially successful, but the tactics that evolved from small southern towns and campus quadrangles proved largely ineffectual when applied to national issues. Blacks, originally in the Student Nonviolent Coordinating Committee (SNCC), discovered that the old tactics and alliances no longer produced desired results. As a consequence, black militants increasingly refused to use totally nonviolent means to achieve their goals. As Lewis Killian argues in this chapter, the change from an evolutionary orientation to a revolutionary one was due to many factors, the most obvious being black pessimism about the rate of progress. Furthermore, many blacks felt that the violence used against them should be returned in kind. In some cases, white protesters followed suit. SDS and similar campus groups, in protesting the war and resisting the draft, began to look beyond parliamentary solutions. At this point the weakly developed reformist programs of the New Left shifted to more traditional Marxist ones. In the course of several campus protests during this period protestors adopted the use of firearms, and confrontations between students and police became more violent. Concurrently, New Left ideology became increasingly revolutionary and reminiscent of the factionalism current in the thirties.

During the SDS Ann Arbor Convention in 1967 two ideological positions emerged. The first, advocated by Progressive Labor Party (PLP) members, was the traditional Marxist program of organizing the working class into a revolutionary force. The counterposition was a quasi–Mills-Marcuse "new working class" formula, which stressed organizing students, intellectuals, and other segments of the techno-structure into a comprehensive movement. The former position was revolutionary, the latter evolutionary. Sociopolitical events of 1968 appeared to have largely discredited the evolutionary position. The presidential campaign of Eugene McCarthy, the Chicago Democratic Convention, and the defeat of the Peace and Freedom Party suggested to many youthful protesters the futility of working within traditional political structures.[17] In 1969 the police occupation of several northern California campuses and the confrontation between the police and students at the Berkeley "People's Park" greatly solidified the PLP's ideological position. In June 1969 this doctrinal struggle came to a head with Marxist elements of SDS allying themselves with PLP and the Worker Student Alliance Caucus (WSAC) to defeat the proponents of the evolutionary or "new working class" position who then walked out of the Chicago SDS convention.[18]

Unlike the Old Left, which was suppressed during the 1950s, the New Left died of internal dissolution with, as we have noted, the futility of the 1968 Democratic party presidential campaign as one factor. Another was the inability of the protesters to find tactics that would end the Vietnam war. The Weathermen's use of

[15] See James O'Brien, "A History of the New Left, 1960–1968," pamphlet.
[16] See Michael W. Miles, *The Radical Probe: The Logic of Student Rebellion* (New York: Atheneum, 1973).
[17] See G. David Garson, "The Ideology of the New Student Left," in *Protest! Student Activism in America*, ed. Julian Foster and Durward Long (New York: William Morrow, and Co., 1970).
[18] See Harold Jacobs, ed., *Weatherman* (Berkeley: Ramparts Press, 1970).

"trashing," or incendiary bombs, cost the Left considerable support within the larger community. Finally, the proliferation of ideological groups on the New Left created an atmosphere of intense sectarianism and internecine conflict.

The turmoil of the sixties and the ethic of "equality" gave rise to what appears to be the dominant form of protest in the 1970s, exemplified by the Women's Liberation Movement. As Jo Freeman states in this chapter, "feminists do not fit into the traditional Left/Right spectrum." However, as Freeman also notes, Women's Liberation has its roots in the radical activities of the sixties. Jessie Bernard also suggests that Women's Lib is a "spinoff" from several new Leftist groups. In response to the disregard shown by SDS for women's concerns, one female member exclaimed, "Men talk about restructuring society, but ask them to make a cup of coffee and all hell breaks loose. Men laugh at changes that would affect half of the world's population. A new society must not perpetuate the inequality of women."[19] Movement women perceived New Left men as behaving like "male chauvinists," with the result that, as Marlene Dixon noted, "Traditional political ideologies and cultural myths, sexual mores and sex roles with them, began to disintegrate in an explosion of rebellion and protest."[20] Although segments of the Women's Lib movement are revolutionary, at least in origin, other portions are fundamentally reformist in nature. The National Organization for Women, which is the largest feminist group, has three hundred chapters with 20,000 members[21] and is essentially concerned with improving employment opportunities for women rather than with changing the entire culture.

NOW appears to be drifting into conflict with more militant and ideologically radical parts of the Women's Liberation cause.[22] In fact, the feminists may be at the same stage in their development as was the civil rights movement when black power emerged as a major theme.[23] Although NOW has achieved much of the legal protection it wished from government, the grievances of many women still remain unresolved. It is quite possible that the women's movement, like the black militants, may seek new and perhaps more radical solutions.

[19] Quoted in Jessie Bernard, *Women and the Public Interest: An Essay on Policy and Protest* (Chicago: Aldine Press, 1971), p. 211.
[20] Marlene Dixon, "Why Women's Liberation," in *Roles Women Play: Readings Toward Women's Liberation*, ed. Michelle Hoffnung Garskof, (Belmont: Brooks/Cole Publishing Co., 1971), p. 167.
[21] Enid Nemy, " 'The Movement . . . Is Big Enough to Roll with All These Punches,' " *The New York Times*, October 2, 1972, p. 46.
[22] Lauri Johnston, "Feminists Score Friedan Article Assailing Movement Disrupters," *The New York Times*, March 8, 1973, p. 46.
[23] See Betty Friedan, "Up from the Kitchen Floor," *The New York Times Magazine*, March 4, 1973, pp. 8ff.

On Being Strangled
by the Stars and Stripes:
The New Left, the Old Left,
and the Natural History
of American Radical Movements

ARMAND L. MAUSS

THE GENESIS OF SOCIAL MOVEMENTS

On the Old Left:

> By giving rise to that curious phenomenon, the American middle-class radical, the student movement (of the thirties) paved the way for that familiar American phenomenon, the post-war version of the successful young man. No matter what the intentions of the Communist and Socialist founders of the student movement may have been, they helped—as, in general, the radical movement in this country has so frequently helped—young people to find their "place" in the very world against which they had first rebelled [Howe & Coser, 1962].

On the New Left:

> . . . blocking the path of the New Left is the culture's skill at amiably absorbing all manner of rebels and turning them into celebrities. To be a radical in America today is like trying to punch your way out of a cage made of marshmallow. Every thrust at the jugular draws not blood, but sweet success; every hack at the roots draws not retaliation, but fame and affluence [Newfield, 1966].

It would seem that there is a certain irony in whatever success is achieved by a radical movement in America, and this irony is as fascinating to social

"On Being Strangled by the Stars and Stripes: The New Left, the Old Left, and the Natural History of American Radical Movements" is reprinted from the *Journal of Social Issues,* Vol. 27, No. 1. (1971). Copyright 1971 by the Society for the Psychological Study of Social Issues. Reprinted by permission of the publisher.

scientists as it may be tragic to the adherents of the movement. Whatever the fate of a radical movement, however, in its genesis it would seem to have much in common with other kinds of social movements. The psychologists and social psychologists who have written about social movements have drawn, broadly, upon the Freudian tradition, and, additionally, upon the perspective of Kurt Lewin. They look, for example, to discrepancies between the "ego-levels" and the "achievement levels" of individuals. Thus Hadley Cantril (1941) finds certain prevalent sources of discontent in the on-going efforts of men to cope with their "ego drives," their pursuit after meaning, and the like. In the same general vein, Hans Toch (1965) focuses on those social and psychological factors that lead certain kinds of people toward a susceptibility or a predisposition to participate in social movements. This is what might be called a microcosmic perspective, looking for the genesis of social movements in what transpires within the psyche and/or within the process of small-scale social interaction. Indeed, the process of socialization itself should be included here, considering that Flacks and Liebman as well as others (Sampson, 1967a) have pointed to the tendency of New Leftists to come from liberal home backgrounds.

Taking a position that is partly psychological and partly sociological, Glock and Stark (1965) find that a "necessary precondition for the rise of any organized social movement, whether it be religious or secular, is a situation of felt-deprivation." They then go on to identify five different kinds of deprivation (only one of which is of an economic nature) and postulate some of the conditions under which any of the five might produce a religious and/or a secular social movement. In this line of thinking, Glock and Stark are somewhat reminiscent of Crane Brinton (1938), whose well-known postulate about the role of frustrated rising expectations in revolutions is certainly applicable also to radical movements more generally. One of the insights of the paper by Demerath, Marwell, and Aiken in the [*Journal of Social Issues*, vol. 27, no. 1, 1971] is the part played by need-fulfillment and personal satisfactions for whites, both in their participation in southern civil rights work and (later) in their withdrawal from it.

Still another perspective (but a complementary one) is the more macrocosmic one of sociologists and political scientists. Here the focus is upon the large-scale social-structural sources of social movements. Smelser, for example (1963), deals with such concepts as structural conduciveness, strains in the system, and the pervasiveness and crystallization of key "generalized beliefs," as factors facilitating the rise of social movements. Along with other sociologists (e.g., Lipset, 1960), Smelser is concerned with the parts played by cultural values and norms in the relations between an emerging movement and its social milieu. Not only do movements characteristically define their own orientations by selective reference to certain societal values or norms, but also there is the interesting question of to what extent a movement can find support (or at least legitimacy) in the underlying political values and norms of the society itself—a point on which turns a basic difference between relatively open societies and the more totalitarian ones. Somewhat more directed toward our own kind of society in particular is the "mass society" theoretical orientation, which postulates that modern industrial mass societies create special stresses and strains because of their unusual cultural heterogeneity and consequent normative ambiguity or anomie; their tendency toward utilitarian and manipulative interpersonal relations, rather than primary ones; and the endemic frustrations among certain segments of the masses, deriving from rising but unfulfilled aspirations (King, 1956; Gusfield, 1968; Sherif & Sherif, 1969).

A more general and abstract (and thus perhaps not too enlightening) explanation for the genesis of social movements is the rather common-sense one expressed by Killian (1964), who says, in effect, that no special theory is required; we must look for the source of movements in the very nature of the social order itself and in the general socialization process. Since no social order can be expected to function equally well for everyone all the time, we can expect a certain amount of dissatisfaction (and therefore incipient radicalism) in any society at any given time, without necessarily postulating a precipitating condition such as heavy repression. This idea would accord with the position of social change theorist Wilbert Moore (1963), who contends that the most realistic model for any society is neither the "consensus" nor the "conflict" model, but simply the model of a "tension-management system."

To be sure, any or all of the general theoretical ideas just reviewed have to be made specific to a given social movement in order to be of any real value in explaining it. We would have to ask, for example, *which* "ego drives," which unfulfilled aspirations, which unmanaged tensions, which specific milieux, etc., have been involved in the rise of the Old Left or of the New Left. A number of the papers in [*JSI*, vol. 27, no. 1, 1971] and elsewhere have addressed such specific questions, explicitly or implicitly (especially the papers by Abcarian, Flacks, Finney, Marx & Useem, Schweitzer & Elden, and Liebman). These papers, and my own earlier one, suggest that there are some definite differences between the Old and New Left with respect to generating factors. In a past issue of this journal (Sampson, 1967a) several articles focused on the college or university milieu as one tending especially to generate the student movement, which we include here in the New Left (Keniston, 1967; Trent & Craise, 1967; Sampson, 1967b). Sampson's paper emphasizes what he calls the "subversive function" of the university setting. This function seems to make an important contribution both to the "motivational base" and to the "ideological base," which must coincide, according to Sherif and Sherif (1969), if a social movement is to arise. The special importance of certain campus atmospheres (irrespective of campus size or other such attributes) in the rise of the New Left is brought out also by Kahn and Bowers (1970). Feuer (1969), in his study of the rise of radical youth movements, finds a tendency for such movements to attach themselves at the beginning to what he calls a "carrier movement"; this reminds us that the New Left, in certain important respects, was spawned and carried for a while by the Old Left. The SDS, after all, arose out of the old League for Industrial Democracy (LID) and indeed held its first meeting at the UAW center at Port Huron, Michigan. Furthermore, the civil rights movement, an Old Left enterprise at the beginning, was a major part of the milieu in which the New Left arose (see Flacks, Mauss, Marx & Useem, Demerath et al.).

THE NATURE AND COMPOSITION OF SOCIAL MOVEMENTS

Receiving as much attention in the literature as the genesis or origins of social movements has been their nature and composition, once they are in progress. There is, to begin with, no shortage of "definitions" offered for a social movement (e.g., Blumer, 1951; Killian, 1964; Sherif & Sherif, 1969; and Gusfield, 1968). We will not consider here as problematical whether the Old and New Lefts qualify as "social movements." They readily meet any of the standard definitions of a social movement, possessing, for example, such characteristics as shared values and goals, in-group feeling, a structure with a kind of organized nucleus or "critical mass" surrounded by a large, fluid, and unorganized aggregate, and so on. Beyond mere definitions, however, there are interesting questions about the structure or "morphology" of a social movement—who are its leaders and its followers, what is the relation between its active nucleus and its periphery, what is its normative and ideological content?

Many of the questions that relate to the composition and morphology of the Old and New Lefts were discussed in descriptive terms in the introductory article to [*JSI*, vol. 27, no. 1, 1971]. It was noted, for example, that the social base of much of the New Left—in contrast to the proletarian and immigrant base of the Old—consists of bourgeois youth and blacks. The respective heroes, models, and leading personalities of the two Lefts were also pointed out. Finney's paper deals in large part with the social class backgrounds from which the early New Leftists presumably came (questioning some of the earlier findings), while the Schweitzer and Elden article involves itself more broadly with the whole social structural base of New Left strength as of 1968. Liebman does much the same kind of thing for the Puerto Rican New Left. These papers can be considered as supplements to the already existing descriptions of the composition of New Left membership and leadership in such works as those of Flacks (1970), Keniston, (1968), and Newfield (1966). These accounts strongly suggest that however limited the social base which first fostered the New Left may have been, the backgrounds of the participants now are quite varied. Similarly, while the Old Left once had a strong proletarian base, that base has since undergone an extensive "bourgeoisification." Such developments in the history of social movements put one in mind of the generalization of Sherif and Sherif (1969) that leaders (and followers?) in any social movement can be expected to come from a variety of social backgrounds—eventually, if not originally—precisely because they are ". . . as much creations of the movement, its motivational base, and its temper at a particular time, as they are creators of the movement." Similar observations are made by Killian (1964).

One of the most interesting and problematic questions about the social composition of the New Left has been the ethnic one, and to a much greater extent than was true for the Old Left. In the late 1920s and early 1930s, efforts were made to recruit blacks to various Leftist causes, especially by the Communist party, which even supported a kind of black separatism for a while. By and large these efforts were not terribly successful among an unaroused (and still predominantly rural) black population (Howe & Coser, 1962). The black segment of the New Left, however, has been a major component from the beginning, specifically since the mid-1960s when blacks began to adopt an increasingly separatist posture and to demand parity instead of paternalism within the movement. From that point on, indeed, it might be argued that we have had *two* New Left movements, one white and one black. While a number of commentators have written about this development (e.g., O'Brien, 1968; Meier, 1970), a much more profound understanding of it is made possible by two articles in [*JSI*, vol. 27, no. 1, 1971]. The piece by Demerath, Marwell, and Aiken makes clear the nature of the strains between the black and white components of the New Left from the earliest days of the movement; Marx and Useem's contribution helps us to see these strains as endemic in any movement which enlists "outsiders" in a liberation program.

The discussion so far has been descriptive, emphasizing an interest in such static questions as the definition of social movements, their typical components, and the extent to which the Old and New Lefts fit the "normal" conception of a social movement. Next we shall undertake a somewhat more analytical and dynamic line of discussion.

THE INTERACTION OF SOCIAL MOVEMENTS AND SOCIETY

It is obvious that little can be understood about any social movement as long as it is considered only in isolation from its host milieu. Killian is one who makes the point that not only is the development of a movement itself critically affected by the surrounding society's reaction to it, but also that "rarely does a social movement leave unchanged the structure of the group in which it arises [1964, p. 454]." A movement is always of an emergent nature, and what happens to its members "as a consequence of their interaction within the movement is vastly more important than the reasons why they first came into the movement [Killian, 1964, p. 445]." Thus the interaction between the society and the movement affects both to some extent.

A number of theoretical positions converge on this interaction process. It was a major concern, of course, for Karl Marx, although the dialectic he saw in this process led to quite a different outcome from the one this paper postulates. Max Weber's classic paradigm followed the transformation of a movement (particularly but not necessarily a religious one) from a charismatic beginning on through to the "routinization" of its charisma, as one accommodation after another is made between the society and the movement. The more thorough and systematic scheme of Ernst Troeltsch set forth the "sect-church" model of the development of religious movements. More recent theorists have explicitly recognized the applicability of the Troeltsch type of model to *secular* movements as well (see Gusfield, 1968; Heberle, 1951, esp. Chapter 15). Following in part from some ideas of Cantril (1941), Hans Toch (1965) has posited a "push-pull" effect in the interaction between the movement and the society, with resultant change in both. Turner and Killian (1957) also comment upon dual changes; they draw upon the work of Brewer (1952) on Methodism and of Messinger (1955) on the Townsend movement, in order to illustrate the process of routinization in movements. Not that routinization is the *inevitable* destiny of every social movement; some, indeed, succeed in revolution and in the establishment of a new regime; others secede and remain aloof; still others simply die out. The nature of the interaction with the society, in any case, appears to be an important determinant of the outcome. Here one is reminded somewhat of the interactionist model which Howard Becker (1963) has put forth to describe the dynamic of labelling and ostracism experienced by the *individual* deviant. Radical social movements also tend to be labelled and ostracized, and, like individual deviants, to respond to this process in certain (usually predictable) ways. The series of responses and counter-responses tells the history of the radical movement, just as it does for the individual deviant.

Those theorists who have studied the careers of social movements over time, then, have all noted that a process of interaction occurs which progressively alters not only the nature and behavior of the movement and the society, respectively, but also the nature of the relationship between them. Each is required to keep changing in response to the other, and each has a dilemma to contend with. For the democratic society, the dilemma is one of accommodating the movement while still containing and controlling it; for the movement, the dilemma is one of maintaining the radical spirit and integrity while still compromising enough to gather maximum support from non-radical sympathizers and sponsors in the society. The latter effort involves, in part, the process observed by Killian:

> Since a movement develops within the context of the society which it seeks to change, and since the members are products of this society, it is constrained to reconcile its values with those of the larger society, no matter how revolutionary it may appear. Hence, it tends to develop explicit values, presented both to members and to nonmembers, which cloak the movement with a mantle of idealism and altruism, if not always of respectability [1964, p. 435].

Another way of stating the same dilemma is to observe (as do the Liebman and the Demerath et al. papers) the difficulty experienced by radical movements in trying both to broaden the recruitment base and to maintain intense commitment to principles.

In this context, the responses of the larger society are critical. If the revolutionary element in the movement becomes prominent and explicit, then the society can be expected to respond with repression. This repression, if sustained, might succeed in eliminating the movement, particularly if the latter is lacking in broad support (see Hakman). At the same time, however, the society will try to win over such support as the movement may have by an effort at co-optation, i.e., ameliorative gestures in the direction of neutralizing the movement's criticisms, combined with propaganda emphasizing the common interests and values which exist between the society and the movement. In the case of movements which are very radical, especially if they are also small in size, there will likely be a greater element of repression than of co-optation (e.g., the American Communist party—Howe & Coser, 1962). With less radical and more respectable movements (e.g., the current ecology-and-environment movement), co-optation is emphasized. Any American movement, however, is faced with the necessity of coping with this "double death-squeeze" of co-optation and repression, and with the dilemma of trying to maintain an identity and an integrity in a relatively permissive society, which awards stars of fame and respectability to its constructive critics but stripes of repression and ostracism to its unreformed radicals. The result seems always (Killian, 1964) to be the demise of the movement in one way or another: (a) elimination through secession or repression or a combination of the two; (b) at the other extreme, successful revolution and seizure of power, followed by the classical Thermidorian reaction (Brinton, 1938), which constitutes in large part a betrayal of the original radical stance and values; or (c) an accommodation with society, in which both sides have made compromises and come to terms with the other's position (e.g., a successful third party in the United States). The irony of the last outcome, of course, is that while it allows the movement some long-range consequence and influence, the very process of institutionalization co-opts it and makes of it a kind of political eunuch. Small wonder that New Left spokesmen of late have warned of this development and decried it (Flacks, 1970; Allen, 1968). Indeed, both the Marx-Useem and the Demerath et al. papers [in *JSI*, vol. 27, no. 1, 1971] show that one of the strains leading to separatism of the black New Left was the increasing fear and suspicion that at length the white New Left would be "bought off" by the system.

STAGES IN THE CAREER OF A RADICAL MOVEMENT

To postulate an interaction process between the movement and the society, in which each experiences a series of changes in response to the other, is to raise the question of stages in the development over time of the movement, and probably of the society too. Such a postulate is neither novel nor particularly profound, and it carries with it many risks, including that of oversimplification and factual distortion (two of the charges made, for example, against Karl Marx's dialectical model). Nevertheless, if we proceed with caution, we may find that looking at radical movements as having "careers" with "stages" has certain heuristic advantages in helping us to interpret the papers in [*JSI*, vol. 27, no. 1, 1971], as well as much of the other literature on the New and Old Left.

A number of scholars have conceived of movements as passing through more or less inevitable—or even predictable—stages (Hopper, 1950; Brinton, 1938; Sherif & Sherif, 1969; King, 1956). Certain other theorists, while perhaps not themselves undertaking a stage-by-stage analysis of movements, have implicitly assumed the existence of such stages in their analyses of changes over time in the style of a movement's chief zealots (e.g., Hoffer, 1951), or of its leaders (e.g., Lang & Lang, 1961; Heberle, 1951; Killian, 1964).

All of the above conceptual schemes carry the intriguing challenge of empirical application to actual historical cases, and some of them (e.g., Brinton's) are convincingly illustrated from history. In general, however, they leave something to be desired for purposes of discussing the Old and New Left. First of all, except for Brinton's, they have not been developed especially for radical movements, but for social movements in general, and a theoretical model which lumps together such diverse movements as, say, Conservation (or Ecology) and Communism (or Socialism), operates at too abstract a level to be very helpful. Secondly, these career models have tended to draw, for their empirical support, upon "successful" movements—

those which have, in some degree, achieved their goals. They give little or no attention to the many movements (notably radical ones) which have died or been destroyed while still struggling. Third, the stages which these earlier career models have postulated have usually been only superficially worked out and the models have involved very few distinct stages (I would say probably too few) considering the lengthy histories that many radical movements have had (e.g., Left-wing radicalism in the U.S.). Finally, seldom have the extant models made clear and explicit what conditions (within and/or without the movement) are associated with change from one stage to the next, an explication which would be the chief value of a career model, according to Turner and Killian (1957).

The career model being postulated here is set forth with the Old and New Left particularly in mind. On the one hand, this makes it especially appropriate to our theme; on the other hand, it may make for some limitations upon its general applicability. I shall be drawing upon (and partially synthesizing) the work of others aforementioned in outlining *five stages* through which American radical movements pass in the natural history of their careers. This five-stage model will be illustrated by references to the histories of the Old and New Left, particularly the latter.

The five stages of the model here being proposed we shall call: (a) incipiency; (b) coalescence; (3) institutionalization; (d) fragmentation; and (e) demise. A growth curve representing this five-stage life-cycle would have a shape approximating the normal curve, with the third stage at the apex.

Incipiency

The *inception* of a radical movement may take place in accordance with any of the sociological or social-psychological postulates discussed above under "the genesis of social movements," but the progression of the movement through its succeeding stages will be the result of the movement's responses to the changing stances which the surrounding society is taking toward it. In general, the continuing stance of any establishment toward a radical movement is one of a mixture of co-optation and repression, as described earlier herein. In viable totalitarian police states (of the kind we have come to associate with a Hitler or a Stalin or a Mao), the mixture is clearly dominated by the element of repression, thus totally eliminating the stimulus of rising expectations—which is why radical movements so seldom get past mere inception in such societies. In liberal democratic societies like our own, however, the establishment's response is typically an indulgent one at the inception of a radical movement, with emphasis upon co-optation and absorption. (Or, in deference to the radical interpretation, we should perhaps say that at the inception stage the repression is more subtle, recognizing that to the radical the co-optation itself is seen as a form of repression.) Of course when we speak of co-optation or repression, we do not necessarily refer only to the responses of the formal social control agencies of government, but rather to the responses of various institutions of the society.

At the outset, then, the discontent (of whatever kind) which provides the radical animus, must express itself in a search for boundaries (within what Newfield—quoted at the beginning of this paper—called a "cage made of marshmallow!"). There is typically a commitment within the movement in its earliest stages to work within the system, since the boundaries of "the system" (at least as they pertain to the particular movement) are not well defined. Such are the conditions surrounding the incipiency stage. The situation within the embryonic movement is reminiscent of what Blumer (1951) has had to say about what he calls *general*, as opposed to *specific*, social movements (and I would suggest that every social movement goes through a "general" phase in Blumer's sense): "groping uncoordinated efforts . . . unorganized, with neither established leadership nor recognized membership, and little guidance or control [Blumer, 1951, pp. 200–201]."

Coalescence

As the various institutions of the society begin to add to their initially indulgent and co-optive efforts a series of ad hoc control (repression) measures, the incipient radical movement is provided with a series of provocations around which to organize for its own defense. This constitutes the stage of *coalescence*, in which the public (or publics) of the incipiency stage now begin to "supplement their informal . . . discussion with some organization to promote their convictions effectively and insure more sustained activity [Turner & Killian, 1957, p. 307]." Typically this means the organization of a number of local and ephemeral ad hoc committees, caucuses, fronts, and the like, here and there around the society. There is not yet any nationally coordinated organization.

Institutionalization

In response to the movement's growing influence, self-consciousness, and potential for trouble-making, the establishment (now particularly the government) begins steadily to increase both its co-optive and its repressive efforts, with the latter now becoming more prominent in the mixture and more formalized. This process brings in the stage of *institutionalization*.

The movement becomes institutionalized in at least two senses. A society-wide coordination of the movement crystallizes for common political action in response to the establishment's "escalation"; this may mean more than one nationwide organization, but there will be a tendency for parallel organizations to have some overlapping in membership. Simultaneously, the society itself devises a series of routine measures for coping with the movement, including new laws and penalties on the one hand, combined with new forms of co-optation, on the other (such as the currying of favor of radical leaders, the formation of new political parties and/or factions within existing parties, etc.).

It is during this third stage that the radical movement enjoys its greatest success: the mass media begin to take it seriously, Leftist politicians within the establishment vie for its favor, and its spokesmen become fashionable (and perhaps well paid) speakers before various aware and concerned citizens' groups. Success for the movement during this stage can also be seen in the legislative arena, where repressive legislation is being increasingly accompanied by ameliorative legislation aimed at some of the criticisms which the movement is making.

Fragmentation

The very success of the institutionalization stage leads to the fourth stage, *fragmentation*. As the movement and some of its leaders gain increasing respectability, they come to have an increasing stake in maintaining the status quo, or at least in not changing it too rapidly. In short, they are "bought off." Radical militancy is reduced also by the realization that some of the radical program has been implemented, or at least picked up as part of the campaign of one or more of the establishment political parties. Increased repression, meanwhile, is making the radical stance more and more costly. It is perhaps inevitable that such conditions should make for a great proliferation within the movement of varied degrees of radicalism, as each radical individual continues to assess and reassess his position vis-à-vis an ever-changing establishment. It is just as inevitable that this proliferation should lead to segmentalization of the movement into small factions (fragments) representing the various degrees of radicalism.

Demise

The final stage of the movement, its *demise*, is from the establishment's point of view only a "mopping up." The various facets of the co-optation process have appropriated most of the movement's effective members and all of its outside societal support, leaving only small bands of true believers to engage in increasingly desperate measures (including violence and terrorism) to try to keep the movement alive. Their behavior alienates them still further from the rest of the society, including their erstwhile radical colleagues, and they are either driven to complete secession from the society or left to face the onslaught of total repression from a now unrestrained establishment backed by a strong public consensus. The "mix" of co-optation and repression with which the establishment first began its approach to the movement has now changed from almost total co-optation to almost total repression.

The stages of fragmentation and demise for a radical movement in this society seem inescapable except in the event that the society should develop the revolutionary conditions outlined by Brinton (1938). Lacking these conditions (as the history of even recent radical movements suggests is the case), we can expect that our society, while it will surely be affected— politically, socially and even culturally—by its co-optation of radical movements, will ultimately absorb and destroy these movements. For, ironically, the greater their success in influencing the society, the more rapid their fragmentation and demise. (This, I would suggest, is precisely the paradox which Flacks has found in the "successful" outcome of the New Left.)

THE FIVE-STAGE MODEL AND THE OLD AND NEW LEFT

It will perhaps be apparent to the reader that the theoretical model which has just been presented was developed with the history of the American Left very much in mind. While it seems plausible to postulate that the model is also applicable to any radical movement in this kind of society (and I do so postulate), the remainder of this paper will attempt to apply the model to the Old and New Left.

Stages in the old left

It is difficult in any absolute sense to decide where to begin the history of the Old Left, and certainly no attempt is being made here to present a comprehensive history. According to one interpretation (Feuer, 1969), the Left prior to the depression of the 1930s (e.g., Intercollegiate Society of Socialists and the League for Industrial Democracy) was always pretty much arrested in what Feuer calls the "circle stage," which seems, from his description, very much like what I am here calling the stage of "coalescence." This would suggest that in the early days of this century the conditions existed for an Old Left to develop that far, but no farther. The outbreak of World War I—accompanied and followed, as it was, by a general campaign of nationalism, nativism, and the like—made for a very repressive atmosphere for anything having an un-American appearance; in addition the general prosperity of the 1920s greatly reduced the potential for widespread discontent. Leftist activities on the college campuses in particular were nearly wiped out in the period around World War I; and Feuer (1969) remarks on the virtual absence of any youthful protestors in the Sacco-Vanzetti affair in 1927.

In the mid- and late-1920s and the early 1930s, a considerable amount of Leftist ferment developed among intellectuals, such as those associated with the journal *New Masses* (e.g., Max Eastman and John Dos Passos). During the same period, however, Communist party efforts among the workers were a complete flop, and their campaign among the youth, the immigrants, and the Negroes was only slightly more successful (Howe & Coser, 1962). All in all, the Old Left does not appear to have gotten past *coalescence* up through the 1920s, and, given the conditions in the society, it would seem to have done well to have gotten that far!

The coming of the depression in the early 1930s, of course, provided the conditions necessary to move the Old Left into the third stage of the model, institutionalization (Feuer, 1969; Howe & Coser, 1962). The old socialist groups, and particularly the Communist party, took on more cogency in the public mind and developed strong organizations. By the mid-1930s, for example, almost the entire student movement had come under the control of the Communist party (Feuer, 1969); after 1935 the Communist-Socialist United Front showed real viability for a while (Howe & Coser, 1962). The New Deal represented an attempt to co-opt the appeal of such radical groups and itself turned noticeably more to the left for a time after 1935 (Howe & Coser, 1962). Furthermore, after a period of pacifism, the Old Left found, with the emergence of Hitler and the Spanish Civil War, foreign causes on which to help build its movement.

The effective co-optation of the Old Left was finally made possible only by the advent of World War II. The Communist segment of the Left was morally compromised by the Hitler-Stalin pact of 1939, and then the war effort brought an end to the depression and thus to much of the appeal of the Leftist organizations. At the same time, the patriotic fervor at that time gave the establishment even more co-optive potential than it would otherwise have had, as even the most radical groups were constrained to rally behind the government. Nevertheless, during and just after the war, the Communists succeeded in making some real inroads into labor organizations.

All in all, the period from about 1932 to 1948 (i.e., including the Henry Wallace campaign) can be called the hey-day of the Old Left; this was the period of its institutionalization, when its organizations were strong and the establishment was forced to reckon with it. The reckoning took the form of both legislative and judicial action [see Hakman in *JSI*, vol. 27, no. 1, 1971], with the establishment and the radicals engaging each other in courtroom conflict. While this judicial process was part of the repression program, it also constituted a kind of co-optation insofar as the Old Left radicals were thereby recognizing and legitimizing the judicial institutions—something which the New Left radicals have been considerably less willing to do. The gain to the radicals (both old and new), however, has been the opportunity to use the courtroom as a proselyting forum.

The following decade saw the *fragmentation* and *demise* of the Old Left. A sure symptom, and part of the process itself, was the series of important defections of radical Old Leftists (in this case mainly Communists) as analyzed in Abcarian's paper in [*JSI*, vol. 27, no. 1, 1971]. New Deal co-optation and repression had been left stronger than ever by World War II. The Communists had been discredited by the changing policies of Stalin during the 1930s and by the outbreak of the Cold War in the late 1940s; "fellow-travellers" (which often meant almost anyone on the Left) came under the same opprobrium. The United Front was destroyed by these developments. Anti-Communist labor leaders began to reverse the temporary Communist successes in that realm, and a generation of students dominated by returning veterans made an unreceptive environment on the campuses. The multi-faceted repression of the McCarthy period represented only the climax of a crescendo of anti-Leftist repression that began in the late 1940s. [See Hakman's paper in *JSI*, vol. 27, no. 1, 1971: the court cases and the litigation which he analyzes constitute a partial chronicle of the program of repression against the radical Old Left.]

Thus, the co-optation of the New Deal period, in both domestic and foreign affairs, rendered the Old Left radicals largely helpless in the face of the repression which followed. Coming out of the McCarthy period, only tame bourgeois radicalisms (e.g., civil rights and peace campaigns) were respectable, and even these forms of "radicalism" were largely co-opted by the government's succession of civil rights measures, beginning in 1954, and by the Nuclear Test Ban Treaty signed less than a decade later.

New left stages

The earliest days of the civil rights movement in the mid- or late-1950s, when blacks and whites, young and old, worked together in the South, define the *incipiency* stage of the New Left. The numbers were small and the organization was feeble, but a movement was starting to grow around the themes of civil rights and peace. The social and intellectual base of this incipient period is well described and analyzed in Finney's paper in [*JSI*, vol. 27, no. 1, 1971]. From precisely the comfortable (but varied) social class background and intellectual libertarianism represented by Finney's sample of Berkeley students came the student cohort who were to go South in increasing numbers during the next stage of the movement and who were to begin the organization of protests against the HUAC, against nuclear testing, and against a foreign policy of interventionism.

The *coalescence* of the New Left begins in the early 1960s with the rise of new (and still rather feeble) organizations like SDS and SNCC, together with a variety of campus-oriented groups at a few of the nation's larger universities, such as SLATE at Berkeley. Liebman's paper deals with the incipiency and coalescence of the student movement in Puerto Rico (FUPI) and indicates some of the reasons why this branch of the New Left has apparently remained pretty well arrested in the coalescence stage. In mainland United States, quite to the contrary, the oft-mentioned combination of repression and co-optation was early apparent and contributed significantly to an even greater coalescence of the New Left. Repression was of a localized and ad hoc nature: the quelling of militant protest at the 1960 HUAC hearings in San Francisco, the steady stream of violence by the establishment against civil rights workers in the South. The beginning of the Kennedy regime in 1961, meanwhile, began a decade in which a New Frontier and a War on Poverty both (a) raised the expectations of idealistic youth and blacks far beyond what was actually to be realized, thus assuring the continuing growth and development of the New Left, and (b) gradually co-opted at least the domestic issues which had brought the New Left into being. Local community projects such as ERAP in the North and the co-ordinating efforts of COFO in the South in 1963 and 1964 (O'Brien, 1968) indicated the ever-increasing coalescence toward a fully national movement that was taking place. The kinds of internal strains and dynamics experienced by the movement as it coalesced can be seen in the article by Demerath et al.; the black-white schism which emerged more fully with the later institutionalization of the movement was apparent even at this early stage.

The New Left's *institutionalization*, with the strengths and the stresses which that stage characteristically brings, began during the early part of 1965, after a period of rapid growth and coalescence (Flacks). It is probable that the escalation, at that same time, of the Vietnam War provided the rallying cause which the New Left needed for full-scale, nation-wide organization. The SDS and virtually all other New Left groups experienced dramatic growth and organizational development during this mid-sixties period; indeed, the strength of the new Peace and Freedom Party by 1968 [see Schweitzer & Elden's paper in *JSI*, vol. 27, no. 1, 1971] was perhaps the surest sign of the institutionalization of the movement, but also of co-optation into respectability by the establishment. Furthermore, in response to the increasingly militant student unrest on the campuses and beginning with the Free Speech Movement in Berkeley at the end of 1964, college administrations, states, and local governments all began to develop coping routines of an increasingly repressive kind—which, as we have said, is the other indication of the movement's institutionalization.

Even as the New Left movement was enjoying its hey-day during the mid-1960s, it was starting to experience the strains resulting from the classical co-optation/repression response of the establishment. The most conspicuous of these was the black-white strain and eventual rupture. The nature of the strain is clearly described in the Demerath, Marwell, and Aiken paper [in *JSI*, vol. 27, no. 1, 1971], whereas the Marx and Useem piece seems to confirm my contention that this kind of strain is probably inevitable when a movement reaches the stage I have called *institutionalization.* What seems to happen is that establishment co-optation (in this instance, the barrage of civil rights legislation in the 1960s), combined with increasingly costly repression, makes the work on behalf of the oppressed less and less attractive to the outsider-idealist (in this case, the white New Leftist), who then channels his idealism into other causes (e.g., anti-war activities). The oppressed segment of the movement (i.e., the blacks) finds the outsider less and less militant, more and more an obstacle in the way of real progress. Marx and Useem show how this tendency split three different radical movements involving oppressed people and their outside benefactors; Demerath et al. closely examine the process during one summer in the mid-1960s. There is a suggestion that perhaps the stage I call *institutionalization* can not be fully reached by the underdog (e.g., the black) segment of a radical movement until the outsiders do depart. Nevertheless, in the case of the New Left, a black/white split was only barely avoided at the 1967 Chicago National Conference for the New Politics, and since that time the black and white segments of the New Left have largely gone their separate ways.

It is the contention of this paper that we are now witnessing the *fragmentation* stage of the New Left, and that the stage of *demise* is not far off. The election of Nixon in 1968 and the establishment's general program of continuing co-optation and repression since that time have created severe problems for the New Left. The Nixon administration has gained widespread credence for its commitments to continue "pushing ahead" in the civil rights area and to end the Vietnam War in the very near future, thus co-opting the two major issues on which the New Left movement was built. Meanwhile militant radical action has been made increasingly costly by repression—ranging from the apparently successful crackdown by Hayakawa at San Francisco State College even to the shooting of students at Kent State University.

The fragmentation process, which began with the black/white split, has proceeded apace. The well-known split in 1969 in the SDS (see Flacks and Schweitzer-Elden) has been accompanied by an increasing "taming" of the less radical SDSrs (the self-styled RYM–II) and the increasing isolation and hunting down of the more extreme "Weatherman" faction (RYM–I). Abbie Hoffman is among those who are critical of the "chickening out" of the less extreme SDS faction (Hoffman, 1969), but the Weathermen are left with few accomplishments excepts act of terrorism, hardly the stuff of which successful movements are built and maintained. RYM–II, realizing the desperation and futility which terrorism represents, disclaims the Weathermen and their activities and tries to distinguish such "bad violence" from "good violence" in the form of ghetto uprisings and student disruptions (see the *San Francisco Chronicle*, 1970b). Tom Hayden (1970), while not willing to condemn the Weathermen, sees the future of the movement as taking the form of "islands" or "free territories" of the revolution, in which the emphasis will be upon building a "revolutionary culture." But such only gives a kind of explicit territorial expression to the very *fragmentation* process characteristic of this stage of the movement.

Another of the SDS founding fathers (Flacks, 1970) also seems to call for a shift in emphasis to cultural "reconstruction"—the "long march," as he calls it, through the culture and institutions of the society—an idea reiterated in his paper for [*JSI*, vol. 27, no. 1, 1971]. This leavening-of-the-loaf approach to revolution, however, inevitably means that the leaven has itself been absorbed, in accordance with the very co-optation process which Flacks [1970 and in *JSI*, vol. 27, no. 1, 1971] discusses and which has concerned us so prominently throughout this paper. One finds the Hayden and Flacks observations reminiscent, furthermore, of those made some time ago by Messinger (1955) on the Townsend movement, that is, a kind of "deflection" from the movement's original central aims as part of the "process . . . of adaptation to decline."

The black segment of the New Left can be expected to decline and fragment more slowly, since its grievances are less easily ameliorated than those on which the white New Left was built. Co-optation, in other words, will take longer. This is partly because fewer blacks than whites in the New Left have bourgeois backgrounds and ties, and partly because cultural and structural characteristics like racism do not yield as readily to change as do, say, military policies (recall Marx and Useem). Nevertheless, the ghettoes have been quiet in recent years—though it would be foolish, of course, to predict no more ghetto violence at all (Banfield, 1970). Young blacks with education (and especially PhDs) are being co-opted by the establishment as rapidly as they can be located, militant or not. Furthermore, although the continued unrest and separatism of the black New Left may at times alienate moderates both black and white, these developments clearly represent a phase in the very process by which other ethnic groups in American history have been assimilated (Banfield, 1970; Handlin, 1951). While, as we have said, it will go more slowly, still the fragmentation of the black New Left can be seen—beginning with the militant and separatist turn of CORE in the late 1960s and the rise of the even more revolutionary Black Panthers during the same period. Now, according to recent reports (see, for example, the *San Francisco Chronicle*, 1971), the Panthers themselves have begun to split into factions of "left" and "right."

If it is yet too early to speak of the total demise of the New Left, then we must at least speak of its moribundity. The relative quiet of the Seattle Seven trials has been an immense contrast to the earlier trials of the Chicago Eight. In similar contrast to the bloodily repressed Cambodia protests of 1970, renewed bombings of North Vietnam and the incursions in Laos in 1971 have brought merely murmurs from the New Left. The Vietnam Committee, which once mobilized hundreds of thousands of war protestors in marches across the land, has disbanded, partly for fear of its own most radical elements and the consequences of their extremism (i.e., severe repression), and partly because (see the *San Francisco Chronicle*, 1970a) there seems no longer to be any "mechanism [through] which to put pressure on the administration," the latter having, we might say, *co-opted* the war issue. A thorough national survey of youth and others about this same time (Converse & Schuman, 1970) finds that there is not, even among the youth, the support for anti-war protest that many had assumed, and that in any case the protest has been based more upon pragmatic than upon moralistic grounds. Thus with a "pragmatic" (i.e., co-opting) administration in the White House, "the net effect of vigorous protest in the streets has been to shift mass opinion toward renewed support of the President [Converse & Schuman, 1970]."

That the same president, fellow-traveller with Spiro T. Agnew, could get completely away with describing his 1971 proposals to Congress as a "New American Revolution" is surely a sign that the establishment's co-optation of the New Left has now extended even to its rhetoric!

REFERENCES

Allen, R. *Dialectics of black power.* (Pamphlet.) Weekly Guardian Associates, 1968.

Banfield, E. *The unheavenly city.* Boston: Little-Brown, 1970.

Becker, H. S. *Outsiders.* New York: Free Press, 1963.

Blumer, H. Collective behavior. In A. M. Lee (Ed.), *Principles of sociology.* New York: Barnes & Noble, 1951.

Brewer, E. D. Sect and church in Methodism. *Social Forces*, 1952, *30*, 400–408.

Brinton, C. *The anatomy of revolution.* New York: Norton, 1938. (Republished: Vintage, 1957.)

Cantril, H. *The psychology of social movements.* New York: Wiley, 1941.

Converse, P. E., & Schuman, H. Silent majorities and the Viet-Nam war. *Scientific American*, 1970, *222* (6, June), 17–25.

Feuer, L. *The conflict of generations.* New York: Basic Books, 1969.

Flacks, R. Young intelligentsia in revolt. *Transaction*, 1970 (June), 47–55.

Glock, C. Y., & Stark, R. *Religion and society in tension.* Chicago: Rand-McNally, 1965.

Gusfield, J. R. The study of social movements. In *International Encyclopedia of the Social Sciences.* New York: Crowell, Collier and Macmillan, 1968.

Handlin, O. *The uprooted.* New York: Grossett and Dunlap, 1951.

Hayden, T. (Untitled) In the *San Francisco Chronicle*, September 15, 1970, p. 8.

Heberle, R. *Social movements.* New York: Appleton-Century-Crofts, 1951.

Hoffer, E. *The true believer.* New York: Mentor Books, 1951.

Hoffman, A. (Untitled) In the *Los Angeles Free Press*, April 12, 1969, p. 12.

Hopper, R. D. The revolutionary process: A frame of reference for the study of revolutionary movements. *Social Forces*, 1950, *28*, 270–279.

Howe, I., & Coser, L. *The American communist party: A critical history.* New York: Praeger, 1962.

Kahn, R. M., & Bowers, W. J. The social context of the rank-and-file student activist. *Sociology of Education*, 1970, *43* (Winter), 1.

Keniston, K. The sources of student dissent. *Journal of Social Issues*, 1967, *23* (3), 108–137.

Keniston, K. *Young Radicals*. New York: Harcourt Brace Jovanovich, 1968.

Killian, L. M. Social movements. In R. E. L. Faris (Ed.), *Handbook of modern sociology*. Chicago: Rand-McNally, 1964.

King, C. W. *Social movements in the United States*. New York: Random House, 1956.

Lang, K., & Lang, G. *Collective dynamics*. New York: Crowell, 1961.

Lipset, S. M. *Political man: The social bases of politics*. Garden City: Doubleday, 1960.

Meier, A. (Ed.) *The transformation of activism*. New York: Aldine Press, 1970.

Messinger, S. L. Organizational transformation: A case study of a declining social movement. *American Sociological Review*, 1955, *20*, 3–10.

Moore, W. *Social change*. Englewood Cliffs, New Jersey: Prentice-Hall, 1963.

Newfield, J. *A prophetic minority*. New York: Signet, 1966.

O'Brien, J. *A history of the new left*. Boston: New England Free Press, 1968.

Sampson, E. E. (Ed.) Stirrings out of apathy: Student activism and the decade of protest. *Journal of Social Issues*, 1967, *23* (3). (a)

Sampson, E. E. Student activism and the decade of protest. *Journal of Social Issues*, 1967, *23* (3), 1–33. (b)

San Francisco Chronicle, April 27, 1970, p. 7. (a)

San Francisco Chronicle, October 17, 1970, p. 4. (b)

San Francisco Chronicle, March 5, 1971, p. 2.

Sherif, M., & Sherif, C. *Social psychology*. New York: Harper and Row, 1969.

Smelser, N. J. *Theory of collective behavior*. New York: Free Press, 1963.

Toch, H. *The social psychology of social movements*. New York: Bobbs-Merrill, 1965.

Trent, J. W., & Craise, J. L. Commitment and conformity in the American college. *Journal of Social Issues*, 1967, *23* (3), 34–51.

Turner, R. H., & Killian, L. M. *Collective behavior*. Englewood Cliffs, New Jersey: Prentice-Hall, 1957.

Social and Cultural Meanings of Student Revolt: Some Informal Comparative Observations*

Richard Flacks

The phenomenon of student rebellion has in the past few years come to appear international in scope. During this period, student demonstrations and strikes have paralyzed universities and shaken the political systems in societies as far apart, culturally and geographically, as Japan and France, Mexico and West Germany, Italy and Brazil, Czechoslovakia and the United States.

The simultaneity of these outbursts and the similarities in style and tactics of the student movements have led many observers to assume that there is a world-wide revolt of the youth, which is new historically, and which derives from a single set of causes.

It is obvious, however, that student movements, acting in opposition to established authority, are not at all new. For example, student revolutionary activity was a constant feature of Russian life during the 19th century. It played a major role in the revolution of 1848 in Central Europe. The communist movements in China and Vietnam grew out of militant student movements in those countries. In Latin America, student movements have been politically crucial since the early part of this century. Youth and student movements were a dramatic feature of life in pre-World War I Germany; the Zionist movement among European Jews had its roots in the German youth movement. Since World War II, student movements have helped bring down regimes in Asia and Latin America. It is clear that the events of recent months are in certain respects merely further expressions

* Paper prepared for presentation at meetings of American Association for the Advancement of Science, Dallas, Texas, December 1968.

of a long tradition of student rebelliousness (cf. Altbach, 1967, for an overview of this tradition).

But just as it would be a mistake to think that the student revolts are historically new, it would also be an error to uphold the conventional wisdom which asserts that youth are "naturally" rebellious, or idealistic. There are, of course, good reasons for believing that some segments of the youth are likely to be particularly disposed to revolt, particularly attracted to new ideas, particularly prepared to take direct action in behalf of their ideals. But it is by no means true that rebellious, experimental, or idealistic behavior is a general characteristic of young people—indeed, it is probably the case that in any historical period the majority of the young, as Bennett Berger has remarked, are not "youthful." Moreover, it is even less true that youthful impulses in support of radical change inevitably take the form of distinct, autonomous political movements against the established political system. For instance, such movements have been quite rare in the U.S. and other advanced Western countries until the present decade. Although significant minorities of students and other young people have been active participants in movements for social change in the U.S., Britain, France, and the smaller capitalist democracies, these societies have not had movements created by and for youth, independent of adult organizations, containing a strong element of rebellion not only against injustice but against the authority of the older generation. The feeling that there is something new about generational revolt is not accurate in global terms; but it is substantially correct for societies like our own.

There is a need for a theoretical framework to account for the emergence of oppositional movements among youth—a framework which can embrace the fact that such movements have become a feature, not only of developing pre-industrial societies, but of apparently stable advanced industrial nations as well. In searching for such a framework, two classical theoretical perspectives might be expected to provide some help. One would be Marxian theory, which, after all, was created in an effort to account for the rise of revolutionary movements in contemporary society. But Marxism, since it emphasizes the role of classes as revolutionary agencies, has a difficult time assimilating student revolutionary action. First, students do not themselves constitute a class. Second, students do occupy class positions, but these are typically privileged ones. Indeed, one fact about the American student movement is that participation in it tends to be associated with high family status and income (Westby and Braungart, 1966; Flacks, 1970), and the same pattern may be found in other countries as well. Thus, a problem for Marxian theory of revolution would be to account for the mass defection of students from their families' class, and for the tendency of privileged youth to identify with the plight of the dispossessed in their society. This is particularly problematical in the advanced industrial societies: here we have a situation in which at the present time organized political and cultural opposition to capitalism appears to be more extensive and militant among students than among workers. There is no straightforward way to derive this fact from the body of Marxian theory.

A second theoretical perspective which one might find useful is that of Parsons. Indeed, one of the few theories about the conditions giving rise to generational conflict is that of Eisenstadt (1956) whose perspective flows directly from Parsons (cf. Parsons, 1962, for a recent formulation).

This perspective focusses less on the revolutionary thrust of student and youth movements than on their functional character. What is most salient to Parsons and Eisenstadt is the formation of distinctive groups or movements among persons at the same stage in the life-cycle. The appearance of such groupings among youth is seen as a consequence of the differentiation of the family from the occupational structure, resulting in a sharp discontinuity between the values and role-expectations operative within the family and those prevailing in the larger society. As youth move out of the family and experience such discontinuities, major problems of socialization are created by the necessity for them to successfully orient toward occupational roles. Such problems are not manageable within the family, not within the institutions of formal schooling. What is needed are institutions which can combine some of the features of family life with those of the occupational structure. Youth groups, youth cultures, and youth movements serve this function of aiding the transition to adulthood by combining relations of diffuse solidarity with universalistic values.

This perspective predicts that the sharper the disjunction between family values and those in the larger society, the more distinctive and oppositional will be the youth culture. In particular, one would expect that students in societies undergoing a rapid breakdown of traditional authority, and in which new bases of legitimation had not yet been established, would most acutely experience problems of achieving adult status and would be most likely to form autonomous, oppositional movements. By the same token, young people in the advanced, stable, industrial, democratic societies, although experiencing marked discontinuity between familial and occupational roles, would not experience the same intense cultural dislocation found in developing countries. For, although familial and occupational roles are disjunctive in advanced industrial countries, families in these societies tend to be congruent in their values and expectations with other institutions. Thus the industrialized societies would exhibit distinctive youth cultures, but these implicitly support other socializing agencies in identity formation and orientation toward adulthood. In short, the Parsons-Eisenstadt perspective leads us to expect student movements in societies where traditional authority is disintegrating under the impact of industrialization, Western ideas, and modernizing trends, and where families continue to adhere to traditional culture. Depicting industrial societies as ones in which both parental and political authority support modernity and change, this perspective leads us to expect a distinctive youth culture, but not an "alienated" oppositional, revolutionary one in societies like our own (Eisenstadt, 1956; Parsons, 1962).

As I have suggested, this perspective was a viable one—until this decade. Now each passing year makes it less and less easy to assume the stability of the developed Western societies, less and less safe to adopt the view that the U.S. represents some culmination point in cultural development, or that there is a fundamental congruence among socializing, political and economic institutions and the values which prevail within them in our society.

A comparative perspective on student movements and generational revolt leads us to seek a theoretical framework which transcends the Marxian view of the sources of revolutionary impulse in capitalistic society, and the Parsonian view that such impulses are not characteristic of advanced industrial society. If such a framework existed it would undoubtedly constitute a synthesis of Eisenstadt's insight that student movements are a symptom of cultural disintegration and the Marxian insight that capitalism and its culture are themselves unstable and capable of being negated.

II

If recent events lead us to discard the view that student movements are characteristically only of societies in which traditional culture and authority are breaking down, we nevertheless ought to be able to specify why such movements have been endemic under such conditions. The Parsons-Eisenstadt hypothesis provides us with at least a partial answer: the university student in an agrarian society is someone who is compelled to abandon the values with which he was raised, who is exposed to a set of new cultural influences but who is becoming an adult in an historical period in which the new values have not been clarified, new roles have not been created, new authority has not been established or legitimated. The student movement, with its diffuse, fraternal interpersonal life, its identification with the masses of the people, its disdain for privilege and authority—combined with a commitment to rationalism, democracy, nationalism and other "modern" values—enables them to develop the political skills and motives which may be necessary to challenge the established elites, enables them to undergo the personal transition which is an aspect of the historical transition through which the whole society is going.

In addition to this hypothesis, which locates the sources of "strain" in the cultural and psychological consequences of modernization, there are additional and equally powerful factors at work in such societies which make such movements extremely likely. (A summary of such factors appears in Lipset, 1968.)

There is, for example, the widely remarked fact that typically in developing countries there is an "overproduction" of educated youth—the available jobs for university graduates often are not commensurate with the training or aspirations they have as a result of their educational attainment. Prospective or actual unemployment, and the frustration of aspiration, is presumably a politicizing experience for many educated youth in such societies.

Another politicizing and radicalizing feature of these societies is the backwardness and authoritarianism of political authority. Political authority in these societies plays a paradoxical role for students; on the one hand, it sponsors the formation and expansion of a university system in order to promote technical progress, while simultaneously it resists the political, social, and cultural transformations which such progress requires. In this situation, students inevitably come into conflict with the state and other established elite institutions. The more intransigent the established elites are with respect to nationalist, democratic, and modernizing aspirations, the more likely it is that the student movement becomes the breeding ground for a "counterelite" and the spearhead of revolutionary politics (Ben-David and Collins, 1967).

Still another factor likely to generate discontent is the quality of life in the universities of these societies. Living and working conditions are likely to be extremely impoverished. The schools are likely to be overflowing; the quality of instruction and facilities for study are likely to be totally inadequate; and material poverty among students is likely to be substantial.

If cultural disintegration, overproduction of the educated, reactionary regimes, and university conditions generate discontent leading to politicization and radicalism, additional factors promote the emergence and growth of autonomous student movements in developing nations. For example, the autonomous character of student movements in these countries is facilitated by the absence of other oppositional forces. To the extent that peasants, workers and other strata are poorly organized or passive or suppressed, students, with their high degree of interaction and their sophistication may become the only group in a society capable of initiating oppositional activity. Moreover, students may have a degree of freedom for political action which is not available to other opposition forces. This freedom may in part be due to the fact that many student activists are the offspring of elite or upper status families, in part because of the recognition of the fact that students are indispensable to the future of the society, in part because of an established tradition of university autonomy which makes it illegitimate for police power to invade the campus. Given the relative leniency toward students and the ambivalence of authorities toward them, instances of repressive action taken against students are likely to be especially discrediting to the regime. Thus, the weakness of other oppositional forces, the wide opportunities for intensive interaction available to students, the large numbers of students likely to be concentrated in particular locales, and the special freedom for political expression which they are likely to have all combine to foster the growth of a student movement as an independent oppositional movement.

The conditions we have been describing may be regarded as the "classic" pattern presaging the emergence of students as a revolutionary force. Put another way, these conditions help us understand why student oppositional movements have been a regular feature of developing societies.

III

Our analysis has suggested that the classical student movement is a symptom of marked cultural incoherence, of political stagnation, and of severe problems of identity for educated youth in the face of the social and technological changes associated with the process of "modernization." Because this analysis emphasizes that student movements are an aspect of the modernization process, it appears to be quite inadequate for accounting for the rise of student movements in societies like our own, which are not agrarian, which are not dominated by traditional culture and authority, which are not struggling to achieve national identity and independence, where democratic, rationalistic and egalitarian values prevail, where families orient their offspring toward active achievement in a technological society, where the freedom to organize political opposition is available and used. At least at first glance one would be led to believe that the advanced industrial capitalist societies of the West would provide the least hospitable soil for a revolt of educated youth.

Yet a student movement has grown up over the past decade in American society. Over these years, it has become increasingly radicalized, and indeed now includes an avowedly revolutionary wing. Like the classical movements, it contains a strong component of generational revolt—that is, of implicit and explicit hostility to the authority of older generations, and an emphasis on the moral superiority of the young as such and on their capacity to be an agency of social transformation. Like the classical movements, the student movements of the West are intensely anti-authoritarian, egalitarian, and populist. They also resemble the classical type in being completely independent of other, "adult" political groups.

Are there any ways to comprehend the appearance of such a movement in American society that will account for its comparability with classical student movements?

The most parsimonious hypothesis, perhaps, would focus on possible similarities between the immediate situation of the student in the advanced industrial societies and in the developing countries. For example, it seems plausible that the rapid expansion of higher education and the great influx of young people to the universities has led to a devolution in the quality of educational institutions and of student life in the U.S. and Western Europe. It is also plausible that the rapid growth in the numbers of educated youth has produced the same kind of sectional unemployment of the educated which is present in the developing nations.

There may be considerable validity to these hypotheses; indeed, much of the commentary on the French student revolt has emphasized these factors as crucial ones. But it is much harder to see how they can be applied to the American case. For instance, data on the distribution of student protest on American campuses quite clearly show that the student movement had its origins at the highest quality state universities and prestigious private universities and colleges, that the movement continues to have its widest following on such campuses, and that it has only recently spread to schools of lower prestige and quality (Peterson, 1966; 1968). There is, in short, a negative correlation between the quality of an institution and the proportion of its student body which is activist, and between the selectivity of an institution and the radicalism of its student body.

It is equally hard to make a case that the student movement in the U.S. originates in overproduction of educated youth. In the first place, there is no dearth of opportunity for college graduates. Still, one might hypothesize that students who are attracted to the movement experience "relative deprivation"—for example, they may be students who cannot hold their own in academic competition. However, the data on student protesters indicate otherwise; there is, in fact, a tendency for activists to have above average academic records in high school and college, and most of the several studies on student protesters indicate they include a disproportionate under-representation of students with poor academic records (Flacks, 1967; 1970). Student protesters come from families with high income and occupational status; they tend to be most prevalent at the top schools; they have above average aptitude for academic work, and perform at above average levels. If there is an overproduction of educated youth in this society at this time, it is hard to see how this would affect the structure of opportunities available to the academic elite from which activists tend to be recruited.

It seems clear that any effort to explain the rise of a student movement in the U.S. must take account of the fact that the movement originated among highly advantaged students, that it did not begin as a revolt against the university, and that its active core contains many students whose aptitudes, interests, values, and origins suggest a strong orientation to intellectual and academic life.

Indeed, one of the most striking findings about American activists has to do with their intellectualism. I refer here not only to the variety of studies which find activists exhibiting intellectual interests and achievements superior to those of the student body as a whole. More persuasive and more sociologically relevant are findings concerning the socioeconomic backgrounds of participants in protest activity. These findings may be briefly summarized as follows: activists are disproportionately the sons and daughters of highly educated parents; in a large proportion of cases, their parents have advanced graduate and professional degrees; a very high percentage of activists' mothers are college graduates; the parents tend to be in occupations for which higher education is a central prerequisite: professions, education, social service, public service, the arts; both businessmen and blue and white collar workers tend to be underrepresented among the parents of activists; family interests—as they are expressed in recreation, or in dinner-table conversation, or in formal interviews—tends to be intellectual and "cultural" and relatively highbrow; these are families in which books were read, discussed, and taken seriously, in which family outings involved museums and concert-halls rather than ball-parks and movies, etc. They were families in which "values" were taken seriously—conventional religion and morality were treated with considerable skepticism, while at the same time strong emphasis was placed on leading a principled, socially useful, morally consistent life. They were, finally, families in which education was regarded with considerable reverence and valued for its own sake, rather than in utilitarian terms.

In short, the student movement originated among those young people who came out of what might be called the "intellectual" or "humanist" subculture of the middle class. In the last two years, it has become considerably more heterogeneous, but it was created almost exclusively by offspring of that particular stratum. (A more detailed review of these findings appears in Flacks, 1970.)

At first glance, it would seem that nothing could be more incomparable than the situation of these middle class American youth and the situation of educated youth in underdeveloped countries. The former, as we have said, can look forward to an array of high status occupational opportunities. Their lives as students are well-subsidized, comfortable, and intellectually rich. Their parents are highly "modern" people, playing central cultural roles, well-informed about and sympathetic with the latest cultural developments. All of this is especially true in comparison with the position of educated youth in developing countries, whose futures are extremely uncertain, whose lives as students are likely to be meager and oppressive, whose families are likely to be locked into traditional ways and attitudes and stand as positive hindrances to the emancipation of their children.

These contrasts are striking, but they may be quite superficial. What I want to do is to restate some of the major factors which we have seen to be central in accounting for the appearance of classical student movements—and try to determine whether comparable factors are at work in American society, especially in relation to the situation of students who come out of the educated middle class.

1. We have said, after Eisenstadt, that a central determinant of the appearance of youth and student movements is sharp discontinuity between values embodied in the family and those emerging in other institutional contexts. From this perspective, as we have suggested, the student movement serves as a "secondary institution"—a way of re-establishing family-like solidarity to ease the achievement of independent adult identities and role-orientations. For youth in developing countries, discontinuity arises because of the fundamental conflict between the traditional orientation of the family and the modernizing orientations encountered in the university and the cosmopolitan community associated with it.

This kind of discontinuity could not be one experienced by the offspring of the educated middle class in America—if anything, students from this stratum are likely to experience less disjunction between familial and university values than any other groups of students. But there are grounds for feeling that humanist youth in America do experience a kind of discontinuity between family and larger society that may have comparable implications for the establishment of identity.

Our studies (cf. Flacks, 1967) of the parents of student activists show that these parents differ from others in the middle class in the following respects:

First, as mentioned above, there is a strong commitment to intellectuality and "culture" and a considerable disdain for mass culture and mass leisure. Their children were expected to be intellectually aware and serious, artistically creative or at least appreciative, serious about education and self-development.

Second, these parents were unusual in their political awareness and their political liberalism. Although they were not necessarily politically active, they tended to stress to their children the necessity for social responsibility and service, and active citizenship, and encouraged their children to support racial equality, civil liberties, and other liberal political goals. In this respect, these families were likely to see themselves, correctly, as different from the vast majority of politically passive or conservative families in their community.

Third, these parents were overtly skeptical about conventional middle-class values, life-styles, and religious orientations. Most of these parents were explicitly secular; those who were actively religious tended to belong to particularly liberal religious denominations or to have a strong social gospel kind of religious commitment. Many of these parents were articulate critics of conventional middle-class mores—by which, in particular, they had in mind sexual repressiveness, materialism, status-striving, and strict methods of rearing children. Many were quite explicit in hoping that their children would be more successful than they had been in leading self-fulfilling, socially responsible lives rather than participating in the "rat-race," the "suburban way of life," the "commercial world."

Finally, these parents tended to express these values implicitly through the structure of the family and the styles of child rearing which they adopted. These were parents who encouraged "self-expressive" and "independent" behavior in their children, who interacted with each other and with their children in relatively "democratic" ways, who refused to impose conventional stereotypes of masculine and feminine conduct on their children (e.g., they tended to foster aesthetic and intellectual interests in their boys and assertive behavior on the part of their girls). It was not that these parents were unusually "permissive" or over-indulgent—for instance, their very explicit expectations about intellectuality and social responsibility indicate that they did not adopt a "laissez-faire" attitude toward their children. But they rather consciously organized family life to support anti-authoritarian and self-assertive impulses on the part of their children and rather clearly instructed them in attitudes favoring skepticism toward authority, egalitarianism and personal autonomy (Flacks, 1967, 1970; Keniston, 1968b).

Now what happens when these intellectual, anti-authoritarian, socially conscious, somewhat unconventional children move on to school and street and peer group? I think it is clear that they are likely to experience a considerable discontinuity between the values they encounter in these settings and the values with which they were raised. They are likely to find authority in school to be petty, arbitrary, repressive. They are likely to feel considerable isolation from the conventional culture of their peers. They are likely to be particularly sensitive to the hypocrisies, rigidities, and injustices of particular institutions and of the society as a whole as they experience it.

Most American youth experience some dislocation as they move from their families into the larger society, if for no other reason than that the rapidity of social change prevents any family from adequately preparing its offspring for the world as it actually is developing, and because proper, moral behavior for children in the American family is inescapably different from proper, moral behavior in the competitive, impersonal society beyond. The existing primary and secondary institutions—school and youth culture—which Parsons and others have expected to be serviceable in easing the transition to adulthood, have failed to incorporate humanist youth, who were in fact raised to question many of the fundamental premises of these institutions. As more and more such youth have entered upon the scene, they have tended to find each other and to create a kind of counter-culture, much as Black urban youth, similarly unincorporated, have created theirs. This new humanist youth culture embodies norms concerning sex-role behavior, worthwhile activity, and personal style which are quite opposed to those which prevail in conventional adolescent society; it expresses values which seem quite subversive of conventional middle-class aspirations, and an attitude toward adult authority which is quite clearly defiant. The American student movement is an expression of that new youth culture, although by no means the only one.

In a peculiar sense, then, the appearance of a student movement and a rebellious youth culture in American society in recent years supports the Eisenstadt hypothesis that such phenomena are rooted in sharp discontinuities between family values and values in the larger society. It is a peculiar kind of support for that hypothesis because, unlike the classical case, the discontinuities we refer to do not have to do with incongruence between a traditional family and a modernizing culture. If anything, the reverse may be the case.

2. As we have suggested, a second major factor contributing to the rise of classical student movements has been the "overproduction" of educated youth—a factor which appears to be largely absent in the American situation. Nevertheless, there are severe problems for humanist youth with respect to vocation. These problems have to do, not with the scarcity of opportunity, but with the irrelevance of the opportunities which do exist. One of the most characteristic attributes of students in the movement (and an attribute which they share with a large number of apolitical students) is their inability to decide on a career or a vocation. This indecision is less the result of the wide range of choices available, than of the unsatisfactory quality of those choices. What is repellant about the existing opportunities is not their incompatibility with the status or financial aspirations of these youth—but that they are incompatible with their ideals. Business careers are rejeced outright as acquisitive, self-seeking, and directly linked to that which is defined as most corrupting in American society. Careers in government or conventional politics are regarded as either self-deluding or "selling-out." Professional careers—particularly such established professions as law and medicine—are attractive to some, but only if one can become a doctor or lawyer outside of the conventional career lines; otherwise such careers are regarded as just as acquisitive as business. Teachers and social workers are seen as agents of social control; a few are attracted to scholarship or science, but with profound anxiety. To take an ordinary job is to give up any chance for leading a free life. In general, embarking on a career within the established occupational structure is regarded as morally compromising because it leads to complicity with established interests or because it requires abandoning personal autonomy or because it draws one away from full commitment to radicalism or because it signifies acceptance of the norms and standards of bourgeois society or because it means risking corruption because of material comfort and security.

Although some of these attitudes are undoubtedly the result of participation in the movement rather than a determinant of such participation, it is clear that an underlying revulsion with conventional adult roles and established, institutionalized careers predates movement involvement for many students. One reason for believing that it does is the fact that such revulsion is observable among young people who do not become political activists; indeed, a widespread restlessness about becoming committed to conventional careers and life-styles is evident on the American campus. This has been particularly surprising for those of us who remember the decade of the Fifties and the prevailing feeling of that era—namely, that affluence was producing a generation which would be particularly conformist, complacent, status-conscious, and bourgeois.

It now appears that the opposite may be equally true. Although people with high status and material security may typically be motivated to maintain their position, it is also the case that being born into affluence can foster impulses to be experimental, risk-taking, open to immediate experience, unrepressed. For some at least, growing up with economic security in families of secure status can mean a weakening of the normal incentives of the system and can render one relatively immune to the established means of social control, especially if one's parents rather explicitly express skepticism about the moral worth of material success. Post-war affluence in our society then has had the effect of liberating a considerable number of young people from anxieties about social mobility and security, and enabled them to take seriously the quest for other values and experiences. To such youth, established careers and adult roles are bound to be unsatisfying. What is the sense, after all, of binding oneself to a large organization, of submitting to the rituals, routines, and disciplines of careerism, of postponing or foregoing a wide range of possible experience—when there is little chance of surpassing one's father, when the major outcome of such efforts is to acquire goods which one has already had one's fill of, when such efforts mean that one must compromise one's most cherished ideals?

In newly-industrializing societies, students became revolutionaries, or bohemians, or free intellectuals and artists, because established careers commensurate with their education had not been created. In our society, large numbers of students do the same, not because opportunities for conventional achievement are absent but because they are personally meaningless and morally repugnant. We began with the proposition that a blockage of economic opportunity for the educated is a determinant of student movements. Our comparative analysis leads us to a reformulation of this proposition—any condition which leads in a weakening of motivation for upward mobility increases the likelihood of student rebellion—such conditions can include either blocked opportunity *or* high levels of material security. In short, when numbers of youth find occupational decisions extremely difficult to make, their propensity for collective rebellion is likely to increase.

3. What we have so far been discussing may be described as a kind of cultural crisis—the emergence of a sector of the youth population which finds its fundamental values, aspirations, and character structure in sharp conflict with the values and practices which prevail in the larger society. We have said that, in certain respects, this conflict is similar to that experienced by youth in societies undergoing rapid transition from traditional to "modern" culture; and in both cases, we find these youth responding to their crisis by banding together in movements of opposition to the older generations and attempting to generate what amounts to a counter-culture.

In some ways this kind of crisis is not new in American society. For more than a century, at least, small groups of intellectuals have expressed their revulsion with industrial capitalism, and the commercialism, philistinism and acquisitiveness they saw as its outcome. By the turn of the century, what had largely been an expression of genteel criticism was supplanted by a more vigorous and intense revolt by some educated youth—expressed through bohemianism and through a variety of political and social reform movements. Indeed, opposition to Victorian morality and business culture has been characteristic of American intellectuals in this century (Hofstadter, 1966); and the emergence of large numbers of humanist youth out of relatively intellectual families is an indication of the impact this opposition has had on the society. What was once the protest of tiny pockets of intellectuals and artists has become a mass phenomenon, in part because the ideas of these earlier critics and reformers were taken up in the universities and became part of the world-view of many members of the educated middle class. These ideas influenced not only sentiments regarding commercialism, material success and intellectuality, they also had a direct bearing on the treatment of women and the raising of children, since an important element of anti-bourgeois thinking had to do with the emancipation of women and the liberation of the child from repressive and stultifying disciplines.

What is new in this decade is, first of all, the degree to which this cultural alienation has become a mass phenomenon—an extensive, rooted subculture on the campus and in major cities, with a wide and steadily growing following. Equally important, the present movement is new in the degree to which it has expressed itself through political opposition—an opposition which has become increasingly revolutionary, in the sense that it has increasingly come to reject the legitimacy of established authority and of the political system itself.

As we have previously pointed out, political rebellion by students in other countries has largely been a response to authoritarian, reactionary regimes—regimes which were incapable of or unwilling to adapt to pressures for modernization, and which tended to meet such pressures by attempting to repress them. Thus, classical student movements tend to arise out of the cultural crisis created by the processes of modernization, and tend to go into active political opposition when the political system stands against those processes.

It is perhaps hard for American social scientists to understand why American students should undergo a similar reaction to the American political system. After all, many of them have spent years demonstrating that the system was pluralist, democratic, egalitarian, and highly flexible; thus, while it may be rational for Russian, Chinese, or Latin-American students to have become revolutionary in the face of tsars, warlords, and dictators, it is, for them, irrational for students in the U.S. and other Western countries to adopt revolutionary stances against liberal, democratic regimes. (For one example cf. Glazer, 1968.)

To understand why the cultural alienation of intellectual youth in America has become politicized and radicalized requires an historical analysis—the details of which are beyond the scope of this paper. Without attempting such an analysis we can, I think, at least point to some of the most relevant factors.

The first point would be that culturally alienated intellectuals in America have not historically been revolutionary. They have, instead, either been anti-political or have placed their hopes in a variety of progressive, reform movements. In part they have been sustained by the view that the national political system, whatever its flaws, had progressive potential because of its democratic character. They have also been sustained by comparisons between the American system and the rest of the world.

During the New Deal and World War II period, a kind of culmination was reached in the formulation of an ideological perspective for the educated class in America. At the heart of this perspective was the view that inequality, injustice, and business culture could be controlled and offset by effective political and social action through the Federal government. The rise of labor as a political force, the passage of social legislation, and the subsidization of reform by the government would create the conditions for a just and humane society. Not incidentally, the expansion of the public sector would also create vast new vocational opportunities for educated people with humanitarian concerns—in education, in social service, in public health, mental health, child care, public planning, and all the rest. Thus the creation of the welfare state and an American version of social democracy was crucial for the expanded intelligentsia, not only because it provided a solution to the social ills that contributed to their alienation, but also because it offered a way to realize themselves vocationally outside of the business economy and in terms of their values. It is perhaps important to mention that it was in this ideological milieu that the parents of the present generation reached maturity.

In the past twenty years, however, two things have been happening simultaneously: on the one hand, the ranks of the educated middle class have greatly expanded, due in considerable degree to government support of higher education and of public sector types of occupations which required advanced education; on the other hand, the social benefits anticipated from this development have not been forthcoming—that is, liberal politics have not eradicated gross social inequality, have not improved the quality of public life, and perhaps above all have not created a pacific, internationalist global posture on the part of the American government. Instead, the educated middle-class person is likely to see his society as increasingly chaotic and deteriorating, to feel that enormous waste of material and human resources is taking place, and to believe that his nation is not a liberalizing force internationally, but perhaps the reverse.

The offspring of this stratum, as they began to throng the nation's universities in the early Sixties, entered political involvement at just the point where their parents had begun to experience disillusionment with progressive ideology. But the early phase of the student movement tended to continue traditional middle-class faith in the democratic process. The New Left, in its beginnings, rejected all received ideology; for fairly obvious reasons, it found neither social democracy, nor Marxism-Leninism, nor liberalism at all adequate foundations for renewing radical politics. Indeed, in an early age, many New Leftists would not have attempted to create a youth-based radicalism at all; they would instead have found their way into one or another established radical or reform movement. It is important to realize that the exhaustion of existing ideologies in post-war Europe and America meant that young people with radical impulses had to start afresh. The starting point in the U.S. was to take democratic ideals seriously; to try to make the system work, by participating in and catalyzing grass-roots protest against glaring injustice—particularly against segregation and the threat of nuclear holocaust. Such an outlook included a fairly explicit expectation that the creation of protest and ferment from below would provide an impetus for major change at the top—on the part of the Federal government (in behalf of the constitutional rights of Negroes, for example) and on the part of established agencies of reform such as the churches, the universities, the labor movement. Until about 1964, this political model seemed to be working to a considerable extent—civil rights laws were passed, the Kennedy Administration was moving toward detente with the Soviet Union, a war on poverty was declared, and a spirit of social renovation seemed to be taking hold in the society. In this situation, the SDS and other student radicals retained a considerable willingness to operate within the conventional political system; it is well to remember for example that in the election campaign of 1964, SDS adopted the slogan, "Part of the Way with LBJ."

The escalation of the war in Vietnam marked a turning point for radical students—it began a process of progressive disillusionment with the political system, a process which, for many, has culminated in a total rejection of its legitimacy. I cannot here recount in any adequate way the series of events which contributed to this process; but it is clear that the war itself was crucial to it, as was the use of the draft to prosecute that war and to "channel" young men educationally and occupationally, as was the failure of the war on poverty (a failure directly experienced by many young activists as they tried to work in poverty areas), as was the transformation of the black movement from a struggle for integration to a far more radical struggle for "liberation" and economic equality, as was the revelation that many universities actively contributed to the war effort and military research, as was the increasing use of the police to suppress protest demonstrations in the streets and on the campuses, as was the failure of the political parties to recognize their liberal, doveish constituencies. In short, for young people who identified with the cause of racial equality, who despised war and militarism, and who had hoped to construct lives based on humane, intellectual, and democratic ideals, by 1968 American society did seem largely reactionary, authoritarian, and repressive. (A more detailed review of this history appears in Skolnick, 1969: 87–105.)

This perception is heightened and reinforced by other, more fundamental beliefs. For example, it is very difficult to accept the amount of squalor, inequality, and misery in this society if one is aware of the fact that the society has the material resources to guarantee a decent private and public life to the whole population. It is very difficult to accept war and the arms race and the expansion of militarism when one is convinced that these institutions have the capacity to destroy the human race. And, finally, it is very difficult to maintain a calm long-run perspective, if one believes that the society has the capacity—in its technology, in its large-scale organizational structure, and in the character structure of millions of its members—to obliterate personal autonomy, individuality, and free expression. Many radical students, in other words, have a profound pessimism about the chances for democracy, personal freedom and peace (for an empirical demonstration of this pessimism, cf. Westby and Braungart, 1970); this pessimism, however, leads toward activism rather than withdrawal because many are convinced that the probable future is not a necessary one. The events of the past four or five years have overwhelmingly confirmed their sense of the main social drift, but what has sustained the impulse to act has been the rapid growth of resistance among many in their generation.

Briefly, then, our argument to this point has been something like the following: the expansion of higher education in our society has produced a social stratum which tends to rear its children with values and character structures which are at some variance with the dominant culture. Affluence and secure status further weaken the potency of conventional incentives and undermine motivations for upward mobility. The outcome of these processes is a new social type or subculture among American youth—humanist youth.

Such youth are especially sensitized to injustice and authoritarianism, are repelled by acquisitive, militaristic, and nationalistic values, and strive for a vocational situation in which autonomy and self-expression can be maximized. They have been politicized and radicalized by their experiences in relation to the racial and international crises, and by the failure of established agencies of renewal and reform, including the universities, to alleviate these crises. They also sense the possibility that opportunities for autonomy and individuality may be drying up in advanced technological societies. One of the reasons that their political expression has taken generational form is that older ideologies of opposition to capitalism and authoritarianism have failed in practice.

We have also been saying that, although it is clear that the situation of these youth is enormously different from the situation of educated youth in underdeveloped countries, there are important analogies between the two. Both groups of youth confront the problem of discontinuity between family tradition and the values of the larger society. Both confront major problems of vocation and adult identity. Both confront political systems which are stagnated and repressive, and find few resources and allies external to themselves as they attempt to change that system.

There is a final issue in the comparative analysis of student movements that I want to raise. In our discussion of the classical movements, we suggested that the appearance of such movements was a clear sign that processes of fundamental social and cultural change were at work, and that these movements were not simply the result of certain pressures operating on a particular group of young people in a society but more importantly were indications that traditional, agrarian society was being transformed by processes of industrialization and modernization. It is clearly important to ask whether the appearance of student movements in advanced industrial societies are similarly signs that a new social and cultural era is struggling to emerge.

There are those who believe that the current crop of student revolutionaries is not the vanguard of a new social order, but rather, in the words of Daniel Bell, "the guttering last gasps of a romanticism soured by rancor and impotence" (Bell, 1968). In this view, student unrest in industrial societies is regarded as analogous to the protests of the first waves of industrial workers who resisted their uprooting by the machine. Now, it is argued, high-status intellectually and artistically inclined youth resist their incorporation into large-scale organizations—an incorporation which, nevertheless, is as inevitable as was the imposition of the factory on the rural lower classes.

Such a view does implicitly recognize that a major social transformation may be in the making. What I find objectionable in it is the implication that the new radicalism of the young is irrelevant to the nature of that transformation.

An alternative view would emphasize the possibility that large scale social, political, and cultural changes are occurring, that these are reflected in the social origins and focal concerns of student rebels, and that the existence of student rebellion may be a determining feature of this process of change.

First, at the cultural level, the student movement and the new alienated youth culture appear to reflect the erosion, if not the collapse, of what might be called the culture of capitalism—that cluster of values which Max Weber labelled the "Protestant Ethic"—a value system which was appropriate for the development of capitalism and the entrepreneurial spirit but which has lost its vitality under the impact of the bureaucratic organization of the economy, the decline of entrepreneurships, and the spread of affluence. The erosion of this culture is reflected in the transformation of family structure and childrearing practices, in the changing relations between the sexes, in the replacement of thrift with consumership as a virtue. As Schumpeter (1950) predicted many years ago, bourgeois culture could not survive the abundance it would generate. Thus, the cultural crisis experienced very sharply and personally by humanist youth really impinges on the whole society. It is a crisis because no coherent value system has emerged to replace what has deteriorated; but it is hard not to believe that the anti-authoritarian, experimental, unrepressed, and "romantic" style of the youth revolt does in fact represent the beginnings of the effort to create a workable new culture, rather than the "last gasps" of the old. Such a view gains support when one observes the degree to which the youth revolt has affected popular culture and attracted the interest, if not the total involvement, of large numbers of young people in his country and abroad.

A second major social change which underlies the student movement is the rise of mass higher education. If the student movement is any indication of the possible effects of higher education, then one might have the following expectations about the coming period. First, the number of people in the middle class with critical attitudes toward the dominant culture will rapidly rise. In my view, critical feelings about capitalist culture—particularly negative attitudes toward symbols and ideology which support competitive striving, acquisitiveness, narrow nationalism, and repressive moral codes—are enhanced by exposure to higher education. Such feelings are further reinforced by entrance into occupations which are structurally not bound into the private, corporate economy—for example, occupations associated with education, social service, social planning, and other intellectual or human service work. These occupations embody values which tend to be critical of the culture and of the going system and tend to have an ethic which emphasizes collective welfare rather than private gain. It is important to recognize that the current student activists were born into the social stratum defined by these occupations, and many students with activist sympathies end up in these occupations. Data collected by Lubell (1968) show a general tendency for students oriented toward such occupations to move toward the left, politically. In a certain sense, then, the student movement may be seen as an outgrowth of a new level of occupational differentiation, i.e., the development of a distinct stratum organized around these occupations. This stratum is one of the most rapidly growing occupational sectors, and its political impact can already be seen, not only on the campus, but in such developments as the "new politics" movement during the recent elections. I am not arguing that this "new middle class" of intellectuals, professionals, upper white-collar workers, technical workers, public employees, etc., is politically homogeneous, or class-conscious, or radical. Indeed, it contains many antagonisms, and its participants are hardly ready for massive collective action, much less the barricades. But it does seem to me that the student movement, with its opposition to nationalism and militarism, its identification with egalitarian deals, and particularly its opposition to bureaucratic and rigid authority in the university represents a militant version of the kinds of attitudes which are increasingly likely to prevail in the stratum to which I am referring. It seems particularly likely that the spread of mass higher education will mean increasing pressure against bureaucratic forms of authority and for "participatory democracy" within the institutions in which the newly educated work. The political trajectory of the educated class will, in large measure, be a function of the responsiveness of the political and economic system to their demands for more rational domestic and international policies, more personal autonomy and participation in decision-making, and a more authentic and humane cultural and public life. More Vietnams, more racial turmoil, more squalor in the cities, more political stagnation, more debasement of popular culture—in short, more of the status quo is likely to increase the availability of members of this stratum for radical politics.

One may continue at greath length to enumerate other cultural and social changes which seem to be implied by the appearance of a student movement in our society. For example, it clearly signifies a process of change in the position of youth in the society—a change which involves protest against the subordination of youth to rigid and arbitrary forms of authority in the school system and in the general legal system, and which also may involve an extension of youth as a stage of life beyond adolescence (Keniston, 1968a). The student movement may also signify a general decline in the legitimacy of military authority and nationalist ideology—a decline associated with rising education levels, with changing character structure, and with the impact of mass communications.

My point in mentioning all of these potential cultural and social transformations is not to stake a claim as a prophet, but rather to urge that we take seriously the possibility that the appearance of student movements in advanced industrial societies really does signify that a new social and cultural stage is in the process of formation. A comparative perspective leads us to that hypothesis, because the classical student movements were, as we have suggested, just such signs. If we were to take the student movement in our own country seriously in this sense, then we would, I believe, be less likely to assume the stability of our social and political order and the cultural system sustaining it, less likely to dismiss campus unrest as a momentary perturbation or a romantic last gasp, less likely to focus on particular tactics and bizarre outcroppings of the youth revolt. Instead, we would open up the intellectual possibility that our kind of society can undergo major transformation, that it can generate, as Marx anticipated, its own "internal contradictions" and "negations," and that the future need not be like the present only more so.

REFERENCES

Altbach, P.
   1967   "Students and politics." Pp. 175–187 in Seymour Martin Lipset (ed.), Student Politics. New York: Basic Books.

Bell, Daniel
   1968   "Columbia and the new left." The Public Interest. (Fall): 61–101.
Ben-David, J., and R. Collins
   1967   "A comparative study of academic freedom and student politics." Pp.
          148–195 in S. M. Lipset (ed.), Student Politics. New York: Basic Books.
Eisenstadt, S. N.
   1956   From Generation to Generation. Glencoe: The Free Press.
Flacks, R.
   1967   "The liberated generation: An exploration of the roots of student pro-
          test." Journal of Social Issues 23 (July): 52–75.
   1970   "Who protests: The social bases of the student movement." Pp. 134–157
          in J. Foster and D. Long (ed.), Protest! Student Activism in America.
          New York: William Morrow and Company.
Glazer, N.
   1968   "Student power at Berkeley." The Public Interest. (Fall): 61–101.
Hofstadter, R.
   1966   Anti-intellectualism in American Life. New York: Vintage.
Keniston, K.
   1968a   "Youth as a stage of life." New Haven: Yale University (mimeo).
   1968b   Young Radicals. New York: Harcourt Brace Jovanovich.
Lipset, S. M.
   1968   "Students and politics in comparative perspective." Daedalus 91: 97–123.
Lubell, S.
   1968   "That 'generation gap.'" The Public Interest. (Fall): 52–60.
Parsons, T.
   1962   "Youth in the context of American society." Daedalus 91: 97–123.
Peterson, Richard F.
   1966   The Scope of Organized Student Protest in 1964–65. Princeton: Educa-
          tional Testing Service.
   1968   The Scope of Organized Student Protest in 1967–1968. Princeton: Edu-
          cational Testing Service.
Schumpeter, J.
   1950   Capitalism, Socialism and Democracy. New York: Harper and Bros.
Skolnick, Jerome
   1969   The Politics of Protest. New York: Simon and Schuster.
Westby, D., and R. G. Braungart
   1966   "Class and politics in the family backgrounds of student political acti-
          vists." American Sociological Review 31 (October): 690–692.
   1970   "Activists and the history of the future." Pp. 154–183 in J. Foster and
          D. Long (ed.), Protest! Student Activism in America. New York: Wil-
          liam Morrow and Company.

The Significance of Extremism in the Black Revolution

LEWIS M. KILLIAN

The term "extremism" is about as vague as a concept can be and can hardly
be classified as a tool for sociological analysis; yet it frequently crops up in
social science writings. It is even vaguer than some other terms which are
used almost synonymously—"radical" and "militant." It differs from these in
that it is more likely to be used in a pejorative sense. Its affective implications are usually much clearer than its ideological referent. Of course, other
terms capable of somewhat more precise definition have also been used
primarily as epithets, such as "communism," "anarchist," "socialism," and in
the years before 1776, "republicanism." The term "fascist," though amenable
to scientific definition, has for many years been employed as a vague, emotional label.

So long as we have social movements centering around bitterly contested,
emotionally charged issues, we can expect to have with us the words "extremism" and "extremist." They reflect the observation by both partisans and
detached observers that a social movement is monolithic neither in leadership nor in ideology. It typically is characterized by a range of values, beliefs, and tactics and a variety of leaders reflecting different orientations and
styles. Some of these are invariably labelled by someone as constituting
"extremism." The interaction between so-called extremists and other actors,
including leaders, followers and opponents of a social movement, as well as
the spectator· public, not only attracts popular interest but is worthy of
sociological analysis. Indeed, popular preoccupation with extremists in the
Black Revolution is in itself a significant topic for investigation.

USAGES OF THE CONCEPT "EXTREMISM"

Although the concept "extremism" is admittedly vague, some effort at definition seems necessary. Rather than undertaking to construct a definition,

we may examine some ways in which the term is implicitly defined in usage. This brief exercise in contextual analysis not only may reveal something of the meaning of the word but also may cast light on the relationship of extremism to a social movement.

One of the most obvious and frequent uses is as a term of opprobrium employed by critics or opponents. Thus, during the 1970 congressional campaign Vice-President Agnew characterized a black democratic candidate, Ronald Dellums, as "a radical extremist," an enthusiastic supporter of the Black Panther Party. Such rhetoric is sometimes employed by spokesmen who are avowed opponents of all that a social movement stands for. More often, however, spokesmen who appear to accord some validity to the movement as a whole and to regard some of its demands as negotiable employ the "extremist" label selectively, directing it at only some leaders. In doing so, they reveal certain important things about their posture *vis-à-vis* the movement. Who they choose as their targets offers important clues as to what issues they regard as negotiable, what tactics they will accept as legitimate, and what personal styles they will tolerate in face-to-face encounters. In many cities in which white authorities have been brought to the point of proposing biracial negotiations because of rising racial tensions, some black leaders have been left out of the parleys partly because they were defined as "extremists." There have been implications that they were unreasonable fanatics with whom one could not negotiate. There may also be an implication, however, that these are the most effective and, therefore, dangerous leaders. An interesting question is what effect such an implication has on the prestige of the "extremist" within the movement.

The second context in which the term is used is closely related to the first. Some aspirants to leadership are labelled "extremists" by competing leaders within the social movement itself. When we examine the history of the Black Protest Movement, the term "moderate" appears almost to be an invention of a sophisticated white resistance which bestows it upon certain black leaders in an attempt to co-opt them. Nevertheless, it seems to become a label which some black leaders must wear, no matter how uncomfortably, because they sense that they are threatened by competitors who are vulnerable to the charge of extremism. One effect of accepting this dichotomy undoubtedly considered by moderate leaders is that it may increase their own acceptability to the authorities or other whites with whom they may interact. If they act on this assumption, however, they encounter the age-old dilemma of whether gains in acceptability are not accompanied by proportional losses in effectiveness.

Another consideration must be how the definition of a leader as "moderate" affects his appeal to his potential followers. The answer is not simple: the black leader who accepts definition as a moderate and brands his competitors as extremists does, obviously, run the risk of being denounced as an "Uncle Tom." There may be compensating gains, however. Myrdal (1944: 771) pointed out that during the era of accommodating black leadership in the South there was great ambivalence towards militant or extremist protest leaders. While blacks in southern communities might secretly admire them for their courage and agree with their demands, they still feared them because of the anger and reprisals that they evoked from whites. Therefore, they continued to follow the less quixotic moderate leaders. This did not signify whole-hearted support of the accommodating leaders, of course.

A third and prolific source of the terms "extremism" and "extremist" is the mass media. Newsmen and commentators seem to select the referents primarily on the basis of the novelty and the drama of the words or actions they thus characterize. They may also be influenced by the vigor of the response which social movement rhetoric or tactics evoke from authorities or the opposition. When the Black Panther Party charges that the federal government is pursuing a policy of genocide, that is dramatic news; but when J. Edgar Hoover declares that the Black Panther Party is a dangerous and subversive organization that, too, makes headlines. In either case, the Panthers get the tag "extremist." One important observation should be made about the relationship of the mass media to extremist leaders and mass preoccupation with them: it is an oversimplification to contend that the mass media create such leaders. The late Whitney Young (1968:45) observed a few years ago that H. Rap Brown had a following of "about 50 Negroes and 5,000 white reporters." In an age of television this is the name of the game. Leaders with a weak and tenuous power base know very well that one way to enhance their visibility and to spread their gospel is by providing the mass media with the kinds of dramatic events that they consider newsworthy. Blacks who do not get invitations to appear on "Meet the Press" on the basis of being invited to the White House or heading "respectable" black organizations may nevertheless appear on the program because of their extremism.

SOCIOLOGICAL REFERENCES TO "EXTREMISM"

As has been suggested, social scientists also use the term "extremism" on occasion. There are two ways in which these writers implicitly or explicitly define "extremism." One usage reflects an implicit, subjective conception of what constitutes the "mainstream" or the "real values" of a movement such as the Black Revolution. There is the implication that the mainstream values, such as integration, are modal among the members of the movement. This conception may also reflect, however, unstated assumptions about values and tactics. Some leaders and their proposals may be classified as "extremist" because they are not in accord with the social scientist's own value premises. Thus a white social scientist who has made a great commitment of energy and emotion to the struggle for racial integration and has defended it as the only "democratic" solution to problems of racial discrimination may cling desperately to the belief that most blacks want for themselves what he wants for them. Thus he may characterize black separatist leaders as "extremists."

A more explicit and objective definition is derived from the use of attitude and opinion surveys to identify the modal attitudes towards values, tactics, and leaders among the putative members of a social movement. Gary Marx (1969) has undertaken to do this in a systematic way for the Black Protest Movement and, in so doing, has come up with a relatively precise characterization of what constitutes "extremism" in the current phase of the Black Revolution, although he does not use this term himself. Up to now what is usually denoted by references to "black extremism" has not been specified, but it is apparent that what Marx identifies as "extreme" or "minority" black attitudes correspond rather closely to those implied in the other usages. He finds, after reviewing 15 studies of black opinion, that black "extremism" incorporates: (1) approval of violence as a tactic in black protest; (2) pessimism about the change that has occurred and is expected to occur in race relations; (3) support for separatist goals as over against integration; (4) hostility to and mistrust of whites rather than the more prevalent "high degree of tolerance of whites;" (5) positive evaluation of black power when it is taken to imply black control of black communities; and (6) support for Stokely Carmichael and the Black Muslims as opposed to the NAACP and Ralph Abernathy (1969:216–231). These 15 studies conducted in 1967 and 1968, supported the conclusions reached by Marx in his own survey carried out in 1964.

In the revised edition of Protest and Prejudice, issued in 1969, Marx (p. 216) adds a postscript in which he grapples with the problem of the relationship to social movements of mass, as opposed to extreme, opinion. While he concludes that mass opinions among blacks have not changed since 1964, he recognizes that during this time a number of new leaders have emerged, have been involved in many dramatic confrontations with authorities, and have achieved high visibility. He notes that there has been "an important shift in tactics and goals on the part of crucial segments of the black movement." Nevertheless, from his analysis one must conclude that the "extremists" by his operational definition cannot be regarded as leaders with mass support. Yet people like Elijah Muhammad, Malcolm X, Stokely Carmichael, H. Rap Brown, Eldridge Cleaver, Huey Newton, Bobby Seale, and Angela Davis still capture popular interest and engage the attention of social scientists.

Some possible explanations of the significance of such extremists readily suggest themselves. One, already alluded to, is that they are merely spectacles thrust into prominence by the mass media. Somewhat similar is the suggestion that their rhetoric is just so much verbal battling with no real significance for the movement, and that their confrontations with authorities constitute deviant behavior from the standpoint not only of the larger society but also of the Black Protest Movement itself. This suggests that they are the lunatic fringe of the movement, who precipitate riots or shootouts and get themselves arrested or killed but really accomplish nothing. This view implies that, in spite of them, the mainstream of the movement, led by moderates, goes on making slow, unspectacular but steady progress. A more negative evaluation of their significance as a lunatic fringe suggests that they actually impede the progress that the movement might be making were it not for the backlash which they evoke. While I will not devote a great deal of attention to this widely-held hypothesis, I do not mean to deny its importance. I am not arguing that "extremism" is "functional" in the sense of promoting the success of a movement. It may destroy a movement. On the other hand, a more positive hypothesis is that the extremists are indeed the vanguard of the Black Revolution, that while they do not have mass support now they will gain it quickly when the crucial time arrives.

I would suggest that the significance of extremists is much more complex

than any of these sweeping propositions imply. My analysis of their significance depends neither on dismissing them as "crazies" nor on romanticizing
them as the "real leaders" of the black movement. Before proceeding to this
analysis, I want to consider what seem to be earlier manifestations of "extremism" in the Black Protest Movement. In some cases what is "moderate"
today constituted the extremism of yesterday. In other cases, what were
defined as extremist leaders have risen and fallen in apparent failure, but
not without having an enduring impact on the movement.

"EXTREMISM" IN EARLIER PERIODS

At the time of its formation in 1909 the NAACP was regarded in many
quarters as a radical, extremist organization. It encompassed the earlier
Niagara Movement whose manifesto was described by Kelly Miller, a prominent black intellectual, as "scarcely distinguishable from a wild frantic
shriek." More importantly, W.E.B. Dubois was a key figure in the new organization. John Hope Franklin (1949:447) states that his mere presence on
the staff "branded the organization as radical from the beginning." It must
be recalled that for at least the first quarter of this century, Booker T. Washington's policy of accommodation represented the respectable style of black
"uplift," not just in the South but even more so in the North. Tuttle (1970:
227–8) in Race Riot, contends that in 1919 the Justice Department used as
one criterion of Black radicalism "the denunciation of Booker T. Washington's racial philosophy." Garfinkel (1968:31) states that during World War
I the protest activities of the NAACP were termed "seditious and enemy
inspired." Needless to say, long after the NAACP achieved a measure of respectability outside the South, it was still regarded in that region as an
extremist organization. In the decade of the 1950's numerous legislative in-
vestigative committees mercilessly harassed its leaders and its members alike
on the pretext that the organization was engaged in subversive activities.
They subpoenaed membership lists, charged officers with contempt for failing to submit them, and sought to make public employees disclose all organizational affiliations as a condition of employment.

As early as the 1920's, however, the leaders of the NAACP were themselves using such adjectives as "extremist," "impractical," "bombastic," and
"vicious" in the effort to meet the challenge that Marcus Garvey presented
them. Apparently Garvey was viewed as a dangerous extremist by white
authorities, also. His UNIA was kept under constant surveillance in New
York by a hostile district attorney; in 1919 the U.S. Department of Justice
cited his newspaper as a purveyor of "radicalism and sedition." When the
U.S. Attorney General moved to destroy the Garvey Movement through a
mail-fraud case, he did so with the public support of Dubois and other
NAACP leaders (Lincoln, 1970:288–91).

The NAACP survived to become a symbol of moderation in the black
movement; Garveyism seemed to be a case of extremism which suffered an
untimely death. Yet it is indeed true, as Lincoln (1970:291) has declared,
that "Garveyism is not dead." It has taken the passage of some 30 years and
the resurgence of black nationalism in the Nation of Islam and the Black

Power Movement to show that the support for Garveyism among blacks was not as evanescent as it appeared.

The weird and intricate dance of "moderates" and "extremists" has continued. One of the severest critics of Garvey in 1922 was A. Philip Randolph. After he launched his March on Washington Movement in 1942, however, he found himself under attack by the NAACP for his "extremism;" he was even accused of "Garveyism!" Randolph had seized the leadership of the Black Protest at a time when the established leaders had reached an impasse in their attacks on job discrimination. Furthermore, he insisted that the movement must be black-controlled. Ironically, in comparison with the black extremists of today, Randolph now must be regarded as once again a moderate.

According to Marx's findings, support for non-violent action as a tactic of the Black Movement is today a feature of mainstream moderation. Yet when the early CORE introduced the tactic and Martin Luther King, Jr., became a national symbol of civil disobedience, nonviolent direct action appeared "extremist" to many leaders of the NAACP, to conservative whites who had become somewhat accustomed to "test-cases" but not to attempts to fill the jails, and even to white liberals. According to Powell (1968:57–62), many white liberals acclaimed the moralistic implications of non-violence but feared and condemned the disruption of coercion which really gave civil disobedience its effectiveness. Powell also contends that it was another almost forgotten "extremist," Robert F. Williams, whose experience and writings moved some CORE leaders toward the conclusion that non-violence might have to be supplemented by violent self-defense, even while they were still publicly preaching non-violence. She adds, "The NAACP suspended him from membership at the same convention at which it upheld, in theory, the right of self-defense" (1969:54).

THE SIGNIFICANCE OF EXTREMISM

This is a very incomplete inventory of leaders and tactics that have at one time or another been regarded as extremist. Nevertheless a few propositions may be advanced about the significance of extremism for a social movement. The first two propositions rest on the assumption that while they are not unimportant, extremist leaders do play a secondary role to moderate leaders.

First, it has often been pointed out by moderate leaders themselves that the existence of extremist leaders makes them appear more reasonable in their demands and thus increases their bargaining power. This follows from a well-established principle of the psychology of perception: extending the anchorage points near the end of a scale changes the value of objects nearer the center of the scale. There is an important corollary to this first proposition. Changing of the anchorage points by the extremists moves other leaders in their direction even though the latter continue to appear moderate. There is no need to review the changes in the postures of the NAACP and the National Urban League that have been made in obvious response to new forms of radicalism in the Black Protest Movement.

Going beyond this interaction between extremist and moderate leaders, the rhetoric and the actions of extremists have other effects on both the leadership and membership of a social movement. The critical and pessimistic attitudes of extremist leaders serve as a constant corrective to what may be illusions of progress which might otherwise cause a relaxation of the struggle. This is done not by just propaganda but even more so by actions, by confrontation. For example, the adamant insistence of the Mississippi Freedom Democratic Party on being seated at the 1964 Democratic Convention served to show how shallow was the commitment of the party regulars, including Hubert Humphrey, to the cause of black rights. The compromise which some moderate black leaders were willing to make at that time was soon to be exposed as of little value when the Johnson administration shifted its emphasis from the war on poverty and racism to the war in southeast Asia. The confrontations of the Black Panthers with the police, particularly the shooting of Fred Hampton, have led all blacks to question the extent of official respect for civil and human rights when blacks are the victims. Even Ralph Abernathy was constrained to accept Hampton as a race hero, despite his well-known opposition to Panther ideology and tactics. That Charles Garry may have exaggerated the number of killings does not change the fact that Roy Innis, Ralph Abernathy, Whitney Young, and Carl Rowan all took his charge seriously. Were the whole charge of federally-inspired "genocide" based on myth, deterioration of confidence in the police is still a reality.

When George Jackson was killed in San Quentin Prison, his mother's first reaction was that the authorities had planned his death, despite their official declaration that he had been shot while attempting to escape. It was not just the bereaved mother and black revolutionaries who saw Jackson as a heroic victim of justice, however. Roger Wilkins (1971), formerly director of the federal Community Relations Service, felt impelled to write a eulogy entitled "My Brother, George." Then in quick succession, subsequent events cast a pall of doubt over the official statements of prison authorities in general. First the officials at Attica were caught in a story which could not be reconciled with a coroner's findings. A few days later, disclosure of the results of the medical examination of Jackson's body lent credence to the charge that his killing may indeed have been unjustified. Not just revolutionary rhetoric but the course of events lends support to the belief that a black skin cancels out a person's civil and human rights at the moment when he most desperately needs their protection.

In creating what often seems to be futile if not suicidal confrontations, extremists serve to identify unresolved, and in that sense crucial, issues still facing the movement. When the police have finally come around to providing protection for non-violent demonstrators, blacks who carry arms for self-defense test the depth of official commitment to equal rights. They ask, in effect, "Do the guarantees of the second amendment apply to black citizens as well as to members of the National Rifle Association?"

Such confrontations also may have the effect, often intended by their initiators, of radicalizing a growing segment of the movement membership and increasing the polarization between the movement and its opposition. Just as the extremist will not be taken in by illusions of progress, he refuses to accept a false peace. Making things worse so that they may get better is a dangerous, often self-defeating strategy, but it is a common one in social movements. The extremist has always been willing to take the gamble, even at the possible cost of his own life.

These consequences of extremism are particularly significant because of their impact on young people who are the most important source of recruits for an enduring social movement. When the kinds of polls that Marx cites are analyzed by age groups, younger blacks almost invariably appear more pessimistic, more alienated, more inclined toward violence, more separatist—in other words, more "extremist"—than the total sample. Regardless of how minor their immediate consequences may be, the dramatic acts of extremists provide young people with novel behavioral models; the propaganda of the extremists suggests to them what the new, "real" issues are and distorts their whole frame of reference in a way that makes it different from that of their elders.

Finally, the activities of extremists have effects on a movement's opposition which may either be positive or negative from the standpoint of the movement itself: the attention of the opposition, like that of the membership, may be forced on new or unresolved issues. While the demands for black control of black schools may have gone against the mainstream emphasis on the desegregation of schools, it has forcefully reminded school administrators of the deplorable conditions that exist in ghetto schools while the debate over integration drags on. Furthermore, the issues that extremists raise may help to create a new sense of injustice even in those who are not part of the movement. For example, had it not been for the seemingly unreasonable demands of the Black Panthers and their supporters for the release of Bobby Seale, such a prestigious white figure as Kingman Brewster would probably never have made his famous statement expressing doubt that a radical black could get a fair trial in an American court. For such a man to make such a statement gave the issue a credibility that the Panthers, Ralph Abernathy, or Roy Wilkins, none of them, could have given it.

Needless to say, the constant, abrasive challenges of extremists to a social order even while it seems to be yielding to moderate demands can have the effect of evoking drastic repression of the whole movement. Marx suggests that one salient characteristic of the extremist is his deep commitment to his cause. Because of this commitment or, if you will, fanaticism, the extremist is willing to take maximum risks. Yet he risks not only his own program and his own personal welfare, but the entire movement. The stakes he plays with are not just his but those of the moderates.

SOME CONSEQUENCES OF EXTREMISM

All of the propositions above may be valid even if so-called "extremists" can be classified only as "would-be leaders," as some sociologists would call them. In suggesting that mass support is of only minor importance to them, I do not want to de-emphasize their significance. There may be two broader, more speculative consequences of extremism in the Black Revolution. One is that, poll results notwithstanding, they may indeed be only the tip of the iceberg, the hard-core minority who could launch a widespread, revolutionary confrontation with white power and quickly amass widespread support once the battle-lines were drawn. There seems to be no black leader today with sufficient charisma to launch such an effort. Yet it should be remembered that one characteristic of many social movements is fluctuations in leadership. "Stars" arise suddenly, as did Marcus Garvey, and as did A. Philip Randolph during the short-lived March on Washington Movement. We may be at the moment in a situation when there is a virtual vacuum in black leadership, one into which a new charismatic leader might move quickly. If such a new leader arises, it is doubtful that he will rely on moral suasion to the extent that Martin Luther King, Jr., did. Regardless of what specific power resources he seeks to mobilize, he will be a "Black Power" leader.

Secondly, because of their pessimism about the rate of progress, their constant de-bunking of illusions of progress, and their preference for coercive tactics, black extremists serve as a constant reminder of the objective condition of black power in the United States. This is the fact that black power still remains fundamentally a veto power. Regardless of the specific tactics that may be employed, the most effective strategy for blacks remains one of coercion.

REFERENCES

Franklin, John Hope
   1947   From Slavery to Freedom. New York: Alfred A. Knopf.
Gamson, William A.
   1968   Power and Discontent. Homewood, Ill.: The Dorsey Press.
Garfinkel, Herbert
   1969   When Negroes March. New York: Atheneum.
Lincoln, C. Eric.
   1970   "Black nationalism: The minor leagues," in Ross K. Baker, ed., The Afro-American. New York: Van Nostrand Reinhold.
Marx, Gary
   1969   Protest and Prejudice. New York: Harper Torchbooks.
Powell, Inge Bell
   1968   Core and the Strategy of Non-Violence. New York: Random House.
Tuttle, William M., Jr.
   1970   Race Riot. New York: Atheneum.
Wilkins, Roger
   1971   "My Brother, George," The New York Times, August 27:31.
Young, Whitney M., Jr.
   1968   "We Need Tangible Victories," U.S. News and World Report, April 22:45.

The Origins
of the Women's Liberation
Movement [1]

JO FREEMAN

The emergence in the last few years of a feminist movement caught most thoughtful observers by surprise. Women had "come a long way," had they not? What could they want to be liberated from? The new movement generated much speculation about the sources of female discontent and why it was articulated at this particular time. But these speculators usually asked the wrong questions. Most attempts to analyze the sources of social strain have had to conclude with Ferriss (1971, p. 1) that, "from the close perspective of 1970, events of the past decade provide evidence of no compelling cause of the rise of the new feminist movement." His examination of time-series data over the previous 20 years did not reveal any significant changes in socioeconomic variables which could account for the emergence of a women's movement at the time it was created. From such strain indicators, one could surmise that any time in the last two decades was as conducive as any other to movement formation.

I

The sociological literature is not of much help: the study of social movements "has been a neglected area of sociology" (Killian 1964, p. 426), and, within that field, virtually no theorists have dealt with movement origins. The *causes* of social movements have been analyzed (Gurr 1970; Davies 1962), and the *motivations* of participants have been investigated (Toch

[1] I would like to thank Richard Albares and Florence Levinsohn for having read and criticized earlier versions of this paper.

1965; Cantril 1941; Hoffer 1951; Adorno et al. 1950), but the mechanisms of "how" a movement is constructed have received scant attention.[2] As Dahrendorf (1959, p. 64) commented, "The sociologist is generally interested not so much in the origin of social phenomena as in their spread and rise to wider significance." This interest is derived from an emphasis on cultural processes rather than on people as the major dynamic of social change (Killian 1964, p. 426). Consequently, even the "natural history" theorists have delineated the stages of development in a way that is too vague to tell us much about how movements actually start (Dawson and Gettys 1929, pp. 787–803; Lowi 1971, p. 39; Blumer 1951; King 1956), and a theory as comprehensive as Smelser's (1963) is postulated on too abstract a level to be of microsociological value (for a good critique, see Currie and Skolnick [1970]).

Part of the problem results from extreme confusion about what a social movement really is. Movements are rarely studied as distinct social phenomena but are usually subsumed under one or two theoretical traditions: that of "collective behavior" (see, especially, Smelser 1963; Lang and Lang 1961; Turner and Killian 1957) and that of interest-group and party formation (Heberle 1951; King 1956; Lowi 1971). The former emphasizes the spontaneous aspects of a movement; and the latter, the structured ones. Yet movements are neither fully collective behavior nor incipient interest groups except in the broadest sense of these terms. Rather, they contain essential elements of both. It is "the dual imperative of spontaneity and organization [that] . . . sets them apart from pressure groups and other types of voluntary associations, which lack their spontaneity, and from mass behavior, which is altogether devoid of even the rudiments of organization" (Lang and Lang 1961, p. 497).

Recognizing with Heberle (1951, p. 8) that "movements *as such* are not organized groups," it is still the structured aspects which are more amenable to study, if not always the most salient. Turner and Killian (1957, p. 307) have argued that it is when "members of a public who share a common position concerning the issue at hand supplement their informal person-to-person discussion with some organization to promote their convictions more effectively and insure more sustained activity, a social movement is incipient" (see also Killian 1964, p. 426). Such organization(s) and other core groups of a movement not only determine much of its conscious policy but serve as foci for its values and activities. Just as it has been argued that society as a whole has a cultural and structural "center" about which most members of the society are more or less "peripheral" (Shils 1970), so, too, can a social movement be conceived of as having a center and a periphery. An investigation into a movement's origins must be concerned with the microstructure preconditions for the emergence of such a movement center. From where do the people come who make up the initial, organizing cadre of a movement? How do they come together, and how do they come to share a similar view of the world in circumstances which compel them to political

[2] "A consciously directed and organized movement cannot be explained merely in terms of the psychological disposition or motivation of people, or in terms of a diffusion of an ideology. Explanations of this sort have a deceptive plausibility, but overlook the fact that *a movement has to be constructed* and has to carve out a career in what is practically always an opposed, resistant or at least indifferent world" (Blumer 1957, p. 147; italics mine).

action? In what ways does the nature of the original center affect the future development of the movement?

II

Most movements have very inconspicuous beginnings. The significant elements of their origins are usually forgotten or distorted by the time a trained observer seeks to trace them out, making retroactive analyses difficult. Thus, a detailed investigation of a single movement at the time it is forming can add much to what little is known about movement origins. Such an examination cannot uncover all of the conditions and ingredients of movement formation, but it can aptly illustrate both weaknesses in the theoretical literature and new directions for research. During the formative period of the women's liberation movement, I had many opportunities to observe, log, and interview most of the principals involved in the early movement.[3] The descriptive material in Section III is based on that data. This analysis, supplemented by five other origin studies made by me, would support the following three propositions:

Proposition 1: The need for a preexisting communications network or infrastructure within the social base of a movement is a primary prerequisite for "spontaneous" activity. Masses alone don't form movements, however discontented they may be. Groups of previously unorganized individuals may spontaneously form into small local associations—usually along the lines of informal social networks—in response to a specific strain or crisis, but, if they are not linked in some manner, the protest does not become generalized: it remains a local irritant or dissolves completely. If a movement is to spread rapidly, the communications network must already exist. If only the rudiments of one exist, movement formation requires a high input of "organizing" activity.

Proposition 2: Not just any communications network will do. It must be a network that is *co-optable* to the new ideas of the incipient movement.[4] To be co-optable, it must be composed of like-minded people whose background, experiences, or location in the social structure make them receptive to the ideas of a specific new movement.

Proposition 3: Given the existence of a co-optable communications network, or at least the rudimentary development of a potential one, and a situation of strain, one or more precipitants are required. Here, two distinct

---

[3] As a founder and participant in the younger branch of the Chicago women's liberation movement from 1967 through 1969 and editor of the first (at that time, only) national newsletter, I was able, through extensive correspondence and interviews, to keep a record of how each group around the country first started, where the organizers got the idea from, who they had talked to, what conferences were held and who attended, the political affiliations (or lack of them) of the first members, etc. Although I was a member of Chicago NOW, information on the origins of it and the other older branch organizations comes entirely through ex post facto interviews of the principals and examination of early papers in preparation for my dissertation on the women's liberation movement. Most of my informants requested that their contribution remain confidential.

[4] The only use of this significant word appears rather incidentally in Turner (1964, p. 123).

patterns emerge that often overlap. In one, a crisis galvanizes the network into spontaneous action in a new direction. In the other, one or more persons begin organizing a new organization or disseminating a new idea. For spontaneous action to occur, the communications network must be well formed or the initial protest will not survive the incipient stage. If it is not well formed, organizing efforts must occur; that is, one or more persons must specifically attempt to construct a movement. To be successful, organizers must be skilled and must have a fertile field in which to work. If no communications network already exists, there must at least be emerging spontaneous groups which are acutely atuned to the issue, albeit uncoordinated. To sum up, if a co-optable communications network is already established, a crisis is all that is necessary to galvanize it. If it is rudimentary, an organizing cadre of one or more persons is necessary. Such a cadre is superfluous if the former conditions fully exist, but it is essential if they do not.

Before examining these propositions in detail, let us look at the structure and origins of the women's liberation movement.

III

The women's liberation movement manifests itself in an almost infinite variety of groups, styles, and organizations. Yet, this diversity has sprung from only two distinct origins whose numerous offspring remain clustered largely around these two sources. The two branches are often called "reform" and "radical," or, as the sole authoritative book on the movement describes them, "women's rights" and "women's liberation" (Hole and Levine 1971). Unfortunately, these terms actually tell us very little, since feminists do not fit into the traditional Left/Right spectrum. In fact, if an ideological typography were possible, it would show minimal consistency with any other characteristic. Structure and style rather than ideology more accurately differentiate the two branches, and, even here, there has been much borrowing on both sides.

I prefer simpler designations: the first of the branches will be referred to as the older branch of the movement, partly because it began first and partly because the median age of its activists is higher. It contains numerous organizations, including the lobbyist group (Women's Equity Action League), a legal foundation (Human Rights for Women), over 20 caucuses in professional organizations, and separate organizations of women in the professions and other occupations. Its most prominent "core group" is the National Organization for Women (NOW), which was also the first to be formed.

While the written programs and aims of the older branch span a wide spectrum, their activities tend to be concentrated on legal and economic problems. These groups are primarily made up of women—and men—who work, and they are substantially concerned with the problems of working women. The style of organization of the older branch tends to be traditionally formal, with elected officers, boards of directors, bylaws, and the other trappings of democratic procedure. All started as top-down national organizations, lacking in a mass base. Some have subsequently developed a mass base, some have not yet done so, and others do not want to.

Conversely, the younger branch consists of innumerable small groups—engaged in a variety of activities—whose contact with each other is, at best, tenuous. Contrary to popular myth, it did not begin on the campus nor was it started by the Students for a Democratic Society (SDS). However, its activators were, to be trite, on the other side of the generation gap. While few were students, all were "under 30" and had received their political education as participants or concerned observers of the social action projects of the last decade. Many came direct from New Left and civil rights organizations. Others had attended various courses on women in the multitude of free universities springing up around the country during those years.

The expansion of these groups has appeared more amoebic than organized, because the younger branch of the movement prides itself on its lack of organization. From its radical roots, it inherited the idea that structures were always conservative and confining, and leaders, isolated and elitist. Thus, eschewing structure and damning the idea of leadership, it has carried the concept of "everyone doing her own thing" to the point where communication is haphazard and coordination is almost nonexistent. The thousands of sister chapters around the country are virtually independent of each other, linked only by numerous underground papers, journals, newsletters, and cross-country travelers. A national conference was held over Thanksgiving in 1968 but, although considered successful, has not yet been repeated. Before the 1968 conference, the movement did not have the sense of national unity which emerged after the conference. Since then, young feminists have made no attempt to call another national conference. There have been a few regional conferences, but no permanent consequences resulted. At most, some cities have a coordinating committee which attempts to maintain communication among local groups and to channel newcomers into appropriate ones, but these committees have no power over any group's activities, let alone its ideas. Even local activists do not know how big the movement is in their own city. While it cannot be said to have no organization at all, this branch of the movement has informally adopted a general policy of "structurelessness."

Despite a lack of a formal policy encouraging it, there is a great deal of homogeneity within the younger branch of the movement. Like the older branch, it tends to be predominantly white, middle class, and college educated. But it is much more homogenous and, unlike the older branch, has been unable to diversify. This is largely because most small groups tend to form among friendship networks. Most groups have no requirements for membership (other than female sex), no dues, no written and agreed-upon structure, and no elected leaders. Because of this lack of structure, it is often easier for an individual to form a new group than to find and join an older one. This encourages group formation but discourages individual diversification. Even contacts among groups tend to be along friendship lines.

In general, the different style and organization of the two branches was largely derived from the different kind of political education and experiences of each group of women. Women of the older branch were trained in and had used the traditional forms of political action, while the younger branch has inherited the loose, flexible, person-oriented attitude of the youth and student movements. The different structures that have evolved from these two distinctly different kinds of experience have, in turn, largely determined the strategy of the two branches, irrespective of any conscious intentions of their participants. These different structures and strategies have each posed different problems and possibilities. Intra-movement differences are often perceived by the participants as conflicting, but it is their essential complementarity which has been one of the strengths of the movement.

Despite the multitude of differences, there are very strong similarities in the way the two branches came into being. These similarities serve to illuminate some of the microsociological factors involved in movement formation. The forces which led to NOW's formation were first set in motion in 1961 when President Kennedy established the President's Commission on the Status of Women at the behest of Esther Petersen,[5] to be chaired by Eleanor Roosevelt. Operating under a broad mandate, its 1963 report (*American Women*) and subsequent committee publications documented just how thoroughly women are still denied many rights and opportunities. The most concrete response to the activity of the president's commission was the eventual establishment of 50 state commissions to do similar research on a state level. These commissions were often urged by politically active women and were composed primarily of women. Nonetheless, many believe the main stimulus behind their formation was the alleged view of the governors that the commissions were excellent opportunities to pay political debts without giving women more influential positions.

The activity of the federal and state commissions laid the groundwork for the future movement in three significant ways: (1) it brought together many knowledgeable, politically active women who otherwise would not have worked together around matters of direct concern to women; (2) the investigations unearthed ample evidence of women's unequal status, especially their legal and economic difficulties, in the process convincing many previously uninterested women that something should be done; (3) the reports created a climate of expectations that something would be done. The women of the federal and state commissions who were exposed to these influences exchanged visits, correspondence, and staff and met with each other at an annual commission convention. Thus, they were in a position to share and mutually reinforce their growing awareness and concern over women's issues. These commissions thus created an embryonic communications network among people with similar concerns.

During this time, two other events of significance occurred. The first was the publication of Betty Friedan's (1963) book, *The Feminine Mystique*. An immediate best seller, it stimulated many women to question the status quo and some to suggest to Friedan that a new organization be formed to attack their problems. The second event was the addition of "sex" to Title VII of the 1964 Civil Rights Act. Many men thought the "sex" provision was a joke (Bird 1968, chap. 1). The Equal Employment Opportunity Commission (EEOC) certainly treated it as one and refused to adequately enforce it. The first EEOC executive director even stated publicly that the provision was a "fluke" that was "conceived out of wedlock" (Edelsberg 1965). But, within the EEOC, there was a "pro-woman" coterie which argued that "sex"

---

[5] Then director of the Women's Bureau.

would be taken more seriously if there were "some sort of NAACP for women" to put pressure on the government. As government employees, they couldn't organize such a group, but they spoke privately with those whom they thought might be able to do so. One who shared their views was Rep. Martha Griffiths of Michigan. She blasted the EEOC's attitude in a June 20, 1966 speech on the House floor (Griffiths 1966) declaring that the agency had "started out by casting disrespect and ridicule on the law" but that their "wholly negative attitude had changed—for the worse."

On June 30, 1966, these three strands of incipient feminism were knotted together to form NOW. The occasion was the last day of the Third National Conference of Commissions on the Status of Women, ironically titled "Targets for Action." The participants had all received copies of Rep. Griffith's remarks. The opportunity came with a refusal by conference officials to bring to the floor a proposed resolution that urged the EEOC to give equal enforcement to the sex provision of Title VII as was given to the race provision. Despite the fact that these state commissions were not federal agencies, officials replied that one government agency could not be allowed to pressure another. The small group of women who had desired the resolution had met the night before in Friedan's hotel room to discuss the possibility of a civil rights organization for women. Not convinced of its need, they chose instead to propose the resolution. When the resolution was vetoed, the women held a whispered conversation over lunch and agreed to form an action organization "to bring women into full participation in the mainstream of American society now, assuming all the privileges and responsibilities thereof in truly equal partnership with men." The name NOW was coined by Friedan, who was at the conference researching her second book. Before the day was over, 28 women paid $5.00 each to join (Friedan 1967).

By the time the organizing conference was held the following October 29–30, over 300 men and women had become charter members. It is impossible to do a breakdown on the composition of the charter membership, but one of the first officers and board is possible. Such a breakdown accurately reflected NOW's origins. Friedan was president, two former EEOC commissioners were vice-presidents, a representative of the United Auto Workers Women's Committee was secretary-treasurer, and there were seven past and present members of the State Commissions on the Status of Women on the 20-member board. Of the charter members, 126 were Wisconsin residents—and Wisconsin had the most active state commission. Occupationally, the board and officers were primarily from the professions, labor, government, and the communications industry. Of these, only those from labor had any experience in organizing, and they resigned a year later in a dispute over support of the Equal Rights Amendment. Instead of organizational expertise, what the early NOW members had was media experience, and it was here that their early efforts were aimed.

As a result, NOW often gave the impression of being larger than it was. It was highly successful in getting publicity, much less so in bringing about concrete changes or organizing itself. Thus, it was not until 1969, when several national news media simultaneously decided to do major stories on the women's liberation movement, that NOW's membership increased significantly. Even today, there are only 8,000 members, and the chapters are still in an incipient stage of development.

In the meantime, unaware of and unknown to NOW, the EEOC, or to the state commissions, younger women began forming their own movement. Here, too, the groundwork had been laid some years before. Social action projects of recent years had attracted many women, who were quickly shunted into traditional roles and faced with the self-evident contradiction of working in a "freedom movement" without being very free. No single "youth movement" activity or organization is responsible for the younger branch of the women's liberation movement; together they created a "radical community" in which like-minded people continually interacted with each other. This community consisted largely of those who had participated in one or more of the many protest activities of the sixties and had established its own ethos and its own institutions. Thus, the women in it thought of themselves as "movement people" and had incorporated the adjective "radical" into their personal identities. The values of their radical identity and the style to which they had been trained by their movement participation directed them to approach most problems as political ones which could be solved by organizing. What remained was to translate their individual feelings of "unfreedom" into a collective consciousness. Thus, the radical community provided not only the necessary network of communication; its radical ideas formed the framework of analysis which "explained" the dismal situation in which radical women found themselves.

Papers had been circulated on women,[6] and temporary women's caucuses had been held as early as 1964, when Stokely Carmichael made his infamous remark that "the only position for women in SNCC is prone." But it was not until late 1967 and 1968 that the groups developed a determined, if cautious, continuity and began to consciously expand themselves. At least five groups in five different cities (Chicago, Toronto, Detroit, Seattle, and Gainesville, Florida) formed spontaneously, independent of each other. They came at a very auspicious moment. The year 1967 was the one in which the blacks kicked the whites out of the civil rights movement, student power had been discredited by SDS, and the organized New Left was on the wane. Only draft-resistance activities were on the increase, and this movement more than any other exemplified the social inequities of the sexes. Men could resist the draft; women could only counsel resistance.

What was significant about this point in time was that there was a lack of available opportunities for political work. Some women fit well into the "secondary role" of draft counseling. Many did not. For years, their complaints of unfair treatment had been ignored by movement men with the dictum that those things could wait until after the revolution. Now these movement women found time on their hands, but the men would still not listen.

A typical example was the event which precipitated the formation of the Chicago group, the first independent group in this country. At the August 1967 National Conference for New Politics convention, a women's caucus

---

[6] "A Kind of Memo," by Hayden and King (1966, p. 35) circulated in the fall of 1965 (and eventually published), was the first such paper.

met for days but was told its resolution wasn't significant enough to merit a floor discussion. By threatening to tie up the convention with procedural motions, the women succeeded in having their statement tacked to the end of the agenda. It was never discussed. The chair refused to recognize any of the many women standing by the microphone, their hands straining upward. When he instead called on someone to speak on "the forgotten American, the American Indian," five women rushed the podium to demand an explanation. But the chairman just patted one of them on the head (literally) and told her, "Cool down little girl. We have more important things to talk about than women's problems."

The "little girl" was Shulamith Firestone, future author of *The Dialectic of Sex* (1971), and she didn't cool down. Instead, she joined with another Chicago woman, who had been trying to organize a women's group that summer, to call a meeting of those women who had half-heartedly attended the summer meetings. Telling their stories to those women, they stimulated sufficient rage to carry the group for three months, and by that time it was a permanent institution.

Another somewhat similar event occurred in Seattle the following winter. At the University of Washington, an SDS organizer was explaining to a large meeting how white college youth established rapport with the poor whites with whom they were working. "He noted that sometimes after analyzing societal ills, the men shared leisure time by 'balling a chick together.' He pointed out that such activities did much to enhance the political consciousness of the poor white youth. A woman in the audience asked, 'And what did it do for the consciousness of the chick?' " (Hole and Levine 1971, p. 120). After the meeting, a handlful of enraged women formed Seattle's first group.

Groups subsequent to the initial five were largely organized rather than emerging spontaneously out of recent events. In particular, the Chicago group was responsible for the creation of many new groups in that city and elsewhere and started the first national newsletter. The 1968 conference was organized by the Washington, D.C. group from resources provided by the Center for Policy Studies (CPS), a radical research organization. Using CPS facilities, this group subsequently became a main literature-distribution center. Although New York groups organized early and were featured in the 1969–70 media blitz, New York was not a source of early organizers.[7]

Unlike NOW, the women in the first groups had had years of experience as local-level organizers. They did not have the resources, or the desire, to form a national organization, but they knew how to utilize the infrastructure of the radical community, the underground press, and the free universities to disseminate ideas on women's liberation. Chicago, as a center of New Left activity, had the largest number of politically conscious organizers. Many traveled widely to Left conferences and demonstrations, and most

---

[7] The movement in New York has been more diverse than other cities and has made many major ideological contributions but, contrary to popular belief, it did not begin in New York. In putting together their stories, the news media, concentrated as they are in New York, rarely looked past the Hudson for their information. This eastern bias is exemplified by the fact that, although the younger branch of the movement has no national organization and abjures leadership, all but one of those women designated by the press as movement leaders live in New York.

used the opportunity to talk with other women about the new movement. In spite of public derision of radical men, or perhaps because of it, young women steadily formed new groups around the country.

Initially, the new movement found it hard to organize on the campus, but, as a major congregating area of women and, in particular, of women with political awareness, campus women's liberation groups eventually became ubiquitous. While the younger branch of the movement never formed any organization larger or more extensive than a city-wide coordinating committee, it would be fair to say that it has a larger "participationship" than NOW and the other older branch organizations. While the members of the older branch knew how to use the media and how to form national structures, the women of the younger branch were skilled in local community organizing.

IV

From this description, there appear to be four essential elements contributing to the emergence of the women's liberation movement in the mid-sixties: (1) the growth of a preexisting communications network which was (2) co-optable to the ideas of the new movement; (3) a series of crises that galvanized into action people involved in this network; and/or (4) subsequent organizing efforts to weld the spontaneous groups together into a movement. To further understand these factors, let us examine them in detail with reference to other relevant studies.

1.   Both the Commissions on the Status of Women and the "radical community" created a communications network through which those women initially interested in creating an organization could easily reach others. Such a network had not previously existed among women. Historically tied to the family and isolated from their own kind, women are perhaps the most organizationally underdeveloped social category in Western civilization. By 1950, the 19th-century organizations which had been the basis of the suffrage movement—the Women's Trade Union League, the General Federation of Women's Clubs, the Women's Christian Temperance Union, the National American Women's Suffrage Association—were all either dead or a pale shadow of their former selves. The closest exception was the National Women's Party (NWP), which has remained dedicated to feminist concerns since its inception in 1916. However, since 1923, it has been essentially a lobbying group for the Equal Rights Amendment. The NWP, having always believed that a small group of women concentrating their efforts in the right places was more effective than a mass appeal, was not appalled that, as late as 1969, even the majority of avowed feminists in this country had never heard of the NWP or the ERA.

References to the salience of a preexisting communications network appear frequently in the case studies of social movements, but it has been given little attention in the theoretical literature. It is essentially contrary to the mass-society theory which "for many . . . is . . . the most pertinent and comprehensive statement of the genesis of modern mass movements" (Pinard 1968, p. 682). This theory hypothesizes that those most likely to join a mass movement are those who are atomized and isolated from "a structure of groups intermediate between the family and the nation" (Korn- hauser 1959, p. 93). However, the lack of such intermediate structures among women has proved more of a hindrance than a help in movement formation. Even today, it is those women who are most atomized, the house- wives, who are least likely to join a feminist group.

The most serious attack on mass-society theory was made by Pinard (1971) in his study of the Social Credit Party of Quebec. He concluded that intermediate structures exerted *mobilizing* as well as restraining effects on individuals' participation in social movements because they formed com- munications networks that assisted in the rapid spread of new ideas. "When strains are severe and widespread," he contended, "a new movement is more likely to meet its early success among the more strongly integrated citizens" (Pinard 1971, p. 192).

Other evidence also attests to the role of previously organized networks in the rise and spread of a social movement. According to Buck (1920, pp. 43–44), the Grange established a degree of organization among American farmers in the 19th century which greatly facilitated the spread of future farmers' protests. In Saskatchewan, Lipset (1959) has asserted, "The rapid acceptance of new ideas and movements . . . can be attributed mainly to the high degree of organization. . . . The role of the social structure of the western wheat belt in facilitating the rise of new movements has never been sufficiently appreciated by historians and sociologists. Repeated challenges and crises forced the western farmers to create many more community in- stitutions . . . than are necessary in a more stable area. These groups in turn provided a structural basis for immediate action in critical situations. [Therefore] though it was a new radical party, the C.C.F. did not have to build up an organization from scratch." More recently, the civil rights movement was built upon the infrastructure of the Southern black church (King 1958), and early SDS organizers made ready use of the National Student Association (Kissinger and Ross 1968, p. 16).

Indirect evidence of the essential role of formal and informal communi- cations networks is found in diffusion theory, which emphasizes the impor- tance of personal interaction rather than impersonal media communication in the spread of ideas (Rogers 1962; Lionberger 1960), and in Coleman's (1957) investigations of prior organizations in the initial development of conflict.

Such preexisting communications networks appear to be not merely valu- able but prerequisites, as one study on "The Failure of an Incipi   cial Movement" (Jackson, Peterson, Bull, Monsen, and Richmond 1960) made quite clear. In 1957, a potential tax-protest movement in Los Angeles gen- erated considerable interest and public notice for a little over a month but was dead within a year. According to the authors, its failure to sustain itself beyond initial spontaneous protest was largely due to "the lack of a pre- existing network of communications linking those groups of citizens most likely to support the movement" (Jackson et al. 1960, p. 40). They said (p. 37) that "if a movement is to grow rapidly, it cannot rely upon its own net- work of communication, but must capitalize on networks already in exis- tence."

The development of the women's liberation movement highlights the salience of such a network precisely because the conditions for a movement existed *before* a network came into being, but the movement didn't exist until afterward. Socioeconomic strain did not change for women significantly during a 20-year period. It was as great in 1955 as in 1965. What changed was the organizational situation. It was not until a communications network developed among like-minded people beyond local boundaries that the movement could emerge and develop past the point of occasional, spontaneous uprising.

2. However, not just any network would do; it had to be one which was co-optable by the incipient movement because it linked like-minded people likely to be predisposed to the new ideas of the movement. The 180,000-member Federation of Business and Professional Women's (BPW) Clubs would appear to be a likely base for a new feminist movement but in fact was unable to assume this role. It had steadily lobbied for legislation of importance to women, yet as late as "1966 BPW rejected a number of suggestions that it redefine . . . goals and tactics and become a kind of 'NAACP for women' . . . out of fear of being labeled 'feminist'" (Hole and Levine 1971, p. 81). While its membership has become a recruiting ground for feminism, it could not initially overcome the ideological barrier to a new type of political action.

On the other hand, the women of the President's and State Commissions on the Status of Women and the feminist coterie of the EEOC were co-optable, largely because their immersion into the facts of female status and the details of sex-discrimination cases made them very conscious of the need for change. Likewise, the young women of the "radical community" lived in an atmosphere of questioning, confrontation, and change. They absorbed an ideology of "freedom" and "liberation" far more potent than any latent "antifeminism" might have been. The repeated contradictions between these ideas and the actions of their male colleagues created a compulsion for action which only required an opportunity to erupt. This was provided by the "vacuum of political activity" of 1967–68.

The nature of co-optability is much more difficult to elucidate. Heretofore, it has been dealt with only tangentially. Pinard (1971, p. 186) noted the necessity for groups to "*possess* or *develop* an ideology or simply subjective interests congruent with that of a new movement" for them to "act as mobilizing rather than restraining agents toward that movement" but did not further explore what affected the "primary group climate." More illumination is provided by the diffusion of innovation studies which point out the necessity for new ideas to fit in with already-established norms for changes to happen easily. Furthermore, a social system which has as a value "innovativeness" itself (as the radical community did) will more rapidly adopt ideas than one which looks upon the habitual performance of traditional practices as the ideal (as most organized women's groups did in the fifties). Usually, as Lionberger (1960, p. 91) points out, "people act in terms of past experience and knowledge." People who have had similar experiences are likely to share similar perceptions of a situation and to mutually reinforce those perceptions as well as their subsequent interpretation.

A co-optable network, therefore, is one whose members have had common experiences which predispose them to be receptive to the particular new ideas of the incipient movement and who are not faced with structural or ideological barriers to action. If the new movement as an "innovation" can interpret these experiences and perceptions in ways that point out channels for social action, then participation in social movement becomes the logical thing to do.

3. As our examples have illustrated, these similar perceptions must be translated into action. This is the role of the "crisis." For women of the older branch of the movement, the impetus to organize was the refusal of the EEOC to enforce the sex provision of Title VII, precipitated by the concomitant refusal of federal officials at the conference to allow a supportive resolution. For younger women, there were a series of minor crises. Such precipitating events are common to most movements. They serve to crystallize and focus discontent. From their own experiences, directly and concretely, people feel the need for change in a situation that allows for an exchange of feelings with others, mutual validation, and a subsequent reinforcement of innovative interpretation. Perception of an immediate need for change is a major factor in predisposing people to accept new ideas (Rogers 1962, p. 280). Nothing makes desire for change more acute than a crisis. If the strain is great enough, such a crisis need not be a major one; it need only embody symbolically collective discontent.

4. However, a crisis will only catalyze a well-formed communications network. If such networks are only embryonically developed or only partially co-optable, the potentially active individuals in them must be linked together by someone. As Jackson et al. (1960, p. 37) stated, "Some protest may persist where the source of trouble is constantly present. But interest ordinarily cannot be maintained unless there is a welding of spontaneous groups into some stable organization." In other words, people must be organized. Social movements do not simply occur.

The role of the organizer in movement formation is another neglected aspect of the theoretical literature. There has been great concern with leadership, but the two roles are distinct and not always performed by the same individual. In the early stages of a movement, it is the organizer much more than any "leader" who is important, and such an individual or cadre must often operate behind the scenes.[8] Certainly, the "organizing cadre" that young women in the radical community came to be was key to the growth of that branch of the women's liberation movement, despite the fact that no "leaders" were produced (and were actively discouraged). The existence of many leaders but no organizers in the older branch of the women's liberation movement and its subsequent slow development would tend to substantiate this hypothesis.

The crucial function of the organizer has been explored indirectly in other areas of sociology. Rogers (1962) devotes many pages to the "change agent" who, while he does not necessarily weld a group together or "construct" a movement, does do many of the same things for agricultural innovation that an organizer does for political change. Mass-society theory makes reference to the "agitator" but fails to do so in any kind of truly informative way. A

---

[8] The nature and function of these two roles was most clearly evident in the Townsend old-age movement of the thirties. Townsend was the "charismatic" leader, but the movement was organized by his partner, real estate promoter Robert Clements. Townsend himself acknowledges that, without Clement's help, the movement would never have gone beyond the idea stage (see Holzman 1963).

study of farmer's movements indicates that many core organizations were organized by a single individual before the spontaneous aspects of the movement predominated. Further, many other core groups were subsidized by older organizations, federal and state governments, and even by local businessmen (Salisbury 1969, p. 13). These organizations often served as training centers for organizers and sources of material support to aid in the formation of new interest groups and movements.

Similarly, the civil rights movement provided the training for many another movement's organizers, including the young women of the women's liberation movement. It would appear that the art of "constructing" a social movement is something that requires considerable skill and experience. Even in the supposedly spontaneous social movement, the professional is more valuable than the amateur.

V

The ultimate results of such "construction" are not independent of their origins. In fact, the attitudes and styles of a movement's initiators often have an effect which lasts longer than they do. Those women and men who formed NOW, and its subsequent sister organizations, created a national structure prepared to use the legal, political, and media institutions of our country. This it has done. The EEOC has changed many of its prejudicial attitudes toward women in its recent rulings. Numerous lawsuits have been filed under the sex provision of Title VII of the Civil Rights Act. The Equal Rights Amendment has passed Congress. Complaints have been filed against over 400 colleges and universities, as well as many businesses, charging violation of Executive Order 11246 amended by 11375, which prohibits sex discrimination by all holders of federal contracts. Articles on feminism have appeared in virtually every national news medium, and women's liberation has become a household word.

These groups have and continue to function primarily as pressure groups within the limits of traditional political activity. Consequently, their actual membership remains small. Diversification of the older branch of the movement has been largely along occupational lines and primarily within the professions. Activity has stressed using the tools for change provided by the system, however limited these may be. Short-range goals are emphasized, and no attempt has been made to place them within a broader ideological framework.

Initially, this structure hampered the development of older branch organizations. NOW suffered three splits between 1967 and 1968. As the only action organization concerned with women's rights, it had attracted many different kinds of people with many different views on what and how to proceed. With only a national structure and, at that point, no local base, it was difficult for individuals to pursue their particular concern on a local level; they had to persuade the whole organization to support them. Given NOW's top-down structure and limited resources, this placed severe limits on diversity and, in turn, severe strains on the organization. Additional difficulties for local chapters were created by a lack of organizers to develop new chapters and the lack of a program into which they could fit. NOW's initiators were very high-powered women who lacked the time or patience for the slow, unglamorous, and tedious work of putting together a mass organization. Chapter development had to wait for the national media to attract women to the organization or the considerable physical mobility of contemporary women to bring proponents into new territory. Locally, women had to find some common concern around which to organize. Unlike that of New York, which had easy access to the national media and many people skilled at using it, the other chapters had difficulty developing programs not dependent on the media. Since the national program consisted almost exclusively of support of legal cases or federal lobbying, the regional chapters could not easily fit into that either. Eventually, connections were made; and, in the last year, national task forces have begun to correlate with local efforts so that individual projects can combine a national thrust with instrumentation on the local level. After initial difficulties, NOW and the other older branch organizations are thriving at this point because they are able to effectively use the institutional tools which our society provides for social and political change. Yet, these groups are also limited by these tools to the rather narrow arenas within which they are designed to operate. The nature of these arenas and the particular skills they require for participation already limit both the kind of women who can effectively work in older branch groups and the activities they can undertake. When their scope is exhausted, it remains to be seen whether organizations such as NOW will wither, institutionalize themselves as traditional pressure groups, or show the imagination to develop new lines for action.

The younger branch has had an entirely different history and faces different prospects. It was able to expand rapidly in the beginning because it could capitalize on the infrastructure of organizations and media of the New Left and because its initiators were skilled in local community organizing. Since the prime unit was the small group and no need for national cooperation was perceived, multitudinous splits increased its strength rather than drained its resources. Such fission was often "friendly" in nature and, even when not, served to bring ever-increasing numbers of women under the movement's umbrella.

Unfortunately, these masses of new women lacked the organizing skills of the initiators, and, because the ideas of "leadership" and "organization" were in disrepute, they made no attempt to acquire them. They did not want to deal with traditional political institutions and abjured all traditional political skills. Consequently, the growth of the movement institutions did not go beyond the local level, and they were often inadequate to handle the accelerating influx of new people into the movement. Although these small groups were diverse in kind and responsible to no one for their focus, their nature determined both the structure and the strategy of the movement. One result has been a very broad-based creative movement to which individuals can relate pretty much as they desire with no concern for orthodoxy or doctrine. This branch has been the major source of new feminist ideas and activities. It has developed several ideological perspectives, much of the terminology of the movement, an amazing number of publications and "counter-institutions," numerous new issues, and even new techniques for social change. The emphasis of this branch has been on personal change as a means to understand the kind of political change desired. The primary instrument has been the consciousness-raising rap group which has sought to change women's very identities as well as their attitudes.

Nonetheless, this loose structure is flexible only within certain limits, and the movement has not yet shown the propensity to transcend them. While rap groups have been excellent techniques for changing individual attitudes, they have not been very successful in dealing with social institutions. Their loose, informal structure encourages participation in discussion, and their supportive atmosphere elicits personal insight; but neither is very efficient in handling specific tasks. While they have been of fundamental value to the development of the movement, they also lead to a certain kind of political impotency. It is virtually impossible to coordinate a national action, or even a local one, assuming there could be any agreement on issues around which to coordinate one.

Individual rap groups tend to flounder when their numbers have exhausted the virtues of consciousness raising and decide they want to do something more concrete. The problem is that most groups are unwilling to change their structure when they change their tasks. They have accepted the ideology of "structurelessness" without realizing its limitations.

The resurgence of feminism tapped a major source of female energy, but the younger branch has not yet been able to channel it. Some women are able to create their own local-action projects, such as study groups, abortion counseling centers, bookstores, etc. Most are not, and the movement provides no coordinated or structured means of fitting into existing projects. Instead, such women either are recruited into NOW and other national organizations or drop out. New groups form and dissolve at an accelerating rate, creating a good deal of consciousness and very little action. The result is that most of the movement is proliferating underground. It often seems mired in introspection, but it is in fact creating a vast reservoir of conscious feminist sentiment which only awaits an appropriate opportunity for action.

In sum, the current status of the women's movement can be said to be structurally very much like it was in its incipient stages. That section which I have called the older branch remains attached to using the tools the system provides, while the younger branch simply proliferates horizontally, without creating new structures to handle new tasks.

REFERENCES

Adorno, L. W., et al. 1950. *The Authoritarian Personality*. New York: Harper.

Bird, Caroline. 1968. *Born Female: The High Cost of Keeping Women Down*. New York: David, McKay.

Blumer, Herbert. 1951. "Social Movements." In *New Outline of the Principles of Sociology*, edited by A. M. Lee. New York: Barnes & Noble.

————. 1957. "Collective Behavior." *Review of Sociology: Analysis of a Decade*, edited by Joseph B. Gittler. New York: Wiley.

Buck, Solon J. 1920. *The Agrarian Crusade*. New Haven, Conn.: Yale University Press.

Cantril, Hadley. 1941. *The Psychology of Social Movements*. New York: Wiley.

Coleman, James. 1957. *Community Conflict*. Glencoe, Ill.: Free Press.

Currie, Elliott, and Jerome H. Skolnick. 1970. "A Critical Note on Conceptions of Collective Behavior." *Annals of the American Academy of Political and Social Science* 391 (September): 34–45.

Dahrendorf, Ralf. 1959. *Class and Class Conflict in Industrial Society*. Palo Alto, Calif.: Stanford University Press.

Davies, James C. 1962. "Toward a Theory of Revolution." *American Sociological Review* 27 (1): 5–19.

Dawson, C. A., and W. E. Gettys. 1929. *An Introduction to Sociology*. New York: Ronald.

Edelsberg, Herman. 1965. "N.Y.U. 18th Conference on Labor." *Labor Relations Reporter* 61 (August): 253–55.

Ferriss, Abbott L. 1971. *Indicators of Trends in the Status of American Women*. New York: Russell Sage.

Firestone, Shulamith. 1971. *Dialectics of Sex*. New York: Morrow.

Friedan, Betty. 1963. *The Feminine Mystique*. New York: Dell.

————. 1967. "N.O.W.: How It Began." *Women Speaking* (April).

Griffiths, Martha. 1966. Speech of June 20, *Congressional Record*.

Gurr, Ted. 1970. *Why Men Rebel*. Princeton, N.J.: Princeton University Press.

Hayden, Casey, and Mary King. 1966. "A Kind of Memo." *Liberation* (April).

Heberle, Rudolph. 1951. *Social Movements*. New York: Appleton-Century-Crofts.

Hoffer, Eric. 1951. *The True Believer*. New York: Harper.

Hole, Judith, and Ellen Levine. 1971. *Rebirth of Feminism*. New York: Quadrangle.

Holzman, Abraham. 1963. *The Townsend Movement: A Political Study*. New York: Bookman.

Jackson, Maurice, Eleanora Petersen, James Bull, Sverre Monsen, and Patricia Richmond. "The Failure of an Incipient Social Movement." *Pacific Sociological Review* 3, no. 1 (Spring): 40.

Killian, Lewis M. 1964. "Social Movements." In *Handbook of Modern Sociology*, edited by R. E. L. Faris. Chicago: Rand McNally.

King, C. Wendell. 1956. *Social Movements in the United States*. New York: Random House.

King, Martin Luther, Jr. 1958. *Stride toward Freedom*. New York: Harper.

Kissinger, C. Clark, and Bob Ross. 1968. "Starting in '60: Or From SLID to Resistance." *New Left Notes*, June 10.

Kornhauser, William. 1959. *The Politics of Mass Society*. Glencoe, Ill.: Free Press.

Lang, Kurt, and Gladys Engle Lang. 1961. *Collective Dynamics*. New York: Cromwell.

Lionberger, Herbert F. 1960. *Adoption of New Ideas and Practices*. Ames: Iowa State University Press.

Lipset, Seymour M. 1959. *Agrarian Socialism*. Berkeley: University of California Press.

Lowi, Theodore J. 1971. *The Politics of Disorder*. New York: Basic.

Pinard, Maurice. 1968. "Mass Society and Political Movements: A New Formulation." *American Journal of Sociology* 73, no. 6 (May): 682–90.

————. 1971. *The Rise of a Third Party: A Study in Crisis Politics*. Englewood Cliffs, N.J.: Prentice-Hall.

Rogers, Everett M. 1962. *Diffusion of Innovations*. New York: Free Press.

Salisbury, Robert H. 1969. "An Exchange Theory of Interest Groups." *Midwest Journal of Political Science*, vol. 13, no. 1 (February).

Shils, Edward. 1970. "Center and Periphery." In *Selected Essays*. Center for Social Organization Studies. Department of Sociology, University of Chicago.

Smelser, Neil J. 1963. *Theory of Collective Behavior*. Glencoe, Ill.: Free Press.

Toch, Hans. 1965. *The Social Psychology of Social Movements*. Indianapolis: Bobbs-Merrill.

Turner, Ralph H. 1964. "Collective Behavior and Conflict: New Theoretical Frameworks." *Sociological Quarterly*.

Turner, Ralph H., and Lewis M. Killian. 1957. *Collective Behavior*. Englewood Cliffs, N.J.: Prentice-Hall.

5: The Radical Right

The Radical Right has customarily been described by social scientists as a "regressive," "resistance," or "reactionary" social movement. This movement, sometimes called the "Right Wing" or "Extreme Right," has generally been depicted as opposing social change or political, technological, and cultural innovations. Gary Rush presents one of the clearest definitions of the Right in America:

> The Extreme Right is a militant and millenarian political ideology, espoused by numerous Right-Wing groups and individuals, which maintains as an ideal the principle of "limited individualism"; this principle being articulated as opposition to "collectivism" in government, international relations, modern social principles, and modern social structure and operation.

Historically, the Radical Right has placed itself in opposition to various meliorative social forces. The decline of the small Main Street entrepreneur and the one-family farm has been a contributing factor leading to the rise of the Right. Political activity on the Right has been motivated by the advent of urban political domination, giant economic conglomerates, the United States as a world power, and the "new morality."[1]

The Radical Right's approach to social and political issues is influenced by two major beliefs: (1) "collectivism" is evil, and (2) a Hobbesian view that humanity is fundamentally selfish and destructive. As William Kornhauser indicates in **Politics of a Mass Society,** the Rightist position has been that increasing industrialization, governmental centralization, and political enfranchisement are forms of collectivization that erode the status of the traditional upholders of culture, freedom, and individual morality.[2] Given its ideological emphasis on the individual, the Right, by and large, attributes modernization to one or another conspiratorial group of individuals who are bent on imposing their will on an unsuspecting populace.

The conspiratorial group identified by the Right has changed over the years. Originally, segments of the post-Revolutionary American states feared an invasion

---

[1] See James McEvoy, *Radicals or Conservatives? The Contemporary American Right* (Chicago: Rand McNally, 1971); also Robert A. Rosenstone, ed., *Protest from the Right* (Beverly Hills, Calif.: Glencoe Press, 1968).
[2] William Kornhauser, *Politics of a Mass Society* (New York: The Free Press, 1959).

by French Jacobins, who were believed to be responsible for the storming of the Bastille. Also in the eighteenth century, the Free Masons, a fraternal guild, became the whipping boys of the traditionalists. In the nineteenth century, ethnic and religious groups, such as the Irish and Catholics, were attacked for supposedly attempting to hand the United States over to the Vatican.[3] After a time, the robber barons and Zionists were pointed to as supposedly spawning Machiavellian plots to take over the nation. The anti-Semitic pamphlet **The Elders of Zion,** which charges an international Zionist conspiracy, was a staple item in fundamentalist Right-Wing circles, such as the Ku Klux Klan and Gerald L. K. Smith's Committee of One Million.

Since 1917, following the October Revolution in Russia, the Right has looked on the "international Communist movement" as the source of most contemporary ills. After the Second World War, Robert Welch, founder of the John Birch Society, and Senator Joseph R. McCarthy both saw Communist infiltration and subversion of the U.S. government as causing set-backs in American foreign policy. McCarthy charged that the fall of China to Communist forces was due to subversion in the State Department. Robert Welch charged that Secretary of State John Foster Dulles had sold Southeast Asian countries "down the river into Communist hands, as cleverly as he knew how and as rapidly as he dared."[4] Domestic events, ranging from fluoridation of drinking water to rock 'n' roll music, have also been viewed by Right-Wing spokesmen, such as Billy James Hargis of the Christian Crusade, as flagrant Communist plots.[5]

The central attitudes of the Radical Right have been cogently presented by Gary Rush in the following essay. He notes that the **Weltanschauung** (world view) of the Radical Right is "atomistic," focusing on the behavior of individuals rather than of institutions. For example, Billy James Hargis attributes the success of the "Red Conspiracy" to individual loss of faith rather than to the failure of social institutions. Large conglomerates and governmental agencies are perceived as products of "grasping robber barons" or "power-mad bureaucrats" rather than as products of particular kinds of social systems. Even when the Radical Right criticises institutional relations it does so from the vantage point of individualism. Opposition to big government and to the welfare programs of national or local governments derives from the belief that individual initiative is thwarted by governmental "intervention." However, as Rush points out, the belief in individualism is limited to those in agreement with the Radical Right and excludes Leftists and members of minority groups. These individuals are viewed as perversely dissatisfied and destructive, thus justifying their repression. Indeed, the police forces of the state are heartily approved by the Radical Right and along with the military establishment are the only agencies of big government that are supported. Both the police and military establishments are seen as performing essentially the same function: protection of the "American way of life" from an external or internal threat.

The Right Wing sees itself as advocating a restoration of the past values and norms "that have made our country great"; its extreme nationalism and patriotism are seen as conferring a kind of legitimacy not found on the Left. For many Americans, the activism of the Right Wing appears to be a patriotic form of protest directed at the preservation of established social arrangements. The Radical Right's claim to be the guardian of tradition provides it with an additional advantage over the Left, for most individuals have some stake in maintaining the status quo. Individuals who feel themselves deprived of former status, or see "rules" of the economic or political "game" being changed to their disadvantage, are apt to

3 Joseph R. Gusfield, *The Symbolic Crusade* (Urbana: University of Illinois Press), 1963.

4 Quoted in Gene Grove, *Inside the John Birch Society* (Greenwich, Conn.: Gold Medal Books, 1969), p. 25.

5 R. Serge Denisoff, *Solid Gold: The Pop Record Industry* (New Brunswick, N.J.: Transaction Books, 1974), Chapter 8.

identify with the regressive policies of the Right.[6] Lewis Corey, in **Crisis of the Middle Class,** suggests that individuals most strongly committed to the existing rules will become politically more active than previously as social change takes place. Lipset, in **Political Man,** also reports that the staunchest supporters of Right-Wing ideologies were previously apolitical and apathetic.[7] The militancy of the New Left in many states has been matched by the growing popularity of Right-Wing candidates.[8] In the thirties, the social and international policies of Franklin D. Roosevelt engendered a plethora of Rightist organizations, such as the Silver Shirts, the Coughlinites, and the American Firsters. In the sixties, the Young Americans for Freedom was organized in response to the Students for a Democratic Society.

As a group of counterorganizations, the Right frequently mobilizes latent public resentment toward the changes advocated by liberal and Left-Wing movements. Both Stouffer and Lipset have found that a large portion of the American electorate has supported some tenets of the Radical Right. In January 1954, for example, a Gallup Poll found that 50 percent of those sampled were in favor of Senator Joseph McCarthy's hearings into communist infiltration of government.[9]

The emergence of Alabama Governor George Wallace's American Independent Party (AIP) provided a rallying point for the Radical Right. Wallace opposed "big" government and business. He could not find "a dime's worth of difference" between the two major political parties. He threatened to toss bureaucrats into the Potomac River. Wallace showed in the 1968 presidential campaign that he was a force to be reckoned with. In 1972, before he was shot in an attempted assassination, Wallace again provided an outlet for Right-Wing sentiment and overall political discontent. Much of the support for his position, as Lipset and Raab show, came from low-income and poorly educated segments of the electorate.

A return to the small-town style of life advocated by the Radical Right would entail an extensive program of decentralization involving social changes as disruptive and dramatic as any favored by the revolutionary Left. The advocacy of the use of force by the Minutemen, the California Rangers, and several segregationist organizations is as dysfunctional to the present political order as that of the most militant sectors of the Left.

In sum, the Radical Right can be viewed as a nativistic opposition movement that places primary emphasis on individual behavior and the maintenance of traditional values. The Right is most disturbed by any social trend toward greater centralization of economic and political institutions. Due to its seeming respectability and its appeal to the past, the Right has a polemical advantage over the **Left.**

6 Everett C. Ladd, "Radical Right: The White Collar Extremists," *South Atlantic Quarterly* 65 (1966): 314–24. See also S. M. Lipset and Earl Raab, *The Politics of Unreason: Right-Wing Extremism in America, 1790–1970* (New York: Harper & Row, 1970).

7 Seymour Martin Lipset, *Political Man: The Social Bases of Politics* (Garden City, N.Y., Anchor Books, 1963), pp. 108–21.

8 Lewis Corey, *The Crisis of the Middle Class* (New York: Covici, Friede, Publishers, 1935).

9 Samuel Stouffer, *Communism, Conformity, and Civil Liberties* (New York: Doubleday and Co., 1955). See also Nelson W. Polsby, "Toward an Explanation of McCarthyism," *Political Studies* (October 1960): 250–71; and S. M. Lipset, *op. cit.*

Toward a Definition
of the Extreme Right*

GARY B. RUSH

A considerable body of literature has accumulated on the phenomenon called, among other terms, The Far Right, The Radical Right, The Right Wing, and The Extreme Right. The term which will be used in the present discussion of this phenomenon will be "Extreme Right" (and the generic form, "Right-Wing Extremism") rather than the more usual "Radical Right." Accepted usage of the term "radical" connotes revolutionary, usually leftist politics. In view of the fact that the Extreme Right lies considerably to the right of center, the author feels that use of the term "Radical Right" contributes to semantic confusion. Moreover, the term "Extreme Right" is consistent with the notion of political extremism. Since the position that the Extreme Right is a form of extremist political expression will be central to this paper, the use of the adjective "extreme" seems more appropriate than that of "radical."

One of the most persistent impressions one gets when reading this literature is that there is a tacit assumption on the part of the writers concerned that everyone knows exactly what is being discussed. Such an assumption may be sufficient for impressionistic observations about the Extreme Right, but if any intensive and scientific study is to be made of this phenomenon, a clear definition of what is to be studied would be in order. No study can claim to be "scientific" unless an explicit definition of the subject to be studied is given. This logical necessity of a definition has been pointed out by Cohen and Nagel:

> Logically, definitions aim to lay bare the principal features or structure of a concept, partly in order to make it definite, to delimit it from

* A revised and expanded version of a paper presented at the annual meeting of the Pacific Sociological Association, Portland, Oregon, April 25–27, 1963. The investigation of which this paper is a part was supported by a Public Health Service fellowship (number MPM 17-207 C1) from the Institute of Mental Health, Public Health Service.

"Toward a Definition of the Extreme Right" by G. B. Rush is reprinted from *Pacific Sociological Review*, Vol. 6, No. 2 (Fall, 1963), pp. 64–73 by permission of the Publisher, Sage Publications, Inc.

other concepts, and partly in order to make possible a systematic exploration of the subject matter with which it deals.[1]

In the present investigation, the focus of attention will be on the psychological rather than on the associational aspects of the Extreme Right. This is deemed advisable because the Extreme Right is composed of *many* groups advocating many *different* (and sometimes opposing) programs. Therefore, although material related to specific Right-Wing organizations will be used for illustrative purposes, no one such organization, or group of organizations, will be used as the basis of this investigation. Instead, we will be concerned with the *ideological* and *attitudinal* nature of Right-Wing Extremism. The relationship between attitude, which lies within the individual, and ideology, which goes beyond the individual, is an inseparable one. Attitudes, in fact, may be regarded as indicators of the individual's ideological system. This frame of reference is exemplified by the way in which these concepts will be used in the present investigation. The term "ideology" will be used as it is defined by Adorno and his associates:

> The term ideology is used in this book, in the way that is common in current literature, to stand for an organization of opinions, attitudes, and values—a way of thinking about man and society. . . . Ideologies have an existence independent of any individual; and those which exist at a particular time are results both of historical processes and of contemporary social events.[2]

As the above definition indicates, attitude is a component of ideology. Usage of the term "attitude" in this investigation will follow that proposed by Krech and Crutchfield, who define attitudes as:

> . . . enduring systems of positive or negative evaluations, emotional feelings, and pro or con action tendencies with respect to social objects.[3]

In light of the foregoing discussion, the problem of the present investigation will be to establish a definition of the Extreme Right—one which defines this phenomenon as an ideology (specifically, as a political ideology), and one which may be operationalized in terms of attitudinal indicators. The first concern of this investigation will be to analyze those definitions of the Extreme Right that are currently in use, with a view to developing a definition capable of meeting these requirements.

CURRENT DEFINITIONS, EXPLICIT OR IMPLICIT

All of the definitions which will be examined here seem to satisfy the requirement of defining the Extreme Right as an ideology. Some explicitly

[1] Morris Cohen and Ernest Nagel, *An Introduction to Logic and Scientific Method*, New York: Harcourt Brace Jovanovich, 1934, pp. 231–232.
[2] T. W. Adorno, *et al., The Authoritarian Personality*, New York: Harper and Brothers, 1950, p. 2.
[3] David Krech, Richard S. Crutchfield, and Egerton L. Ballachey, *Individual in Society: A Textbook of Social Psychology* (a major revision of *Theory and Problems of Social Psychology* by David Krech and Richard S. Crutchfield), New York: McGraw Hill Book Company, Inc., 1962, p. 139.

contain the terms "ideology" or "movement," the latter of which, in the impressionistic sense of the word, connotes an ideological organization of beliefs, values, opinions, feelings, etc. about some social object. Others imply the concept of ideology in the use of words such as "dissent," "discontent," "conviction," and so forth. However, all of these definitions contain shortcomings with respect to the definiens, not the least of which is the inclusion of terms too vague to be expressed in operational terms. This emphasis on operationalism is not meant to imply, of course, that operational definitions are the only kind that have a place in sociological research. In any investigation of social phenomena one has to begin somewhere, and certainly a logical starting point is an *ad hoc* classification of what is to be studied. This kind of definition facilitates the meaningful organization of the researcher's observations and helps him to limit his analysis to the specific problem at hand. However, such an approach to the definitional question is not sufficient for more systematic investigations requiring explicit indicators of the subject under study.

Thus, although the definitions considered here serve to focus attention on certain characteristics of the Extreme Right, they all suffer shortcomings which invalidate them for the particular purposes of the present investigation. These definitions may be grouped according to three weaknesses: phenomenological misinterpretations, lack of equivalence between the definiendum and the definiens, and vague or obscure referents.[4]

1. Phenomenological misinterpretations in the following definitions arise from two sources—either their authors failed to take into account certain properties of the Extreme Right in their analyses, or events subsequent to the formulation of the definitions have rendered them invalid. The first definition to be considered is the following statement regarding Right-Wing groups:

> What all these groups are at heart is the same old isolationist, Anglophobe, Germanophile revolt of radical Populist lunatic-fringers against the eastern, educated, Anglicized elite.[5]

First, while it is true that certain points advocated by Right-Wing groups are isolationist in nature (*e.g.*, withdrawal from the United Nations), this concept seems inconsistent with the aggressive militancy of the Extreme Right about foreign affairs. This militancy goes beyond the position of a "world-wide Monroe Doctrine," and would have the United States be the aggressor nation in war against the Communist bloc. Second, whereas American Populism of the late 1880's was basically a revolutionary agrarian movement, directed largely against urban interest groups, it is doubtful that "populist" can adequately define the Extreme Right of today. Although considerable support for the Extreme Right comes from rural areas of the South and the Mid-West, it also draws a great deal of support from the

---

[4] The second and third of these points are discussed in Cohen and Nagel, *op. cit.*, pp. 238–241. The authors also draw attention to the problems of circular definitions and definitions expressed in negative terms. However, neither of these two problems are evidenced in the definitions considered in this section.

[5] Peter Viereck, "The Revolt Against the Elite," in Daniel Bell (ed.), *The New American Right*, New York: Criterion Books, 1955, p. 95.

urban upper classes (*e.g.*, business executives, entrepreneurs, and the D.A.R.).

This problem of defining the Extreme Right in terms of opposition to the upper classes also characterizes Parsons' definition of McCarthyism, which may be taken as an example of Extreme Right expression. In Parsons' terms, McCarthyism was:

> . . . both a movement supported by certain vested-interest elements *and* a popular revolt against the upper classes.[6]

As will be demonstrated later in this paper, a major characteristic of the Extreme Right is its opposition to certain socialistic trends in modern society. The bureaucratic control and management and the higher tax rates that are concomitant with this modern trend would conceivably tend to alienate the upper classes, particularly the "ragged aristocracy," from the main stream of American politics, at least from an economic point of view. Thus, there would appear to be greater justification for placing the old, elite classes on the same side of the political fence as the Extreme Right, rather than in opposition. This nature of Extreme Right support is documented by Janson and Eismann, who observe:

> First to produce a sizeable following for the Far Right were the Southern and Southwestern bastions of religious fundamentalism and political conservatism and the upper-class suburbs of urban areas.[7]

A final point regarding Parsons' definition is his reference to "vested-interest elements." This concept would be difficult to interpret in operational terms, since Parsons does not indicate what these elements are, nor the nature of their interests.[8]

The last definition of this type to be considered is explicitly-stated and was arrived at through an extensive survey of the literature.

> In summary, the American Right Wing may be said to include all those who share the conviction that the relationship of government to the individual should be severely limited.[9]

Although this definition is accurate as far as it goes, it only partially characterizes the phenomenon of the Extreme Right. Its limitation becomes evident when we observe that extremist opposition to government is contradicted by the fact that the Extreme Right tolerates or even encourages "big government" in matters of national security or national defence. Moreover, this definition would also characterize left-wing anarchists.

2. The rule regarding equivalence between the definiendum and the definiens is expressed by Cohen and Nagel as follows:

[6] Talcott Parsons, "Social Strains in America," in Bell, *op. cit.*, p. 136.
[7] Donald Janson and Bernard Eismann, *The Far Right,* New York: McGraw-Hill Book Company, Inc., 1963, p. 7.
[8] Although this point actually belongs in the section on "vague or obscure referents," it was included here to avoid repetition and confusion.
[9] Ralph E. Ellsworth and Sarah M. Harris, *The American Right Wing: A Report to the Fund for the Republic,* Washington, D.C.: Public Affairs Press, 1962, p. 41.

A definition must give the essence of that which is to be defined. The definiens must be equivalent to the definiendum—it must be applicable to everything of which the definiendum can be predicated, and applicable to nothing else.[10]

Of the definitions reviewed, two do not appear to meet this requirement. The first is given by Hofstadter who defines the Extreme Right as a:

> . . . dissent . . . [which] can most accurately be called pseudo-conservative . . . because its exponents, although they believe themselves to be conservative and usually employ the rhetoric of conservatism, show signs of serious and restless dissatisfaction with American life, traditions and institutions.[11]

Hofstadter's net would appear to be cast too wide to catch only the Extreme Right. Believing oneself to be a conservative, and being dissatisfied with American life, traditions and institutions could conceivably characterize the political attitude of many conservatives who are not Right-Wing Extremists. However, before summarily rejecting the concept of "pseudo-conservative," a closer investigation of who the pseudo-conservative is should be made. The concept is taken from Adorno, who defined the pseudo-conservative as follows:

> The pseudo-conservative is a man who, in the name of upholding traditional American values and institutions and defending them against more or less fictitious dangers, consciously or unconsciously aims at their abolition.[12]

This definition, like so many of a psychological nature, falls far short of one which can be operationalized in sociological terms. What are "traditional American values and institutions" and "more or less fictitious dangers"? Do all those who uphold these values and institutions and defend them against dangers, fictitious or otherwise, aim at their abolition? Conversely, do those who aim at their abolition uphold and defend them? Too much latitude is given by the phrases "more or less" and "consciously or unconsciously." Hofstadter himself asks, and answers, the question of who is a pseudo-conservative:

> Who is the pseudo-conservative and what does he want? It is impossible to identify him by class, for the pseudo-conservative impulse can be found in practically all classes in society, although its power probably rests largely upon its appeal to the less educated members of the middle class. The ideology of the pseudo-conservative can be characterized but not defined, because the pseudo-conservative tends to be more than ordinarily incoherent about politics.[13]

Thus, aside from the basic problem of lack of equivalence in Hofstadter's

---

[10] *Op. cit.*, p. 238.
[11] Richard Hofstadter, "The Pseudo-Conservative Revolt," in Bell, *op. cit.*, pp. 34–35.
[12] *Ibid.*, p. 35. The original source is Adorno, *et al.*, *op. cit.*, p. 676.
[13] *Ibid.*, pp. 35–36.

definition, it would appear that the problems inherent in operationalizing the concept of "pseudo-conservative" itself further rule against the use of this definition in the present investigation.

The other view of the Extreme Right which falls into this category is one given by the Marxist historian Aptheker in his discussion of McCarthyism:

> [McCarthyism] . . . is the name of an ultra-reactionary, a fascist, political movement whose main stock-in-trade is anti-Communism . . . McCarthyism is American fascism.[14]

Although "anti-Communism" is a recurrent theme in the expressions of Extreme Right groups, it is not sufficient as the central criterion for defining the Extreme Right. There are many individuals and groups in this country who are anti-Communist, even militantly so, who are not Right-Wing Extremists. The pitfall of defining the Extreme Right in terms of "anti-Communism" is that of "mistaking the symptom for the disease." Notwithstanding the fact that anti-Communism is one of the many attitudinal characteristics of the Extreme Right, the label of "Communist" is also a convenient and culturally approved brush with which to tar many other elements in the society in order to legitimate the extremist's opposition to them. An additional point in Aptheker's definition may be referred to here, although it actually relates to the problem of phenomenological misinterpretation. The point is that Aptheker's definition of McCarthyism as American fascism might be difficult to document. To be sure, McCarthy's demagoguery was reminiscent of Hitler's, and much of McCarthy's overt following came from those who had supported fascist and semi-fascist movements in the thirties and forties. However, as Richard Rovere points out, there are crucial points on which the differences between Hitler and McCarthy are more striking than the similarities.

> Hitler had a program for the coming millennium; McCarthy had no program for tomorrow morning. Hitler's aim was to win control of the machinery of state; it is still arguable as to whether McCarthy was up to anything of quite this magnitude. He never encouraged direct action by his followers; he did not organize uniformed groups or even raggle-taggle street fighters. Politically, he never tried to organize outside the existing party structure, and there are reasons for supposing that he never intended to do so.[15]

Commenting on McCarthy's political philosophy, Rovere writes:

> He was not, for example, totalitarian in any significant sense, or even reactionary. These terms apply mainly to the social and economic order, and the social and economic order didn't interest him in the slightest. If he was anything at all in the realm of ideas, principles, doctrines, he was a species of nihilist; he was an essentially destructive force, a revolutionist without any revolutionary vision, a rebel without a cause.[16]

[14] Herbert Aptheker, *The Era of McCarthyism*, New York: Marzani and Munsell, Inc., 1962, pp. 146, 152.
[15] Richard H. Rovere, *Senator Joe McCarthy*, Cleveland, Ohio: The World Publishing Company (Meridian Books), 1960, p. 19.
[16] *Ibid.*, p. 8.

Thus, at least to the extent that McCarthyism may be regarded as an example of Extreme Right expression, the use of the terms "anti-Communist" and "fascist" would appear inappropriate in defining the phenomenon under study.

3. Four additional definitions may be considered under the heading of "vague or obscure referents." By this is meant the introduction in the definiens of substantive examples which are not supported by reference to a reality situation, or the use of vague and general concepts which are not clearly defined or established in prior or subsequent discussion. The first definition of this type to be considered is one advanced by Daniel Bell. He describes the Extreme Right as an example of:

> . . . protest movements . . . [of] new divisions [within the society] created by the status anxieties of new middle class groups. . . .[17]

Thus, Bell seems to be defining the Extreme Right in terms of "status politics." This concept is not uncommon in political sociology, and has been advanced by writers such as Daniel Bell, Richard Hofstadter, and S. M. Lipset. Lipset has defined the term as follows:

> Status politics . . . refers to political movements whose appeal is to the not uncommon resentments of individuals or groups who desire to maintain or improve their social status.[18]

This concept may have considerable utility as an "orienting" concept for the present investigation.[19] A major problem in Bell's definition, however, is created by the use of the terms "new divisions" and "new middle class groups." The nature of these new divisions within society is not made clear, nor is there any evidence given to indicate that they really exist. If such heuristic constructs are to have utility in scientific research, there must be some way of "grounding them in reality." Since this has not been done in Bell's discussion his definition would not appear suitable for the purposes of the present investigation. Moreover, Bell's statement does not comply with the logical conditions of a definition since he confounds definition with hypothesis. That is, the statement, "created by the status anxieties of new middle class groups," seems to be an implicit hypothesis.

Riesman and Glazer view Right-Wing Extremism as an expression of the discontent of what they call the "discontented classes."[20] This discontent centers in the new middle class which has evolved as a result of fifteen years of prosperity. This definition suffers from the same shortcoming as Daniel Bell's. That is, there is no elucidation of what are the "discontented classes" and no evidence is given to indicate that such classes really exist.

[17] Daniel Bell, "Interpretations of American Politics," in Bell, *op. cit.*, pp. 5, 29.
[18] S. M. Lipset, "The Sources of the 'Radical Right,'" in Bell, *op. cit.*, p. 168.
[19] This paper is part of a larger research project, in which a "status crystallization" model is used to predict the incidence of Right-Wing Extremist political attitudes with respect to individuals. The orienting nature of the concept of "status politics" refers to its apparent relationship to the concepts of "status crystallization" and "status inconsistency.
[20] David Riesman and Nathan Glazer, "The Intellectuals and the Discontented Classes," in Bell, *op. cit.*, p. 61.

Lipset, in his paper in the Bell volume, makes no attempt at a formal definition of the Extreme Right. However, he does state:

> These [right-wing] groups are but one more manifestation of American political and moral activity, much like the popular attempts to ban liquor, gambling, or immorality in comic strips.[21]

This definition could have value in studying Right-Wing Extremism since it suggests that attention should be focused on the moralistic elements in this type of political behavior. However, its application would require a prior definition of the vague term, "political and moral activity," which is not given in Lipset's discussion.

In another paper, published elsewhere, Lipset defines the Extreme Right, specifically McCarthyism, as an:

> . . . irrational protest ideology [espoused by discontented] . . . declining 'liberal' classes living in declining areas.[22]

In addition to the questionable utility of the term "irrational" (*i.e.*, against what criteria is the rationality of the Extreme Right to be judged?), the reference to "declining 'liberal' classes" poses the same problem as the previous definitions in that there is little or no evidence given to indicate that these social groups actually do exist and can be clearly identified.

In summarizing this review of definitions of the Extreme Right, the following points may be made.

1. Very few *explicit* definitions of the Extreme Right have been made to date.

2. A number of *implicit* definitions may be drawn out of the existing literature on the Extreme Right.

3. Many of these definitions have a potentially valuable "orienting" function in that they direct attention to certain significant characteristics of the Extreme Right.

4. For a number of reasons, none of the definitions in their present form adequately define the Extreme Right for the purposes of the present investigation. Either because of phenomenological misinterpretations, lack of equivalence between the definiendum and the definiens, or the use of vague or obscure referents, none of the definitions could be readily expressed in operational terms.

In view of these considerations, the next task must be to define the Extreme Right in terms that will permit representation by operational indicators.

TOWARD A DEFINITION OF THE EXTREME RIGHT

A basic assumption of the present investigation is that the Extreme Right is essentially political in nature. The fact that this country has a two-party political system tends to obscure the possibility that a variety of political

---

[21] S. M. Lipset, *op. cit.*, p. 181.
[22] S. M. Lipset, "Social Stratification and 'Right-Wing Extremism,'" *British Journal of Sociology*, 10 (December, 1959), p. 28.

attitudes can and, in fact, do exist. In countries having a multi-party system, such as France, institutionalized channels of expression for various types of political attitudes are manifest. Consequently, a wide range of political attitude is laid open to investigation by an equally wide range of political behavior. In the American political system, on the other hand, splinter parties operating through alternative channels of political expression have not been successful in gaining direct political power, and are either short-lived or doomed to obscurity. The necessity for the two dominant political parties to compete for the support of a heterogeneous electorate tends to reduce the difference between them, and institutionalized channels of extremist political expression are forestalled from developing within the existing political framework since they would be antithetical to the necessary "middle of the road" posture of both parties.[23] The militancy and millenarianism of the Extreme Right reflect the "crises of legitimacy" to which this element in the American political system is exposed. Frustrated in gaining access to formal and institutionalized political power, the Extreme Right has pinned its hope on a policy of militant and unilateral action designed to bring about desired changes in the political system in a not-too-distant millenium.[24]

Further evidence of the political nature of the Extreme Right lies in the fact that most of the changes which extremist groups advocate are designed to be implemented primarily through the political framework of society. In addition, the Extreme Right seeks alignment with institutionalized conservative political forces. This is evidenced, for example, in Right-Wing support for Senators Goldwater, Tower, and Eastland.

In sum, then, the Extreme Right may be regarded as an as yet non-institutionalized political ideology. The use of the term "ideology" here is in the sense in which it is defined earlier—an organization of attitudes, opinions, and values about society. In the literature on social movements, ideology is usually distinguished from the specific program of change that a group advocates as, for example, in the following statement from Turner and Killian:

> At the outset we may distinguish the particular program of change that a movement advocates from the conception of society through which it justifies that program. The latter we shall call the *ideology* of the movement . . . .[25]

This conception of ideology will thus permit a study of the attitudinal char-

[23] Daniel Bell, in "Interpretations of American Politics," *op. cit.*, pp. 4–5, discusses this situation as follows:

"Perhaps the most decisive fact about politics in the United States is the two-party system. Each party is like some huge bazaar, with hundreds of hucksters clamoring for attention. But while life within the bazaars flows freely and licenses are easy to obtain, all trading has to be conducted within the tents; the ones who hawk their wares outside are doomed to few sales. This fact gains meaning when we consider one of the striking facts about American life: America has thrown up countless social movements, but few political parties; in contradiction to European political life, few of the social movements have been able to transform themselves into political parties."

[24] This problem of inability to gain formal political power and recognition is discussed in S. M. Lipset, *Political Man*, Garden City, New York: Doubleday and Company, Inc., 1960, chapter III, "Social Conflict, Legitimacy, and Democracy," pp. 77–96.

[25] Ralph M. Turner and Lewis M. Killian, *Collective Behavior,* Englewood Cliffs, New Jersey: Prentice-Hall, Inc., 1957, p. 331.

acteristics of the Extreme Right without going into a detailed analysis of the content of the *programs* of Right-Wing groups. The utility of this approach has been referred to earlier in this paper.

The next phase of this investigation will be to establish, by the process of "intuitive induction,"[26] a definition capable of being operationalized which will delimit the Extreme Right from other phenomena. To this end, we shall attempt to discern a number of the outstanding characteristics of the Extreme Right. The most extensive survey of such characteristics published to date is that of Ellsworth and Harris.[27] To those which they have identified, I have added a number drawn from my own surveys of available literature.[28] The initial investigation took the form of a content analysis of this material to determine what the Extreme Right advocated or supported and what they opposed or rejected. As might be expected, a considerable overlapping of the attitudes expressed by different groups and individuals occurred. However, some twenty-eight relatively distinct attitudes, mostly negativistic, appeared manifest. A preliminary inspection of these attitudes suggested that they fell under four general headings.[29] These hypothesized categories and the attitudes constituting them are as follows:

I. *Attitudes regarding government:*
    Opposition to strong central government.[30]
    Belief in strong government and leaders, but at the local level.

[26] Basically, this process consists of making empirical observations of a phenomenon in order to arrive at a basic knowledge of it. For a discussion of this form of reasoning, see Morris R. Cohen and Ernest Nagel, *op cit.*, pp. 273–275.

[27] Ralph E. Ellsworth and Sarah M. Harris, *op. cit.*

[28] A comprehensive list of more than 1800 Right-Wing Groups is given in *The First National Directory of "Rightist" Groups, Publications and Some Individuals in the United States,* fourth edition, Los Angeles: Alert Americans Association, 1961. The major sources investigated in the present survey are speeches made by acknowledged Extreme Right spokesmen; pamphlets published by *America's Future, Inc.,* New Rochelle, New York; pamphlets published by *Bible Recordings, Inc.,* Baltimore, Maryland; transcripts of testimony given before the *House Committee on Un-American Activities;* radio broadcasts and newsletters of *The 20th Century Reformation Hour,* Rev. Carl McIntire, Director, Collingswood, New Jersey; "Dawn," a monthly newspaper published by *Independence Foundation, Inc.,* Portland, Indiana; the "Blue Book" and monthly bulletins published by *The John Birch Society, Inc.,* Belmont, Mass.; Frank J. Donner, *The Un-Americans,* New York: Ballantine Books, 1961; Gene Grove, *Inside the John Birch Society,* Greenwich, Conn.: Fawcett Publications, 1961; Telford Taylor, *Grand Inquest,* New York: Ballantine Books, 1961; Richard Vahan, *The Truth About The John Birch Society,* New York: McFadden Books, 1962; Donald Janson and Bernard Eismann, *The Far Right, op. cit.*

[29] A subsequent cluster analysis of attitudinal indicators, too extensive to report in the present paper, substantiated the division of Extreme Right attitudes into these four categories.

[30] It must be borne in mind that this opposition is selective. The Right-Wing Extremist's conception of the function of the state is not unlike that of the classical liberal who saw the state as a protector of property and a preserver of order, much like a night watchman, rather than as an entity which imposed positive obligations upon individuals. Thus, the extremist's major opposition to the federal government is in those areas where he is told what he *should do* (*e.g.,* desegregation). On the other hand, Right-Wing support is given to strong government in matters pertaining to security (*e.g.,* congressional investigating committees). For an interesting discussion of this conception of the state, see Harry K. Girvetz, *From Wealth to Welfare: The Evolution of Liberalism,* Stanford, California: Stanford University Press, 1950, pp. 68–78.

Dissatisfaction with the United States Supreme Court.
Opposition to the Federal Reserve System.
Conviction that there is corruption in government.
General distrust of the federal government.
Opposition to increased government spending, higher taxes.
Opposition to metropolitan government.
Opposition to urban renewal.

II. *Attitudes regarding international relations:*
Opposition to foreign entanglements.
Dedication to an "America First" approach.
Opposition to the United Nations.
Opposition to foreign aid, Point Four Programs, NATO, etc.

III. *Attitudes regarding modern social principles:*
Opposition to modern education.
Opposition to racial integration.
Suspicion of international collectivism (*e.g.*, the Common Market).
Militant anti-Communism.
Political cynicism.[31]
Opposition to "social gospel" Protestantism.

IV. *Attitudes regarding modern social structure and operation:*[32]
Opposition to socialized medicine.
Opposition to collective bargaining.
Support of "right to work" proposals.
Support of "free enterprise."
Opposition to "full employment."
Opposition to the "welfare state."
Opposition to federal aid to health and education.
Suspicion of modern "progressive" innovations.[33]

The main theme running through these attitudes appears to be a general opposition to certain forms of "collectivism." This view is strengthened by a review of statements made by some of the leaders of Extreme Right groups. Robert Welch, for example, devotes all of section two of his *Blue Book* to the "cancer of collectivism,"[34] Leslie Fleming, President of the Oregon John Birch Society, states that the program of the Society is ". . . individuality opposing collectivism,"[35] and R. K. Scott, President of America's Future,

---

[31] This attitude refers primarily to the attitudes and motivations of politicians and to the operation of the political system in general rather than to any specific political issue.

[32] A distinction should be drawn between this category and the preceding one regarding "modern social principles." The latter refers primarily to a generalized attitudinal framework through which the Right-Wing Extremist regards his society. "Modern social structure and operation," on the other hand, refers more to specific programmatic policies, particulary those of the contemporary liberal state.

[33] *E.g.*, fluoridation, psychiatry, pastoral counseling, mental health programs, mental hospitals, etc.

[34] Robert Welch, *The Blue Book of the John Birch Society*, sixth printing, 1961, Section Two, "But Let's Look Deeper . . . ," pp. 41–55.

[35] Excerpted from the transcript of a speech delivered by Leslie Fleming, President of

Incorporated, writes of his organization's ". . . unbending opposition to all forms of collectivism including the communist conspiracy."[36] The kinds of collectivism opposed by the Extreme Right are primarily Communism and the type of contemporary liberalism practiced in the United States. With a few notable exceptions (such as the Tennessee Valley Authority and the Bonneville Power Administration), contemporary American liberalism does not tend toward governmental ownership and management of the means for the production and distribution of goods. Rather, the governmental role in the economy tends more toward increasing control and regulation while relying, for the most part, on a market system economy and its corollaries of private property and private profit.

In addition to this control or regulatory aspect, Extreme Right opposition also extends to an underlying philosophy of contemporary American liberalism—one which may be called the "ameliorative" or welfare function of the state. This function refers not only to an acceptance of responsibility on the part of the state for the basic well-being of its members, but also to systematic planning aimed at providing fuller lives for *all* members of the state. Extreme Right antagonism to this kind of welfare function, or "quasi-paternalism," reflects not only a practical opposition to taxation—a requisite for the financing of welfare and aid programs—but also a belief that man will not be motivated to work unless he suffers deprivation. This belief has its roots in the *classical* liberal view of the psychological nature of man.[37] According to this view, man is motivated by self-interest ("egoism") or pleasure ("hedonism"). From this, it follows that purposive activity must somehow be induced and that unless some enticement is offered by way of pleasure or advantage man will remain apathetic and inert ("quietism"). However, man is also basically rational ("intellectualism"). Given a choice of alternatives, reason will balance the quality of pleasure or pain involved, and conduct will follow that course of action which carries the greatest pleasure or the least pain. In order to motivate man to purposive activity, the pains of deprivation must therefore exceed those of work. If, on the other hand, public welfare and assistance programs permit man to consume without toiling, the pleasures derived will be so great as to encourage perpetual indolence.

It is against the collectivistic or socialistic principles of contemporary American liberalism that the main force of Extreme Right expression is directed. Since a great deal of the policy of the present liberal government is based on these principles, it is understandable that the federal government should be a primary target of the Extreme Right. However, tendencies toward socialism at *any* governmental level are decried. At the state level, public (*i.e.*, governmental) management of state supported institutions (par-

---

the Oregon John Birch Society, at Clark College, Vancouver, Washington, February 26, 1962. Published in *Pace: The Emerald Features Supplement*, University of Oregon, Thursday, May 17, 1962, under the following affirmation: "This is the views (sic) of myself and the John Birch Society. LESLIE FLEMING (signed), Box 3174, Eugene, Oregon, May 5, 1962."

[36] Quoted from a personal communication received from R. K. Scott, President of *America's Future, Incorporated*, 542 Main Street, New Rochelle, New York, March 12, 1963.

[37] For a full discussion of the nature of this view and its consequences for classical liberal thought, see Harry K. Girvetz, *op. cit.*, esp. pp. 7–27 and 28–42.

ticularly educational institutions) is closely scrutinized. At this level, however, extremists must walk a very thin line since "States' Rights" is a battle cry against the extension of federal government power. Socialistic tendencies at the local government level (such as urban renewal—a joint federal-local project—and metropolitan government) are also opposed by the Extreme Right, primarily for tactical reasons. This is understandable in light of the extremist conviction, articulated by [Radical Right] spokesmen such as [ministers] Carl McIntire, Billy Hargis, Fred Schwartz and [ex-FBI agent] W. Cleon Skousen, that the fight against collectivism must begin at the local or "grass roots" level.

At the international level, the greatest source of concern to the Extreme Right is the United Nations and America's participation in it. In the eyes of the extremist, that body is collectivism incarnate, and practically every group on the Extreme Right has expressed vehement opposition to it. American aid to foreign countries is also protested, being regarded in the same light as social welfare on the domestic scene.

The militant anti-Communism of the Extreme Right can also be understood under this frame of reference, since the Right Wing considers that Communism is either the polar extension of socialism, or, what is worse, that socialism is merely Communism by another name. This approach to the anti-Communism of the Extreme Right also explains the bias against intellectuals, liberals, modernists, and progressives. Since these are the main groups advocating socialism, it is understandable that they be labelled as "Communist" and treated as such.

By the same token, it is natural that most of the modern philosophies and programs advocated by these liberal groups be suspect in the eyes of the Extreme Right. Thus, "progressive education," a modern innovation, is regarded by the extremists as a means through which the socialistic, liberal elements in the society are attempting to indoctrinate the younger generation with their insidious beliefs. Higher education, primarily in the liberal arts and the social sciences, is also a target of the Extreme Right. Similarly, modern innovations such as pastoral counseling, mental health programs, psychiatry, mental hospitals, and even fluoridation are all regarded as part of a modern collectivistic conspiracy.

What the extremist proposes as an alternative to this collectivism is a political state in which the individual is the final arbiter of truth. A consistent and militant theme in the agitation of the Extreme Right is for the individual to awake, to arouse himself from the apathy to which he has been led, to be aware of the dangers which surround him, and to take action against those dangers, as well as against the leaders who have brought him to this pass. The notion of an enslaved people dominated by corrupt leaders is a recurrent one in Extreme Right expression. The Right-Wing Extremist views his world in terms of a simplistic, black-and-white dichotomy. In his eyes, an impersonal, rationalized, complex, technical, bureaucratic "society" is destroying the simple virtue of man as an "individual."[38]

[38] This extremist "world view" has been recognized by several of the contributors, in their 1962 articles, to Daniel Bell (ed.), The Radical Right (The New American Right expanded and updated), Garden City, New York: Doubleday and Company, Inc., 1963. See for example, Daniel Bell, "The Dispossessed," pp. 1–38; David Riesman,

Given this picture of the extremist "world view," the philosophy underlying the Extreme Right may be discerned. The essence of this philosophy
lies in the Right-Wing Extremist's *atomistic,* as opposed to *organicist,* view
of the relationship between man and society. "Atomism" refers to the conception that the whole is nothing more than the sum of its parts. "Organicism," on the other hand, refers to the conception of the whole as
something more than the sum of its constituent parts—a reality *sui generis.*
Applied to society, "atomism" is the view that individuals make society;
"organicism" is the view that society makes individuals.[39] Girvetz has summarized the atomistic philosophy as follows:

> The classical liberals, in accord with their atomistic outlook, re-
> garded social institutions as the handiwork of pre-existing individuals
> whose characteristic mental and emotional endowments antedate the
> social arrangements into which these individuals enter. Even rights
> are often regarded as natural, that is to say, as antedating the state.
> Social arrangements affect individual human nature only superficially.
> They are additative and artificial, and their importance is largely nega-
> tive, an importance which consists mostly of removing obstacles which
> might prevent individuals from achieving complete self-expression. The
> relationship between individuals and society is an external one; the
> individual with his various propensities and faculties is given, and
> society is an arrangement of convenience, whereby faculties operate
> more effectively and propensities are more likely to find fruition. To
> repeat, social institutions are created by the fiat of self-contained in-
> dividuals; they are instruments, even expedients, which the individual
> can employ or discard without fundamentally altering his own nature.[40]

This quotation, although somewhat extensive, is included in its entirety because of its central importance to the thesis which is being developed in
these pages. This atomistic philosophy, together with the classical psychological view of the nature of man discussed earlier, constitute the basic
identifying characteristic of the Extreme Right—a characteristic which will
be referred to herein as "individualism." Individualism is defined by Webster
as:

> A theory or policy having primary regard for individual rights, spe-

---

"The Intellectuals and the Discontented Classes: Some Further Reflections," pp.
115–134; Talcott Parsons, "Social Strains in America: A Postscript," pp. 193–199.

[39] Theories of society based on these polarities have characterized almost the entire history of social thought. Although their roots go back into classical philosophy, the
development of atomism and organicism may be conveniently traced from their
Eighteenth Century formulations. The former is evidenced in the writings of men
such as Hobbes (1588–1679), Rousseau (1712–1778), Burke (1729–1797), Bentham
(1748–1832), and, in its Nineteenth Century specification, Spencer (1820–1903).
Organicism may be traced through the writings of Locke (1632–1704), Hume (1711–
1776), Blackstone (1723–1780), DeMaistre (1754–1821), DeBonald (1754–1840),
Comte (1798–1857) and Durkheim (1855–1917). The empirical validity of such
polarities is an academic problem, and one which need not concern us here. What is
essential is the fact that the Right-Wing Extremist *does view his society in these terms.*
That he does so has important implications for the study of his attitudes and behavior,
for, as W. I. Thomas has pointed out in his concept of "definition of the situation,"
what men believe to be true are true in their consequences.

[40] Harry K. Girvetz, *op. cit.,* p. 23.

cifically one maintaining the independence of initiative, action and interests. . . .[41]

This individualism is not unlike that discussed by Max Weber in his essay on the Protestant Ethic.[42] Specifically, it is epitomized in the Ascetic Protestant attitude that the success or failure of every man, both in this world and in the next, rests on his own individual initiative. This is the attitude which finds expression in the Right-Wing Extremist's opposition to "assistance" programs and his abhorrance of the maxim, "from each according to his ability, to each according to his need." It is from the expression of this attitude by Right-Wing Extremists that many writers deduce the notion of "regression" as a dominant characteristic of the Extreme Right—a desire to return to the nineteenth century. In maintaining this principle of individualism in opposition to what has earlier been described under the heading of "collectivism," the Right-Wing Extremist is opposing a system which would not only take away the fruits of one's labors (through taxation) to distribute it to those who did nothing to earn it (through social welfare), but would also restrict (through government control) one's prerogative to act in his own best interest in all matters.

The form of individualism which is advocated by the Extreme Right is selective in nature. First, independence of initiative, action and interest would not be extended to all individuals or groups. Minority groups would be excluded, as would those individuals who did not share the Extreme Right's opposition to collectivism (such as modernists and liberals). Second, the infringement of individualism would be tolerated in those situations where intervention and/or control may be regarded as furthering the aims and interests of the Extreme Right. This explains the Extreme Right's Janus approach to the federal government. For example, while federal intervention in school desegregation is regarded as an infringement of States' Rights and is thus vigorously opposed, the granting of federal defence contracts is seen as a benefit to the economic situation of the state, and the federal control accompanying such a form of intervention is overlooked. Moreover, strong government control is advocated by the Extreme Right in matters pertaining to the "police function" of the state for the protection of property, the preservation of order, and the maintenance of security, both internal and external. Thus, as indicated earlier, the Extreme Right supports the F.B.I. and congressional investigating committees. Toleration of collectivism is also extended to corporate "big business," which the Extreme Right courts as a source of economic support. It may be said that the Extreme Right opposes collectivism by proposing individualism, *except* in those areas where collectivism can be rationalized as furthering extremist interests.

The foregoing discussion of the nature of the Extreme Right may now be summarized, preparatory to establishing a definition of this phenomenon. Throughout this discussion, the concepts of "collectivism" and "individualism" have been used extensively. Unfortunately, no one word can completely express the complexities of a phenomenon such as the Extreme Right. How-

[41] *Webster's New International Dictionary of the English Language,* second edition, unabridged, Springfield, Massachusetts: G. and C. Merriam Company, 1935, p. 1268.
[42] Max Weber, *The Protestant Ethic and the Spirit of Capitalism,* translated by Talcott Parsons, New York: Charles Scribner's Sons, 1958.

ever, it is hoped that the particular contextual meaning of these terms, as they are applied to this study of the Extreme Right, has been made clear in the preceding pages. By "collectivism" we mean primarily the "quasi-paternalistic" welfare functions of twentieth century American socialism, and, on the international scene, Communism. Thus, Right-Wing opposition is directed primarily against government, whose function it is to administer aid and welfare programs. This opposition to government is not universal, however, since the Extreme Right tolerates and even supports certain functions of the state (such as the "police function" and the maintenance of the "market-place economy"). Corporate business which, in the classical "laissez-faire" sense, may be regarded as detrimental to the individualism of entre-preneurial business, is also spared extensive Right-Wing attack primarily because it is a potential source of economic support for Extreme Right groups. It has been proposed that the Extreme Right opposes this form of collectivism by advocating "individualism." This latter term, as it is used in this investigation, also has a certain restricted meaning. This principal of individualism has its basis in the classical "atomistic" view of society—the view that social institutions are subordinate to the individual. Thus, the Extreme Right tolerates those functions of the state that protect the interests and conditions of the individual. The individualism advocated by the Extreme Right is limited, however, since the right to act in one's own best interests would not be extended to all individuals. Those who would subvert what the Right-Wing Extremist regards as "the greatest good," (e.g., liberals and leftists), as well as the non-productive and shiftless members of the society (e.g., most minority group members), would not be afforded the privileges of individualism.

In conclusion, it is proposed that the Extreme Right be defined as follows:

> The Extreme Right is a militant and millenarian political ideology, espoused by numerous Right-Wing groups and individuals, which maintains as an ideal the principle of "limited individualism"; this principle being articulated as opposition to "collectivism" in government, international relations, modern social principles, and modern social structure and operation.

By focusing thus on the ideological aspects of the Extreme Right, rather than on individual groups of this persuasion, it should be possible to delineate more sharply the attitudinal indicators of this phenomenon, thus facilitating the scientific study of it.

Populist Influences on American Fascism

VICTOR C. FERKISS

The doctrinal roots of American fascist thought have long remained obscure for reasons inherent in recent American history itself. Essentially fascist popular movements grew up in America during the period 1929–41 at a time when American publicists and intellectuals were rediscovering America in their reaction to the growth of fascism and nazism abroad. Increased regard for American tradition among hitherto alienated intellectuals made them reluctant to admit that movements such as those led by Huey Long, Father Coughlin, and Gerald L. K. Smith were not the result of temporary psychological aberrations on the part of the masses but were, instead, the culmination of an ideological development stemming from such generally revered movements as Populism and "agrarian democracy." For them fascism was by definition un-American.

The sentimental quasi-Marxism of many influential writers reinforced this refusal to search for the roots of American fascism in American political history. When not dismissed as exotic imports, fascist ideas were held to be hothouse plants carefully nurtured by domestic capitalists bent on cultivating their own financial gardens while Western civilization was at stake in a death struggle waged by the democratic masses against the new barbarism.

American fascism, however, was a basically indigenous growth. When Anne Morrow Lindbergh spoke of a "Wave of the Future" as American as a New England autumn,[1] she was not so much expressing a hope as enunciating a fact.

AMERICAN FASCISM DEFINED

Any search for the roots of American fascism must necessarily be preceded by a clear understanding of the essential features of the movement. Few

[1] Her general thesis is expounded in *The Wave of the Future* (New York: Harcourt Brace Jovanovich, 1940).

"Populist Influences on American Fascism" is reprinted from the *Western Political Quarterly*, Vol. X, No. 2 (June, 1957) by permission of the University of Utah, copyright owners.

definitions of fascism are without their ardent supporters and violent de-
tractors. Because of space limitations, the definition used herein can only
be explicated, not defended.

We hold that the essential elements of fascism in the American context
are:

(1) An economic program designed to appeal to a middle class composed
largely of farmers and small merchants which feels itself being crushed between big business—and especially big finance—on the one hand, and an industrial working class which tends to question the necessity of the wage
system and even of private property itself on the other. Such an economic
program will include violent attacks against big business and finance—particularly the latter—and will advocate their control by the government in
the interest of the farmer and small merchant.

(2) Nationalism. International co-operation is held to be a device by
means of which supranational conspirators are able to destroy the freedom
and well-being of the people. A desire to stay aloof from foreign affairs is
the American (and English[2]) fascist substitute for imperialism, and any
imperialistic venture undertaken by either of these countries will ordinarily
be denounced as a conspiracy engineered by selfish economic interests. Areas
or groups with extensive foreign contacts are suspect and are feared as
beachheads of the antinational conspiracy, and venom which elsewhere is
directed against foreign powers is in America directed against such groups
as the Jews. Certain conservative social and religious beliefs are identified
as essential parts of the national heritage and attacks on them are considered
de facto evidence of activity on the part of the conspiracy.

(3) A despair of liberal democratic institutions, resulting from the belief
that the press and the other communication media have been captured by
the enemy, as have the two major political parties. Political power is held
to belong to the people as a whole and is considered to be best exercised
through some form of plebiscitary democracy. Leaders with a popular mandate will sweep aside any procedural obstacles to the fulfillment of the
popular will, and will purge those institutions which stand in the way of the
instantaneous attainment of popular desires. The destruction of liberal institutions such as the press and an independent legislature is not a desired
end in itself, but is a necessary means for protecting the nation and effectuat-
ing those economic reforms which the popular will demands.

(4) An interpretation of history in which the causal factor is the machinations of international financiers. The American Revolution, the fight of
Jackson against the bank, and Lincoln's war against the South and its British
allies are all considered episodes in the struggle of the people against the
"money power." International finance is held responsible for the "crime of
'73," entry into World War I, and the 1929 Depression. Communism is the
creation of international finance and a system in which the money power
strips off the mask of sham democracy and rules nakedly. A Communist
state naturally results when the concentration of economic power in the
hands of a few members of the international conspiracy reaches its logical
terminus.

The congruence of this body of doctrine with that of the various Euro-

[2] For the English attitude see Oswald Mosley, *The Greater Britain* (London: British
Union of Fascists, 1932), p. 146, *ca.*

pean fascist movements, especially in the period before they came to power, is virtually complete. The only important differences are the fact that in American (and English) fascism there is virtually no pseudo-mystic exaltation of the State as such, and that nationalism takes the form of isolationism rather than imperialism. In American fascism a strong state is held to be a necessary means rather than an end in itself; it is required in order that the will of the sovereign people may prevail over the conspirators and the corrupted. And, as noted above, nationalism takes the form of isolationism since America needs no foreign empire, and intervention in World War II would be at the behest of those wishing to defend "pluto-democracy" against the rising friends of the people, the fascist powers.

How this creed, on which all the segments of the American fascist movement were in basic agreement, arose logically from the Populist creed, and how the American fascist leaders attracted substantially the same social groups and sectional interests as had Populism is the burden of this paper.

THE POPULIST MESSAGE

Populism is used herein as a generic term to denote not merely the People's party, or Populism properly so-called, but such closely allied movements as the Greenback party, the Bryan free silver crusades, La Follette Progressivism, and similar manifestations of primarily agrarian revolt against domination by Eastern financial and industrial interests.[3]

The Populist economic program was, of course, tailored to the needs of the farmers of the prairies. The class struggle throughout American history has traditionally been waged not by laborers against employers, but by debtors against creditors. Agrarian discontent had a long history prior to the Civil War. Following that conflict the West was opened to settlers under the Homestead Act. These settlers needed money for capital and were dependent upon the railroads to sell their goods. The value of money appreciated so greatly that they had difficulty in paying their debts. The railroads, controlled by Eastern financial interests, were able to exploit them. The local governments and press were to a considerable extent the creatures of Eastern money, as were most of the local banks. A struggle began for a government which would regulate credit and control the railroads so that the settlers might prosper as middle-class landowners. This struggle reached its climax in Bryan's campaign of 1896 and abated thereafter as a result of the increasing amount of gold in circulation.

---

[3] The best history of the Populist movement is still John D. Hicks, *The Populist Revolt* (Minneapolis: University of Minnesota Press, 1931). See also Russell B. Nye, *Midwestern Progressive Politics* (East Lansing: Michigan State College Press, 1951).

For a summary of Populist doctrine see E. R. Lewis, *A History of American Political Thought from the Civil War to the World War* (New York: Macmillan, 1937), pp. 291–305; Frank L. McVey, "The Populist Movement," *Economic Studies,* I (1896), 133–209; and Carl C. Taylor, *The Farmers' Movement, 1620–1920* (New York: American Book Co., 1953), pp. 281–317.

Economic program

The motives of these Populists were similar to those which produced the rank-and-file twentieth-century American fascist. The Populists' aim was not the destruction of capitalism as they knew it, but was rather its preservation and extension. They were interested in protecting capitalism and the small entrepreneur from abuse at the hands of the monopolist and the banker. Populism was a middle-class movement; the Populists saw in Eastern finance capitalism a force which, unless controlled, would destroy their status and reduce them to proletarians.

The Populist economic program centered about the need for public control of credit. Senator Peffer of Kansas described the Populist economic creed in the following words:

> If there is any part of the Populist's creed which he regards as more important than another, and which, therefore, may be taken as leading, it is that which demands the issue and circulation of national money, made by authority of the people for their use, money that they will at any and all times be responsible for, money that persons in business can procure on good security at cost, money handled only by public agencies, thus doing away with all back issues of paper to be used as money.[4]

The extent of Bryan's faith in cheap credit as a panacea is reminiscent of the Chartist faith in universal suffrage as the sovereign remedy for social ills: ". . . When we have restored the money of the Constitution all other necessary reforms will be possible; but . . . until this is done there is no other reform that can be accomplished."[5]

This, then, was the most important plank in the Populist economic platform—the restoration to the people of their "sovereign power" to control money; private control is held to be a violation of the Constitution and a usurpation of a governmental function. In addition, the railroads and similar interests must also be controlled by a strong, central government capable of crushing the selfish few in the interests of the nation as a whole.

> Populists believe in the exercise of national authority in any and every case where the general welfare will be promoted thereby. . . .
>
> Populism teaches the doctrine that the rights and interests of the whole body of the people are superior, and, therefore, paramount to those of individuals. The Populist believes in calling in the power of the people in every case where the public interest requires it or will be promoted.[6]

Public power will protect the national interest against the selfish few.

Though the People's party flirted with the labor theory of value their inferences from it resembled those of Locke rather than those of Marx. Populism was no attack on private property or the wage system. It was the at-

---

[4] At Des Moines, Iowa, August 18, 1897; quoted in "Populism, Its Rise and Fall" by Senator Peffer, *Chicago Daily Tribune*, July 7, 1899, p. 12.
[5] Bryan's "Cross of Gold" speech, July 9, 1896; reprinted in William J. Bryan, *The First Battle* (Chicago: W. B. Conkey Co., 1896), p. 204.
[6] Senator Peffer, *op. cit.*

tempt of its adherents to retain the former and avoid becoming subject to the latter; hence Populism's lack of sympathy for and appeal to urban labor. Despite some concessions during the 1896 campaign, Bryan's appeal to the voters, even the Eastern workers, was to put their trust in free silver as the basic solution to all of their difficulties.[7]

Nationalism and anti-semitism

Nationalism was to be found in Populism principally in the form of a suspicious isolationism which regarded foreign involvements as inimical to the national interest and as existing solely to promote the interests of Eastern capitalists. Economic nationalism was reflected in Peter Cooper's proposal for protective tariffs,[8] and Populists often advocated severe restrictions on immigration.[9]

The protest against financial interests was frequently associated with a hatred of cities as centers of exploitation and of moral as well as political corruption. Nationalistic impulses cloaked themselves in the garb of sectionalism and Bryan referred to the East as "the enemy's country."[10] Dwight MacDonald has noted that because of the varied national origins of its population, its geographic isolation, and its relatively higher standard of living, the venom of American nationalism will ever be directed against New York City, "which is properly and correctly considered an outpost of Europe on this continent."[11] Populist and, later, fascist nationalism confirms this judgment.

The final ingredient of Populist nationalism was the anti-Semitism endemic throughout the rural West. The correlation between hatred of Jews (though in a mild form and wholly without dialectical formulation) with sentiment for Bryan has been noted by Professor Oscar Handlin.[12] The prairie farmer associated the Jew with the merchant, the financier, and the corrupt and domineering Eastern city.

Populist racial hostility was directed against those believed capable of destroying the small farmer's economic status and way of life. To the Midwesterner, the Negro presented no problem since he was not physically present and since he (unlike the Jew) could hardly be pictured as scheming to undermine the position of Midwestern farmers and shopkeepers from afar.

---

[7] Richard Hofstadter, *The American Political Tradition* (New York: Vintage Books, 1954), pp. 190–91.

[8] Vernon L. Parrington, *Main Currents in American Thought* (New York: Harcourt Brace Jovanovich, 1930), III, 279–82.

[9] William B. Hesseltine, *The Rise and Fall of Third Parties* (Washington: Public Affairs Press, 1948), p. 17. McVey traces the evolution of this and other major Populist planks, *op. cit.*, p. 142.

[10] Hofstadter, *op. cit.*, p. 194.

[11] *Fascism and the American Scene* (New York: Pioneer Publishers, n.d.), p. 10.

[12] "How U.S. Anti-Semitism Really Began," *Commentary*, XI (1951), 541–48. See also the perceptive discussion of Populist anti-Semitism and its relationship to the concept of "history as conspiracy" in Richard Hofstadter, *The Age of Reform* (New York: Knopf, 1955), pp. 60–93.

  The anti-Semitism of the Populists is also discussed by John Higham, "Anti-Semitism in the Gilded Age: A Reinterpretation," *Mississippi Valley Historical Review*, XLIII (1957), 559–78.

In the South, the situation was more complex. At first white and Negro farmers stood together in a common economic struggle against "the interests." However, it was not too long before the xenophobic feelings to which Populist orators appealed in their attempts to arouse the "red-necks'" opposition to the interests endangered this small-farmer solidarity. Hatred of the different could focus on the black skin of the Negro as well as on the uncalloused hands of the white plantation owner, and the enemies of Populism were not tardy about taking advantage of this fact to divide their foes. Before long such ardent Populist leaders as Senator "Pitchfork Ben" Tillman of South Carolina and Senator Tom Watson of Georgia (earlier a friend of the Negro) became standard-bearers of violent racist doctrines. Eventually hatred of the Negro replaced hatred of the interests as the main subject of demagoguery among Southern poor-whites, and, save in Louisiana which had never experienced a fully developed Populism, the American fascist message of later years fell on ears deafened by the loud cries of the white supremacists.

Plebiscitary democracy

Populism's predisposition to anti-Semitism and to nationalism and its suspicion of the corruption of urban life are all tendencies opposed to those trends which issue in democratic socialism in the humanist tradition; these proclivities more closely coincide with the patterns of conservative or fascist social beliefs. There is a tendency on the part of observers to overlook the true import of these propensities because of the role played by Populist and Progressive movements in the development of American democracy. To these movements America largely owes, for better or for worse, the direct primary, popular election of senators, the initiative, the referendum and recall, and the Wisconsin tradition of clean, efficient government, conducted with the assistance of experts.

Yet some qualifications must be made of the popular conception of Populism as a democratic or liberal force. First, the agrarian trend toward political reform was rarely based upon any broad ideas about human freedom or the fuller human life. Populist-inspired reforms were instrumental. The farmer wanted particular political changes because he felt they were needed to effect the defeat of the "money power" and to gain for farmers certain direct economic benefits. From their support of these measures we cannot infer a willingness on the part of the Populists to support egalitarian measures which would conduce to the benefit of others with different substantive aims.

Secondly, all these reforms serve to strengthen not liberalism but direct, plebiscitary democracy. They are designed to make the will of the majority immediately effective and to sweep away intervening institutions such as the legislatures, the older political parties, and the courts, which have all been corrupted by the money power. The Populist condemnation of the older parties is significant:

> We charge that the controlling influences dominating both these
> parties have permitted the existing dreadful conclusions to develop

> without serious effort to prevent or restrain them. Neither do they now promise us any substantial reform. They have agreed together to ignore, in the coming campaign, every issue but one. They propose to drown the outcries of a plundered people with the uproar of a sham battle over the tariff, so that capitalists, corporations, national banks, rings, trusts, watered stock, the demonetization of silver, and the oppressions of the usurers may all be lost sight of. They propose to sacrifice our homes, lives and children in order to secure corruption funds from the millionaires.[13]

If the existing parties are controlled by a gigantic conspiracy and the nation is at the mercy of an "international gold trust"[14] then the trust's opponents cannot be expected to treat these conspirators in quite the fashion one would treat honest dissenters. The rhetoric of "Bloody Bridles" Waite and Mary Ellen Lease is strong even for their times.[15] It bespeaks an unwillingness to compromise, a crusading zeal, and an inability to conceive of a sincerely motivated opposition that ill befits any group participating in parliamentary democracy. So, too, the oft-repeated charge that the press is controlled by special interests, whether true or not, leaves the way open for insuring "true" freedom of the press through the enactment of measures which might endanger freedom of speech as it has traditionally been understood in Anglo-Saxon law.

William Jennings Bryan many years later was to shed light on the devotion of the Populist crusade to liberal institutions when he held that the people in prosecuting Scopes were simply asserting their right "to have what they want in government, including the kind of education they want."[16] The people are the rulers and "a man cannot demand a salary for saying what his employers do not want said."[17]

In short, Populist political thought is compatible in spirit with the plebiscitary democracy of a Huey Long or a Hitler. This is not to say that Populists and Progressives universally opposed free speech as such or that Weaver, Lindbergh, Sr., or the elder La Follette would ever have seized power and then denied to the opposition an opportunity to regain power through constitutional means. They did believe that the opposition, including the press, was corrupt and antisocial; but they still believed that an aroused people could regain control of the government from the selfish few who had usurped it. It is only with the passing of time that Populism degenerates into fascism and comes to believe that the power of the enemy and his ability to corrupt the people is so great that constitutional institutions are a useless sham and that the people can only effectuate their will by modifying these institutions in form or spirit in such a manner as to deny their use to the conspiratorial enemy.

---

[13] Omaha Platform of July 4, 1892; quoted by Peffer, *op. cit.*, June 11, 1899, p. 23.
[14] J. C. Sibley of the American Bimetallic party; quoted *ibid.*, June 15, 1899, p. 7.
[15] The remark earning Governor Davis H. Waite of Colorado this picturesque sobriquet is quoted in Nye, *op. cit.*, p. 137. For a typical Lease speech see Taylor, *op. cit.*, pp. 283–84.
[16] Hofstadter, *op. cit.*, p. 204.
[17] *Ibid.*

THE DEGENERATION OF POPULISM

The degeneration of Populism into incipient fascism can be explained by the rebuffs and defections it suffered during the early years of the twentieth century. These reverses and the resulting fragmentation of its constituency meant the periodic peeling away of its more liberal elements. The Populist creed aroused no interest in serious American intellectual circles.[18] Populist economic literature was driven underground and there it remained. Out of contact with criticism, Populist doctrine became ever more extreme, developing a fondness for strange jargon and historical apocrypha and the belief that the real truths about modern history were being completely suppressed by the press and the universities. The arguments, the rhetoric, and the historical theories do not emerge again until they are incorporated in the literature of Coughlinism[19] and the pamphlets of Ezra Pound.[20]

As Populism's hope of achieving political power waned, its adherents grew more dogmatic and its doctrines more inflexible. Cut off from the main stream of American life, Populists developed not merely their own economics but their own history, and, through intellectual inbreeding, retained and strengthened all their ancient hatreds. The most significant developments in this process were the break with urban liberalism and the development of an intransigent nationalism.

At the turn of the century the Populists were already unhappy about the failure of organized labor to support the Bryan crusade. The alleged betrayal of the Populists by Theodore Roosevelt widened the political rift between the Westerners and urban reformism. The Populists accused Roosevelt of waging a sham battle against finance and of having cruelly deceived La Follette regarding the 1912 presidential nomination.[21] The resulting split drained from Populism many internationalists and humanists, who thereupon cast their lot permanently with the urban liberal movement, leaving the Populist forces even more regional and agrarian than they had previously been.

In 1912 Populist and Progressive support was divided between Roosevelt and Woodrow Wilson. The reforms Wilson inaugurated were heartily applauded by many Populists. Others, particularly the more doctrinaire, felt that his banking reforms especially were a snare and delusion. The major break came over Wilson's internationalist foreign policy. Many of the more internationally-minded Progressives stood by Wilson, but most of the Midwestern and Southern inheritors of the Populist tradition violently opposed his foreign policy and suffered the consequences. La Follette was branded

---

[18] Brooks Adams is an exception to this generalization. Although not a Populist sympathizer, he held many parallel views and had independently developed a monetary explanation of historical causation. *The Law of Civilization and Decay* (2d ed.; New York: Knopf, 1903).

[19] Most noteworthy is the periodical *Social Justice* (Royal Oak, Michigan: Social Justice Pub. Co., 1936–42).

[20] See especially *America, Roosevelt and the Causes of the Present War* (London: Peter Russel, 1951), *Gold and Work* (London: Peter Russell, 1951), *An Introduction to the Economic Nature of the United States* (London: Peter Russell, 1950), *A Visiting Card* (London: Peter Russell, 1952). These are postwar translations and reprints of works by Pound originally printed in Fascist Italy.

[21] See the narratives in Hesseltine, *op. cit.*, chap. ii, and Nye, *op. cit.*, chap. vi.

pro-German because of his isolationism, and the young Huey Long with difficulty secured the acquittal of his political idol, Louisiana State Senator S. J. Harper, accused of sedition for attacking the role of the financiers in Wilson's wartime administration.[22] There was a general tendency to treat Populism and pro-Germanism as synonymous. This attitude drove the remaining Populists into the nationalist camp, a result not impeded by the prominence of Wall Street among the forces advocating American intervention abroad.

Illustrative of the condition in which Populism now found itself is the history of the North Dakota Non-Partisan League, a radical farmers organization favoring state banking and state handling of crop storage. The League was founded in 1915 by Arthur C. Townley, a Socialist, and William Lemke, a young lawyer who while still in college had said, "if I can find out what people hate most I can build a new political party around it."[23] The hatred Lemke found was hatred of European capitalism and of the "war-party" in Washington and New York, and on this base the League was built. The League was widely opposed as seditious, and organizers were sometimes run out of town by patriotic mobs. Nonetheless, the League flourished. It dominated political life in North Dakota for many years and was influential in the politics of neighboring states as well.

In the House of Representatives, the fight against Wilson's foreign policy was led by the most radical of the Populist survivors, Charles A. Lindbergh, Sr., of Minnesota. Lindbergh did much to synthesize the Populist interpretation of history. In his speeches and books he traced the machinations of the "money-power" back as far as the Civil War, pointed up their responsibility for "internationalism," and portrayed them as leading the nation into World War I to protect Britain, head of the international financial trust.[24] This thesis was not generally popular and the double-barreled charge of economic radicalism and treachery was leveled against it.

Other Populists suffered physical violence for speaking out against internationalism. Ernest Lundeen, later a Farmer-Labor senator from Minnesota and a close associate of Nazi agents, was driven out of a Minnesota town in a locked refrigerator car as a result of his denunciation of the League of Nations.[25]

But Populism survived this persecution. Its effect was mainly to strengthen the alliance between nationalistic isolationism and hatred of finance capital-

[22] Forrest Davis, *Huey Long* (New York: Dodge Pub. Co., 1935), pp. 70–71.

[23] Quoted in Samuel Lubell, *The Future of American Politics* (New York: Harper, 1951), p. 138.
On the League see Andrew A. Bruce, *Non-Partisan League* (New York: Macmillan, 1921); Herbert E. Gaston, *The Nonpartisan League* (New York: Harcourt Brace Jovanovich, 1920); Taylor, *op. cit.*, pp. 421–69; Charles Edward Russell, *The Story of the Non-Partisan League* (New York: Harper, 1920); and Theodore Saluotos and John D. Hicks, *Agricultural Discontent in the Middle West, 1900–1939* (Madison: University of Wisconsin Press, 1951), pp. 149–218; Harold S. Quigley, "The Non-Partizan League," *The Unpartizan Review*, XIV (1920), 55–75.

[24] See his books, *Banking and Currency and the Money Trust* (Washington: National Capital Press, 1913), *The Economic Pinch* (Philadelphia: Dorrance, 1923), and *Your Country at War and What Happens to You after a War* (Philadelphia: Dorrance, 1934).

[25] *New York Times*, September 1, 1940, p. 6. On his Nazi connections see John Roy Carlson, *Under Cover* (New York: Books, 1943), p. 415.

ism, the Eastern urban liberals, and the press. Belated revenge was enjoyed by the Populists when, in 1934, Senator Gerald Nye of North Dakota (a product of Non-Partisan League politics and a former associate of the French biological elitist Alexis Carrel in a plan to institute a guild system in the United States[26]) headed a Senate committee which proved to the satisfaction of many that financial and industrial interests dragged nations into wars for the sake of larger profits.

A last attempt at uniting the Populist holdouts and the Eastern urban liberals was made in 1924, when, in conjunction with the Socialist party and the American Federation of Labor, the Progressive party ran a ticket composed of Bob La Follette for President and Burton K. Wheeler (Democratic senator from Montana) for Vice-President. The ticket received slightly less than five million votes, largely in the Middle and Far West,[27] but the dissatisfaction which produced this ticket was soon swallowed up in the wave of normalcy.

THE EMERGENCE OF AMERICAN FASCISM

Normalcy was not to last, and its demise witnessed the rise of many popular leaders armed with programs for change. In the social matrix of the Depression, the New Deal, and the shadow of World War II, various intellectual and popular leaders developed doctrines which were the American equivalent of European fascism and national socialism. These doctrines were influenced to some extent by such European ideas as syndicalism, distributism, the Papal social encyclicals, and fascism proper. But the most important single ingredient in this new creed was American Populism brought up to date—taking into account new social conditions and problems and informed by a despair of achieving its ends within a liberal constitutional system— but nonetheless directly derived from the older brand.

It is as difficult to pinpoint the essence of fascist doctrine as it is to supply a satisfactory one-sentence definition of Populism, and the history of the American fascist movement, with its shifting personal and electoral alliances, is at least as complex as that of Populism. There is, however, a remarkably coherent common core of doctrine uniting such widely divergent intellectuals as the economist Lawrence Dennis[28] and the poet Ezra Pound, and fascism as a popular movement, from its emergence under Senator Long and Father Coughlin in 1930 to its demise under Gerald L. K. Smith in 1946, was united by a common conception of what constituted the principal problems and in what direction a solution to them ought to be sought. These formulations include virtually all the old Populist doctrines and there is little in them which could not have been foreseen as a logical development of the Populist creed under the impact of the altered conditions of twentieth-century American life.

---

[26] *American Review*, II (1934), 509.

[27] Nye, *op. cit.*, pp. 341–42.

[28] Dennis' most important writings are *The Coming American Fascism* (New York: Harper, 1936) and *The Dynamics of War and Revolution* (New York: The Weekly Foreign Letter, 1940).

Economic program

The American fascist economic program, like that of Populism, advocates the use of strong governmental controls in a few key areas in order to protect a middle class of independent farmers and shopkeepers from becoming impoverished proletarians as a result of the "boom and bust" business cycle which, it is maintained, is engineered by the Eastern bankers for their own enrichment. But fascism's program was designed to appeal not merely to the rural interests but also to those members of the urban lower-middle class (especially the white-collar workers) who were unwilling to identify themselves with organized labor and feared its power almost as much as they feared that of big business.

The program is again based on a monocausal interpretation of economic problems which makes it possible to apply simple, once-and-for-all solutions. For Huey Long the solution is a demagogic Share-Our-Wealth program, designed to make "Every Man a King" through the redistribution of wealth and the prevention of its concentration in the hands of the few by means of restrictions on big business. Most fascists have chosen the old Populist remedy—control of the monetary supply so as to stabilize the ratio between goods and prices and to destroy the usury of private banking which, it is held, is the source of the concentration of economic power.

Populist economics is revived *in toto* by the fascists, and the claim is openly made that the fascists[29] are the inheritors of the Populist mantle. The core of the fascist program is exemplified in the Nye-Sweeney bill (H.R. 6382) introduced in Congress in 1935 at the behest of Father Coughlin. Its purpose as stated in its preamble was:

> . . . To restore to Congress its constitutional power to issue money and regulate the value thereof; to provide for the orderly distribution of the abundance with which a beneficent Creator has blessed us; to establish and maintain the purchasing power of money at fixed and equitable levels; to increase the prices of agricultural products to a point where they will yield the cost of production plus a fair profit to the farmer; to provide a living and just annual wage which will enable every citizen willing to work and capable of working to maintain and educate his family on an increasing level or standard of living; to repay debts with dollars of equal value; to lift in part the burden of taxation; and for other purposes.[30]

Monetary manipulation is still (as it was for Bryan) the sovereign remedy.

The program of the National Union for Social Justice, which remained the official Coughlinite program even after the demise of the National Union,[31] closely paralleled that of the Farmer-Labor party, and, on matters other than money reform, it was as vague and shifting as Bryan's program

---

[29] It should be noted that no figure discussed in this article, except as otherwise noted, ever applied the label "fascist" to himself.

[30] Quoted in Richard M. Boeckel, "Father Coughlin *vs.* the Federal Reserve System," *Editorial Research Reports*, II (1936), 275.

[31] Founded in 1936, the Union had been reorganized and gradually abandoned during 1938–39; however, it was not formally dissolved until 1944. *New York Times*, August 18, 1944, p. 15.

had been. Gerald L. K. Smith made a return to "constitutional money" the heart of the economic program of his America First party.[32] Ezra Pound, the grandson of a pioneer Idaho money-reformer, became a Social Credit advocate in England and anticipated the fascist tendencies of the movement as a whole by early embracing fascism as the best means to monetary reform.[33] "USURY," he thundered, "is the Cancer of the World, which only the surgeon's knife of Fascism can cut out of the life of nations."[34] Pound's voluminous economic writings are almost wholly devoted to the advocacy of public control of credit to defeat the money power and of fascism as the necessary means to this end. The evils of usury and the necessity of monetary reform are the themes of his most important poetic works.

Huey Long was pledged to enact the Nye-Sweeney bill if he became President.[35] William Dudley Pelley was an ardent money reformer,[36] and the anti-Semitic agitator, Joe McWilliams, was a preacher of the gospel of money reform.[37] Seward Collins, while drawing most of his ideas from Southern agrarianism and distributism, accepted the basic thesis of American fascism that finance capitalism is destroying private property, and hailed fascism as Europe's revolt against "capitalism, the usurper."[38] Even the sophisticated Lawrence Dennis, who attacked Long and Coughlin in violent terms for their oversimplifications and naïve solutions,[39] agreed that the private taking of interest was intolerable, that credit fluctuation was a major cause of the depression, and that Long and Coughlin were the greatest teachers of economics that the American people had—far superior to the "kept" academic economists.[40]

Save for Dennis and Coughlin, American fascists generally offered money reform as the sole economic plank in their program for social reform, since for them it was the issue on which all other economic reforms hinged. This concentration on monetary reform fostered the fascist view that capitalism and communism are basically similar in that both concentrate all economic power in the hands of a few. For the fascist the evils of capitalism and communism can be avoided only through the creation of a strong state. The state will then be able to intervene to save private property from becoming concentrated in the hands of the few through social control of those eco-

---

[32] The platform of the America First party appears as an insert in Smith's periodical, *The Cross and the Flag*, Vol. III (October, 1944).

[33] Pound's shift from Social Credit to fascism is discussed in his "A Social Creditor Serves Notice," *Fascist Quarterly*, II (1936), 492–99. For a summary of Pound's shifting and often only semi-coherent political ideas, see Victor C. Ferkiss, "Ezra Pound and American Fascism," *Journal of Politics*, XVII (1955), 173–97. On the development of the Social Credit movement as such see C. B. Macpherson, "The Political Theory of Social Credit," *Canadian Journal of Economics and Political Science*, XV (1949), 378–93.

[34] *What is Money For?* (London: Peter Russell, 1951), p. 12.

[35] Huey P. Long, *My First Days in the White House* (Harrisburg: Telegraph Press, 1935), pp. 34–36.

[36] See his *No More Hunger* (Asheville: The Pelley Publishers, 1936), especially pp. 27–30.

[37] Under the auspices of the Midwest Monetary Foundation, later called the Institute for American Economics. Henry Hoke, *Black Mail* (New York: Readers Book Service, 1944), p. 56; E. A. Piller, *Time Bomb* (New York: Arco Pub. Co., 1945), p. 68.

[38] "The Revival of Monarchy," *American Review*, I (1933), 252.

[39] See his "Debunking Father Coughlin," *Awakener*, I (February 1, 1934), 1.

[40] *The Coming American Fascism, op. cit.*, pp. 164–65, 227.

nomic mechanisms which are used by the usurious international bankers to destroy their economic competitors and to control both the nation's economy and its government. Although the mania for seeing monetary reform as a social panacea also possessed the early National Socialist party and the work of Sombart attacks finance as "unproductive,"[41] the interest of American fascist popular leaders in the control of credit is directly traceable to the influence upon them of the American Populist tradition.

Coughlin in his later phase expanded his program to include explicitly what was always implicit in the work of Lawrence Dennis—an economy organized in the form of a corporate state, an arrangement which allegedly would give labor a share in the control of industry, rationalize production, and protect the public against exploitation by capitalist and union alike.[42] Pound sees in the corporate state a return to the occupational representation which he feels was a basic feature of American federalism as conceived by the founding fathers.[43]

The controlled corporate economy was regarded with some suspicion by Long and Smith, who thought it sounded too much like NRA[44] to appeal to their farm followers, but it was undeniably compatible with their desire for an economy in which the most important function of the state would be to protect the middle class against organized capital and organized proletariat alike. The American fascist state which Smith and Long visualized would destroy usury and nationalize credit and possibly a few utilities, and thus protect private property while, of course, retaining the ability to regulate it when necessary for the public good.

Nationalism and anti-semitism

American fascist nationalism is also of a piece with the nationalism of the Populists. Save for Dennis' desire to make American influence felt in Latin America,[45] where he had served in the Foreign Service, imperialism is no part of American fascist doctrine. The emphasis is upon the material and moral superiority of America. She needs a strong defense but should remain aloof from foreign quarrels. Nationalism takes the form of doctrinaire iso-

---

[41] For Sombart's ideas see his *The Quintessence of Capitalism,* trans. and ed. by M. Epstein (London: T. F. Unwin, 1915).

[42] Coughlin describes his projected corporate state in *Social Justice,* I, N.S. (April 4, 1938), 11, 14; II, N.S. (December 19, 1938), 14; III, N.S. (January 30, 1939), 7.

[43] A *Visiting Card, op. cit.,* p. 15.

[44] Commenting on a summary of the Papal social encyclicals, which he admitted he had not read, Long said, "I don't know anything about it, but it sounds like NRA. If it's NRA, I'm against it." J. I. Salter, "The Passing of Huey Long," *Dalhousie Review,* XV (1936), pp. 446–47. Clearly, Long's ideal was the small-owner utopia of the Populists rather than the minutely organized and regulated corporate state. See Long's own (ghost-written) account of his ideas in *Every Man a King* (New Orleans: National Book Co., 1933) and *My First Days in the White House* (Harrisburg: Telegraph Press, 1935).

[45] Dennis' criticisms of U.S. policy can be found in "Revolution, Recognition and Intervention," *Foreign Affairs,* IX (1931), 204–21; "Nicaragua: In Again, Out Again," *ibid.,* 496–500; and "What Price Good Neighbor," *American Mercury,* XLV (1938), 150–58.

lationism in which the Populist monetary interpretation of history is used to explain current international problems and to indicate their proper solution. Thus World War II is held to be simply a plot on the part of the Wall Street-London group of international bankers to use the common people of the Western nations to defeat the revolt against banker domination being led by Italy and Germany.

Pound says: "After the assassination of President Lincoln no serious measures against the usurocracy were attempted until the formation of the Rome-Berlin axis;"[46] and, "this war is part of the secular war between usurers and peasants, between the usurocracy and whomever does an honest day's work with his hands."[47] Coughlin's *Social Justice* maintained that Hitler and the fascists were "the champions of Christian social order against the forces of anti-Christian chaos,"[48] and that "it would be better for the world that Germany should win the war rather than the Allies"[49] because they were fighting the good fight against the international bankers' conspiracy.

Dennis was active in holding that the fascist powers should be allowed to win their battle against dying capitalist democracy and that America should not interfere.[50] Long, had he lived, would doubtless have continued to be as ardently isolationist as he had been when he claimed that the League of Nations was controlled by "the European enemies of this country."[51] Save for the emotional nationalistic rallies of Smith's Christian Nationalist party, American fascists vented their nationalism in a negative manner, attacking the Western democracies, seeking to keep America out of World War II, and proclaiming all internationalist movements, from Union Now to communism, to be fronts for the international bankers and world Jewry.

While the only anti-Negro agitation in the American fascist movement is to be found in Smith's later period and not at all in the other major fascist ideologues, anti-Semitism is rampant. The Jew is branded a national enemy and is identified with the banker, the communist, and the antinationalist. Alleged Jewish racial solidarity is claimed to be not merely a link that reinforces the economic ties of international finance, but one which binds such seemingly disparate but actually compatible groups as the international capitalists and the communists in common cause against the American nation and people. This anti-Semitic agitation ranges from Dennis' remarks distinguishing between Americans and "Jews living in America"[52] to the paranoic diatribes of Pound, although save for Pound and a few street agitators like McWilliams, all the important American fascists denied they were anti-Semitic, just as they denied they were fascist. Thus another Populist predilection was resurrected in a more violent form—the identification of Jews, New York, and international finance. To this, fascism added the identification of all three with communism.

As was true of Populism, American fascism not only failed to attack con-

---

[46] *Gold and Work*, p. 7.
[47] *America, Roosevelt and the Causes of the Present War*, p. 5.
[48] Editorial, I, N.S. (April 11, 1938), 6.
[49] *Ibid.*, V, N.S. (June 10, 1940), 5.
[50] See especially "After the Peace of Munich," *American Mercury*, XLVI (1939), 12–21.
[51] *American Progress*, II (February 1, 1935), 9–10.
[52] "Propaganda for War: Model 1938," *American Mercury*, XLIV (1938), 3.

servative middle-class social mores but claimed to be their defender against the corrupt press which served the ends of the alien conspiracy. Indeed both the Reverend Mr. Smith and Father Coughlin, like many of their supporters, were men of the cloth.

Plebiscitary democracy

The American fascist ideal of plebiscitary democracy was best exemplified by Huey Long, who used the mandate given to him by the voters as an excuse to create a rubber-stamp legislature, pack the courts, and attempt to intimidate the press. Said Long:

> Down in Louisiana we have no dictatorship, but what I call a closer response to the will of the people. It is a government of initiative and referendum. We called a convention to amend the Constitution, and when these amendments were approved by the people, we merely called the legislature together to pass enabling acts. Everything that has been done in Louisiana is merely to carry out the will of the people as expressed in the amendments to the constitution. That's not a dictatorship.[53]
>
> They [the legislature] look to somebody to get up the program for them; they're committed to the general program and so we get through with it without squandering the State's time and money.[54]

Father Coughlin's "People's Lobbies" had as their purpose the election of similar legislatures. William Lemke promised the voters in 1936 that when Congress was convened:

> I will inform them that the Union Party platform, having been endorsed in the election, is the mandate of the people, and therefore must be enacted into law during my term as president. I will insist upon this even if I have to keep Congress in session continuously for four years.[55]

Dennis and Pound both saw a need for a strong leader to protect the people from the selfish few, and denied any value to liberal institutions, behind which, they alleged, the special interests hid. Dennis wrote:

> Most of the rules of liberalism which are most touted as safeguarding popular rule merely insure the rule of the rich, powerful, irresponsible, and selfish who, under liberalism, can produce expressions of popular will and opinion to suit their selfish interests at the rate of so many dollars a given unit of expression of popular opinion or will.[56]

The old Populist theme that liberal institutions and the party system are the tools of the rich is now echoed by people who, unlike the early Populists, have despaired of capturing or reforming them. The use of force to ensure

[53] Quoted, *New York Times*, February 10, 1935, sec. 6, p. 3.
[54] Quoted in Davis, *op. cit.*, p. 35.
[55] Campaign statement quoted in *Social Justice*, II (October 19, 1936), 5.
[56] *The Coming American Fascism, op. cit.*, p. 198.

the triumph of the popular will, which in the Populist era meant the employment of mob violence to prevent sheriffs' sales of mortgaged property, will in the new dispensation be the prerogative primarily of various storm troop and youth movements such as those developed by Smith and Coughlin.

Political action

The influence of Populism in the generation of American fascism can be illustrated by political as well as by intellectual similarities. A high degree of correlation has been shown to exist between the vote given La Follette in 1924 and Lemke in 1936 and the counties which withdrew their support from the Democratic party in 1940 because of opposition to its foreign policy but returned to the fold in 1948.[57] Samuel Lubell has stressed the importance of the Germanic ethnic origin of the populations of these areas and concludes that their support of Populist candidates in the past was the result primarily of isolationist and pro-German sympathies rather than of their economic beliefs.[58] Yet their desertion of the Republicans in 1948 is an indication that on economic questions they favor a less conservative approach than that advocated by the G.O.P. A real alliance between the peculiar kind of anticapitalist feeling exploited by Populism and an ardent nationalism exists in these areas even if for a time the foreign policy issue was given primacy. It must also be remembered that Populist lack of sympathy for organized labor and for Marxian socialism could well cause rejection of Marxist-oriented Farmer-Labor candidates without implying any alliance with economic liberalism in the Manchester sense. Though the enormous Long and Coughlin audiences continued to support the New Deal in the 1936 elections, the vote Lemke received revealed an irreducible core of support for fascism among erstwhile Populist constituencies and among their newly developed allies in certain segments of the urban lower-middle class.

The death of Huey Long in 1935 deprived American fascism of its most politically eligible candidate; Father Coughlin's National Union for Social Justice collapsed after the defeat of Lemke; and under the spur of war preparations economic conditions were improving. Fascist leaders had to search for new issues and new political figures with which to make their bid for power. Nationalism was to be the dominant issue, but the development of anti-Semitism and an increased emphasis on foreign policy did not mean that Populist economic doctrine was to be ignored or replaced and Populist historical theory was to prove useful in providing a rationale for isolationism.

Many monetary reform advocates like ex-Senator Owen[59] and Professor Soddy[60] maintained their connections with the fascist movement and aug-

[57] Lubell, *op. cit.*, pp. 129–57, 211–14.

[58] *Ibid.*, pp. 132–46.

[59] Robert F. Owen (Democrat of Oklahoma), head of the Senate Banking and Currency Committee in Wilson's administration, author of the foreword to Gertrude Coogan, *Money Creators* (Chicago: Sound Money Press, 1935), and frequent contributor to *Social Justice*. See that periodical, III (May 31, 1937), 15; III (June 14, 1937), 15, etc.

[60] Frederick R. Soddy, Nobel Prize winner in Chemistry, 1921, author of various books on "money reform." An Englishman, he contributed frequently to *Social Justice*, sign-

mented its strength and dynamism, and most fascist leaders could be numbered among the supporters of "money-reform."[61] Symbolically, Jacob Coxey,
the old Populist veteran, in 1939 told a gathering that Hitler was doing the
world a service by ridding Germany and Europe of the power of usury.[62]

But the big issue of the moment was foreign policy. The controversy over
intervention in World War II gave the native fascists an issue on which to
seek popular support and political power. The America First Committee
provided the culture in which the seeds of American fascism were to grow.

THE AMERICA FIRST COMMITTEE

The America First Committee was the successor of earlier isolationist
movements which for various reasons had not gained much popular support.
Founded by a wealthy young Yale student under the aegis of liberal faculty
members, the Committee drew much of its financial support from businessmen, but these were only a small and unrepresentative segment of the business community and the majority of them were Midwesterners. Most of the
large donations seem to have come from a few individuals[63] and should
probably be interpreted as expressing individual nationalism rather than as
signifying a trend in politico-economic relationships. But if the national
committee was heavily weighted with the names of businessmen (largely
in an attempt to fill the treasury), both the rank and file of the AFC and the
political leaders who belonged to the group were persons of a different
stripe.

It would be false to call the AFC a fascist organization, just as it would
have been false to call the Wallace Progressive party of 1948 a communist
organization.[64] In neither case were the leaders fascists or communists in
organizational affiliation. In neither case did the leaders accept all the doctrines of fascism or communism. Neither the Progressive party nor the AFC
based its appeal on its affiliation with these ideologies, nor were most of
their supporters adherents. Nonetheless, both movements represented bids

---

ing a contract for a 52-week series in the reorganized *Social Justice* of 1938. See that
periodical, V (January 24, 1938), 4.

[61] The extent of the interpenetration of the American fascist and monetary reform
movements is indicated throughout the text of the *Honest Money Year Book and
Directory, 1940* (Chicago: Honest Money Founders, 1939), which contains articles
and/or quotations from Soddy, Owen, Preston Bradley, Bismarck, and Hitler, among
others. The list of monetary reform leaders in the Directory section includes Father
Coughlin, Robert Noble, Gerald P. Winrod, Seward Collins, William Dudley Pelley,
Mrs. Huey P. Long, and a host of lesser lights.

Not all American monetary reformers were pro-fascist, of course, but the need the
nonfascists felt to resist the pro-fascist tendencies of many in the movement is in itself
illustrative of the role of the old Populist battle cries and warhorses in American
fascism. For an antifascist statement by a monetary reform leader see Gorham Mun-
son, "Ezra Pound and the Dean of Canterbury," *Dynamic America*, XIII (December,
1941), 8, and "Money Reform Simpletons," *ibid.*, XII (April, 1941), 20.

[62] Quoted in *Social Justice*, III, N.S. (June 19, 1939), 13.

[63] Wayne S. Cole, *America First: The Battle Against Intervention, 1940–1941* (Madison:
University of Wisconsin Press, 1953), pp. 31–33.

[64] See Charles Angoff, "Wallace's Communist Front Party," *American Mercury*, LXVII
(1948), 413–21, 756–57.

for power by ulterior forces. Just as the dynamism and the local organizational strength of the Progressives came from openly communist or fellow-traveler organizations, so the strength of the AFC came from the fascists. As Wallace could easily have gone down the road to Marxism, so also the leaders of the AFC were the soil from which a fascist movement would be most likely to spring; the AFC approach to political issues was, on the whole, compatible with that of fascism, just as Wallace's program was in its broad outlines compatible with that of the communists. As the Progressives favored the Soviet Union, so the AFC favored the fascist powers and increasingly accepted support and ideas from the American adherents of Germany and Italy.

The America First Committee probably had a membership of 850,000 or so, concentrated in the Midwest and in a few large Eastern and Far Western cities.[65] A considerable proportion of its chapters were dominated by fascists or their friends, despite the efforts of many of the local AFC leaders. In Southern California the organization was largely dominated by known Nazis; in San Francisco, both Coughlinites and Nazis figured prominently among the membership.[66] The Pontiac, Michigan, chapter was controlled by the fascist National Workers League.[67] The Brooklyn, New York, chapter was little more than the Christian Front by another name,[68] and an official of the large New York chapter, Judge Mildred Dugan, said: "Eighty percent of the membership is Coughlinite, and there isn't the least doubt in my mind that at the present rate the anti-Semites and Coughlinites will come out on top eventually."[69] When an attempt was made to bar Coughlinites from the AFC such a storm of protest arose from them and from the non-Coughlinite leaders who knew they needed Coughlinite support that the idea was dropped. General Wood and Mrs. Burton K. Wheeler publicly apologized for any friction which might have resulted from the suggestion.[70] Coughlinism was officially within the pale.

Consideration of the leadership pattern within the AFC is also instructive. Opposition to World War II provided the AFC with an issue which elicited the active support of conservative nationalists like Congressman Hamilton Fish. But the brunt of the speechmaking was borne by men like Senators Gerald Nye and Burton K. Wheeler (for many years a shining example of the perfect statesman in the estimation of *Social Justice*).[71] Phil La Follette was usually on the road speaking, imparting his vision of the New America that could be built on this continent. At a rally at the Brooklyn Academy of Music he told his Christian Front audience that he had last been in that building during a campaign speech his father gave there in 1924; the invocation which preceded the young La Follette's address was pronounced by

---

[65] Cole, *op. cit.*, pp. 30–31.

[66] Joint Fact-Finding Committee on Un-American Activities in California, *Un-American Activities in California*, Report to the California Legislature, 55th Session (Sacramento: State Printing Office, 1943), pp. 273–81.

[67] Carlson, *op. cit.*, p. 260.

[68] Personal observation, 1941.

[69] Carlson, *op. cit.*

[70] Cole, *op. cit.*, p. 137.

[71] For example, *Social Justice*, V, N.S. (March 18, 1940), 20; VII, N.S. (February 17, 1941), 8–9.

Father Edward Lodge Curran, Coughlin's eastern deputy.[72] The wave of the future was taking shape in American politics. Almost all the old Progressives who had not drifted into the social democratic camp were bitter isolationists. Some were extremely frank in stating their views: Old Non-Partisan-Leaguer William Langer of North Dakota told his Senate colleagues that Dennis, McWilliams, and their fellow prisoners were just "good American patriots."[73] Thus far had the Populist definition of American nationalism evolved.

The America First Committee's most popular speaker was Charles A. Lindbergh (son of the Populist Congressman). Lindbergh had carried the memory of his father's struggles with him from his early years. In Europe he had come under the influence of racial theorists[74] and later had collaborated in scientific experiments with elitist Alexis Carrel.[75] He was now telling America that it was useless to try to help the Western nations stem the force of National Socialism. In Des Moines, Iowa, in September, 1941, his career as an orator reached its climax. He told his audience: "The three most important groups who have been pressing this country toward war are the British, the Jewish and the Roosevelt administration."[76] With regard to the Jews, he maintained, "Their greatest danger to this country lies in their large ownership and influence in our motion pictures, our press, our radio, and our government."[77] This was his father's old indictment of the "money power" of the East transfigured. Populism had blossomed into fascism. There was much adverse comment just as there had been when Coughlin had earlier propounded this thesis. But, strikingly, the lines of the AFC held. No major figure repudiated Lindbergh.[78] The America Firsters simply replied that, regardless of the charges, the AFC was not anti-Semitic—a familiar refrain.

The area of fascist resonance within pure isolationism began to grow.[79] On March 4, 1941, Senator Rufus Holman (Republican, Oregon) said in the Senate:

> I doubt if the right is all on one side among the present belligerents. At least Hitler . . . has broken the control of the international bank-

[72] Personal observation, 1941.
[73] Carlson, *The Plotters* (New York: Dutton, 1946), p. 166.
  Dennis, McWilliams and a number of small-fry fascists were indicted in 1944 by the United States government for conspiracy to commit sedition. During the course of the lengthy trial the presiding judge died, a mistrial was declared, and the charges were dropped. The defendants' interpretations of the trial are to be found in Lawrence Dennis and Maximilian St. George, *A Trial on Trial* (N.P.: National Civil Rights Committee, 1946).
[74] See his "Aviation, Geography and Race," *Reader's Digest*, XXXV (November, 1939), 64–67.
[75] The scientific fruit of this collaboration is found in Alexis Carrel and Charles A. Lindbergh, *The Culture of Organs* (New York: Hoeber, 1938). Carrel's social philosophy is expounded in *Man the Unknown* (New York: Harper, 1939).
[76] Cole, *op. cit.*, p. 144.
[77] *New York Times*, September 12, 1941, p. 2.
[78] For a description of the America First Committee reaction see Cole, *op. cit.*, pp. 145–54. One Jewish leader, Lessing Rosenwald, resigned.
[79] For instance, long after Coughlin's anti-Semitic campaign was in full swing, Senator Arthur Capper of Kansas, an old veteran of the early Populist-Progressive movement, wrote to *Social Justice* to the effect that he read it weekly and it was to be commended for doing "a great job." V, N.S. (May 20, 1940), 14.

ers and traders over the rewards for the labor of the common people of Germany.

In my opinion it would be advantageous if the control of the international bankers and traders over the wages and manner of living of the people of England could be broken by the English people and if the control of the international bankers and traders over the wages and savings and manner of living of the people of the United States could be broken by the people of the United States.[80]

Archbishop Francis L. Beckman of Dubuque, a close friend of Coughlin, told a national radio audience: "This war is nothing more or less than a struggle to re-establish the shattered boundaries of international finance, and other things international, in countries which have had their fill of them and do not want them any more."[81] An organ of the isolationist "Mothers" movement noted: "The fact that we lack vital constitutional money now is due chiefly to the crafty Jews and other money changers who have continually bribed, in various ways, a majority of our legislators to betray their trust."[82] In the House of Representatives John Rankin, though not an AFC member, did his bit by making several speeches condemning Jewish international bankers as the real "war-mongers."[83] The fascist approach to international relations was filling in the gaps in the ideology of the new movement.

Other steps taken at this time were also leading in the direction of the development of a full-blown fascist creed. It was alleged that a prime element in the conspiracy against American isolation was the Jewish-dominated motion picture industry. Senator Nye, with the backing of the AFC leadership, began to press for a congressional investigation of the moviemakers as war propagandists. Wendell Willkie, who had repeatedly been subjected to abuse by *Social Justice*, had his revenge when, acting as counsel for the industry, he discredited the investigation as anti-Semitic in inspiration and it was dropped.[84] However, the fact that such an investigation was proposed is an interesting commentary on the place of free speech in the new ideology. While it is true that the motion pictures have not until recently been considered entitled to the same protection under the First Amendment as the press,[85] it is obvious that this move could have provided an opening wedge for a program designed to reduce the influence and interfere with the activities of those who were deemed to be exercising their control over communications in an "irresponsible" manner. This investigation could well have

[80] Carlson, *Under Cover*, p. 138.
[81] Quoted in *Social Justice*, VIII, N.S. (August 11, 1941), 13. See also *Time*, XXXVIII (August 4, 1941), 44–46.
[82] *Women's Voice*, August 26, 1943, quoted in *New Masses*, L (April 3, 1944), 6.
[83] Carlson, *Under Cover*, pp. 233–34; *Social Justice*, VII, N.S. (May 12, 1941), 14.
[84] See "Gerald P. Nye" in *Current Biography 1941*, p. 621; *New York Times*, Septembei 2, 1941, p. 19; September 10, 1941, p. 1; September 14, 1941, p. 20.
[85] See as an introduction to the problem "Motion Pictures and the First Amendment" ir "Notes," 60 *Yale Law Journal*, 696–719 (1951).

Recent attacks on the motion picture industry differ from the AFC-inspired attack: of the '40's in that the focus of the attack has been primarily upon the politica affiliations of individual performers rather than directly upon film content. In addition the AFC viewed the motion picture companies themselves as the enemy, while of late the companies have been the blacklisters' active allies. See John Cogley, *Report ot Blacklisting I: Movies* (N.P., The Fund for the Republic, 1956).

set a pattern for rule if the America First Committee had ever achieved national political power.

Gaining power was indeed the objective of the AFC. "We shall clasp hands at the polls in 1942," Charles Lindbergh said in one of his last addresses,[86] and just prior to Pearl Harbor the AFC began to take steps to turn itself into a political party for the elections of 1942.[87] Vast mailing lists were compiled by congressional district.[88] A "pre-convention" conclave was held in Indiana under the management of Phil La Follette.[89] Father Coughlin had already predicted that the coming years would see the birth in America of a victorious National Socialist party, with the accent on the "nationalist."[90] Nationalism would indeed have been the dominant issue, but it is highly probable that had the party received an opportunity to develop fully it would, despite some conservative backing, have supported a socioeconomic program similar to that advocated by the Coughlinites and the National Progressives.[91] Plans apparently called for Phil La Follette to be the party's presidential candidate. Lindbergh, however, would be "party leader"[92] and the real star of the show. Around him would be grouped the followers of Coughlin in the local AFC chapters and the Gerald L. K. Smith coterie, who would early join the coalition. In the background would be such figures as Joe McWilliams,[93] waiting in the wings for his cue, and Lawrence Dennis, quietly and discreetly offering advice from the prompter's box.

The attack on Pearl Harbor put an end to these plans and the legions scattered. Only the die-hards remained at work, and many of them had their labors interrupted by the hand of the law. Senator Nye collaborated with Smith,[94] who was the first in the field with a new "America First" party. Coughlin continued to communicate with his Mothers' groups. Senator Lundeen's widow toured the country for Smith's America First party, and her marriage to Senator Holman was a nationalist social event duly reported in *The Cross and the Flag*.[95] The fascists, the money-reform men, and the isolationists met in search of common ground. Langer was reportedly working for a coalition of these elements during 1943.[96] The na-

---

[86] Michael Sayers and Albert E. Kahn, *Sabotage! The Secret War against America* (New York: Harper, 1942), p. 240.

[87] Noted with approval in *Social Justice*, VIII, N.S. (November 24, 1941), 7.

[88] Sayers and Kahn, *op. cit.*, p. 253; also personal observation, 1941.

[89] *Ibid.*, p. 240.

[90] Carlson, *Under Cover*, p. 253.

[91] The National Progressive party was an abortive political experiment organized in 1938 by Phil La Follette. See regarding the party and public reaction to it, Philip La Follette, "They Wanted Something New," *Nation*, CXLVII (1938), 586; "The La Follette Progressives" in "The Fortune Survey," *Fortune*, XVIII (October, 1938), 90–92; Hesseltine, *op. cit.*, pp. 55–56; Lubell, *op. cit.*, pp. 144–45; and Nye, *op. cit.*, 372–74. Following its swift demise the National Progressive movement received unstinting praise from Coughlin's *Social Justice*, VII, N.S. (April 7, 1941), 13.

[92] Sayers and Kahn, *op. cit.*

[93] On his career and views see Carlson, *Under Cover*, pp. 83–85, and R. L. Taylor, "Reporter at Large: The Kampf of Joe McWilliams," *New Yorker*, XVI (August 24, 1940), 34–39.

[94] Carlson, *Under Cover*, pp. 293, 319.

[95] Vol. III (1944), p. 425.

[96] John L. Spivak, "Senator Langer's Secret Meeting," *New Masses*, L (April 3, 1944), 3–8. Langer denied the charges, saying he and this group were discussing old-age

tionalist, Senator Robert R. Reynolds (Democrat, North Carolina), was active with money of his own; Smith, however, was wary, holding that Reynolds was too reactionary to attract much public support.[97] The Greenback party, vestigial Populist survival, nominated for President in 1944 one Leo Donnelly, M.D., a former Coughlinite official.[98]

In 1944 a Congress of Monetary Organizations was held at the so-called "Women's White House" in Cleveland. It was a picture in miniature of the death of an era. The aged and ageless Jacob Coxey wandered forlornly through the vast rooms,[99] while Smith and the outright Nazis quarreled over position. Joseph Scott, publisher of *Money* and employer of Joe McWilliams, was elected president of the Congress and the gathering dispersed to go home and wait for better days.[100] But by 1946 it was evident that better days were not imminent.

THE FUTURE OF AMERICAN FASCISM

The war years dealt a blow to the forces of Populism and fascism from which (unlike the situation after World War I) recovery seems unlikely. Senators Wheeler, Nye and the late Rush Holt were defeated at the polls and have been unable to regain office. Langer still survives: he was one of three senators to vote against ratification of the United Nations Charter (the other two were the old Progressive Hiram Johnson and the former Farmer-Laborite Henrik Shipstead).[101] But Langer is now only a quaint individualist rather than a spokesman for a social and political movement.

Sympathetic interest in the ideology of Populism is at a low point. Liberal Progressive historians like Hesseltine still may complain that Franklin Roosevelt did not solve the banking problem;[102] nonetheless, Roosevelt did so complicate the situation by dividing fiscal functions between the Federal Reserve and the Treasury that it would be well-nigh impossible to make the problem of credit control a clear-cut political issue. The great apostles of monetary reform are dead politically, and soft versus hard money has subsided into merely one of many policy differences between Republicans and Democrats, one element in the problem of how to adjust the dials in a controlled economy.

---

pensions, the improving of race relations, and "other liberal measures dear to the late Senator Norris." *Ibid.*, p. 4.

[97] Dorothy Roberts, "Feuds Among the Fascists," *New Masses*, LVII (November 20, 1945), 14.

[98] Dorothy Roberts, "Old Anti-Semites in New Clothes," *New Masses*, LVII (October 20, 1945), 8.

[99] Carlson, *The Plotters*, p. 186.

[100] For a description of this meeting see *ibid.*, p. 186 ff.; Roberts, "Old Anti-Semites," *op. cit.*, "Feuds among the Fascists," *op. cit.*, and "Blueprints for Pogroms," *New Masses*, LVII (October 30, 1945), 6–9. This meeting symbolizes the close of an era which began in 1933 with a similar gathering of Populist-fascist oriented critics of capitalism. See on the earlier meeting Harold Loeb and Selden Rodman, "American Fascism in Embryo," *New Republic*, LXXVII (1933), 185–87.

[101] Following the breakup of the old Farmer-Labor party during the war years, Shipstead ran on the Republican ticket and was officially a Republican at this time.

[102] Hesseltine, *op. cit.*, p. 83.

The farmers have decided that their need is not fundamental reform of the system, but that log-rolling for price supports will do, and they have been absorbed into the great push-and-pull of America's quasi-syndicalist economy. Despite price fluctuations the "Farm Bloc" is now mainly a "have" group, even in the states of the Middle Border.

The urban adherents of such leaders as Father Coughlin are now also largely numbered among the "haves" and are little interested in schemes for social reform. In recent years they constituted an important segment of the following of Senator Joseph McCarthy,[103] a man who employed many of the same general tactics as their former leaders but who lacked their racial and economic programs. Some surviving fascist leaders such as Gerald L. K. Smith now devote most of their time to agitating against the United Nations.[104] Others concentrate on such peripheral targets as UNESCO and progressive education.[105] Most of those who figured in the fascist movements of the thirties, however, have melted into the mainstream of the contemporary "radical right."[106]

The American fascist movement dissolved because the radical right appropriated its demagogic nationalism and anticommunism and because its Populist-inspired economic panaceas lost their relevance and appeal as a result of changes in the conditions of American life. For these reasons it seems unlikely that American fascism will ever again be able to attract a substantial popular following.

[103] On the role of Father Coughlin as a link between Populism and McCarthyism see Peter Viereck, "The Revolt against the Elite," in Daniel Bell (ed.), *The New American Right* (New York: Criterion Books, 1955).

Ironically, McCarthy gained his entree into the political limelight by defeating Robert M. La Follette, Jr., in the Republican primary of 1946 with the aid of the votes of Democrats and left-wing labor, led by communists seeking revenge on La Follette for his isolationism and anticommunism. See Jack Anderson and Ronald W. May, *McCarthy: The Man, the Senator, the "Ism"* (Boston: Beacon, 1952), pp. 101–5.

[104] For Smith's activities between 1946 and 1953 see Ralph Lord Roy, *Apostles of Deceit* (Boston: Beacon, 1953), pp. 59–76.

[105] Allen Zoll, an associate of Dennis, Smith, and Coughlin, has turned up in the fight against "progressive" and "subversive" education. *New York Times,* February 21, 1950, p. 29; May 9, 1950, p. 35.

[106] On the contemporary political right-wing movements see Seymour Lipset, "The Sources of the 'Radical Right' " in Bell, *op. cit.*

The Wallace Whitelash

SEYMOUR MARTIN LIPSET
and EARL RAAB

The American Independent Party of George C. Wallace brought together in 1968 almost every right-wing extremist group in the country, and undoubtedly recruited many new activists for the rightist cause. Today many of the state parties organized under this aegis have formal legal status and have announced that they intend to nominate candidates for state and local office during the next few years in an effort to build the party. George Wallace himself has sent out a clear signal that he has plans for the future. He has begun to mail the *George Wallace Newsletter* monthly to a mailing list of over one million names which had been assembled during the election. The old address for Wallace activities was Box 1968, Montgomery, Alabama. It is now Box 1972.

The effort to maintain and build the party, however, faces the perennial problem of ideological extremist movements—splits among its supporters. Even during the 1968 campaign, sharp public divisions over local-versus-national control occurred in a number of states, usually because complete control over the finances and conduct of the party's work was kept in the hands of coordinators directly appointed by Wallace and responsible to the national headquarters in Montgomery. In some states, two separate organizations existed, both of which endorsed the Wallace candidacy but attacked each other as too radical. Since the 1968 election, two competing national organizations have been created and again each is attacking the other as extremist.

The group directly linked to Wallace has had two national conventions. The first, held in Dallas in early February, attracted 250 delegates from forty-four states and set up a group known as The Association of George C. Wallace Voters. The Dallas meeting was attended by a number of top Wallace aides, including Robert Walters, who represents Wallace in California; Tom Turnipseed, a major figure in the Wallace presidential effort since it started; Dan Smoot, the right-wing radio commentator; and Kent Courtney, the editor of the *Conservative Journal*. The same group met again on May 3 and 4 in Cincinnati, and formally established a new national party to be called the American Party. A Virginian, T. Coleman Andrews, long active on the ultraconservative front, was chosen as chairman. Wallace gave his personal bessing to the new party and its officers. One of his Montgomery aides, Taylor Hardin, who maintains a national office with twenty employees in Montgomery, indicated that the party would have a considerable degree of "central control."

The competing national group met in Louisville on February 22, 1969, and established a new national conservative party to be composed largely of autonomous state parties. As if to emphasize the extent to which it fostered local control, this organization called itself The National Committee of the Autonomous State Parties, known as the American Independent Party, American Party, Independent Party, Conservative Party, Constitutional Party. This group, or constellation of groups, was united in its opposition to domination by Wallace and his Montgomery aides. Although the former candidate received compliments at the convention, the delegates were much more concerned with building a movement that was not limited to his supporters in 1968. The national chairman of the new group, William K. Shearer of California, editor of the *California Statesman,* had already broken with Wallace during the campaign on the issue of local autonomy. At the Louisville convention, Shearer said:

> Governor Wallace has not shown any interest in a national party apart from a personal party. A candidate properly springs from the party and not the party from the candidate. The party should not be candidate-directed. While we have great respect for Mr. Wallace we do not think there should be a candidate-directed situation. We want our party to survive regardless of what Mr. Wallace does.

The Shearer group also appears to be more conservative on economic issues than the Wallace-dominated one. During the convention, Wallace was criticized for being "too liberal" because of his advocacy during the campaign of extended social security and farm parity prices.

The leaders of each faction claim that the other includes extremists. Robert Walters attacked Shearer's group as composed of "radicals and opportunists" and as having "a pretty high nut content." Shearer, on the other hand, has said that he finds many in the Wallace-dominated party "not too savory."

The publications of the competing groups indicate that each is supported by viable segments of the 1968 party. The Shearer national committee, however, is clearly much weaker financially, since the Wallace national group retained a considerable sum from the 1968 campaign for future activities. It is also unlikely that they can attract many Wallace voters against the opposition of the candidate. The competition for support, however, does give each group an immediate function; and both national organizations appear to be busy holding state and local conventions designed to win over those who were involved in the presidential campaign.

Who *did* support George Wallace in 1968? A detailed answer to that question will perhaps tell us more than anything else about his chances for the future, as well as about the potentiality of right-wing extremism in America.

Election Day results confirmed the basic predictions of the preelection opinion polls. George Wallace secured almost ten million votes, or about 13.5 percent of the total voting electorate. He captured five states with forty-five electoral votes, all of them in the Deep South: Mississippi, Georgia, Alabama, Louisiana and Arkansas. With the exception of Arkansas, which had gone to Johnson in 1964, these were the same states Barry Goldwater won in that year. But Wallace lost two states carried by Goldwater—South Carolina, the home state of Nixon's Southern leader, the 1948 Dixiecrat candidate, Strom Thurmond, and Arizona, Goldwater's home state.

Since the support for Wallace seemingly declined considerably between early October and Election Day, falling from about 21 percent to 13 percent, an analysis of his actual polling strength is obviously important. Fortunately, the Gallup Poll conducted a national survey immediately after the election in which it inquired how respondents voted and whether they had supported another candidate earlier in the campaign. The data of this survey were made available by the Gallup Poll for our analysis. They are particularly useful since it would appear that most voters who had supported Wallace, but shifted to another candidate, did report this fact to Gallup interviewers. Thirteen percent indicated they had voted for Wallace, while another 9 percent stated that they had been for him at an earlier stage in the campaign.

From the national results among whites, it is clear that the data are heavily influenced by the pattern of support in the South. Wallace's voters were most likely to be persons who did not vote in 1964, or who backed Goldwater rather than Johnson. The pattern of an extremist party recruiting heavily from the ranks of nonvoters coincides with the evidence from previous extremist movements both in this country and abroad. Wallace also clearly appealed to those in smaller communities, and his strength was greatest among those with the least education. With respect to income, his backers were more likely to come from the poorer strata than the more well-to-do, although he was slightly weaker among the lowest income class—under $3,000—than among the next highest. He was strongest among those in "service" jobs, a conglomerate which includes police, domestic servants and the military. Of the regular urban occupational classes, his support was highest among the unskilled, followed by the skilled, white-collar workers, those in business and managerial pursuits, and professionals, in that order. The number of farmers voting for Wallace was relatively low, a phenomenon stemming from differences between farmers in the South and in the rest of the country. Among manual workers, Wallace was much weaker with union members than nonunionists.

The voting behavior with respect to other factors also corresponds in general to preelection predictions. Wallace was backed more heavily by men than by women, a pattern characteristically associated with radical movements, whether of the left or right. Surprisingly, young voters were more likely to prefer him than middle-aged and older ones, with the partial exception that voters in the twenty-five-to-twenty-nine-year-old category were a bit more likely to prefer Wallace than the twenty-one-to-twenty-four-year-old age group. Religion also served to differentiate: Wallace received a higher proportion of the votes of Protestants than Catholics—a product of his strength in the predominantly Protestant South.

Viewed nationally, however, the pattern of support for Wallace is a bit deceiving since so much of his support was in the South. He carried five Southern states and received a substantial vote in all the others, plus the border states. To a considerable extent, his movement in the South took on the character of a "preservatist" defense of Southern institutions against the threat from the federal government. In most Southern states, it was a major-party candidacy. In the rest of the country, however, the Wallace movement was a small radical third party, organized around various extreme right-wing groups. While it obviously gave expression to racial concerns, it also included a number of other varieties of the disaffected. One would expect, therefore, differences in the types of voters to whom he appealed in the different sections.

The variations are apparent along a number of dimensions. Northern Wallace voters were more likely to come from the ranks of identified and committed Republicans than were those from the South. Thus in the South, a much larger proportion of people who were identified as Democrats (37 percent) than as Republicans (10 percent) voted for him. Conversely in the North, a slightly larger segment of the Republicans voted for him than did Democrats. This emphasis is reversed, however, with respect to the 1964 vote. In both sections, larger proportions of Goldwater voters opted for Wallace than did Johnson supporters. Relatively, however, he did better among the Southern Goldwater voters. The seeming contradiction may be explained by the fact that Wallace did best among "independents," and that there were proportionately many more independents in the South than in the North. Southern independents presumably are people who have opted out of the Democratic party toward the right, many of whom voted for Goldwater in 1964 and Wallace in 1968. His greatest support, both North and South, of course, came from the ranks of those who did not vote in 1964. Almost half of the Southern nonvoters in the 1964 election who voted in 1968 chose Wallace.

The effect of the social-stratification variables were relatively similar in both parts of the country. In general, the better-educated, the more well-to-do and those in middle-class occupations were less likely to vote for Wallace than voters in the lower echelons.

As far as religion is concerned, nationally, Wallace appeared to secure more support among Protestants than Catholics, but a sectional breakdown points up the fact that this was because of the relatively small Catholic population in the South. Outside of the South, Wallace secured more support from Catholics than from Protestants. The pattern appears to be reversed in the South, but the number of Catholics in the sample is too small to sustain a reliable estimate. What is perhaps more significant than the Catholic-Protestant variation is the difference among the Protestant denominations. Wallace's greatest backing, North and South, came from Baptists, followed by "other," presumably mainly fundamentalist sects which have a history of disproportionately backing right-wing groups. Wallace, after all, became the protector of the "Southern way of life" and the status of those who bear it, not only for Southerners, but for Southern migrants to the North. This, apart from education, is one significance of the disproportionate support of Wallace by Northern Baptists.

As noted earlier, perhaps the most surprising finding of the polls was the consistent report by Gallup, Harris and the Michigan Survey Research Center that youth, whether defined as twenty-one to twenty-four or twenty-one to twenty-nine years old, were more favorable to the third-party candidate than those in older age groups. Two special surveys of youth opinion also pointed in this direction. One was commissioned by *Fortune* and carried out by the Daniel Yankelovich organization among 718 young people aged eighteen to twenty-four in October 1968. It revealed that among employed youth 25 percent were for Wallace, as compared with 23 for Humphrey, 31 for Nixon and 15 without a choice. Among college students, Wallace received 7 percent of the vote. A secondary analysis of this survey indicated that class and educational level differentiated this youth group as well. Thus 31 percent of young manual workers who were the sons of manual workers were for Wallace, as contrasted with but 6 percent among nonmanual workers whose fathers were on the same side of the dividing line. A pre-election survey by the Purdue Opinion Poll among a national sample of high school students, reported that Wallace had considerable strength among them as well: 22 percent backing, which came heavily from members of Southern and economically less affluent families.

This "shift to the right" among youth had first been detected among young Southerners. Although various surveys had found a pattern of greater youth support for integration in the South during the forties and fifties, by the 1960's this finding had been inverted, according to two NORC polls reported by Paul Sheatsley and Herbert Hyman. They suggested that Southern youth who grew up amid the tensions produced by the school integration battles reacted more negatively than the preceding generations who had not been exposed to such conflicts during their formative political years. And as the issue of government-enforced integration in the schools and neighborhoods spread to the North, white opinion in central city areas, which are usually inhabited by workers, also took on an increased racist character.

What has happened is that increasing numbers of white young people in the South and in many working-class districts of the North have been exposed in recent years to repeated discussions of the supposed threats to their schools and communities posed by integration. They have been reared in homes and neighborhoods where anti-Negro sentiments became increasingly common. Hence, while the upper-middle-class scions of liberal parents were being radicalized to the left by civil rights and Vietnam war issues, a sizable segment of Southern and Northern working-class youth were being radicalized to the right. The consequence of such polarizations can be seen in the very different behavior of the two groups in the 1968 election campaign.

The indications that the Wallace movement drew heavily among youth are congruent with the evidence from various studies of youth and student politics that suggests young people are disposed to support the more extreme or idealistic version of the politics dominant within their social strata. In Europe, extremist movements both of the right and left have been more likely to secure the support of the young than the democratic parties of the center. Being less committed to existing institutions and parties than older people, and being less inured to the need to compromise in order to attain political objectives, youth are disproportionately attracted to leaders and movements which promise to resolve basic problems quickly and in an absolute fashion.

So much for those who actually voted for Wallace. Equally significant are those who supported Wallace in the campaign but didn't vote for him. Presumably many who shifted from Wallace did so because they thought he could not win, not because they would not have liked to see him as President. This is the uneasiness of the "lost vote." There is also the "expressive" factor, the votes in polls which do not count. Casting a straw vote for Wallace was clearly one method of striking a generalized note of dissatisfaction in certain directions. But since total considerations take over in the voting booth, the nature of the defections becomes one way to measure these dissatisfactions in various quarters. On another level, there is the factor of the social reinforcements that may or may not exist in the voter's milieu and are important for the ability of a third-party candidate to hold his base of support under attack.

In general, Wallace lost most heavily among groups and in areas where he was weak to begin with. Individuals in these groups would find less support for their opinions among their acquaintances, and also would be more likely to feel that a Wallace vote was wasted. In the South, however, almost four-fifths of all those who ever considered voting for Wallace did in fact vote for him. In the North, he lost over half of his initial support: only 43 percent of his original supporters cast a ballot for him. Similarly, Baptists and the small "other" Protestant sects were more likely to remain in the Wallace camp than less pro-Wallace religious groups.

There were certain significant differences in the pattern of defections with respect to social stratification. In the South, middle-class supporters of Wallace were much more likely to move away from him as the campaign progressed. He wound up with 90 percent of his preelection support among Southern manual workers, and 61 percent among those in nonmanual occupations. In the North, however, Wallace retained a larger proportion of his middle-class backers (52 percent) than of his working-class followers (42 percent).

The data from the Gallup survey suggest, then, that the very extensive campaign of trade-union leaders to reduce Wallace support among their membership actually had an effect in the North. Almost two-thirds (64 percent) of Northern trade-union members who had backed Wallace initially *did not* vote for him on Election Day. A similar pattern occurred with respect to the two other measures of stratification, education and income. Wallace retained more backing among the better-educated and more affluent of his Northern supporters, while in the South these groups were much more likely to have defected by Election Day than the less educated and less privileged.

The variations in the class background of the defectors in the different sections of the country may be a function of varying exposures to reinforcing and cross-pressure stimuli in their respective environments. On the whole we would guess that middle-class Wallace supporters in the North came disproportionately from the group of persons previously committed to extreme rightist ideology and affiliations. Wallace's support among the Northern middle-class corresponds in size to that given to the John Birch Society in opinion polls. If we assume that most people who were pro-Birch were pro-Wallace, then presumably Wallace did not break out of this rela-

tively small group. And this group, which was heavily involved in a reinforcing environment, could have been expected to stick with him. In the
South, on the other hand, he began with considerable middle-class support
gained from people who had been behind the effort to create a conservative
Republican Party in that section. The majority of them had backed Barry
Goldwater in 1964. This large group of affluent Southern Wallace-ites encompassed many who had not been involved in extremist activities. And it
would seem that the efforts of the Southern conservative Republicans
(headed by Strom Thurmond) to convince them that a vote for Wallace
would help Humphrey were effective. Conversely, among Northern manual
workers an inclination to vote for Wallace placed men outside the dominant
pattern within their class.

Which of the other two candidates the Wallace defectors voted for clearly
depended on background. Three-fifths of those who shifted away from Wallace during the campaign ended up voting for Nixon. But those Wallace
backers who decided to vote for one of the major-party candidates almost
invariably reverted to their traditional party affiliation. The pattern is even
clearer when Southern Democrats are eliminated. Among the twenty-nine
Northern Democrats in our sample who defected from Wallace, 90 percent
voted for Hubert Humphrey. Humphrey recruited from among the less
educated and poorer Wallace voters, Nixon from the more affluent and better-educated.

The pattern of shifting among the Wallace voters points up our assumption that Wallace appealed to two very different groups: economic conservatives concerned with repudiating the welfare state, and less affluent
supporters of the welfare state who were affected by issues of racial integration and "law and order." As some individuals in each of these groups felt
motivated to change their vote, they opted for the candidate who presumably stood closer to their basic economic concerns. The data also point up
the difficulty of building a new movement encompassing people with highly
disparate sentiments and interests.

After specifying what kinds of groups voted for whom, the most interesting question still remains, especially with respect to deviant and extremist
political movements such as Wallace's: What creates the differentials within
each of these groups? Why, in other words, do some members of a group
vote for a particular candidate, but not others? Quite clearly, members of
the same heuristic group or class may vary greatly in their perception of the
world, and will therefore differ as to political choice. Since candidates do
differ in their ideology and position on particular issues, we should expect
that the values of the electorate should help determine which segments of a
particular stratum end up voting one way or another.

Data collected by the Louis Harris Poll permit us to analyze the connection between political attitudes and voter choice in 1968. The Harris data
are derived from a special reanalysis of the results of a number of surveys
conducted during the campaign that were prepared by the Harris organization for the American Jewish Committee. Based on 16,915 interviews, it
points up consistent variations. The question that best indicated differing
political attitudes among those voting for a given candidate was one in the
Harris survey that asked, "Which groups are responsible for trouble in the

country?" Choices ranged from the federal government to Communists, students, professors, Jews and others.

The findings of the Harris organization clearly differentiate the supporters of the different candidates in 1968 and 1964. On most items, the rank order of opinions goes consistently from right to left, from Wallace to Goldwater to Nixon to Johnson to Humphrey. That is, the Wallace supporters show the most right-wing opinions, while the Humphrey ones are the most left. As a group those who voted for Goldwater in 1964 are somewhat more "preservatist" than the Nixon supporters in 1968. There is, of course, a considerable overlap. Since none of these items bear on attitudes toward the welfare state, what they attest to is the disdain which rightists feel toward groups identified with social changes they dislike.

The Wallace supporters differ most from the population as a whole with respect to their feelings toward the federal government, Negroes, the Ku Klux Klan and, most surprisingly, "ministers and priests." Although Wallace himself did not devote much attention to attacking the liberal clergy, his followers were seemingly more bothered by their activities than by those of professors. Although the electorate as a whole was inclined to see "students" as a major source of trouble, Wallace backers hardly differed from the supporters of the two other candidates in their feelings. As far as we can judge from these results, they confirm the impression that Wallace appealed strongly to people who identified their distress with changes in race relations, with federal interference, and with changes in religious morality. It is of interest that the Wallace supporters in the South and those in the non-South project essentially the same pattern. The Southern differential is very slight with respect to blaming Negroes, still slight but higher in blaming clergymen, and higher yet in blaming the federal government.

Fears that Wallace would convert his following into an extraparliamentary influence on the government and terrorize opponents by taking to the streets —fears based on statements that Wallace himself made during the campaign —have thus far proved unwarranted. Wallace seems largely concerned with maintaining his electoral base for a possible presidential campaign in 1972. The effort to continue control of the party from Montgomery seems to be dedicated to this end.

The existence of local electoral parties, even those willing to follow Wallace's lead completely, clearly poses a great problem for him. Wallace's electoral following is evidently much greater than can be mobilized behind the local unknown candidates of the American Party. To maintain the party organizations, they must nominate men for various offices. Yet should such people continue to secure tiny votes, as is likely in most parts of the country, Wallace may find his image as a mass leader severely injured. He seems to recognize this, and though concerned with keeping control over the party organization, he has also stressed the difference between the "movement" and the "party," describing the two as "separate entities" which agree on "purposes and aims." Wallace is emphatic about this: "The *movement* will be here in 1972. The *movement* is solvent and it will be active." Speaking at the Virginia convention of the American Party in mid-July of 1969, he said, "A new party ought to go very slow. It ought to crawl before it walks. It ought to nominate a candidate only if he has a chance to be elected." In

Tulsa, he again warned his followers to move slowly, if at all, in nominating Congressional and local candidates. He argued that if he was elected President in the future he "wouldn't have any trouble getting support from Congress, because most of its [major party] members were for the things [I'm] for."

One aspect of the nonparty "movement" may be the reported expansion of the Citizens Council of America, whose national headquarters is in Jackson, Mississippi. Its administrator, William J. Simmons, helped direct Wallace's presidential campaign in Mississippi, where he received 65 percent of the vote. In June 1969, Simmons said, "There has been no erosion in Wallace strength. Wallace articulates the hopes and views of over 99 per cent of our members. This state is not enchanted with Nixon, and Wallace sentiment is very strong indeed." He also reported that the Council, mainly concerned with the maintenance of segregation in the schools, had expanded "as a result of backlash generated by campus riots and better grassroots organizational work." The impetus of the Wallace campaign remains one reservoir of future organization strength for Wallace.

Moreover, Wallace has attempted to maintain his ties to other groups whose members had backed him in 1968. The Birch Society's principal campaign during 1969 has been against sex education and pornography; Wallace devoted a considerable part of his talks during the year to the subject. In addition, he publicly embraced for the first time the ultraconservative "Christian Crusade" of Billy James Hargis by attending its annual convention.

In his speeches and *Newsletter* Wallace has retained the same combination of "preservatist" moralism and populist economic issues that characterized his presidential campaign. On the one hand, he continues to emphasize the issues of "law and order," "campus radicalism," "military failures in Vietnam," and "the need for local control of schools." On the other hand, speaking in Tulsa, one of the principal centers of the oil industry, he called for tax reform that would benefit the little man, adding that "the 27½ percent oil depletion allowance ought to be looked into." He argued that we must "shift the [tax] burden to the upper-class millionaires, billionaires and tax-exempt foundations." Since this kind of rhetoric flies in the face of the deep-dyed economic conservatives among his supporters, such as the Birchers, it is clear that Wallace's grab bag of appeals still suffers from the same sort of contradictions that characterized it in 1968—contradictions, it might be added, which have characterized most other right-wing extremist movements in American history.

Another problem that Wallace faces comes from supporters who want to build an extremist movement rather than an electoral organization for one man's candidacy. This can be seen in the activities of an autonomous youth organization, the National Youth Alliance, formed by those active in Youth for Wallace. As of September 1969, the NYA claimed 3,000 dues-paying members recruited from the 15,000-person mailing list of the Youth for Wallace student organizations. The group has a more absolutist and militant character than either adult party, and it is much more unashamedly racist. Members wear an "inequality button" emblazoned with the mathematical symbol of inequality. Among other things, the Alliance advocates "White studies" curricula in colleges and universities. According to its national organizer,

Louis T. Byers, "The purpose of these will be to demonstrate the nature of mankind. The equality myth will be exploded forever." In an article describing its objectives the then-national vice-president, Dennis C. McMahon, stated that NYA "is an organization with the determination to liquidate the enemies of the American people on the campus and in the community." The tone of this pro-Wallace youth group sounds closer to that of classic fascism than any statements previously made by Wallace's associates. As McMahon wrote,

> The National Youth Alliance is an organization that intends to bury the red front once and for all . . . The NYA is made up of dedicated, self-sacrificing young people who are ready to fight, and die if necessary, for the sacred cause. . . .
>
> Now is the time for the Right Front terror to descend on the wretched liberals. In short, the terror of the Left will be met with the greater terror of the Right . . . Tar and feathers will be our answer to the pot pusher and these animals will no longer be allowed to prowl and hunt for the minds of American students. . . .
>
> A bright future full of conquest lies ahead of us . . . Soon the NYA will become a household word and the Left will be forced to cower in the sewers underground as they hear the marching steps of the NYA above them.

The racism of NYA leaders includes approval, if not advocacy, of virulent anti-Semitism. Its national headquarters in Washington distributes literature by Francis Parker Yockey, including his book *Imperium*, which defines Jews, Negroes, Indians and other minorities as "parasites" in the Western world. The five members of its adult advisory board have all been involved in anti-Semitic activities. Two of them, Rivilo P. Oliver and Richard B. Cotten, were forced out of the Birch Society because of their overt racist and anti-Semitic views. A third, retired Rear Admiral John Crommelein, ran for President on the anti-Semitic National States Rights Party ticket in 1960; while a fourth, retired Marine Lieutenant General Pedro A. Del Valle, is an officer of the Christian Educational Association, which publishes the overtly anti-Semitic paper *Common Sense*. The fifth member of the board, Austin J. App, former English professor at LaSalle College, is a contributing editor to the anti-Semitic magazine *American Mercury*.

Perhaps most interesting of all the problems that Wallace will have to deal with is the fact that the national chairman of his American Party, T. Coleman Andrews, has publicly advocated the Birch Society's version of that hoary international conspiracy, the historic plot of the Illuminati. The Illuminati, which was an organization of Enlightenment intellectuals formed in Bavaria in 1776, and dissolved, according to historical record, in 1785, has figured in the conspiratorial theories of assorted American right-wing movements as the insiders behind every effort for religious, economic and social reform since the 1790's. In recent times both Father Coughlin, the former right-wing extremist of the 1930's, and Robert Welch, the head of the Birch Society, have explained various threats to "the American Way"—from the French Revolution to the Communist movement—as well as the behavior of most key officials of the government, as reflecting the power of this secret cabal of satanically clever plotters. In a newspaper interview following the establishment of the American Party in May, Andrews bluntly announced:

I believe in the conspiratorial theory of History . . . [The Birch Society has been] responsible, respectable. . . . Recently, the Birch Society has begun to prosper. People are beginning to see that its original theories were right . . . There is an international conspiracy.

Though George Wallace himself has never publicly stated a belief in the conspiracy of the Illuminati (he prefers to talk about the role of Communists, pseudo-intellectuals and the Council on Foreign Relations), the formal organization of his personally controlled national party is headed by a man who has no such hesitation. On May 26, 1969, Wallace formally sanctioned the American Party as the political arm of the movement and said that if he ran for President again it would be under the American Party's banners.

However, while the pulls toward the conspiracy theory and toward ideological racism are evident in the background, the logic of the Wallace-ite movement and its future as a mass movement obviously rests on other foundations. S. M. Miller points out that many had been shocked by "the attraction of George Wallace as a presidential candidate to a large number of union members . . . racism appeared to be rampant in the working class. When the vote came, however, racism seemed to have receded before economic concerns." Their disaffection remains, nevertheless. As Miller writes, "About half of American families are above the poverty line but below the adequacy level. This group, neither poor nor affluent, composed not only of blue-collar workers but also of many white-collar workers, is hurting and neglected." It is the members of this group that the Wallace-ite movement must grow on if it is to grow, not so much out of their ideological racism as out of their general sense of neglected decline.

Whether the Wallace movement itself will have returned to full or fuller electoral vigor by 1972 depends on a number of factors which emerge from an examination of America's right-wing extremist past. Determinative—not just for the Wallace movement but for any extremist movement—will be the larger historical circumstances. The disaffection of the white working class and lower-middle class has been noted; if that disaffection grows, and *at the same time* the pressures of an increasingly disaffected black population increase, the soil will of course be fertile for a George Wallace kind of movement. It is the pressure of the emergent black population that provides an essentially preservatist thrust to the social and economic strains of the vulnerable whites. Whether the major political parties can absorb these concomitant pressures in some pragmatic fashion as they have in the past is another conditional factor, which is also partly dependent on historical development.

Wallace, however, is clearly preparing to use another issue in 1972—the responsibility for American defeat in Vietnam. Like others on the right, he has repeatedly argued that if the U.S. government really wanted to win the war, it could do so easily, given America's enormous superiority in resources and weapons technology. Consequently, the only reason we have not won is political: those who have controlled our strategy consciously do not want to win. But, he argued recently, if it "should be that Washington has committed itself to a policy of American withdrawal, irrespective of reciprocal action on the part of the enemy, in effect acknowledging defeat for our forces, which is inconceivable, we feel that such withdrawal should be swiftly accomplished so that casualty losses may be held to a minimum." And in late 1969 he left for a three-week tour of Vietnam and Southeast Asia, announcing that he would run in 1972 if Vietnam was turned over to the Communists "in effect or in substance." Clearly Wallace hopes to run in 1972 on the issue that American boys have died needlessly, that they were stabbed in the back by Lyndon Johnson and Richard Nixon.

In order to do so, however, Wallace must keep his movement alive. As he well recognizes, it is subject to the traditional organizational hazards of such a movement, notably fragmentation, and the ascendancy of overt extremist tendencies that will alienate the more respectable leadership and support. During the year following the 1968 election, he performed as though he understood these hazards well. He has attempted to keep his organization formally separated from the fringe groups and the more rabid extremists, even those who were in open support of him. In a letter sent to key Wallace lieutenants around the country, asking about the local leadership that might be involved in the next Wallace campaign, James T. Hardin, administrative assistant to Wallace, carefully emphasized that "perhaps of greatest importance, we would like your opinion as to those who demonstrated neither ability nor capability to work with others and who were, in fact, a detriment to the campaign . . ."

Whether Wallace can succeed in avoiding the organizational hazards of which he seems aware, and whether historical circumstances will be favorable, is of course problematical. But whether his particular movement survives or not, George Wallace has put together and further revealed the nature of those basic elements which must comprise an effective right-wing extremist movement in America.

6: Repression
of
Dissent

The major problem of any social movement is survival in a hostile world. Political visionaries and idealists are increasingly considered "social deviants," as Horowitz and Liebowitz indicate. Once labeled as "deviants," radicals are stigmatized and subjected to various societal sanctions. The more extreme or radical the movement, the greater the likelihood that it will be judged "deviant" and generate strong negative reactions.

Every society labels its deviants, either through public opinion or political institutions. Public opinion may judge a group as deviant, and the operations of the group may then be restricted. Demonstrations and meetings, for example, may either be banned through judicial action or made purposely difficult by law-enforcement agencies. Such measures serve to limit the ability of a movement to survive.

As a Supreme Court justice once remarked, a people's most valuable possession is "the right to prevent self destruction." This assumed right legitimates the exercise of repressive power in the guise of "protecting" the existing order. The use of law-enforcement agencies against political organizations, however, presents a dilemma to the authorities in the United States. Political dissidence is protected by law; people and organizations have the constitutional right to assemble, dissent, and speak out against what they consider to be "injustice." This form of political activity cannot be legally tampered with unless it is deemed beyond the protection of the Constitution. As can be easily seen, it is useful for the authorities to apply the stigma of "criminality" to radical groups. The options for action against such movements greatly increase when they can be thought of as criminal.[1]

The labeling of the American Communists as "subversive" and the charge that they engaged in various espionage activities enabled the U.S. government to treat the political organization as a criminal one. This allowed the government to resort to otherwise proscribed activities in its effort to destroy the CPUSA. As Shannon demonstrates in this chapter, the CPUSA was an easy target. Not only did many people already view the CPUSA as criminal, but the Party's rigid adherence to the shifting line put forth by the Kremlin alienated many potential supporters.[2] Hence, there was little broad-based opposition to the government's abrogation of the civil rights of individuals suspected of being Party members. More recently, organizations such as the Weathermen, Black Muslims, and Black Panthers have been subjected

---

[1] For examples, see R. Serge Denisoff and Charles H. McCaghy, eds., *Deviance, Conflict, and Criminality* (Chicago: Rand McNally and Co., 1973), pp. 239–330.
[2] Theodore Draper, *American Communism and Soviet Russia* (New York: Viking Press, 1960).

to somewhat similar treatment by the government. Leaders of radical movements have been publicly accused of immorality, theft, and other deviant acts.[3] A movement's life style may be labeled deviant also: "It's all part of the Godless, atheistic, homosexual, drug-smoking, free love, hippie conspiracy to overthrow the government by force and violence."[4] Threats of violence provide the government with the excuse to arrest and harass groups it disapproves of, even when in some cases the groups are legally innocent of any wrongdoing.[5]

The use of a deviance tag can sometimes backfire, since protest activity is at least theoretically protected by law. A movement can become "an underdog" and gain the sympathies of nonpolitical people.[6] As Rodney Stark shows, the "police riot," the use of unwarranted force by the police, can shift culpability from the protester to the legal authorities. Many students were "radicalized" during the late sixties by government excesses against demonstrators at Columbia, Cornell, and Kent State.

Violent confrontations involve an exchange of risk for both sides in a conflict. On the one hand, a confrontation places an insurgent movement in a position where it can be shattered by exposing its members to being beaten, jailed, and sometimes killed. The ability of the movement to disperse, regroup, and resume its activities after such treatment is questionable. On the other hand, violent repression is the ultimate weapon of government. As with other ultimate weapons, its use may precipitate a desperate situation. A prolonged and unresolved confrontation can result in a state of "internal war" that may, in time, lead to revolution.[7]

Violence, when not used judiciously, can call into question the legitimacy of the government. Large-scale arrests of peaceful dissenters, imprisonment without trial, and arbitrary killings undermine faith in the regime. Indeed, these acts highlight the existing strains between the ruled and the ruler, and violence itself can become a major political issue. Its very use then becomes counterproductive. When the legitimacy of the state has deteriorated, violence may not be sufficient to maintain power, as was the case in Cuba prior to Fidel Castro and in Russia prior to Lenin. At the very least, successful revolutions indicate that the use of governmental violence is not always an adequate response to the pressure for social change.

3 See Colin Miller, "The Press and the Student Revolt," in *Revolution at Berkeley*, ed. Michael V. Miller and Susan Gilmore (New York: Dell Books, 1966), pp. 313–48.
4 See Charles E. Moore, "Anarchy on the Campus," *The Police Chief* 32 (April, 1965): 48–60; and Michael E. Brown, "The Condemnation and Persecution of Hippies," *Transaction* 6 (September, 1969): 33–46.
5 See Rodney Stark, *Police Riots: Collective Violence and Law Enforcement* (Belmont, Calif.: Focus Books, 1972); and C. R. Hormachea and Marion Hormaches, eds., *Confrontation: Violence and the Police* (Boston: Holbrook Press, 1971).
6 Jerry L. Avorn et al., *Up Against the Ivy Wall: A History of the Columbia Crisis* (New York: Atheneum, 1968); and William Barlow and Peter Shapiro, *An End to Silence: The San Francisco State Student Movement in the '60s* (New York: Pegasus Books, 1971).
7 Harry Eckstein, "On the Etiology of Internal Wars," *History and Theory* 4 (1965); 133–63.

Social Deviance
and Political Marginality:
Toward a Redefinition
of the Relation Between
Sociology and Politics

IRVING LOUIS HOROWITZ
and MARTIN LIEBOWITZ

THE WELFARE MODEL OF SOCIAL PROBLEMS

The study of social deviance within American sociology has traditionally been based on a model that consigns delinquent behavior to the instruments of social welfare. This model has sought to liberalize the visible agencies of social control (the police, judiciary, and welfare agents) by converting them from punitive instruments into rehabilitative instruments. This underlying premise that punishment and rehabilitation are the only two possible responses to deviance yields the conventional tendency to evaluate deviant behavior in *therapeutic* rather than *political* terms.[1]

The rehabilitation model seeks a more human redefinition of the moral code as its long-range goal. Its short-range goal is to indicate the superordinate role that agencies of social control adopt in prescribing subordinate status to deviants. Coser has recognized this role conflict in the welfare orientation to poverty when he indicated that "in the very process of being helped and assisted, the poor are assigned to a special career that impairs their identity and becomes a stigma which marks their intercourse with others."[2]

---

[1] See, for example, Gwynn Nettler, "Ideology and Welfare Policy," *Social Problems*, 6 (Winter, 1958–59), pp. 203–212; also see his "A Measure of Alienation," *American Sociological Review*, 22 (April, 1957).

[2] Lewis A. Coser, "The Sociology of Poverty," *Social Problems*, 13 (Fall, 1965), p. 145.

However serviceable this model has been in the past, and notwithstanding its use in resisting encroachments on the civil liberties of accused deviants, the social welfare model does not exhaust present options—either on logical or pragmatic grounds. A relationship among equals is possible only in democratic politics, where conflicts are resolved by power rather than *a priori* considerations of ascribed status. Only in such politics can deviants attain the status of legitimate combatants in social conflict.

POLITICAL REQUISITES OF SOCIAL PROBLEMS

In the traditional welfare model, deviant behavior is defined as a social problem. This definition implies several important assumptions about the nature of deviance. First, it takes for granted that deviance is a problem about which something should be done. Second, it assumes that deviance is a public problem, which means that social agencies have the right to intervene. Finally, deviance is treated as a social problem in contradistinction to a political issue. Thus decisions concerning it are relegated to administrative policy rather than to the political arena. As a result, deviance is handled by experts instead of being debated by the very publics who are supposedly menaced.

These beliefs about the nature of deviance have scant empirical justification. They derive from no intrinsic characteristics of deviance. Rather, they are normative statements about how deviant behavior should be treated. Bernard has shown a singular appreciation of this.

> Values are inherent in the very concept of social problems. The conditions that are viewed as social problems are evaluated by the decision-maker as bad, as requiring change or reform. Something must be done about them. The reason for coming to the conclusion may be humanitarian, utilitarian, or functional. In any case, a system of values is always implicit, and usually quite explicit.[3]

In this framework, identifying the values of the decision-makers is crucial. As Becker indicates, if we take the above seriously, the selection of decision-makers who define deviance as a social problem is a political process, not only a value problem.

> The question of what the purpose or goal (function) of a group is, and, consequently, what things will help or hinder the achievement of that purpose, is very often a political question. Factions within the group disagree and maneuver to have their own definition of the group's function accepted. The function of the group or organization, then, is decided in political conflict, not given in the nature of the organization. If this is true, then it is likewise true that the questions of what rules are to be enforced, what behavior regarded as deviant and what people labeled as outsiders must also be regarded as political.[4]

[3] Jessie Bernard, "Social Problems as Problems of Decision," *Social Problems,* 6 (Winter, 1958–59), pp. 212, 215.
[4] Howard S. Becker, *The Outsiders,* New York: Free Press, 1963, p. 7.

The decision to treat deviance as a social problem is itself a political decision. It represents the political ability of one group of decision-makers to impose its value sentiments upon decisions concerning deviance. The anomaly is that although the political decision has been to treat deviance as a non-political problem, deviance persists as a political problem. A comprehensive analysis of deviance must include political factors by determining which decision-makers define deviance as a social problem, and indicate why they consider deviance a problem. Lemert was almost alone among the sociologists of the past decade to contend that deviance does not pose an objectively serious problem.

> In studying the problem-defining reactions of a community, it can be shown that public consciousness of "problems" and aggregate moral reactions frequently center around forms of behavior which on closer analysis often prove to be of minor importance in the social system. Conversely, community members not infrequently ignore behavior which is a major disruptive influence on their lives. We are all too familiar with the way in which populations in various cities and states have been aroused to frenzied punitive action against sex offenders. Nevertheless, in these same areas the people as a whole often are indifferent toward crimes committed by businessmen or corporations—crimes which affect far more people and which may be far more serious over a period of time.[5]

A CONFLICT MODEL OF DEVIANCE

Deviance is a conflict between at least two parties: superordinates who make and enforce rules, and subordinates whose behavior violates those rules. Lemert noted the implications of this conflict for understanding the sources of deviance.

> Their common concern is with social control and its consequences for deviance. This is a large turn away from older sociology which tended to rest heavily upon the idea that deviance leads to social control. I have come to believe that the reverse idea, *i.e.*, social control leads to deviance, is equally tenable and the potentially richer premise for studying deviance in modern society.[6]

The conflict model implies alternative formulations of deviance as a problem: the deviant behavior itself, and the actions of rule-makers to prevent such behavior. The political climate prescribes both what conflicts will occur between deviants and non-deviants, and the rules by which such conflicts will be resolved. The struggle of groups for legitimation thus constitutes an integral part of deviant behavior.

Deviance has been studied by employing a consensus welfare model rather than a conflict model because, for the most part, decision-making

[5] Edwin M. Lemert, *Social Pathology*, New York: McGraw-Hill, 1951, p. 4.
[6] Edwin M. Lemert, *Human Deviance, Social Problems and Social Control*, Englewood Cliffs, N.J.: Prentice-Hall, 1967, p. 5.

concerning deviance has been one-sided. The superordinate parties who regulate deviance have developed measures of control, while the subordinate parties, the deviants themselves, have not entered the political arena. The conflict, though existent, has remained hidden. As Becker correctly notes, this leads to a non-political treatment of deviance:

> It is a situation in which, while conflict and tension exist in the hierarchy, the conflict has not become openly political. The conflicting segments or ranks are not organized for conflict; no one attempts to alter the shape of the hierarchy. While subordinates may complain about the treatment they receive from those above them, they do not propose to move to a position of equality with them, or to reverse positions in the hierarchy. Thus, no one proposes that addicts should make and enforce laws for policemen, that patients should prescribe for doctors, or that adolescents should give orders to adults. We call this the *apolitical* case.[7]

As the politicization of deviance develops, this apolitical case will become atypical—the hidden conflict will become visible and deviants can be expected to demand changes in the configuration of the social hierarchy.

Although there has been scattered intellectual opposition to asylums in the past, patients have never been organized to eliminate or radically alter mental hospitals; addicts, to legalize drug use; or criminals, to abolish prisons. Synanon, a center formed by addicts to treat drug addiction, is a striking exception to this pattern. Staffed completely by former addicts, it has no professional therapists. Thus, it represents an insistence that deviants themselves are best able to define their own problems and deal with those problems. Ironically, while Synanon challenges both the right and the competency of professional therapists to intervene in the lives of addicts, it has not discarded the value premises of an adjustment therapy. Nonetheless, as Yablonsky indicates, this marks a departure from the conventional welfare model.

> Over the past fifty years, the treatment of social problems has been dropped into the professional lap and has been held onto tightly. The propaganda about the professional's exclusive right to treat social problems has reached its high mark. The professionals, the public, and even patients are firmly convinced that the only "bona fide" treatments and "cures" available come from "legitimate professionals" with the right set of degrees.[8]

Even where deviant social movements have become powerful, they have avoided political participation as special interest groups. For instance, Synanon has acted politically only when new zoning codes threatened its very existence. The politicization of deviance is occurring, as groups like homosexuals and drug addicts pioneer the development of organizational responses to harassment. A broad base for the political organization of devi-

[7] Howard S. Becker, "Whose Side Are We On?," *Social Problems*, 14 (Winter, 1967), pp. 240–41.
[8] Lewis Yablonsky, *The Tunnel Back: Synanon*, New York: Macmillan, 1965, p. 368.

ants now exists, and demands for the legitimation of deviant behavior will increasingly be made.

The political questions inherent in a conflict model of deviance focus on the use of social control in society. What behavior is forbidden? How is this behavior controlled? At issue is a conflict between individual freedom and social restraint, with social disorder (anarchy) and authoritarian social control (Leviathan) as the polar expressions. The resolution of this conflict entails a political decision about how much social disorder will be tolerated at the expense of how much social control. This choice cannot be confronted as long as deviance is relegated to the arena of administrative policy-making. For example, public schools are perceived as a repressive institution by many Negro youths, yet there is no political option of refusing to attend or radically altering them. This problem is now being raised by Black Power advocates who demand indigenous control over schools in Negro ghettos despite the city-wide taxation network.

POLITICAL MARGINALITY AND SOCIAL DEVIANCE: AN OBSOLETE DISTINCTION

Conventional wisdom about deviance is reinforced by the highly formalistic vision of politics held by many social workers and sociological theorists. This view confines politics to the formal juridical aspects of socal life, such as the electoral process, and to the maintenance of a party apparatus through procedural norms. In this view, only behavior within the electoral process is defined as political in character, thus excluding from the area of legitimacy acts of social deviance.[9]

In its liberal form—the form most readily adopted by social pathologists —the majoritarian formulation of politics prevails. This is a framework limited to the political strategies available to majorities or to powerful minorities having access to elite groups.[10] The strategies available to disenfranchised minorities are largely ignored and thus the politics of deviance also go unexamined. The behavior of rule-makers and law enforcers is treated as a policy decision rather than as a political phenomenon, while a needlessly severe distinction is made between law and politics. Analyses of political reality at the level of electoral results help foster this limited conception of politics. Consequently, the shared inheritance of sociology has placed the study of deviant behavior at one end of the spectrum and the study of political behavior at the other.

Conventional non-political responses on the part of sociology were possible largely because the political world itself had encouraged this kind of crisp differentiation between personal deviance and public dissent. Political

[9] See Angus Campbell *et al.*, *The American Voter*, New York: Wiley, 1960; V. O. Key, *Public Opinion and American Democracy*, New York: Alfred Knopf, 1961; Seymour Martin Lipset, *Political Man*, Garden City, N.Y.: Doubleday, 1960; Samuel Lubell, *The Future of American Politics*, New York: Harper, 1952.

[10] C. Wright Mills, "The Professional Ideology of Social Pathologists," *Power, Politics, and People,* Irving Louis Horowitz, editor, New York and London: Oxford U., 1963, pp. 525–552.

deviance is a concept rarely invoked by politicians because the notion of politics itself implies the right of dissent. Lemert points out that this has not always been true for radical political deviants.[11] There is a history of punitive response to political deviants in this country, involving repression of anarchists, communists, socialists, and labor organizers. This has spread at times to a persecution of liberal groups as well. What characterizes the "McCarthy Era" is not the hunt for radicals, but rather a broadening of the definition of radicals to include all sorts of mild dissenters. Only on rare occasions has political deviance been defined as a major social problem requiring severe repression. Thus, with the possible exception of anarchists, communists, and socialists (and sometimes even including these groups in the political spectrum normally defined as legitimate), there is no way of dealing with political life as a deviant area. The nature of American political pluralism itself promotes dissent, at least in the ideal version of the American political system. The onus of responsibility in the castigation of a political victim is upon the victimizer. Rights and guarantees are often marshaled on behalf of a widening of the political dialogue. Indeed, the definition of American democracy has often been in terms of minoritarian supports rather than majoritarian victories.

The area of deviance is not covered by the same set of norms governing minority political life. The source of responsibility for deviant behavior, whether it be drug addiction, homosexuality, alcoholism, or prostitution is not borne by the person making the charges but rather is absorbed by the victims of such charges. The widespread recognition of the juridical shakiness of the deviant's position serves to privatize the deviant and embolden those who press for the legal prosecution of deviance. While the right to dissent politically is guaranteed (within certain limits), the right to dissent socially is almost totally denied those without high social status.

One simple test might be the perceived reactions toward political radicalism in contrast to social deviance. If one is accused of being an anarchist there may actually accrue a certain "halo effect" to the person so charged. Perhaps a charge of naiveté or ignorance might be made against the politically marginal man, but not a censorious response demanding non-political behavior.

In the area of deviance, if there is a self-proclamation of drug addiction or alcoholism, the demand for therapeutic or punitive action comes very quickly. If one admits to being a drug addict, there is an attempt to remove the curse from everyday life so that at least the visibility of deviance is diminished.

The line between the social deviant and the political marginal is fading. It is rapidly becoming an obsolete distinction. As this happens, political dissent by deviant means will become subject to the types of repression that have been a traditional response to social deviance. This development compels social scientists to reconsider their definitions of the entire range of social phenomena—from deviance to politics. Wolfgang and Ferracuti have taken an important first step toward an interdisciplinary study of social violence.[12]

[11] Edwin M. Lemert, *op. cit.*, pp. 203–209.
[12] Marvin E. Wolfgang and Franco Ferracuti, *The Subculture of Violence*, London and New York: Tavistock, 1967, pp. 1–14.

For the social sciences, this implies a new connection between social problems and political action. The old division between the two can no longer be sustained. In terms of theory, the new conditions throw into doubt the entire history of political science as an examination of the electoral situation, and of social problems research as a study of personal welfare. If politics is amplified to incorporate all forms of pressure (whether by deviants or orthodox pressure groups) to change the established social order, and if sociology is redefined to include pressure by deviants to redesign the social system so that they can be accepted by the general society on their own terms, then there is a common fusion, a common drive, and a common necessity between sociology and political science, not only on the level of empirical facts, but on the level of scientific interpretation.

Some sociologists have already adapted to this new situation. Cloward's work in organizing welfare recipients is a particularly striking effort, which is an outrageous idea to both the classical Capitalist and Socialist doctrines.[13] This marks the first time that a sociologist has organized welfare recipients. This enlargement of roles demonstrates that changes are occurring in what constitutes political life and social work.

There are several other important directions that applied sociologists might follow: drug addicts might be organized to alter laws concerning drug use; students might be organized to change the character of schools; and mental patients might be organized to change the way they are treated. In each of these cases, change would be initiated from below by members of subordinate marginal groups. This would be in sharp contrast to the conventional elitist pattern of politics, where decisions are made from above by members of the prevailing majority. This is the primary distinction between the existing political party style and the political outsider style that is currently emerging.

THE POLITICIZED SOCIAL DEVIANT

A serious dilemma for many deviant and marginal groups alike is their failure to perceive any main line organizations (either overtly political or social) as providing the sort of universal legitimation which governed an earlier, more tranquil period in American history. The entire gamut of formal and informal organizations seems arrayed against the kind of deviant particularisms expressed by hippies, hell's angels, or acid heads. Thus, the sub-groups, whether of deviant lower-class origins or marginal middle-class origins, begin to align themselves with each other and against the mainstream of American life. A new set of cultural heroes, dance forms, art forms, coalesce to define not just a classical generational revolt for the rage to live, but for a particularistic expression of immediate personal liberation as a prelude to distant public equalitarianism.

The key demonstration effect that such individualistic responses may prove extremely effective, even if they involve small numbers, is the rise of guerrilla insurgency as a military style in the underdeveloped areas. If

[13] See Richard A. Cloward and Richard M. Elman, "Advocacy in the Ghetto," *Trans-Action*, 4 (December, 1966), pp. 27–35.

"colored people" can conduct protracted struggles in Asia and in Africa, why can't the same sort of struggles be conducted from the rooftops of Watts and Newark? Indeed, the expanding internationalization of the deviant and marginal groups can best be appreciated in new cultural heroes such as Franz Fanon, Malcolm X, and others connected to the demi-monde of the Black Power movement. The seeds of this were long ago raised in the works of Padmore and DuBois, when they urged precisely such ideological linkages with revolutionary forces elsewhere in the world—particularly in Pan-Africanism. What was absent before was the mechanism for success— and in the guerrilla style, this mechanism, this critical missing ingredient, was finally supplied, and the linkage made complete.

The area of Negro struggles is a particularly fertile source for re-evaluating the relationship between deviance and politics. Originally, there was a clear distinction between vandalism for personal gain and an act of organization for political gain. When the political life of Negroes was circumscribed by the NAACP, it was clear that political life entailed normative behavior within the formal civic culture. Similarly, it was clear that acts of personal deviance fell outside the realm of politics. Indeed, there was little contact between Negro deviants and participants in the civil rights protest.

The rise of civil disobedience as a mass strategy has blurred this distinction. Such disobedience entails personal deviance to attain political ends. Regardless of the political goals involved, it is a conscious violation of the law. The treatment of civil disobedience in the courts has therefore been marked by ambiguity. It is difficult to predict whether it will be treated as a political act of insurrection or a simple personal violation of the law. Many law enforcement officials see no distinction between civil disobedience and crime, and blame the ideology of law-breaking inherent in civil disobedience for rising crime rates and the emergence of race riots.[14]

In turn, these officials may be responding to the large scale denial by Negroes of the traditional police role as keeper of social order. This can perhaps best be gauged not only in the expressed attitudes of political leaders from governors down to sheriffs, but indirectly as well, i.e., by the inability of local gendarmeries to cope with Negro mass rioting. The Watts riots of August 1965 were, in this connection, prototypical of the current breakdown in traditional forms of police legitimacy. In that riot, which lasted four days, witnessed 34 deaths and 1032 injuries, and saw 4000 arrests made, the key fact was the role of the National Guard in quelling the riot. The Los Angeles police were thoroughly unable to cope with a situation once it achieved paramilitary proportions. This lesson has clearly not been lost on Negro ghetto communities elsewhere in the United States.

Confining ourselves to the cluster of race riots which took place in the months of June and July of 1967, we can see how Watts heralded a new stage in the relationship between deviance and politics. In the main riot areas of Chicago, Cleveland, Cincinnati, Buffalo, and Newark (we will disregard for present purposes the satellitic riots which took place in the smaller centers of Plainfield, Louisville, Hartford, Prattville, and Jackson) the following characteristics were prevalent in each community during the riot:

[14] In this connection, see Stanley Lieberson, "The Meaning of Race Riots," *Race,* 7 (1966), pp. 371–378.

(a) Each city requested and received National Guardsmen to restore social order. Correspondingly, in each city, the police proved ineffectual in coping with the riots once the shield of legitimation was removed.

(b) In each city, there were deaths and serious injuries not only to the rioters but to the established police and invading guardsmen.

(c) In each city, the riots lasted more than one day, the duration of the riots lasting from two to seven days. This indicates the guerrilla-like nature of the struggle.

(d) In each case, the triggering mechanism for the riot was an altercation involving police officials (usually traffic patrolmen) and Negroes accused of reckless driving, driving without a license, or driving under the influence of alcohol.

(e) In each case, the major rioting took place during summer months, when the normal load of Negro male unemployed are swelled by students and teenage former students not yet relocated.

(f) In each city, property damage was extensive, with the sort of sniper tactics and scorched earth policies usually associated with so-called wars of national liberation.

(g) In each case, the major rioting seemed to lack official civil rights organization sponsorship.

The following chart gives some indication of the character and extent to which the conflict model dominates current Negro deviance-marginality.

TABLE I   Major Negro Riots in Urban Ghettos

DATE	PLACE	KILLED	INJURED	ARRESTED	NATIONAL GUARD*	RIOT DURATION (DAYS)	PROPERTY DAMAGE (THOUSANDS)
8/65	Watts (LA)	35	1000+	4000+	14,000	5	$50,000+
7/66	Cleveland	4	55	275	nd	5	4,000+
6/67	Buffalo	—	68	182	500	4	100+
6/67	Cincinnati	1	50	300	1,100	2	2,000
7/67	Chicago	2	100+	500+	4,200	4	nd
7/67	Newark	24	1150	1600+	3,375	6	15,000+
7/67	Detroit	36	1500+	2665+	13,000**	5	500,000+

* National Guard figures exclude City Police.
** Includes 8,000 National Guard and 5,000 Federal Troops.
  Source: Compiled from *New York Times Index*.

The parallel with what Eckstein has termed "internal violence,"[15] and what is more customarily referred to as guerrilla warfare,[16] is clear. What this amounts to is a military rather than a civil definition of the situation in racial

[15] See Harry Eckstein, *Internal War*, New York: Free Press, 1964; and for a more specific account, Harold Black and Marvin J. Labes, "Guerrilla Warfare: An Analogy to Police-Criminal Interaction," *American Journal of Orthopsychiatry*, 37 (July, 1967), pp. 666–670.
[16] See Irving Louis Horowitz, "The Military Elite," in *Elites of Latin America*, Seymour Martin Lipset and Aldo Solari, editors, New York and London: Oxford U., 1967.

ghettoes. The essential deterrent was raw fire power rather than the legitimated authority of the police uniform. Under such circumstances, the established welfare distinction between juvenile delinquency and guerrilla
warfare means very little.

The rapidly rising crime rates indicate a further ambiguity in the traditional formulation of social deviance. It is of decreasing *sociological* importance whether "crime" is perceived as an act of politics or deviance. The
consequences are the same in either case: cities are becoming increasingly
unsafe for whites, and white-owned businesses are suffering mounting losses.
Whether it is political insurgency or traditional crime, the consequences
remain the same—a disruption in the legitimation system of American society.

THE DEVIANT POLITICAL MARGINAL

At the opposite pole—namely minoritarian politics—a similar set of am-
biguities plague those in search of precise boundary lines. An example is the
behavioral pattern of the Left wing. Among the radical youth of the thirties
certain characteristics clearly emerged: a relatively straitlaced "Puritan"
ethos concerning sexual mores; a clear priority of politics over personal life—
what might be called the ascetic purification of self—and a concern for a
relatively well defined ideology, combined with encouragement for all to
participate in the life of the working classes. The radical Left of an earlier
generation shared with the dominant cultural milieu a distinct, even an intense, disaffiliation from deviant patterns. Indeed, the Old Left pointed to
social deviance as illustrative of the moral degeneration of bourgeois society.
The need for social revolution came about precisely because the existing
social order was considered incapable of controlling social deviance. Thus,
the demands of the traditional Left were not very different from establishment demands with respect to social deviance.

This contrasts markedly with the position of the New Left on conventional indicators of deviance. First, they exhibit substantial positive affect
toward an extreme and libertarian ethos replacing Puritanism. Second, there
is an identification with deviant forms stemming from a continued affiliation
with the "beatnik" movement of the fifties. There has been a considerable
absorption of the Beat Generation of the fifties into the Activist Generation
of the sixties. The ideology of the New Left, insofar as it has clear guidelines, is based on freedom from repression. It has both political and social
components: freedom for the Negro from the effects of racial discrimination;
freedom for the student from the constraints of university regulations; freedom for the young generation from the demands of their elders; and freedom for politically powerless groups from the growing authority of the centralized State. In this sense, Freud feeds the ideology of the New Left at
least as much as Marx defined the ideology of the Old Left.

The traditional notion of a noble affiliation of radical youth with the working class has already dissolved in favor of a highly positive response to deviant and marginal groups in American society. There is a relative unconcern
for the traditional class formations engaged in the struggle for upward mobility. If there is a hero, it is the alienated man who understands what is
wrong and seeks escape. Often, escape takes the form of social deviance,

which is considered no worse than the forms of behavior which are traditionally defined as normative. The traditional hero has been supplanted by the anti-hero who wins and attains heroic proportions by not getting involved in the political process. This anti-hero is defined by what he is against as much as by what he is for; he is for a world of his own, free from outside constraints, in which he is free to experiment and experience.

What this means operationally is that the line between Left-wing political behavior and personal deviance has been largely obliterated. Nowhere has this been more obvious than in the student protest movement, where it is impossible to separate the deviant student subculture from the substantive demands of the student revolt. Spence accurately describes the significance of this student movement at the University of California at Berkeley.

> This was the first successful student strike at a major university in the United States. But more important, this was the first significant white-collar rebellion of our time. These sons and daughters of the middle class demonstrated and walked picket lines, not behind the moral banner of the oppressed Negro, but on the basis of their own grievances against a system that had deprived them of their rights of responsibility and self-expression.[17]

The student rebellion underlies a major thesis herein proposed, since it led not to organized political responses of a conventional variety, but rather to a celebration of deviance itself as the ultimate response to orthodox politics. Stopping "the operation of the machine," which for Mario Savio "becomes so odious, makes you so sick at heart that you can't take part; can't even tactically take part," led to only one conclusion: "the machine must be prevented from running at all."[18] It is interesting that victory was not defined as taking over the operations of the machine, not in the classical capture of organized political power, but rather in non-participation and in non-acceptance. Savio himself, as if in conscious defiance of Michel's "iron law," simply refused to participate in any leadership functions in the Berkeley post-rebellion period. The definition of victory then is in the ability of marginal groups to disrupt the operations of political power either in its direct parliamentary form or in surrogate forms.

Among young members of the New Left, draft evasion has become an important form of deviance. The number of people who adopt the traditional political path by refusing to serve and going to jail as political prisoners is small compared to the number who adopt the deviant path, using mental illness, homosexuality, or drug addiction (whether these be real or feigned) to avoid serving. In effect, they are taking advantage of the prevailing established norms toward deviants. However, this path is made much more accessible with the merger of Leftist politics and social deviance, since only politics can transform private desires into public principles.

An important social characteristic of the New Left is its self-definition as a "swinging" group, or conversely, not being "square." This new definition

[17] Larry D. Spence, "Berkeley: What It Demonstrates," *Revolution at Berkeley,* Michael V. Miller and Susan Gilmore, editors, New York: Dell, 1965, p. 217.
[18] Jack Newfield, *A Prophetic Minority,* New York: New American Library, 1966, p. 27; on this general theme, see Irving Louis Horowitz, "Radicalism and Contemporary American Society," *Liberation,* 10 (May, 1965), pp. 15–18.

of Leftism is also a central definition of the deviant subculture. So it is that Berkeley and Watts became the symbols of the twin arms of radical politics: the university campus and the Negro ghetto. Even in terms of social psychological definitions of friends and foes the line between the political Left and social deviance is now largely transcended. Thus, there is a deep distrust of formal politics and of the people who operate within the bureaucratic channels of the political apparatus. This definition of friends and foes is obvious at Berkeley, where many students feel that they cannot trust anyone over 30.

The Right-wing movement in America also illustrates this perspective. The Old Right was characterized by extreme antipathy for any kind of promiscuous behavior or overtly immoral behavior. The American Right viewed with alarm attacks upon law-enforcement officials. The Old Right perceived itself conventionally as a paragon of law enforcement. This is the core around which the Right wing has traditionally been established. But a phenomenon such as the Minutemen reveals a spinoff from law-abiding to direct action approaches to politics. The Minutemen, for example, are encouraged to acquire possession of fully automatic weapons, even though many such weapons are forbidden to individuals by law. They are urged to join the National Rifle Association to become eligible for rifles and handguns at cost as well as free ammunition. The Minutemen *Handbook* contains lessons on such subjects as "Booby Traps," "Anti-Vehicular Mines," and "Incendiary Weapons Composition." The self-made saboteur is encouraged to improvise lethal weapons. Espionage and infiltration of established political groupings are also encouraged. A sub-unit is called the Minutemen Intelligence Organization, in possession of a fairly sophisticated organization, not unlike those of paramilitary units.[19]

Breakaway segments of the New Right, like their opposite numbers in the New Left, are concerned with redefining the relationship of the person to the legal code in very loose terms. The appeals to youth are in terms of training in weaponry rather than in law. When confronted by the law, the Minutemen dissolved their public leadership and created a new underground leadership. This phenomenon could be an extreme situation in American life precisely because so many armed forces veterans may be attracted to such a combination of politics and deviance. A situation has arisen in which the use of weapons for personal enjoyment, such as in hunting, has been fused—particularly in the releases of the American Rifleman's Association—with the uses of weapons for protection against criminals, and assistance to police authorities. Political conflict may become marked by opposing marginal political groups confronting each other in armed conflict, with the legitimated State agencies of power the enemy of both.

THE POLITICS OF DEVIANT VIOLENCE

In a previous section we drew attention to the growing Latinization of Negro riots and student revolts in the present period. This was done in terms

[19] See William W. Turner, "The Minutemen: The Spirit of '66," *Ramparts*, 5 (January, 1967), pp. 69–76.

of rough macroscopic data. Here we wish to underscore this point by taking closer note of the workings of the new style of subculture in America. The largest Negro gang in Chicago, the Blackstone Rangers, is a clear example of the breakdown in the distinction between crime and marginal politics, as well as the course which the politics of marginality is likely to follow. The Rangers act as an autonomous group, in conflict with both local residents and police. The strategies employed in this conflict indicate the style of the new politics. They entered into negotiations with the Chicago police, and reached a satisfactory settlement: they agreed to surrender their weapons and stop fighting other gangs if the police would drop certain charges against their leaders and disarm a rival gang.

Negotiation of this sort is a major strategy of international politics, although it has seldom been used to resolve conflicts involving marginal domestic groups. The negotiation process itself entails the recognition that marginal groups represent legitimate political interests. So far, the art of negotiation has not been adequately developed for dealing with such situations, just as it has not been adequately developed for dealing with unconventional international conflicts.

The problem posed by marginal groups like the Rangers is not yet viewed as a political problem to be solved by political strategies. When police violated the negotiated settlement, the Blackstone Rangers planned to file suit in the Federal Courts to prohibit a pattern of harassment. It is novel for such deviant groups to engage in political conflict with legitimate agencies like the police. But it does indicate a step beyond the "good bad boy" approach of social welfare.

There is a growing impulse to develop political means of resolving conflicts that involve marginal groups, as an alternative to the military means that have thus far prevailed. The Woodlawn Organization, composed of local residents, received a federal grant of $927,341 to work with gangs like the Rangers and the Disciples. The Chicago police raided the first meeting between the gang leaders and leaders of the Woodlawn Organization, demonstrating a conflict between advocates of a political solution and proponents of what amounts to a military solution to the gang problem.[20] In the absence of acceptable political solutions, it is probable that increasing reliance upon domestic military solutions will be sought—just as the failure of political solutions internationally often leads to pressure for quick military solutions.

This trend toward marginal politics reflects a rejection of conventional political styles that have proven unsuited to the needs of marginal groups. In the past, the powerless had recourse to two choices for political action: legitimate means, to which they do not have sufficient access, and by which they invariably lose; or accessible but ineffective illegitimate means that bring little structural change. Marginal minorities are now searching for the development of political means that are both accessible and effective. It is probable that these new styles will be illegitimate rather than legitimate, and that the distinction between social deviance and political insurgency will be further reduced.

Race riots differ from both orthodox politics and personal delinquency. They offer some important insights into these new styles. Race riots have an

---

[20] Rowland Evans and Robert Novak, "The Negro Gangs," *Herald Tribune, International Edition*, July 5, 1967.

ideological core, while many other forms of collective behavior do not. They are avowedly political, organized, and purposeful. Typically, deviant acts like theft, assault, and homocide have none of these attributes. For these reasons, race riots may be closer to organized unconventional warfare than they are to conventional crime. Once perceived in this way, they constitute a powerful if latent political weapon.

At present, in most American cities a relatively small police force can effectively control the populace. But this is true only as long as police are accorded legitimacy. When conflicts are defined totally in terms of power and force rather than authority and legitimacy, as during race riots, they cannot effectively maintain control. For this reason, riots constitute a major departure from established patterns of interaction between police and deviants. Deviants are not organized to battle police, and they have no ideology which labels police as enemies to be attacked and destroyed. Police have legitimacy as long as deviants avoid rather than attack them. However, police traditionally mount an organized collective effort against deviants, who typically respond only as unorganized individuals. The existing conflict is a one-sided war. The emergence of a bi-lateral conflict situation promises to be a major development in the link between politics and deviance. Race riots are the first indication of this change.[21]

This conflict can take several alternative forms: on a *minimax* scale there could be de-escalation to the English system, in which both Negro militants (or deviants in general) and police would not carry arms; at the other end, there could be escalation to race riots, which are sporadic and constitute a relatively unorganized set of events. Beyond sporadic racial strife lies the possibility of sustained conventional war. This is most closely approximated in American history by the Indian Wars and the Civil War. Presently, unconventional warfare is coming into focus. The latter two possibilities indicate how social deviance could spill over into insurrectionary politics, given both the peculiar racial division which exists in American society and the consistent exclusion of marginal groups from political and social legitimacy.

This marginal style of politics is being adopted by groups of all "extreme" ideological persuasions. Marginals of both the Left and Right fear the growing power of the centralized government, which they feel will be used to repress them, and are opposed to the consolidation of power by the majority. This commonality is demonstrated by the high amount of social interaction that occurs, in places like Greenwich Village and Berkeley, between politically opposed deviant groups. Even such political opposites as the Hell's Angels and opponents of the Vietnam War shared a common social network in California. Their political enmity was matched by their similar enjoyment of deviant social patterns.[22]

The clearest example of this movement toward violence, and one easily overlooked, is the reappearance of assassination as a political style, coupled with the inability to know whether Left, Right, or Deviant is spearheading this style. It is almost impossible to say whether the assassination of John F. Kennedy or Malcolm X was a deviant act or a political act. No group took

---

[21] See Ed Cray, *The Big Blue Line: Police Power vs. Human Rights,* New York: Coward-McCann, 1967, p. 121.

[22] See Hunter S. Thompson, *Hell's Angels: The Strange and Terrible Saga of the Outlaw Motorcycle Gangs,* New York: Random House, 1966, pp. 231–257.

responsibility for the assassinations as overt political acts, and the assassins did not link the deaths to ideological demands. Without taking into account the breakdown in the distinction between politics and deviance, the meaningfulness of both sociology and political science is seriously compromised.

MARGINAL SECTORS AND DEVIANT VALUES

Applied social science must take account of this new view of marginality in American life. If any group has emerged as the human carrier of the breakdown between political and private deviance, it has been the *lumpenproletariat,* or the non-working class. This group has replaced the established working and middle classes as the deciding political force in America. Lang and Lang point out,[23] in their discussion of collective dynamics, that this is precisely the condition which breeds collective deviance.

> Ordinarily the cleavages within a society are between clearly constituted social strata or between parties whose special interests seek recognition within a broader framework of order. But when the cleavages occur between constituted authority and those who do not accept it, or between those who feel unable to share in them, one can refer to the condition as one of widespread and general alienation.

The army of marginally employed comprises a significant segment of *both* politically radical and socially deviant cultures. If the bureaucracy grew disproportionately to all other classes in Western Europe, the disproportionate rise of the marginally employed characterizes contemporary America. This group, rather than disappearing or, as Marx would have it, becoming a social scum to be wiped out by revolution, grows ever larger. At a practical level, there is now a new and powerful intermediary class that performs vital roles in the authoritarian political system, while at the same time it sets the style for a new libertarian morality.

The boundaries of American politics reflect the growing affluence which typifies the American social structure. However, a significant minority of disaffected marginals exists in the midst of this affluence. It is becoming increasingly clear that these marginals threaten to destroy the fruits of general affluence, and indeed threaten to disrupt the entire system. Increasing crime rates are merely the first indicator of this situation. Race riots are a more serious indicator of the inability of the political system to maintain an equilibrium despite the general affluence.

The overlap of deviance and marginality is well captured in a current book on the Hell's Angels. The Hell's Angels—with the Swastika, German helmet, and Iron Cross as their main symbols—differ but slightly from the pseudo-Maoist organizations of the Left. Without wishing to equate Maoists with either Minutemen or Hell's Angels, it is clear that each of these groups is marginal and deviant with respect to established political norms. Further, it is difficult to give conventional definitions to those holding a gun in one hand and a flower in the other.

[23] Kurt Lang and Gladys Engel Lang, *Collective Dynamics,* New York: Thomas Y. Crowell, 1961, p. 18.

The Angels have given up hope that the world is going to change for them. They assume, on good evidence, that the people who run the social machinery have little use for outlaw motorcyclists, and they are reconciled to being losers. But instead of losing quietly, one by one, they have banded together with a mindless kind of loyalty and moved outside the framework, for good or ill. They may not have the answer; but at least they are still on their feet. It is safe to say that no Hell's Angel has ever heard of Joe Hill or would know a Wobbly from a bushmaster, but there is something very similar about their attitudes. The Industrial Workers of the World had serious blueprints for society, while the Hell's Angels mean only to defy the social machinery. There is no talk among the Angels of building a better world, yet their reactions in the world they live in are rooted in the same kind of anarchic, para-legal sense of conviction that brought the armed wrath of the Establishment down on the Wobblies. There is the same kind of suicidal loyalty, the same kind of in-group rituals and nicknames, and above all, the same feeling of constant warfare with an unjust world.[24]

The policy response to this dilemma has been the Welfare State: an attempt to "cool out" the marginal underclass and minimize the potential danger it poses. It is an attempt to avoid the consequences of large-scale marginality without making any social structural changes. Schatzman and Strauss contend that this welfare style deals with the problem by avoiding its political implications.

America pours its wealth into vast numbers of opportunity programs to achieve its goals and names almost any conceivable group, event, or thing a social problem if it can be seen as threatening the achievement of these goals. Hence its concern for the culturally deprived, the under-achievers, the school dropouts, the job displaced, the aged, the ill, the retarded, and mentally disturbed. This concern goes beyond that of the nineteenth century humanitarians who involved themselves with the underprivileged out-groups on moral grounds. Now all these aggregates are seen as special groups whose conditions are intolerable to society, if not actually threatening, in light of today's social and economic requirements.[25]

This attempt to depoliticize a highly political problem has proved inadequate. The welfare solution has not erased the consequences of having a growing number of disaffected people in the midst of general affluence. Indeed, the very existence of affluence on so wide a scale creates demands that parallel those made by the "poor nations" on the "rich nations." Because of this, a political attempt to solve the problem is bound to emerge. If this attempt is not initiated from above within the legitimate political or electoral apparatus, it will be generated from below and probably take illegitimate para-military forms.

The implicit exchange system which formerly existed between the very poor and the very rich in American society was simple: "don't bother us and we won't bother you." In exchange for the poor not disturbing the rich, the wealthy provided just enough money for the poor to live at Ricardian sub-

[24] Hunter S. Thompson, *op. cit.*, pp. 265–266.
[25] Leonard Schatzman and Anselm Strauss, "A Sociology of Psychiatry," *Social Problems*, 14 (Summer, 1966), p. 12.

sistence levels. This exchange has been the basis of American social work, and continues to define the boundaries of the welfare system. The rich have only vaguely appreciated the magnitude of the poor's potential power, and their ability to disrupt the entire system. For their part, the poor only vaguely appreciate the power at the disposal of the rich, which accounts for the suicidal characteristics of many race riots.

This interchange system is now being threatened. The poor are gradually developing an appreciation of their own power, while at the same time they have a greater appreciation of the power held by the rich. For their part, the rich are becoming more aware of the power available to the poor, as seen in the generalized fear created by rising crime rates and race riots. In short, there is a greater polarization of conflict between the two classes.

The primary political problem of deviance can be framed as a Hobbesian dilemma. Hobbes sought the creation of the State as a solution to the problem of social disorder, in which individuals war with each other in pursuit of their individual interests. The dilemma is that the creation of the State creates a problem of social control. The solution to the problem of chaos or the *Anarch* is the *Leviathan*. But the *Leviathan* is the *totalitarian* State. Indeed, totalitarianism is the perfect solution to the problem of disorder. The dilemma for those who consider social problems obstacles to be overcome is that any true overcoming of social problems implies a perfect social system. And this entails several goals: first, the total institutionalization of all people; second, the thoroughgoing equilibrium between the parts of a system with respect to their functioning and the functioning of other sectors; third, the elimination of social change as either a fact or value. Thus, the resolution of social problems from the point of view of the social system would signify the totalitarian resolution of social life.

The political problem posed by deviance is how to avoid social disorder while at the same time avoiding the problem of total social control. It is a dilemma precisely because of the impossibility of solving both problems simultaneously. Political decisions about deviance must reflect judgments about the relative dangers of these two problems, and must constitute a weighing process based on ethical no less than empirical considerations.

Connections between deviance and politics take place most often when a society does not satisfactorily manage its affairs. For better or worse, a well-ordered society is one that can impose a distinction between responses to deviance and responses to marginality. Antecedents for the linkage of deviance and marginality exist in two "conflict societies." In the eighteen nineties in Russia, the Narodnik movement was directly linked to the movement toward personal liberation. In Germany of the nineteen twenties, the "underground" movement, aptly summed up by the Brecht theater, Nihilism, and amoralism, gave rise to both the Nazi and Bolshevik political tendencies. The merger of the Beat Generation and the current Radical Student movements reveals this same pattern of connecting political revolution with demands for personal liberation.

These examples indicate how the fusion between deviant behavior and political processes is a prelude to radical change. If the fusion of politics and deviance is the herald of revolution, or at least indicates a high degree of disassociation and disorganization within the society, then radical changes in the structure of American social and political life are imminent.

What takes place in personal life has major political ramifications in contemporary society. American life has been resilient enough to forestall a crisis in treating marginality until now. This is a testimonal to the flexbility of the American system of political legitimation. But it might well be that the extent of deviance in the past was not sufficient to cause more than a ripple in the political system.[26] In the emerging system, with automation and cybernetics creating greater dislocation and marginal employment, personal deviance may generate a distinct transformation in normal political functions; it marks the point at which the political system cannot cope with deviant expressions of discontent.

A political description of this condition begins with the inability of American society to resolve political problems that are important to *marginal* people. Almost one-third of the potential voting population does not vote, and is therefore without even the most minimal political representation.[27] The fact that these disenfranchised people have important problems in common that cannot be managed within existing arrangements creates a volatile situation.

Political styles evolve that are not presently labeled as political behavior, much as race riots are not now generally considered political behavior. These new styles are characterized first, by a rejection of the legitimacy of the existing political system (the challenge to the rules by which the game is now played); second, by a rejection of compromise as a political style; and third, by a willingness to oppose established authority with illicit power in order to change not merely the rules but the game itself. Ends will attain a primacy over means, whereas a concern with the legitimacy of means has traditionally characterized American politics. Direct expressions of power might assume a more important role than legitimate authority in resolving important conflicts.

Political legitimacy is itself subject to change in order to meet the demands of a society in which social deviants and political marginals have become more, rather than less, important in determining the structure of American society.

[26] Rex Hopper, "Cybernation, Marginality, and Revolution," *The New Sociology,* Irving Louis Horowitz, editor, New York and London: Oxford U., 1964, pp. 313–330.
[27] See E. E. Schattschneider, *The Semi-Sovereign People,* New York: Holt, Rinehart, and Winston, 1960, pp. 97–114.

The Communist Party and Anti-Communism

DAVID SHANNON

In 1949 and 1950, the disillusion, frustration, and anxiety that had been building in the United States over the Communist issue at home and abroad burst into full, angry reaction. Each year since the war was one of shock, but 1949 and 1950 were traumatic even for that trying era.

By then the world was clearly divided into three camps—the Communist world, led by the Soviet Union; the Western world, led by the United States; and the "neutralist" Afro-Asian bloc—and the cold war was sharp. Some events of 1949 led many Americans to think they were losing the cold war, and many people thought the reverses were as much the result of internal betrayal as of foreign Communist strength.

In the spring of 1948, Chiang Kai-shek had controlled about three-fourths of China's territory and two-thirds of its population. The next year, Mao Tse-tung's Communist forces drove Chiang and his Nationalists to Formosa. Shanghai obviously would not now become what Senator Kenneth Wherry had so wildly predicted—"just like Kansas City."[1] In September 1949, President Truman announced that the Russians had exploded an atomic bomb. It was now apparent that Soviet bombers could destroy the industrial centers of the Western European nations, which had been brought into a military alliance with the United States earlier in the year. Further than that, as many an American recognized when he awakened in the night at the sound of an airplane over his home, it was possible now for the Russians to bring nuclear destruction to the United States itself.

Americans were bewildered, angry, and resentful. A few years earlier, when their fascist enemies were near defeat, the chances of postwar peace and international harmony had seemed bright. But there was no real peace, no harmony, and now another hostile dictator had power to hurt America such as Hitler had never possessed. Assured by some military leaders and others in 1946 that only American technology and science were capable of discovering the "secret" of atomic fission, many people now leaped to the conclusion that only Communist espionage, disloyalty, treachery, and a bungling, "soft-on-Communism" administration could account for the Russians having the bomb. And when Klaus Fuchs confessed to atomic espionage and the Rosenbergs were convicted, these dark conclusions were confirmed in some people's minds.

In 1946, there had been a spy sensation when the Canadian Government exposed an espionage ring which had operated during the war. In 1947, there had been the confusing Eisler case. Contemporaneous with the revelation of the Russian bomb was the story of Judith Coplon's passing classified information to Valentin Gubichev of the Soviet Embassy. The biggest headlines about espionage at the time, however, concerned the affair of Whittaker Chambers and Alger Hiss.

The Hiss case marked the end of one era and the birth of another. The whole Hiss story as it slowly unfolded was so bizarre—involving microfilms hidden in an abandoned dumb-waiter and a pumpkin, Oriental rugs, an old Woodstock typewriter, a Model A Ford, and two very strange men—that one would reject the story as too wild if one read it as mystery fiction. The evidence in the case was extremely complicated, but the main point is that relatively few Americans formed their judgment of Hiss and Chambers—at least their first judgment—on the basis of the evidence. The personalities and appearances of the two men, their careers, and the kinds of people they symbolized, rather than the evidence, influenced the judgment of most people—that, and whether one regarded himself as a friend or an opponent of the New Deal.

The Hiss case began during the 1948 campaign, when Chambers, once a Communist and a Bohemian writer, later a spy for the Soviets, and later still a senior editor of *Time*, charged that Alger Hiss, to all appearances the prototype of the young, competent, well-educated, idealistic, and liberal lawyer and junior New Deal administrator, had been a member of the Communist Party from at least 1934 to 1938. Chambers made his charges before the House Committee on Un-American Activities, whose chairman then was J. Parnell Thomas, of New Jersey. But the most prominent member of the committee in the Hiss case was a young politician-on-the-make from southern California, Richard M. Nixon. Nixon was a freshman congressman at the time, having defeated the veteran liberal Democrat Jerry Voorhis in the 1946 Republican landslide.

Faced with a libel suit brought by Hiss, Chambers broadened his charges against him, asserting now that Hiss had helped him covertly transmit classified State Department documents to agents of the Soviet Government. He produced the "pumpkin papers," and a New York grand jury indicted Hiss for perjury, the statute of limitations preventing an indictment for espionage, and early in 1949 the case went to trial. The trial ended in July with a hung jury, eight to four for conviction. A second jury found Hiss guilty, and he received a five-year sentence.

More important to us here than the details of the Hiss case was its impact upon American public opinion. The case brought to the public in a dramatic way a realization of the strength of Communism in America in the previous decade, and the contemporary political implications of the case tended to exaggerate Communist influence in 1949. President Truman during the 1948 campaign referred to the Hiss affair as a "red herring" designed to distract voters from the inadequacies of the "awful Eightieth Congress," and the public came to see the case as a struggle between Nixon, the symbol of aggressive Republicanism, critical of all things New Deal, and Hiss, the symbol of the bright young New Deal intellectual. When more evidence was brought to light and Hiss was finally convicted, more was at stake than his own career. The New Deal and the kind of liberalism it represented were now suspect to many a person who had voted for Roosevelt; and some New Deal critics, always ready to impute the worst to "that man" and what he symbolized, now felt vindicated. Then Secretary of State Dean Acheson, dapper, urbane, suspect in some quarters anyway because of his Ivy League polish, in an impolitic but compassionate statement said he would not "turn my back on Alger Hiss." Many people concluded that subversion was still rife in the federal government.

The jury found Hiss guilty on January 21, 1950. On February 3, Klaus Fuchs confessed in London. On February 9, at Wheeling, West Virginia, Joseph R. McCarthy, then a relatively unknown first-term senator [from Wisconsin], asserted he had "here in my hand" a list of 205—or 57, as later speeches put it—names who were known to Acheson to be Communist Party members and who were nevertheless still working in the State Department. The era of McCarthyism was born. It was a violent child, destined to live about a half-decade.

McCarthyism was a whole complex of attitudes, some of them contradictory. It was militant anti-Communism, but it was also unreasoning fear and hysteria about Communism, both at home and abroad. It was exploitation of popular fear and frustration about Communism for partisan political advantage, but it was also a more general political irresponsibility. It reflected isolationist attitudes toward Europe—but not toward Asia—yet played upon the nationalist feelings of European immigrants whose homelands were behind the Iron Curtain. It was anti-intellectual, both in the sense of exalting the irrational and in the sense of animosity toward intellectual and cosmopolitan people. It appealed to the prejudices and frustrations of the relatively poor as well as to the fears of the *nouveaux riches,* particularly Texas oil millionaires. Above all, McCarthyism was an acceptance of the idea that the end justifies the means, and end being power and the eradication of the Communists, who themselves believed that the end justifies the means.

Senator McCarthy did not invent McCarthyism, and his abrupt political decline after his repudiation by the Senate in December 1954 did not absolutely end the phenomenon. Nevertheless, McCarthy—as did Hiss—came to symbolize more than he actually was. The years of the height of McCarthyism saw many wild and improbable developments. The American people swung frantically with an anti-Communist bludgeon. They used the rapier very little. The bludgeon hurt the Communists, but it hurt a great many anti-Communists too. In the effort to save democracy and liberty from Communism, the American people outraged democracy and liberty themselves. At both popular and official levels, Americans violated both the spirit and the letter of the Bill of Rights.

The federal government, under the administration of both Truman and Eisenhower, pursued an extensive campaign against Communism at home and abroad. The Truman administration instituted a security program to root out subversives from government, and the Eisenhower administration widened its scope. Congressional committees investigated almost everything and received many headlines. Congress passed new anti-Communist legislation, for example the McCarran Internal Security Act of 1950, which among other things provided for concentration camps for the internment of Communists in the event of war. And the Department of Justice brought many prosecutions under the Smith Act of 1940. By the end of 1954, ninety-two Communist leaders had been indicted and tried under that act. Four others were indicted but were fugitives at the time of their trials. Of this total of ninety-six, only three were acquitted. One died during trial, and five others had their cases severed because of poor health.

State and local governments and the people generally were also active in the anti-Communist crusade. A few states prosecuted Communists under "little Smith acts." Many instituted non-Communist oaths as a condition of public employment. At the state level, officials were apt to be extreme, even sometimes a little silly, in their anti-Communism. One member of the Indiana Textbook Commission, for example, wanted to ban school readers that included Robin Hood stories, perhaps on the theory that the Sherwood outlaw was an anticapitalist precursor of Marx and Lenin. Indiana also required professional boxers to take a non-Communist oath before practicing their trade in the Hoosier State. But government officials were only a little wilder, if any, than the public at large. The Cincinnati Reds became the Redlegs. Social clubs ostracized members who were suspected of Communist sympathies. An association of chess players expelled an officer thought to be a Communist.

American public opinion had been hostile to the Communists ever since they came into being during and just after World War I. Apparently, however, the experience of being a wartime ally of the Soviet Union softened that hostility, and immediately after World War II, American Communists enjoyed greater good will—or, rather, less ill will—from the public at large than ever before or since. A 1940 public-opinion survey indicated that nearly three-fourths of the population favored a law to forbid membership in the Communist Party. In 1946, fewer than half the people favored such action. But soon public opinion was to change again. By the early 1950's, Americans were unwilling to tolerate Communists. A careful survey made in the early summer of 1954 revealed that about three-fourths of the people favored stripping admitted Communists of their citizenship, and about one-half thought they should be jailed.[2]

All this anti-Communism hurt the Communist Party. The party suffered badly. Hampered by legislation, vulnerable to prosecution, and the object of the public's intense hostility, the Communists were in no position to advance their political program nor to expand their organization. In this climate of opinion, the opportunities for an actual, living, active Communist were limited indeed. Forces and conditions outside the party, in the real world—what Communists call the "objective situation"—put the American Communists on the defensive. The Communists had to be more concerned with their party's survival than with its advancement, and they quite naturally tended to isolate themselves from the harsh world.

Yet it was not the "objective situation" alone that brought the Communist Party to a moribund and feeble condition. When Communist parties die, or nearly die, a large part of the final illness is self-inflicted. Not even the "objective situation" of Hitler's Germany killed the German party. Years of intellectual malnourishment and ill-advised self-medication with magic rituals, complete with incantations and exorcism of demons, take their toll.

EXPECTATIONS OF FASCISM AND WAR

The Communists had two closely related ideas about the immediate future during the years of McCarthyism that underlay their line and activities on almost all matters. These basic assumptions were that the United States was on the verge of fascism nationally and on the precipice of total nuclear war internationally.

The villains, of course, were "American imperialism," "Wall Street," "the monopolies." The twin dangers of war and fascism were but two sides of the same imperialist coin. Imperialism, "especially American imperialism," was "incurably warlike." But the American masses—"labor and progressive-minded Negro and white masses"—opposed war, as did, of course, the Communist Party, the "vanguard" of the working class. The imperialists, according to Communist writers, then, had to make America fascist to put over their war program: ". . . the purpose of the fascist trend is to hasten the preparation for a war seeking Wall Street's world domination."[3]

The Communists deluded themselves with the thought that they were in actual fact the vanguard of the working classes and that they were so regarded by "Wall Street." From this delusion arose their belief that all measures directed against Communists or the party were but the opening wedge of fascism, of a program of imperialism to destroy American democracy, annihilate the labor movement, reverse the direction of the Negro toward full equality, and coerce the population to an acceptance of total war. "The anti-Communist drive cannot and will not be limited to Communists," wrote the veteran Communist Will Weinstone in 1950. "The Communists are singled out for attack first of all because they are staunch fighters for peace against a ruling class gone war mad; because they are unyielding battlers for democracy against a bourgeoisie which is turning to fascism and hates and fears every vestige of democracy. . . . But while the main edge of the onslaught is directed against the Communists . . . the anti-Communist crusade is seeking to speed the destruction of all working-class, militant, progressive organizations, and to gag all decent people." The Communists thus saw themselves in the heroic posture of the Dutch boy with his finger in the dike. If they faltered, if they were defeated and silenced, all was lost, not only for them, but for "all decent people."

The party leadership's position on whether or not war and fascism were inevitable was another of their several Scylla-Charybdis constructions. The "correct" line was that the party must sail between the Scylla of underestimating the danger the imperialists represented and the Charybdis of considering war and fascism inevitable. The consequences of Scylla were obvious, and Charybdis "can only lead to paralysis in action, to waiting about and even to feelings of hopelessness, and to attempts at liquidationism of the Party in practice."[4]

In actual practice, as apart from what they said, the party's leaders operated on the assumption that war and fascism were extremely likely if not inevitable. Their arguments admitted of no other logical conclusion. If the imperialists had their way, they would bring war and fascism. If their drive for world domination were blocked by the Soviet "peace camp," they would make war out of frustration. Either successful or unsuccessful in their expansionist program, the imperialists would bring fascism and war. The Communists had themselves in a tight intellectual box. While exhorting the membership not to let up the fight against war and fascism, which the membership might do if told the twin evils were inevitable anyway, the leadership instituted internal party reorganizations based upon the premise of the extreme likelihood of war. Surely the party's internal purges and the decision to go "underground" (to be described in the next chapter) were designed to ride out the storm of an imminent war and accompanying fascism.

There is more than a little irony in the denouement in the mid-1950's. By then the danger of war had subsided—because of changed Russian leadership and policy—and McCarthyism had declined to relative insignificance. But the American Communists, huddled in their storm cellars, talking only among themselves, had nothing to do with this outcome. All in all, the Communists' campaign against war and fascism was quite ineffective. Their worst fears—indeed, their expectations—did not materialize. The Communists were ineffective because they alienated non-Communist opponents of war and reaction and because the insincerity of their posture as civil libertarians and defenders of freedom was transparent.

A few examples will illustrate. Labor leaders, Communists thought, should be their allies. But Foster called C.I.O. and A.F. of L. leaders "blatant supporters of the current employers' program . . . splitting unions and breaking strikes at the behest of the State Department . . . tools of the warmakers." Will Weinstone called Phil Murray a "slanderer" pursuing "a craven policy."[5] Negro leaders also felt the Communist lash. Communists attacked Dr. Ralph J. Bunche "for his services to the Western imperialist warmongers," and called the anti-Communist George Schuyler "a true lackey of the monopolists."[6] Nor were Communists likely to get sympathetic understanding or co-operation from the liberal wings of the Democratic and Republican parties, which the Communists attacked more vigorously than they did those parties' conservative wings. When Truman vetoed the McCarran Act, Will Weinstone said that Truman was just as bad as McCarran and did not really want to defeat the measure. His veto was "only for the record and to 'appease' and deceive the masses."[7] And back in 1946, Wisconsin Communists in the U.A.W. West Allis local had supported McCarthy, then an unknown conservative circuit-court judge, against the liberal Senator Robert M. La Follette, Jr., in the open Republican primary. The *Daily Worker* was clearly delighted with La Follette's defeat.[8]

The Communist effort to pose as defenders of the Bill of Rights was ridiculous to anyone who knew their record on freedom within the party, let alone Communist unwillingness to grant civil liberty to their enemies. When the Supreme Court announced its decision in the Dennis case, upholding the constitutionality of the Smith Act, the party's national committee issued a statement which among other things urged the American people to "speak out together in defense of the Constitution and the Bill of Rights" and declared the party would "not capitulate to the bookburners."[9] The appeal had a hollow ring to people who remembered that the Communists had supported the prosecution of the Minneapolis Trotskyists under the same Smith Act in 1942 and had reaffirmed that position in July 1949 even while the first Communist Smith Act trial was in progress.[10] In 1946, the party had tried to get what it called "poison books" removed from the library shelves of New York's public schools. The *Daily Worker* was particularly opposed to an allegedly anti-Negro novel called *Lanterns on the Levee,* by William Alexander Percy.[11]

In fact, the Communists had several times used precisely the same kind of illiberal tactics and methods that the McCarthyites used. In 1946, the Communists heard that old White Russian General Anton Denikin had been admitted to the United States. They demanded that the Immigration Service explain itself and deport the man.[12] And they had pushed the guilt-by-association device to extreme lengths to smear an enemy. A *Daily Worker* story in 1946 by William Allan, a Detroit U.A.W. Communist, about Walter Reuther is a case in point. Reuther, as head of the U.A.W. committee on social security, had negotiated on a group-insurance plan with "one Leo Perlman, former Czech social Democrat, who likes to be called a doctor and an insurance actuary, though he is neither." Perlman's firm was the Trade Union Casualty Co., which had associations with another insurance firm called Continental Assurance Co., which was "connected through interlocking directorates with the Chicago packing houses, Elgin Watch Co., large Illinois banks and International Harvester." There was thus a link between Reuther and Chicago capitalists. But Allan pushed the association one step farther. On the board of Continental Assurance was the uncle of the first national secretary of America First. Thus Reuther was also consorting with Nazis. This tenuous commercial and avuncular relationship was "evidence" for Communist support of the Thomas-Addes faction of the U.A.W.[13]

The Communists invoked the memory of Jefferson and Madison when the court upheld the Smith Act. The tragedy was that the times called for genuine, rather than cynical, defenders of the Jefferson-Madison tradition of civil liberty.

THE SMITH ACT CASES

In 1940, during the period of the Nazi-Soviet pact, President Roosevelt signed the Alien Registration Act, generally known as the Smith Act, for its sponsor, Representative Howard Smith, of Virginia. The measure's Title I forbade, upon pain of fine up to $10,000 and imprisonment up to ten years, "knowingly or willfully" advocating, abetting, advising, or teaching the "duty, necessity, desirability, or propriety" of overthrowing or destroying by force or violence the United States Government or American state and local governments. Title I also forbade organizing or attempting or helping to organize "any society, group, or assembly of persons who teach, advocate, or encourage the overthrow or destruction of any such government by force or violence; or becomes or is a member of, or affiliates with, any such . . . [organization], knowing the purposes thereof." The act had first been invoked in 1942 against eighteen Trotskyists. The Eighth Circuit Court of Appeals upheld the conviction and the Supreme Court denied certiorari. Also, during the war there had been an indictment of thirty alleged Nazi sympathizers under another section of Title I, pertaining to inciting disloyalty in the armed forces. The presiding judge died after seven hectic months of trial, and the case was dropped, only to be revived in 1945. In November 1946, the District of Columbia Court of Appeals dismissed the indictment.

One other relevant background case involved William Schneiderman, chairman of the California Communists. The case was a denaturalization proceeding not involving the Smith Act. In 1943, the Supreme Court ruled that the government had not proved by "clear, convincing, and unequivocal evidence" that the Communist Party in the five years before 1927 had advocated violent or forceful overthrow of government.[14]

Then on July 20, 1948, the Department of Justice sought and obtained from a federal grand jury in New York City an indictment against the twelve members of the national board of the Communist Party under Title I of the Smith Act. The twelve national board members were: William Z. Foster, Eugene Dennis (born Francis X. Waldron, Jr.), John B. Williamson, Jacob Stachel, Robert G. Thompson, Benjamin J. Davis, Jr., Henry Winston, John Gates (born Israel Regenstreif), Irving Potash, Gilbert Green, Carl Winter, and Gus Hall (born Arno Gust Halberg). The specific charges against them were that they had conspired with one another "and with divers other persons to the Grand Jury unknown" to dissolve the Communist Political Association and to reconstitute the Communist Party of the United States, "a society, group, and assembly of persons who teach and advocate the overthrow and destruction of the Government . . . by force and violence," and then knowingly and willfully had caused to be taught and advocated such overthrow and destruction by force or violence. The indictment did not allege the defendants had committed any overt revolutionary act—only teaching and advocating. In other words, they were not charged with a conspiracy to overthrow the government; they were charged with conspiracy to form a party to teach and advocate overthrow of the government. The twelve defendants were arrested without incident in July and were released upon bail. At the beginning of the trial, the case against Foster was severed because his health was frail.[15] Since then, the government has occasionally reconsidered trying Foster, but each time it has let the matter drop because Foster's health has deteriorated further.

The trial opened January 17, 1949, before Judge Harold R. Medina in the federal court building, Foley Square, New York City. The trial lasted nine months, dragging through an exceptionally hot summer, and did not end completely until October 21. It was, in the words of one constitutional historian, "certainly among the most turbulent and hectic in American court annals."[16] The defendants engaged five principal attorneys: George W. Crockett, Richard Gladstein, Abraham J. Isserman, Louis F. McCabe, and Harry Sacher. Dennis acted as his own attorney. In the words of Judge Augustus Hand, the conduct of the defense attorneys at the trial was "wilfully obstructive." Despite several warnings from Medina that their conduct was contemptuous, the defense attorneys persisted in baiting the trial judge and accusing him of seeking publicity, of partiality toward the prosecution, and of racial prejudice. In June, Judge Medina declared defendants Hall and Winston in contempt, and the party organized a demonstration of pickets on Foley Square and a Union Square rally of protest. At the trial's end, Judge Medina cited the defense attorneys for contempt, found them guilty, and sentenced them to imprisonment without giving them an opportunity to reply. The Court of Appeals, by a 2 to 1 vote, upheld the contempt conviction, as did the U.S. Supreme Court, by a vote of five to three. Justices Black, Douglas, and Frankfurter dissented, and Justice Clark did not participate.[17]

It was clear from the beginning of the trial that the Communists' strategy in the courtroom was to use the case as a sounding board for its general position and program and to attempt to portray American justice as a sham. For the first several weeks of the trial, the Communists challenged the validity of the jury panel, asserting that the method of selecting jurors systematically excluded Negroes, the poor, and working people. The open purpose of this unsuccessful gambit was, in Foster's words, to put "the Government, not the Communists . . . on trial."[18] But the courtroom strategy was only part of a larger strategy: to arouse mass protest against the government's case in order to pressure the administration to drop its prosecution and actually to build the party and the movement in the process.

Soon after the trial opened, the Communist national committee made a full-page announcement in the *Worker*. The headline was "THE HERESY TRIAL HAS BEGUN." A subhead continued, "But this 20th century Political Inquisition is not proceeding according to bipartisan plan. In the courtroom the accused have become the accusers." In a box on the page was an outline of general strategy: "HERE IS OUR PLAN FOR A NATIONWIDE CAMPAIGN TO QUASH THE HERESY INDICTMENTS AND PRESERVE THE BILL OF RIGHTS: 1) Speak To the People, For the People Will Decide. . . . Get All Within The Sound of Your Voice to Pass Resolutions And Send Telegrams To Attorney General Tom Clark. . . . 2) Give The People Something To Read And Pass On To Others. . . . 3) Show The People How To Act Together. . . . 4) Ask The People To Pass The Ammunition. . . . 5) Build While You Convince." A few weeks later the veteran party war horse Elizabeth Gurley Flynn wrote in one of her frequent "pep talk" articles, "There is no more telling offensive to defend the leaders of the Party . . . than for the Party to grow right now in the very period of the court trial."[19]

The party's strategy did not work. The defendants and their counsel did not present the kind of a case to persuade a jury, and the party's activities outside the courtroom neither helped the party grow nor aroused public opinion in the defendants' behalf. Indeed, the party could not even count on its usual friends. The party had difficulty raising money for trial expenses. One of the party fronts, the Civil Rights Congress, began a campaign in the summer of 1948 to raise $250,000. By the following February, it had collected only $74,095.45. (The way this sum was spent is further evidence of the party's strategy: only $25,592.05 went for legal defense; the balance was spent on "mass agitation, tours, conferences, printing, etc.")[20] The party's defenders complained of public apathy. As "The Thin Man," Dashiell Hammett, put it, "We had a lot of people going around saying, 'I don't care how it comes out just so they get it over with.' " He blamed the "imperialist press" for this apathy.[21]

The prosecution in the trial presented a three-pronged case. It dealt at length with the circumstances under which the party had been reconstituted in 1945; it introduced as evidence of intent to overthrow the government several "classics" of Marxism-Leninism-Stalinism published or taught by the party; and it presented thirteen former Communists and F.B.I. "plants" who testified that the "classics" had been taught or that the defendants had otherwise taught and advocated overthrow of the government.

The Communist strategy not only failed in the courtroom, it failed also to arouse any widespread concern in the public at large for the civil-liberties issues involved in the case. Indeed, the Communist antics in the court tended to prevent such general concern. Their tactics certainly were not well calculated to attract non-Communists and anti-Communists to the defense of free speech for Communists, though the Supreme Court ruled in 1957 that the case did involve principles of free speech.

Perhaps the most important aspect of the trial was Judge Medina's charge to the jury. The prosecution had concerned itself only with evidence about Communist speeches and publications, the advocacy of overthrow of government, rather than overt action leading to such overthrow. Yet the first amendment to the Constitution clearly guarantees free speech and a free press, which has been judicially construed to mean no limitations unless the speech or publication presents a "clear and present danger" to the safety of the republic. Judge Medina bridged the gap between illegal action and constitutionally guaranteed speech by charging the jury that the defendants could be found guilty if they found that the defendants intended to overthrow the government by violence and force "as speedily as circumstances permit." And he removed the clear-and-present-danger issue from the jury's consideration by stating that, as a matter of law, "there is sufficient danger of a substantive evil."

The jury found the eleven defendants guilty as charged. Judge Medina sentenced them to $10,000 fines and five years' imprisonment, except for Robert Thompson, whose record of heroism in the army prompted the judge to reduce his imprisonment to three years. The defendants appealed, and in 1950 the Court of Appeals, Judge Learned Hand writing the opinion, upheld the conviction. The Supreme Court granted certiorari, and, in June 1951, found the Smith Act constitutional and upheld the convictions. Justices Black and Douglas dissented, and Justice Clark did not participate.

The Supreme Court's decision in the Dennis case is an extremely important one in the nation's constitutional history, but it need not detain us here. Suffice it to say that the opinions were varied and complicated and that the vote of the court represented an unprecedented judicial approval for restriction of speech. It is interesting to note that Justice Douglas's dissenting opinion referred to the Communists as "miserable merchants of unwanted ideas," and that two of the majority justices, Frankfurter and Jackson, wrote that the Smith Act, while constitutional, was an ill-advised and ineffective method of combating Communism.[22]

The Department of Justice sought and secured indictments of many other Communist leaders after the Supreme Court upheld the convictions of the top eleven leaders. On March 10, 1952, Philip Frankfeld, his wife, and four other Maryland Communist leaders were brought to trial in Baltimore. All were found guilty and sentenced to $1,000 fines and from two to five years' imprisonment. Ironically, the *Daily Worker* announced Frankfeld's expulsion from the party and his wife's removal from leadership just three days before the trial began. The party's leadership accused him of "defeatism," of writing and circulating among the membership a pamphlet counter to the line of the party, and "moral degeneracy and corruption . . . double-dealing and deception."[23] Such charges certainly smacked of the party's own "thought control."

In a trial in Los Angeles beginning on February 1, 1952, and ending August 5, William Schneiderman, Oleta O'Connor Yates, Dorothy Healy, and eleven other top California Communists were convicted under the Smith Act. Although convicted, the California Communists conducted quite a different kind of defense from the one in the first trial. These defendants, in June 1957, became the first Smith Act group to receive a favorable decision from the Supreme Court.

The most widely publicized of these "second-string" prosecutions was *United States* v. *Elizabeth Gurley Flynn, et al.*, sometimes known as the "second Foley Square trial." In this trial, thirteen Communists were convicted, but a new development was Judge Edward J. Dimock's directed acquittal of two of the defendants, Isadore Begun and Simon W. Gerson, on the grounds that insufficient evidence had been presented to connect them to the indicted conspiracy. Subsequently, the convictions of two other defendants, Alexander Trachtenberg and George Blake Charney, were set aside and new trials ordered when the testimony of the principal witness against them, Harvey Matusow, was revealed to be questionable at best.

Prosecutions and convictions of "second-string" and even "third-string" Communist leaders continued through 1953 and 1954. Seven were convicted in Honolulu, five in Pittsburgh, four in Seattle, six in Detroit, five in St. Louis, and nine in Philadelphia. In all these cases there was but one acquittal.

What were the effects on the Communist Party of all these prosecutions, convictions, and imprisonments? (The question of the wisdom of the Smith Act prosecutions, which involves an assessment of their impact on civil liberties, is another question.) Certainly prosecutions under the Smith Act did not kill the party, for it was still a going concern after the frequency of new indictments declined about 1955. In that year, the F.B.I. estimated the party had 22,663 members.[24] Membership strength shrank considerably after the 1949 trial, but the party's most important membership loss did not come until 1956 and 1957, after the Smith Act prosecutions had almost ceased.

It is impossible precisely to measure the various factors causing the decline of the Communist Party in the early 1950's and say that this or that causal factor was responsible for *x* percentage of the party's deterioration. Smith Act prosecutions were only one among many actions and conditions that hurt the party. Among others were the further deterioration of Russian-American relations during the Korean war, the continued health of the American economy, and, perhaps most important, the ill-advised actions of the Communist Party itself.

The prosecutions obviously hurt the party. It was forced to spend for legal defense a great deal of money it would otherwise have spent for offensive, rather than defensive, activity. The trials consumed a great deal of the Communists' time and energy, which they would have preferred to use otherwise. It has been asserted that the Smith Act convictions "beheaded" the party, leaving the rank and file without effective leadership. Unquestionably, the imprisonment of the abler and more experienced leaders damaged the party's efficiency, but the most important party leader, William Z. Foster, actively led the party despite the poor health that prevented the government from pushing his prosecution. There is no reason to believe that the main direction of the party would have been different had the imprisoned leaders remained active in the leadership. The party's decision to go "underground" in 1949 and 1950, related of course to the Smith Act prosecutions, probably damaged party efficiency more than the leaders' imprisonment. It is unlikely that a considerable number of Communists severed their party connection because of fear of prosecution. Only one of the convicted Communists, Barbara Hartle, convicted at Seattle in 1953, renounced the party before the Communists' 1956 crisis, and she related that her indictment prompted her to stay in the party longer than she would have otherwise. It may even be true that the prosecutions led members to resolve to stick with the party, come what may.

"PEACE" AND WAR

In the late 1940's and early 1950's, the most prominent feature of the American Communists' outward face was their "peace crusade." "Peace," by which the Communists actually meant unstinting agreement with the foreign policy of the Soviet Union, had long been a prominent Communist demand. But in 1949 and early 1950, "peace" became the ideological hook upon which all else hung.

Foster expressed the notion of the centrality of the "peace" issue clearly in a message to the party's national committee. "Under no circumstances should we neglect the mass struggles over wages, unemployment, Negro rights, and fascism: but we must recognize that these are all bound up with the fight against war. Everything depends upon our success in this all-inclusive key struggle. To mobilize the masses to fight for peace should be the very center of the work." Then, in a passage that illustrated the party's ambiguous position on the inevitability of war, he advised that the "peace crusade" must be a long-term campaign, if not one of indefinite duration. "Regardless of any agreements that may be made to soften the cold war . . . the war danger will continue to exist. . . . That is because of the incurable warlike character of imperialism, especially American imperialism. The war danger will last as long as capitalism does, and we must orientate upon this realization . . . the fight for peace must be in the center of all our Party's work."[25]

The party's first big peace project was the Scientific and Cultural Conference for World Peace, usually called the Waldorf Peace Conference, in March 1949. An organization called the National Council of the Arts, Sciences, and Professions, composed of former Progressive Citizens of America members for the most part, officially sponsored the conference, but the Communists actually organized the affair. The conference attracted an impressive list of intellectuals as participants, indicating that as late as the spring of 1949 the influence of Communists in the non-Communist Left was far from extinguished.[26] In October, the party inspired the formation in Chicago of the National Labor Conference for Peace, and in December, it was behind a weekend peace rally in New York City's Manhattan Center.[27]

The Communist peace campaign began in earnest in the spring of 1950; the immediate occasion for the stepped-up program was the job of getting

American signatures to the so-called Stockholm Peace Petition. In March, the Permanent Committee of the World Peace Congress met at Stockholm and drafted the appeal. The chairman of this committee was the French scientist and Communist Frederic Joliot-Curie, now dead; the vice-chairman was a non-Communist former assistant attorney general of the United States, O. John Rogge. Other American delegates were Albert Kahn and Johannes Steel. The petition itself was an innocuous condemnation of the use of atomic bombs, which several million Americans might have endorsed had it not been for the petition's international Communist sponsorship. It did not call for the abolition of nuclear testing. The Russians still had a lot of testing to do.

O. John Rogge's story was interesting. Rogge had criticized both American and Russian imperialism at a peace conference in Mexico City in 1949, and the Communists called him a slanderer. In early March 1950, before the Stockholm meeting, he agreed to serve as legal counsel for Tito's Yugoslavia in the United States, and he registered with the Department of Justice as required by the Foreign Agents Registration Act of 1938. Still he went to Stockholm. At a meeting of the World Peace Conference in Warsaw in November 1950, Rogge gave a speech in which he vigorously condemned Soviet imperialism. His speech caused a scene of memorable proportions. An American delegate, Charles P. Howard, who had given the keynote speech at the 1948 Progressive convention, called Rogge "not only a lawyer for Tito but . . . the advocate for the slaveholder Jefferson Davis . . . and of King George III." The staff of the Cominform's newspaper was violent in condemnation of Rogge.[28]

In order to reach their goal of five million signatures to the Stockholm petition by October 24, United Nations Day, the Communists staged the kind of organizational campaign at which they once excelled. They used their influence in the trade unions they still dominated; they created new front groups (Harlem Women's Committee on Peace, Veterans for Peace, U.S. Youth Sponsoring Committee for the World Peace Appeal); they organized conferences with noble titles; and they exploited their old front groups, like the American Slav Congress. But their effort failed to achieve the goal. At the end of the campaign, the Communists claimed only two and one-half million signatures, and that figure was unquestionably padded.[29]

Before the petition campaign was over, the United States was actually engaged in armed conflict with Communists in Korea. Early in the morning of June 25, 1950, North Korean troops crossed the thirty-eighth parallel, the boundary between the American and Russian occupation zones set by the Potsdam Conference, in a large-scale, obviously long-planned invasion of South Korea. Almost immediately, the United States, independently and through the United Nations, went to the aid of the South Koreans; within a matter of days, American soldiers were being killed as the North Koreans pushed on south.

The American Communists now faced a new situation, but the fundamentals of their position on the Korean war had already been decided. As early as 1947, the party press had begun to publish paeans to the Soviet-supported North Koreans and condemnations of the American-supported government of Syngman Rhee in South Korea. The North Koreans were peaceful and democratic; Syngman Rhee was a reactionary puppet of Wall

Street.[30] Curiously, there had even been foreshadowings of some of the details of the party line on the Korean war. On the first anniversary of V-J Day, *New Masses* had carried an article on bacteriological warfare with ideas that would in time come to fruition in such *Daily Worker* headlines as "REPORT U.S. PLANES DROP MORE GERMS ON KOREA," "BACTERIOLOGICAL WAR CRIMINALS," and "EYEWITNESS DESCRIBES GERM BOMB."[31]

The Communists claimed that the whole Korean affair was part of a conspiracy of Wall Street and its agents in Washington and Seoul. In a "plot . . . as thoroughly planned as . . . the Japanese seizure of Mukden in 1931," Wall Street had entrusted Syngman Rhee to arrange the incident. John Foster Dulles was "the trigger man." The party secretariate issued a statement that even had Dulles "standing in the front lines of the puppet government trenches, giving them their marching orders." Dulles was indeed an awful person in the Communist press. The Cominform called him, under the headline "JOHN FOSTER DULLES, BANKER, SLAVEOWNER, WARMONGER," "one of the more sinister members of the imperialist gang of misanthropic fiends."[32] According to the Communists, North Korea had not invaded South Korea. Quite the reverse. Troops of "the quisling South Korean government" had "crossed all along the 38th parallel and penetrated one kilometer into North Korean territory."[33]

The purposes of the whole Wall Street plot, the Communists maintained, were the "colonial enslavement" of all East Asia and the establishment in Korea of "powerful bases from which to make war upon the new China and the Soviet Union."[34] The North Korean "guards," as the party press first called them, had foiled the imperialist plot with strong resistance. Then they counterattacked. Within six weeks, they controlled nearly all the Korean peninsula, and the "guards" became "Korean people's liberation forces." How the North Koreans were able, without previous planning and careful and extensive preparations, to launch such a major offensive was a military question the Communists did not answer—or even consider. The intervention of American-U.N. forces on a large scale, the subsequent expulsion of the North Korean army from South Korea, and the carrying of the war north of the thirty-eighth parallel only served to confirm for the Communists their interpretation of the whole conflict.

Almost from the beginning of the Korean war, there was a difference of opinion about war aims and strategy between President Truman and General Douglas MacArthur, commander of the U.N. forces in Korea. Truman wanted no more than a limited war; he tried to restrain his colorful and outspoken general, who was for more adventurous policies even should they risk involvement for the United States in a general war with Communist China or the Soviet Union. The Truman-MacArthur differences became impossible to ignore or compromise in the spring of 1951, and in April, the president removed the general from command.

The MacArthur ouster prompted a few Communists to reassess their interpretation of the Korean war, as well it should have. If the Truman administration were bent on a war of conquest in the Far East, why should it risk political disaster with the removal of the bellicose and politically important MacArthur? No important Communist, apparently, at that time prepared any thorough critique of the whole party position on war, imperialism, and American foreign policy. But at least one, Joseph Starobin, foreign editor of the *Daily Worker* and secretary of the party's commission on peace activities, quietly and privately expressed his doubts to party leaders about the validity of the party line. Neither Starobin nor anyone else led any large-scale agitation in the party. The rank and file and most leaders had no knowledge of any dissent in the national office.[35]

Lest anyone else should develop heretical ideas about the party's line, Eugene Dennis wrote a letter to the party membership on the MacArthur affair, in which he upheld the old line in no uncertain terms. The Truman-MacArthur controversy was of no real significance, wrote Dennis. The differences between the president and the general were only over tactics and pace. "The Truman Administration continues to move in its own aggressive way and at its own pace toward a global war . . . under the guise of opposing a 'third world war,' of waging a 'limited war,' the Truman Administration continues to pursue Wall Street's aggressive war policy, a criminal policy which . . . if unchecked, can only lead . . . to a third world war." The party must not relax, must not let up the struggle against a general war. Henceforth, ordered Dennis, every item *"of every Party agenda in every leading committee and club must be linked with . . . an all-out struggle and campaign against the Truman and MacArthur war policies."*[36]

The Communists failed to modify their position on Korea in the slightest. Through the long truce negotiations, conducted intermittently from July 1951 until the armistice two years later; through a Presidential election in which Foster called General Eisenhower "Wall Street's speed-war candidate";[37] through the gradual but steady fading away of old soldier MacArthur, the Communists incessantly maintained that Washington was about to launch a new world war of imperialistic conquest. Even when the final armistice was signed, the party's national committee declared that the peace was only a partial victory over "the plans of Wall Street to establish its world domination through war." Foster, never one to allow a fact to upset his theory, found little solace in the armistice. The "Wall Street planners of a third world war," he told his readers, "have been trying (and still are) to make another Spain in Korea." The State Department will yet "try to sabotage the [Korean] peace."[38]

The most important effect of the party's whole peace crusade in the long run was that it further contributed to its isolation from the publics it needed for sustenance. Besides all their work in especially constituted peace organizations—they scorned the established peace organizations such as those of religious groups and the Fellowship for Reconciliation and were in turn scorned by them—the Communists tried to use their influence in organizations founded for some other purpose. In trade unions, for example, the Communists regarded a leader's position on foreign policy as a touchstone. "A labor leader is a progressive to the degree that he stands for peace . . . and co-existence with the Soviet Union. He is a reactionary to the extent that he stands for . . . the war drive of U.S. imperialism and its anti-Soviet foreign policy. No matter how militant . . . on other questions, to the extent that he supports the war drive, he is a reactionary."[39] Communists applied the same test to Negro leaders. When the national leaders of the N.A.A.C.P. supported the Korean war, the Communists accused them of selling out for "a few paltry jobs [in] the operation of Point Four in Africa."[40] And, as will be seen in greater detail later, the Communists in the

Progressive Party insisted on their position on Korea, precipitating a crisis in the Progressive organization that left it without a prominent non-Communist leader. The root of the matter was that the party accorded conformity to the international Communist line a higher priority than its own viability.

A few Communists dimly perceived the effects of the party's parochialism. There was even a guarded and fuzzy warning in the party's official magazine.[41] But warnings from their own ranks did not change party policy. The Communists were not fully to realize the consequences of their sectarianism until they were jarred by events in the Soviet Union.

With a more astute peace program, one less obviously a reflection of Russian foreign policy, the Communists might have gained some strength or at least slowed their decline. For there was widespread opposition to war in the United States as well as widespread opposition to Communism. A large part of the population was anxious and frustrated about the Korean war. Ironically for the Communists, popular desire for peace expressed itself in the election of a Republican administration, an administration headed by a war-hero five-star general and a Vice-President who made his mark in politics as a professional anti-Communist.

THE LAST DAYS OF THE PROGRESSIVE PARTY

After Wallace's showing in the 1948 elections, the Communists were slow to lose their illusions about the Progressive Party being a "mass party of the working class." Communists deplored the electorate's commitment to the major political parties and tried to convince themselves that sentiment for the Progressive Party's program was growing even if the party was not. But in 1950, they had to admit that "there is not yet a mass third party in America."[42]

Despite the ineffectiveness of the Progressive Party and despite the fact that any realistic appraisal of its future would not indicate growth, the Communist Party continued until after the 1952 elections to support and dominate the Progressive Party. The Communists, too, continued their relationship with the A.L.P. in New York, which supported the Progressives in national elections. With each group, the Communists continued their support because these "progressive" political organizations represented the best instruments then available to the Communists for amplifying the general Communist program. Within the Progressive Party and the A.L.P., there were still some leftist non-Communists, residues of the popular frontism of the mid-1930's, who would tolerate the Communists and respond to such general slogans as "Peace, Democracy, and Socialism."

Early in 1950, Henry Wallace belatedly tried to change the popular impression that the Communists controlled his party lock, stock, and barrel. At the second national convention of the party, in Chicago, Wallace said that the failure of the first convention to adopt the "Vermont resolution" denying blanket endorsement of the foreign policy of any nation had been a mistake. He went on to warn that Progressives should not take any positions that would give observers "the slightest, legitimate reason for believing that any working member of our Party puts Rome, Moscow or London ahead of the United States."[43] The convention went on to declare in one of its resolutions that the United States and the Soviet Union had both "made mistakes" in foreign policy.

This was mild enough. Neither Wallace nor the convention seriously criticized Soviet foreign policy or began any movement to remove Communists from influence within the Progressive Party. The Communists, nevertheless, refused to overlook the Progressives' slight reproach to Communist orthodoxy. The *Daily Worker* took the Progressive convention to task. "What happened at the Progressive Party convention," National Committeeman Gil Green instructed his comrades, "cannot be condoned."[44] Thus bucked up, the Communists in the Progressive Party were in no mood to compromise when the outbreak of war in Korea came.

Within a few days after the administration's decision to go to the aid of the South Koreans, the executive committee of the Progressive Party called a meeting of the full national committee for July 15. The smaller group then began on July 6 a series of sessions in preparation for the meeting of the full committee. In these meetings it became obvious that the differences over the Korean war between Henry Wallace on the one hand and the Communists and pro-Communists on the other were too great to be compromised.

There were five meetings of the executive committee before it finished drafting a statement on Korea. Not all members of the committee attended all the sessions. The members most consistent in attendance were C. B. Baldwin, Progressive Executive Secretary; James Durkin, President of the Communist-dominated United Office and Professional Workers of America; the playwright Lillian Hellman; Vito Marcantonio, the A.L.P.'s congressman; John McManus, Editor of the *National Guardian;* Paul Robeson; Arthur Schutzer, Executive Secretary of the A.L.P.; Alfred K. Stern; Henry Wallace; and Walter Wallace, who has since testified that he was then a member of the Communist Party.[45] Others who attended meetings but were not committee members were John Abt, Vaughn Albertson, Louis Burnham, Lydia D'Fonseca, and Mrs. Martha Dodd Stern.[46] After the Sterns refused to return to the United States from Mexico in the spring of 1957 to appear before a grand jury investigating espionage, Boris Morros, an American counterspy, implicated Mrs. Stern in espionage. The daughter of the late Professor William E. Dodd, American Ambassador to Germany in the 1930's, and her husband then fled to Czechoslovakia.[47]

There was a wide gulf between Henry Wallace's estimate of the Korean conflict and that of the rest of the executive committee, but Wallace's dissent from the statement drawn by the committee was not stated clearly and decisively in the committee's meetings. At the end of the July 10 meeting, according to the minutes, Wallace even expressed "provisional agreement" with the drafted statement but would reserve final decision until the next morning. The next morning, he telephoned Baldwin to say that he could not agree to the statement unless it contained four major modifications. These modifications would have changed the entire direction of the statement. The committee declined to make the changes, and thus, on July 11, 1950, Wallace severed his connection with the Progressive Party.[48]

On July 15, the entire Progressive national committee met, and by a vote of 32 to 2 adopted the statement with which Wallace could not agree. The two dissenters were Clark Foreman, of the Southern Conference of Human

Welfare, and Thomas Emerson, of the Yale University law faculty. Henry Wallace did not attend the meeting because he had already in effect left the party. The statement condemned Truman's directive commanding the fleet to defend Formosa, urged that Communist China be admitted to the United Nations, and urged the U.N. Security Council to "issue appropriate orders and adopt measures" to end the hostilities and then increase economic and technical assistance in Asia. On the same day, Wallace issued a statement to the press in which he put responsibility for the conflict on the Soviet Union. "We must continue our fight . . . in South Korea until such time as Russia is willing to use her influence to stop the fighting and start . . . UN negotiations. . . . I say that Russia could stop the fighting now if she wished to do so."[49]

From the summer of 1950 on, the strength of the Progressive and American Labor parties steadily waned. The Korean war polarized political opinion: the general public more and more identified the policies of these parties with sympathy for the Soviet Union, and the Communists and fellow travelers in these parties were less and less inclined to compromise. The Progressives and Communists in California, for example, condemned Mrs. Helen Gahagan Douglas vociferously in her race against Richard M. Nixon in 1950 because she supported the war.[50] In the same election, Vito Marcantonio made "peace" the main issue of his campaign and was defeated by a fusion candidate. The 1952 Progressive Party national candidates—Vincent Hallinan for President and Mrs. Charlotta Bass for Vice-President—where almost unknown. Hallinan, a cousin of Ireland's Eamon de Valera, was a wealthy San Francisco Left Wing lawyer; Mrs. Bass had worked closely with the Communists.[51] The Hallinan-Bass ticket received only 140,023 votes, about one-fifth of 1 percent of the total vote. Well over half the Progressive vote came from New York City, Los Angeles, and the San Francisco Bay area.[52]

After the 1952 election, it became obvious to the Communists that to continue their third-party gambit was fruitless. The "mass party of peace" had become just another Left Wing sect, only slightly larger than the Communist Party itself. The extent to which the Communists controlled the Progressive organization and the American Labor Party is seen in the subsequent history of those parties when the Communists pulled out: the Progressives disappeared altogether, and the A.L.P. failed to get enough votes in 1954 to stay on the ballot.

THE C.I.O. EXPULSIONS

The C.I.O. began in a small way to expell the Communist-controlled unions the very month Truman trounced Dewey and Wallace. The end of the road for the C.I.O. Communists was in sight after the Portland, Oregon, C.I.O. convention in late November 1948. The convention summarily ended the jurisdictional dispute between the Left-led Farm Equipment Workers (F.E.) and the U.A.W. by ordering F.E. to merge its 65,000 members into the Reuther organization within sixty days. When the F.E. leaders refused, the U.A.W. raided F.E.'s members, and F.E. disappeared anyway. At the Portland convention, President Murray gave three small Communist unions a stern lecture on their inadequacies as trade unions and threatened to deal with them more harshly in the future. These unions—the United Office and Professional Workers, the United Public Workers, and the Food and Tobacco Workers—had organized only a tiny fraction of the workers in their industries.[53]

The Communist unions did not stand together at the Portland convention. The leaders of the Food and Tobacco Workers, the Furriers, and the Marine Cooks and Stewards, all with much stronger Communist support in the rank and file than most Left unions, fought back at the anti-Communist C.I.O. leadership. They submitted and voted for a set of resolutions that sounded like a summary of the Communist line.[54] But the leaders of the bigger Left unions, more vulnerable to attack from their non-Communist rank and file, tried to compromise. Delegates from U.E., I.L.W.U., and the Furniture Workers voted for the C.I.O. majority resolution and even for the resolution rescinding the charter of the Communist-run New York City C.I.O. Council —to the exasperation of the Communist labor secretary.[55] Albert Fitzgerald, President of U.E. and the presiding officer of the Progressive convention four months before, voted for a resolution endorsing the Marshall Plan in the C.I.O. executive board and delivered a self-effacing speech on the convention floor: "I tell you frankly I do not give a damn for Russia. . . . Vishinsky and Molotov are engaging themselves in saber rattling and war mongering. . . . If President Truman makes a sincere effort to carry out his promises . . . I will tell the Progressive Party to go to hell."[56] Through such tactics, Fitzgerald managed to postpone C.I.O. action against his union and even remain a C.I.O. vice-president—for another year.

After the convention, the party's leadership stiffened the resistance of the C.I.O. Left unions. Early in January 1949, delegates of eight Communist unions met in New York and announced a "rank and file unity plan."[57] In the spring, the Communists refused a compromise in the Transport Workers Union, which, according to Mike Quill's account, would have given them a large minority on the union's executive board and the post of national secretary-treasurer. The party preferred to fight it out with Quill for a majority of the executive board. Quill utterly routed the Communists after this challenge. At the next national convention of the T.W.U., the Communists won no national offices and not a single seat on the executive board.[58] In May, the officers of nine Left unions voted as a bloc against the C.I.O. executive-board decision to withdraw from the World Federation of Trade Unions.[59] In June, the Communists, in an effort to give better co-ordination to the Left unions, started a new monthly magazine, the *March of Labor*.

Perhaps the best example of the Communists' decision not to compromise —even to counterattack and take the consequences—was in U.E., by far the most important of the Communist-controlled unions. The Communists had effectively controlled U.E. since 1941, when they elected James Matles and Julius Emspak to national office. The slow-moving and slow-thinking Albert Fitzgerald, President of the union, was not a Communist; he was only a "front man" for the Communists who ran the union. At U.E.'s national convention in Cleveland in September 1949, the Communist leadership encountered for the first time an effectively organized anti-Communist opposition, led by James B. Carey. The Carey forces represented most of the big U.E. locals, but Matles and Emspak had a majority at the convention through their control of the many small locals. The Communists got their slate of national officers elected and their resolutions adopted. Then they counter-attacked. They began a purge of the anti-Communists by amending the union's constitution to empower the general executive board to bring charges against and expel individual members. The amendment empowered the Communist national U.E. officers to eliminate their opponents even when their opponents had the support of their locals.[60]

Even after the C.I.O.'s Portland convention, the Communist unions might have been able to survive in the C.I.O. if they had behaved circumspectly. After the Communist activities in 1949, however, the C.I.O. leadership resolved to make quick work of them. At the Cleveland C.I.O. convention in November 1949, the national C.I.O. majority effectively ended all Communist influence in the national body. By a large vote, the convention amended its constitution to make Communists or those who consistently followed the Communist line ineligible for C.I.O. national office, including membership on the executive board. The convention itself then expelled U.E., saying that it was no more than "the Communist Party masquerading as a labor union." The convention then amended its constitution again to empower a two-thirds majority on the executive board to expel "or take any other appropriate action against" any union whose policies and activities "are consistently directed toward the achievement of the program or purposes of the Communist Party."[61]

Soon after the convention, the C.I.O. executive board, through a series of subcommittees, began hearings on charges against the Left Wing unions. The pattern in all the hearings was to prove that the union, through its publications and resolutions, had consistently followed each turn in the Communist party's line, a relatively easy matter to prove. The C.I.O. did not try to prove that the union leaders were members of the Communist Party, a task which would have been considerably more difficult, if not impossible, but would have been irrelevant anyway. By the late spring of 1950, the C.I.O. executive board had expelled nine Communist-led unions. Communist influence in the C.I.O. was all but completely eliminated. Any Communists left were either rank and filers or, at most, local officers who thereafter could sing the party tune only softly.[62]

Being cut off from the rest of the labor movement was a severe handicap for the Communists and the unions they controlled, but worse was to come. The C.I.O. granted charters to new unions to compete with the expelled unions or allowed established C.I.O. unions to raid the Communist unions' membership. Within a few years, the Communist unions, assaulted by raid after raid, had dwindled away. By 1956, the only Communist unions with anything like their strength before expulsion were the Bridges union and Mine, Mill. A new union in the electrical industry, the International Union of Electrical, Radio and Machine Workers (I.U.E.), the Machinists (I.A.M.), and the A.F. of L.'s International Brotherhood of Electrical Workers had all but eliminated the once-powerful U.E.[63] The Bridges union and Mine, Mill were able substantially to retain their old strength because of special circumstances. Harry Bridges, despite, rather than because of, his politics, is a popular figure among West Coast dock workers. His generation of dock workers will not forget his heroic role in the 1934 dock strike, and Bridges runs a union that "delivers" in the Gompers "bread and butter" sense. There are two reasons for Mine, Mill's survival. It has a heritage of radical rhetoric that goes back to William D. ("Big Bill") Haywood and the Western Federation of Miners, for one thing, and employers prefer Mine, Mill to unions, such as the United Steelworkers, that might give them greater opposition at the bargaining table. Thus, Mine, Mill is a peculiar combination of a Red and a company union.[64]

In Communist theory, the workers in basic industry are supposed to be the core of their party's strength, the revolutionary proletariat. Until 1949–50, the Communists looked at the two million members in the unions they controlled and, with a bit of optimistic self-delusion, saw themselves as the vanguard of the working class. But by the mid-1950's, the membership of Communist-controlled unions had shrunk to about 200,000, about one-tenth of the former membership, less than 1 per cent of total American trade-union strength. Any group that professes to speak in the name of the working class with as little power in that class as the Communists have demonstrated speaks with a hollow ring indeed.

THE ROSENBERG CASE

The exclusion of Communist influence from the mainstream of the American labor movement, the prosecutions under the Smith Act and other governmental anti-Communist programs, the deflation of the Progressive and A.L.P. popular fronts, and the general anti-Communist sentiments of the public, together with certain internal activities of the Communist organization, considerably reduced the strength of the Communist Party. Any index of the party's health shows a sharp decline from about 1949 to about 1953. In early February 1950, F.B.I. Director J. Edgar Hoover testified to a Congressional appropriations committee that there were at that time 54,174 members of the Communist Party. In 1953, he reported that party membership was 24,796, more than a 50-per-cent decline in three years.[65] In 1950, the general manager of the *Daily Worker* in his annual sworn circulation statement reported his paper's average circulation as 20,336, and the Sunday edition (the *Worker*) as 67,199. In 1953, these figures had fallen to 10,443 and 28,822 respectively.[66]

Despite the party's weakened organizational strength, despite the almost universal disapproval of Communist doctrines by the American people, despite the inhibitions upon Communists when they operated in public, the Communists still were able in the early 1950's to make of the Rosenberg affair one of the biggest, noisiest, and most successful propaganda campaigns in Communist Party history.

In early February 1950, Klaus Fuchs, a German-born physicist who as a naturalized British subject had worked in the United States during the war on the atomic-bomb project, was arrested for espionage. Fuchs confessed to the English authorities and told them what he knew of espionage. His testimony implicated Harry Gold, an American, who soon confessed to his role as a courier for a spy ring. Gold pleaded guilty in the Philadelphia courtroom of Federal Judge James P. McGranery, and was sentenced to thirty years' imprisonment. This sentence was the maximum imprisonment; the law provides for "death or imprisonment for not more than thirty years."

Gold told the F.B.I. all he knew about the ring and implicated Julius Rosenberg, a Communist engineering graduate of the City College of New York; Julius Rosenberg's wife, Ethel; Ethel Rosenberg's brother, David Greenglass, a skilled machinist; Morton Sobell, a college classmate of Rosenberg; and Anatoli A. Yakovlev, a Russian national then presumably in the Soviet Union. When Gold's arrest was announced to the press, the *Daily Worker,* under the headline "FBI WHIPS UP NEW 'ATOMIC SPY' HOAX," declared, "By an obvious 'coincidence,' the arrest of Gold was timed to knock off the front pages the return tomorrow of United Nations Secretary-General Trygve Lie and his anticipated report of Soviet proposals to end the cold war."[67]

Greenglass confessed and revealed all he knew, as had Fuchs and Gold before him. The Rosenbergs and Sobell were indicted in August 1950, and their trial began in New York City in the court of Federal Judge Irving R. Kaufman on March 6, 1951. The burden of the prosecution's case was the testimony of Harry Gold and David Greenglass. The revelations of these two witnesses were partially confirmed by the testimony of others. The Rosenbergs denied everything. Ethel Rosenberg, when asked before the grand jury if she knew Gold and Yakovlev, had declined to answer on the grounds that her testimony might be self-incriminating. At the trial she denied she knew Yakovlev or had ever seen Gold before. Sobell pleaded not guilty, but did not take the witness stand at all; he said nothing to the jury whatsoever. The trial consumed three weeks. On March 29, 1951, after deliberating seven and one-half hours, the jury announced its verdict: the Rosenbergs and Sobell were guilty as charged. The Rosenbergs' attorney, Emmanuel H. Bloch, thanked the court, the prosecuting attorney and his staff, and F.B.I. members for their courtesies during the trial. He told the jury he was satisfied that it had examined the evidence "very carefully." Judge Kaufman sentenced the Rosenbergs to death and Sobell to thirty years' imprisonment. David Greenglass received a sentence of fifteen years' imprisonment.

The Communist press did not carry one word about the Rosenbergs until after they had been found guilty and had been sentenced. A person in the unenviable position of receiving news only from the *Daily Worker* would not have known until the day after they were sentenced that the Rosenberg case even existed. Nor did the party's Civil Rights Congress come forward to raise bail for the Rosenbergs after their arrest. When the Communists finally mentioned the case, they did not deny the Rosenbergs' guilt. The first mention, a news story, asserted that the Rosenbergs were being made scapegoats for the Korean war. An editorial three days later took the position that the sentence was what one would expect from a government "which is refusing to negotiate peace in Korea." The whole case, according to the editorial writer, was an effort "to turn the hatred of 57,000 American casualties away from the war makers in Washington toward Jews and Communists. Not since the days [of] the Czars . . . and Nazis . . . has this pogrom tactic been so brazenly used." But there was no accusation of a judicial frame-up.[68] No newspaper asserted that the Rosenbergs were innocent until four months after the end of the trial, and the charge that the Rosenbergs had been framed came then, not from the Communist press, strictly speaking, but from the fellow-traveling *National Guardian,* a publication of the New York A.L.P. begun for the Wallace movement in 1947.[69]

Why the Communists were so reticent about the Rosenberg case at first is an interesting subject for speculation. It seems likely that the Communists were quiet about the case until they were confident that the Rosenbergs were not going to confess to espionage, as had Fuchs, Gold, and Greenglass before them. To have organized and launched a big amnesty campaign and have it undermined by a confession would have been disastrous.

On November 8, 1951, seven months after the Rosenberg trial, while the case was being appealed, a group that called itself the National Committee to Secure Justice in the Rosenberg Case opened a bank account in New York City. The committee did not announce its formation until almost two months later. The president of the organization was Louis Harap, Editor of the Communist magazine *Jewish Life*. The chairman was Joseph Brainin. The most active directors of the committee were its executive secretary, David Alman, and his wife, Emily, who served as national treasurer. Alman had been a paid staff member of the New York Civil Rights Congress and the American Peace Crusade. The sponsors of the committee were a mixture of active party members, such as Herbert Aptheker, and intellectuals with several past associations in party fronts, such as W. E. B. DuBois, a few of whom enjoyed national prominence.[70] This committee organized and coordinated the pro-Rosenberg campaign throughout the country.

For its first several months, the Rosenberg committee's effort failed to generate much excitement except among small leftist groups in a few big cities ever ready to respond to such appeals. In the late fall and early winter of 1952, the committee stepped up its activities with more mass meetings, delegations to Sing Sing, where the Rosenbergs were imprisoned, and pickets outside the White House gates. Simultaneously, Rosenberg committees appeared in Paris and London. From then until the Rosenbergs' execution on June 19, 1953, the campaign operated at fever pitch.

Circumstantial evidence indicates that there was a relationship between the intensification of the Rosenberg campaign both in the United States and in Europe and the case of Rudolph Slansky in Czechoslovakia. Slansky and thirteen other defendants were tried in Prague, November 20–27, 1952, and eleven of the defendants were hanged six days later. All but three of the fourteen were Jewish, and there were distinctly anti-Semitic overtones to the prosecution. Among other things, Slansky was charged with "Jewish bourgeois nationalism." The Communists everywhere were quick to deny they were anti-Semitic—they were only anti-Zionist, they asserted—but they clearly linked the Rosenberg and Slansky cases in an apparent attempt to divert attention from the Prague trial. Jacques Duclos, the French Communist leader, went so far as to say, "The conviction of U.S. atom spies Julius and Ethel Rosenberg was an example of anti-Semitism but the execution of eight Jews in Czechoslovakia last week was not."[71]

The French Communists achieved much more spectacular results with their pro-Rosenberg campaign than did their American comrades. Exploiting the legacy of the Dreyfus case of more than a half-century before, the French Rosenberg agitation emphasized the assertion that the couple were victims of anti-Semitism, a charge the major American Jewish organizations consistently rejected. Such prominent non-Communist French leaders as Cardinal Feltin, Archbishop of Paris, Edouard Herriot, President of the National Assembly, four former premiers of France, and Vincent Auriol, President of the Republic, took part in appeals for the Rosenbergs.[72] Undoubtedly, the Rosenberg agitation in France heightened anti-American sentiment, as it was intended to do.

In the last frantic days of the American pro-Rosenberg campaign, which featured motorcades, special "Rosenberg trains" from New York to Washington, and "round-the-clock vigils" outside the White House, there occurred a little-publicized incident that indicated that the Rosenberg committee and the Communists were determined to run the clemency campaign entirely by themselves and wring from it the greatest possible propaganda value. The incident involved Irwin Edelman, of Los Angeles, an erratic leftist expelled from the Communist Party in 1947. In November 1952, Edelman published a pamphlet entitled *Freedom's Electrocution*, which quite agreed with the Communist line on the Rosenberg case except that it was critical of the conduct during the trial of the Rosenbergs' counsel, Emmanuel H. Bloch. Soon after the pamphlet's publication, Edelman was expelled from the Los Angeles Rosenberg Committee.[73] The *National Guardian* refused to accept an advertisement for the pamphlet, and a letter in the *People's World* urged that Edelman be ignored.[74] Edelman interested two lawyers, Fyke Farmer, of Nashville, and Daniel G. Marshall, of Los Angeles, in his indictment of Bloch and in his suggestion that the Rosenbergs should have been tried under the Atomic Energy Act of 1946 rather than under the Espionage Act of 1917. Under the 1946 act, the death penalty or life imprisonment may be imposed only when intent to injure the United States is proved and only by recommendation of the trial jury. Using Edelman's argument, Farmer and Marshall, on June 13, 1953, five days before the Rosenbergs' scheduled execution, filed with Judge Kaufman a petition for a writ of habeas corpus. Bloch declined to co-operate with Farmer and Marshall and wired Judge Kaufman to state his refusal to be associated with the petition. Judge Kaufman denied the petition on June 15. Bloch refused again to co-operate with Farmer and Marshall when they tried to interest the Supreme Court in their argument. On June 17, two days after the Supreme Court had recessed for the summer, Justice William O. Douglas granted a stay of execution after hearing the Edelman argument. The court reconvened in extraordinary session the next day. The following day, June 19, the court vacated Justice Douglas's stay of execution. That evening, shortly after eight o'clock, the Rosenbergs were executed.[75] The Communists and the Rosenberg committee had been determined to keep the Rosenberg case activity in their own hands, where they could control it, even if this end meant rejection of a legal argument that had sufficient merit to persuade a justice of the nation's highest court to call the court into extraordinary session.

The primary motive of the Communists in the Rosenberg agitation in the United States was to broadcast the Communist opinion, central to their whole political line, that the government of the United States was controlled by "fascists" who sought to involve the nation in war, destroy the labor movement, abrogate civil liberties, eliminate dissent, and persecute minority groups. For Communists, already persuaded to the party's line, the Rosenberg case served as confirmation, and the defense agitation served to deepen personal commitments. And non-Communists moved to sympathy for the Rosenbergs by humanitarian considerations afforded the Communists an opportunity for indoctrination. From the first editorial on the Rosenberg case to the blast when the couple was executed, the Communists hammered away with the argument that the Rosenbergs were sentenced to death as a step toward outright fascism. The facts of the case itself got short shrift in Communist pages. The Rosenberg affair, the Communists repeated, was a device to channel "the hatred of the American people for the Korean war, for the 'inevitable atomic war' line of the atombomb maniacs . . . against the working-class vanguard, the Communists, the Negro and Jewish people, the labor and progressive forces generally." The Rosenbergs' trial and conviction was nothing but "a political plot to assist in advancing the McCarthyite pro-fascist reign of fear in the United States, to brutalize the population, and get it to accept the further fascization of the United States without resistance." Thus, the Communists asserted, to defend the Rosenbergs was not only humanitarian, but it was self-defense against fascism, essentially patriotic protection of American democracy. "There must be a halt to the Hitlerization of America by the Eisenhower-Brownell-J. Edgar Hoover forces working hand in glove with the swastika-minded McCarthy and his goons."[76] The opening-wedge-of-fascism theme dominated appeals directed to organized labor and to Jews, both groups that had good reasons to fear fascism. The theme permeated even the sentimentally murky poems and songs of the Rosenberg campaign.[77]

Why was it that the Communist Party, declining in size and power even while it led the Rosenberg agitation, was able to create such a big amnesty campaign and then bombard the campaign's followers with the usual Communist propaganda line? Why was it that thousands of non-Communists came sincerely to believe that the Rosenbergs had been framed, despite a trial at which defense counsel expressed no complaint about procedure and despite over two years of appeals, motions for retrials, petitions for habeas corpus, and applications for reduction of sentence which were heard seven times by the Court of Appeals and seven times by the Supreme Court? Part of the answer lies in the fairly widespread opposition to capital punishment. And a large part of the answer lies in part of the American heritage. There were skeletons in America's closet. There had been cases of injustice in the courts and discrimination against minorities. It was not difficult to persuade some people that what had happened before was happening again. Had there been no Sacco-Vanzetti case and no Mooney-Billings case and had no American Jew ever suffered persecution, it is not likely that the Rosenberg defenders would have received a serious hearing. This the Communists realized, and they worked mightily to inflate the Rosenberg case into an American Dreyfus affair. Therein lies the real tragedy in the Rosenberg case. The sins of the past are not easily lived down.

This, then, was the outward face of the Communist Party in the late 1940's and early 1950's. It clearly was in retreat. American public opinion had reached an unprecedented pitch of opposition to Communists and their ideas. The government's prosecution of Communist Party leaders and the kind of defense that the party elected to make against the prosecution had resulted in an important handicap to the party's efficiency. The manner in which the party conducted its "peace" campaign had further isolated it from the non-Communist Left and from the movement for Negro equality, and the Communists' "hard" line had contributed to the decline of the Progressive Party and the elimination of Communist influence in the decisions of the C.I.O.

Facing attack from government, from the trade unions, and from the public in general, the Communists endeavored to appear as militant advocates of freedom and justice, as defenders of the Jeffersonian tradition of civil liberty. They sought to be regarded as the innocent victims of a society that had lost its restraint and that had forgotten a noble tradition of due legal process and fair play toward dissenters from majority attitudes. The Communists and their organizations obviously were the victims of a reaction that was sometimes disrespectful of the highest traditions of law and justice, but they were hardly innocent victims.

REFERENCES

1. Eric F. Goldman, *The Crucial Decade: America, 1945–1955* (New York: Knopf, 1956), pp. 116–17.
2. For further details see Hadley Cantril, ed., *Public Opinion, 1935–1946* (Princeton: Princeton University Press, 1951), pp. 130–1; Samuel A. Stouffer, *Communism, Conformity and Civil Liberties: A Cross-Section of the Nation Speaks Its Mind* (Garden City: Doubleday, 1955), pp. 43–4.
3. William Z. Foster, "Keynote Message of Greetings to the Plenum," *PA*, XXIX (May 1950), p. 11; Michael Bianca, "How To Fight McCarthyism," *ibid.*, XXX (Oct. 1951), p. 23.
4. William Weinstone, "The Fight to Repeal the Legislative Blueprint for Fascism," *ibid.*, XXIX (Oct. 1950), pp. 35, 43; see also Alexander Bittelman, "Who Are the Conspirators?," *ibid.*, XXX (July 1951), p. 21; Gus Hall, "The Present Situation and the Next Tasks," *ibid.*, XXIX (Oct. 1950), p. 7; William Z. Foster, in "Is the United States in the Early Stages of Fascism?," *ibid.*, XXXIII (Nov. 1954), pp. 4–21, concluded that at that time, while the Senate was in the process of censuring McCarthy, fascism was a growing danger.
5. Foster in *Wkr,* Jan. 15, 1950; Weinstone, *op. cit.,* p. 38.
6. Abner Berry in *DW*, Oct. 2, 1950; James W. Ford, "The Communist Party: Champion Fighter for Negro Rights," *PA*, XXVIII (June 1949), p. 48.
7. Weinstone, *op. cit.,* p. 40.
8. James Rorty and Moshe Decter, *McCarthy and the Communists* (Boston: Beacon, 1954), p. 150; *DW*, Aug. 15, 1946, and Rob F. Hall, "The People Won't Mourn La Follette," *ibid.*, Aug. 19, 1946.
9. "America's Hour of Peril—Unite! Save Democracy and Peace!," *PA*, XXX (July 1951), pp. 1–8.
10. Editorial, "The Trap against Unity," *DW*, July 14, 1949.
11. *DW*, Jan. 12, 1946.
12. *Ibid.*, Feb. 1, 1946.
13. *Ibid.*, Aug. 5, 1946.
14. *Digest of the Public Record of Communism in the United States* (New York: Fund for the Republic, 1955), pp. 194–6.
15. New York *Times,* Jan. 18, 19, 1949.
16. C. Herman Pritchett, *Civil Liberties and the Vinson Court* (Chicago: University of Chicago Press, 1954), p. 233.
17. *Ibid.*, pp. 233–6, 280 note 7.
18. *DW*, Feb. 25, 1949.

19. *Wkr*, Jan. 30, 1949; *DW*, March 22, 1949.
20. *Wkr*, Sept. 19, 1948; Elizabeth Gurley Flynn in *ibid.*, April 3, 1949.
21. See his introduction to George Marion, *The Communist Trial: An American Crossroads* (New York: Fairplay Publishers, 2d ed., 1950).
22. For a critical discussion of the constitutional issues involved in the decision see Pritchett, *op. cit.*, pp. 71–7.
23. *DW*, March 7, 1952.
24. Subcommittee . . . of the Committee on the Judiciary, United States Senate, 84th Cong., 1st sess., Committee Print, *The Communist Party of the United States of America . . . A Handbook for Americans* (Washington, D. C., 1955), p. 34.
25. Foster, "Keynote Message of Greetings to the Plenum," *PA*, XXIX (May 1950), pp. 10–11; see also *DW*, March 21, 1950.
26. Committee on Un-American Activities, House of Representatives, 81st Cong., 2d sess., House Report No. 1954, *Review of the Scientific and Cultural Conference for World Peace Arranged by the National Council of the Arts, Sciences and Professions and Held in New York City, March 25, 26, and 27, 1949*. This report has utility, but it is a typical report of this committee in that its emphasis was on lists of names rather than analysis.
27. *DW*, Oct. 3, Dec. 5, 6, 1949.
28. *Ibid.*, Nov. 21, 1950, Nov. 14, 15, 1951; *Wkr*, Sept. 11, 1949; *For a Lasting Peace, For a People's Democracy!*, March 31, Nov. 24, 1950.
29. *DW*, May 18, 21, 23, June 14, 1950; *Wkr*, June 11, Oct. 1, 1950; *Labor Fact Book 10* (New York: Labor Research Association, 1951), p. 26.
30. *Wkr*, May 18, 1947, March 28, 1948; *DW*, Sept. 29, Oct. 11, 14, 19, 30, 1947.
31. Dyson Carter, "New Ways of Killing," *New Masses*, Sept. 3, 1946; *DW*, March 19, 20, April 9, 1952.
32. Frederick Vanderbilt Field, "Wall Street's Aggression in Korea and the Struggle for Peace," *PA*, XXIX (Sept. 1950), p. 15; for secretariat statement, "Halt Wall Street Aggression in Asia!," *ibid.*, XXIX (Aug. 1950), p. 2; *For a Lasting Peace, For a People's Democracy!*, Sept. 22, 1950.
33. *DW*, June 26, 1950.
34. Betty Gannett, "Wall Street's War against the Korean People," *PA*, XXIX (Aug. 1950), p. 7; Field, *op. cit.*, p. 26.
35. Interview with Joseph Starobin, Oct. 1, 1956; Joseph Starobin, "A Communication," *PA*, XXXVI (Jan. 1957), pp. 60–2.
36. Eugene Dennis, "The MacArthur Ouster: A Letter to the Members of the Communist Party, U.S.A." *PA*, XXX (May 1951), pp. 3, 6. Italics in original.
37. *Wkr*, July 13, 1952.
38. *DW*, July 28, 30, 1953.
39. John Swift, "Some Problems of Work in Right-Led Unions, II," *PA*, XXXI (May 1952), p. 32. Not to be confused with the "John Swift" articles of 1953. "John Swift" was clearly a pen name.
40. *DW*, June 29, 1950.
41. Joseph Rockman, "Tasks in Broadening the Fight for Peace," *PA*, XXXI (June 1952), pp. 15–29. "Rockman"—another obvious pen name—pointed out that sectarianism hurt the party cause in the peace movement. In his sharpest sentence he wrote that "We place an impossible task for ourselves if we . . . insist that the Negro people fight for peace under the leadership of the Left or not at all" (p. 29).
42. Gus Hall, "Through United Front Struggle to Peace," *ibid.*, XXIX (May 1950), p. 37; Hall, "The Present Situation and Next Tasks," *ibid.*, XXIX (Oct. 1950), p. 21. Each of these articles was a report to the national committee.
43. Wallace speech at second national convention of Progressive Party, Ashland

Auditorium, Chicago, Feb. 24, 1950, Progressive Party press release in library of Philip Jaffe, Stamford, Conn.

44. *DW*, March 30, 1950; see also William Z. Foster in *ibid.*, March 3, 1950.

45. *Ibid.*, July 30, 1957, for denunciation of Walter Wallace.

46. "Minutes of the Meetings of the Executive Committee of the Progressive Party on the Situation in Korea and China, July 6, 8, 9, 10, 11, 1950," mimeographed documents in library of Philip Jaffe, Stamford, Conn.

47. New York *Times*, April 26, Aug. 18, 19, 21, 1957, Jan. 3, March 16, 1958.

48. "Minutes," July 10, 11, 1950. See note 46.

49. "Minutes of Special Meeting of National Committee, Progressive Party, 13 Astor Place, New York City, July 15, 1950"; Wallace's press release of same date. Both in library of Philip Jaffe, Stamford, Conn. See also Wallace's brief account of his leaving the Progressives in "Henry Wallace Tells of His Political Odyssey," *Life*, May 14, 1956, pp. 183–4.

50. *Daily People's World*, Oct. 10, 1950.

51. In January 1952, for example, she appeared on a program with *DW* staff writers Joseph North and John Pittman to increase the paper's circulation— *DW*, Jan. 18, 1952.

52. Richard M. Scammon, comp. and ed., *America Votes: A Handbook of Contemporary Election Statistics* (New York: Macmillan, 1956), pp. 33, 259, 421–2.

53. Max M. Kampelman, *The Communist Party vs. the C.I.O.: A Study in Power Politics* (New York: Praeger, 1957), pp. 157–8.

54. *Wkr*, Dec. 19, 1948.

55. John Williamson, "Two Conventions of Labor: The Situation in the Trade Union Movement," *PA*, XXVIII (Jan. 1949), p. 35.

56. *Proceedings*, Tenth Constitutional Convention, Congress of Industrial Organizations, 1948, pp. 281–2.

57. *Wkr*, Jan. 9, 1949.

58. *Proceedings*, Eleventh Constitutional Convention, Congress of Industrial Organizations, 1949, pp. 272–3. For background on the Quill union and its peculiar combination of Irish Catholic membership and Left leadership, see James J. McGinley, S.J., *Labor Relations in the New York Rapid Transit Systems, 1904–1944* (New York: King's Crown, 1949), pp. 316–25.

59. *DW*, May 20, 1949. For background on W.F.T.U., see Kampelman, *op. cit.*, pp. 233–45.

60. *Proceedings*, Fourteenth Convention, United Electrical, Radio, and Machine Workers of America (U.E.), Cleveland, 1949, pp. 205–25.

61. *Proceedings*, Eleventh Constitutional Convention, C.I.O., 1949, pp. 240, 281, 288, 302, 305.

62. Kampelman, *op. cit.*, pp. 167–222.

63. Even the *DW*'s labor columnist, George Morris, saw U.E.'s situation as hopeless. See *DW*, Sept. 28, 1956.

64. Vernon Jensen, *Nonferrous Metal Industry Unionism, 1932–1954* (Ithaca: Cornell University Press, 1954), p. 305.

65. *Testimony of the Director on February 3 and February 7, 1950 . . . on the 1951 Appropriation Estimates for the Federal Bureau of Investigation*, Department of Justice, 1950; *Digest of the Public Record*, p. 550.

66. *DW*, Oct. 4, 1950, Oct. 2, 1953; *Wkr*, Oct. 8, 1950, Oct. 11, 1953.

67. *DW*, May 25, 1950.

68. *Ibid.*, April 6, 9, 1951.

69. *National Guardian*, Aug. 15, 1951.

70. Committee on Un-American Activities, House of Representatives, *Trial by Treason: The National Committee to Secure Justice for the Rosenbergs and*

Morton Sobell (Washington: Government Printing Office, 1956), pp. 13, 15–24.

71. For Communist denials of anti-Semitism, see Klement Gottwald, "The Prague Treason Trials," *PA*, XXXII (Feb. 1953), pp. 46–50; and Samuel Rosen, "Zionism and Bourgeois Nationalism," *ibid.*, XXXII (June 1953), pp. 38–48, and (July 1953), pp. 57–65; Jacques Duclos quotation from Robert B. Glynn, "*L'Affaire Rosenberg* in France," *Political Science Quarterly*, LXX (Sept. 1955), p. 509.

72. Glynn, *op. cit.*, pp. 514–15.

73. Irwin Edelman, "An Open Letter to the Rosenberg and Sobell Friends," undated one-page mimeographed flier. Internal evidence indicates the "letter" was written between June 19 and July 16, 1953. For this document I am indebted to Mr. Edelman.

74. Edelman, "The Rosenberg Case: Some Observations," *Contemporary Issues* (London), V (Oct.-Nov. 1954), p. 319. This article indicates that Edelman had some highly unusual ideas, to say the least. In the article, he argued that Bloch, the Communists, and the F.B.I. conspired to execute the Rosenbergs. Nevertheless, he did suggest a legal argument which a Supreme Court justice thought warranted consideration.

75. S. Andhil Fineberg, *The Rosenberg Case: Fact and Fiction* (New York: Oceana, 1953), pp. 110–13; Edelman, "The Rosenberg Case," *loc. cit.*, p. 319.

76. Communist Party national committee, "The Rosenbergs: Heroes of Democracy," *PA*, XXXII (July 1953), pp. 2–3.

77. *DW*, Feb. 16, 25, June 22, 1953; Edith Segal, *Give Us Your Hand! Poems and Songs for Ethel and Julius Rosenberg in the Death House at Sing Sing* (New York: National Committee to Secure Justice in the Rosenberg Case, 1953).

Collective Police Violence

RODNEY STARK

. . . the police were seen throwing rocks at fleeing citizens from roof-tops. . . .

I. WHAT IS A POLICE RIOT?

Readers of the Kerner Commission Report[1] or the Skolnick Report[2] or any of dozens of other books, reports, and articles on recent events in black ghettos or during student and anti-war demonstrations will have recognized that sometimes police behavior is indistinguishable from that attributed to rioters. It is not merely that sometimes the character of the police response in certain situations provokes riots, which it does, but that on some occasions the police seem to be *the major or even the only* perpetrators of disorder, violence, and destruction. *Such occasions are police riots.*

Recently police riots have often followed a ghetto disturbance or a confrontation with demonstrators. For example, two consecutive riots occurred in Newark during July 1967. Although the first was perhaps provoked by police, the rioters were ghetto blacks. But in the second, police officers were seemingly the only important participants. During the first riot, blacks damaged and destroyed white-owned stores. During the second, policemen damaged black-owned stores. Indeed, the second riot was only distinguishable from the first by a much higher casualty rate and by the fact that the rioters wore uniforms, were better armed and equipped, were paid by the public, and were immune from prosecution. This same pattern has occurred fairly often: in police- and National Guard–controlled territory in the later stages of the Detroit riot, and—according to the findings of a grand jury—in Paterson, N.J. during July 1968, to cite only two examples.

It must be recognized that sometimes the police behave in a disorderly way through panic and confusion, as when they shoot wildly and at each other in response to imaginary snipers.[3] But a true police riot is not simply an incident of bumbling or confusion—although certainly these factors may

[1] *Report of the National Advisory Commission on Civil Disorders* (New York: Bantam Books, 1968).
[2] Violence Commission, *The Politics of Protest* (New York: Ballantine Books, 1969).
[3] A virtually definitive study was prepared by the Stanford Research Institute for the Kerner Commission: Arnold Katz, *Firearms, Violence and Civil Disorders* (Menlo Park, Calif.: Stanford Research Institute, 1968), no. MU–7105.

be present; it must involve a certain degree of intent to employ excessive force.

Nor is a police riot simply a fight between the police and a crowd. No reasonable person questions the right of the police to use necessary force (although on some occasions when justified force has escalated a crisis, the wisdom of using force may be questioned). Thus, when the lives of police or the lives of others are actually endangered by crowd behavior or when the police are otherwise unable to effect arrests for significant offenses, their use of the amount of force required can in no sense be called a police riot. Such police violence is legitimate. An event may only be called a police riot when the police during the incident collectively violate reasonable standards governing the lawful use of force.

Full-scale police riots are not a unique form of police violence. As they will be treated in this study, a police riot is simply the most elaborate and extreme form of *collective violence*[4] by the police, differing only in degree and scope from an event in which only several policemen launch an attack on several citizens.

It must be recognized, however, that this study will not attempt to account for all varieties of the excessive use of force by the police. I shall exclude instances that can be explained on purely individual grounds, such as when a policeman beats a citizen against whom he has a private grudge, or a beating administered by a psychopath in uniform. I shall also ignore such institutionalized forms of police brutality as the "third degree," which is motivated by a desire to obtain speedy confessions and convictions, or brutality that is used primarily to punish offenders whom it would be difficult or unpleasant to prosecute, as is sometimes done with sex offenders.[5] All of these are important abuses of police power and ought to be suppressed. However, they do not constitute instances of collective behavior, and the reasons they occur are better understood. Collective outbursts by the police are currently more inexplicable and more dangerous. In addition, evidence . . . suggests that perhaps the majority of police violence these days is collective, not idiosyncratic.

An event is a police riot when roving bands of *policemen set upon nonprovocative persons and/or property in an excessively violent manner.* When only one small group of policemen sets upon citizens and/or property in a single location it may be useful to call this a *police attack.* A *police riot* is any such event involving *two or more attacks.*

Nonprovocative persons are those who represent no significant threat to life, physical safety, or property (at least before the police set upon them). . . . A young man standing on the steps of his home who gives "the finger" to passing police may insult their pride and provoke their wrath, but his actions are not provocative in the sense of providing a legitimate justification for being dealt with violently. Such a young man may be subject to arrest for his behavior, but to beat him or shoot him is legally and morally indefensible and constitutes a police attack. Similarly, carrying a picket sign advocating a cause with which the police disagree, having long hair, or being

---

[4] My use of the term "collective outbursts" or "collective behavior" follows the work of Neil J. Smelser, *Theory of Collective Behavior* (New York: The Free Press, 1963).

[5] See William A. Westley, "Violence and the Police," *American Journal of Sociology*, 59 (July 1953), pp. 34–41.

black may provoke the police, but is not legally provocative. Furthermore, nonviolent acts of civil disobedience may be unlawful, but they do not justify force other than that needed, for example, to carry away limp arrestees to jail.

One clear indicator that a police attack or riot has occurred is when persons are assaulted by the police and abandoned without being arrested, in other than a situation where arrest is impossible (for example, when police are too busy defending themselves or protecting life to make arrests). Often, of course, police do make arrests during a riot or attack. Indeed, they ordinarily justify their use of force by charging those on whom they have used force with acts of provocation such as resisting or fleeing arrest. Admittedly, often the police are justified in bringing such charges. However, when a citizen is beaten or shot and simply abandoned (when an arrest could have been made) the matter is unambiguous. If their use of force was legitimate, then the police were guilty of extreme dereliction of duty in not making an arrest. If the victim was not guilty of an offense that justified the use of force against him, then the police behavior was clearly felonious.

A second indicator of a police riot or attack is when police destroy or damage property without filing a report attributing this action to the necessities of duty. Even when filed, such reports can be fraudulent, but when none is filed, the grounds for calling the destruction wanton and unlawful seem clear.

II. THE PROTOTYPE POLICE RIOT: AN ESCALATION MODEL

Police riots don't simply occur out of nowhere. They develop from a relatively common set of circumstances and escalate through a typical series of stages. An explication of these stages provides a fuller understanding of what police riots are and how and why they occur.

Stage 1: Convergence

A police riot can occur only if a relatively large number of civilians and policemen are present at the same time in a fairly restricted area. There must be someone for the police to riot (or counter-riot) against, and there must be enough policemen present to engage in rioting. It is difficult to say with any precision how many civilians and how many policemen are necessary in order to produce a police riot. I have heard of incidents involving only 40 or 50 civilians and 10 policemen. But ordinarily police riots have involved more than 100 policemen and at least 400 civilians. The convergence of large numbers of civilians and policemen in a single location is hardly unusual, and only infrequently results in a police riot (or any kind of riot). Most such convergences are simple crowd control and traffic direction operations produced by such events as parades and sporting events. Such convergences nearly always remain routine.

Stage 2: Confrontation

The potential for escalation into violence greatly increases, however, when convergence is accompanied by a conflict of interest, mutual hostility, or divergent definitions of appropriate behavior between the police and the civilians.

Three typical sources of confrontations are:

1. An incident, involving one or a few civilians and several policemen, attracts a crowd sympathetic to the civilians which in turn draws a large number of policemen to the scene in support of their fellow officers. This is typical of the genesis of ghetto confrontations and is also fairly common on college campuses.
2. A crowd gathers for a demonstration or protest march which offends the ideals of the police or which is designated by the police as illegal or potentially disruptive. The importance of police views of such events for the creation of confrontation is demonstrated by the differences when similar events (or the same event) are treated as a traffic problem on the one hand and an illegal assembly on the other. On several occasions peace marches lacking parade permits have been treated as merely traffic problems in Berkeley, but as illegal assemblies once across the boundary into Oakland. Trouble occurred only in Oakland.
3. Police are drawn to public recreational gatherings (such as love-ins, street dances, rock festivals, outdoor beer busts, and the like) which are judged by the police to be illegal, immoral, or a public nuisance.

The majority of confrontations do not escalate further. In order for escalation to continue, one or both sides must take action.

Stage 3: Dispersal

The potential conflict inherent in confrontations is activated if the police attempt to end the incident by dispersing the civilians. This decision may be forced upon the police by hostile or dangerous actions of the crowd. For example, the crowd may endanger the police by throwing bottles and bricks or by attempting to disrupt police lines. Or the crowd may endanger property, perhaps by smashing store windows. But frequently the decision to disperse the crowd is not forced upon the police by the action of the civilians. That is, for all that an assembly may be illegal (lacking proper permits) or distasteful, it poses no immediate threat to public safety or property. In such situations sometimes the police choose to disperse the crowd.

Stage 4: The utilization of force

Sometimes crowds disperse upon command or in response to police deployment and threats of arrest or gas. Sometimes they do not—often enough because of faulty police deployment they *cannot*. When they do not, and if dispersal remains the tactical goal, force is used by the police; police lines may advance brandishing riot batons; they may use these batons, tear gas, or firearms. The amount of force is usually increased as dispersal proves difficult to achieve. The more it is increased, the greater the likelihood that an excessive amount will be used. . . . Police commanders tend to maximize rather than minimize the use of force in order to maximize officer safety and to maximize dispersal. This is also true of individual officers. Furthermore, . . . police command control and tactical integrity tend to collapse in contact with crowds and as greater force is employed. Thus, once introduced, *the use of force by the police tends to escalate rapidly into excessive use.* This is especially likely if the crowd offers any significant resistance (either real or symbolic) and/or if the crowd is made up of kinds of persons who arouse police hostility (blacks, students, radicals, and so on).

Stage 5: The limited riot

When excessive use of force by the police becomes relatively widespread during a dispersal action, this constitutes a police riot. It is typified by the break-up of police formations into autonomous groups chasing fleeing civilians and charging into clusters of a crowd, beating people up. Sometimes this also involves uncontrolled use of tear gas, primarily in punitive ways (e.g., throwing canisters into homes and stores), and occasionally has escalated into wild shooting sprees (mainly during ghetto riots, but also at Jackson State and during Berkeley's People's Park incident). Whatever the level of violence reached, if the police cease their attacks when crowd dispersal is complete or very shortly thereafter, this is a limited police riot—limited to the single scene and incident.

Stage 6: The extended police riot

In the aftermath of crowd dispersal, sometimes police riots do not stop. They may continue for several more days. If the initial riot and dispersal occurs on the home "turf" of the crowd—if a confrontation develops into a police riot in an area where the citizens live or typically congregate—a ghetto neighborhood, a student living area, a campus—then police attacks tend to continue well beyond the conclusion of dispersal. In part this is because in a sense the dispersal can never be complete. The targets of police wrath remain close by in their homes and shops. Furthermore, it is only under such conditions that the police are able to continue their riot once dispersal is complete. When a police riot occurs on neutral grounds—for example, in a downtown area—typically the civilians disperse to widely scattered places. The police have nowhere to go to continue the fray. But when police hostility can be attached to a neighborhood the possibility of continuing the attacks remain available. Thus, in Newark, police attacks on persons and property continued in the neighborhood of the disturbance several days after the rioting by blacks had ceased. In Berkeley, in the event to be discussed below, the initial confrontation and dispersal occurred on a Friday night, but heavy police action against the student community continued through Monday. It is also sometimes the case that continuing police rioting against such a neighborhood results in generating new crowds and new confrontations, thus renewing the cycle for some days. This is often what happens in campus situations.

The phases through which events move from convergence to an extended police riot indicate that there are a number of contingencies or decision points along the way. Much of the remainder of this study will be devoted to understanding why events so often take the particular turn they do and lead to police riots. It is also clear in this prototype that police riots grow out of interaction between the police and a group of citizens. Obviously, if civilians never provided the police with a confrontation or were always easily dispersed without force, police riots would be unlikely to occur. This is an unreasonable expectation, and ultimately civilian behavior—while it may contribute greatly to the likelihood of police rioting—does not explain or justify it. The mere fact of violence between citizens and the police does not constitute a police riot. The police must employ unnecessary, unlawful, and willful violence if we are to call an event a police riot. That can never be blamed on the victims of police riots, only on the police.

This prototype is intended primarily as a sensitizing device to critical questions of why police riots occur and what the phenomenon of a police riot is like. I now describe two specific police riots in order to provide the reader with a more concrete sense of the sequence of escalation and the behavior of police and citizens.

The first of these riots occurred in Los Angeles in the summer of 1967 during an anti-war march. It was a limited police riot which ended when the remnants of the crowd managed to depart for their homes. The second occurred in Berkeley during the summer of 1968 in the heart of the student living area. It was an extended riot. I have chosen to recount these two cases in considerable detail primarily because they were among those which were the subject of lengthy investigations. In most other instances of police riots one can only make educated guesses from fragmentary evidence about what happened. This is particularly true of police riots in minority communities. But except for the fact that guns were not used and no one was killed, these two police riots typify what I have been able to observe or reconstruct about the patterns of mass police misbehavior in other incidents.

LOS ANGELES

> As I tried to get Laurie [her 4-year-old] away, I found a cop towering over me. "I can't move back, my little girl's brace is caught," I said. "What the hell do I care," he replied, and hit me over the head with his night stick, knocking Laurie and myself to the pavement.

On the evening of June 23, 1967, President Johnson attended a $500-a-plate fund-raising dinner at the Century Plaza Hotel in Los Angeles. It was still some months before the nation would begin to realize that the war in Viet Nam had cost Johnson his renomination to a second term—the Tet offensive and the New Hampshire primary would not take place until after Christmas. Still, the anti-war movement was developing rapidly.

A few weeks before the dinner members of the Peace Action Council, which had operated for nearly a year as a loose confederation of local anti-war groups, began to plan what they hoped would be their first sizable peace march. The demonstrators would parade past the hotel while the President was speaking.

As they planned, so did the police. Unable to block a parade permit, the police laid on ultra-tight security measures. Flaws in these measures, compounded by faulty decisions at the scene, produced first a confrontation, then dispersal, and then one of the bloodiest police riots ever unleashed on the peace movement.

In the event the police literally ran amok. They beat, herded, and abused a helpless, nonviolent crowd, composed mainly of terrorized, white, middle-class adults, who police actions prevented from dispersing. Infants, cripples, pregnant women, the very elderly—none was immune as the crowd was beaten from one cul-de-sac to another while motorcycles and squad cars careened among them.

In the aftermath of the riot, a vigorous public protest was launched, and, when an official investigation was not forthcoming, the American Civil Liberties Union of Southern California initiated a painstaking inquiry into what happened. More than 500 persons submitted written statements to the ACLU—some of them passers-by who had never been part of the protest march. A month after the incident, the ACLU published its report: *Day of Protest, Night of Violence.*[6] In reconstructing this police riot I have made considerable use of this document. I also conducted interviews with some participants, particularly with members of the Los Angeles Police Department. These interviews with the police unfortunately were off the record, and I may not quote them directly.

In what follows I first sketch the sequence of what happened. Then I try to assess the extent and the character of the police violence. Finally, I try to suggest why the police acted as they did.

What happened?

The gathering place for the march was Cheviot Hills Park, about a mile from the Century Plaza Hotel. By the day of the march the plan was to walk to the hotel and back again to the park. This was not a very good plan, but it was the only one available. A variety of plans proposing dispersal areas beyond the hotel and a rally *to draw people on from the hotel to the dispersal area,* had been rejected by the police and the hotel. This ultimately proved disastrous, at least for the demonstrators.

The crowd began to gather during the afternoon. The march was to begin at 7:30 p.m. From 5:00 o'clock on the crowd swelled rapidly as people arrived from work. It was a very good-natured and relaxed crowd. It was made up of the kind of people who knew nothing of police violence, who were accustomed to proper, even cordial interaction with the police. They

---

[6] American Civil Liberties Union, *Day of Protest, Night of Violence* (Los Angeles: Sawyer Press, 1967). Unless otherwise noted, all quotations in this section are from this document.

were white, middle-class Americans. Many were business or professional men. Many were housewives. There were a great number of children and babies—many of whom were pushed along the parade route in strollers and buggies. There were, of course, a good number of students and some in hippie dress. But overall it was, as one observer described it, "one of the Goddamnedest most respectable crowds you could imagine. I mean it was mainly Beverly Hills solid types, all those cute, earnest women and guys in the $40 shoes."[7]

The pre-march rally began at 6:00. Dr. Benjamin Spock spoke quietly and persuasively about the immorality of the war. Muhammed Ali, recently stripped of his heavyweight title because he refused induction—"I got no quarrel with them Viet Cong"—advised the rally to remain nonviolent.

At 6:30, while the speeches continued, white-helmeted policemen accompanied a civilian through the park. He handed out leaflets. These were copies of a restraining order obtained that morning in Santa Barbara which barred demonstrators from committing a whole series of acts—many of which it is unreasonable to suppose they would have done. They were barred from using stink bombs, smoke-making devices, "loosing any animal on the premises" of the hotel, and so on. They were also enjoined from congregating in front of the hotel or entering any private property within the hotel complex.

Upon receipt of a leaflet some members of the crowd left thinking the march itself had been banned. It hadn't. But it had been made considerably more dangerous. For the police also barred all sound trucks from the parade, thus destroying the ability of parade leaders to communicate with, direct, or, eventually, to warn off the marchers. Some hand bull horns were passed out among monitors. These proved inaudible. Worse yet, it was impossible to get the word to the monitors about what directions they ought to give over their bull horns. Still the crowd was jovial and confident. Most people felt they didn't really need monitors to walk in a short parade.

By 7:00 the now 15,000 persons in the park began to line up in preparation for the march. Immediately, the police cracked down, giving a major hint of what was to come—"This is an illegal assembly. Your parade permit does not go into effect until 7:30." Fearing a confrontation, the march leaders got people to fall out of ranks and mill about until the appointed time when standing abreast would be legal.

At 7:30 the march began forming up again and the first ranks moved out the gate of the parking lot of the park. Here a Toyota pickup truck with sound equipment tried to join the parade. The truck was manned by several radicals who wanted to urge the crowd to engage in a massive sit-in once they reached the hotel. Parade monitors formed a linked-arm circle around the truck while the marchers flowed by in order to keep the truck out of the demonstration. The monitors took this action both because sound trucks were illegal and they feared their permit might be cancelled and because they did not want such advocates of civil disobedience associated with the parade.

The police noted the incident and moved in. Told what was going on, a sergeant said, "All right, we'll handle it." And they did. The sergeant mo-

---

[7] Confidential interview conducted by the author.

tioned the truck out of the parade line and the driver signaled compliance and began to slowly turn the truck out of the march. Then an officer broke from the police lines and began to bash out the windows of the truck with his baton. Other police bolted and followed him and also began to smash the truck—on the doors, the windows, the body. Others followed. The police pulled people from the cab of the truck and beat them in front of the crowd. Several persons in the rear of the truck were beaten severely. "A policeman broke his club over someone, and then grabbed a picket sign and continued slashing at people with it."

> . . . the police came after the boy and girl on the back of the truck. They hit them with their night sticks, knocked them down, and pulled them off the back of the truck. At this point I could no longer see the blows land but the night sticks kept coming up above the side of the truck and down again, up and down again.

The police then beat everyone within reach around the truck, dragged several people off, beating them as they went, grabbed and beat and kicked several monitors and finally retired.

The behavior of the police in this incident was a preview of what was to come. The police seemed very angry. They erupted into violence or abuse easily. Numerous other early incidents of club waving, dangerous driving, and the like were reported. At 6:30 that evening a column of patrol cars, loaded with five officers to a car, on their way to the hotel stopped at a traffic light. On that particular corner four young Cal Tech students were distributing leaflets about an upcoming love-in. They good-humoredly offered them to the officers. Those in the first two cars took them and laughed. Then as traffic began to move, an officer reached out of the third car as it slowly passed. One youth handed him a leaflet. Suddenly the officer lunged out with his nightstick which he had hidden below window level and slammed the boy on the wrist. Officers in the following car yelled curses and an officer in the next car, now moving perhaps at 20 miles an hour, leaned out and swung with his club as he passed. He missed. But he would have many better targets later. Some tension built in the crowd as a result of police behavior and demeanor. But still, most seemed to expect no real trouble.

Meanwhile at the hotel, 1,300 police officers with another 200 in reserve had been assembled to seal the hotel off from the marchers. The first sign that police planning—despite an inch-thick special manual (*Century City '67*) prepared for the occasion—was ill-conceived was the fact that several thousand spectators, both sympathetic and antagonistic to the march, were permitted to gather in front of the hotel. Later, police proclaimed it was illegal to stand in front of the hotel, but by that time the crowd had already greatly contributed to clogging the route of the march past the hotel. For several hours those in front of the hotel had merely been requested to remain on the sidewalks by the police. The injunction obtained earlier, prohibiting congregating in front of the hotel, was not announced or enforced at a time when it might have still been possible for the spectators to leave.

And so on came the marchers. They had no internal communications. They had been denied a suitable dispersal area beyond the hotel. They were

not marching past the hotel *to* somewhere, for they had been denied permission to hold a post-march rally. As a march leader put it:

> There was no focal point beyond the hotel to attract those in the
> march. . . . Therefore, the hotel itself became the focal point.

Furthermore, it turned out to be virtually impossible for the marchers to
pass the hotel. Passage was partly blocked by the crowd in front of the hotel.
As the march approached, the police who had been positioned to keep the
spectators on the sidewalks were withdrawn and the crowd permitted to
spill into the street. Worse yet, the police positioned themselves at a critical
bottleneck and blocked the only remaining space through which the march
could have continued. As the march piled up and people began to mill
around in front of the hotel the police continued steadfastly to block the
traffic lanes through which it could have moved on through. There was no
way to proceed, and no way to contact the line of march to halt. So the
march continued to arrive and the crowd got denser. In effect, the police
had created the very thing they said they most feared. They had stopped the
march in front of the hotel and created a huge crowd. It would have been
hard enough to keep the crowd moving in the best of circumstances. After
all it was the presence of the President that had brought out so large a
gathering in the first place. And the President was in the hotel. The hotel
was the magnet. Given a predisposition for the crowd to be drawn to the
hotel, police actions which greatly impeded the march made the creation of
a large crowd certain.

As the crowd continued to build up in density, approximately 25 more
militant demonstrators conducted a brief sit-in. The press of the crowd
broke it up within five minutes. There simply was too little room.

The police felt something had to be done. They had no intention of permitting 15,000 people to stage a protest rally in front of a hotel in which the
President was speaking. The police were probably right in wanting to avoid
this situation. The reasonable course, however, would have been to open adequate passage for the march to leave the front of the hotel and direct the
marchers out of the area. But reason was lacking. Instead, at 8:25, Captain
Louis Sporrer took the microphone of the police sound van and announced
that the assembly was illegal since, by stopping, the demonstrators had violated the terms of their parade permit. Quite true. He then ordered the
crowd to disperse, *but he gave no instructions on how the marchers were to
comply with this order. In fact the police had no adequate plan by which
the march could disperse.* They simply confronted the front of the march in
an area where all routes, except to the rear, were blocked or so clogged as to
allow only a trickle of traffic. They seem to have wanted the parade to turn
around on itself. Those in front could not accomplish this. The rear echelons
coming along the route were not blocked off and turned back, but continued unsuspectingly to pour in, thus successively telescoping the line of
marchers into a dense congregation in front of the hotel. In desperation to
somehow comply with police orders some monitors instructed those near
them in the crowd to march in circles (and thus keep moving). Impasse.
Ahead as unyielding line of police. To the west was another line. To the
east was a very steep embankment down from an overpass additionally

blocked by a guard railing. To the rear only a sea of on-coming marchers unaware of why the parade was congregating in front of the hotel. Indeed, at this time police reinforcements blocked the last trickle of marchers edging by their lines.

The police asked the impossible. Of course they failed to get compliance. But they were determined none the less. They used motorcycle wedges to force an open space between the crowd and police lines. But as soon as they were opened, the density of the crowd forced those in front back close to the police again.

Then the police struck. They turned dazzling spotlights into the crowd and wadded in swinging. They beat everyone they could reach while the crowd reeled back into tighter compression. Women and children were being pushed down underfoot, screaming. Attorney Judith Atkinson offered this description:

> As the press of the crowd grew thicker, there were times when my feet were not on the ground. I was being carried along by the crowd. . . . People in front of us began to fall down. . . . As I turned around at this point, I saw a cop strike a white-haired, about sixty-year-old lady behind me with his club because she could not move forward. Cops to my right were now freely hitting and striking all people in front of them, prodding them as you would cattle, and I heard one cop as he struck a woman say, "They want to come to the show, but they don't want to pay the price."

After the initial charge the whole affair became a nightmare for the demonstrators. Most were forced to flee down a steep embankment (45° slope) into an underpass. The police bullied them over the edge. Many fell. The crowd was beaten and shoved hither and yon.

But once down the slope into the underpass they were again boxed in. Eventually, baton-wielding lines of policemen beat them back up the steep slope which was covered with slippery ice plant. The crowd formed human life lines and passed infants, children, and the elderly up the slope. The police beat whomever they could reach.

Finally, the crowd was cleared from the hotel area. Women seeking lost children were turned away from the site. Police lines began to move into the surrounding neighborhood and on towards the park. Demonstrators were harassed wherever police found them. Some were chased into Beverly Hills. Others were diverted from parking areas where their vehicles were parked. All groups larger than five were considered an illegal gathering. This was interpreted to mean no more than five could ride in a single automobile and led to many car stops. Police violence was directed at anyone still seen to possess a picket sign. Innocent passers-by were sometimes pulled from their cars and beaten or harassed.

The extent of police brutality

In the aftermath of the police riot no systematic effort was made to determine the number of people beaten by the police or the number who were injured. This would have been extremely difficult to accomplish, since many suffered cuts and bruises for which they did not seek medical attention and many went to private physicians and clinics throughout the Los Angeles area. Nevertheless, early press accounts reported that 30 persons were treated at UCLA's emergency room. Furthermore, statements submitted to the ACLU give some hint of the widespread injuries inflicted by the police. One hundred and seventy-eight persons reported injuries to the ACLU. Forty said they were hit on the head by police, 16 reported blows on the back or kidneys, and 97 reported blows on the neck, arms, legs, or chest.

The eyewitness accounts make it clear that a very large number of persons were beaten. Under the circumstances it is difficult to believe that any appreciable amount of the police use of force was justified.

Reading the various eyewitness accounts one can only conclude that most of the policemen who came into contact with the civilians used their clubs willfully and needlessly and that they hit about as many people as they could. The stories of elderly ladies and pregnant women being beaten and trampled were numerous, indicating the police were on a rampage against the crowd and had lost their heads entirely. It would serve no purpose to recount a litany of horror stories here. But considering what took place it is extremely fortunate that a number of people weren't killed.

Why did it happen?

Two main issues arise about why this police riot occurred. First, why was police planning so grotesquely inadequate? Second, once the confrontation had developed why did the police behave so brutally?

The first of these questions has to do with a faulty assumption about the kinds of people who opposed the war at that time and thus a serious underestimation of the size of crowd to expect. This in turn bears greatly on the second issue. The kind of people the police expected to turn out were those the police particularly hated and those who the police believed would pose a substantial threat to their safety. In addition to all of this, the police were anxiety-ridden by the fact that they were protecting the President of the United States. All of these factors led to the violence of the police once the situation developed.

In summer 1967, the Los Angeles police, like many Americans, believed that people who actively opposed the war were kooks, radicals, hippies, and subversives. But, while polls showed that a majority of Americans had not yet turned against the war, they also showed that a substantial minority (at least a third) did oppose the war at that time. This did not enter into police planning, however. They relied on the fact that earlier demonstrations against the war in Los Angeles had never drawn more than several thousand people. They recognized that a chance to protest directly against President Johnson would increase the size of the crowd, but I have been told that they did not expect many more than 5,000 persons to turn out. Three times that many did.

In judging anti-war sentiments to be deviant, they also assumed that those protesting would be deviants—hippies, students, radicals. This influenced their judgment of the threat of the marchers. It also, I believe, made them more intransigent in their predemonstration negotiations with the protest committee. From the beginning they pushed the demonstrators around. They were uncooperative in helping find march plans which would minimize the chance for confrontation or the need for dispersal and violence. It is a simple axiom of parade management that there must be dispersal areas, adequate route supervision, and the like. The police vetoed available dispersal areas and when the time came denied the parade organizers the use of sound systems to direct the march. They seem to have felt that the march should not occur, and when they found they had no choice but to permit it, essentially refused to condone it. Possibly they believed that the kinds of people they would be dealing with ought to be harassed and even set upon for their affront to the President, to "the boys over there," and to the civic reputation of Los Angeles.

In any event, I have been told that the plans for crowd control did not envision so large a crowd and that the police got caught short and were unable to improvise adequate tactics on the spot. Later, the then Police Chief Reddin said he gave the order to disperse the crowd when he looked down from a ninth story hotel window and saw a bulge in the crowd. Presumably from such a vantage point he might have worked out a dispersal route as well.

Amateurish intelligence work prior to the march helped the police misread the size and character of the crowd they would be facing. A private detective, hired by attorneys for the hotel, attended planning sessions conducted by the parade organizers and returned with lurid tales of conspiracies and diabolical plans: to unleash mice, cockroaches, and stinkbombs in the hotel, and other such outlandish schemes. The meetings were in fact open to the public and many of the detective's stories were based on suggestions offered by members of the audience. None was ever taken seriously by the planning committee.

However, such tales seem to have reinforced police beliefs that they were dealing with kooks and subversives. Certainly these impressions were widespread among the rank-and-file officers assigned to control the crowd. The rash of early violence and anger, long before the parade got anywhere near the hotel, indicated police sentiments and intentions. Statements submitted to the ACLU are filled with quotations of the police indicating they regarded the crowd as made up of disreputable people: "Get that damn Jew," "A bunch of dirty, Goddamned communists," "Animals and commies, that's all they are."

Finally, it is clear that the police were especially anxious because they were charged with the protection of the President of the United States. The major concern in their planning was to provide an impassable defense of the hotel. Thus officers with high-powered rifles were stationed on tall buildings throughout the area. A military helicopter hovered above the hotel armed with 20mm. cannon. The deployment of 1,300 officers was designed to defend the hotel against assault, not to facilitate dispersal or order.

The police view of their responsibility is perhaps best summarized by the words of one young officer to a housewife as police were forcing the crowd down the slope to the underpass:

I asked [him] why they were so violent; he was shaking with fear when he answered, "I'd push you off that cliff if I had to. The President's here."

BERKELEY

A young black addressing a street meeting in the aftermath of the conflict:
Now you whites been done like we been done for years!

On a Friday evening (June 28, 1968), 124 Berkeley policemen, augmented by 32 police reservists, 10 University of California campus policemen, and 110 Alameda County Deputy Sheriffs, forcibly dispersed—with tear gas, riot batons, kicks, stones, and curses—a peaceful crowd of several hundred persons gathered on Telegraph Avenue, some of whom were listening to speeches in support of the French student strike. Thus ended a long era of good feeling between the community and the police, based to a considerable extent on the neutral policies of the police, who had previously dealt with rallies purely in terms of crowd and traffic control, regardless of political content.

During the long weekend disturbance that ensued, the conflict escalated. The first stones were thrown at the police. Gas cannisters were caught and hurled back. More beatings and gassing by the police occurred and eventually turned into what can only be described as a police rampage against unarmed and mainly nonprovocative citizens. For several nights many policemen were lawless, dangerous rioters against a terrorized community.

What follows is an attempt to recreate and analyze what happened during this police outburst. The account is based mainly on the work of a short-lived, experimental Crisis Research Team which I organized just as the trouble began. This team of seven observers (including myself) conducted a close-up study of the Berkeley crisis as it occurred.[8] Members were on the streets throughout the crisis trying to keep track of events, running from the police, being gassed, talking to people, and making notes as best they could. In addition, the team conducted interviews with police officials, all members of the city council, businessmen, witnesses, victims, newsmen, clergymen, radical organizers, physicians, and nurses at area emergency hospitals—more than 500 persons in all. To augment these materials, 177 affidavits filed with the Berkeley Citizen Complaint Center of the American Civil Liberties Union were made available (without names).[9] In all, accounts by 221 persons who claimed to be victims or witnesses of police violence were available for analysis. This account also draws upon statements issued by a number of citizens and organizations, testimony before the city council, reports written by the mayor and by the city manager, and press and television stories.

The report is divided into three parts. The first is a chronological story of what happened. The second draws upon the reports of victims and witnesses to provide some conception of the frequency and variety of police rioting.

[8] I wish to thank team members Ruth White, Andrea Saltzman, Henry Schroerluke, Steve Hart, Nigel Young, and David Minkus.
[9] An ACLU staffmember checked against our list of interviewees in order to avoid any duplication, omitting ACLU affidavits of anyone we had interviewed.

The third explores briefly why the police acted against the crowd in the first place.

What happened?

On June 19, 1968, the Young Socialist Alliance (YSA) applied to the City of Berkeley for a sound amplification permit for Telegraph Avenue—the heart of the campus community—for the evening of Friday, June 28. The permit was granted. Then the YSA announced that the sound amplification would be used for speech making at a rally to demonstrate solidarity with French students who had just lost their strike after narrowly failing to bring down the de Gaulle government. City officials countered that a sound permit was not sufficient, but that YSA would also need a permit to hold a street rally.

The YSA refused to request such a permit. Their leader, Peter Camejo, told a meeting of the city council on June 23 that under recent Supreme Court decisions on the right of free assembly such a permit was not legally required and that YSA would hold the meeting without one to challenge the local ordinance. This did not automatically necessitate a confrontation; rallies without permits are not unknown in Berkeley and in the past had been dealt with amicably by the police. Later police claimed that Camejo and the YSA were trying to produce a confrontation with the police, hence their refusal to apply for a permit. But, whatever Camejo might have wished, from past experience it is hard to believe that he could have had much reason to suppose he would be able to produce a confrontation.

In any event, publicity for the rally proceeded via sound trucks, handbills, and the underground press. It promised to be a typical Berkeley rally, which up to that time had been nothing more than long successions of speakers, some articulate, some not. Indeed, in this case there was not even an important local issue to turn out a crowd.

Meanwhile there were some sounds from city hall and police headquarters which in retrospect could have been a warning that this rally would be different. Several statements were released to the press that the rally was illegal, or that it would be illegal if the crowd grew beyond the sidewalks and into the street, thus blocking traffic. But this did not seem too grave a prospect. There would be monitors to direct the crowd, as there always are at Berkeley rallies. And besides, some clogging of the street is common on Telegraph Avenue on weekend evenings. Indeed, it was widely recognized that the YSA was holding the rally on Telegraph Avenue because of a justified lack of confidence in their ability to *attract* a large crowd—thus they were going where a crowd would be whether or not there was a rally. This becomes important shortly in assessing just how many people actually attended the rally, and thus in evaluating the police reaction.

But in addition to issuing statements about the potential illegality of the rally, unique preparations were being made by the police. Several days before the event the Berkeley police had decided they would use their mutual assistance pact with neighboring law enforcement agencies to assemble a large enough force to handle a riot. In the past no such action had been taken. Later I shall try to explain, based on interviews with Berkeley police commanders, why they decided that this particular rally was intrinsically much more dangerous than dozens of previous rallies which had been treated as simple crowd and traffic management problems and which had not prompted them to gather more than several dozen officers.

On the evening of the rally, 276 officers had been gathered to deal with the rally. Policemen controlled all rooftops along that section of Telegraph Avenue where the rally was to be held.

The rally began at 8:00 p.m. with the usual impassioned and somewhat boring speeches. As usual for a Friday night, the streets were packed with people. It was difficult to estimate how many people were actually attending the rally. At any given moment there were perhaps a thousand people in the block where the rally was going on. But many of them stopped and listened for a few minutes and then moved on. Others clearly were not interested at all, but were headed for the bookshops, coffee houses, and movies which are the heart of the Avenue scene. The consensus among Crisis Team observers and persons later interviewed was that there were about 200 people present who were serious about attending the rally and another two or three hundred mildly interested passers-by.

Until 8:50 p.m. the rally proceeded uneventfully. The presence of large police formations in nearby side streets had not yet come to be regarded with alarm in Berkeley. The monitors kept the streets clear and directed traffic. All was normal. And after the first several speakers the crowd began to dwindle significantly. As one respondent put it later, "I mean everybody was sympathetic with the French students but after you've said that, so what? I mean it wasn't like we could do anything. And, well, everybody has heard Camejo dozens of times. He doesn't grow on you."

At that point an unidentified young man suddenly urged the crowd to "liberate" the street. Presumably he was trying to put a bit more life into the sagging rally. About 200 people followed him into the street, despite protests by the monitors.

Berkeley Police Chief William Beall promptly declared the rally an illegal assembly, which, by blocking the street, it had become. Camejo exhorted the people to move back onto the sidewalk and asked the chief whether the rally might continue if they did so promptly. Beall retired to consult with his commanders. The crowd returned to the sidewalk, having blocked the street for approximately five minutes.

Then Chief Beall returned—the street was empty—and said no, the meeting was now illegal and must disperse. Several minutes later, at 9:00 p.m., police formations moved onto Telegraph Avenue, split the crowd, and pushed it onto two groups. City Manager William Hanley stated in his report to the city council that "by 9:30 the police lines were holding 200 people on Telegraph Avenue between Dwight [Way] and Blake [Street] and another 150 on Haste [Street] west of Telegraph." The situation remained static for awhile with some verbal abuse shouted at the police by a few members of the crowd while others attempted negotiations to resolve the situation. One group who tried to negotiate was made up of about a dozen persons, most of them Berkeley clergymen who typically volunteer as monitors for rallies, but also included City Councilman Daniel Dewey. Finally, as the police moved forward, this group interposed itself between a police line and part of the crowd. Councilman Dewey (who said he was present because he felt it important that council members observe demonstrations and rallies in Berkeley) said he and the clergymen linked arms and backed down the Avenue ahead of the oncoming police line out of concern "that the crowd be pushed back as nonviolently as possible."

When police lieutenant Charles Plummer approached the line, several clergymen tried to discuss the situation with him. He responded, "That's enough talk," and clubbed at their clasped hands with his bull horn. Lieutenant Plummer is a huge man, and he had little difficulty breaking the line of clergymen.

Then came a barrage of gas. A retired police commander with considerable experience in managing crowds both here and abroad was an eyewitness to police tactics at this point. In his judgment the use of gas was either done with extraordinary incompetence or with the intention of punishing the crowd, because the gas was thrown *behind* the crowd making them approach the police, and no dispersal routes had been left open. "The crowd could not disperse because the police had them boxed in," he said. In fact for some time, while the police had been seemingly demanding the dispersal of the crowd prior to the use of gas, dispersal had not been permitted by the police.

Choking in the gas, the previously passive crowd made desperate attempts at flight. Many were beaten by the police as they did so. After this came the first police rampage. Bands of policemen on foot and five to a car roved the South Campus area. Private residences were gassed. The Free Church and YSA headquarters were gassed. Unsuspecting crowds leaving movie theaters were gassed, clubbed, and even made to run gauntlets of club-swinging policemen. People were beaten in a seemingly random way, without any attempt being made to arrest them. (The second section of this account provides details and statistics on police attacks. I am concerned here only to provide a general outline of events.)

As the police violence erupted there came the first signs of fighting back. Some rocks were thrown at policemen—although as will be discussed later some of the rocks were thrown from the rooftops *by* policemen! Some building materials were dragged into the street to suggest barricades, and a number of trash cans (perhaps nine in all) were dragged into the street and set afire.

Well before midnight the streets were empty except for the police.

Saturday was another day. Residents of the South Campus area awoke to a still heavy pall of tear gas. As Telegraph Avenue came to life there was considerable anger and tension. Over breakfast in the cafés along the Avenue people recounted their experiences of the night before, read press accounts, and wondered what it all meant. Technically illegal or not, a peaceful and rather ordinary Berkeley rally had been broken up. Such a thing had never happened before. Many were inclined to put the blame on Alameda County Deputy Sheriffs, who, while they had yet to earn their dangerous and brutal reputation in subsequent Berkeley crises, were thought to be hostile to the Berkeley scene. Still, Berkeley officers had led and made the decisions. It was hard for many to accept this—relations with the Berkeley police had historically been benign. The normal Saturday crowds developed on the Avenue, but were infused with outrage, fear, and uncertainty.

By 3:00 p.m. leaflets were being circulated calling for a mass meeting under Young Socialist Alliance auspices at the intersection of Bancroft Way and Telegraph Avenue—the intersection adjacent to the Sproul Plaza entrance to the University of California campus. A second group—The Resistance, a small organization of street radicals—announced that a street dance would be held at the location of Friday night's rally.

At 7:00 p.m. the YSA "mass meeting" began with perhaps 200 persons. Speakers demanded that the city condone this peaceful rally and also open Telegraph Avenue for a street party on July 4th. Several speakers displayed gas masks and told where they could be bought. At 8:00 p.m. the rally voted to march down Telegraph to The Block, scene of the previous night's action. By 8:30 about 600 persons had gathered on The Block. Meanwhile, at 7:15 the Berkeley police had recalled all off-duty officers, requested reinforcements from the Alameda County Sheriffs, the California Highway Patrol, and the Oakland Police Department, and alerted the National Guard and all local hospitals. Subsequently the fire department and the public works department were asked to stand by.

This night the crowd was significantly different from that of the night before. There were many fewer middle-class and "straight" people. There were more juveniles—some who had come from Oakland and Richmond to "see what was happening." Traffic was directed off Telegraph by members of the crowd. Several small barricades were constructed to close off The Block. Several people painted peace symbols on the street and sidewalk with spray paint. A rock band played, and many danced. A few—perhaps 40—listened to the speeches. As is normal during such impromptu street dances, it was not uncommon to see people smoking marijuana.

While the rally of the night before failed to stop or gather a really sizable crowd, rock bands and a street dance are always successful in doing so on Telegraph Avenue, especially on a Saturday night. By 9:30 p.m. perhaps as many as 2,000 people were taking part. Periodically, rumors circulated that the police were about to attack. But none appeared. Some said this was proof that Friday night was due to the Alameda Sheriffs. Things seemed back to normal.

This was faulty judgment. The police were in fact busy. They set up check points a few blocks from the scene and closed all exits from the area, diverting traffic. At 10:45 they gassed the first aid station at the Free Church.

By 11:00 the crowd began to diminish. The illegal assembly had seemingly been condoned for three hours. The police maintain they warned the crowd that they were an illegal assembly at 11:08. Perhaps they did, but no Crisis Team observers, members of the crowd we contacted later, or members of the press said they had heard such an announcement. Be that as it may, at 11:30 the police struck suddenly, violently, and in great numbers. Lines of riot-equipped policemen moved on the crowd from three sides throwing great numbers of tear gas cannisters. The crowd withdrew north along the Avenue back towards the university. The side streets were blocked —it was the only direction in which movement away from the gas was possible. Along the way large numbers of the ordinary Saturday night crowds which clog Telegraph were forced with them. As they neared the University the crowd was boxed in by another line of policemen advancing from the campus. The melee began.

Gas was everywhere. Demonstrators, street dancers, and great numbers of ordinary citizens tried desperately to flee. All exits were blocked, and flight required passing through police lines. In doing so, many citizens were beaten. There were 273 policemen in action. Many broke ranks and went on beating sprees. Sometimes squad-sized groups of officers chased and beat citizens.

Little knots of the most militant demonstrators reacted by breaking store windows and setting fire to trash cans. Others threw stones. An empty house owned by the University and scheduled for demolition was set afire.

At midnight someone threw a Molotov cocktail at a highway patrolman near the campus. He suffered serious burns on his lower legs. In the confusion of the moment a rumor seems to have rapidly spread among the police—possibly transmitted erroneously over the police radio—that the patrolman had lost his genitals as a result of the firebomb and was near death. This produced the most furious outburst of police violence during the entire crisis. The Crisis Team investigation located 27 persons who reported having been beaten *unconscious and left* by roving bands of policemen on Saturday night following this incident, and clearly only a relatively small proportion of victims were interviewed. All familiar with the American police recognize that injury, danger, or other difficulties suffered by a fellow officer galvanize the police. In this instance they had already been sporadically attacking the crowds. They were angry already. Thus, the attack on the officer with its attendant horrid rumors drove some policemen nearly berserk. The furious attacks which will be discussed shortly continued well into the night as did some further window breaking and stone throwing by militants. Police attacks were not particularly aimed at the militants (who were hard to catch). Instead, the police vented their rage on the community as a whole. And consequently it was mainly nonmilitants, often people standing in front of their homes or walking from restaurants, theaters, or a late session in their University labs and offices who took the brunt of the police violence.

At 3:30 Sunday morning a curfew was proclaimed for the South Campus area to be in effect from 7:00 p.m. to 6:00 a.m.

Sunday was a day of meetings and community mobilization. The demand for a July 4th street celebration, raised the night before, was widely agreed upon by those attending.

Meanwhile, during the afternoon policemen were deployed in substantial numbers along Telegraph Avenue. The curfew was extended from the South Campus area to include the campus itself.

At 6:00 p.m., approximately 300 people gathered in a park across from the city hall. It was a disorganized meeting. Berkeley Mayor Wallace S. Johnson joined the crowd and was spat upon. Some members of the crowd urged that he be beaten, others protected him. He left. At 7:00 p.m. many drifted away from the park meeting. Half an hour later a small band of militants marched from the park up University Avenue. Their passage was marked by window breaking in business establishments and some rock throwing.

This foray was met by police—approximately 700 of whom were gathered through the mutual aid arrangements. At 9:00 p.m. the curfew was extended to the entire city, but only enforced in the South Campus area. There were many fewer beating incidents. Instead the police began making arrests: 123 were picked up, four times as many as had been arrested during the first two days of the crisis.

Despite the relative calm, the massive police presence, and the curfew, several remarkable beating incidents occurred Sunday night. A restaurant was entered, damaged, and a young man dragged out, beaten, and left in the gutter. Two black men, one of them a minister, were chased and beaten by perhaps 50 officers. (Both incidents are taken up in greater detail below.)

From Monday on, street action cooled while community action heated up. At 8:00 p.m. to 6:00 a.m. curfew was in effect until Tuesday. There were a few dispersals of small groups gathered on Telegraph. There were a few more beatings. But the episode had run its course. However, marathon city council meetings began. The council demanded a report on police action from the city manager. Hundreds of citizens recounted their experiences to the council during public sessions. The curfew was cancelled. Attention focused on the demand for a Fourth of July street party. After much discussion the council granted a permit when Avenue businessmen and a number of clergy supported the demand, requested a permit, and undertook to monitor the event.

On July 4th a huge day-long rally was held. Thousands danced, ambled the Avenue, and listened to the rock bands. The crowd constituted a huge solidarity gathering of the University community—young and old, straight and hippie, moderate and radical. The police were nowhere in sight. There was no disorder.

The extent of police violence

The preceding section sketched a considerable amount of violent police misconduct during this episode in Berkeley. Admittedly, there was also citizen misconduct. I hardly challenge the right of the police to move against such misconduct using the force necessary to make arrests or to preserve life. What is at issue is police behavior far beyond the bounds of such justification. I shall now establish that, whatever else may have occurred in Berkeley during this period, the police rioted.

As will be shown, police violence took two main forms. One involved lines of policemen charging, chasing, and beating unresisting persons on the street. The other involved four or five policemen piling out of a squad car to chase and beat citizens without provocation. In both kinds of incidents the victim was usually beaten and left lying where he fell while the police ran on or got back in their cars to seek new targets. Very few of those beaten were arrested; thus not even trumped up charges were used by the police to disguise their attacks. The hit-and-run attacks made from automobiles usually began after crowds had been dispersed and were especially frequent after midnight Saturday night.

In all, 37 citizens were treated for injuries at local hospitals—six for fractures, two of the skull. A much larger number were treated at impromptu first-aid stations, several of which were subsequently gassed and attacked by the police. Others were treated by private physicians.

In what follows, data from interviews with witnesses and victims will be presented to establish three main points about the nature and extent of police violence:

1. Tear gas was not simply used as "the best available means for dispersing crowds and controlling mass violence in a quick, decisive manner with a minimum risk of physical injury" as claimed in a report on the episode by the city manager. It was extensively used as a weapon of reprisal and terror against nonprovocative individuals and against the community as a whole.
2. Policemen indiscriminately beat nonprovocative persons, often in hit-and-run gang attacks, and engaged in various other indefensible forms of physical brutality.
3. Policemen systematically issued contradictory and impossible commands, made repeated threats, used abusive and obscene language, and otherwise employed terror tactics.

From its initial use against the crowd on Friday night, tear gas was *mainly* utilized as punishment and to create, not to disperse, potentially dangerous confrontations. I have earlier reported the expert judgment of a former police commander on the initial use of gas: that the crowd was not hostile and constituted no threat to the police; that the crowd was boxed in and thus the gas could not disperse them, only set them in motion within police lines; and that the gas was thrown at the back of the crowd, thus making it advance on the officers using the gas. Later in the evening a number of other gas attacks were reported.

Persons attending a dance at the student union and a movie on campus were tear-gassed as they attempted to leave. A professor who was at the movie reported that those in attendance had received no warning of the altercation going on several blocks away. He said, "old people and children were gassed, and gas was fired into a crowd near the student union that had made no provocative gestures, but had stopped, realizing that Telegraph Avenue was impassable."

Interviewers were told of a number of private residences that had been gassed, as were several emergency first aid stations, one at the headquarters of the Young Socialist Alliance, the other in the Free Church. Clergymen present at the Free Church reported that a number of canisters of tear gas were thrown down the entryway to the church on several occasions Friday night. The Rev. Jock Brown was badly beaten by a policeman as he stood at the entrance of the church directing injured persons inside. On one occasion two police officers in gas masks broke in the back door of the church, shouted unintelligibly, and then left. Later police broke into the church sanctuary, and then also withdrew.

On Saturday night the Free Church was again a scene of gassing. Later, Police Chief William Beall, Mayor Johnson, and "ten to fifteen officers" all in gas masks came to the side door of the church and "pushed their way in." Drawers and desks were searched. The police showed no warrant; indeed, the chief reportedly refused to speak to church leaders. The mayor and the police then withdrew without action or comment.

A convalescent home was also reported gassed, as were a number of private residences. Several witnesses described the following use of gas: a number of people were at a party in an apartment house on Haste Street (a block from Telegraph Avenue). A black girl at the party noticed police officers beating two black men on the street below. She and two young men shouted from the balcony of the apartment that the police should stop. No one recalls now exactly what was said, or whether obscene language was used. But the police reaction was to launch a tear gas canister up onto the balcony. The girl sustained cuts and burns on her legs which required medical treatment and, of course, all suffered from tear gas fumes.

Three reporters for the *Daily Californian* reported that they were caught up in the flight of people after police began their most savage outburst of beatings following the injury of a highway patrolman by a gasoline bomb. To escape they ran into an alley which turned out to be dead end. Police then fired four tear gas grenades at these three people.

At approximately 1:45 a.m. a policeman broke a large plateglass window at a bookstore. The building was then gassed.

Although the city manager said no gas was used Sunday night, interviewers received testimony that it had been used several times. One complainant charged that a private dwelling was gassed without cause. Another claimed he was gassed at 11:00 p.m. on Telegraph Avenue at a time when he was the only person on the street!

This pattern of gas use by the police makes it clear that they used gas to vent their rage, rather than using it according to accepted tactics. If these actions do not speak with sufficient force, we have testimony on the loud words used by the police about gas. In one incident an officer entered a private establishment which was serving as a first aid station. An employee told the officer that if he didn't have a warrant he would have to leave. According to several witnesses the policemen then brandished a tear gas canister and said, "I don't need a warrant; I've got a tear gas bomb. Would you like that?"

In a similar incident a policeman who was asked to leave a restaurant by its owner waved a gas canister and responded: "Shut up, you motherfucker, or we're going to blow up your restaurant."

Nevertheless, gas was not the main resource of the police. Half of the witnesses and victims interviewed reported beatings. For Saturday night alone the Crisis Team obtained 50 accounts of being beaten. Only one of these victims was arrested. The others were beaten and left.

In a great many incidents, persons were set upon by roving groups of policemen—either moving on foot or in squad cars. These were not forays into crowds or groups of demonstrators. Some victims were pedestrians walking residential streets, some were standing outside their homes, others stood in small knots of bystanders watching the scene. Five persons reported being attacked by groups of officers on foot on Friday night, seven on Saturday night. We received accounts of six incidents Friday night in which police jumped from their vehicles to beat one or more persons. Thirty-one such separate incidents were reported to us for Saturday night and eight more on Sunday and Monday nights.

In a typical incident police would drive up in their car and suddenly slam on the brakes when one or more of the five officers in the vehicle spotted someone or something which aroused him. The officers would scramble out of the car and run up to (or after) a victim, beat him with their batons, then return to their car and drive off. Frequently the target of the police beating was left lying unconscious, sometimes bleeding profusely from scalp lacerations. No one saw police issue either warnings or commands in any of these situations. Indeed, in most incidents witnesses stated that the police said nothing at all, except for some yelling of obscenities.

The typical victim was male, although perhaps surprisingly a third of the victims on whom we have information were female. More than half of the victims we interviewed were over 25 years of age. And most were "straight" in appearance. These last two findings may have been produced by a reluctance of younger and "hipper" people to be interviewed. A good many persons refused to be interviewed—some because they felt it would be futile (and perhaps they were right), others because they were suspicious that we might be fronting for the police. Thus, it must be kept in mind that these data probably considerably underestimate the actual number of police beatings. Crisis Team observers saw a number of beating incidents which later did not turn up in complaints and thus are not included in the statistics.

All witnesses and observers agree there were very few black persons present on the streets in the South Campus area during the weekend. Nevertheless, Crisis Team observers believed that the police were particularly likely to pick out any black they saw in choosing whom to chase or beat. It was reported that alerts were given over the police radio to be on the lookout for Black Panthers and other black militants. Reportedly police were warned to watch for Eldridge Cleaver especially.

Despite the fact that few blacks were present two of them were victims in one of the most flagrant and widely publicized incidents. A young black man, Raymond "Gypsy" Williams, was chased by approximately 50 police officers for more than a block down Telegraph Avenue on Sunday evening. They caught him just beyond Channing Way and beat him bloody and senseless (he had allegedly made an obscene gesture to a policeman). A black minister—in clerical collar—who attempted to intercede was clubbed down and arrested. About a score of newsmen witnessed this event, many of them photographing and filming it. The police then turned on them and smashed several cameras.

Also on Sunday night the Forum affair occurred—films of which shocked Bay Area viewers. Approximately eight policemen charged into the Forum restaurant–coffee house after a young man had allegedly shouted an insult at them. The police knocked down the railing in front of the outdoor coffee area, rushed inside pushing over tables and shouting angry curses, caught the offending youth, dragged him out under a rain of blows, and then discarded him unconscious and bleeding in the gutter.

The ratios of attacker to victim—perhaps 50 to 1 in the case of Gypsy Williams, and 7 or 8 to 1 in the case of the Forum victim—were not atypical. Most respondents claimed that the attacking groups of police officers greatly outnumbered the size of the civilian group set upon. On Saturday night, when the largest number of beating incidents occurred, there were 31 reported incidents of police attacks on persons who were either alone or accompanied by fewer people than there were attacking officers. Of course, not all officers in such groups always struck blows. Some stood and shouted encouragement. Some held victims while others beat them. Some were too slow to reach the victim before fleeter colleagues had finished the job. And some officers appeared to find the whole affair disgusting and simply stood to the side.

Most of the victims claimed they had not engaged in any illegal acts and furthermore that their presence in the area where they were beaten was not connected with the demonstration. Seventy-two persons who claimed to have been victims of police assaults claimed they had taken no part in any of the action during the four-day period. Eighteen victims reported to have been threatened, struck, gassed, or arrested while standing in close proximity to, or inside, their home or that of a friend.

On Friday night police attacks were confined to the Telegraph Avenue vicinity, but on Saturday beatings were reported as far as five blocks west of Telegraph and ten blocks south of Haste Street. On Sunday, beatings were dispersed throughout the South Campus area.

On Saturday night several locations were particularly frequent scenes of police action. One of the most dangerous places to have been was the intersection of Telegraph and Parker. Seven respondents, including one clergyman, reported a series of beatings at this location over a period of two hours, during which perhaps 30 individuals were attacked. Here is one victim's description of the action as he wrote it up in a publicly released statement:

> Saturday night, having been out of town all day and at home all evening, I went out a little after midnight when fire engines went up our street. I did not know the demonstrations were still going on in any form. A few blocks from my own home, standing with a group of my neighbors, most of them middle-aged family types like myself, we saw Berkeley police attack and brutally beat a boy and two girls on the far side of Telegraph at Parker; the boy was clubbed repeatedly as he lay on the ground, kicked and stomped; the girls were "merely" clubbed as they dragged themselves along the ground, screaming. Our group made no hostile or provocative gesture, though a few people shouted, "stop it." A moment later we were charged by three *carloads* of blue-uniformed police who roared across the sidewalk, cutting us off from any escape. No order to disperse had even been given, though a Berkeley police officer had been standing no more than 20 feet from us during all of this. The police piled out of the cars, clubbed us, and cursed us. I myself was clubbed as I ran.

Another bad scene on Saturday night was the dark parking lot behind a restaurant which is located on Telegraph Avenue. The restaurant was teargassed and patrons fled the gas through the rear door into the parking lot. Here club-swinging policemen set upon them. One male student claims he was beaten by six policemen who attacked without warning. He suffered a fractured arm and required stitches in his head. A 34-year-old male claimed that he and 14 others were directed by one group of policemen to leave by a particular route only to be beaten by other policemen when they did so. He also required medical treatment for cuts. These are only the most seriously injured of many complainants from this particular episode.

Police also forced a number of citizens to run the gauntlet—to run past a line of policemen who struck at them as they passed. We received eyewitness accounts of three such incidents on Friday night and four on Saturday. We suspect that this may have been the work of one group of policemen.

I have no way of knowing how many times they engaged in such perform-ances.

On Saturday night the police were seen throwing rocks at fleeing citizens from rooftops overlooking Telegraph Avenue. This activity was reported in the British press and a British reporter provided us with an affidavit signed by 17 persons who claimed to have seen this occur. The reporter collected these witnesses on the spot while he was himself watching the police throw down rocks and a few tear gas canisters.

And finally we received assorted complaints of police-perpetrated damage to property. A policeman was seen knocking in a window at a bookstore. Others broke down the Forum's wroughtiron railing. Several persons re-ported damage to their residences after the police had forced their way in-side. A number of others claimed that police beat their automobiles with riot batons, causing dents and breaking headlights. Several photographers had their cameras smashed. Others were forced to ruin their film. Two per-sons claim the police intentionally stepped on and smashed their glasses. In all, 16 respondents charged police with property damage.

Had we had more resources and more rapport we could have documented many more cases of police misbehavior during this four-day crisis. But it hardly seems necessary. Even a small portion of what we did record would be sufficient to establish that the police in Berkeley rioted.

Many will object that this report is biased because it does not provide a detailed account of violence and dangerous acts by citizens against the police. But the hostile actions of the citizens, whatever they may have been, are beside the point. I have not discussed actions taken by policemen to pro-tect themselves or others from physical harm. I have discussed police attacks on persons who, whatever else they might have done to enrage the police, posed no threat. No one yet has died of being called a pig (although some may have died for saying it). Thus the police behavior, exemplified by beat-ing persons and leaving them without bothering to make an arrest—when it would have been simple to throw the victim into the back of the police car and haul him off to jail—or making middle-aged couples run a gauntlet, was criminal, brutal, and immoral regardless of what other citizens may have done elsewhere.

Regardless of how many people steal, it is the job of the police to catch them, not become thieves themselves.

Why did the police act?

No one really expected the police to move against the rally on Friday night. By doing so the police turned some portion of a peaceful crowd into militant antagonists and severely damaged public confidence at least within the University community. The police also initiated an escalating pattern of violence and counterviolence that has continued ever since. It is important to try to understand why the police chose this course not only for what it tells us about this particular event, but for what it tells of police ideology and tactical conceptions more generally. The Berkeley Police Department has long been regarded as a model of police excellence. Chief Beall was fond of saying that no department in the country had had so much experience in crowd and rally management and none had so successfully averted trouble in such situations. Until Friday, June 28, 1968, this was unquestionably true. Thus, if it could happen in Berkeley it could happen anywhere. Why did it happen?

Looking back, it is clear that one factor in the police decision was a growing hostility towards the Telegraph Avenue youth scene. Hippie dress, marijuana, radical politics, uninhibited public behavior, interracial couples all offended police prejudices, values, and conceptions of proper order. . . . Furthermore, the Avenue is usually very crowded. More people are drawn to it than can fit the sidewalks and there is no open space to relieve the congestion (a major factor in the People's Park conflict a year later). With the collapse of the San Francisco Haight–Ashbury hippie community under the pressures of the police, tourists, drugs, and rough elements, there has been some relocation to Berkeley. And as arrest and crime statistics show, petty thieves and toughs from elsewhere in the Bay Area have been attracted to Berkeley by its openness and excitement and have exploited the scene to commit burglary, theft, robbery, and rape. Even though the police know that the South Campus area residents are the victims, not the perpetrators of crime, they have reacted to the rising incidence of crime by proposing the easiest solution: remove the youth culture instead of protecting it. This tactic manifested itself in considerable police harassment—papering the area with jay-walking tickets, for example, or backing urban renewal schemes to physically obliterate the student scene. Thus, prior to the decision to disperse the crowd there had been a growing "turf" dispute between the residents of the South Campus area and the police. Quite simply the police took on the role of outsiders trying to take control of an area in which the residents had an extremely strong sense of community as well as commitment to a relatively unique culture. Through the ensuing friction the police came to be more and more alarmed about the challenge to their authority and more and more convinced that the Avenue was a growing peril to order, safety, and just plain decency.

Reflecting this attitude among the police is the fact that words such as "creep" and "freak" have been used almost routinely over the police radio to refer to South Campus people. (Recently, the new chief of police has asked his men to stop using these terms.)

This helps to account for why the police were so brutal after the action began, but it does not adequately account for the decision of police commanders to act in the first place. After all, the action did not begin accidentally or in the heat of the moment. Considerable preparations had been made—scores of outside officers had been gathered, riot equipment had been issued, rooftops had been secured, and so on. What led the police to believe that they would or should need such preparations?

Interviews with police commanders elicited a murky and mysterious notion of a grave threat which they believed was going to materialize during what everyone else expected to be another ordinary Berkeley demonstration. These tales were told by the police with much indirection, innuendo, and knowing looks. It took some time to catch on to what they were talking about. But once I did it became possible for me, and for other interviewers, to test the interpretation which follows and to have it confirmed by the answers given.

In my interview with the chief of police, the first policeman to whom I talked after the episode passed, I laid out the puzzle as I saw it. What had made him think there was likely to be a great deal of trouble at the Friday night rally? What led him to prepare so large a force this time when previously only a few Berkeley officers had sufficed?

The chief responded in terms of a very mysterious "Them." He had made such preparations because of "Them." "They" were planning to move into the situation and exploit it to produce a violent outburst. "They," obviously, were people who wanted to launch the revolution. But who were they? I began by working through the various groups taking part in the rally and in the Avenue scene more generally. "They" were not Peter Camejo and his small band of Young Socialist Alliance members, according to the chief. He just snorted when I asked. He indicated that the department had dealt with Camejo and various Berkeley politicos for years, and like everyone else in Berkeley knew perfectly well that Camejo is harmless. Well then, were "They" the street people—the floating hippie population? At this point I got the distinct impression the chief thought I was hopelessly uninformed. "I am not talking about Berkeley people," he said at that point. "They have never been a real problem for us."

As our conversation continued I kept sliding back to who "They" were. It began to dawn on me that the chief believed that some outside band of anarchists, who knows from where, were secreted in Berkeley waiting for the YSA rally to run up the black flag and overturn law and order. Subsequent interviews with other police commanders and city council members turned up additional clues. FBI agents had been briefing the Berkeley police on the impending appearance in Berkeley of radicals from out of state. One council member said the FBI had informed the Berkeley police that people were planning to fly in from Chicago, New York, and New Orleans for the Friday night rally. Others said the FBI had warned of spotting vehicles in Berkeley belonging to campus radicals and various politicos from the East (in fact, such people normally come to Berkeley during the summer and many people from Berkeley ordinarily turn up in the East during the summer). For these and undoubtedly other reasons the Berkeley police became convinced that the YSA rally was the time when radicals were going to rise up. Consequently, they prepared to meet the trouble.

From then on, police preparations and expectations followed a self-fufilling course. . . . Arriving prepared for a major confrontation, the police found simply an ordinary and not very well attended Berkeley rally. But instead of concluding they had misjudged the situation, they concluded that they were being outmaneuvered. They maintained their original assessment, believing that because they had taken precautions the radicals had decided to postpone their outburst until another time when the police were not prepared to deal with them. Like any good tactician the chief apparently decided that if a battle were inevitable it had best be fought at a time and place of his choosing. I am convinced that the chief, suffering under the strain of expecting considerable trouble sometime soon, decided to make a demonstration of his strength and resolve the trouble while he had the manpower available. I believe he felt that such a demonstration would be chastening to the majority of the crowd, who in his judgment did not intend to engage in or support violence, and thus in the future those bent on disorder would not be able to exploit large crowds. Subsequently, when violence begot violence, the police took that as confirmation of their original suspicions—those who fought back, who threw rocks and pop bottles, who set trash cans afire, who broke windows, were "Them." There is, of course, a much simpler explanation of the citizen violence. "He who sows the wind shall reap the whirlwind." But the police reject such a possibility, preferring implausibly complicated conspiracy theories instead. As Chief Beall told the city council, "If we had not escalated our level of force as the demonstrators escalated their violence, we would have lost the city."

After the initial move against the crowd, the police continued to make preparations and tactical decisions which greatly increased the likelihood of violence, especially violence on the part of police officers. While watching police preparations Saturday night—they were loading cars with rifles and shotguns, putting large amounts of ammunition and gas into their trunks, deploying some mortars, placing snipers on rooftops—a British correspondent said to a Crisis Team observer, "They must be planning to fight a war." Understandably, policemen tend to judge the potential danger of a situation on the basis of the preparations made to deal with it, and they subsequently respond on the basis of their initial judgments. Thus preparations made "to be on the safe side" often increase the danger. Certainly bringing in large numbers of officers from outside Berkeley increased the sense of crisis among both the police and the citizens. Furthermore, these extra officers greatly overloaded the communications system and caused a breakdown in the command structure. There simply were not enough commanders to go around. In addition these outside officers were less accustomed to, and thus much more provoked by, the costumes and customs of the South Campus community. All of these factors played a part in producing the police riot.

Nevertheless, for all that Chief Beall decided, perhaps unwisely, to utilize his large and partly borrowed force to disperse the crowd and to continue massive police action, it would be extremely unfair to a responsible man to suggest that he either expected or encouraged the violent behavior of the police which followed. He did not. Nor, despite his unwillingness to publicly condemn what occurred or to take action against officers who committed brutal acts (for reasons which apply to most police commanders), . . . was he unaware of what had actually happened.

This is clear in the excerpts presented below from a memorandum prepared for Chief Beall by the police sergeant he appointed to conduct an investigation of police behavior during the crisis. The results of this official police investigation, which were not made publc at the time, confirm my account of a police riot. Indeed, it is an adequate summary of what I have written:

Memorandum dated August 21, 1968 [The following are excerpts]:

General Observations

Most casualties and complaints arise out of the same tactical situation . . . the dispersal technique employing a (1) one-handed riot baton method by an officer in a (2) squad formation (often without a squad leader of supervisory rank) resulting in a (3) blow to the head of a recalcitrant civilian.

Both civilians and officers have reported observing a sort of "one-upmanship" phenomenon in squads without leaders of a supervisory rank. Each officer seems not to want anyone to feel that he is less zealous than anyone else in the squad, and in tense encounters, a spiralling force-level was observed.

Over 50 percent of the civilian casualties were head injuries, and all but two of these were caused by a riot baton.

None of the complainants stated that they felt that they had been singled out on the basis of their appearance, nor did they feel that they were the objects of a campaign of vengeance. The most common observation was that the police appeared to have "gone berserk" or "lost their cool" or otherwise acted in a nonrational way.

It is the opinion of the undersigned that this impression is due to a number of factors, but principally to (1) the inherent nature of a "brush-fire" operation, and (2) a lack of squad discipline due in turn to either (2a) the absence of a supervisory squad leader or (2b) the lack of civil disturbance training *in squads*. . . .

D. The observation was frequently made by civilians and officers that persons were ordered to disperse, but were hindered in so doing by our deployment, forcing them in some cases to "run the gauntlet."

E. A paradox is created when persons are ordered to disperse and then their resistance is met with a level of force which incapacitates them.[10]

---

[10] Quoted in James W. Smith, *The Park*, unpublished report prepared with the cooperation of the Berkeley Police Department for the Lemberg Center for the Study of Violence, 1970.

Politics of Confrontation

H. L. NIEBURG

There is no secret about the problems of our time: the oppressive discipline of world responsibility and permanent international crisis, the growing divisions between social groups, the alienation of the young, and the cleavages between city and suburb, black and white, rural slum and urban citadel of wealth and power, the decay not only of cities but also of towns and villages somehow passed by in a subsidized power economy. We know these things in the specifics of everyday life and as the problems of public policy that all institutions and groups confront daily. In politics there is no such thing as an abstract problem. Nothing becomes a problem until someone ripples the glassy surface of the social process.

A "social problem" is recognized and generalized when the available bargaining equations and established channels for adjustment fail to reflect the actual bargaining resources of the parties, forcing some groups to use pressure to get further adjustments. Problems become urgent and difficult when new constituencies, whose viability and legitimacy are still unrecognized by established power groups, become capable of exerting pressure upon the body politic. Demand for recognition and access to positive transactions through peaceable and constructive channels become the compelling goals of the new constituency. It must find its spokesmen and leaders while it develops the capability for coordinated and unified action and reaction. Those who aspire to lead must convince both those who will be led and those outside who already hold the formal and informal vantages of society. The first responses of the establishment are to deny the viability of new constituencies, to counter its emerging unity with evasion and tokenism, to use its police power vindictively, and to bend and waive its formal values adroitly in order to buy off or disarm the emerging leadership.

In short, the first requirement of new constituencies is confrontation, which inevitably introduces the danger of escalation on both sides. The viability of all the parties is under challenge, and the degree of violence is the result of the action-reaction patterns which, for whatever reasons, appear. The perils thereby evoked are an essential aspect of the learning process both for uniting the emerging constituency and for preparing established groups to admit an outsider into the magic circle of their social, economic, and political institutions.

. . . The function of the police powers of the state is to maintain a threshold of force that deters or contains latent antisocial acts of individuals and groups. Some element of personal dislocation and anomie exists in the best managed and most equitable societies. Even when isolated outbreaks contain germs of larger social issues, they may be contained at acceptable costs by the measured application of appropriate police power. This is the normal function of the state in dealing with private violence. So long as this task is managed at acceptable risk and cost, police power protects most of the members of the community and enjoys general support.

This kind of violence may be termed *frictional.* To minimize and control it is the legitimate purpose of the police power. Political grievances are forced into peaceable channels and eventually adjusted through debate, legislation, public policy, and private contract.

The characteristic pattern of contemporary riots, however, has shown a tendency toward violent counterescalation against police action by elements of both Negro and white communities. While white violence has been limited, Negro violence escalates in response to police action, often with general support from the black community and with enhanced responsiveness, organization, and danger of future outbreaks. This phenomenon is different in kind from frictional violence. The capability of infinite escalation heightens the risk and increases the cost to society beyond acceptable levels; most important, it destroys the efficacy of normal methods of police power. This kind of violence must be termed *political.* It addresses itself to changing the very system of social norms that police power is designed to protect. It focuses grievances in recurring, deliberate, or spontaneous acts of violence perpetrated even at great risk and cost to the actors. The peaceable procedures of political adjustment fail to divert the escalation, whether because they are closed, discredited, halting, or simply untried.

The peculiar pattern of major social upheaval and political confrontation arises from the fact that normal police security methods become counterproductive; they merely solidify the capability and likelihood of disruption by groups which are increasingly polarized and alienated. Treating such outbreaks as frictional violence tends to create a vicious circle of violence and counterviolence which may discredit responsible leadership on both sides and make further disruption and alienation inevitable. It is these risks and costs that endow such violence with political efficacy and induce the general community to look for other remedies, not only through escalation of force but also through modification first of access to peaceable channels of adjustment and eventually of the norms of social relationships.

In the face of major political violence, the prevailing consensus of interest and power groups must choose between social-economic-political adjustments and the unpromising course of infinite escalation of force. However spontaneous, isolated, and emotional the incidents that trigger the circle of disruption, they impose an iron choice; the prevailing social order has no third course in sight.

We witness the phenomenon anew each year; it grows more perilous as imitative outbreaks proliferate, not only in the summer and by race, but throughout the seasons and as a model for disruptive action by groups of other kinds. One can readily recognize a distinctive political element which rioters seem instinctively to feel. A Dutchman who rioted against

Nazi occupation during World War II noted that, like American Negro rioters, the Dutch rioters were "filled with elation by the fact that they were doing something." There was a community feeling that combined hope, impatience, and impulsiveness. They looted "to obtain trophies, not to get merchandise they could use profitably. Loot has to have symbolic value; strictly utilitarian goods are set on fire!" (Boeke, 1967, p. 577).

Scientific literature makes much of "social stress," "precipitating events," and the "contagious" quality of panic, terrorism, and other forms of extreme behavior (Abrahamsen, 1960, pp. 23–26). These are useful concepts, but they need to be fixed within social and political matrices in order to be of diagnostic value. Many studies demonstrate that social stress can be a factor of cohesion as well as of division. Under the discipline of external war, the rates of both suicide and murder fall (although suicide falls at a sharper rate than murder). The real test of social cohesion occurs under conditions of relative relief of stress. Latent divisive forces are suddenly discharged; long deferred demands for social change suddenly assert higher priorities than do discipline and unity.

Stress is not uniformly distributed in society and thus endows bargaining relationships with different degrees of commitment and urgency. If the main function of government is to "allocate values," then the inverse of that function is to "allocate stress." Groups without access to the formal process of values always get more than their share of stress; forms of direct action and political protest may be viewed as efforts to reallocate stress. Political assassination may be viewed as an act of retaliation designed to induce panic in others to match the panic already felt by the assassin; he seeks to inflict his own predicament upon others, to enlarge and legitimatize it. Langston Hughes said,

> Seems like what makes me crazy has no effect on you.
> I'm gonna keep on doing until you're crazy too.

And Dick Gregory: If the "white power structure" does not share its garbage trucks with us, "we gonna share our garbage with you!"

In the same way, urban renewal programs administered by bankers, realtors, politicians, and universities sharpen stress in the lives of slum dwellers. These programs obliterate the territory of the poor and turn it over to middle-class town houses and high-rise apartments (with token public housing carefully placed near a boundary), erasing informal ecological systems of social integration and community and liberating highly energized search behavior on the part of the displaced.

Black rioting in the 1960s has been shown by every study to be highly selective and politically acute in the choice of targets: loan companies, exploitative merchants (whose business was based upon the garnishment code), substandard tenements, "Burn, baby, burn," and attacks upon firemen have been described as "instant urban renewal"; in the sense that this method reallocates stress, the description merits consideration. The role of police terror—the "incident" which triggered the ballooning sequel—gives most of these events the character of prison uprisings. Self-consciousness and black unity were forged more effectively than in all the Selma marches. Many blacks and whites welcomed a violent test, the former to isolate and gal-

vanize the community behind more militant leadership, the latter to eliminate the troublemakers and impose superior force in order to destroy, once
and for all, the viability of the emerging movement.

This process has aided, not halted, the emerging unity of the black community. The bargaining position and demands of this new constituency are
now highly viable, and therefore it must now be dealt with in other ways,
including full admission for some blacks into the routine, day-by-day bargaining systems of recognized and established groups.

No precipitating event is significant unless all the factors are present,
ready to react—in which case a great variety of events may be equally
capable of catalytic action. Social contagion is a familiar process. When it
is transitory, it is called "fadism"; and when after a long period it proves of
enduring value, it becomes "tradition." There is obvious fadism in all social
behavior, including suicide, crime, and political action. Men socialize each
other and continuously test new forms of adaptive behavior, some of which
wax and wane peripherally and shallowly, while others leave a residue of
enduring institutionalized culture. The tides of social change are always
influenced by creative individual acts that possess great expressiveness and
communicability in terms of changing social values. Imitation and mimicry
are forms of social learning having a functional effect, giving form (what
might be called *behavioral direction*) to emerging values that are widely
shared (Tarde, 1912, pp. 339–40). An important contributory condition to
extreme behavior is the existence of social or group preconceptions of situations that require and elicit extreme responses (Lindesmith and Strauss,
1949, p. 332).

To analyze contagion and precipitating events, we must look to conditions that endow them with efficacy. To comprehend and deal with a pattern
of political assassination, we must ask: How is assassination learned and
reinforced? Why and for whom does such behavior become adaptive and
functional? If indeed assassination should become a fad or a tradition, this
would suggest conditions of deeply divided legitimacy, including incipient
or actual warfare between large social groups. Once such a pattern is established, it suggests that less provocative forms of political action have lost
efficacy and that, for some, only sensational political murders are still potent
as rallying symbols and as attacks on the social viability of others.

Among current conditions and events that generate violence, four factors
are worthy of attention:

1. The rapidity and magnitude of social change, uprooting of populations,
   obsolescence of institutions, of capital investment, deepening relative
   deprivation, and unfulfilled expectations.
2. The requirements and tasks of war and diplomacy, which generate and
   legitimize patterns of violence and intensify the use of formal restraints
   as means of social control.
3. The Vietnam war, both as a condition and as a precipitant—because of
   the lack of success of U.S. policies and arms, the bitter issues raised by
   the draft, economic inflation, and other social costs, and, most important, the loss of legitimacy by national government.
4. The black rebellion, which provides the model and the inspiration of
   extreme political tactics because of the efficacy of such tactics in

achieving Negro demands, in pillorying and exploiting the guilty conscience of white America, and in challenging the tokenism and evasion which characterized the response to earlier nonviolent methods.

All these factors are pertinent to the increasing incidence of political violence in America. However, uprooting by social change, war and diplomacy, and Vietnam are judged to be largely background factors capable of inducing a variety of nonviolent outcomes. Rather, *the pattern and history of black militancy is judged the active ingredient and most salient precipitant of violence.* It is this factor that has catalyzed and directed new norms of political behavior, endowing them with legitimacy, demonstrating their bargaining value to other groups, and eliciting retaliatory behavior.

THE RAPIDITY OF SOCIAL CHANGE

Marshall McLuhan attributes current unrest and its modes of behavior to changes in technology. Violence, he says, "is an involuntary quest for identity." Every new technology sets off this quest. "Violence is directed toward image-making, not goals. . . . The Columbia students have no goals, neither do the Negroes. As long as we provide them with new technology, they must struggle for a new image" (McLuhan, *New York Times,* May 26, 1968, p. 72). He writes, "When one has been hurt by new technology, when the private person or the corporate body finds its entire identity endangered by physical or psychic change, it lashes back in a fury of self-defense" (McLuhan, 1968, p. 97).[1]

McLuhan gives us a significant and important half-truth. He emphasizes the point that is too readily neglected, namely, that technology is the physical environment—that human culture has created and exists within a largely culture-created set of boundary conditions which minimize and modify the relation of social groups to the physical environment. Only occasional catastrophies of air, water, earth, and fire rupture the encapsulated, manmade world which has become the environment of human existence. Technology plays an important role in defining the tasks of culture, in providing a kind of ecological reality principle within which the options of human organization must operate.

Beyond this, McLuhan's classical simplicity is inadequate. Modern civilization and organized human groups are complex living organisms of which the technological and physical environment is as much a response as it is a condition. The direction of technology is not an abstract process, but responds to and reflects the interests and desires of those who exercise political, social, and economic power (Jacob Schmookler, 1966). The McLuhan thesis ("The Technological Imperative" cited by Galbraith) is widely shared by a coalition of aerospace industries, engineering companies, universities, government planning agencies, and so on, which look for the solution to

[1] "When our identity is in danger, we feel certain that we have a mandate for war. The old image must be recovered at any cost. But, as in the case of 'referred pain,' the symptom against which we lash out may quite likely be caused by something about which we know nothing. These hidden factors are the invisible environments created by technological innovation" (McLuhan, 1968, p. 97).

every problem in the invention of new technology to bypass the "insoluble" human element of social problems. In the past such bypasses have served to enlarge the disparity of power between the technology coalition and the rest of us, generating many of the concrete problems we now face.

To prescribe a technological solution for technologically induced problems is to continue a self-serving process that has become increasingly sterile. The rate of "blind technological innovation" is already rapid and the ability of the technology coalition to foresee the results of cheap technological fixes is questionable. Attempts to isolate and treat the accessible physical parameters of contemporary problems will have peripheral benefits at best, serving the interests of prevailing power groups but leaving the basic social equations, the development of a new capability for social bargaining by previously submerged social groups, to fester and pullulate beneath the surface, eventually to break through and deface even the brightest and most gracious structures of our society.

It is not necessary to embrace the technology thesis in order to assess the tendency of technology to dehumanize our institutions. Hardware turnover is merely one dimension of the uprooting and turbulence of the modern age. The breakup of the family as a social group, working mothers, moonlighting fathers, the increase in all forms of crime, the vast movement and mixing of populations due to war as well as industrial development, urbanization, mental illness, permissiveness, secularism, drug addiction—all are aspects of the pathology of our times. Along with the weakening of family and informal, internalized controls comes a compensatory increase in reliance upon formal, external controls by all institutions, social, economic, and political. Large, impersonal corporations, government bureaucracies, faceless, hostile, and unfamiliar policemen strive to contain the exploding disruptions of social change; by their very method such impersonal forces generate resistance and challenges.

Jacques Ellul describes the impact of automation upon man's work, one of his primary means of self-expression and identity:

> . . . man was made to do his daily work with his muscles; but see him now, like a fly on flypaper, seated for eight hours, motionless at a desk. Fifteen minutes of exercise cannot make up for eight hours of absence. The human being was made to breathe the good air of nature, but what he breathes is an obscure compound of acids and coal tars. He was created for a living environment, but he dwells in a lunar world of stone, cement, asphalt, glass, cast iron, and steel. The trees wilt and blanch among sterile and blind stone facades. Cats and dogs disappear little by little from the city, going the way of the horse. Only rats and men remain to populate a dead world. Man was created to have room to move about in, to gaze into far distances, to live in rooms which, even when they were tiny, opened out on fields. See him now, enclosed by the rules and architectural necessities imposed by over-population in a twelve-by-twelve closet opening out on an anonymous world of city streets (Ellul, 1967, p. 321).

It is not only the pace of life, and the increased insecurity that attends it, which dehumanizes, but also the monotony, meaninglessness, and anonymity of the forces that we reckon with in our daily lives. Everything is swept up by vast, impersonal, seemingly reachless, insensitive, implacable, and impregnable agents and agencies about which the individual can do nothing. To those locked in a Kafkaesque, bureaucratic prison world, the violence of a Mike Hammer or a James Bond becomes an adaptive fantasy and a model for self-defense. "Murder and capital punishment are not opposites that cancel one another but similars that breed their kind" (Shaw, 1903, p. 232). Violence is glorified in all the media of popular culture, and Gestapo types become the Good Guys. As in the turbulence of nineteenth-century European revolutions, the criminal becomes a romantic hero and the social misfit a prophet. The stock heroes of television drama and the movies have undergone a subtle change during the last generation. The nineteenth-century "rational man" (Nero Wolfe or Ellery Queen, both Sherlock Holmes types who solve crimes by the exercise of logic, aiding the duller but sympathetic police officials) has been replaced by sociopathic lone avengers who, against the wishes and interests of dumb and corrupt officials, out-plunder and out-sex everyone in sight. They beat the criminal by criminal methods in the name of abstract justice or merely for sadistic fun.

The cowboy is now rarely a simple champion of the good; he has been transformed into an opportunistic antihero, a moral loner flawed by life but justified in amorality by his bravura style, physical prowess, and basic honesty. In the words of Robert Warshow, ". . . it is not violence at all which is the point of the Western movie, but a certain image of man, a style, which expresses itself most clearly in violence" (Warshow, 1962, p. 7). When the antihero gets it in the end, we are left with the implication that not he but the world has gone wrong. The villain of the piece is often the counterpart of a hero-antihero, a "hip killer" who also has style and a code of honor based upon opportunism and physical prowess. The plot frequently contains a moment of truth: the protagonist and the villain confront each other and recognize an unspoken bond even though each must try to kill the other. Such fantasies probably vent more violence than they induce. Certainly they reflect conditions of antisocial behavior rather than causing it.

In real life, however, the children of the middle classes in great numbers have adopted the tradition of the slums that jail is not only honorable but a necessary stopping place in personal development and peer recognition. Sexual intercourse in public, nudity, illegal traffic in dope, and attacks on policemen have for some become forms of neoromantic revolutionary action. Manipulation of people "as though they are things" has been cited by Martin Luther King and others as being as much responsible for the perpetuation of grief and misery in our cities as the absence of wealth. We are baffled by the dropping out from establishment values of vast numbers of people of all social classes and ages, especially those who are beneficiaries of the comforts, conveniences, and wealth generated by an expanding economy.

Mumford, always the incisive diagnostician, see "a pathology that is directly proportionate to the overgrowth" of the metropolis, "its purposeless materialism, its congestion, and its insensate disorder, . . . a sinister state" that manifests itself in the enormous sums spent on narcotics, sedatives, stimulants, hypnotics, and tranquilizers, not alone by the hippie generation but by a great mass of middle-class adults, in an attempt to adjust to the vacuous desperation and meaningless discipline of their daily lives (Mumford, 1967, pp. 194–95).

Hiding behind palace guards of computers, punch cards, and automated production lines, giant authoritarian corporations, systems engineers, and managers create a spiritually empty drive for production and gadgetry, mobilizing all our lives to tasks that are meaningless to most of the people and thus generating alienation and estrangement. Droves of people withdraw defensively into the trance of drugs or television, or strike back wildly at the faceless social distance that destroys the possibility of creative human confrontation. The soldier activating electronically controlled missiles has no basis for empathy with his target; the industrial manager prefers to automate rather than deal with union grievance committees; state legislators delegate the problems of traffic control and waste disposal to systems engineering firms rather than deal face-to-face with the refractory human element of county boards, mayors, aldermen, and citizens.

Modern society imposes an unbearable burden on human empathy, generating personal anomie and search behavior attempts to contrive new principles of community, as well as extremes of political action. Alienation and denial of the legitimacy of the whole society become necessary defense mechanisms. New subcultures search for first-hand experience, personal integrity, and real refreshment in a world destroyed by suffocating abundance.

The dropping out of the young can be looked upon as the white equivalent of the Negro conversion from killing each other to killing policemen. The tendency of some of the most articulate dropouts to identify their situation with that of the Negro reflects both an attempt to exploit the efficacy and threat of black violence and a borrowing of the trappings, if not the reality, of black dynamism and insurgency.

The result of social alienation is increased reliance on external restraints and formal controls, methods which do not operate effectively in the absence of informal group reinforcement. Vast numbers who are poorly integrated are therefore "most likely to aggravate conflict beyond the bounds of normal disagreements" (Berelson and Steiner, 1964, p. 61).[2] In their excellent study of suicide and homicide, Henry and Short observe that "when external restraints are weak, aggression generated by frustration will be directed against the self, and when external restraints are strong, aggression generated by frustration will be directed outwardly against another person" (Henry and Short, 1954, p. 17).

The United States faces some curious paradoxes. The most productive economy in history stagnates at a high level and intensifies, rather than allays, social cleavages. The most democratic society in history witnesses political opportunities rejected in favor of violent protest. A high level of abundance and material well-being generates anger among the poor and

[2] "When community members are highly involved with the community per se, identifying their own future with that of the community, that identification . . . appears to modify and constrain the disagreement. People who feel apart, and unidentified, are quickest to overstep the bounds of legitimate methods and carry the dispute into disruptive channels. When there are few or none who are identified, then there are essentially no norms to restrain the opposing sides. Conversely, if most people and organizations in the community are identified with community as a whole, then the potentially disruptive effects of the dispute are felt by all; there are conscious attempts at reconciliation" (Coleman, 1957, p. 21).

terrible anxieties for the middle classes, especially the young. A sophisticated, advanced civilization reenacts the dilemmas of a banana republic and makes a mockery of the fondest doctrines of economic development and political stability. If for no other reason, the nation owes a considerable debt to the young radicals whose confrontation tactics are proving that MAN is not ready to become an acronym for Meaningless Archaic Nonentity! They are forcing personal confrontations on a society that has done everything possible to standardize people into interchangeable parts.

WAR AND DIPLOMACY

These characteristics of culture in the United States constitute a cluster of variables having two major impacts upon the norms of political behavior. First, they intensify the rapidity of social change and the uprooting of established institutions. War, hot or cold, and permanent international crisis thrust upon the nation unavoidable tasks and priorities of defense preparedness and international responsibility. In an atmosphere of tension and crisis, all elements of spatial and social mobility are accelerated, solid social structures are dismantled and new ones jerry-built. Populations and life situations are scattered by the winds of events. Insistent demands of national security disrupt the order of personal life and rest the whole social balance upon the shifting knife-edge of each new foreign crisis.

Second, war and diplomacy provide a pattern of national behavior which by its very nature legitimizes violence in all its forms. This necessarily must inflame private behavior, raise the level of social irritability, and weaken inhibitions against personal violence. In addition to the two great wars of this century, the world since 1945 has seen 12 limited wars, 48 coups d'état, 74 rebellions for independence, 162 social revolutions, and vast numbers of racial, religious, and nationality riots (see Sanger, 1967). Respectable men in the nation's highest offices play the game of "Chicken" with brinkmanship nuclear diplomacy, and the same sport tends to become commonplace in all kinds of domestic political situations. Guns become status symbols and elemental protection for homeowners and shopkeepers, just as missiles do for nations. Ministers, teachers, and leaders urge the people to peaceable conduct and love while at the same time they support mutilation and murder abroad. Confrontation diplomacy pursued in the national interest cannot help but proliferate confrontation politics among interest groups at home. Gestapos, GPUs, CIAs, espionage, subversion, and all forms of official undergrounds facilitate and legitimize a social and political underground at home.

Such facts of life, indisputable and honored, make it easy for many people, especially those whose interest it serves and those who are young, to accept uncritically the scenario of an international assassination chain carried out under official auspices. The script reads from Lumumba to Diem, Diem to John F. Kennedy, John F. Kennedy to Malcolm X (who commented about Kennedy's death that "the pigeons have come home to roost"), Malcolm X to George Lincoln Rockwell, to Martin Luther King, to Robert F. Kennedy . . . and the next act in the series is already in preparation. Thus the series is legitimized. Thus it becomes reasonable and necessary that the next great political sensation involve another major assassination. Thus the pattern is generalized and escalated as other groups and individuals, aspirants to political attention and efficacy, deliberate which victim deserves and will best serve their purpose to get into the act.

Hannah Arendt calls our time "a period . . . of bloody imperialist adventures" which give rise to a moral dissent which is "treated with open contempt by the administration." Taught in the school of the civil-rights movement, the opposition "took to the streets, more and more embittered against the system as such" (Arendt, 1968, p. 24). Western self-righteousness in two world wars imposed formulas of unconditional surrender and total victory, in the name of which whole societies were smashed in Europe by bitter-end warfare, and in Japan by saturation fire-bombing climaxed by Hiroshima and Nagasaki. Long ago George F. Kennan argued the difficulty with which mass societies, especially democratic ones, conduct international diplomacy and wage war. Unless the nation is whipped into an ideological crusade, limited war and limited diplomacy (measured against political objectives) are virtually impossible to sustain. If this dismal assessment is correct, it might be said that an essential link exists between domestic violence and violence unleashed abroad: the latter must overreact in order to be justified to American public opinion; this in turn facilitates overreaction on the part of those who oppose what they consider the unwarranted use of force.

THE LINGERING UNSUCCESS OF VIETNAM

Vietnam is frequently cited as the most immediate precipitating event in the whole pattern of violence sustained and legitimized by contemporary war and diplomacy. Much of the so-called moral issue which surrounds opposition to the war is attributable to the failure of policy to achieve minimal U.S. objectives at acceptable risk and cost within a tolerable time, rather than to the substance of U.S. policy in Southeast Asia. Be that as it may, the term "credibility gap" is essentially a way of describing the loss of legitimacy of the national government and the incumbent administration. All kinds of unresolved issues, some related, others remote to Vietnam, share in the collapse. The critics and opponents generalize their assault, exploiting the disaster of official policy as a means to attack and weaken the "establishment." Every disaffected group sings the unsuccess of Vietnam in order to advance and argue its own values and to assert its own new principles of reintegration and legitimacy.

Certainly major failures of national policy have the effect of weakening the legitimacy of institutions and leaders. The direction of the revolt, however, reflects all kinds of conflicts that preceded Vietnam and that do not require a major foreign policy failure for validation. The Vietnam issue may really be just a target of opportunity. This is not to minimize the fact that the war has intensified all the elements of an uprooted society. The requirements of military service, the tremendous mobilization of national resources and money, the wave of inflation, with consequent dislocation of lives and savings for vast numbers of middle-class Americans, and the postponement of positive public programs to deal with competing priorities—all have embellished existing tensions and tendencies with a galloping fire. In this sense, Vietnam may be considered both a precipitating event and a background condition.

The role of the precipitant of violence may vary enormously in significance; we can assess its causal importance only in terms of the whole dynamic system of which it is a part. To quote MacIver, "The causal efficacy we impute to any factor will always be contingent not only on the other factors, but also on the dynamic interdependence of them all within the total situation. It is only as a temporary heuristic expedient that we can select any item as 'Cause' and speak of the rest as 'conditions'" (MacIver, 1964, p. 425).

None of the factors or conditions noted above, taken separately or together, are sufficient to cause extreme political behavior and violence. The increasing incidence and incipient normalization of violence by many different groups require something more—a demonstration of its efficacy as a form of social bargaining.

THE BLACK REBELLION

It is in the black rebellion that such tactics have emerged as most efficacious. Here they have achieved a degree of legitimacy which invites imitation by every excluded social group, ranging from the Students for a Democratic Society to American Indians, Puerto Rican high-school students, and teachers. A specific coincidence of historical circumstances has made the time ripe for Negro self-consciousness and concerted social action and has also predisposed other claimants for political access to emulate Negro success.

No hypothesis of "organized conspiracy" and "outside agitators" is required to explain the clear pattern of escalated violence and counterviolence that has accompanied the search for identity, organization, and leadership by the black community. Nor is the theory of relative or absolute deprivation a satisfactory explanation. Rather, the direction of the black power movement has been largely a result of the response by dominant white power groups to early low-risk tactics of nonviolence. The process by which radical militants achieved legitimacy and entered the mainstream of Negro leadership has been largely dependent on the tokenism, evasion, and resistance which discredited the legalistic approach of the NAACP and the nonviolent methods of Martin Luther King. To the shame of the white community and its leadership, riots and insurrectionary sniping are accomplishing breakthroughs that seemed impossible before the long hot summers of the early 1960s. Even backlash and the rise of white extremism confirm and augment the efficacy of black militancy, endowing it with a defensive justification and raising the level of cost and risk for the whole society, thereby forcing the middle to seek real social adjustments as the only means of isolating, limiting, and containing the dangers of continued escalation.

Like the decades of violence that accompanied the organizing phase of the labor movement, the initial series of confrontations between the black community and the police represented an organizing phase whose primary function was to unite the Negro community and discredit both white liberals and Uncle Toms who had previously claimed to act on its behalf. "Black is beautiful," black power, and black separatism are tactics of unification rather than program goals.

In their initial response to militancy, white policemen sought to punish the whole community, treating all Negroes, including bystanders, as rioters and looters—as if, by terrorism, to teach the whole black community the futility of violence. This was a test of legitimacy which the white policemen lost; instead, their actions aided and abetted the organizing process. Training programs were put into effect to teach police and the National Guard to deal with rioters selectively, in an effort to isolate lawbreakers. Aggressive and terroristically inclined policemen were removed from ghetto assignments, and other efforts were made to legitimize antiriot measures—for example, new forms of token participation in policy-making, poverty programs, and police review boards.

To a certain extent these measures succeeded. They forced militants into more extreme tactics which divided the Negro community. However, these actions were not all of one piece, and, by and large, the conditions of social exclusion and isolation remained in force for most Negroes. Once again, the power structure played into the hands of the most militant. The division of the black community aided the process of tightening militant control, splitting off mostly those already discredited by the failure of legalistic and political tactics. As was noted by the Kerner commission, the gap between black and white is widening despite Negro gains.

Most of the adjustments have been token or abortive. Every institution in the nation is anxious to train, hire, and upgrade Negroes in white-collar, professional, and junior executive jobs, but these jobs are not numerous, and blue-collar and unskilled employment is unstable and shrinking. At the lower levels, most of the work produced by crash programs involves "dead-end" jobs which only serve to confirm black alienation. Jobs on the higher social scales still tend to be for purposes of display in the front office and in full-page ads in slick magazines. Manipulation from the top down—paternalism—is still the rule. General Motors and Xerox are using a few black faces as a way of writing "soul brother" on the door in hopes that marauding bands of the still excluded group will pass them by. Negroes still account for most of the executions carried out for capital crimes, while white criminals wait on deathrow for long years until a court or governor finally commutes their sentences. Negroes may escape from the old ghetto compound, but the city itself becomes an enlarged ghetto encircled by white suburbs with token integration, civil defense armies, all-white poilce forces, and armed housewives. The tax base of the cities erodes as industry follows its executives and blue-collar workers out of the city; mercantile business disperses and clusters in shopping centers. Years ago, cities ruled by white majorities fought for adequate apportionment and representation in state legislative bodies, jealously resisting programs for metropolitan and county-wide government; now, as the suburbs become the locus of power, reapportionment of state legislatures is achieved for suburbs at the expense of cities. Programs for metropolitan government suddenly seem politically feasible as a means to circumvent black political control of cities.

The disparity between city and suburb goes far beyond race and income.

Every available indicator of economic activity dramatizes the deteriorating competitive position of the city—medical care, hospital facilities, private and governmental services of all kind, unemployment (which is double that of suburbs), disease and death rates, decline of housing, streets, and the rate of gas-line leaks and explosions.

A major reason why more enlightened police tactics have so far failed to end extremist black provocation is that tactics of limited force are difficult to implement and ineffective against sniping and guerrilla tactics. There are extremists in every community. By reacting against a whole community in order to deal with isolated acts of provocation (as has historically been done), the power structure endowed extremists, both white and black, with a power over events they could attain in no other way. Even today almost any irresponsible teenager holds in his hands the power to start an incident at any time. Escalation and counterescalation are built into the situation, and the Negro community is forced to support the acts of its own extremists. For decades police have responded to the acts of Negroes (including children) as though a state of undeclared war existed between the two communities. They interpreted their duty as requiring them to intimidate and terrorize at every opportunity, creating an automatic riot syndrome which could be triggered by any claimant to leadership, irresponsible youth or irresponsible policemen. It was and still is impossible for policemen to arrest one black man without having to deal with all the bystanders as though they were equally guilty. One cannot undo in a year or even a decade the automatic syndrome which a century of police terrorism put into the hands of the newly awakened militant leaders.

Lynching and the murder of civil-rights workers lost their efficacy in the South in the early stages of the civil-rights struggle. If three civil-rights workers are murdered today, ten more appear tomorrow. If one uppity nigger is lynched, ten more aggressively taunt their white masters the next day. In the 1960s, police terrorism has equally lost its efficacy in the cities of the North; however, black militancy continues to enjoy the new-found efficacy of extreme tactics, programs, and paramilitary brigades—both to maintain unity of new organizations behind new leaders and to facilitate bargaining with dominant social groups.

The year 1968 has been saluted as the year in which no major riot occurred. The great cities that had exploded during the previous five years were quiet except for isolated sniping attacks and hit-and-run guerrilla actions against police and property. Only a number of middle-sized hinterland cities, previously untouched, experienced the familiar pattern of burning, looting, and attacks on white motorists and police.

Many explanations have been offered for the relative calm. The black community has now achieved self-consciousness and a capability for acting in concert, and new forms of activism are underway. "Operation Breadbasket," growing out of the Chicago program of the Southern Christian Leadership Conference, and similar organizations in the style of Saul Alinsky, are creating new institutions to administer private and public ventures and initiating every kind of pressure activity which will yield concrete and specific results: use of rent strikes by tenants' unions to enforce sanitary and fire codes against absentee landlords; pooling of savings to establish Negro-owned businesses, housing projects, credit unions, savings and loan associations, and banks; forcing white merchants to take in Negro partners or face total boycott, if not worse; blocking bill collectors and repossession artists, welfare investigators, vice squads, and narcotics agents from operating in the area; establishing unofficial intracommunity peace-keeping forces; providing all kinds of local services (job placement, education, family counseling). There is a general demand that traditional white-controlled agencies be withdrawn and that their places be taken by emerging community-controlled institutions with public funding and grants of formal authority. Black dependence on traditional white political machines is finally breaking down and new-breed blacks are gradually acquiring political office. Similar changes are occurring in labor unions, but more slowly.

These are the most positive results of polarization of black and white communities; if they achieve real efficacy of social bargaining, they bode well for the future—even though the changes in store for America, such as decentralization of schools, will present hazards and challenges.

Another side of the coin is the less positive but probably essential black capability for terrible counterescalation of violence against any renewed provocations. Fear of and respect for this capability, exercised at greast cost in Watts, Detroit, and Newark, serves as the underlying incentive for white power groups, no longer able to send police into the ghetto at will, to tolerate and encourage more positive assertions of black power in ongoing formal institutions.

The experience of the riots has not only unified the black community but also professionalized its security forces. Battle plans and capabilities are now in readiness. Newly formed commando groups with arms and uniforms, Black Panthers, the Black Liberation Front, and other organizations are a professional paramilitary vanguard. Policemen, bill collectors, and non-soul-brother social workers find it virtually impossible to operate in the ghetto without a safe-conduct pass from the informal militia. A television repairman or a social worker may get a pass, but many others find it very difficult, especially if they come armed and in uniform. Even the provocation of a sniping incident no longer leads to wholesale police invasions, for fear of broadening resistance and thus precipitating an uncontrolled, ravaging situation—this time with organized black troops coming from other cities to bomb and sabotage city water supplies and electric generators, and possibly with hit-and-run attacks in the suburbs. In the words of fugitive Eldridge Cleaver:

> Guerrilla warfare has traditionally been conceived and developed to deal with exactly this kind of situation—the presence of massive occupying forces on the one hand and the existence, on the other hand, of sizable numbers of people who are not going to confront those forces full-face but will strike swiftly at times and places of their own choosing. Works on guerrilla warfare have been widely circulated, and a lot of people understand that it doesn't take millions of people to undermine the stability of the American economic system in that way. That's what's at stake—the stability of the system (Cleaver, 1968, p. 94).

The underlying (and now mostly passive) capability of escalated violence provides the substratum which holds the community together and liberates it from traditional occupation and intervention by the dominant white majority. The traditional uses of force and violence are working with great political efficacy, serving to induce peaceable accommodations rather than necessarily triggering a merciless civil conflagration. Decades—indeed, centuries—of deprivation, repression, and harassment have given blacks the resources and deep commitment necessary to out-escalate the white community and thereby attain recognition for the legitimacy of their demands. The process has worked, and others hasten to apply the lesson. Racial violence has had therapeutic value for both the Negro and the white community. This is clear in the Kerner commission studies as well as in the consensus of black opinion.

However, the changed posture has, like all bargaining transactions, ambivalent effects. First, there is the ominous possibility that future violence will be more far-reaching and unmanageable than the riots of recent years. If the process of escalation is once again evoked, we may have occasion to look back on Watts, Newark, and Detroit as "the good old days"! This ever present possibility has the incidental side effect of allowing a minority of young black militants to strut and taunt the white community at every opportunity as if to grind white pride into humiliation. Invited to confer with university presidents, city councilors, television MCs, they begin by calling their hosts "pigs" who will be destroyed when the time is right. At universities throughout the country, black student unions demand not only courses in Afro-American history and culture, but also relief from grades and abject apologies and confessions by college administrators for white racism. How can a university president refuse to negotiate just because he is called "pig," when he believes the alternative is escalated violence and counterviolence with no clear resolution in sight except massive outside police presence, which may destroy the university quite as completely as could ransacking students.

The Columbia-Berkeley model and the ghetto riots terrify authority and encourage a brutal travesty of legitimate demands for reform. Ghetto rumblings and white guilt, much of which is warranted, create a condition as unreal and unproductive as the old system of tokenism. It may be that new tests of unity, determination, and purpose are in the offing as the very success of the black rebellion stiffens backs in both communities.

The second effect of the new bargaining capability is, while ambivalent, more hopeful. Tokenism carried far enough becomes real integration, on the job, in government and politics, if not in neighborhoods or country clubs. All the new institutions arising under black initiative and leadership will inevitably become formalized vantage points for social, economic, and political bargaining, not in abstractions and slogans but in the nitty-gritty that constitutes assimilation. Programs for integration have now apparently been deferred while a stage of voluntary separate development and self-rule enables the American Negro to establish a collective identity of his own. Eventually it may no longer be necessary to insist on black pride and "Black is beautiful." Americans, both black and white, will live it by treating each other as individuals and human beings rather than as symbols of hostile communities. Social integration may come quietly and solidly on the basis of individual freedom and opportunity rather than through programs based on color. For the present, there is widespread incentive in the black community to continue to marshal its forces, removing the remnants of formal exclusion and inferiority while bargaining for other forms of access.

These contrary trends, taken together, are substantial grounds for optimism. Most studies of the black community indicate that in the mass the Negro is far less revolutionary in his outlook than some of his more militant spokesmen. "While there is no doubt that Negroes want change and some of them are prepared to do desperate things to bring it about, the changes they have in mind are essentially conservative in nature. The great majority do not propose to withdraw from America; they want equal status in it" (Campbell and Schuman, 1968, p. 61). Furthermore, much initiative still lies in the hands of dominant power groups who, quite apart from racist sentiments, cannot ignore the real bargaining power achieved by the black community. A united black community is bound to have a good effect in inducing the kinds of change which ultimately will make "blackness" relevant neither for the nationalists nor for the bigots.

MIMICRY AND INSTANT REVOLUTIONS

Two tendencies are now at work for other groups as well: an effort to exploit potential black violence for their own purposes, and imitation of the pattern of protest as the means of unifying other claimant groups and winning attention for their demands.

Just as every energetic pressure group capitalized for years on the Cold War, the Soviet sputnik triumph, the space gap, the Chinese peril, the international Communist conspiracy, just as educators, scientists, industrialists, and military men all offered special-interest formulas to save the nation, so the explosions in the ghetto have provided new self-serving slogans for all groups. A massive black army of potential seditionists, saboteurs, and Mau Mau terrorists is evoked for a wide variety of ends.

Prevailing power groups exploit the urban tragedy to maintain their own advantages, reiterating that the path to progress is via more money invested in scientific and technical innovation, new government contracts to renew the slums, operate job camps, train and rehabilitate black workers, and maintain an expanding economy based on government subsidies and tax advantages, all of which will bring about a painless solution without curtailing existing property rights, righting social inequities, or modifying the disparities of political power.

So too, teachers and public employees escalate the use of strikes and demonstrations. The welfare poor and college youth exploit the methods and summon the image of the black rebellion, suggesting that denial of their claims will lead to the same escalation that only the numbers and solidarity of the black community so far make credible. A violent confrontation between Vietnam protestors and police raises the specter of an even more dangerous uprising in the black ghetto, now no longer disorganized and self-distructive, but galvanized under paramilitary organizations.

In this setting, violent confrontation becomes more frequent. All kinds of groups seek organization and legitimacy by probing and testing the established authorities and searching for opportune issues around which to rally and extend their leadership. The escalation of sensation will, they hope, win political efficacy by evoking the dangers of reciprocal extremism. It is said that all things happen at least twice. Dissenting groups all around the world have learned the words and are singing "We Shall Overcome." Huk insurgent groups, calling themselves "Beatles," grow in size and make daring attacks against Philippine troops in Central Luzon, while their balladeers sing Muddy Waters and Chuck Berry songs. Sometimes imitation converts the brilliant and the tragic into the farcical and the stupid: witness recent destructive rampages by elementary school children in Boston, Chicago, and New York City.

In much the same way, young, white, middle-class rebels adopt the successful tactics of the blacks, searching for rallying cries and issues (student power, sexual freedom in the dorms, drugs, Vietnam) with which to unify a constituency and win legitimacy. In effect, they seek once again to exploit the sacrifices of the black community for their own purposes. Rennie Davis, Yippie activist, articulated the method in the *Village Voice:* "The goal? A massive white revolutionary youth movement which, working in parallel cooperation with the rebellions in the black communities, could seriously disrupt this country, and thus be an internal catalyst for a breakdown of the American ability and will to fight guerrillas overseas" (Davis, *Village Voice,* October 10, 1967, p. 2).

Traditional "rites of spring" of the young become stylized beer riots in LaCross, Wisconsin, beach riots at Fort Lauderdale, occupation of university buildings, disruption of classes, and more. Assassination and counterassassination of college student leaders, as well as of government officials, has long been a feature in many Latin American countries. It can happen here! We already have witnessed bombings and burnings on several campuses. Just as strikes and purposeful property damage are filtering down through the high schools and grade schools, so extreme forms of escalated violence can spread throughout the society if we are imprudent enough to let it happen. The power to direct and control these events lies more in the hands of the powerful than it does in the rallying cries and ambitions of the powerless.

The black rebellion has created an atmosphere of anxiety and incipient terror which is making possible important, but not necessarily positive, social adjustments. This national mood creates opportunities for all those with a grievance to take advantage of the beseiged and embattled condition of traditional power groups. There are many just causes and real problems which give rise to dissent. However, there is also much that is shallow and transitory. After a well-publicized kidnaping, all kinds of people send their own ransom notes trying to cash in. Similarly, in a period of general anxiety, all kinds of people use innuendo and direct threats to exploit the opportunities created by the acts of others. Anonymous telephone and letter threats of assassination proliferate, but they have little social effect.

The best way to dampen pseudo-terrorism is to deal effectively with the roots of real terrorism; the best way to limit the mimic search for instant revolution is to deal effectively with the sources of real dissent. This may require a showdown to test the legitimacy of demands, and thus may deny automatic efficacy to extreme tactics. Courage and cool assessment of one's own resources are indispensable to formal authorities. However, superior force alone plays into extremist hands; to deny efficacy to violent tactics and leadership requires genuine validation of other channels of protest, two-way communication, and social change.

While many have learned the lesson of black power—intransigence and stylized violence—not all the imitations are meaningless and marginal. Much of the search behavior of contemporary youth can have great reintegrative power for the whole society. Has monogamy failed? Have universities failed? Is there a need to improvise new bases of community to replace the fragmented anomie that exists in the rootless suburbs? Are job and work still adequate bases of human identity in an age of automated abundance? Is it perhaps true that the Protestant ethic *is* ready for the dustbin, and that some new ethic based upon consumption, self-indulgence, and sensuality is ripening? Is the time ripe for dismantling the great concentrations of power imposed by sheer machine production and the nation-state system? These are real questions; they deserve to be approached with open minds and a willingness to permit experimentation and social invention by those who would change the accepted order.

Irving Kristol declares that the hippies and associated sects are the only truly radical groups in American society today because "they are dropouts from the revolution of rising expectations and reject the materialistic ethos that is the basis of the modern social order." However, he despairs that simple hedonism can make a radical alternative viable. The self-proclaimed radicals are mainly concerned, like the rest of us, with consumption, "even if they prefer sex and drugs" rather than detergents and automobiles (Kristol, 1968, pp. 174–75).

Revolution is a serious business. Apart from the black rebellion, how serious and cataclysmic is this "era of confrontation politics"? How well will SDS stand up to the backlash of an S. I. Hayakawa? There is an ersatz quality in the new middle-class underground. The safety valves of American pluralism are still functioning and rob it of much of its steam. If the new underground were truly revolutionary, would we see Head Shops selling trinkets in every respectable suburb? Would Country Joe and the Fish or the Fugs be building up investment portfolios? Would Tom Hayden and Abbie Hoffman be making the rounds of the radio and television talk shows? Would underground newspapers (full of Zen Buddhism and four-letter words) have a national news service?

DEATH AND TRANSFIGURATION

Attempts to obliterate all occasions and possibilities of political and personal violence are unrealistic and even dangerous. Any effort by the state to obtain an absolute monopoly over violence leads inexorably to totalitarian repression of all activities and associations which may, however remotely, create a basis of antistate or anti-establishment action. The logic of such attempts generates a strong counterreaction. In addition to forcing opposition into the most extreme channels (the very thing the state seeks to eliminate), a repressive system threatens the freedom and safety of every citizen. A democratic system must preserve the right of organized action by private groups and accept the risks of an implicit capability for violence. By permitting a pluralistic base, the democratic state enables potential violence to have a social effect and to bring social accommodation with only token and ritual demonstrations, facilitating a process of peaceful political and social change.

The good society must learn to manage constructively some degree of violence and potential violence. Communities can endure even with societies practicing organized murder in their midst, providing the institutions of the whole maintain their legitimacy and are able to isolate and control the effects of antisocial actions. One can never hope to eliminate completely anonymous telephone or letter threats to authors, public personalities, and people who get their names in the paper. Political assassination cannot be eliminated once and for all by any preventive measures which are not even more dangerous to the health and survival of the nation. Attempts to make violent confrontations impossible are incompatible with a free political process and may in fact enhance the probability of a coup d'état. The most anxious man in a totalitarian system is the dictator, just as the most anxious man in a prison is the warden.

However, it is possible for society to manage its problems in such a way that no single man can change history with a single bullet. The inefficacy of political extremism is the best safeguard against the danger that an isolated act will begin a self-perpetuating series and provide a pattern for political success.

At all times, even in a healthy society, the whole spectrum of political options is occupied by groups and individuals who claim leadership and legitimacy. The best way to keep the extremes of the spectrum from overwhelming the center is to improve the efficacy and legitimacy of such modes of political action and leadership as will deescalate latent threats of violence and facilitate social change and political integration of new groups. The very success of peaceable modes of bargaining constitutes a prediction of futility for extremist modes. When violence occurs, the vast multitudes of the nation will support the actions of the state in limited and reasonable deterrence, localization, and, when necessary, containment by appropriate and measured, but not overreactive, means of force. George Wallace's threat to run his car over demonstrators tends to escalate and legitimize political violence. Mayor Daley's instruction to police to "shoot to maim" looters has the same effect. Government must learn the value of nonviolence as an appropriate tactic of control in certain conditions where violence, even the superior violence of the state, will not work.

It is a simple matter to make a theoretical diagnosis of the conditions and causes of political violence. It is much more difficult to know, as a matter of practical policy, how to avoid social trials by ordeal. How does government terminate and stabilize a period of search behavior and confrontation? How to conserve and integrate adaptive social innovations? How a social process starts and spreads has been much more studied than how it terminates. A process may cease because it has exhausted itself. Some processes may go on indefinitely, ceasing only with the disappearance of the groups whose interests they served or opposed. In some cases, a process provides built-in opportunities at which it can be deliberately stopped or redirected. What should be done in a situation where high-risk political confrontation is already well established and seemingly irreversible (a situation which the nation has not yet reached)?

One can create countertendencies to dampen extreme oscillations. This calls for highly creative political action and leadership, not only from leaders of prevailing cadres and groups, but on every level of social and political organization in both the formal and the informal polity. This kind of action may not be as difficult as it appears. There is a strong tendency in social life toward humanizing power, toward creating conditions of predictability and order in the midst of change, and avoiding the danger created for all by efforts to apply overextreme penalties and measures to some. One of the great facts of American response to the recent series of political assassinations has been the tendency of the community to unite against all varieties of extremism, to seek new routes of conciliation and social reform. This is a built-in corrective which, with a little luck, can see us through grave situations.

The rise of revolutionary conditions testifies to the absence or disuse of other channels of political change. Political leaders must keep such alternatives alive and responsive to claims by newly articulate groups. Organized conflict groups tend to use less violent means of combat and bargaining than those which lack organization; therefore, we must seek institutions which offer representation and identity to groups that might otherwise remain inchoate and therefore unstable.

The nation-state is a complex living organism whose growth tends to respond to the interests and desires of those who exercise political, social, and economic power. Most of the great political problems that confront us arise when a previously submerged group acquires new capability for social bargaining. Institutions that serve only established and prevailing power groups will always leave basic social equations to fester beneath the surface of established power. Our institutions must aim at the discovery of new constituencies and new routes of access by which they can generate their own leadership. This is a very real challenge to our ingenuity as political innovators.

In terms of political power, there are no abstract issues, only "who gets what, when, and how?" and "who's doing what to whom?" All situations, however desperate they may be to some, are manageable and tolerable for those who do not suffer them. So long as slum occupants confined their crimes to the ghettos, internalized the disarray of their lives through mental disease or use of narcotics, there was no problem for most of the society. However, with the arrival of self-consciousness, militancy, and incipient organization, the heat is on. Metropolitan pathology ceases to be an abstract issue to be safely exploited, studied, and pacified; it has become the most authentic confrontation of our day. The same might also be said of other new groups that are winning self-identity and organization. When this happens, cheap fixes and evasions no longer serve. Even counterinsurgency and police repression become provocative, ineffective, and self-defeating. Procrastination, tokenism, all the tricks in the old political bag are bankrupt and outworn culturally, morally, economically, and politically. Those who are already articulate and enjoy some assets of social bargaining have a responsibility to save themselves by saving all.

On the other hand, it is futile to sentimentalize either problems or remedies. Conflict, like the search for order and stability, is inevitable in social life. When the priorities of one conflict are somehow terminated, we can be certain that others will take their place, and that they will be as dangerous and insoluble as the ones they replace. To live is to grow, to grow is to strive, to strive is to struggle. We must be sophisticated enough to understand the imperfect justice of all human relations, past, present, and future. It is the unfinished nature of our task that generates the dynamics of politics and gives individual freedom its meaning. Justice is not to be had for any except as the rigors of political bargaining give it status and degree for those who prevail in the shifting compromises of the bargaining process.

Problems of race, like other problems, may be insoluble in the short run. The best we can hope for is to create a sense of movement and a faith in the ultimate efficacy of political solutions. A sense of movement toward solutions is the great thing that generates excitement and nourishes hope. It is the ultimate means of preserving the legitimacy of a whole society.

There has never been a time which was not intensely difficult and perplexing for most of the people of the world. Today's problems always appear immense, while those that appeared the same way a year before are largely forgotten. Is the prevalence of confrontation politics a sign and a mark of schism in the soul of America? The impending end? The answer to this naive and alarmist question is a paradox: conflict is always present in human relations and constitutes a great force in keeping things loose, capable of adaptation and adjustment, ready to endure other trouble-making generations. Political confrontation is "what societies do instead of committing suicide" (Kopkind, 1968, p. 54). Death and transfiguration are the counter-motifs of life and growth.

REFERENCES

Abrahamsen, David. *The Psychology of Crime.* New York: John Wiley & Sons, Inc. 1960.

Arendt, Hannah. "Lawlessness Is Inherent in the Uprooted," *New York Times Magazine,* April 28, 1968.

Berelson, Bernard, and Gary A. Steiner. *Human Behavior: An Inventory of Scientific Findings.* New York: Harcourt Brace Jovanovich, Inc., 1964.

Boeke, Jan. Letter to the Editor, *Science,* November 3, 1967.

Campbell, Angus, and Howard Schuman. "Racial Attitudes in Fifteen American Cities," *Supplemental Studies for the National Advisory Commission on Civil Disorders.* Washington, D.C.: United States Government Printing Office, 1968. Pp. 1–67.

Cleaver, Eldridge. "A Candid Conversation with the Revolutionary Leader of the Black Panthers," *Playboy,* December 1968, pp. 89–108, 238.

Coleman, James S. *Community Conflict.* New York: The Free Press, 1967.

Ellul, Jacques. *The Technological Society.* New York: Random House, Inc., 1964.

Henry, Andrew F., and James F. Short, Jr. *Suicide and Homicide: Some Economic, Sociological, and Psychological Aspects of Aggression.* New York: The Free Press, 1954.

Kopkind, Andrew. "Are We in the Middle of a Revolution?" *New York Times Magazine,* November 10, 1968, pp. 54–59, 64–69.

Kristol, Irving. "The Old Politics, The New Politics, The *New* New Politics," *New York Times Magazine,* November 24, 1968.

Lindesmith, Alfred, and Anselm Strauss. *Social Psychology.* New York: The Dryden Press, 1949.

MacIver, R. M. "The Role of the Precipitant," in Etzioni, 1964, pp. 421–26.

McLuhan, Marshall. *War and Peace in the Global Village*. New York: McGraw-Hill Book Company, 1968.

Mumford, Lewis. *The Myth of the Machine. Technics and Human Development*. New York: Harcourt Brace Jovanovich, Inc., 1967.

Sanger, Richard H. *Insurgent Era*. Washington, D.C.: Potomac Books, Inc., 1967.

Schmookler, Jacob. *Invention and Economic Growth*. Cambridge, Mass.: Harvard University Press, 1966.

Shaw, George Bernard. "The Revolutionist's Handbook," in *Man and Superman*. Cambridge, Mass.: The University Press, 1903. Pp. 177–224.

Tarde, Gabriel. *Penal Philosophy*. Trans. R. Howell. Boston: Little, Brown and Company, 1912.

Warshow, Robert. *The Immediate Experience*. New York: Doubleday & Company, Inc., 1962.

7: Revolution

As George Pettee notes in his essay included here, revolutionary activity has interested political thinkers since classical times. Given this prolonged interest, it is understandable that the word "revolution" should have developed an enormous variety of uses, some of which have been pointed out by Crane Brinton.[1] Exploiting its romantic overtones, advertising men speak easily of "revolutions" in fashion, automotive design, and interior decoration. On a somewhat more serious level, radical changes in scientific thought or artistic styles have also been called revolutionary. It therefore behooves us to note that our use of the word is restricted to the political context.

But even within the political context, the word has a greatly varied usage. **Coups d'état,** violent changes of political leaders without significant changes in political institutions or the distribution of power, have often been described as revolutions by writers on the subject. Indeed, nonviolent parliamentary changes of government have also been called revolutions by political essayists. During the 1950s the American electoral process was widely regarded as constituting a "permanent revolution." Brinton has recalled with some amusement that the Daughters of the American Revolution looked on the actions of their forebears with pride and on the comparable actions of the Russians in this century with horror. Perhaps more in the nineteenth and twentieth centuries than at any previous time the term has acquired a wide range of private meaning for many individuals. Albert Camus, for example, found in the revolutionary act the means of breaking through the isolation of the individual and the grounds for making moral judgments in a universe deprived of absolute criteria.[2] Terry Hoy states that in Camus' view "authentic rebellion is an affirmation" and should be distinguished from totally destructive revolutions, which Camus thought of as a perversion of the rebellious impulse.

Camus was not the only thinker who sought redemption through revolution. Long before him, Marx and Engels, like the utopian socialists they repudiated, looked to revolution as the catalyst for increased humanization of labor and social relations. To Marx, revolution follows from the "Law of Immiserization," the progressive worsening of the conditions of labor. The process of immiserization would unite the working classes, he argued, and bring them to the revolutionary action that leads to a total transformation of society. In their rousing conclusion to the **Communist Manifesto** Marx and Engels asserted:

> The Communists disdain to conceal their views and aims. They openly declare that their ends can be attained only by the forcible overthrow of all existing social conditions. Let the ruling classes tremble at Communist revolution. The proletarians have nothing to lose but their chains. They have a world to win.[3]

1 Crane Brinton, *The Anatomy of Revolution* (New York: Vintage Books, 1959), pp. 3–5.
2 Albert Camus, *The Rebel: An Essay on Man in Revolt* (New York: Alfred A. Knopf, 1956).
3 Karl Marx and Frederick Engels, *The Communist Manifesto* (New York: International Publishers, 1948).

Marx's theory of revolution deals with both subjective and objective conditions.[4] T. Robert Gurr has clearly summarized the objective aspect of Marx's theory:

> Marx finds revolution essentially a function of economic change, specifically the development of contradictions between productive forces of society and the relations of classes to production. There are a succession of historically inevitable stages of economic organization, the penultimate of which, bourgeois capitalism, gives way to the classless society of the workers.[5]

The subjective aspect of Marx's theory centers on the development of "class consciousness" among the workers. As their conditions deteriorate, according to Marx, the proletariat develops a revolutionary class consciousness that will ultimately demand the overthrow of the exploitative capitalist system.[6] In large part Lenin's conception of Marxist tactics dealt with this subjective aspect, focusing on propaganda and agitation as the key to revolutionary success.

In his "Theories of Revolution," Lawrence Stone points out that subjective as well as objective aspects are incorporated in many current explanations of revolution. As he notes, Crane Brinton isolated several characteristics common to the four revolutions he studied. Of these, two might be considered subjective: the alienation of the intellectual and the loss of self-confidence within the ruling elite. The other characteristics are more objective and include the stage of economic development within the prerevolutionary society, class antagonisms, and governmental ineptitude in administration and the use of force.[7]

Stone observes that "the recognition of a lack of harmony between the social system on the one hand and the political system on the other" is fundamental to all analyses of revolution. This recognition of disharmony is present whether or not a particular analysis stresses objective or subjective factors. Barrington Moore, for example, proposes the view that revolution is an attempt at "the forced reintegration of society around new or partially new patterns of behavior."[8] Revolution is an ideologically grounded quest for power that occurs under conditions of "external shock or internal decay." Social or psychological circumstances, he continues, create discontent in individuals and groups. These discontented people seek power in order to do "what should be done to correct" the condition that is perceived as "wrong."[9] On the other hand, Chalmers Johnson, whom Stone considers overly "objective," regards revolution as the result of dysfunctions within society of sufficient magnitude to cause violence. As Stone notes, Johnson contends that if the social strains are profound enough they "may cause the sense of deprivation, alienation, anomie to spread into many sectors of society at once, causing what Johnson calls multiple dysfunction, which may be all but incurable within the existing political system."

Revolutions seek to bring about total or absolute change in the power relationships that obtain within society. As Eugene Kamenka defined the term:

4 C. Wright Mills, *The Marxists* (New York: Dell Publishing Co., 1962).

5 T. Robert Gurr, "The Revolution—Social-Change Nexus," *Comparative Politics*, J 3, (April 1973): 359–92.

6 See Robert C. Tudker, *The Marxian Revolutionary Idea* (New York: W. W. Norton & Co., 1969).

7 Brinton, *op. cit.*, pp. 250–53.

8 Barrington Moore, Jr., "Notes on the Process of Acquiring Power," in *Political Power and Social Theory* (New York: Harper Torch Books, 1965), pp. 1–29.

9 See James Davies, *When Men Revolt and Why* (New York: The Free Press, 1971); and Clifford T. Paynton and Robert Blackey, eds., *Why Revolution? Theories and Analyses* (Cambridge, Mass.: Schenkman Publishing Company, 1971). As suggested in an earlier chapter, the internal and the external needs of a social movement are frequently dysfunctional and contradictory. For example, the Left Wing stresses adopting a "correct position" which generally isolates it from those it wishes to organize.

> Revolution is a sharp, sudden change in the social location of political power, expressing itself in the radical transformation of the process of government, of the official foundations of sovereignty or legitimacy and of the social order.[10]

Revolutions, hence, are characterized by the transfer of power from one social group to another, usually through force or violence. Various significant factors have been thought to precede revolutionary action on a wide scale, but there is considerable disagreement about which of these is of paramount importance. Marx, Brinton, and others see economic fluctuations and the increasing nonlegitimacy of the existing government as necessary preconditions for revolution. Even among these theorists, however, there is considerable disagreement. Marxists argue that economic conflict between classes plays the primary causal role in revolution. Brinton and those who follow him advocate a thesis of "relative deprivation" or rising expectations which is at odds with the immiserization model urged by the Marxists. Both Marx and Brinton posited economically advanced societies as the necessary framework for revolution, while others, such as Lewis Corey and Erich Fromm, argue that economic decline and status crises bring about revolution. Corey and Fromm, as well as many other observers, note that the "decline of the middle class" leads to the development of revolutionary Right-Wing movements.[11] Richard Bendix, however, concluded in his analysis of the rise of the Nazi Party that other factors besides the deprivation of the German middle class brought Hitler to power.[12] Still other observers suggest, as Lawrence Stone noted, that revolutionary temperaments are the primary source of major social unheavals.

We are thus left with the question of whether social conditions or revolutionary consciousness cause revolutions.[13] However the question may be answered, the phenomenon of revolution is with us still and in all likelihood will continue to be problematic for both society and those who study society.

---

[10] Eugene Kamenka, "The Concept of a Political Revolution," in *Revolution Memos VII*, ed. Carl Friedrich (New York: Atherton Press, 1966), p. 124.

[11] Lewis Corey, *The Crisis of the Middle Class* (New York: Covici, Friede, Publishers, 1935); and Erich Fromm, *Escape From Freedom* (New York: Holt, Rinehart and Winston, 1941).

[12] Richard Bendix, "Social Stratification and Political Power," *American Political Science Review* 6 (1952): 357–75.

[13] See T. Robert Gurr, *Why Men Rebel* (Princeton: Princeton University Press, 1970).

Albert Camus:
The Nature of
Political Rebellion

TERRY HOY

It is often observed that the modern age is characterized by a decline of belief in supernatural authority or higher law, as well as a growing disillusionment with scientific reason as a means of defining the ethical foundations of political life. This has fostered the growth of relativist, subjective interpretations of political value which has been viewed with both optimism and alarm. On the one hand, it is defended by those who point to the fact that it has meant the emancipation of man from ideological traditions and dogmas which have often been utilized as defense of political injustice and tyranny; it has nourished libertarian, individualist tendencies in modern life. On the other hand, the rejection of belief in higher law or objective moral standards, it is often argued, paves the way for nihilist ideologies, which would enthrone the supremacy of irrational impulse and force as the ultimate arbiter of political value.

Thus a basic problem of modern man is whether or not it is possible to give rational meaning and value to his existence in an age whether there is no longer confidence that reason can establish absolute or objective truths. This problem takes on special significance where it is concerned with defining the nature and conditions of political revolt and protest. That is, if man, alone, is the sole creator of his values and purposes, does this mean that his freedom is unlimited? Does it imply the nihilist logic that anything is therefore possible—including revolutionary violence and terrorism? Is it possible, in other words, to recognize limits on the exercise of freedom without appeal to higher law or objective truth? Is it possible to define the positive, humane substance of rebellion, as a protest against injustice and tyranny, without embracing the logical extreme of nihilist rebellion?

It is this problem which has been given significant expression in the writings of Nobel prize winner Albert Camus. What is of special significance in Camus' analysis of this question is his effort to show that political rebellion, as the demand for freedom against tyranny and oppression, is incompatible with the ideology of revolutionary nihilism; and that although rebellion involves the negation of belief in God or higher law, it is not a doctrine that sanctions the nihilist creed that everything is possible—including murder or suicide. For authentic rebellion, as opposed to revolutionary nihilism, is an affirmation, as well as negation; an affirmation that the individual person has a worth that should be respected and valued. Revolutionary movements, by deifying the state or "historical destiny," by justifying political terrorism and violence, thus betray the true meaning of rebellion.

In considering Camus' treatment of this problem it is convenient to consider separately three phases of his general argument: first, his characterization of the human condition as an encounter with "absurdity"; secondly, his discussion of revolutionary political nihilism as a false or perverted deduction from the awareness of the absurd; thirdly, his attempt to reconcile absurdist reasoning with the principle of human dignity and limited freedom.

I

The central concern of Camus is the question of how man can give meaning to his life in an "absurd" universe; where the individual becomes conscious that life has no meaning or objective value. The first step, in attempting to answer this problem, is for the mind to distinguish what is true from what is false, but this proves to be a futile endeavor. It was Aristotle, Camus contends, who has best demonstrated this futility. For by asserting that all is true, we assert the truth of the contrary assertion and consequently the falsity of our own thesis. And if we say that all is false, that assertion is itself false. If we declare that solely the assertion opposed to ours is false, or else that solely ours is not false, we are nevertheless forced to admit an infinite number of true or false judgments. For the one who expresses a true assertion proclaims simultaneously that it is true and so on *ad infinitum.* Today people despair of absolute knowledge. Nor can one place any confidence in science:

> You enumerate its laws and in my thirst for knowledge, I admit they are true. You take apart its mechanism and my hope increases. At the final stage you teach me that the wonderous and multi-colored universe can be reduced to the atom, and that the atom itself can be reduced to the electron. All this is good and I wait for you to continue. But you tell me of an invisible planetary system in which electrons gravitate around a nucleus. You explain this world to me with an image. I realize that you have been reduced to poetry. I shall never know. Have I time to become indignant? You have already changed theories. So that science that was to teach me everything ends up in hypothesis, that lucidity founders in metaphor, that uncertainty is resolved in a work of art.[1]

Thus man is confronted with an absurd universe; a horde of irrationals has sprung up and surrounds him until his ultimate end. And what is absurd is the confronting of this irrational, and the wild longing for clarity. The plane

[1] Albert Camus, *The Myth of Sisyphus and Other Essays* (New York: Vintage Books, 1959), p. 15.

of history, declares Camus, illustrates the essential passion of man torn between his urge towards unity and the clear vision he may have of the world closing in on him. "The absurd is born of this confrontation between human need and the unreasonable silence of the world."[2]

It is the concept of the absurd which is the foundation for Camus' analysis of the nature of political rebellion. In his book *The Rebel* Camus attempts to show how the awareness of the absurd (in its perverted and destructive form) becomes a sanction for political nihilism. Camus notes two types of destructive rebellion; metaphysical and historical. Examples of metaphysical rebellion are illustrated in such figures as the Marquis de Sade; the character of Ivan in *Brothers Karamazov;* and in Nietzsche. Sade embodies the absolute negation in the name of nature; the lawless universe where the only master is inordinate energy and desire; the law of the world is nothing but the law of force. Sade preaches the morality of an aristocratic class who would keep the majority in total subjection. Thus, two centuries ahead of time, Sade extolled totalitarian societies in the name of unbridled freedom.

With Ivan Karamazov, declares Camus, the history of contemporary nihilism begins. "If there is no virtue, there is no law. Everything is permitted."[3] In Nietzsche nihilism becomes fully conscious for the first time. Rebellion begins with "God is dead." Christianity is decadent: socialism and humanitarianism are degenerate forms of Christianity, betraying life and nature; substituting ideal for real ends; enervating both the will and imagination. Rid of God and moral idols, then man is alone; without a master. Man thus must create his own values; he becomes a heroic superman dominated solely by the will to power. At this point, Camus contends, metaphysical rebellion proves disastrous to freedom and leads to the justification for tyranny and servitude. It is then that the spirit of metaphysical rebellion openly joins forces with revolutionary movements. For revolution, according to Camus, is the logical consequence of metaphysical rebellion. "Every action of rebellion expresses a nostalgia for innocence and an appeal to the essence of being. But one day nostalgia takes up arms and assumes responsibility of total guilt, in other words adopts murder and violence."[4] Rebellion in itself is limited in scope; it is no more than an incoherent pronouncement. Revolution, on the contrary, originates in the realm of ideas. Specifically it is the injection of ideas into historical experience, while rebellion is only the movement that leads from individual experience to the realm of ideas. Here we have the attempt to shape actions to ideas to fit the world into a theoretical frame.

It is the phenomena of *historical* rebellion which Camus believes is the characteristic quality of revolutionary political movements of the modern world. The year 1789 is the starting point of modern times, because men of this period wished to introduce on the historical scene the forces of negation and rebellion which had been the essence of intellectual discussion in the previous centuries. Rousseau's general will became the gospel of revolutionary impulse: "the new religion whose God is reason confused with nature and whose representative on earth, in place of the king, is the people considered as an expression of the general will."[5]

[2] *Ibid.,* p. 21.
[3] Albert Camus, *The Rebel* (New York: Vintage Books, 1956), p. 57.
[4] *Ibid.,* p. 105.
[5] *Ibid.,* p. 115.

Rousseau, according to Camus, is the first man to justify the death penalty in a civil society, and the absolute submission of the subject to the authority of the sovereign. The year 1789 became the enthronement of Rousseau's principle: the infallibility of the general will as the expression of truth and virtue. State terrorism, in the name of the general will, becomes legitimate and necessary. No dissension of factions can be tolerated. "A patriot is he who supports the Republic in general; whoever opposes it is a traitor."[6]

In Hegel we find the fullest embodiment of historical rebellion. German philosophy substituted for the abstract reason of Rousseau, which soared above the phenomena related to it, a reason incorporated in historical events. Revolutionary movements of the twentieth century have borrowed from Hegel this vision of history without any kind of transcendence, dedicated to perpetual strife and struggle of wills bent on seizing power. Although twentieth-century ideologies have rejected the idealism of Hegel, they have borrowed from Hegel the emphasis upon history as the ultimate arbiter of good and evil, and the absolute state as the incarnation of historical destiny. "Cynicism, the deification of history and of matter, individual terror and state crime, these are the inordinate consequences that will now spring, armed to the teeth, from the equivocal conception that entrusts to history alone the task of producing values and truth."[7]

Russian nihilism of the 1860's is viewed by Camus as a further example of historical rebellion. It enthroned reason and self interest as ultimate values. But instead of skepticism, it chose to propagate a doctrine and embraced socialism. Like all adolescent minds, they simultaneously experienced doubt and the need to believe. Bakunin embodies this contradiction. He rejected Hegelianism, but his passion for religious freedom lead to an emphasis upon revolution as the incarnation of good. The statutes of the International Fraternity which he edited in 1864–67, established the absolute subordination of the individual to the central committee. He hoped to see the liberation of Russia produce a strong dictatorial power, supported by an elite of enlightened partisans—thus anticipating Leninist doctrine. In Russian terrorist doctrines of the 1870's one finds an expression of totalitarian gospel of the twentieth century. For those who dedicate themselves to revolution, according to Nechaev, everything is permitted. "Revolution must have neither romantic relationships nor objects to engage his passion. Every part of him should be concentrated in one passion: the revolution."[8]

All modern revolutions, Camus points out, have ended in the reinforcement of the power of the state: 1789 brings Napoleon; 1848, Napoleon III; 1917, Stalin; and later Mussolini and Hitler. Fascist ideology, however, does not merit the title of revolution, for it lacks the ambition of universality. This is because fascism deified irrational elements of the nihilist inheritance, instead of deifying reason. This is to be found in its extolling of the elemental forces of the individual; the dark power of blood and instinct, the biological justification of all the worst things produced by the instinct of domination. Yet Mussolini makes use of Hegel, and Hitler of Nietzsche, and in this sense, fascism belongs to history of rebellion of nihilism. "They were

[6] *Ibid.*, p. 126.
[7] *Ibid.*, p. 146.
[8] *Ibid.*, p. 160.

the first to construct a state on the concept that everything is meaningless, and history is only written in themes of the hazards of force."[9]

But it is Marxism, rather than fascism, which represents the fullest expression of revolutionary ideology in the twentieth century, with a doctrine and movement based on definitive revolution and final unification of the world. Marx destroys, even more radically than Hegel, the transcendence of reason, and hurls it into the stream of history. Marx was genuinely concerned for the dignity of man. He rebelled against degradation of workers to the level of a commodity and of objects. But the Nietzschean tragedy is evident again in Marx. The aims and prophecies are human and liberal, but the reduction of every value to historical terms leads to dire consequences. Marx thought that the end of history would be moral and rational. "But when good and evil are reintegrated in time, and confused with events, nothing is either good nor bad, but either premature or out of date."[10]

It was Lenin who shaped Marxism into a revolutionary weapon which repudiated the limits of formal morality, identifying revolutionary action with the strategy and expedience for seizure of political power. This led Lenin to justify the repressive power of the state to achieve the aims of communism. Thus the regime of Russian Stalinism, as an implementation of Leninist principles, witnessed the establishment of a totalitarian political system in which all ideological dissent was crushed, police terrorism enthroned, and private relations subordinated to an inhuman abstract world of power and calculation.

II

Camus' analysis of revolutionary political movements show how negation of belief in transcendental values leads to the justification of political tyranny and totalitarianism. Revolutionary ideologies of the modern world are the expression of a moral nihilism which proceeds from the logic that since there are no objective values, then everything is permitted, including murder. Thus, the awareness of the absurd, when we first claim to deduce a rule of behavior from it, makes murder seem a matter of indifference. If we believe in nothing; if nothing has any meaning; if we can affirm no values whatsoever, then everything is possible. There is no pro or con; the murderer is neither right nor wrong. But Camus attempts to show that absurdist analysis, in its most important deduction, finally condemns murder, and repudiates the logic of revolutionary political nihilism. How does Camus arrive at this conclusion? The initial premise is that where one accepts the concept of the absurd; where he confronts it squarely and honestly he cannot, without being contradictory, embrace the logic of murder or suicide. Why? Because in being fully conscious and aware of the absurd, I am aware of the impossibility of reducing the world to rational solutions; this is the only thing that I know: my appetite for unity and the impossibility of reducing the world to rational principle. As such, this constitutes commitment to the absurd as a principle; I cannot mask it, escape it, or deny any one of its terms. Therefore, I cannot accept the logic of murder or suicide, for this would, in effect,

[9] *Ibid.*, p. 178.
[10] *Ibid.*, p. 209.

drown the absurd; it would nullify and destroy its very meaning. From this conviction, I am led to the recognition that human life is the only good, since it is precisely life that makes the absurdist logic possible, and since without life, the absurdist wager would have no basis. "To say that life is absurd the conscience must be alive. . . . From the moment that life is recognized as good, it becomes good for all men."[11]

It is on the basis of this reasoning, then, that revolutionary political actions stand condemned, for it betrays the authentic meaning of rebellion as an affirmation, as well as renunciation. A slave, for example, who has taken orders all his life, suddenly decides that he cannot obey some new command. But by saying "no" the slave is not only making a negation, he is also affirming that there is something in him that is worth while, and that there is a point beyond which an oppressive authority cannot be tolerated. In this sense the rebel affirms something which is the common ground of all men.

It is for this reason that revolutionary action, according to Camus, is not compatible with the authentic meaning of rebellion. Revolution, it was seen, justifies political terrorism and murder. But murder and rebellion are contradictory. For rebellion (in its authentic sense) is a force of life and not death; it is a logic of creation and not destruction. If it is to remain authentic, it must be the father to the "yes," as well as to the "no" that nihilist interpretation isolates in rebellion. Historical revolution, therefore, betrays rebellion, because it supposes the absolute malleability of human nature and its possible reduction to the condition of a historical force. "But rebellion in man is the refusal to be treated as an object and to be reduced to simple historical terms. It is the affirmation of a nature common to all men which eludes the world of power."[12]

Rebellion therefore, is not a claim to absolute freedom. Rebellion, itself, aspires only to the relative. It supposes a limit at which the community of man is established. Its universe is the universe of relative values. It is here, Camus believes, that rebellion cannot exist without a strange form of love.

> Those who can find no rest in God, or in history, are condemned to live for those who, like themselves, cannot live; in fact for the humiliated . . . Rebellion proves that it is the very movement of life and that it cannot be denied without renouncing life. Its purest outburst, on each occasion, gives forth to existence. Thus it is love or fecundity, or it is nothing at all. Revolution without honor, calculated revolutionary movements which, in preferring an abstract concept of man to a man of flesh and blood, denies existence as many times as is necessary, puts resentment in place of love. . . . It is no longer either revolution or rebellion, but rancor, malice and tyranny.[13]

III

Camus focuses attention on a basic ideological problem of twentieth-century political thought. What is the value and contribution of his analysis? So far as practical political implications are concerned, Camus' argument cannot be considered wholly satisfactory. Camus recommends political mod-

[11] *Ibid.*, p. 6.
[12] *Ibid.*, p. 250.
[13] *Ibid.*, p. 305.

eration, in contrast to revolutionary political action, and he has advocated socialist planning along the Scandinavian model, as well as the strengthening of trade-union activity. But Camus' views on contemporary political affairs, vigorously expressed in his journalistic writings,[14] embody an uncompromising commitment to moral principle which tends to alienate him from contemporary realities of power politics. This is illustrated, for example, in his repudiation of European governments for acceptance of Franco Spain into UNESCO; his emphasis upon a politics of nonviolence; his insistence that the only solution to the danger of atomic war between East and West is the establishment of a democratic world government.[15] Here, Camus is vulnerable to the charge that he is taking refuge in a purist, utopian idealism out of touch with problems of practical politics.

But it may be said, in defense of Camus, that he does not pretend to be a practical politician, and that he should be judged on the merits of his ethical position. Here one may at least concede the general validity of his conviction that authentic rebellion must acknowledge the value of human dignity and freedom, and that these values are betrayed by extremist forms of revolutionary political action. The more basic question is whether Camus has succeeded in establishing that these values can be given a philosophical foundation which does not require appeal to objective or transcendental truth. Now obviously, Camus' contention that matters of political value cannot be given rational or objective certitude is of course debatable (although here he is in company with highly influential intellectual tendencies such as logical positivist analysis). But it is not the point here to debate the issue of whether an objective value theory is possible. What is more important is Camus' reasoning that although it is not possible to define human existence in terms of objective or transcendental values, this does not justify nihilist reasoning that anything is possible; but that on the contrary, it leads to a respect for human dignity and limited freedom. Is Camus entitled to this deduction? Camus suggests that where one fully acknowledges and accepts the absurd; when one makes this into a principle, then one cannot, without contradiction, sanction murder or suicide, since this would nullify or destroy the absurd: one is then betraying his own principles.

But the crucial question is whether Camus is entitled to say that the recognition of absurdity as a logical or factual condition of my existence leads to the recognition of human dignity freedom as a value. In other words, can one deduce an *ought* from an *is;* a *value* from a supposed *fact.* Here Camus is vulnerable to the criticism made by logical positivists, such as Ayer, who contends that Camus is getting involved in what is essentially a metaphysical question about which philosophical analysis is impossible.[16] One does sense that despite Camus' refusal to appeal to metaphysics or to religious faith, he is actually committed in somewhat those terms. That is, one senses that there are two dimensions to Camus for which he does not quite succeed in providing a philosophical bridge. One side of Camus is his attachment to

---

[14] Camus contributed actively to the newspaper *Combat* during the period 1944–48. A selection of his editorials has been brought together in a single volume entitled: *Actuelles* (Paris: Libraire Gallimaird), 1950. A second volume contains other articles and interviews during the period 1948–53.

[15] See *Actuelles,* I, 160–74; 183–207.

[16] A. J. Ayer, "Novelist-Philosophers," *Horizon,* VIII (March 1946) 155–168.

the importance of reason and lucidity. Although there are no objective a priori values which reason can establish, one must, nonetheless, live in terms of what reason can illuminate; one is not entitled to an irrational leap into faith. But the other side of Camus is his obvious passionate and emotional commitment to human freedom and dignity; his hatred of tyranny and oppression. It is this side of Camus where one senses an intensity of commitment which strikes one as something more than a cool logical deduction from his philosophical concept of the absurd.

But such criticism, while it points up an apparent paradox or dilemma in Camus' philosophy, does not do him justice. For if one agrees that objective or a priori values are not possible, then it is difficult to see how one can logically avoid the dangers of ideological nihilism, unless one argues somewhat in the terms which Camus suggests (however inadequate this may be). There are, of course, other alternative positions if one wishes to repudiate the appeal to reason altogether. From the standpoint of logical positivists this amounts to the contention that the kinds of questions Camus is asking are not amenable to philosophical inquiry at all, and that we must accept the fact that value judgments about the meaning of individual existence are ultimately irrational in character. In this case we are apparently left with the choice of either assuming a deterministic explanation in regard to ethical choices (environmental conditioning, childhood training, etc.) or we affirm a religious faith as an alternative to reason. Good arguments can be made for either of these possibilities, but they are not satisfactory where one insists (as Camus does) that one cannot escape or evade responsibility by assuming a deterministic or irrational explanation for individual choice and decision.

It is here that Camus' argument reveals its true merits. Camus insists upon the point that in recognizing the limits of reason we do not therefore negate it. The one thing we do know is our appetite for unity, and yet the impossibility of reducing the world to rational principle. We must live with what we know. We cannot escape into faith, for this would be to retreat in face of what the mind has brought to light. Here we are called upon to adopt the logic of the absurd man, who is conscious that reason cannot give him certainty, but who insists that he must live without appeal.

> At a certain point on his path the absurd man is tempted. History is not lacking in either religions or prophets, even without Gods. He is asked to leap. All he can reply is that he doesn't fully understand, that it is not obvious. Indeed he does not want to do anything but what he fully understands. . . . Hence what he demands of himself is to live *solely* with what he knows, to accommodate himself to what is, and to bring in nothing that is not certain. He is told that nothing is. But that is at least a certainty. And it is with this that he is concerned; he wants to find out if it is possible to live *without appeal.*[17]

Perhaps Camus does not establish that this is possible. Perhaps it is true (as we are often told) that man cannot live without appeal to religious faith; to higher law, or to some kind of external authority. One cannot say that Camus settles this question, but he has confronted it with imagination, courage, and honesty.

[17] Camus, *The Myth of Sisyphus and Other Essays,* p. 39.

Revolution—Typology and Process

GEORGE PETTEE

Revolution has been a subject of interest to political philosophy ever since political thought in our Western tradition had its origins. The intensity of the interest has varied, however. It was strong in the classical period, when revolutions in the city-states were frequent, sometimes progressive or fruitful, often destructive or regressive, and commonly bitter and bloody. Interest lagged in the Middle Ages, but was reborn when the Italian cities renewed those conditions in which factional strife and intercity rivalry provided conditions conducive to political malaise. During this period revolution served sometimes as a corrective, but often only as an aggravation. Machiavelli, in his *Discourses,* is generally preoccupied with revolution, or with its opposite, the problem of political stability. Since his time revolution and stability have always rated the attention and effort of political thinkers.

The great period of strife which we call the Reformation widened the horizon. Political thought throughout Europe was at a most intense level of activity, and with or without the label "revolution," the problem of violent change of government, its justification or its lack thereof, its occasions and its causes, lay in the center of concern for the designers of just government, and for the factional arguments of monarchomachists and antimonarchomachists, Jesuits and Calvinists and Politiques.

The thinking of the Politiques, and such doctrines as those of Althusius on the social-political structure of the state, found a laboratory in England. Here the issue of the relative power of the Crown and Parliament became crucial to the solution of the clash of churches, and to the relationship between England and Scotland. This was the situation that called forth the principles of Hobbes, that the state is always necessary and always better than factional strife, and those of Locke, that government exists by basic constitutional agreement, with a right of revolution as redress for violation of the contract. Since then also, revolution has been subject to theoretical treatment by jurisprudence as well as by political thought.

The American Revolution passed with little fresh impact on thought, partly because the men who conducted it were well aware of Locke, and

able to translate the concept of the "right of revolution" into a highly pertinent interpretation of a new situation, as they did in the Declaration of Independence. It was the first major instance of separation of a colony of
Europe from European authority; America was truly a colony, that is, a
people derived by migration rather than by conquest. It was also an example
of a case in which a people able to expel the government of the colonial
empire was also well able to govern itself.

After the American Revolution came the French Revolution. Both bore
the name of revolution. Beyond that, they had little in common. The French
Revolution was an explosive release of energy, in a country growing in all its
powers, destroying a system of authority that had failed to grow in capacity
to function as a state. It brought not one but a dozen violent shifts of power.
It brought the Rights of Man, and eventually the Code Napoléon. It released
a reign of terror; drew upon itself the intervention of all conservative
powers, and its military rejoinder shook the whole structure of Europe. In
the world of thought it put forth doctrines that echoed Locke and Rousseau,
and tried to echo Montesquieu on the design of a government. It left the
fundamental repudiation of privilege and the affirmation of some sort of
equality so established that they could not be effectively denied thereafter,
though much more than a century has passed and practice has not yet come
into full stride with those theories.

The French Revolution also provoked the thought of Burke and von
Gentz. They saw the shallowness of its utopianism and its sham aspects, and
its destructiveness to the fibers of stability and confidence in a well-ordered
society. Burke confidently downgraded the physical power of Revolutionary
France, seeing the wreck of its economy in its credit structure, and failing to
see its booming growth of energy. But he also saw and lamented that "in
ability, in dexterity, and in the distinctness of their views, the Jacobins are
our superiors." (Second Letter on the Proposal for a Peace with the Regicide
Directory of France.) After Napoleon had departed the scene and something called "Restoration" had occurred, there was left a strong residue of
conviction that revolution can be necessary and justified, though also that its
excesses can be deplorable.

There followed shortly the succession of revolutions in Spanish America
that made all the area from Mexico to the Argentine free of rule by Spain.
By 1830 there was a new round of outbreaks in Europe, and in 1848 a more
pronounced one showed how powerful were the forces whose political character was *not* effectively geared to the half-modernized governments of that
time.

On the side of political action there was an advance of parliamentary
forms of government. This was overshadowed, however, by the implementation of nationalism, especially in Italy and in Germany. As an idea, nationalism
was not a well-rooted branch of political theory; it was rather a necessary
replacement for the Divine Right of Kings. It had the force of reality; a
national people could be a new basis of political accounts. The growth of
nationalism throughout Europe did as much to liquidate the stubborn residues of feudalism as did the idea of democracy.

Out of the experiences of 1830 and 1848 there arose seriously analytic
considerations of the causes of revolution, and of a stable political system
immune to revolution. The idea of stability had been dealt with at length

by Aristotle and by Machiavelli, but not in the context of the industrial revolution. The idea of revolution similarly had lacked the insights afforded by
the changes of property and production organization that occurred in the
late eighteenth and early nineteenth centuries. Marx, Engels, and others
wrote perceptive short historical accounts of several crises, as we would
call them, in the middle of the century. At the same time Disraeli and his
government were constructing an articulated system of power that made the
English people a major organ of the English State and assured the State's
continuing responsiveness. This work had started far earlier of course, as
Namier has done much to show (*Crossroads of Power*, 1962, and other works
on British political development), and it still awaited Bagehot to explain
the design after the construction.

Marx went on, of course, to create a vast ideological superstructure
founded on materialism as philosophic base, on the dialectics of action and
reaction in historical sequence, on the role of the proletariat as the embodiment of virtue and enlightenment, and on revolution as the handmaid of
progress.

This construction contained elements well suited to the needs and purposes of Lenin. Marxism was for him something like a staff college, where
he learned to analyze a situation and mastered the tactics of revolutionary
action. Here emerged the revolutionary technique, which could be combined
with the intrinsic occasion and purpose for a true revolution, or could be
separated from it as an effective instrument in a power struggle for the
world, with little regard for the merit of an occasion for its use. Russia had
a revolution, the greatest since the great French Revolution. It was preceded
by a decay of effectiveness in government comparable to that in the Old
Regime in France. Lenin was skillful and successful in seizing power, and
then in consolidating the one-party Communist system, which hardened into
Stalinism.

The period between the wars had much to teach about revolutions. The
First World War had brought a great revolution in Russia and less drastic
ones in several other nations, including Germany, Austria, Hungary, and
Turkey. Soon there was the Kuomintang victory in China. Lawrence of
Arabia had raised a revolution of national liberation among the Arabs, and
found the truth that the expulsion of alien rulers can be accomplished by a
people long before they can rule themselves. That lesson had been writ
large in Latin America earlier, but it was not read and understood. It is
still being written, and perhaps we have begun to read it. Meanwhile such
writers as Laski went on examining the principles of revolution and finding
the argument for the justice of revolution inescapable, given the possibilities
of failure by an old regime and of lethargy and stupidity in a ruling class.
One important new observation was made however, by Duguit and by
Seldes. Each of them pointed out, though in different contexts and different
idioms, that the modern industrial state is simply too delicate an organism
to permit revolution à la France. The disruption of the modern social services would bring a paralyzing economic collapse that would make the
luxury of such violence and disorder as in the classic revolutions impossible.

The last three decades have produced a new mass of experience, and new
realms of thought. Hitler conducted a revolution in Germany, using the
opportunity afforded by the great economic depression, and Nazism thor-

oughly alienated all those who had clung to the doctrine that revolution is probably just and necessary. The prosecution of revolutionary tactics by the Communists was all too evidently focused on world power, and all too evidently separate from the intrinsic needs or causes of historical revolution. Because of these obvious abuses of revolutionary technique, modern thinkers are more willing to lend a hand to the analysis of problems of counterinsurgency than their immediate predecessors were. Revolution seems farther away than ever before in those most advanced nations which, according to Marxism, should be most ripe for it. The means and methods of stable constitutional government, adaptable to changing problems, with an increasingly well-integrated linkage of government to people, seem to be making headway. Russian and Chinese Communists still conduct subversion, but not in full harmony. There are few books that offer clear theoretical propositions in this situation, but vast activities are predicated on the feasibility of conducting affairs generally in nations, and between them, so that all necessary measures can be taken. Weak regimes exist in many places, but they are not left to their own resources, economic or intellectual. One of the deepest tenets of the time is that the old-fashioned revolution is no longer needed as "the locomotive of history," that revolution leads only to tyranny, and that constitutional democracy need not fail. The Chinese Communists of course feel differently. The ideas that win will be those that win in the world of action.

TYPES

In order to discuss revolutions more clearly it is essential to define some classes. For initial purposes the following types serve fairly well to separate likes from unlikes.

A type that may be called the private palace revolution occurred many times in earlier history, but is less common today. The story told by Shakespeare of the murder of Duncan by Macbeth, and Macbeth's succession, is an illustration. It was conducted within one building; it involved very few people; the public had no information of it until after the fact. The general cultural circumstances were permissive, but the causes lay within the personalities of Macbeth and his wife.

Another type is the public palace revolution. These have occurred many times from our oldest to our most recent history. The event is more elaborate and much larger in scale than in the private type. Typically, there may be movements of troops about a city and a small battle at the palace. The public knows that something is going on, but it did not initiate the event, and takes little part in it. The causation is involved with economic and political issues, but at the level of organized factions. It is not linked to major economic and social contradictions. The new rulers are not altogether outsiders to the prevailing ruling class; and the new regime and old regime are not very different. Although the term *coup d'état* is used rather loosely, its most frequent and significant manifestations belong to this public palace revolution type. One need not look far away in time for good examples. They have occurred in Korea, in Vietnam, in Iraq, in Syria, in Brazil, and in several other countries.

Next in significance, of the recognized types, is the rebellion of an area against rule by the government of another country. Such a movement arises from large-scale social factors, involves large-scale military action, or at least the realistic threat of such action, and strong popular support. It is generally regarded as right and just. It reflects a considerable cultural advance by the rebellious people. A people submissive to foreign rule has become hostile to such rule, able to defy it, capable of expelling it, and to some unspecified degree, capable of providing a government for itself.

It is difficult to think of a case of rebellion that was not preceded either by the conquest of the rebellious people, or by true migratory colonization. Conquest is seldom mentioned in the context of revolution, yet it would seem as revolutionary, in the nonmilitary sense, for the conquered, as is rebellion for the liberated. Since history is predominantly told by the winners in such events, there is a bias here. We know of the conquest of Peru from Spanish sources rather than from Inca sources, and the violent revolution that was inflicted on the Incas passes as an incident of Spanish expansion. So for Clive in India, or Cecil Rhodes in South Africa. Yet these imposed revolutions are important, for they measure the condition of a people at one time as subjugable, just as their rebellion at a later time measures their emergence to a higher level of competence and activity.

The most important of the recognized types, however, is the type of which the French and the Russian Revolutions are the classic examples. They may be called the great national revolutions. One could almost regard one of them as a rebellion without spatial separation of the rebellious from the former rulers. Changes have occurred; a people that was subjugable has grown out of its passivity. A ruling class, separated from a formerly passive people by the privileges of power and property and culture, has remained isolated, has decayed in function, in leadership capacity, and in motivation toward measures needed for the growth and advancement of the society or community. Here we have a mass phenomenon, a people rejecting its government and the ruling class. It moves by plan, but the events constantly contradict the plans, and the results can be measured only long after the event. The social and political structure is drastically reorganized. Not every law is changed, but very great changes in the laws do occur, and public law is almost entirely changed. There is widespread violence, acute bitterness, brutality, and intense mass emotion. The process is in some respects like the business cycle, a mass action by a great number of individuals, with the course and outcome on a basis that is statistically and historically logical, *but not understood by the participants.*

There is one more class of historic event which is rarely mentioned in discussion of revolution, but which may deserve an important place in such a discussion. This I will call, for the sake of a label, a systemic revolution. The "system" referred to is not the internal social and political system; rather it is the system of state organization, the type state, for a wider human area than a single state.

Within Western history we have had several distinct state systems. In the earliest historical times there were tribes, and at quite an early time there were empires, originating in the Near or Middle East. Then there arose, in Greece and in nearby Asia Minor, and elsewhere about the Mediterranean littoral, the city-state. There were numerous examples of this type of political organization. The rise of the city-states reached a phase at which the Empire of Persia attempted to suppress the Greek cities. Persia was defeated. So for a time, some centuries before, and a little time after, there was the city-state system. Its strength, its progress, its growth, all led to conditions in which its supersession was inevitable. Great processes of change, with great wars and much violence, intervened between the time when the city-state flourished and the next time of stability, under the Augustan settlement of the Roman Empire. Thucydides recognized these civil wars as the first great revolutionary wars. They came in series, because the sides did not well understand what they were fighting about. So there were several Peloponnesian Wars, followed by several Punic Wars, and several Roman "social wars."

The change from the state system at the time of Pericles to that at the time of Augustus stands as the first great systemic revolution of which we know much detail. The second is the one we call "the fall of Rome." The third, oddly, we know as "the Renaissance and the Reformation." The fourth we think of mainly by its wars, World War I and World War II.

For each of these it is easy to identify an *ancien régime*, and (except for the last case) easy to identify a postrevolutionary system. Each involved exceptionally severe wars, recognized later as of civil war character in many respects. Each was conducted to a great extent, including the conduct of its wars, under ideas and doctrines that had little relevance to its main political effect. Each affected a human area recognized as constituting a cultural community, though a larger and less intense one than has generally been organized as a single state (with the exception of the case of Rome). In each case, a state system stood as the political order for the larger community, as a single state may stand for a smaller and more closely knit area.

CHARACTERISTICS

The classes are not absolute, they make a continuum. Those most typical of their own classes are markedly different. Those on the margins are close to the nearest specimens in the next class. There is a need to classify, but neither need nor reason for rigidity.

If the classification makes sense, then the characteristic features of a revolution will vary a great deal according to class. The characteristic traits of the great national revolutions such as the French or the Russian are more complex and significant than those of conquest, rebellion, or palace revolution.

Given a revolution and the hypothesis of social causation, we have first to scrutinize the prerevolutionary society. This is not as easy as it sounds and historians have given rather scanty effort to it. But we do have the ordinary record of what may have seemed either a dull period, as in France, or a period much concerned with extraneous matters, as in Russia. In retrospect, however, a great deal of memoir material is produced, and is added to evidence from sources ignored in their own time, and recognized only by hindsight. Various men did say in France that the system was decrepit. Madelin quotes Calonne, in the sharp language of a good policy memorandum:

> France is a kingdom composed of separate states and countries, with mixed administrations, the provinces of which know nothing of each other, where certain districts are completely free from burdens the whole weight of which is borne by others, where the richest class is the most lightly taxed, where privilege has upset all equilibrium, where it is impossible to have any common rule or common will: necessarily it is a most imperfect kingdom, very full of abuses, and in its present condition impossible to govern.
> —Louis Madelin, *The French Revolution*, p. 11.

This is a description of the decay that created the opportunity for new ideas to come in all at once, without earlier assimilation. Also, note well, the faults in France that Calonne emphasized were most definitely absent from the restored regime after the revolution was over. The sheer disorder and the lack of power of reform had been most thoroughly done away with. There is less than due emphasis in the histories on these aspects of the revolution.

Less specifically, in a prerevolutionary society there is a general alienation of public feeling. The state structure has failed to change with the times; and regions and classes alike feel antagonism to the government and to each other. Anomie is a good short name for it. But anomie implies a lack of spirit. The lack of spirit is more apparent than real, as becomes all too evident when the backed-up flood is released.

Low synergism, or high entropy, could also serve as terms for the condition. The state of society is one of general frustration or cramp. The system of laws and administration does not make it easy to do constructive things. Enterprise is stifled. And enterprise is there; it is not a passive or inert society. Among the important observations is the fact that there is not less but more wealth than formerly, though less than there should be. There is also more talent and more education than formerly, though less than there should be and less well employed than it should be. The society is ready for greater economic and cultural progress, and needs a better order. Meanwhile the overt symptoms emerge, including the transfer of the loyalty of the intellectuals, expressed in satire and criticism. The Cahiers of 1789 and the elections for the Third Estate expressed the downright depth of feeling.

In the same period, before the revolution, when the need for reform is widely felt and widely recognized, various efforts at reform are made. But the issues involved are complex and controversial, the sources of favorable power are prevented from making the necessary changes. Needs are not clearly formulated or their formulation gains little support. Political leaders of great talent and energy appear, but they lose the support of the ruling groups and, in turn, the support of the formal source of authority, the King or the Czar. Strafford in England, Turgot and Necker in France, Stolypin in Russia, and others, all had careers that proved that the old system was past reform, even for a man of the highest caliber. While the legend is strongly laid that all prerevolutionary authorities are inept, incompetent, stupid, or frivolous, the record is also clear that the system did not fail without the struggle of one or a few great men to save it, and their defeat.

The failure of the great prerevolutionary reformer-conservative is of course a very important detail. This, if anything, measures the decrepitude of the ruling system, and the disparity between its effectiveness and the activities required.

Sometime after the defeat of the major reformer comes a breakdown of the state. A revolution may have been predicted by this stage; yet the real start comes unannounced. The incapacity of the state to deal with some simple fact brings a crisis; the demand that something be done reveals that some new agency must be created, and suddenly men know that a revolution has begun. In France, the financial breakdown of the treasury brought a need for new fiscal measures, so the Estates General had to be called, after more than a century without it. The immediate bargaining between the powers, the Estates and the Crown, brought the order for dissolution; and this order, in turn, brought the rebellious Tennis Court Oath, which Brinton identified as the real beginning of the revolution.

Just after a revolution has begun, and the participants have become aware of its onset, there has been a sort of era of good feeling. Enthusiasm and optimism and friendly feelings and mutual congratulations on the happy state of affairs are expressed on all sides. This lasts until urgent problems present themselves, new controversies emerge, and the struggle for policy turns into a struggle for power. The time of good feeling is brief.

Thereafter there is an extraordinarily energetic ideological period. The revolution has all the marks of being highly doctrinaire. The question is, Just what doctrine does it follow? In retrospect there is far more than enough doctrine, and an active, intellectually kinetic swarming of ideas. This ideological life serves the purpose of examining all relevant ideas, experimenting with many possible systems. Every possible speech is made. The influence of ideas is quite apparent afterward, but this is partly because hindsight has enabled us to select the influential speeches and writings and ignore the others. The French Revolution, with its succession of factions, its series of constitutions, and its numerous palace revolutions or *coups d'état*, is the best example of this. If they were all disciples of Rousseau or of the Encyclopedists, still they guillotined each other.

Every one of the great revolutions has seen more than one fundamental *coup d'état* to effect a shift in power. There were only a few of these in the English case, though Pride's Purge was clearly one. There were few again in the Russian Revolution, though there was a near success by Kornilov before the Bolshevik coup in October, and earlier, the Soviets had exercised power simultaneously with the regular government. In France there was a long succession of power shifts, of which the great coup of the 9th Thermidor ending the Reign of Terror, and the 18th Brumaire, when Bonaparte seized power, are only the most famous.

These mark a condition not anticipated in the first glow of success. The conduct of the revolution has become a subject for wide and bitter divergence. The illegal seizure of power is now a tactical measure. Civil war is at least latent, if not acute, and there may be several. Issues are regional as well as national, and where they are regional the territorial basis for civil war is good. So England fought a long and complex civil war, with established fronts through long winters; France fought a most savage civil war in the Vendée; the Russian Bolsheviks had to fight civil wars all around, in the Ukraine, in Siberia, in the Caucasus.

Civil wars have one certain effect: there is a winner and a loser. The winner retains the means to enforce his power over the loser and the terms are unconditional surrender. Some of the losers emigrate, some are dead, some are jailed, and some are pacified. There are many factors that can distort the result, but generally the side that can prove it is the stronger can win, and the victor belong the spoils.

A period of foreign intervention frequently accompanies the civil wars. England and to some extent Russia are exceptions to this rule. In the case of England, Richelieu had enough to do in France and in Germany without attempting adventures in England, and most of the rest of Europe was busy with the Thirty Years' War during the early years of the Great Rebellion. In Russia, the Bolsheviks were in power for a year before the Armistice ended World War I. The victorious Western allies had ample means to intervene in Russia in 1919, but little clarity of policy or motivation to do so. There was intervention, but not to much effect. France was quite a different case. The revolution in France challenged the foundations of all the European order. The concept of nationalism was useful; but republicanism, the abolition of feudalism, regicide, and expropriations were scandalous and subversive. France found herself at war with all Europe from 1792 intermittently until 1815. Those wars made the revolution more European, and less exclusively French. And they served to motivate the organization of effort that left France the most unified of nations.

During civil wars there is a great deal of violence, and much of it is not conducted by the rules of civilized warfare. Civilians murder troops; ambush is commonplace; conspiracies are everywhere, and are suspected even where they don't exist. Methods of the police state are added to the partisan or guerrilla warfare; the argument for terror and counterterror is raised and followed. The system of investigation and trial is overloaded, and special courts and procedures of summary nature are instituted. The French Revolutionary Tribunal and the Russian Cheka are matched in other revolutionary crises, as in Spain in 1936. This period of partisan strife and terror contributes to the strength of the apparatus available to the victorious regime thereafter, and for the readiness of all concerned to abate the struggle.

At last there is a postrevolutionary society. The new regime is securely founded, and has proven its ability to make good its power by force. The fulfillment of a revolutionary plan is only started, if ever there was one. The greatest changes are the elimination of a vast mass of old abuses and old barriers to economic life, the reshuffling of property, and the replacement of nearly all the former ruling class by a new one. It distorts the point to call this a ruling class. It is surely the class composed of those who take part in ruling the society, but it may be drawn from various classes by any other definition. At any rate, the new men have made good their claims in a stiff competition; they are not there because their fathers were. Then there can be a restoration, as in France, but the restoration is only of an apparent form of government. The new linkage between government and society, once established, cannot be quickly done away. A regime in the *old* form can more or less govern the *new* state, but the ills that Calonne described cannot be brought back.

When the revolution is past men are not hesitant to describe it in definite terms. They recount its causes and purposes, identify the ideas that influenced it, see the result of the trial of power, the successes and mistakes of leaders. There is one difficulty. They go on writing books about the revolution, and as soon as there are many books there are many variations in the account given. Paul Farmer's study of the history of the French Revolution as written by French historians constitutes one of the most important observations on revolution that can be made. He shows that each of the successive schools of French opinion that have existed since it occurred has produced a different version of it, and that an objective history, therefore, has yet to be written. Perhaps it needs greater events than the Revolution to release the enduring tensions that distort interpretation. But history is conducted in extensional life and reality, and the simply true history may well be a Utopian illusion, without at all implying that history is thereby devalued. One of the most important aspects of the French Revolution or any other event is, for us, its effect on ourselves and our circumstances. So we may still find history useful, though it go on changing forever.

The great changes of state system have not been type classified in any familiar school of thought. However, when examined they have surprisingly many of the traits that might be expected.

In each of them there has been a mighty series of wars. In the first, those wars went on from the time of Pericles to the time of Augustus; then there were the wars we call the barbarian invasions. The third systemic change was the religious wars of the Reformation, and in the most recent case we have, so far, World War I and World War II.

Each of the systemic revolutions started from a well-defined general political system of a very wide human area. In some respects the cultural level of the whole area was similar. The area involved in the revolution has been cognate with the type of culture area with which Spengler and Toynbee have been concerned. Only in the case of the Roman Empire was a state system established in the form of a single formally organized state and government.

In each case the need for a change of system was somewhat apparent before the change occurred. Thucydides was filled with a sense of the vast and tragic alteration of the Greek community in the Peloponnesian Wars. He also saw the curious lack of decision in the first war, and the unrecognized, unresolved tensions that required the second phase of what he insisted was a single war divided only by a "treacherous truce." So with the Punic Wars, they were fought in series because the issue was not understood in the first one. With the social wars of Rome too, only the succession of several wars could bring a final settlement.

The last phase of the classical systemic revolution that submerged the city-state in the Roman Empire has been very well portrayed by Ronald Syme, in his too little known book *The Roman Revolution* (1939). The evidence he offers shows how a new state arose, displacing the city of Rome itself as a community, as a state, and as a government.

The exceptional case of course is the fall of Rome. That has been given a degree of attention as great as it deserves, but scarcely yet in the manner of modern analytic social science. There was of course a decay in Rome, in discipline and capability. There was also a rise of capability in the barbarians; they were more formidable than the Gauls, whom Caeser defeated so handily. Yet they were of lower organization and technology than Rome. (A striking fact is that, though the Romans made bricks throughout the period of the Empire, medieval Europe was without new brick for centuries.)

So there was a systemic revolution. It adapted a state system suitable to the new peoples planted on the remains of Rome, from Britain to the Balkans. This system, which we call feudalism, linked the administration of land, to the administration of territory; *dominium* was what we think of as property ownership and government combined, and it was qualified by the higher dominium of an echelon of power, from baron to count to duke to king to emperor. There was also the parallel power of the Church. This is not the place for any extended treatment. It is only necessary to identify this as a state system, different from Rome, and different because its peoples could not operate the Roman one, and needed one fitted to their competence.

The Renaissance and Reformation is the set of words with which we obscure the revolution or transition from the medieval to the modern state system. Before it there was the *ancien régime*, the medieval system; after it there was the Europe of the Baroque, the Europe of the Peace of Westphalia, the Europe of Cromwell, of Richelieu, of Shakespeare, of Galileo and Newton, and of Bodin and Locke and Hobbes.

These great changes have not been classified as have the great national revolutions, and they have been immune to some of the tendencies exhibited in interpreting the others. It has not been charged that they were planned and executed by a conspiratorial faction. They have not been conducted by men preaching relevant theoretical doctrine. Not that theoretical doctrine was absent, it was rife enough in all cases. The speeches in Thucydides, the memoirs of Caesar, the vast outpourings of books and pamphlets of the eighteenth century, and the flood of divergent doctrines in this century are ideological and doctrinaire and theoretical, but for the most part they do not even talk about the major effect of all the events with which they are concerned. It was only long afterward that men recognized that a new system had replaced Rome or that the nation-state was a new thing replacing the system of medieval Europe.

The great civil wars of the unrecognized systemic revolutions have had many of the traits that set other great civil wars apart from ordinary wars between states. They surpass international wars in severity and brutality and in the degree of exhaustion of the loser. They are marked by technical and tactical advances, with major changes in the military art. Thucydides noted all these characteristics, and Caesar and Theodoric and Gustavus confirmed them. They are marked also by confusion about ends; announced strategic objectives turn out to be unimportant, and the mightiest efforts are spent for ends that are defined only afterward. The close is the complete defeat of the loser, with formal revolution imposed; that is, the removal and replacement of the government and the ruling class. As in the American Civil War, the victory of the North settled a question about the system of sovereignty, so did the defeat of Hitler, and so, had it occurred, would his victory have, also. Further, and again this accords with Thucydides, the absolute power exerted in the wars is astonishingly great. Athens and Sparta each put more power into the struggle with each other than all Greece together had displayed against Persia. The Roman system, in its last social wars, fought both sides in wars greater than the Punic Wars. The wars of religion in the revolution called the Reformation were civil wars of Europe, and were greater and more radical than any wars before them. In all of them the establishment, when peace returned at last, was something new, so different from the conscious purposes that those gave no hint of what had really happened.

It is almost commonplace today to affirm that we are in a world revolution, or that the world wars had the character of civil wars. The only large-scale theory for a world revolution, however, has been the Marxist one, and the rejection of that theory leaves the recognition of world revolution without articulate explanation. To relate it to a class of such occurrences at least invites a free intellectual run of analytic observation and analysis and opens the way to theory.

This world revolution of the present is the first in which all the world has been engaged. By implication of its politics it is bringing a new state system. By implication of technology, it must also bring a general peace. And a stable peace must mean giant changes in the capacity for change without war. The work has already gone far. The great actors on the scene were typical nation-states as late as 1914, and already they are cosmopolitan states of far larger scale, the U.S. and the U.S.S.R., with China looming as another, and the fourth beginning to coalesce out of the old system in Europe. These greater states do not promise peace of themselves; but that becomes a necessity, and a promise. The late John von Neuman offered as clear a version of this necessity and promise as has been seen in his article "Can We Survive Technology?" (*Fortune* magazine, June 1955).

IMPLICATIONS FOR METHOD

This description of types and of mechanisms is not meant to be taken as rigid or conclusive. Any classification system serves to assist analysis and further study, and having done so it may always prove open to correction or improvement. However, even the simplest classification carries some implications for method on the one hand, and for the analysis of causes and mechanism on the other.

If revolutions occur in the classes described, and somewhat in the manner described, then the procedure to advance our understanding might include, among other things, the following:

The theoretical studies on revolution should be confronted with the historical studies, to see if the reactions described by the historians can be fitted to the models structured by the theorists.

Several good examples of the same class should be examined to see if one exhibits details not observed in the other, or if two or several afford a richer basis for analysis than one. Several might be used especially as a means of eliminating what might seem a key phenomenon in one but is absent, or unimportant, in another.

The theories of the nature of society and man, the vessel and the material of revolutions, should be confronted with the facts and theories of revolution.

This will enable us to discover the contradictions or confirmations between the two sets of theories and, by coordinating them, clarify both.

From revolutions of one class we should look to revolutions of another class to see if the differences in the process support the distinction of classification. Discrepancies should be targets of attention.

The terminology should be redressed to reduce the obscuration of the essential by the peripheral concerns of those who selected older terms.

Each individual situation should be examined in as wide a range as possible in the study of any revolution, to permit the discovery of joint factors of causation among supposedly disparate elements.

In the study of revolution we should take what men say as evidence of what they think they are doing, but not as a true indicator of the forces at work, or of the causes and effects of the process.

Theories of
Revolution

LAWRENCE STONE*

In attacking the problem of revolution, as most others of major significance in history, we historians should think twice before we spurn the help offered by our colleagues in the social sciences, who have, as it happens, been particularly active in the last few years in theorizing about the typology, causes, and evolutionary patterns of this particular phenomenon. The purpose of this article is not to advance any new hypothesis, but to provide a summary view and critical examination of the work that has been going on.

The first necessity in any inquiry is a careful definition of terms: what is, and what is not, a revolution? According to one view, it is change, effected by the use of violence, in government, and/or regime, and/or society.[1] By *society* is meant the consciousness and the mechanics of communal solidarity, which may be tribal, peasant, kinship, national, and so on; by *regime* is meant the constitutional structure—democracy, oligarchy, monarchy; and by *government* is meant specific political and administrative institutions. Violence, it should be noted, is not the same as force; it is force used with unnecessary intensity, unpredictably, and usually destructively.[2] This definition of revolution is a very broad one, and two historians of the French Revolution, Crane Brinton and Louis Gottschalk, would prefer to restrict the use of the word to the major political and social upheavals with which they are familiar, the "Great Revolutions" as George S. Pettee calls them.[3]

Even the wider definition allows the historian to distinguish between the seizure of power that leads to a major restructuring of government or society and the replacement of the former elite by a new one, and the coup d'état involving no more than a change of ruling personnel by violence or threat of

* I am grateful to Professors Cyril E. Black, Arno J. Mayer, and John W. Shy for some very helpful criticisms of this article.

[1] Chalmers Johnson, *Revolution and the Social System*, Hoover Institution Studies, III (Stanford 1964).
[2] Sheldon S. Wolin, "Violence and the Western Political Tradition," *American Journal of Orthopsychiatry*, xxxiii (January 1963), 15–28.
[3] Brinton, *The Anatomy of Revolution* (New York 1938); Gottschalk, "Causes of Revolution," *American Journal of Sociology*, L (July 1944), 1–8; Pettee, *The Process of Revolution* (New York 1938).

violence. This latter is the norm in Latin America, where it occurred thirty-one times in the ten years 1945–1955. Merle Kling has arrived at a suggestive explanation of this Latin American phenomenon of chronic political instability, limited but frequent use of violence, and almost complete lack of social or institutional change. He argues that ownership of the principal economic resources, both agricultural and mineral, is concentrated in the hands of a tiny, very stable, elite of enormously wealthy monoculture landlords and mining capitalists. This elite is all-powerful and cannot be attacked by opposition groups within the country; externally, however, it is dependent on foreign interests for its markets and its capital. In this colonial situation of a foreign-supported closed plutocracy, the main avenue of rapid upward social mobility for nonmembers of the elite leads, via the army, to the capture of the government machine, which is the only accessible source of wealth and power. This political instability is permitted by the elite on the condition that its own interests are undisturbed. Instability, limited violence, and the absence of social or institutional change are therefore all the product of the contradiction between the realities of a colonial economy run by a plutocracy and the facade of political sovereignty—between the real, stable power of the economic elite and the nominal, unstable control of politicians and generals.[4]

The looser definition of revolution thus suits both historians of major social change and historians of the palace coup. It does, however, raise certain difficulties. Firstly, there is a wide range of changes of government by violence which are neither a mere substitution of personalities in positions of power nor a prelude to the restructuring of society; secondly, conservative counterrevolutions become almost impossible to fit into the model; and lastly, it remains hard to distinguish between colonial wars, civil wars, and social revolution.

To avoid these difficulties, an alternative formulation has recently been put forward by a group of social scientists working mainly at Princeton. They have dropped the word "revolution" altogether and put "internal war" in its place.[5] This is defined as any attempt to alter state policy, rulers, or institutions by the use of violence, in societies where violent competition is not the norm and where well-defined institutional patterns exist.[6] This concept seems to be a logical consequence of the preoccupation of sociologists in recent years with a model of society in a stable, self-regulating state of perpetual equipoise. In this utopian world of universal harmony, all forms of violent conflict are anomalies, to be treated alike as pathological disorders of a similar species. This is a model which, although it has its uses for analytical purposes, bears little relation to the reality familiar to the historian. It looks to a society without change, with universal consensus on values, with complete social harmony, and isolated from external threats; no approximation to such a society has ever been seen. An alternative model,

---

[4] "Toward a Theory of Power and Political Instability in Latin America," *Western Political Quarterly*, IX (1956).

[5] Harry Eckstein, ed., *Internal War* (New York 1964), and "On the Etiology of Internal War," *History and Theory*, IV, No. 2 (1965), 133–63. I am grateful to Mr. Eckstein for allowing me to read this article before publication.

[6] The formula has been used by a historian, Peter Paret, in *Internal War and Pacification: The Vendée, 1793–96* (Princeton 1961).

which postulates that all societies are in a condition of multiple and perpetual tension held in check by social norms, ideological beliefs, and state sanctions, accords better with historical fact, as some sociologists are now beginning to realize.[7]

The first objection to the all-embracing formula of internal war is that, by covering all forms of physical conflict from strikes and terrorism to civil war, it isolates the use of violence from the normal processes of societal adjustment. Though some of the users of the term express their awareness that the use of violence for political ends is a fairly common occurrence, the definition they have established in fact excludes all times and places where it *is* common. It thus cuts out most societies the world has ever known, including Western Europe in the Middle Ages and Latin America today. Secondly, it isolates one particular means, physical violence, from the political ends that it is designed to serve. Clausewitz's famous definition of external war is equally applicable to internal war, civil war, or revolution: "War is not only a political act, but a real political instrument; a continuation of political transactions, an accomplishment of them by different means. That which remains peculiar to war relates only to the peculiar nature of its means."[8]

It is perfectly true that any means by which society exercises pressure or control, whether it is administrative organization, constitutional law, economic interest, or physical force, can be a fruitful field of study in its own right, so long as its students remain aware that they are looking at only one part of a larger whole. It is also true that there is something peculiar about violence, if only because of man's highly ambivalent attitude towards the killing of his own species. Somehow, he regards physical force as different in kind from, say, economic exploitation or psychological manipulation as a means of exercising power over others. But this distinction is not one of much concern to the historian of revolution, in which violence is a normal and natural occurrence. The concept of internal war is too broad in its comprehension of all types of violence from civil wars to strikes, too narrow in its restriction to normally nonviolent societies, too limited in its concern with one of many means, too arbitrary in its separation of this means from the ends in view, and too little concerned with the complex roots of social unrest to be of much practical value to him.

The most fruitful typology of revolution is that of Chalmers Johnson, set out in a pamphlet that deserves to be widely read.[9] He sees six types, identified by the targets selected for attack, whether the government personnel, the political regime, or the community as a social unit; by the nature of the carriers of revolution, whether a mass or an elite; and particularly by the

[7] Barrington Moore, "The Strategy of the Social Sciences," in his *Political Power and Social Theory* (Cambridge, Mass., 1958); Ralph Dahrendorf, "Out of Utopia: Toward a Reorientation of Sociological Analysis," *American Journal of Sociology*, LXIV (September 1958), 115–27; C. Wright Mills, *The Sociological Imagination* (New York 1959); Wilbert E. Moore, *Social Change* (Englewood Cliffs 1963). It should be noted that both the equilibrium and the conflict views of society have very respectable ancestries. The equilibrium model goes back to Rousseau—or perhaps Aquinas; the conflict model to Hobbes, Hegel, and Marx.

[8] Quoted in Edward Mead Earle, ed., *Makers of Modern Strategy* (Princeton 1943), 104–5.

[9] *Revolution and the Social System.*

goals and the ideologies, whether reformist, eschatological, nostalgic, nation-forming, elitist, or nationalist. The first type, the *Jacquerie,* is a spontaneous mass peasant rising, usually carried out in the name of the traditional authorities, Church and King, and with the limited aims of purging the local or national elites. Examples are the Peasant Revolt of 1381, Ket's Rebellion of 1549, and the Pugachev rebellion in Russia in 1773–1775. The second type, the *Millenarian Rebellion,* is similar to the first but with the added feature of a utopian dream, inspired by a living messiah. This type can be found at all times, in all parts of the world, from the Florentine revolution led by Savonarola in 1494, to the Anabaptist Rebellion in Münster led by John Mathijs and John Beukels in 1533–1535, to the Sioux Ghost-Dance Rebellion inspired by the Paiute prophet Wovoka in 1890. It has attracted a good deal of attention from historians in recent years, partly because the career of Hitler offered overwhelming proof of the enormous historical significance of a charismatic leader, and partly because of a growing interest in the ideas of Max Weber.[10] The third type is the *Anarchistic Rebellion,* the nostalgic reaction to progressive change, involving a romantic idealization of the old order: the Pilgrimage of Grace and the Vendée are examples.

The fourth is that very rare phenomenon, the *Jacobin Communist Revolution.* This has been defined as "a sweeping fundamental change in political organization, social structure, economic property control and the predominant myth of a social order, thus indicating a major break in the continuity of development."[11] This type of revolution can occur only in a highly centralized state with good communications and a large capital city, and its target is government, regime, and society—the lot. The result is likely to be the creation of a new national consciousness under centralized, military authority, and the erection of a more rational, and hence more efficient, social and bureaucratic order on the ruins of the old ramshackle structure of privilege, nepotism, and corruption.

The fifth type is the *Conspiratorial Coup d'État,* the planned work of a tiny elite fired by an oligarchic, sectarian ideology. This qualifies as a revolutionary type only if it in fact anticipates mass movement and inaugurates social change—for example the Nasser revolution in Egypt or the Castro revolution in Cuba; it is thus clearly distinguished from the palace revolt, assassination, dynastic succession-conflict, strike, banditry, and other forms of violence, which are all subsumed under the "internal war" rubric.

Finally, there is the *Militarized Mass Insurrection,* a new phenomenon of the twentieth century in that it is a deliberately planned mass revolutionary war, guided by a dedicated elite. The outcome of guerrilla warfare is determined by political attitudes, not military strategy or matériel, for the rebels are wholly dependent on broad popular support. In all cases on record, the ideology that attracts the mass following has been a combination of xeno-phobic nationalism and Marxism, with by far the greater stress on the

---

[10] N. R. C. Cohn, *Pursuit of the Millennium* (New York 1961); Eric J. Hobsbawm, *Primitive Rebels* (Manchester 1959); S. L. Thrupp, *Millennial Dreams in Action,* Supplement II, Comparative Studies in Society and History (The Hague 1962); A. J. F. Köbben, "Prophetic Movements as an Expression of Social Protest," *Internationales Archiv für Ethnographie,* xlix, No. 1 (1960), 117–64.
[11] Sigmund Neumann, quoted in Chalmers, 2.

former. This type of struggle has occurred in Yugoslavia, China, Algeria, and Vietnam.

Although, like any schematization of the historical process, this sixfold typology is concerned with ideal types, although in practice individual revolutions may sometimes display characteristics of several different types, the fact remains that this is much the most satisfactory classification we have so far; it is one that working historians can recognize and use with profit. The one obvious criticism is semantic, an objection to the use of the phrase "Jacobin Communist Revolution." Some of Johnson's examples are Communist, such as the Russian or Chinese Revolutions; others are Jacobin but not Communist, such as the French Revolution or the Turkish Revolution of 1908–1922. It would be better to revert to Pettee's category of "Great Revolutions," and treat Communist revolutions as a subcategory, one type, but not the only type, of modernizing revolutionary process.

Given this classification and definition of revolution, what are its root causes? Here everyone is agreed in making a sharp distinction between long-run, underlying causes—the preconditions, which create a potentially explosive situation and can be analyzed on a comparative basis—and immediate, incidental factors—the precipitants, which trigger the outbreak and which may be nonrecurrent, personal, and fortuitous. This effectively disposes of the objections of those historians whose antipathy to conceptual schematization takes the naïve form of asserting the uniqueness of each historical event.

One of the first in the field of model-building was Crane Brinton who, as long ago as 1938, put forward a series of uniformities common to the four great Western revolutions: English, French, American, and Russian. These included an economically advancing society, growing class and status antagonisms, an alienated intelligentsia, a psychologically insecure and politically inept ruling class, and a governmental financial crisis.[12]

The subjectivity, ambiguity, and partial self-contradiction of this and other analyses of the causes of specific revolutions—for example the French Revolution—have been cruelly shown up by Harry Eckstein.[13] He has pointed out that commonly adduced hypotheses run the spectrum of particular conditions, moving from the intellectual (inadequate political socialization, conflicting social myths, a corrosive social philosophy, alienation of the intellectuals) to the economic (increasing poverty, rapid growth, imbalance between production and distribution, long-term growth plus short-term recession) to the social (resentment due to restricted elite circulation, confusion due to excessive elite recruitment, anomie due to excessive social mobility, conflict due to the rise of new social classes) to the political (bad government, divided government, weak government, oppressive government). Finally there are explanations on the level of general process, such as rapid social change, erratic social change, or a lack of harmony between the state structure and society, the rulers and the ruled. None of these explanations are invalid in themselves, but they are often difficult or impossible to recon-

[12] *Anatomy of Revolution.*
[13] "On the Etiology of Internal War."

cile one with the other, and are so diverse in their range and variety as to be virtually impossible to fit into an ordered analytical framework. What, then, is to be done?

Fundamental to all analyses, whether by historians like Brinton and Gottschalk or by political scientists like Johnson and Eckstein, is the recognition of a lack of harmony between the social system on the one hand and the political system on the other. This situation Johnson calls *dysfunction,* a word derived from the structural-functional equilibrium model of the sociologists. This dysfunction may have many causes, some of which are merely cyclical, such as may develop because of personal weaknesses in hereditary kingships or single-party regimes. In these cases, the revolution will not take on serious proportions, and will limit itself to attacks on the governing institutions, leaving regime and society intact. In most cases, however, including all those of real importance, the dysfunction is the result of some new and developing process, as a result of which certain social sub-systems find themselves in a condition of relative deprivation. Rapid economic growth, imperial conquest, new metaphysical beliefs, and important technological changes are the four commonest factors involved, in that order. If the process of change is sufficiently slow and sufficiently moderate, the dysfunction may not rise to dangerous levels. Alternatively, the elite may adjust to the new situation with sufficient rapidity and skill to ride out the storm and retain popular confidence. But if the change is both rapid and profound, it may cause the sense of deprivation, alienation, anomie to spread into many sectors of society at once, causing what Johnson calls multiple dysfunction, which may be all but incurable within the existing political system.

In either case the second vital element in creating a revolutionary situation is the condition and attitude of the entrenched elite, a factor on which Eckstein rightly lays great stress. The elite may lose its manipulative skill, or its military superiority, or its self-confidence, or its cohesion; it may become estranged from the nonelite, or overwhelmed by a financial crisis; it may be incompetent, or weak, or brutal. Any combination of two or more of these features will be dangerous. What is ultimately fatal, however, is the compounding of its errors by intransigence. If it fails to anticipate the need for reform, if it blocks all peaceful, constitutional means of social adjustment, then it unites the various deprived elements in single-minded opposition to it, and drives them down the narrow road to violence. It is this process of polarization into two coherent groups or alliances of what are naturally and normally a series of fractional and shifting tensions and conflicts within a society that both Peter Amman and Wilbert Moore see as the essential preliminary to the outbreak of a Jacobin Revolution.[14] To conclude, therefore, revolution becomes *possible* when a condition of multiple dysfunction meets an intransigent elite: just such a conjunction occurred in the decades immediately before the English, the French, and the Russian Revolutions.

Revolution only becomes *probable* (Johnson might say "certain"), however, if certain special factors intervene: the "precipitants" or "accelerators." Of these, the three most common are the emergence of an inspired leader

---

[14] Amman, "Revolution: A Redefinition," *Political Science Quarterly,* LXXVII (1962).

or prophet; the formation of a secret, military, revolutionary organization; and the crushing defeat of the armed forces in foreign war. This last is of critical importance since it not only shatters the prestige of the ruling elite, but also undermines the morale and discipline of the soldiers and thus opens the way to the violent overthrow of the existing government.

The first defect of Johnson's model is that it concentrates too much on objective structural conditions, and attempts to relate conditions directly to action. In fact, however, as Eckstein points out, there is no such direct relationship; historians can point to similar activity arising from different conditions, and different activity arising from similar conditions. Standing between objective reality and action are subjective human attitudes. A behaviorist approach such as Brinton's, which lays equal stress on such things as anomie, alienation of the intellectuals, frustrated popular aspirations, elite estrangement, and loss of elite self-confidence, is more likely to produce a satisfactory historical explanation than is one that sticks to the objective social reality. Secondly, Johnson leaves too little play for the operation of the unique and the personal. He seems to regard his accelerators as automatic triggers, ignoring the area of unpredictable personal choice that is always left to the ruling elite and to the revolutionary leaders, even in a situation of multiple dysfunction exacerbated by an accelerator. Revolution is never inevitable—or rather the only evidence of its inevitability is that it actually happens. Consequently the only way to prove this point is to indulge in just the kind of hypothetical argument that historians prudently try to avoid. But it is still just possible that modernization may take place in Morocco and India without revolution. The modernization and industrialization of Germany and Britain took place without revolution in the nineteenth century (though it can be argued that in the latter case the process was slow by twentieth-century standards, and that, as is now becoming all too apparent, the modernization was far from complete). Some think that a potentially revolutionary situation in the United States in the 1930's was avoided by political action.

Lastly it is difficult to fit into the Johnson model the fact that political actions taken to remedy dysfunction often themselves precipitate change. This produces the paradoxical hypothesis that measures designed to restore equilibrium in fact upset equilibrium. Because he begins with his structural-functional equilibrium model, Johnson is a victim of the fallacy of intended consequences. As often as not in history it is the *unintended* consequences that really matter: to mention but one example, it was Louis XVI's belated and half-hearted attempts at reform that provoked the aristocratic reaction, which in turn opened the way to the bourgeois, the peasant, and the sans-culotte revolutions. Finally the dysfunction concept is not altogether easy to handle in a concrete historical case. If societies are regarded as being in a constant state of multiple tension, then some degree of dysfunction is always present. Some group is always in a state of relative deprivation due to the inevitable process of social change.

Recognition of this fact leads Eckstein to point out the importance of forces working *against* revolution. Historians, particularly those formed in the Western liberal tradition, are reluctant to admit that ruthless, efficient repression—as opposed to bumbling, half-hearted repression—involving the physical destruction of leading revolutionaries and effective control of the media of communication, can crush incipient revolutionary movements. Repression is particularly effective when governments know what to look for, when they have before their eyes the unfortunate example of other governments overthrown by revolutionaries elsewhere. Reaction, in fact, is just as infectious as revolution. Moreover diversion of energy and attention to successful—as opposed to unsuccessful—foreign war can ward off serious internal trouble. Quietist—as opposed to activist—religious movements may serve as the opiate of the people, as Halévy suggested about Methodism in England. Bread and circuses may distract popular attention. Timely—as opposed to untimely—political concessions may win over moderate opinion and isolate the extremists.

Basing himself on this suggestive analysis, Eckstein produces a paradigm for universal application. He sees four positive variables—elite inefficiency, disorienting social process, subversion, and available rebel facilities—and four negative variables—diversionary mechanisms, available incumbent facilities, adjustive mechanisms, and effective repression. Each type of internal war, and each step of each type, can, he suggests, be explained in terms of these eight variables. While this may be true, it is fair to point out that some of the variables are themselves the product of more deep-seated factors, others mere questions of executive action that may be determined by the accidents of personality. Disruptive social process is a profound cause; elite inefficiency a behavior pattern; effective repression a function of will; facilities the by-product of geography. One objection to the Eckstein paradigm is therefore that it embraces different levels of explanation and fails to maintain the fundamental distinction between preconditions and precipitants. Secondly, it concentrates on the factors working for or against the successful manipulation of violence rather than on the underlying factors working to produce a revolutionary potential. This is because the paradigm is intended to apply to all forms of internal war rather than to revolution proper, and because all that the various forms of internal war have in common is the use of violence. It is impossible to tell how serious these criticisms are until the paradigm has been applied to a particular historical revolution. Only then will its value become apparent.

If we take the behaviorist approach, then a primary cause of revolutions is the emergence of an obsessive revolutionary mentality. But how closely does this relate to the objective material circumstances themselves? In every revolutionary situation one finds a group of men—fanatics, extremists, zealots—so convinced of their own righteousness and of the urgent need to create a new Jerusalem on earth (whether formally religious or secular in inspiration is irrelevant) that they are prepared to smash through the normal restraints of habit, custom, and convention. Such men were the seventeenth-century English Puritans, the eighteenth-century French Jacobins, the twentieth-century Russian Bolsheviks. But what makes such men is far from certain. What generates such ruthlessness in curbing evil, such passion for discipline and order? Rapid social mobility, both horizontal and vertical, and particularly urbanization, certainly produces a sense of rootlessness and anxiety. In highly stratified societies, even some of the newly-risen elements may find themselves under stress.[15] While some of the *arrivistes* are happily

---

[15] Émile Durkheim, *Suicide* (Glencoe 1951), 246–54; A. B. Hollingshead, R. Ellis, and

absorbed in their new strata, others remain uneasy and resentful. If they are snubbed and rebuffed by the older members of the status group to which they aspire by reason of their new wealth and position, they are likely to become acutely conscious of their social inferiority, and may be driven either to adopt a pose *plus royaliste que le Roi* or to dream of destroying the whole social order. In the latter case they may try to allay their sense of insecurity by imposing their norms and values by force upon society at large. This is especially the case if there is available a moralistic ideology like Puritanism or Marxism to which they can attach themselves, and which provides them with unshakable confidence in their own rectitude.

But why does the individual react in this particular way rather than another? Some would argue that the character of the revolutionary is formed by sudden ideological conversion in adolescence or early adult life (to Puritanism, Jacobinism, or Bolshevism) as a refuge from this anxiety state.[16] What is not acceptable is the fashionable conservative cliché that the revolutionary and the reformer are merely the chance product of unfortunate psychological difficulties in childhood. It is possible that this is the mechanism by which such feelings are generated, though there is increasing evidence of the continued plasticity of human character until at any rate postadolescence. The main objection to this theory is that it fails to explain why these particular attitudes become common only in certain classes and age groups at certain times and in certain places. This failure strongly suggests that the cause of this state of mind lies not in the personal maladjustment of the individuals or their parents, but in the social conditions that created that maladjustment. Talcott Parsons treats disaffection or "alienation" as a generalized phenomenon that may manifest itself in crime, alcoholism, drug addiction, daytime fantasies, religious enthusiasm, or serious political agitation. To use Robert Merton's formulation, Ritualism and Retreatism are two possible psychological escape-routes; Innovation and Rebellion two others.[17]

Even if we accept this behaviorist approach (which I do), the fact remains that many of the underlying causes both of the alienation of the revolutionaries and of the weakness of the incumbent elite are economic in origin; and it is in this area that some interesting work has centered. In particular a fresh look has been taken at the contradictory models of Marx and de Tocqueville, the one claiming that popular revolution is a product of increasing misery, the other that it is a product of increasing prosperity.

Two economists, Sir Arthur Lewis and Mancur Olson, have pointed out that because of their basic social stability, both preindustrial and highly industrialized societies are relatively free from revolutionary disturbance.[18]

E. Kirby, "Social Mobility and Mental Illness," *American Sociological Review,* xix (1954).

[16] Michael L. Walzer, "Puritanism as a Revolutionary Ideology," *History and Theory,* iii, No. 1 (1963), 59–90.

[17] Parsons, *The Social System* (Glencoe 1951); Merton, *Social Theory and Social Structure* (Glencoe 1957), chap. 4.

[18] W. Arthur Lewis, "Commonwealth Address," in *Conference Across a Continent* (Toronto 1963), 46–60; Olson, "Rapid Growth as a Destabilizing Force," *Journal of Economic History,* xxiii (December 1963), 529–52. I am grateful to Mr. Olson for drawing my attention to Sir Arthur Lewis's article, and for some helpful suggestions.

In the former societies, people accept with little question the accepted rights and obligations of family, class, and caste. Misery, oppression, and social injustice are passively endured as inevitable features of life on earth. It is in societies experiencing rapid economic growth that the trouble usually occurs. Lewis, who is thinking mostly about the newly emerging countries, primarily of Africa, regards the sense of frustration that leads to revolution as a consequence of the dislocation of the old status patterns by the emergence of four new classes—the proletariat, the capitalist employers, the urban commercial and professional middle class, and the professional politicians—and of the disturbance of the old income patterns by the sporadic and patchy impact of economic growth, which creates new wealth and new poverty in close and conspicuous juxtaposition. Both phenomena he regards as merely transitional, since in a country fully developed economically there are strong tendencies toward the elimination of inequalities of opportunity, income, and status.

This model matches fairly well the only detailed analysis of a historical revolution in which a conscious effort has been made to apply modern sociological methods. In his recent study of the Vendée, Charles Tilly argues that a counterrevolutionary situation was the consequence of special tensions created by the immediate juxtaposition of, on one hand, parish clergy closely identified with the local communities, great absentee landlords, and old-fashioned subsistence farming, and, on the other, a large-scale textile industry on the putting-out system and increasing bourgeois competition.[19] Though the book is flawed by a tendency to take a ponderous sociological hammer to crack a simple little historical nut, it is nonetheless a suggestive example of the application of new hypotheses and techniques to historical material.

. Olson has independently developed a more elaborate version of the Lewis theory. He argues that revolutionaries are déclassé and freed from the social bonds of family, profession, village or manor; and that these individuals are the product of rapid economic growth, which creates both *nouveaux riches* and *nouveaux pauvres*. The former, usually middle-class and urban artisans, are better off economically, but are disoriented, rootless, and restless; the latter may be workers whose wages have failed to keep pace with inflation, workers in technologically outdated and therefore declining industries, or the unemployed in a society in which the old cushions of the extended family and the village have gone, and in which the new cushion of social security has not yet been created. The initial growth phase may well cause a decline in the standard of living of the majority because of the need for relatively enormous forced savings for reinvestment. The result is a revolution caused by the widening gap between expectations—social and political for the new rich, economic for the new poor—and the realities of everyday life.

A sociologist, James C. Davis, agrees with Olson that the fundamental impetus toward a revolutionary situation is generated by rapid economic growth but he associates such growth with a generally rising rather than a generally falling standard of living, and argues that the moment of potential revolution is reached only when the long-term phase of growth is followed

[19] *The Vendée* (Cambridge, Mass., 1964).

by a short-term phase of economic stagnation or decline.[20] The result of this "J-curve," as he calls it, is that steadily soaring expectations, newly created by the period of growth, shoot further and further ahead of actual satisfaction of needs. Successful revolution is the work neither of the destitute nor of the well-satisfied, but of those whose actual situation is improving less rapidly than they expect.

These economic models have much in common, and their differences can be explained by the fact that Lewis and Olson are primarily concerned with the long-term economic forces creating instability, and Davis with the short-term economic factors that may precipitate a crisis. Moreover their analyses apply to different kinds of economic growth, of which three have recently been identified by W. W. Rostow and Barry Supple: there is the expansion of production in a preindustrial society, which may not cause any important technological, ideological, social, or political change; there is the phase of rapid growth, involving major changes of every kind; and there is the sustained trend toward technological maturity.[21] Historians have been quick to see that these models, particularly that of Rostow, can be applied only to a limited number of historical cases. The trouble is not so much that in any specific case the phases—particularly the last two—tend to merge into one another, but that changes in the various sectors occur at irregular and unexpected places on the time-scale in different societies. Insofar as there is any validity in the division of the stages of growth into these three basic types, the revolutionary model of Olson and Lewis is confined to the second; that of Davis is applicable to all three.

The Davis model fits the history of Western Europe quite well, for it looks as if in conditions of extreme institutional and ideological rigidity the first type of economic growth may produce frustrations of a very serious kind. Revolutions broke out all over Europe in the 1640's, twenty years after a secular growth phase had come to an end.[22] C. E. Labrousse has demonstrated the existence of a similar economic recession in France from 1778,[23] and from 1914 the Russian economy was dislocated by the war effort after many years of rapid growth. Whatever its limitations in any particular situation, the J-curve of actual satisfaction of needs is an analytical tool that historians can usefully bear in mind as they probe the violent social upheavals of the past.

As de Tocqueville pointed out, this formula of advance followed by retreat is equally applicable to other sectors. Trouble arises if a phase of liberal governmental concessions is followed by a phase of political repression; a phase of fairly open recruitment channels into the elite followed by a phase of aristocratic reaction and a closing of ranks; a phase of weakening status barriers by a phase of reassertion of privilege. The J-curve is ap-

---

[20] "Toward a Theory of Revolution," *American Sociological Review*, xxvii (February 1962), 1–19, esp. the graph on p. 6.

[21] Rostow, *The Stages of Economic Growth* (Cambridge, Mass., 1960); Supple, *The Experience of Economic Growth* (New York 1963), 11–12.

[22] Hobsbawm, "The Crisis of the Seventeenth Century," in T. H. Aston, ed., *Crisis in Europe, 1560–1660* (London 1965), 5–58.

[23] *La Crise de l'Économie française à la fin de l'Ancien Régime et au début de la Révolution* (Paris 1944).

plicable to other than purely economic satisfactions, and the apex of the curve is the point at which underlying causes, the preconditions, merge with immediate factors, the precipitants. The recipe for revolution is thus the creation of new expectations by economic improvement and some social and political reforms, followed by economic recession, governmental reaction, and aristocratic resurgence, which widen the gap between expectations and reality.

All these attempts to relate dysfunction to relative changes in economic prosperity and aspirations are hampered by two things, of which the first is the extreme difficulty in ascertaining the facts. It is never easy to discover precisely what is happening to the distribution of wealth in a given society. Even now, even in highly developed Western societies with massive bureaucratic controls and quantities of statistical data, there is no agreement about the facts. Some years ago it was confidently believed that in both Britain and the United States incomes were being levelled, and that extremes of both wealth and poverty were being steadily eliminated. Today, no one quite knows what is happening in either country.[24] And if this is true now, still more is it true of societies in the past about which the information is fragmentary and unreliable.

Secondly, even if they can be clearly demonstrated, economic trends are only one part of the problem. Historians are increasingly realizing that the psychological responses to changes in wealth and power are not only precisely related to, but are politically more significant than, the material changes themselves. As Marx himself realized at one stage, dissatisfaction with the status quo is not determined by absolute realities but by relative expectations. "Our desires and pleasures spring from society; we measure them, therefore, by society, and not by the objects which serve for their satisfaction. Because they are of a social nature, they are of a relative nature."[25] Frustration may possibly result from a rise and subsequent relapse in real income. But it is perhaps more likely to be caused by a rise in aspirations that outstrips the rise in real income; or by a rise in the *relative* economic position in society of the group in question, followed by a period in which its real income continues to grow, but less fast than that of other groups around it. Alternatively it may represent a rise and then decline of status, largely unrelated to real income; or if status and real income are related, it may be inversely. For example, social scientists seeking to explain the rise of the radical right in the United States in the early 1950's and again in the early 1960's attribute it to a combination of great economic prosperity and an aggravated sense of insecurity of status.[26] Whether or not this is a general formula for right-wing rather than left-wing revolutionary movements is not yet clear.

Moreover the problem is further complicated by an extension of the reference-group theory.[27] Human satisfaction is related not to existing conditions but to the condition of a social group against which the individual measures his situation. In an age of mass communications and the wide

[24] Gabriel Kolko, *Wealth and Power in America* (New York 1962); Richard M. Titmuss, *Income Distribution and Social Change* (London 1962).
[25] Davis, 5, quoting Marx, *Selected Works in Two Volumes* (Moscow 1955), 1, 947.
[26] Daniel Bell, ed., *The Radical Right* (Garden City 1963).
[27] Merton, chap. 9.

distribution of cheap radio receivers even among the impoverished illiterate of the world, knowledge of high consumption standards elsewhere spreads rapidly, and as a result the reference group may be in another, more highly developed, country or even continent. Under these circumstances, revolutionary conditions may be created before industrialization has got properly under way.

The last area in which some new theoretical work has been done is in the formulation of hypotheses about the social stages of a "Great Revolution." One of the best attacks on this problem was made by Crane Brinton, who was thinking primarily about the French Revolution, but who extended his comparisons to the three other major Western revolutionary movements. He saw the first phase as dominated by moderate bourgeois elements; their supersession by the radicals; a reign of terror; a Thermidorian reaction; and the establishment of strong central authority under military rule to consolidate the limited gains of the revolution. In terms of mass psychology he compared revolution with a fever that rises in intensity, affecting nearly all parts of the body politic, and then dies away.

A much cruder and more elementary model has been advanced by an historian of the revolutions of 1848, Peter Amman.[28] He sees the modern state as an institution holding a monopoly of physical force, administration, and justice over a wide area, a monopoly dependent more on habits of obedience than on powers of coercion. Revolution may therefore be defined as a breakdown of the monopoly due to a failure of these habits of obedience. It begins with the emergence of two or more foci of power, and ends with the elimination of all but one. Amman includes the possibility of "suspended revolution," with the existence of two or more foci not yet in violent conflict.

This model admittedly avoids some of the difficulties raised by more elaborate classifications of revolution: how to distinguish a coup d'état from a revolution; how to define the degrees of social change; how to accommodate the conservative counterrevolution, and so on. It certainly offers some explanation of the progress of revolution from stage to stage as the various power blocs that emerge on the overthrow of the incumbent regime are progressively eliminated; and it explains why the greater the public participation in the revolution, the wider the break with the habits of obedience, and therefore the slower the restoration of order and centralized authority. But it throws the baby out with the bathwater. It is impossible to fit any decentralized traditional society, or any modern federal society, into the model. Moreover, even where it might be applicable, it offers no framework for analyzing the roots of revolution, no pointers for identifying the foci of power, no means of distinguishing between the various revolutionary types, and its notion of "suspended revolution" is little more than verbal evasion.

Though it is set out in a somewhat confused, overelaborate, and unnecessarily abstract form, the most convincing description of the social stages of revolution is that outlined by Rex D. Hopper.[29] He sees four stages. The first is characterized by indiscriminate, uncoordinated mass unrest and dis-

---

[28] "Revolution: A Redefinition."
[29] "The Revolutionary Process," *Social Forces*, xxviii (March 1950), 270–79.

satisfaction, the result of dim recognition that traditional values no longer satisfy current aspirations. The next stage sees this vague unease beginning to coalesce into organized opposition with defined goals, an important characteristic being a shift of allegiance by the intellectuals from the incumbents to the dissidents, the advancement of an "evil men" theory, and its abandonment in favor of an "evil institutions" theory. At this stage there emerge two types of leaders: the prophet, who sketches the shape of the new utopia upon which men's hopes can focus, and the reformer, working methodically toward specific goals. The third, the formal stage, sees the beginning of the revolution proper. Motives and objectives are clarified, organization is built up, a statesman leader emerges. Then conflicts between the left and the right of the revolutionary movement become acute, and the radicals take over from the moderates. The fourth and last stage sees the legalization of the revolution. It is a product of psychological exhaustion as the reforming drive burns itself out, moral enthusiasm wanes, and economic distress increases. The administrators take over, strong central government is established, and society is reconstructed on lines that embody substantial elements of the old system. The result falls far short of the utopian aspirations of the early leaders, but it succeeds in meshing aspirations with values by partly modifying both, and so allows the reconstruction of a firm social order.

Some of the writings of contemporary social scientists are ingenious feats of verbal juggling in an esoteric language, performed around the totem pole of an abstract model, surrounded as far as the eye can see by the arid wastes of terminological definitions and mathematical formulae. Small wonder the historian finds it hard to digest the gritty diet of this neo-scholasticism, as it has been aptly called. The more historically-minded of the social scientists, however, have a great deal to offer. The history of history, as well as of science, shows that advances depend partly on the accumulation of factual information, but rather more on the formulation of hypotheses that reveal the hidden relationships and common properties of apparently distinct phenomena. Social scientists can supply a corrective to the antiquarian fact-grubbing to which historians are so prone; they can direct attention to problems of general relevance, and away from the sterile triviality of so much historical research. They can risk new questions and suggest new ways of looking at old ones. They can supply new categories, and as a result may suggest new ideas.[30]

[30] See Werner J. Cahnman and Alvin Boskoff, eds., *Sociology and History: Theory and Research* (New York 1964); H. Stuart Hughes, "The Historian and the Social Scientist," *American Historical Review*, LXVI, No. 1 (1960), 20–46; A. Cobban, "History and Sociology," *Historical Studies*, III (1961), 1–8; M. G. Smith, "History and Social Anthropology," *Journal of the Royal Anthropological Institute*, XCII (1962); K. V. Thomas, "History and Anthropology," *Past and Present*, No. 24 (April 1963), 3–18.